THE BEVERLEY COLLECTION OF GEMS AT ALNWICK CASTLE

'This splendid volume for the first time makes accessible a noble collection of the highest importance, combining stunning new photographs with erudite, yet accessible, scholarship. Ancient, Renaissance, and more recent cameos and intaglios – along with their colourful histories – will delight and inform all readers who have an interest in engraved gems, classical art and the history of virtù.'

Kenneth Lapatin, Curator of Antiquities, J Paul Getty Museum, Los Angeles

---

'In their most welcome book the authors have given the world something of a lost treasure. The creation of the Beverley Collection was an exceptional chapter in the history of British gem collecting, yet many of the pieces remain relatively unknown. Here we find fine enlarged colour photographs, with casts and impressions where needed, and all the items presented are of exceptional quality. The cameos and intaglios range from antiquity to the early nineteenth century, from a meticulously cut Etruscan scarab (dating from around 400 BC), through late Republican and imperial Roman gems on which the merry world of Bacchus and Venus is so prominent, to Neo-classical works like the touching scene of Hercules with the dying Amazon queen Hippolyta. Striking portraits catch the eye, like the late Hellenistic Alexander the Great, two of the Emperor Tiberius, a portrait of the First Duke of Northumberland – father of Lord Algernon Percy – and the Emperors Necklace of garnet cameo portraits of the Twelve Roman Caesars, dating from the early nineteenth century. Some pieces, we see, had distinguished former owners. For example, the cameo of the baby Bacchus between a satyr and Silenos from the collection of Pope Paul II passed to the collection of Lorenzo di Medici, and bears the owner's stamp; several cameos are from the collection of Cardinal Grimani (1461–1523), among them the Augustan capricorn-rider whose pose appears to have inspired Michelangelo's figure of Adam on the Sistine Chapel ceiling; and a sard from the Grave of the Scipios in Rome was given by Pope Pius VI in 1790. It is not only the gem-specialists among classical archaeologists and art-historians, or students of the reception of antiquity and history of collecting, who will study this publication with the greatest interest, but all lovers of antiquity and art: they will delight in the mastery of the gem-engraver, the beauty of his works and the variety of subjects portrayed, all presented here so captivatingly and so splendidly.'

Erika Zwierlein-Diehl, Honorary Professor of Classical Archaeology, Bonn University

THE BEVERLEY COLLECTION OF GEMS AT ALNWICK CASTLE

DIANA SCARISBRICK,
CLAUDIA WAGNER
AND JOHN BOARDMAN

in association with The Beazley Archive

PWP

Published in 2017 by Philip Wilson Publishers
an imprint of I.B.Tauris & Co Ltd
London • New York

www.philip-wilson.co.uk

ISBN 978 1 78130 044 2

Designed and typeset by Christopher Bromley
Printed and bound in China by 1010 Printing

The Philip Wilson Gems and Jewellery Series, 2

FSC
www.fsc.org
MIX
Paper from responsible sources
FSC® C016973

CONTENTS

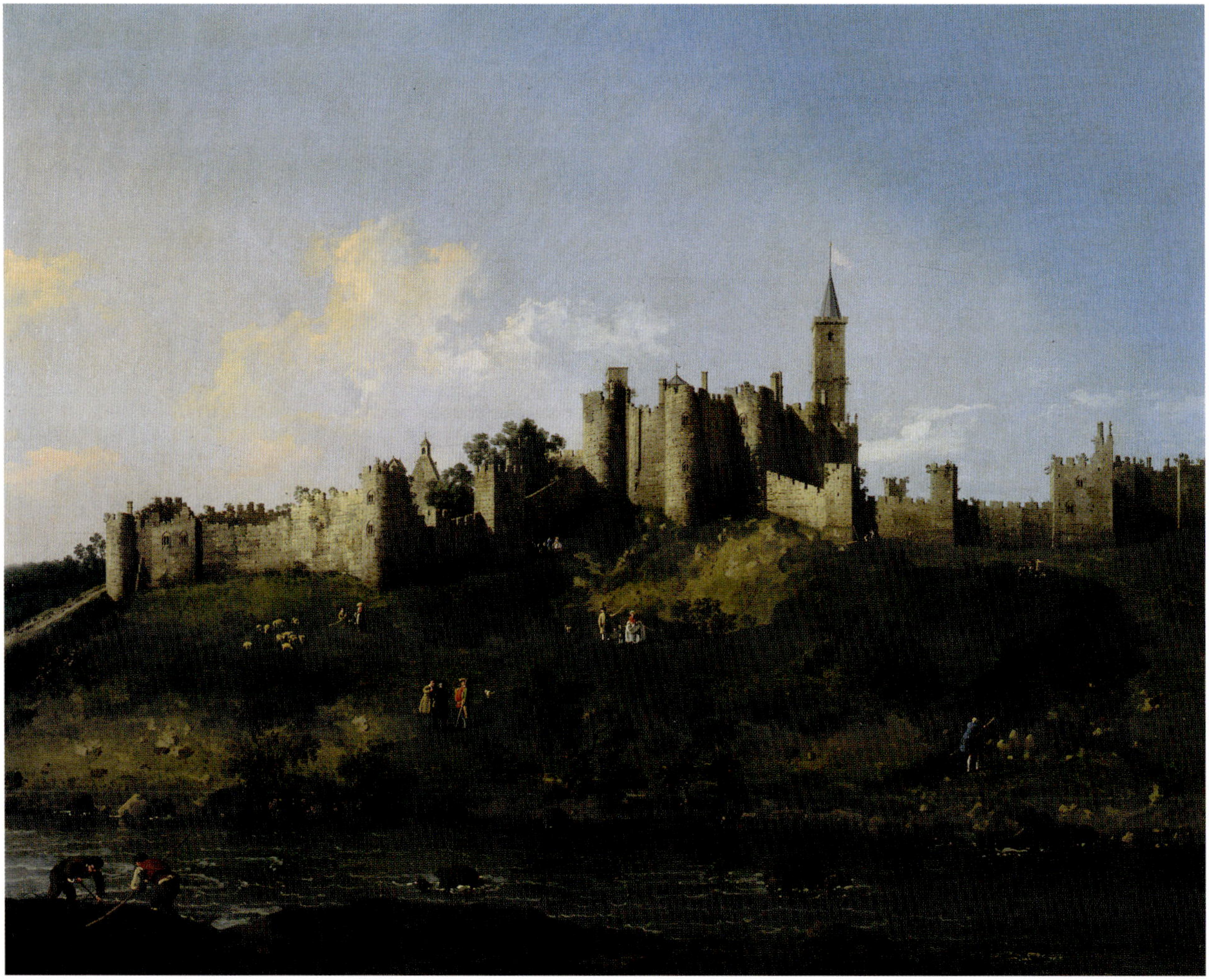

Fig 1: Alnwick Castle in Northumberland; by Canaletto Giovanni Antonio Canal (1697–1768), painted in 1752. (Collection of the Duke of Northumberland, Alnwick Castle.)

PREFACE

Alnwick Castle was built as a border fortress against the Scots in the twelfth century, if not earlier, standing in Northumberland near the coast, halfway between Newcastle and Edinburgh. It became the seat of the Percy family, Earls of Northumberland, and remains in Percy family hands to the present day. It was substantially enlarged in the fourteenth/fifteenth century and stands now as a prime example of robust stone defensive architecture. Its interior was reworked by Robert Adam in the later eighteenth century in the Strawberry Hill style, and has been much adjusted since to present one of the most impressive castle exteriors and interiors in Britain, much visited and admired.

The Alnwick collection of gems is one of the most important in Britain still in private hands, to rank beside the Devonshire gems at Chatsworth and, in its day, the Marlborough Collection at Blenheim Palace, now dispersed; and it remains intact and cared for. Recently several of its more important pieces formed a major part of an exhibition on the Art of Gem Engraving, in Japan (*AGE*), arranged by Diana Scarisbrick, but the collection is not at present displayed in the Castle. The Beazley Archive's mission to make such collections known to scholars has been notably advanced by the 12th Duke's readiness to let a team from the Beazley Archive in Oxford visit, work on, photograph and make impressions of the collection, published here. We are grateful for his hospitality and the close and friendly collaboration of Clare Baxter (Collections & Archives Manager) and Lisa Little (Library & Documentation Officer, Christopher Hunwick Archivist). The text is a collaborative work by all the named authors, with Diana Scarisbrick especially working on the archives, and Claudia Wagner the photography, both also on the text. Adriano Aymonino kindly provided information about the 1st Duchess' Collection. We are indebted also to Erika Zwierlein-Diehl, Carina Weiss and Erika Simon for their comments on several pieces. The documentation and research for this publication were conducted at the Beazley Archive (Classical Art Research Centre) at Oxford University.

Abbreviations

AGDS:	*Antike Gemmen in deutschen Sammlungen*
AG:	A. Furtwängler, *Die antiken Gemmen* (Leipzig 1900).
AGE:	*The Art of Gem Engraving from Alexander the Great to Napoleon III* (Fukuoka 2008).
Beazley, *LHG*:	J.D. Beazley, *The Lewes House Collection of Ancient Gems* (Oxford 1920; revised and updated edition by J. Boardman, Oxford, Beazley Archive 2002).
Berlin:	*Antike Gemmen in deutschen Sammlungen* II (Munich 1969).
Bober/Rubinstein:	P.P. Bober and R. Rubinstein, *Renaissance Artists and Antique Sculpture* (Harvey Miller 1986).
Bracci 1784:	D.A. Bracci, *Memorie degli antichi incisori* (Florence 1784).
Cades:	Tommaso Cades collection of casts 'Beverley Gems.'
Cades, Cent.:	Cades, Centurie I–IV as listed in *Bullettino dell'Instituto di Corrispondenza Archeologica* 1831, 1834. Impressions: a set in Göttingen.
Cambridge:	M. Henig, *Classical Gems: Fitzwilliam Museum* (Cambridge 1994).
Charlesworth:	D. Charlesworth, 'Roman Jewellery found in Northumberland and Durham', in *Archaeologia Aeliana* Ser. 4, 39 (1961) 1–36.
Classicism:	*Classicism to Neo-classicism. Essays dedicated to Gertrud Seidmann* (eds M. Henig, D. Plantzos, Oxford BAR 793, 1999).

Content:	M. Henig, *The Content Cameos* (Oxford 1990).
Dacos et al. 1972:	*Il Tesoro di Lorenzo il Magnifico: Le Gemme* (eds. N. Dacos, A. Giuliano, U. Pannuti, Florence 1972).
Dacos et al. 1973:	N. Dacos in *Les Arts à la Cour des Papes pendant le XVe et le XVIe siècle* (eds. N. Dacos, A. Giuliano, U. Pannuti, Florence 1973).
Eichler/Kris:	F. Eichler and E. Kris, *Die Kameen im Kunsthistorischen Museum* (Vienna 1927).
Ficorini 1757:	F. de Ficorini, *Gemmae Antiquae Litteratae* (Rome 1757).
Geneva:	M.L.Vollenweider, *Catalogue raisonné des sceaux, cylindres, intailles et camées. Musée d'Art et d'Histoire de Genève* I, II, III (Mainz 1976–83).
Gennaioli 2010:	R. Gennaioli, *Pregio e bellezza: Cammei e intagli dei Medici* (Florence 2010).
Giuliano, *Cammei*:	A. Giuliano, *I Cammei della Collezione Medicea nel Museo Archeologico di Firenze* (Rome 1989).
Hadjadj 2007:	Reine Hadjadj, *Bagues Merovingiennes* (Paris 2007).
Hamburg:	with *Hanover* q.v.
Hanover:	*Antike Gemmen in deutschen Sammlungen* IV (Munich 1975).
Hollis 1780:	F. Blackburne, *Memoirs of Thomas Hollis* (London 1780).
Hull Grundy 1984:	H. Tait et al., *The Art of the Jeweller: A catalogue of the Hull Grundy Gift to the British Museum* (London 1984).
Inst. Imp.:	*Impronti del Istituto.* These are 171 impressions almost certainly by Cades but issued separately from and after the main German Institute in Rome series (which includes many of them), and labelled 'Beverley.'
Kagan:	J. Kagan, *Gem Engraving in Britain from Antiquity to the Present* (Oxford, Beazley Archive 2010).

Kagan/Neverov 2000: J. Kagan and O. Neverov, *Splendeurs des Collections de Catherine II de Russie* (Paris 2000).

King 1872: C.W. King, *Antique Gems and Rings* I (text), II (plates) (London).

King 1885: C.W. King, *Handbook of Engraved Gems* (London).

Knight: Alfred E. Knight, *The Collection of Camei and Intagli at Alnwick Castle known as 'The Beverley Gems' a Descriptive Catalogue based upon Manuscript Notes in the possession of His Grace the Duke of Northumberland* (privately printed 1921). Gem numbers here preceded by K are those of his catalogue.

Kris 1929: E. Kris, *Steinschneidekunst in der italienischen Renaissance* (Vienna 1929).

Lang, *Wissen*: J. Lang, *Mit Wissen geschmückt? Zur bildlichen Rezeption griechischer Dichter und Denker in der römischen Lebenswelt* (Wiesbaden 2012)

LIMC: *Lexicon Iconographicum Mythologiae Classicae* (Zurich/Munich 1981–99).

Lippert: P.D. Lippert, *Dactyliothec: Sammlung geschnittener Steine der Alten aus denen vornehmsten Museis in Europa zum Nutzen der schönen Künste und Künstler in zwey tausend Abdrücken* (1766/7). Two volumes, I, II, and a Supplement in three sections, IIIA, IIIB, IV.
This was a second edition of a shorter, more summary catalogue.

Lippold: G. Lippold, *Gemmen und Kameen des Altertums und der Neuzeit* (Stuttgart 1922).

London, Dalton: *Catalogue of the Engraved Gems of the Post-Classical Periods* (London 1915).

London, Walters: H.B. Walters, *Catalogue of the Engraved Gems and Cameos in the British Museum* (London 1926).

Marlborough:	J. Boardman et al., *The Marlborough Gems* (Oxford 2010).
Mariette 1750:	P.J. Mariette, *Traité des pierres gravées* (Paris 1750).
Megow:	W.-R. Megow, *Kameen von Augustus bis Alexander Severus* (Berlin 1987).
Moret, *Palladion*:	J.-M. Moret, *Les pierres gravées antiques représentant le rapt du Palladion* (Mainz 1997).
Munich:	*Antike Gemmen in Deutschen Sammlungen* I. 1–3 (Munich 1968).
Oxford:	J. Boardman and M.L. Vollenweider, *Catalogue of the Engraved Gems and Finger Rings, Ashmolean Museum Oxford* (Oxford 1978).
Pannuti, *Napoli*:	U. Pannuti, *La Collezione glittica. Museo archeologico nazionale di Napoli* (Rome 1994).
Paoletti:	L.P.B. Stefanelli, *La collezione Paoletti, Stampi in vetro per impronte di intagli e cammei* I (Museo di Roma, 2007); II (Museo di Roma 2013). Cited by Paoletti's volume and number.
Pistrucci 1989:	L.P.B. Stefanelli, *I Modelli in Cera di Benedetto Pistrucci, Bollettino di Numismatica* (Rome 1989).
Plantzos:	D. Plantzos *Hellenistic Engraved Gems* (Oxford 1999)
Pope-Hennessy 1965:	J. Pope-Hennessy, *Renaissance Bronzes: Reliefs, Plaquettes, Statuettes from the Samuel H. Kress Collection 9* (London 1965).
Rollett 1874:	H. Rollett, *Die drei Meister der Gemmoglyptik: Antonio, Giovanni und Luigi Pichler* (Vienna 1874).
Santarelli 1981:	M. Casarosa Guadagny, *Ritrattini in cera d'epoca classica. La collezione Santarelli e un appendice sulle cere antiche del Museo Nazionale di Firenze* (Florence 1981).
Seidmann 1987:	G. Seidmann, *Nathaniel Marchant, Gem Engraver 1739–1816* (The Walpole Society, London 1987).

SG. Imp.:	The Sangiorgi collection of impressions of Beverley gems.
Spier, *Getty*:	J. Spier, *Ancient Gems and Finger Rings* (Malibu 1992).
Spier, *Gulbenkian*:	J. Spier, *A Catalogue of the Calouste Gulbenkian Collection of Gems* (Calouste Gulbenkian Museum 2001).
Spilsbury:	John Spilsbury, *A collection of fifty prints from antique gems. In the collections of the Right Honourable Earl Percy, the Honourable C.F. Greville, and T.M. Slade Esquire. Engraved by Mr. John Spilsbury* (John Boydell, London 1784, 1785) – only four items (his nos 11, 16, 33, 38) are at Alnwick.
Tassie:	R.E. Raspe, *A Descriptive Catalogue of a General Collection of Ancient and Modern Engraved Gems, Cameos as well as Intaglios, taken from the most celebrated cabinets in Europe, and cast in Coloured Pastes, White Enamel and Sulphur, by James Tassie, Modeller, arranged and described by R. E. Raspe and illustrated with Copper Plates* (London 1791).
Vico:	*EX GEMMIS ET CAMEIS ANTIQUORUM ALIQUOT MONUMENTA AB AENEA VICO PARMEN INCIS Perillustri et Exccellent D D Dominico Panarolo Rom. In Patrio Lyceo Medicine Professor. Io Dominicus de Rubeis D.D.* Engravings of cameos in the collection of Cardinal Domenico Grimani (1461–1523).
Vollenweider:	M.-L. Vollenweider, *Die Steinschneidekunst und ihre Künstler in spätrepublikanischer und Augusteischer Zeit* (Baden-Baden 1966).
Wagner-Boardman:	C. Wagner and J. Boardman, *A Collection of Classical and Eastern Intaglios, Rings and Cameos* (Oxford, Beazley Archive 2003).
Weber 1992:	I. Weber, *Kostbare Steine: Die Gemmensammlung des Kurfürsten Johann Wilhelm von der Pfalz* (Munich 1992).
Weber 1995:	I. Weber, *Geschnittene Steine des 18. bis 20. Jahrhunderts* (Munich 1995).

Weber 1995: I. Weber, *Geschnittene Steine aus altbayerischem Besitz* (Munich 2001).

Wien: E. Zwierlein-Diehl, *Die antiken Gemmen des Kunsthistorischen Museums in Wien* I-III (Munich 1973–91).

Würzburg: E. Zwierlein-Diehl, *Glaspasten im Martin-von-Wagner Museum der Universität Würzburg* I (Munich 1986).

W.Tassie: The Tassie company impressions collected after 1791, given by William to the National Portrait Gallery in Edinburgh. A manuscript catalogue of the set is in Cambridge (Fitzwilliam Museum 41.NK5517.T2): http://www.beazley.ox.ac.uk/gems/WilliamTassie/.

Yuen 1997: T. Yuen, 'Glyptic Sources of Renaissance Art' in *Engraved Gems, Revivals and Survivals* (ed. C.M. Brown, Washington 1997; Washington Studies in the History of Art 54) 136–157.

Zazoff 1983: P. Zazoff, *Die antiken Gemmen* (Munich 1983).

Zazoff, *ES*: *Etruskische Skarabäen* (Mainz 1986).

Zerner 1969: H. Zerner, *The School of Fontainebleu* (London 1969).

Zwierlein-Diehl 2005: E. Zwierlein-Diehl, 'Gemmen mit Künstlerinschriften', in *Meisterwerke* (Symposion anlässlich des 150. Geburtstages von Adolf Furtwängler; Freiburg im Breisgau, ed. V.M. Strocka).

Zwierlein-Diehl, *AGN*: E. Zwierlein-Diehl, *Antike Gemmen und ihr Nachleben* (Berlin 2007).

Throughout the text the catalogue numbers are cited in **bold**.

Measurements in the catalogue are in mm.

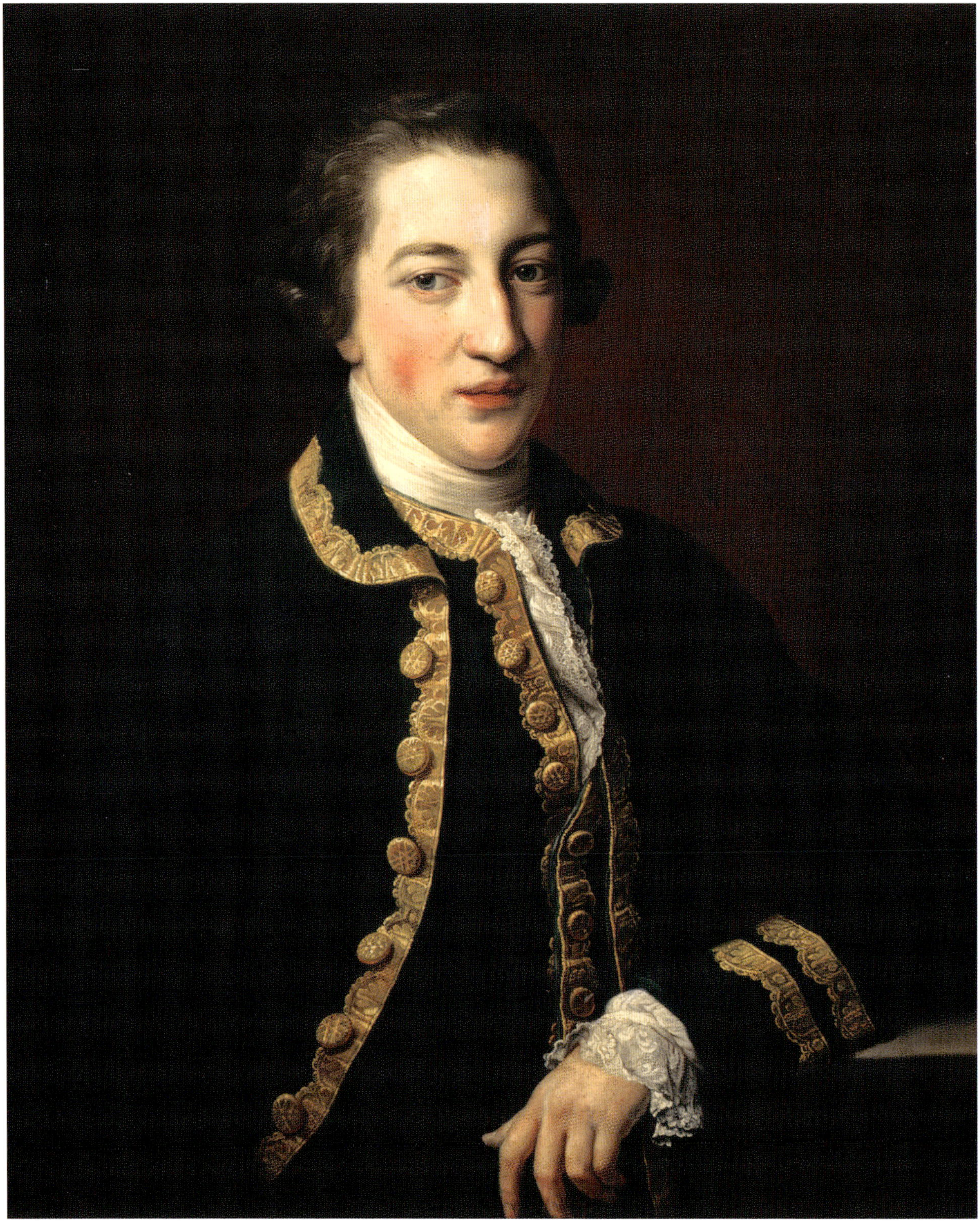

Fig. 2: Portrait of Lord Algernon Percy, later 1st Earl of Beverley; by Pompeo Batoni (1708–1787), signed, Rome; painted c. 1773.
(Collection of the Duke of Northumberland, Alnwick Castle.)

THE BEVERLEY GEMS

Although known as 'the Beverley Gems', because associated with Lord Algernon Percy, 1st Earl of Beverley (1749–1830), the collection of cameos and intaglios at Alnwick Castle also reflects the involvement of other family members, especially the 1st Duke and Duchess of Northumberland. This remarkable art-loving couple, prominent in 18th-century English political, social and court life, married in 1740. He was Sir Hugh Smithson (1715–1786), a Yorkshire gentleman, who, after a visit to Italy in 1733–4 with a tutor, was elected a Fellow of the Society of Antiquaries and Founder Member of the Society of Dilettanti in recognition of his interest in classical art and antiquities. Quite unexpectedly his wife, the blue-blooded Lady Elizabeth Seymour (1716–1776), became, through the death of her young brother Viscount Beauchamp (1725–1744), heiress to the great estates of the Earls of Northumberland and of her father, the 7th Duke of Somerset (1684–1750). Sir Hugh not only increased this great fortune but was also active in national affairs. After serving as Viceroy of Ireland from 1763–65, he was created Earl Percy and Duke of Northumberland by George III in 1766, and Lord Lovaine in 1784, with a special remainder to his second son, Lord Algernon Percy. The principal family residences were the palatial Northumberland House in London, Syon House, the 'maison de plaisance' by the Thames, and Alnwick Castle. Together they patronised the architects James Paine and Robert Adam, the artist Canaletto, and a host of others to embellish these houses and fill them with the finest works of art and antiquities obtainable in Europe.[1] The Duchess, who had a collection of engraved gems, kept them close at hand, next to her bedroom at Northumberland House, as noted by Thomas Martyn, *The English Connoisseur* (1766): 'Lady Northumberland's closet is a repository of curiosities and contains a fine collection of pictures, among them the famous Cornaro family by the celebrated Titian.'[2] The gem collection comprised 37 cameos, 19 intaglios, paste facsimiles of which 22 were made by Dr Quin,[3] and two others by James Tassie. According to the provenances listed by the Duchess, most were gifts from her family: husband, brother Viscount Beauchamp, grandfather the 'proud Duke of Somerset', and her intellectual mother and father. Others were given by friends: Mrs Wyndham, Lord Greville, future Earl of Warwick, Lord and Lady Kerry and the diplomat Sir Thomas Robinson,

1. A. Aymonino, 'The *Musaeum* of the 1st Duchess of Northumberland (1716–76) at Northumberland House in London: an Introduction', in *Women Patrons and Collectors* (eds S. Bracken, A.M. Galdy, A. Turpin, Newcastle 2012).

2. Thomas Martyn, *The English Connoisseur; containing an Account of Whatever is Curious in Painting Sculpture etc in the Seats of the Nobility and Principal Gentry of England both in Town and Country*, vol. 1 (London 1766) 191. His large collection is listed by Tassie; he was a botanist, classical scholar, travelled in Italy, and wrote *Gentleman's Guide Through Italy* (London 1701) with John Lettice, also *Antiquities of Herculaneum* (London 1773).

3. Dr Henry Quin (1718–91), an Irish physician in Dublin, Ireland, held the position of Professor of the Practice of Physic at the medical school of Trinity College, and was elected President of the College of Physicians between 1758 and 1781.

a Yorkshire neighbour, and brother-in-law of another gem collector, the 4th Earl of Carlisle. One of her finest cameos, the sardonyx 'Fall of Phaeton' (**12**), was presented to her in Cologne by the Archbishop Elector, Maximilian Friedrich von Königsegg-Rothenfels (1761–84). Her interest in engraved gems was shared by the Duke, who had acquired in Florence a sardonyx cameo portrait of Britannicus, 'from the collection of the Dukes of Mantua', which was exhibited at the Society of Antiquaries[4] and cannot now be found, although Alnwick has a copy of it as a red jasper intaglio (**225**), and still at Alnwick there are several 'gifts from my Lord': a jacinth Cleopatra commesso (**1**), his intaglio portrait, which is not signed, but could have been engraved by Lorenz Natter (**244**). In addition he gave her Robert Wray's intaglio of The Fair Laundress (**111**), after a drawing by Giles Hussey, a Jacobite artist much patronised by the Duke, Carlo Costanzi's copy of the Strozzi aquamarine Medusa intaglio (**252**), a cornelian intaglio of Meleager (perhaps **156**) and two cameos, one of Caius Caesar (**69**) and another taken to represent Jupiter and Juno (**76**). Also at Alnwick is a sard intaglio of Hercules and Hippolyta (**142**), bought from the Barberini collection by James Byres who sold it for the much talked-about price of £300 to the Indian nabob Paul Benfield, who presented it to Lord Beverley,[5] presumably in the hope of obtaining some political favour. Sixty years later, when Hugh Percy, Bishop of Carlisle, who had inherited the Beverley Gems, wished to sell, the market had changed: the gem engraver Benedetto Pistrucci valued the stone at £150 only and thought it would be difficult to find a buyer.[6]

Notwithstanding their responsibilities at court and in politics, the Duke and Duchess did not neglect their children's education and passed on to them their interest in classical art. The elder son, Hugh, the future 2nd Duke of Northumberland, was sent on the Grand Tour with his tutor, Mr Lippyeatt, in 1761–3, when he bought pictures and was painted by Nathaniel Dance and Pompeo Batoni. To accompany the second son, Algernon, on his travels abroad, they engaged Louis Dutens (1730–1812), a Huguenot diplomatist, man of letters and numismatist, who had become a friend. He describes how the Duke 'universally acknowledged to be the most magnificent nobleman in England … had read (my) work in favour of the ancients, complimented me upon it, invited me to dinner, and made me so welcome that in a short time I found myself almost as well established in his good graces as if I had passed my life with him.'[7] Dutens was also flattered by the attention paid him by the Duchess, 'of the highest birth, descended from Charlemagne through the marriage of Agnes de Percy with Joscelin de Louvain in 1168'. She enjoyed his company: 'I appeared to her as if I had never known any other employment: and in the evening I partook of her social amusements and studied every means of adding to her pleasures,' and he acquiesced: 'As I was not displeased with pomp and grandeur and was treated as a favourite

4. Minutes of the Society of Antiquaries, 16 June 1785: 'Mr. Brand exhibited for his Grace the Duke of Northumberland a beautiful cameo on sardonyx of the head of Britannicus of most exquisite workmanship.'

5. Although Knight says Benfield gave the stone to the 1st Duke, this does not seem correct, since the note below refers to 'my father sixty years ago' and therefore must have been written by one of Lord Beverley's children, presumably Hugh Percy who inherited the collection. For Benfield, see A. Spencer (ed.), *Memoirs of William Hickey*, vol. 3, 1782–90 (London 1922) 98, attacked by Edmund Burke 'in Parliament as a notorious defaulter, who had embezzled large sums from his employer's money which came into his hands from the official situations he had filled, had basely and iniquitously robbed and plundered the Nabob of Arcot and was in many respects the greatest delinquent that ever left India'.

6. Northumberland Archives, hand-written note (Hippolyta is here called Melanippe).

7. L. Dutens, *Memoirs of a Traveller Now in Retirement*, vol. 2 (London 1806) 97–101.

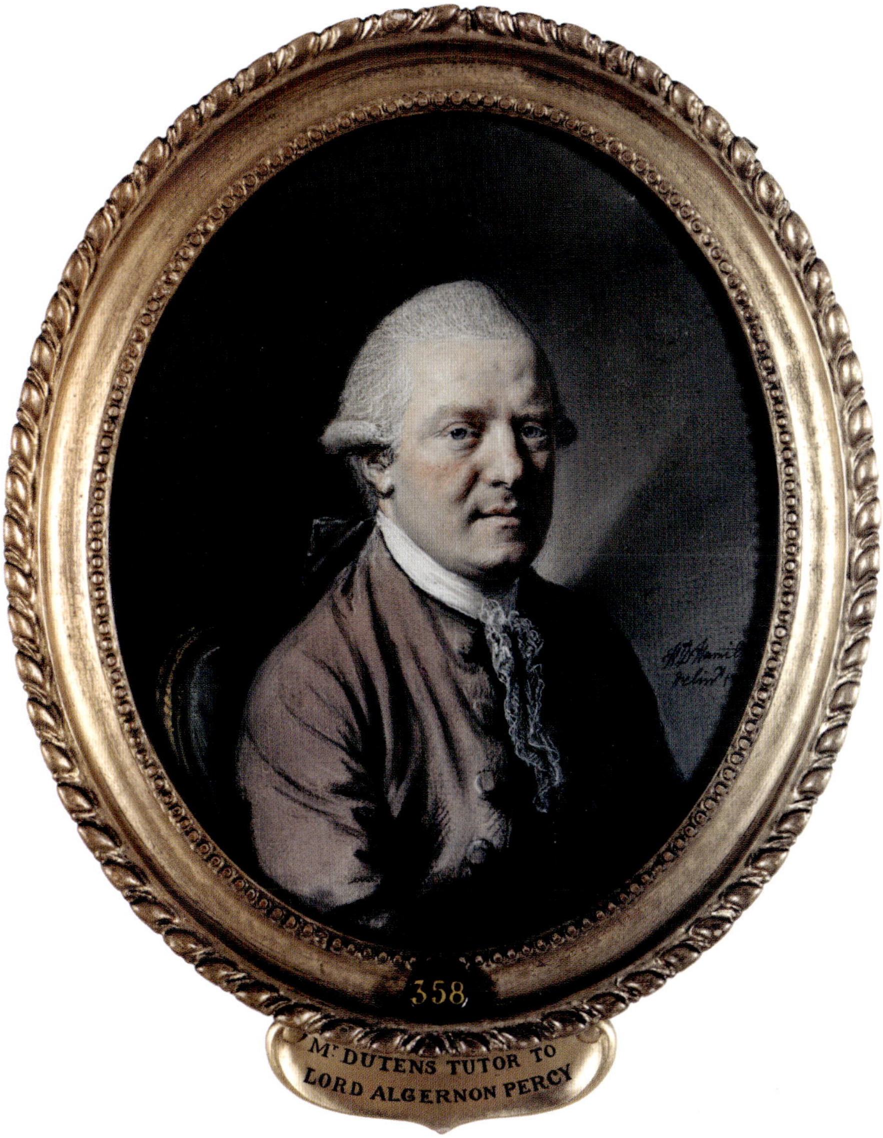

Fig. 3: Portrait of Louis Dutens (1730–1812), diplomat and author; by the Irish portraitist Hugh Douglas Hamilton (c. 1724–1808), painted c. 1773. (Collection of the Duke of Northumberland, Alnwick Castle.)

of the house I gave myself up to this family with all the attachment which the most decided fondness could acquire.' Observing that 'she amused herself by collecting prints and medals and by making other collections of various sorts,' he made himself useful by acting as an agent.[8] In these happy circumstances, when asked to escort Lord Algernon to France in 1766, he did not hesitate, for the Eton schoolboy who had inherited the 'politeness of father combined with that interesting obligingness which his mother knew so well how to show to her friends' was 'lively, gay, did not dislike parade and splendour, evinced great taste in his expenditure, and took particular pleasure in showing his liberality'. Next, came the visit to Italy in 1768–9, and Dutens, who had never had the means to venture south of Turin, now, 'as a partisan of the ancients', made the most of their time there. In all, tutor and pupil spent four years together, travelling through France, Genoa, Florence, Rome, Naples, Venice, Milan, Turin, Germany, and finally settling in the Vienna of the Empress Maria Theresa from October 1769 to March 1771, studying art and history and meeting everywhere outstanding political and intellectual figures, including the philosopher Voltaire, the Swiss scientist Haller and the Austrian statesman Prince Kaunitz.

It was through this Grand Tour experience that Dutens succeeded in giving his young charge, whose ruling passion was dogs, horses and hunting, what was to become the interest in cameos and intaglios that resulted in the formation of the Beverley Gem Collection. In this respect the achievement of Dutens was echoed by Goethe, who, on his arrival in Rome in November 1786, wrote to a friend that 'in earlier years I had the odd notion that nothing would please me more than to be taken to Italy by some knowledgeable man, say an Englishman, well versed in art and history.'[9] The warm friendship continued after Lord Algernon's marriage in 1775 to Isabella Burrell, and the three, who travelled to Italy in 1782–3, remained in close touch, testified by a frequent exchange of letters.[10] After Duchess Elizabeth died in 1776, it was Isabella who took her place in Dutens' affections: for him she was the model for married women, 'making all around her happy, with her simplicity of manner, affability of conversation'.

The Welsh landscape painter, Thomas Jones (1742–1803), observed how during the second half of the 18th century in Rome the young English milords 'moved in a circle of superior splendour surrounded by a group of satellites under the denomination of travelling tutors, antiquarians, dealers in virtù, English grooms, French valets and Italian running footmen'.[11] As one of these privileged gentlemen and supervised by Dutens, Lord Algernon, who visited all the great monuments of the city and the surrounding Campagna, developed a taste for antiquity, as well as enjoying the Carnival and the hospitality of the Roman nobility. Nothing was omitted. They relied on the experience of the Scottish dealer and antiquary, James Byres (1734–1817), established in Rome for thirty years and described by Dutens as

8. Northumberland Archives, Letter, 4 Febuary 1769, from Dutens to Rev. Thomas Percy, 'the Medals which I purchased yesterday for her Grace of the Present Pope (Clement XIII) and one or two of the Pretender's family wanted in her collection.' He not only acted as her agent in forming her collection of medals but also ivories, 'basso relievos' and promised to look for bronzes.

9. J.W. von Goethe, *Italian Journey* (Princeton 1994) 109, quoted in M.D. Sánchez-Sáuregui and S. Wilcox, eds. *The English Prize, the Capture of the Westmoreland: An Episode of the Grand Tour. Exhibition Catalogue* (Yale 2012).

10. Northumberland Archives. Typescripts kindly provided by Chris Hunwick, Archivist.

11. 'Memoirs of Thomas Jones', *The Walpole Society*, 32 (1951) 71.

'très honnête et habile homme, grand connoisseur et très grande enthousiaste des beautés que renferment cette superbe ville' ('a clever and reliable man, a great connoisseur and enthusiast for all the wonders of this splendid city'). They saw much of the connoisseur Cardinal Albani (1692–1779), the 'oracle of good taste', who did not like the French and preferred the English, the Duchess de Bracciano, the Marchioness Boccapaduli and Signora Maria Pizzelli. It was the same in Naples where Sir William Hamilton, the British ambassador and aesthete, not only showed them his own collections, but introduced them to the Bourbon court and the local nobility. Again in Florence, through the English representative Sir Horace Mann, they had access to all the treasures of art in public and private hands. For Dutens the purpose of all these encounters and studies was to instil in Lord Algernon 'le goût et le discernement du beau', and make of him 'un vrai connoisseur des arts qui voit l'ouvrage d'un grand maître et en saisit au premier coup d'oeil le mérite et les beautés' ('the taste for and judgment of the beautiful, and to make of him a true connoisseur of the arts, capable of grasping at first sight the quality and beauty of the works of a great master').

Having given Lord Algernon a thorough grounding in classical art, Dutens next succeeded in impressing on him the significance of the smaller vestiges of antiquity, for, as he explained: 'Even while we admire what remains of the great works of antiquity we should also not exclude the smaller which also illustrate the marvellous artistic skills of the ancients.'[12] He must have been referring to engraved gems which, because of their durability, had survived in better condition than much of the architecture, painting and sculpture, and in sufficient quantities to illustrate, albeit in miniature, the portraits of the illustrious Greeks and Romans, their religion, their history and culture. Through their excellent connections he and Lord Algernon had access to the gem collections everywhere: in Rome, the Vatican, and Barberini, Strozzi and Bracciano families; in Naples, the duc de Caraffa Noia;[13] in Florence, the Grand Duke of Tuscany. These set the standard for Lord Algernon's acquisitions. While in Rome they could buy from James Byres and his partner Christopher Norton, and also from Thomas Jenkins (1722–98), a Welshman who was alleged to have his own workshop forging ancient gems in the Colosseum.[14] According to Thomas Jones, Jenkins 'by purchasing and selling at his own prices Old Pictures, Antique Gems and Sculpture with the profits of a lucrative banking house – was enabled to vie with the Roman nobility in splendour and magnificence.'[15] Since Lord Algernon was rich, he could purchase almost anything he pleased, his only rivals being Russians, usually collecting on behalf of Catherine the Great. As the news spread, gems were offered from various parts of Italy, and it was a Neopolitan courier who brought him an amethyst fragment intaglio of the head of Hercules (or Omphale), signed by the great Dioscourides (**91**).

12. L. Dutens, *Découvertes attribuées aux Modernes*, vol. 2 (Paris 1766) 219: 'Si nous admirons les Anciens dans les monuments qui nous restent de leurs grandes entreprises, nous n'avons pas moins occasion de les admirer dans la dexterité et l'habileté merveilleuse de leurs Artistes dans des entreprises d'une espèce toute opposée. Leurs travaux en petit méritent aussi notre attention.'

13. Giovanni Carafa (1715–68), Duca di Noia, Professor of Mathematics at Naples University, collected Greek vases displayed in his library, absorbed into that of the King of Naples, also natural history, art works, antiquities. Our Prometheus intaglio (**129**) has this provenance. The Egyptian scarabs he sold to Sir William Hamilton are now in the British Museum. Cf. C.L. Lyons, 'The Museo Mastrilli and the Culture of Collecting in Naples 1700–1755' *Journal of the History of Collections* 4.1 (1992) 1–26.

14. J.T. Smith, *Nollekens and His Times* (London 1898) 222.

15. 'Memoirs of Thomas Jones' (see n. 11), 94.

It is significant that a high proportion of his purchases, like this Hercules, were damaged, but Lord Algernon was taught by Dutens that the beauty of these exquisite fragments mattered more than their condition. Some he left in their fragmentary state, others were filled in with gold, for, as Dutens said, 'la beauté de la gravure méritoit la réparation en or' ('for its fine quality the engraving deserved to be restored in gold'). Although aware of the flourishing school of contemporary engraving, Lord Algernon's preference was always for the ancient gems, following Dutens, who declared that 'Nos graveurs en pierres fines n'approchent point encore de la beauté des gravures des anciens artistes don't il nous restent des ouvrages en pierres gravées et en camées si recherchés pour la beauté et la finesse d'exécution' ('The modern engravers cannot match the finesse and beauty of the cameos and intaglios of the ancient artists which are so sought after today'). They made an exception of Giovanni Pichler: 'né a Rome d'un père allemand a été le plus habile graveur en pierres fines parmi les modernes sans excepter Natter. Il a plus d'un autre approché de la perfection des anciens. Je lui ai entendu dire qu'avec tout l'application qu'il avait toujours mise a imiter les grandes maîtres de l'antiquité il n'osait pas se flatter que le meilleur de ses ouvrages arrivât à égaler leurs ouvrages médiocres. Son ambition étoit cependant de travailler à faire quelque chose qui pût être cru antique' ('Born in Rome, the son of a German father, he is certainly the most talented of all the modern gem engravers, not excepting Lorenz Natter. More than any other he approaches the perfection of the ancient masters. I have heard him declare that try as hard as he could to reach their standard, he had to admit that even his very best work was only as good as an average ancient gem. However, his dream was to produce a gem that would be believed to be ancient').[16] Another exception was made of Nathaniel Marchant (1730–1816), who was in Rome 1773–88. From him Lord Algernon acquired, besides other gems, a cornelian intaglio bust of Antinous (**101**), copied from the marble relief 'au dessous d'une cheminée que les connoisseurs estiment a juste titre le plus beau relief de l'antiquité' ('now placed on the wall above a chimney piece, connoisseurs consider it the finest of all the reliefs surviving from antiquity') in the Villa Albani, the Temple of Taste. As for the gems dating from the Renaissance in the collection, in most cases the high quality matches that of those believed to be ancient.

Catherine the Great of Russia has been mentioned, and her voracious collecting of gems had its effect on the composition of the Beverley collection. She heard of the collection and in 1786, through her agent in Britain, Count Semyon Vorontsov, she paid an undisclosed sum for 'the best' of them (Kagan 156). Many of the Beverley gems thus went to St Petersburg, where they can be recognised as 'ex-Beverley'. Catherine complained that she had not in fact been sent 'the best', and here the role of James Tassie has to be considered. Tassie had worked for a while with Dr Quin in Dublin, where they

16. L. Dutens, 'Dutensiana' in *Mémoires d'un voyageur qui se repose*, vol. 3 (Paris 1806) 171–3.

had perfected a means of copying ancient gems in a paste-glass. Several of Quin's paste gems were in Lady Elizabeth's collection. When Tassie returned to London he started a collection of moulds from which he could produce the paste gems for sale. His first catalogue, of 1775, contained 3106 items, of which only one was declared a 'Percy' (his no. 956). He moved to Edinburgh and in 1791 published a new catalogue, of 15,800 pieces, described by R.E. Raspe (also the author of Baron Munchhausen's adventures). In it are listed many in the collection of Lord Algernon Percy, with the comment that part of the collection was now in Russia. Many of those in St Petersburg are indeed fine, but Algernon's finest, notably the cameos from the Rohan-Chabot collection, were only acquired after the date of Catherine's purchase. Her complaint was based on what she saw of Tassie's collection – she was his patron and encouraged his enterprise. Tassie's catalogue included many of the gems still at Alnwick, those that went to St Petersburg, and a number of others that have yet to be located. The whereabouts of these is not known – lost, given away or sold, but so far as we can see not in any sale catalogue or collection known to us. We shall publish separately these travelled and lost gems.

At Alnwick few intaglios in the collection remain in their original settings, because they were almost always melted down for their value as bullion. An exception is the ring said to be from the tomb of one of the Scipios, set with a cornelian intaglio of Victory (**166**). In 1783, after the publication of his genealogy of the Scipios, Louis Dutens was presented with this ring by Pope Pius VI (reigned 1775–99) through the intermediary of the Superintendent of Antiquities, G.B. Visconti, who had discovered it in the tomb, which is in the Vatican.[17] In his turn Dutens gave the ring to Lord Algernon, whose grandson, the 6th Duke, valued it so highly that in 1867 he paid for copies to be made: one is in the Fitzwilliam Museum,[18] another was sent to the Vatican antiquary's grandson, Pietro Ercole Visconti.[19] A Renaissance style ring with the bezel supported by a group of lively putti, is in the sculptural style associated with Benvenuto Cellini (**251**). The quality of the 18th-century ring settings designed for the gems is excellent. Most are surrounded by severe Roman borders, as recommended for collectors by P.J. Mariette, but others are more decorative, suggesting that they were not just kept in a collector's cabinet but were displayed by both men and women. There is evidence too that Lord Algernon liked to seal his correspondence with a gem set in a signet ring, kept ready for use on his finger,[20] and when writing to Isabella, Dutens often adds a comment on her seals and his own. His verdict on the Genius of Prudence, which sealed Lady Beverley's last letter from Naples in 1802, was frank: 'tolerable, not well finished, a little affected in the attitude', and another time he writes 'my mask and everything that I have is much at Lord Algernon's service and he may command it when we meet. The weather is so hot it melts all seals so I could not well inspect your last, and I suppose that my fine great grass-

17. Northumberland Archives, Add. Mss. F/20/1 (322) etc., letters from James Byres to Dutens saying Visconti had asked him to despatch the ring, which he would do through Sir Horace Mann in Florence; from G.B. Visconti to Dutens, draft of Dutens' letter thanking the Pope with 'autant de vénération que de reconnaissance' for the gift. Dutens account 'Memoirs of the late Rev. Lewis Dutens' was published posthumously in *The Gentleman's Magazine* (1812) vol. 82, Part 2, 391–7.

18. *Cambridge* no. 837.

19. Northumberland Archives, Add. Mss. F/95 (430), thanking the Duke for'la bellissima imitazione dell'antico anel'. Visconti appreciates it for its archaeological and family interest, and because it is a reminder of a happy period in Roman life, unfortunately vanished.

20. Northumberland Archives, Add. Mss. F/39/1 (321), letter to George Percy 1782, sealed with an intaglio of a horse grazing.

hopper that will seal this will reach you flat as a pancake.'[21] In recognition of their importance, several ancient cameo portraits (**58, 64, 65** and the scene of the return of Ulysses, **7**) are mounted, probably by the London jeweller, Rundell, Bridge and Rundell, in gold frames within the lids of lightweight tortoiseshell snuff boxes and bonbonnières for Lord Beverley to carry in his pocket. Famous for the elegance and suavity of his manners, he would choose the right moment to show off one of these rarities so that the miniature marble-like heads and 'Ulysses telling his story' would provide a talking point with other collectors. Since there is a pin fitted on the back of the magnificent cameo of the young Octavian/Augustus marking the victory of Actium, set in a decorative octagonal gold frame outlined in royal blue enamel, this indicates that it was also taken out of the cabinet and worn as a brooch (**6**), as was the majestic sixteenth-century Cleopatra commesso (**1**).

Whereas most of the Grand Tourists were only buying works of art as mementoes of their travels in Italy and did not continue to collect them, Lord Algernon's interest in engraved gems was to endure. Away from Italy there were still purchases to be made in London, which was rapidly establishing itself as a centre of the art market. From the many letters Dutens wrote to Lord Algernon and his wife it is clear that he acted as an extra pair of eyes and ears for them, acquiring books for their library as well as buying gems on their behalf. He viewed the auction sales, where he dismissed most gems available as 'modern trash, disgusting to look at'. After a view of antique rings at Christie's in March 1790, said to be from a French nobleman, he reported, 'There was not one antique amongst them and the Modern were, every one, some of the vilest stuff I ever saw so that I did not stay for the sale.' He discusses the possibility of purchasing a Maecenas portrait from the Sir Thomas Rumbold sale of 18 February 1792, and various other gems from the collection of James Hugh Smith Barry, a protégé of Charles Towneley, on 15 February 1802. Sulphurs and impressions were exchanged with Towneley and another keen collector, the Rev. Clayton Mordaunt Cracherode.[22] In March 1801 he acquired for £350 the very fine fragmentary Livia cameo (**74**) from Sir William Hamilton, whose wedding with Emma he attended in 1791.[23] Others were bought from Charles Greville, Sir William's nephew, and from T.M. Slade.[24] His friendship with the dealers of Rome continued as they made a point of visiting their English clients at home. In June 1787 James Byres and his partner Christopher Norton brought a box to London containing six fine intaglios including 'Satyress with baby satyr in her hands, a subject that is as scarce as it is well treated'. From them he purchased for £120 on 3 September 1791 the delightful 'Toilette of Bacchus' from the collections of Pope Paul II and of Lorenzo de'Medici (**10**), and enthuses 'a very elegant cameo. The composition is beautiful, the fawn is much in the same attitude as Achilles in the death of Patrocles of as exquisite workmanship: and yet was if shown to any one who is

21. Northumberland Archives, n.d. but before 1786.

22. *Ibid.*, letter from Dutens, 3 July 1788: 'Mr. Towneley who is in raptures with Lord Lovaine's purchase of Jenkins's ring, showed an impression of it to Cracherode who admires it exceedingly. Both applied to me for a sulphur of it.'

23. *Ibid.*, 19 March 1801: letter from Dutens to Lady Beverley: 'Sir William Hamilton has brought only two or three cameos and no intaglios. One of the cameos is a beautiful head of Livia on a fine sardonyx of three colours, the Veil is made out of the first layer, the face of fine white is the second and the third of a fine black is the ground – £350. The other is a very fine Bacchante head and body down to the hips, white and black, £400.'

24. See Spilsbury.

not a connoisseur the first reflexion would be not on its beauty but 'oh! Laud! It is crac'd and may be afterwards: what a pity it is crack'd.' He would certainly have seen Thomas Jenkins, who also brought objects for sale to England, reporting on 3 July 1788 that 'I have not seen him but Mrs. Damer told me he has some beautiful cameos.' The London shops were not neglected. Dutens mentions gems bought at William Pickett of The Golden Salmon, Ludgate Hill, from a Mr Martin, broker of King Street, Covent Garden,[25] and a Morland who was selling a cameo for the maintenance of a 'poor deranged French emigrant'. Always an admirer of Giovanni Pichler, he advises the acquisition of a Pichler jacinth of Venus rising from the sea, on sale for 30– 25 guineas at jeweller Lever in Bruton Street, Golden Square, and in 1788 and 1789 asks Nathaniel Marchant to give Lord Algernon first refusal of any gems he has for sale. Also contemporary are the cameos set in two rings marking the death in 1789 of Mrs Burrell, grandmother of Lady Beverley and of her sister, wife of the 2nd Duke of Northumberland. These memorial gems may well have been executed in London following the advice of Dutens (**54, 55**).

Another important source emerged as a result of the French Revolution, which brought emigrants to England hoping to sell engraved as well as precious stones. Dutens watches out for the arrival of the antiquarian Abbé Tressan 'with Cargo of Medals and Antiques', and asks the Vicar General of the Archbishop of Bordeaux (from whom he had acquired a Tiberius cameo for £40) to 'beat the drum amongst emigrants for who has cameos to sell'. From the French expert Alphonse Miliotti came Lord Beverley's greatest coup, the acquisition of the cameos acquired in 1790 from the connoisseur duc de Rohan-Chabot (d. 1807), published in the sixteenth century by Aenea Vico (except for **20**), from the collection of Cardinal Grimani (**3**, **6–9**, **20**, **34**). According to Dutens, Miliotti, in charge of the collection of the Prince de Conti, was highly regarded in France where 'he has put them here quite in the taste of antiques and there are now a great number of collectors who have some very fine things.'[26]

Detained in France after the rupture of the Treaty of Amiens, widowed in 1812, plagued by gout and ill health, Lord Beverley seems to have remained there, living quietly first at Moulins, then at Le Mans near Nice, until he died in 1830. His eldest son George looked after his business affairs, and as the surviving correspondence contains almost no references to acquisitions of works of art, there is no proof that Lord Beverley bought the Girometti cameo figure of Napoleon at the height of his glory (**2**), which could have entered the Northumberland collection at the same time as the set of Napoleonic medals.[27] However, it is hard to believe that he gave up completely after thirty years dedicated collecting. The gems were bequeathed to his younger son, Hugh, Bishop of Carlisle (1784–1856), and impressions were made of them by Tommaso Cades in 1834 so as to diffuse knowledge of the collection.[28] As for George,

25. Northumberland Archives, Add. Mss. F/14/1, letter from Dutens, relating to the discovery of a Lucretia carved in a ruby, bought from Mr Martin's, broker's shop 'where I have found Treasures of Antiquity. Take notice of my seal it is a Lucretia of the best Greek work, on a rubi worth a mountain of gold, there is nothing in the King of France's collection equal to this.'

26. Northumberland Archives, letter from Dutens to Lady Algernon Percy from Paris, n.d.

27. European Historical Medals From the Collection of His Grace the Duke of Northumberland, London, 3 December, 1980. A Fine Series of Silver Medals from A.-L. Millin de Grandmaison *Medallic History of Napoleon*, part 1, (London 1819) nos 344–90.

who inherited the Beverley title and in 1865 was to succeed as 5th Duke of Northumberland at the age of 87, in a letter of 1782 Lord Beverley refers to the boy's love of antiques and sends him a 'very pretty antique ring'. School reports from Eton praise his mastery of 'the Greek and Latin authors, Homer, Virgil, Horace, Lucian, Euripedes and Cicero' and he grew up to be very scholarly, served as a Trustee of the British Museum for many years, and was a friend of W.R. Hamilton,[29] who had assumed the role of Dutens as friendly adviser. With his wife and daughter Louisa he visited Rome and Naples frequently in the 1820s and 1830s, and kept a detailed day by day account of the antiquities and monuments he saw, referring to Latin texts and Edward Gibbons' *Decline and Fall of the Roman Empire*. We also know that he bought gems, for in August 1834 he lists 29 gems 'bought by me'. His main source was the well-known Roman dealer, Francesco Capranesi of the via Condotti no. 43, though he also made several acquisitions in Vicenza as well as a chalcedony head of Somnus discovered by a peasant girl near Bracciano, offered by her brother. He describes each stone, the subject depicted, the material and the price paid. Some were given to his friends, such as his Northumberland neighbour, Lord Howick, who succeeded his father as the 3rd Earl Grey in 1845, and received a Venus and Cupid intaglio. At the end of the list he makes it clear that he made these gifts because he regarded this collection 'not as heirlooms, but his own property' to dispose of as he wished.[30] In these circumstances it is unlikely that any of his gems are now at Alnwick, and none of those in the 1834 list can be identified. However, having grown up with his father's collection and knowing it well, he notes that a nicolo intaglio of a 'sheep with a poppy', from Vicenza, was another version of the Beverley gem found in an Essex field (**264**). He must surely have been disappointed by his father's bequest of the gem collection to his younger brother, for there can be no doubt of his deep attachment to classical art and Roman civilisation. Using the words of the dramatist Vittorio Alfieri to express his regret at leaving the city after the Carnival in 1823, he laments: 'infelice che sono oggi, parto da Roma.'

Some gems, kept separate from the Beverley Gems, were discovered by the 10th Duke in 1979,[31] which therefore had been omitted from Alfred Knight's catalogue (1921). A few were part of the collections of the 1st Duchess and of Lord Beverley, but some may also have been acquired by other members of the family who also had a penchant for gems. The box contained, for instance, the citrine hour-glass shaped seal (**280**) engraved at one end with a bee, symbol of diligence, and the other with a coronet and initial P: this would have hung on a chain beside the watch of Earl Percy (1792–1816), later known as Lord Prudhoe (1816–47), and who succeeded as 4th Duke (1847–1865). Although the golden age of discriminating connoisseurship was passing, and public institutions were taking the place of the aristocratic buyer of antiquities, fashionable women continued to display engraved gems in up-to-date jewelled

28. *Bullettino dell'Instituto di Corrispondenza Archeologica* (Rome 1834) includes Beverley Gems in the catalogue of impressions newly acquired by the German Institute in Rome from Tommaso Cades.

29. W.R. Hamilton (1777–1859), Secretary to Lord Elgin, in 1816, obtained the Rosetta Stone in Egypt for the British Museum, friend of Benedetto Pistrucci (1783–1855) who engraved his cameo portrait, ambassador to the court of Naples 1822–25, founder of the Royal Geographical Society in 1833, Trustee British Museum 1838–54.

30. Northumberland Archives DP/DS/3/16. Among the 'Old lists of gems' put together by the 7th Duke in 1899.

31. Private communication, dated 26 March 1979, to the present writer. In another letter dated 1987 he wrote: 'I found another small box of unmounted gems.' These could be the glass copies of the portrait gem of the 1st Duke, buried with the Duchess; see below, Glass Intaglios.

settings. Charlotte Florentia, wife of the 3rd Duke, who is recorded as buying an onyx cameo ring surrounded by diamonds from Rundell, Bridge and Rundell in 1825, owned a cameo portrait of Queen Elizabeth I in a Holbein-esque pendant which is listed in her inventory of 1836 but is now missing, and a splendid parure, the necklace set entirely set with garnet cameos of the twelve Roman Emperors, the earrings and the belt clasp or brooch with a bust of the Sun god, and the top and drop earrings with busts of the Muses, both inscribed; this is still at Alnwick (see below, the Emperors Necklace). Her enthusiasm for engraved gems compares with that of the empress Josephine, who introduced the fashion for them during the Empire. As a young woman, the Duchess wore a cameo parure to the Duchess of Richmond's ball held in Brussels on the eve of the Battle of Waterloo. This consisted of five brooches, each set with a cameo bust of a woman with a diamond border, a pair of earrings, a smaller diamond and cameo brooch, and a necklace with five cameos in blue enamel and pearl frames linked by pearl chains. She bequeathed it to her niece, Lady Williams.[32]

Yet the story does not end with Charlotte Florentia's cameo jewellery. In 1879 the 6th Duke, grandson of the 1st Lord Beverley, agreed to buy the gems from Bishop Hugh's son, Algernon Charles Heber Percy (1812–1901), at a figure fixed by the British Museum, thus saving the collection from a possible dispersal,[33] as had been the fate of the Marlborough Gems. This decision to keep the Beverley Gems at Alnwick as a monument to the taste and learning of his enlightened family certainly justified Archbishop Benson's high opinion of the 6th Duke: 'he was always trying to do the right thing.'

(D.S.)

32. Sold, Christie's, London, *Jewels and Jewellery*, 14 July 1948, lot 79a.

33. The collection of casts and a mahogany collector's cabinet remained with the Heber Percy descendants until sold at Christie's, London, 1 November 1990, lots 16–28.

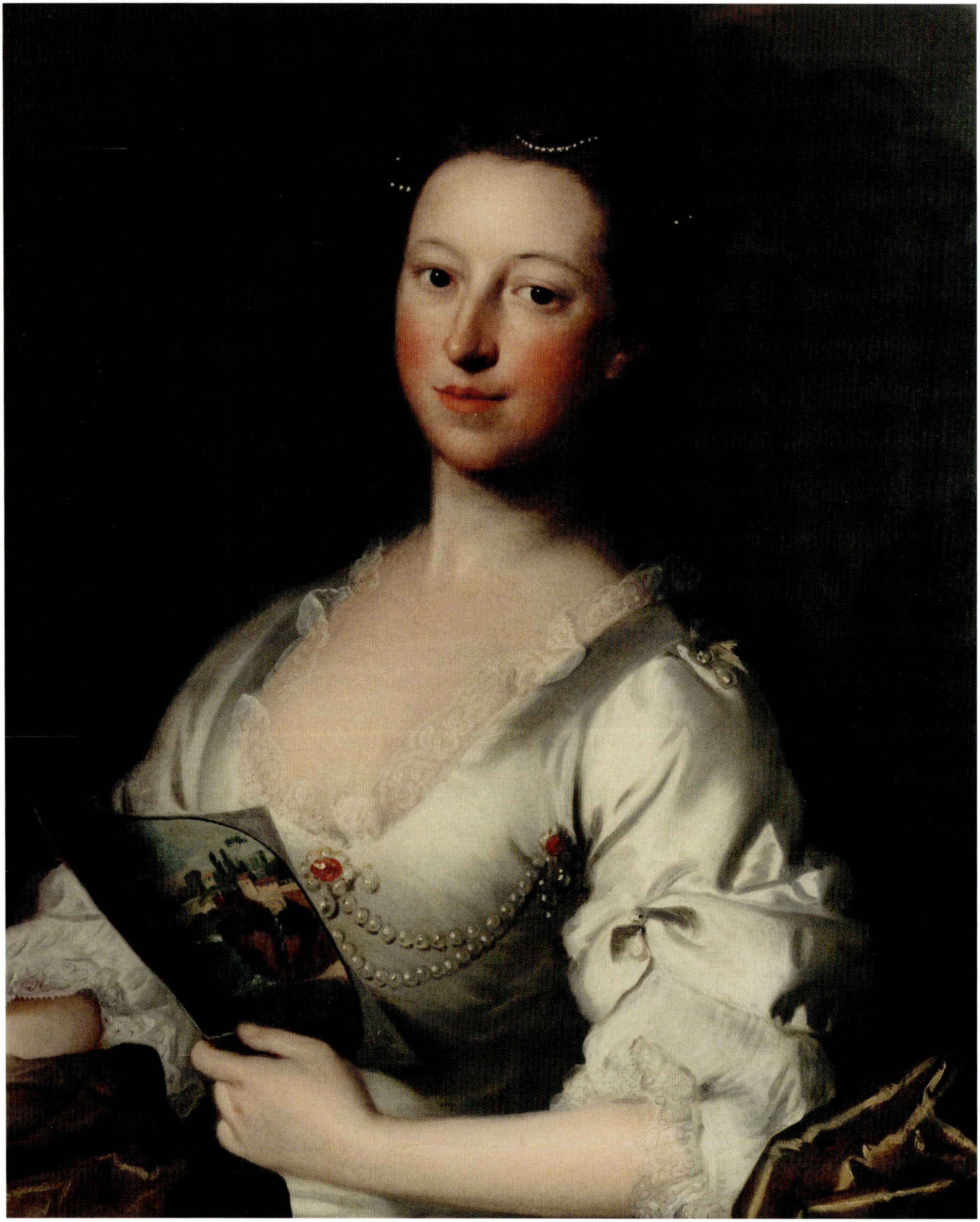

Fig. 4: Portrait of Elizabeth Percy (née Seymour), later 1st Duchess of Northumberland; by Allan Ramsay (1713–1784), painted in 1739. (Collection of the Duke of Northumberland, Alnwick Castle.)

THE 1ST DUCHESS' COLLECTION

Elizabeth Seymour Percy (1716–76), the 1st Duchess of Northumberland (the third creation of the dukedom title), was, on her marriage, already an heiress of the Percy family, who were for centuries Earls of Northumberland. Thus, her husband, Hugh Percy, became Earl, then 1st Duke, of Northumberland when her father died in 1766. Hugh was born Hugo Smithson. A cameo portrait of a youth by Giles Hussey appears on a paper, labelled 'Britannicus. Gemma antiqua exscalpt apud Hugonem Smithson Baronett.' This cameo is no. 1 in the Duchess' catalogue, where it is said to be from the collection of the Dukes of Mantua (i.e. formerly from the Gonzaga collection, on which see *Marlborough* ch. 1); and in the intaglio copy **225.** It was prepared for a publication but never used.

The Duchess collected gems, and there is a list of 37 cameos and 19 intaglios in her possession at Northumberland House in London, recorded by her in her nine-volume *Musaeum Catalogue* (transcribed below). Of her collection only six can be identified (some tentatively) in Knight's catalogue or at Alnwick. She also collected Tassie cameos. Most of her collection was sold at auction in the twentieth century, Northumberland House having been demolished in 1874 after parts of her collection had been distributed to Syon House, Alnwick and 17 Princess Gate, London. We are much indebted to Dr Adriano Aymonino (Buckingham University) for information about this catalogue and his publications about the Duchess' collection: A. Adriano, 'The *Musaeum* of the 1st Duchess of Northumberland (1716–1776) at Northumberland House in London: an Introduction' in *Women Patrons and Collectors* (eds S. Bracken, A.M. Galdy, A. Turpin, Newcastle 2012).

Dnp Ms 124, Musaeum Catalogue V: Cameo's, Intaglias, Bas Reliefs. Bronzes, Busts, Statues

CAMEOS

1. Head of Britannicus. Collection Dukes of Mantua. Gift of My Lord. Antique. Agathonyx. [see our **225**, a copy]
2. Ditto of Caius Caesar in a Ring. Gift of my Lord. Ditto [i.e., 'Antique']. Onyx. [our **69**]
3. Jupiter and Juno Ditto. Gift of My Lord. Antique. Onyx.
4. A female head in an old gold setting with two pearls. Antique. Onyx.
5. Cleopatra with ye Asp. My Lord. Antique. Jacynth. [probably our **1**]
6. A sleeping Dog in a ring. Given by My Fathers. Antique. Onyx.
7. An Amazon. Given by Mrs. F. Wyndham. Oyster shell.
8. Head of a Black with a Diamond collar in a ring. Onyx. Price £10.10.
9. George ye 2nd a la Romaine set with Emerald and Diamonds. Onyx.
10. St Cecilia playing on an Organ. Given by My Mothers. Flint.
11. An Old Man's Head in a Bonnet. Onyx.
12. Alexander the Great after the Antique. By Dr Quin. Enamel.
    [Dr Quin of Dublin invented a technique of creating glass copies of cameos. Tassie was for a while his assistant and helped perfect the techniques which Tassie employed for his sets of impressions and casts. His skills are commented on favourably by Raspe in Tassie, p. lviii.]
13. Antinous. Dr Quin. Enamel.
14. Antoninus Pius. Dr Quin. Enamel.
15. Aristophanes. Dr Quin. Enamel.
16. Cupid and Psyche. Dr Quin. Enamel.
17. Diomede. Dr Quin. Enamel.
18. A Faun. Dr Quin. Enamel.
19. Hercules young. Dr Quin. Enamel.
20. Ditto with a Lion's Skin. Dr Quin. Enamel.
21. Ditto with a large Beard. Dr Quin. Enamel.
22. The fall of Phaeton. Given me by the El[ecto]r [of] Cologne. Antique. Onyx. [our **12**]
23. Livia. Dr Quin. Enamel.
24. Stosch's famous Medusa. Dr Quin. Enamel.
25. Ditto less. Dr Quin. Enamel.
26. Minerva. Dr Quin. Enamel.
27. Ditto less. Dr Quin. Enamel.
28. A Muse a sitting figure. Dr Quin. Enamel.
29. Head of Plato, full faced. Dr Quin. Enamel.
30. Priam a profile. Dr Quin. Enamel.
31. Head of a Priest. Dr Quin. Enamel.

32. A Shell. Dr Quin. Enamel.

33. A kneeling figure of a Spartan soldier. Dr Quin. Enamel.

34. A Vestal an antique Figure. Dr Quin. Enamel.

35. Augustus and Livia. Given by Sir Thomas Robinson. Antique. Alabaster.

36. [bis]. 3 Profiles. Given by Lord Grevile. Onyx.

37. Orus [?] with 5 figures. Given by Lord Grevile. Onyx.

INTAGLIAS

38. Head of Titus. Given by my Granfathers. Antique. Black Agatha.

39. A Bacchante. Gift of my Lord. Antique. Beryl.

40. Hebe an entire figure. After the antique. Cornelian.

41. An Infant Hercules strangling ye Serpents. Copy from the K. of France. Paste.

42. Mars and Venus. Given by my Brothers. After ye Antique. Cornelian.

43. Leda and the Swan a large Blood Stone handle. Onyx.

44. Meleager. Gift of My Lord. Cornelian. [cf. our **156**]

45. Head of Lord Northumberland a l'Antique. White Cornelian. [cf. our no. **244**]

46. Ditto of M. Antoninus Large. Gift of My Mothers. Cornelian.

47. Ditto of Hussey's Washerwoman. Gift of My Lord. By Mr Wray. White Cornelian. [our **111**]

48. Medus from the Antique. Gift of My Lord. By Gobbo Costanzi. Cornelian. [see our **252**]

49. Head of Abubcher the Reverse Arabic Characters. Cornelian. [our **281**]

50. Heads of Socrates and Plato after the Antique. Paste.

51. A Figure suppos'd Phenician found in Irel[an]d. Extr[eme]ly Ancient. Onyx.

52. Head and Shoulder of Leander. Kerry Stone. [cf. our **230**]

53. Minerva a whole figure. Given by My Fathers. Antique, Bloodstone.

54. A little Genius with a Cornucopia. Given by My Fathers. Antique. Cornelian.

55. A Cock and a Cornucopia. Given by My Fathers. Black Agate.

56. A Shepherd piping to his Dogs. Cornelian.

RECORDS OF BEVERLEY GEMS, CASTS, ETC.

Apart from Tassie's set, other early collections of casts and impressions of the gems are known. A private collection in Italy (formed by the distinguished collector G. Sangiorgi) has a set of 187 casts, mounted in two boxes, with a Catalogue in Italian. Of these all but 26 can be identified at Alnwick. The set is not dated but is clearly 18th century. The casts are here referred to as SG.Imp. They are described as *Collezione di No. 187 Impronti cavate da Gemme incise della Collezione del Sigr. Conte di Beverley; No. 179 delle quali sono Gemme antiche, e No. 8 moderna, incise dai Incisori de nostri tempi, i piú distinti.* We are indebted to Annamaria Sangiorgi for the loan of these casts. In 1785 J. Spilsbury published *A collection of fifty prints from antique gems. In the collections of the Right Honourable Earl Percy, the Honourable C.F. Greville, and T.M. Slade, Esquire. Engraved by Mr. John Spilsbury.* Of these three (his nos 38, 41, 42) only one (our no. **136**) was at that time in the Percy collection, which, however, acquired others engraved by Spilsbury (our nos **77, 97, 124, 221**).

Tomasso Cades, an engraver of Rome, made a substantial collection of impressions, the original set of which is in the German Institute in Rome. There was a separate set made of the Beverley gems alone, 171 pieces, of which seven are not at Alnwick. References here are to the latter set (designated as Inst.Imp.). A comparable collection made in Italy by the brothers Paoletti includes in its first four volumes 28 Beverley gems, of which four are not at Alnwick. In the Cades set all gems appear in relief: cameos are casts of the original gem, intaglios casts of the impression.

In the mid-19th century Professor Nevile Story-Maskelyne pioneered the use of electrotyping for making accurate copies of gems and cameos. For his work see *Marlborough* 116–17. He must have visited Alnwick, since there are many electrotype copies of Alnwick cameos and intaglios in the collection of his impressions and electrotypes in the Beazley Archive, Oxford. They display detail very clearly and show the gem as direct copy of the original. Some are figured here if they seem to add something to our understanding of the motifs. In one case he went a stage further and produced a brassy electrotype in intaglio of a cameo (our **58**). We have occasionally added a picture of our own plasticine impression to some of the intaglios.

In 1921 Alfred D. Knight published privately *The Collection of Camei and Intagli at Alnwick Castle known as 'The Beverley Gems.' A descriptive Catalogue based upon Manuscript Notes in the possession of His Grace the Duke of Northumberland*. This included 210 items, the majority of which are illustrated in small photographs of originals (cameos) and casts. He includes comment on the history of some pieces and speculates about some subjects. His work is adequate without being thorough. There are now 281 items at Alnwick and it is not clear how many of these were acquired before or after Knight's catalogue.

The collection has not gone unnoticed by scholars. The Rev. C.W. King included drawings of many in his various books devoted to 'Antique Gems and Rings' in the later 19th century. Adolf Furtwängler refers to and illustrates pieces in the collection in his great study of ancient gems (1900), and later scholars have referred to pieces, usually knowing them only from publication, a notable exception being Marie-Louise Vollenweider, who visited the collection and took photographs for her gem books. The fullest modern presentation of gems at Alnwick has been the selection in the exhibition in Japan in 2008, *The Art of Gem Engraving* (here *AGE*) by Diana Scarisbrick, in which 76 items are illustrated in colour.

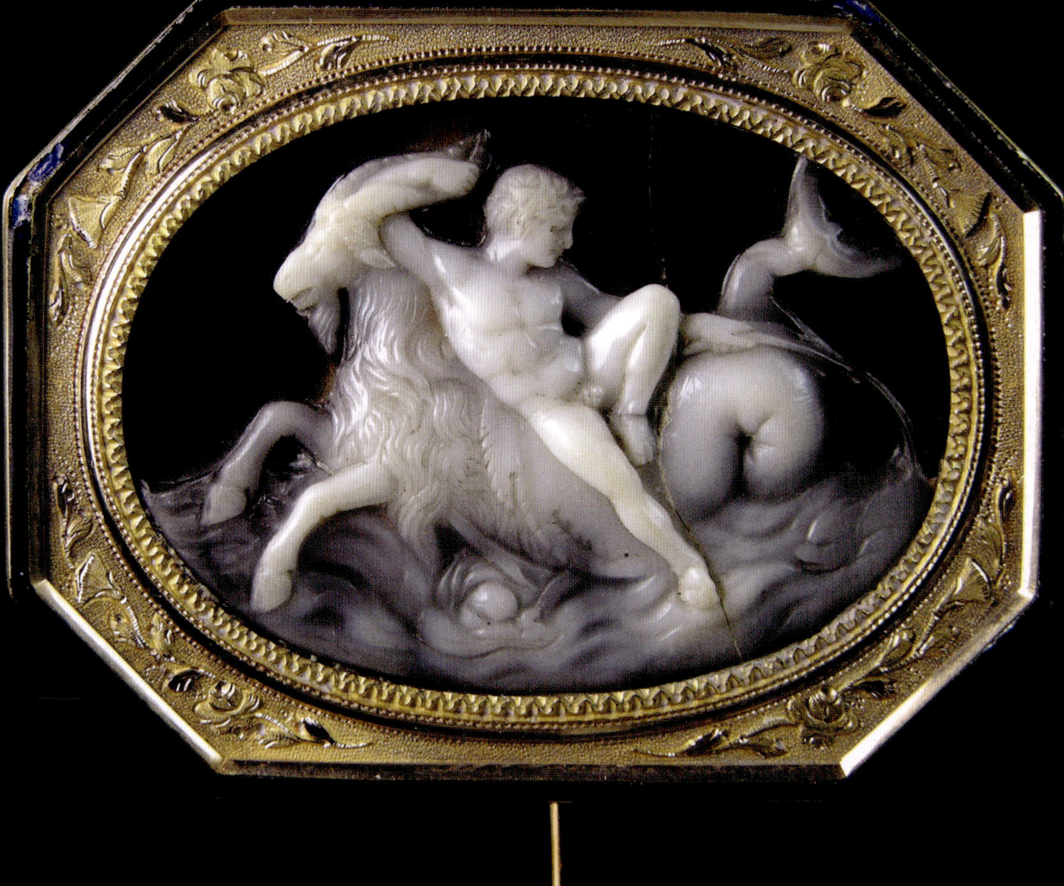

CATALOGUE OF THE GEMS AT ALNWICK CASTLE

CAMEOS

INTAGLIOS

THE EMPERORS NECKLACE

GLASS PORTRAITS

The collection at Alnwick comprises all the 'Beverley Gems' published by Knight in 1921 and 71 others.

We have not here kept the Knight pieces separate, since it cannot be assumed that all the others were acquired after Knight's book. In our publication the pieces are designated with the five-figure numbers of an Alnwick inventory and with Knight's numbers (prefix K). The gems are not at present exhibited and are kept in a number of boxes with trays.

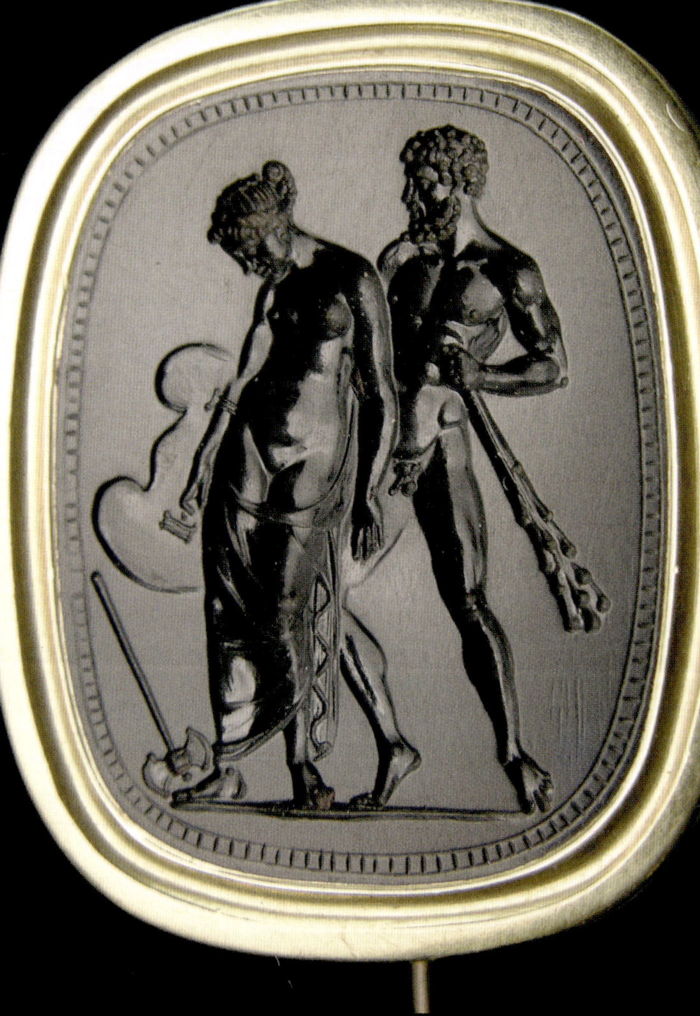

CAMEOS

WITH ARTISTS' NAMES (ANCIENT AND MODERN)

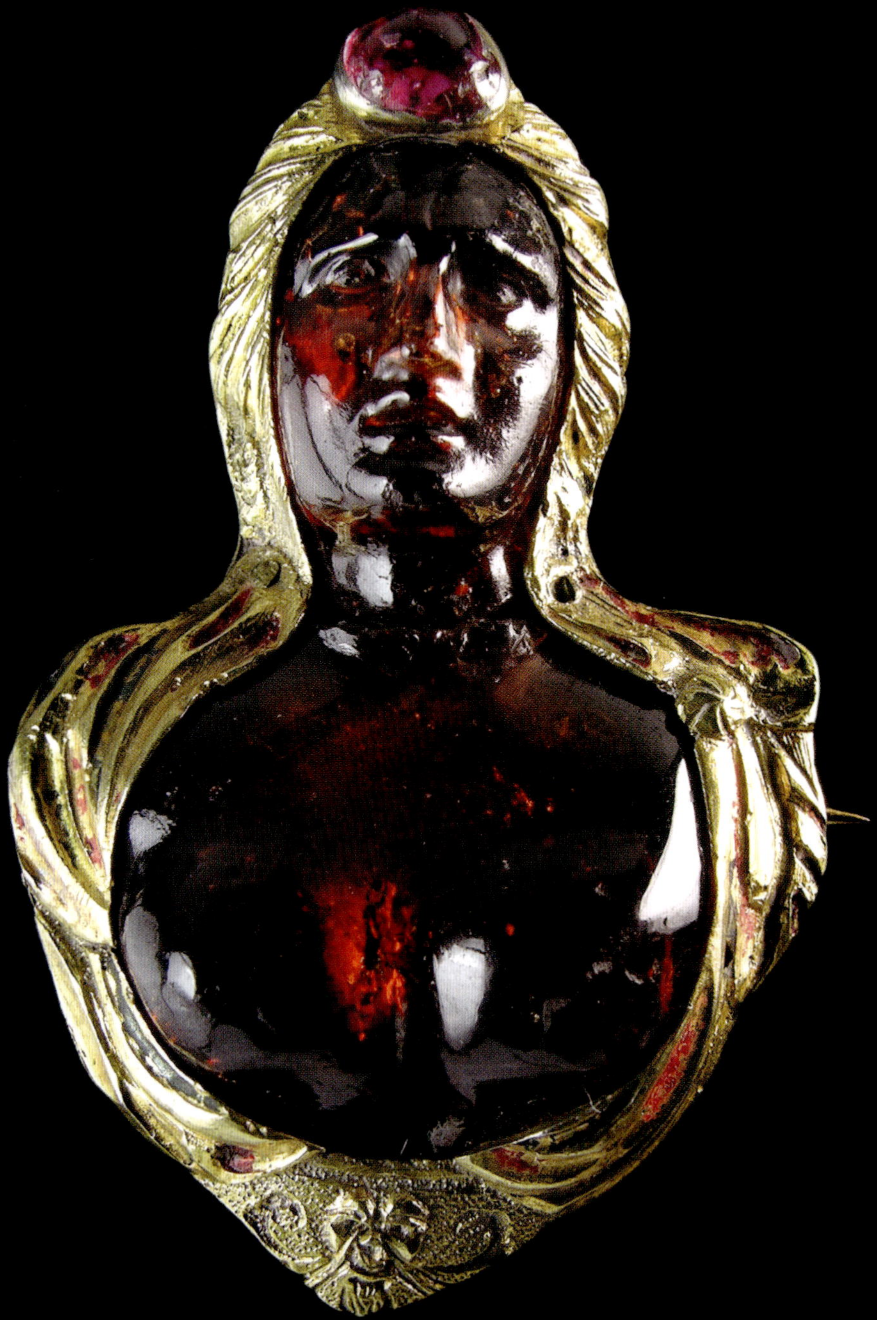

1

(10546) K8
Jacinth, ruby and gold, enamelled, set on a gold clasp; at either side of the neck there are attachments for a hoop (?)
Height 38

Tassie 12472 ('Mr Martyn', a London dealer); in the 1st Duchess' collection (no. 5; 'given by My Lord'); *AGE* no. 116 (as 'Venus').

The bust of a woman, naked, her hair and dress rendered in gold, knotted at the shoulder, a cabochon ruby set in her hair. The folds of her dress and the hair are enamelled in black and red. The belt front is patterned with a facing grotesque head and scrolls in low relief on a stippled ground. Marks between and below her breasts may indicate that a snake, an asp, probably made from enamelled gold, had been attached there, making the figure a Cleopatra, which is how she was described in the 18th century. She has an appropriately pained expression. (Alternatively the marks might have been from a garland, as on the rock crystal bust: Giuliano, *Cammei* p. 132, Florence). Inscribed on the flat gold back NASSARO.

Matteo del Nassaro worked in Italy and France, notably on cameos. Zerner 1969 illustrates examples of the heroic theme of Cleopatra as interpreted by the printmakers of the School of Fontainebleau, The Master L.D. (no. 24), Jean Mignon (no. 31) and Domenico del Barbieri (no. 8). This example is a *commesso*, a combination of carving and goldsmithing. For Nassaro see G.Vasari, *Le Vite de' più eccellenti pittori, scultori, ed architettori*, 1568 (enlarged edition): 1913 translation by Gaston C. de Vere, VI, 75–82. A comparable piece in St Petersburg (from the collection of St Morys, Paris, 1792) is a hessonite bust of a woman set in silver and gold, taken to be made in Augsburg and the setting in Milan (about 1560).

By Matteo del Nassaro (1515–47/8).

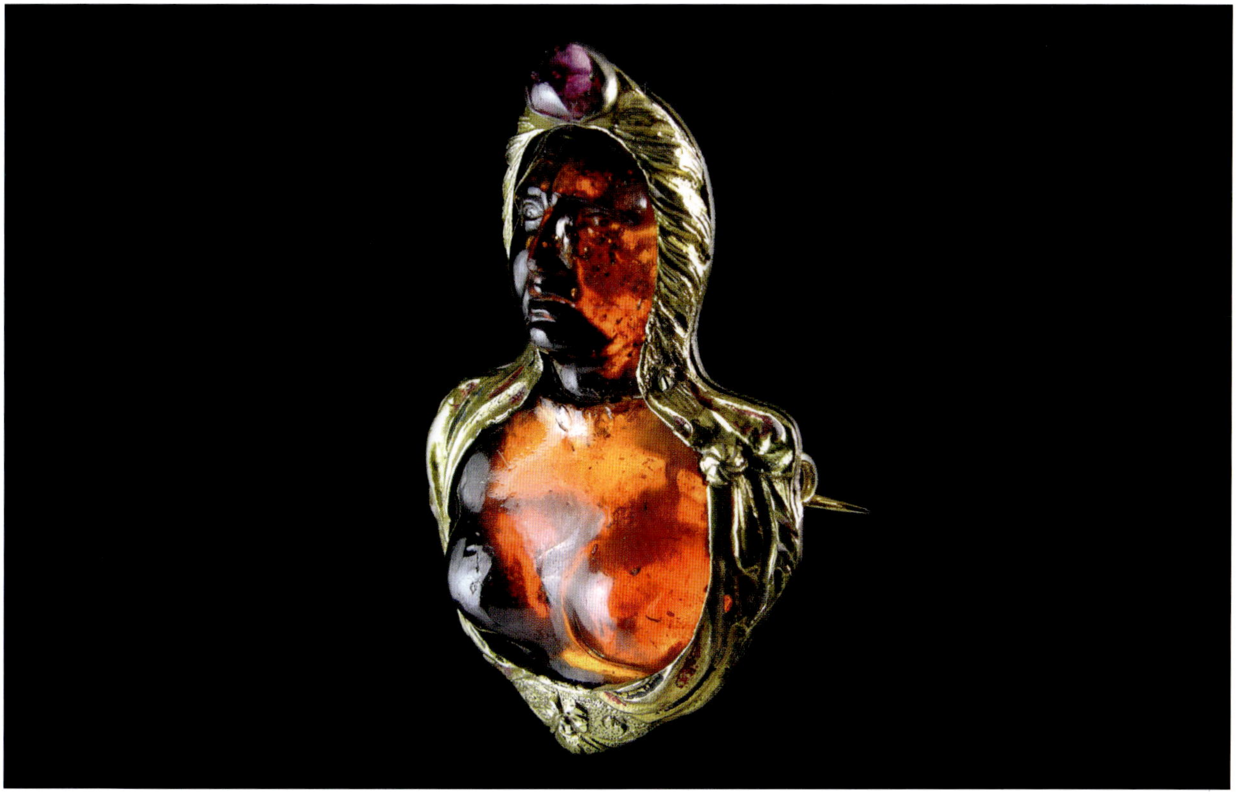

2

(10547) K9 (pl. 1)
Sardonyx, white/mottled brown, polished convex back, set in a gold pendant with stippled border
53 x 41

AGE no. 77; Kagan 2010, 156-7, fig. 8.30.

The Emperor Napoleon. He stands naked, but for a fig leaf, a brooched cloak over his left arm (its clasp at his armpit), which is raised holding a baton. On his outstretched right hand he holds a globe surmounted by the small figure of Victory holding a wreath, and the prop beside him is a tree stump with a sword and baldric draped over it. The cameo is signed GIROMETTI at the left border. Ground line.

A copy of the statue (1806) by Canova, of which the colossal marble version is now in the staircase hall of Apsley House, London, having been bought by the British Government in 1816 for £3,000 and given to the Duke of Wellington. The bronze version is in Milan. Napoleon had disliked the statue and hid it in the Louvre. Wellington also disliked the statue and placed it where it was not too conspicuous and could be damaged (see J. Boardman in *Reception of Classical Art* (ed. D.C. Kurtz, Beazley Archive 2004, 61, pl. 57). Napoleon is said to have wanted to be represented as Mars the peacemaker, but in effect he is simply a victor.

Giuseppe Girometti was a distinguished Roman engraver, and Napoleon was one of his patrons. There is an almost exactly similar cameo of the figure by Benedetto Pistrucci (d. 1855), who also made a cameo with the figure standing in a chariot and led by a flying Victory: Pistrucci 1989, II 81–2, nos 17 (Walker Art Gallery, Liverpool), 18 (Cab. des Médailles, Paris). A collection of Napoleonic medals was acquired by either Lord Beverley or his brother, the 2nd Duke (1786–1817).

By Giuseppe Girometti (1780–1851).

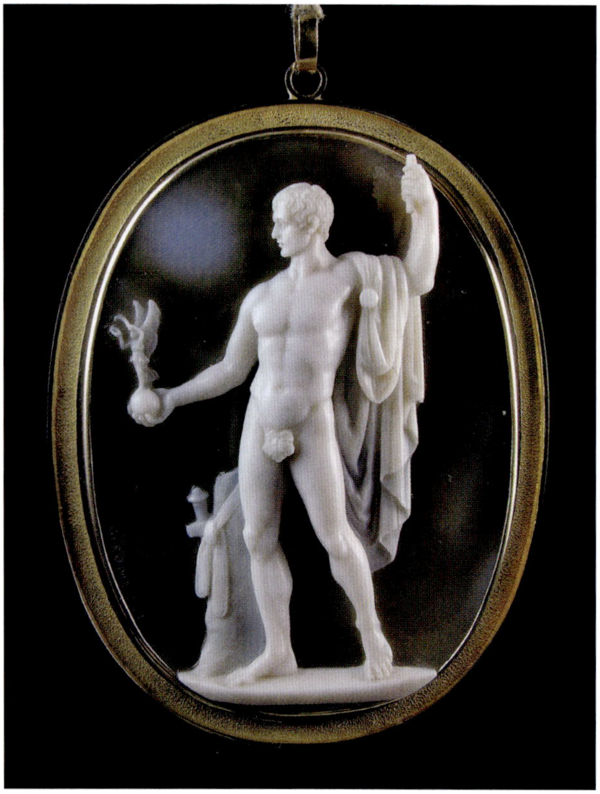

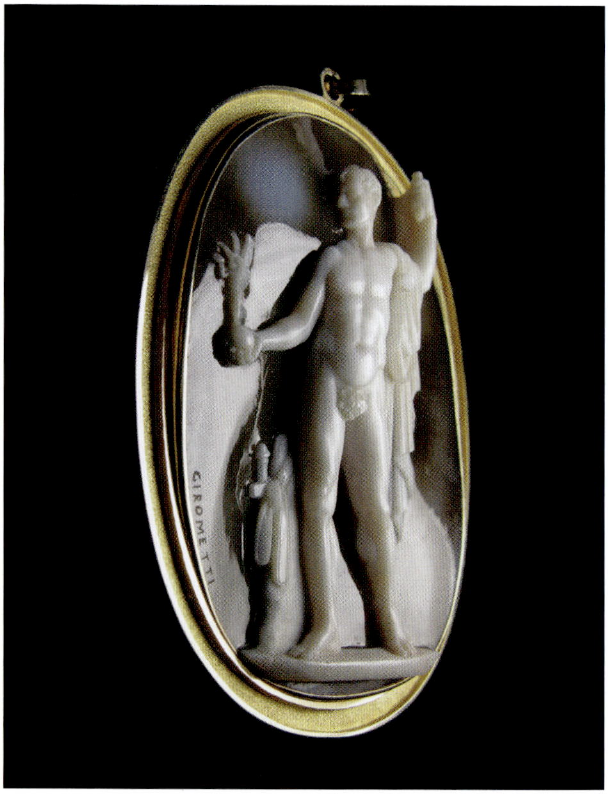

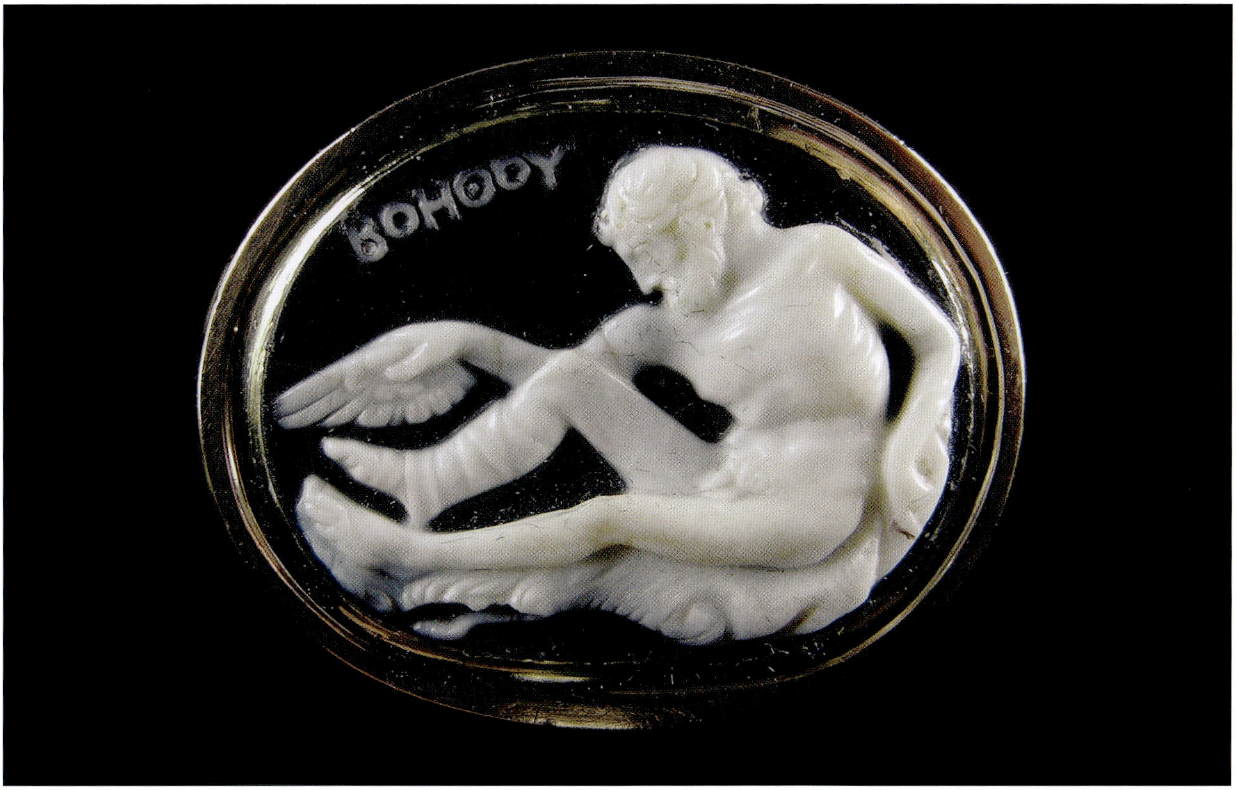

3

(10580) K42 (pl. 2)
Sardonyx, white/brown, set on a plain gold ring
20 x 16

Once Cardinal Grimani Collection; Vico, pl. 29.1, omitting inscription and taking the figure for a *philosophus stoicus*; SG.Imp. 100; Tassie 9357 ('en France'); Inst. Imp. no. 19; Cades, Cent. III, 83; King 1872, pl. 45.4; *AG* pl. 57.3; *LIMC* VII, 380, no. 34; Zazoff 1983, pl. 54.7; Zwierlein-Diehl, *AGN* 69–70, pl. 61.243; *AGE* no. 298.

Philoctetes, seated on an animal skin, fans his bandaged leg and poisoned foot with a feather. Inscribed in relief BOHΘOY, 'by Boethos'. Ground line.

An important Hellenistic cameo, the signature in relief, not incised. For the type compare *Berlin* no. 396; Lippold, pl. 41.15. An Etruscan version, Zwierlein-Diehl, *AGN* pl. 80.344. Copied by Renaissance artists: A.M. Schulz, *Giammaria Mosca* I (1998), 65–6, fig. 42; and for the pose and the left arm, by Michelangelo (see Sutherland op. cit. (below, on our **6**, 16f.)).

2nd century BC.

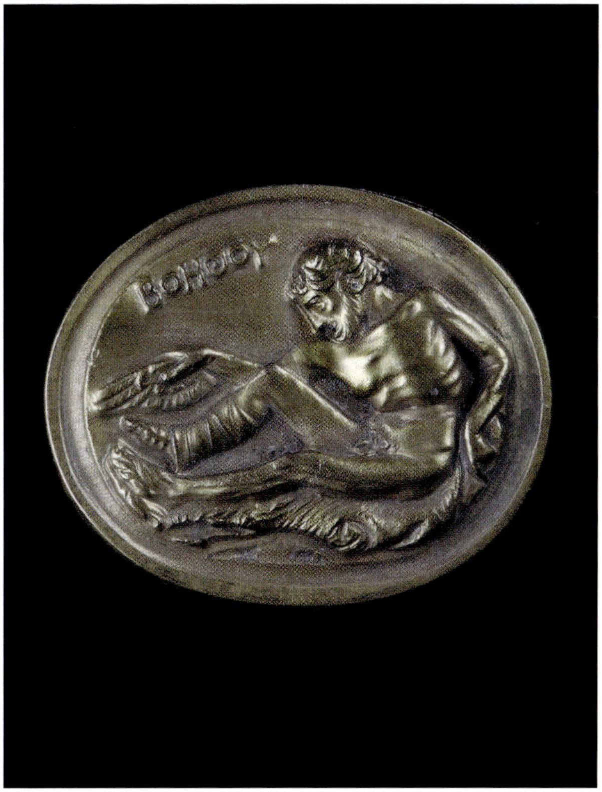

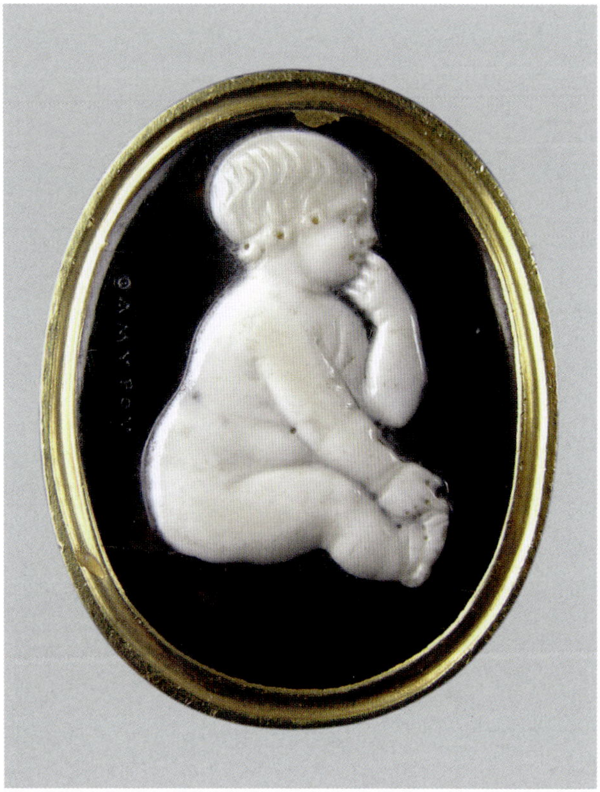

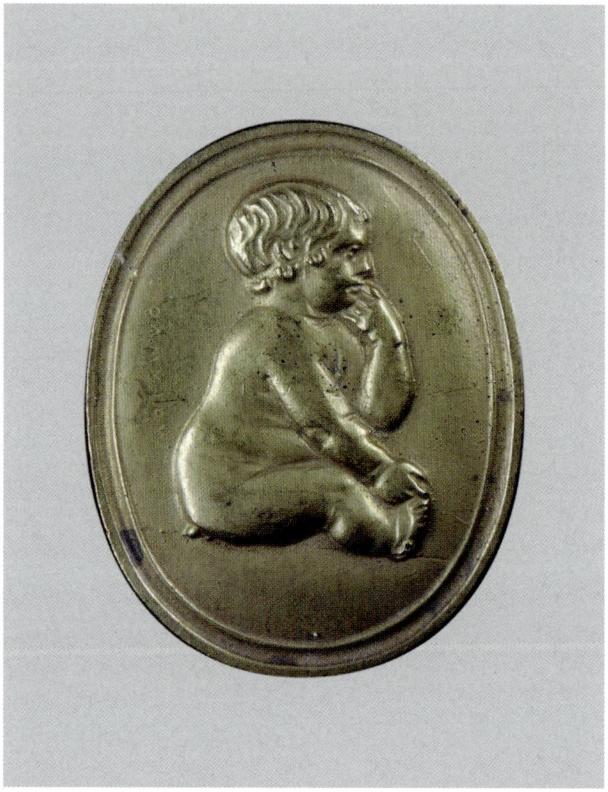

4

(10558) K20 (pl. 2)
Sardonyx, white/brown, polished flat back, set on a plain gold ring; the stone was cut off under the figure, where there may have been a lotus and replaced
23 x 17

SG.Imp. 143; Inst.Imp. no. 14; Paoletti I, I.681; Lippold, pl. 152.6; W.Tassie 123; Vollenweider, pl. 28.3,4; E. Zwierlein-Diehl, 'Thamyras-Gemmen', in H.-U. Cain et al. (ed.), *Beitr. zur Ikonographie und Hermeneutik, Festschrift N. Himmelmann* (Mainz 1989) 428, pl. 68.4 (on the name and date).

Harpocrates seated in the same pose as on our **49**, but his head is purely classical, without the hair lock, but with a central plait on his crown. An incised ground line. With the signature ΘΑΜΥΡΟΥ, 'by Thamyras'.

Thamyras was a gem engraver from the Augustan period (circle of Dioskourides). The name was much used in the 18th century (see E. Zwierlein-Diehl, op. cit., 425–31).

2nd/1st century (except inscription?).

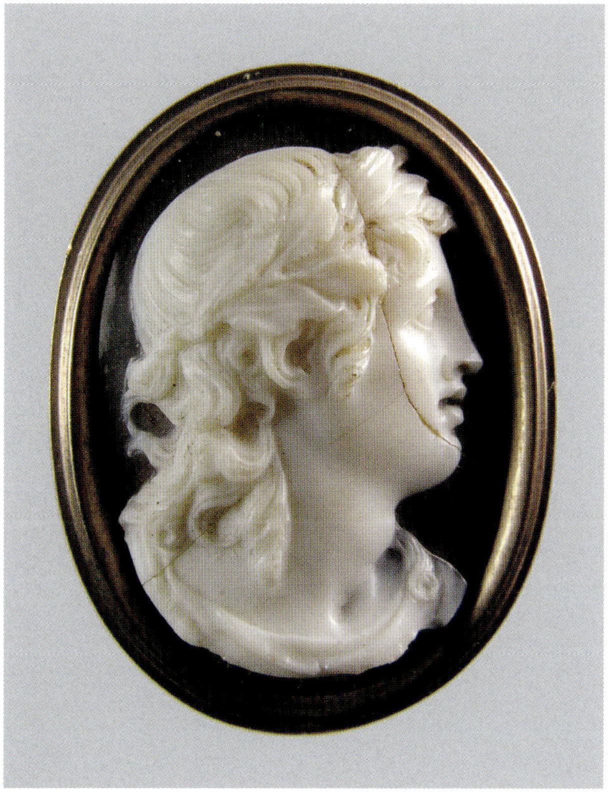

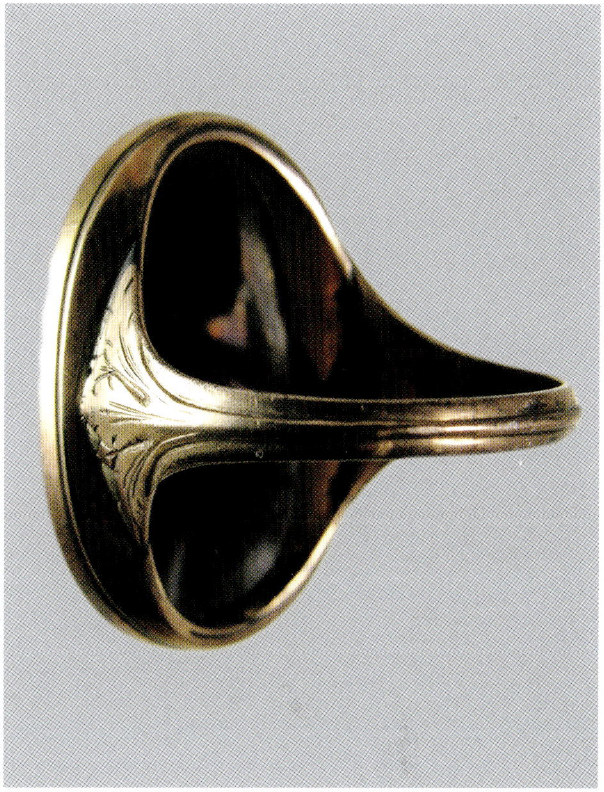

5

(10742) K204 (pl. 1)
Sardonyx, white/brown, set in a gold ring with leafy terminals
26 x 18

Head of a laureate Apollo with dress at his neck. Signed below the neck BHRINI.

Antonio Berini was a pupil of Giovanni Pichler and a prolific engraver who enjoyed the patronage of Luigi Sommariva.

By Antonio Berini (1770–1861).

GROUPS AND FIGURES

Several of the ancient cameos at Alnwick are from Renaissance collections and their subjects were the direct inspiration for the classicising works of various prominent Renaissance artists, including Michelangelo: see the discussion in Yuen 1997, esp. 140–7 (where the Knight pictures are copied, 142, fig. 13), and Sutherland (below, on our **6**). The most notable (**3, 6–9, 20, 34**) were in the collection of Cardinal Grimani (1461–1523), and several were engraved and published by Aenea Vico. On the Cardinal's collection see M. Perry, 'Cardinal Grimani's legacy of ancient art to Venice', *Journal of the Warburg and Courtauld Institutes* 41 (1978) 215–44, and for the group, J. Spier in *Classicism* 207, with fig. 6 and nos 21–2 for another example (*London*, Walters no. 3768; Hermaphrodite, Pan and satyr). On political motifs on gems of the Augustan period see also C. Maderna-Lauter in *Kaiser Augustus und die verlorene Republik* (Antikenmuseum, Berlin 1988) 441–73.

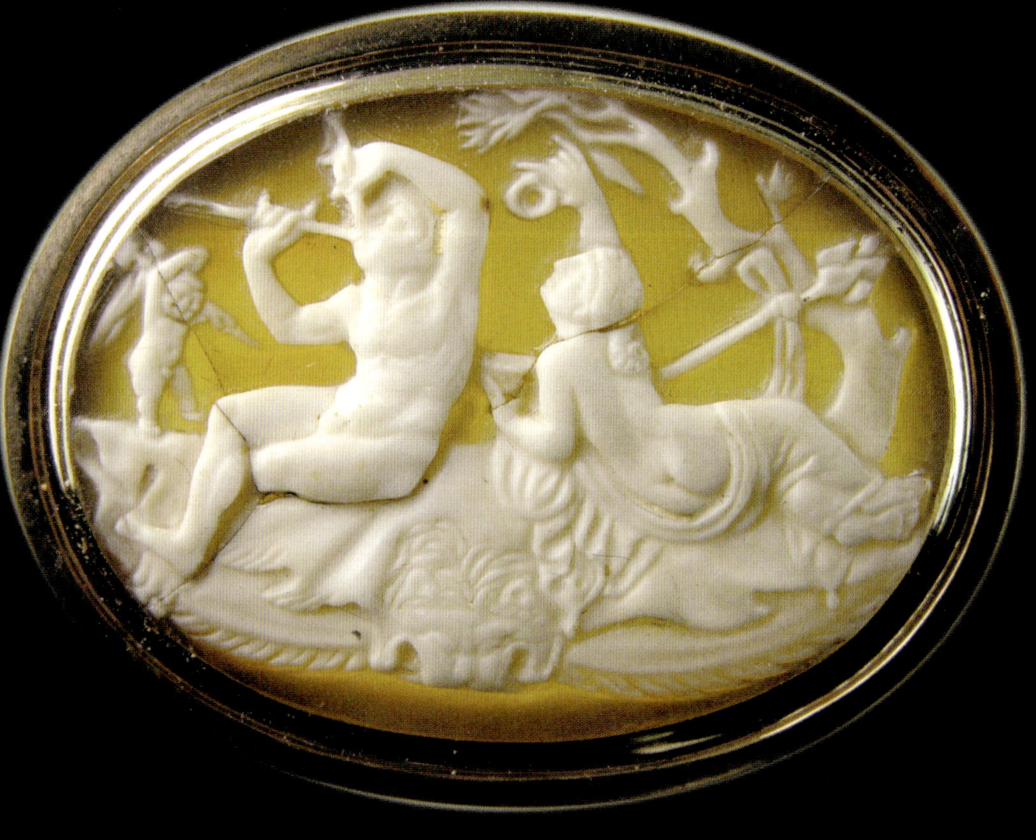

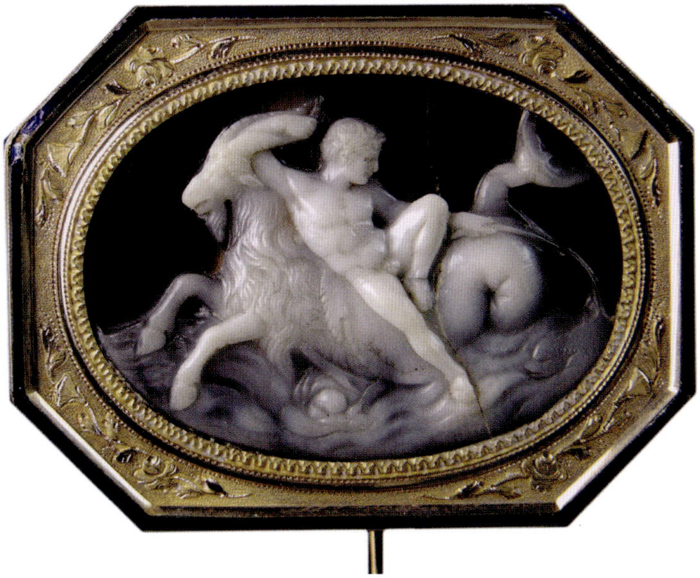

6

(10734) K196 (pl. 1)
Sardonyx, white/brown, polished convex back, set in an octagonal gold frame on a pin
32 x 23

Once Domenico di Piero (d. 1479); Cardinal Grimani Collection; Vico, pl. 33.1, where taken for Palaemon (who was associated with Daedalus, Vulcan and Athena) and shown beside a Daedalus gem, captioned *'Palemon et Dedalus excellentiam artis rapresentantes'*, and with the verse *'Quis vult Aequorum superare Palemona nando Vincet quis doctum Dedalon ingenio?'*; SG.Imp. 51; Inst.Imp. no. 3; Cades, Cent. IV, 13 *(satiro)*; King 1872, I, p. 254; *AG* pl. 50.46; Lippold, pl. 6.9; Vollenweider, 60, pl. 61.1,2; E. Simon, *Augustus* (Munich 1986) 158–9, fig. 210; Zwierlein-Diehl, *AGN* 130, 422, pl. 111, fig. 517; Yuen 1997, 144–5, fig. 17; Megow, 172–4, A33, pl. 7.20; *AGE* no. 10; B.D. Sutherland, 'Cameo Appearances on the Sistine ceiling', *Source: Notes in the History of Art* 2013, 14, fig. 1.

A naked youth riding a capricorn (goat-fish) over waves. He clasps one of the creature's horns and is fishing with a rod, which curves as it catches a small dolphin at the right. He is sitting on a hide with a serrated edge. Below him is the head of another dolphin.

Vollenweider (accepted by Megow) sees here the portrait of the young Octavian/Emperor Augustus, Capricorn being his birth sign, and the scene recalling his sea victory at Actium (31 BC). There is strong evidence that the victory was celebrated on cameos; see T. Hölscher, *Klio* 67 (1983) 81–102. Zwierlein-Diehl, op. cit., takes the figure for a Pan fishing, seeing pointed ears and horns (as had others); we think that neither pointed ears nor horns are intended, but the cutting of the hair is rather confused and that ears and horns, if intended, would have been more explicit. A Pan, however, is intended on the version on an hexagonal carnelian intaglio from Augsburg (Zwierlein-Diehl, op. cit., fig. 516). Vollenweider attributes the carving to Dioskourides. Sutherland points out that this Grimani/Vico gem must have been known to Michelangelo in Rome, and inspired his pose for Adam on the Sistine Chapel ceiling. The pose and subject are also far more vaguely recalled on a Renaissance cameo with Europa on the bull, and a relief with a child on a sea-horse (Yuen 1997, 199, fig. 5, and 145, fig. 18).

About 30 BC.

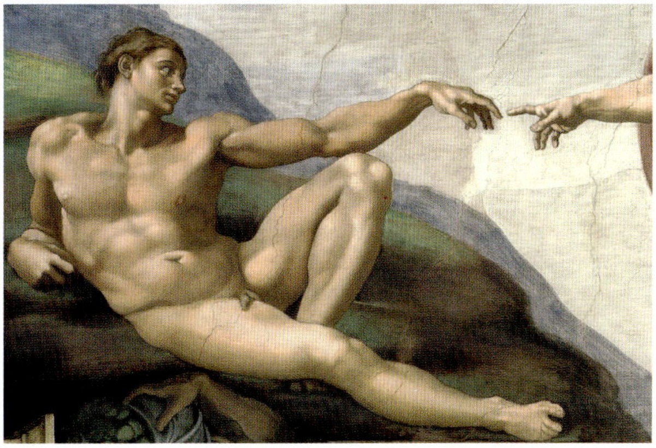

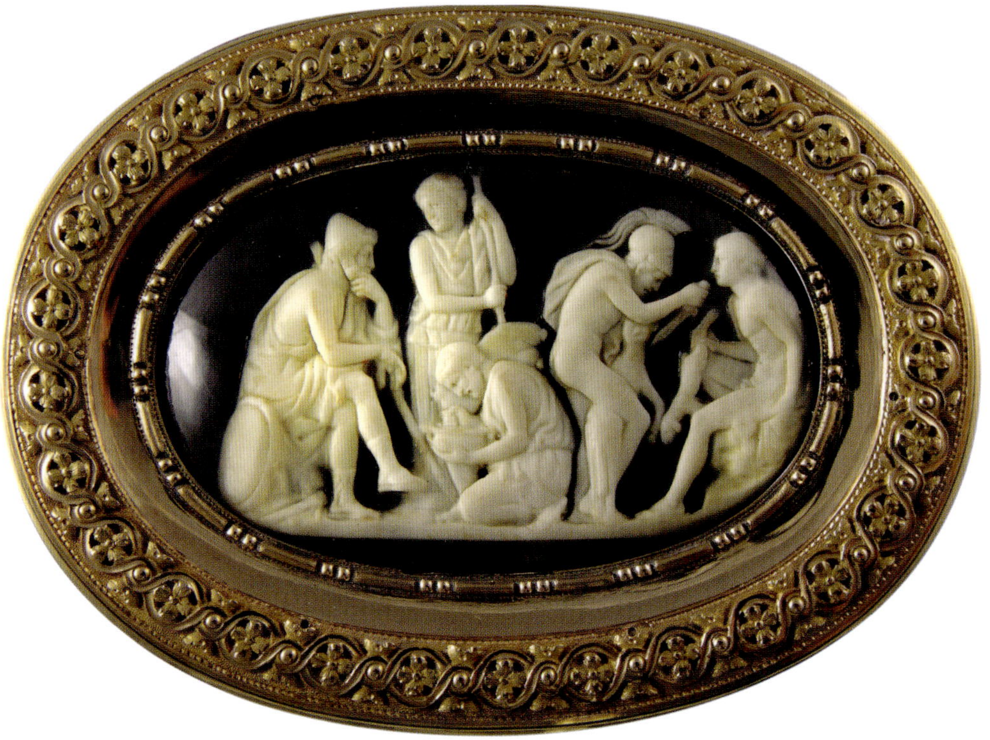

7

(10735) K197
Sardonyx, pale brown, polished flat back, set in the lid of a tortoiseshell and gold snuffbox
39 x 25

From the Cardinal Grimani Collection. Vico, pl. 5 (labelled *Dis Manibus Sacrum* with the verse *Hic munere Bacchi Invocat infernos Manes hic sanguinie sacro* as if a sacrifice to underworld gods); Inst.Imp. 20; *AGE* no. 295.

The return of Ulysses. Ulysses, wearing a pilos cap, short dress and boots, hand to his chin and leaning on a staff, is seated on rocks with a shield against them and a scabbard and baldric below. Before him the swineherd Eumaeus in short dress kneels to pour from the skin over his shoulder into a pot; behind him stands a woman dressed in a peplos, leaning on a spear, with dressed hair. At the right a man, naked but for helmet and cloak over one shoulder, is killing a ram held between his legs, with a short sword, and before him is seated another youth, naked, seated on dress on a rock, holding a dead lamb. Ground line.

The scene is based on that narrated in *Odyssey* Book 21, lines 189–353 (Eumaeus and Philoetius), the figures at the right possibly indicating sacrifice or, more probably, a meal. The scene is also depicted, slightly differently, on a cameo in Vienna (Eichler/Kris, no. 234), and on others, in the Hermitage and Paris (Kagan/Neverov 2000, 132, no. 147/54), where Ulysses is shown without his pilos cap.

16th century.

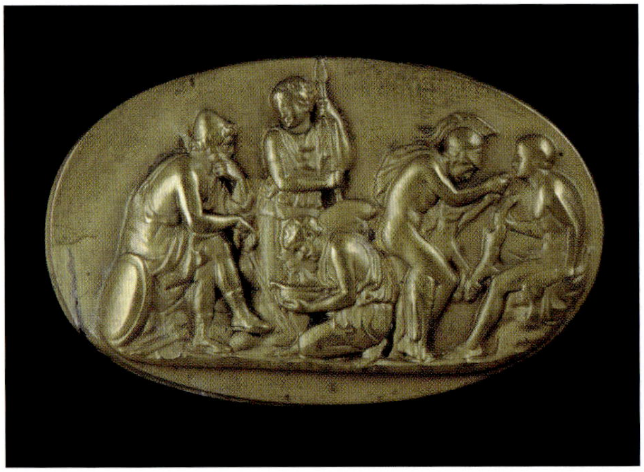

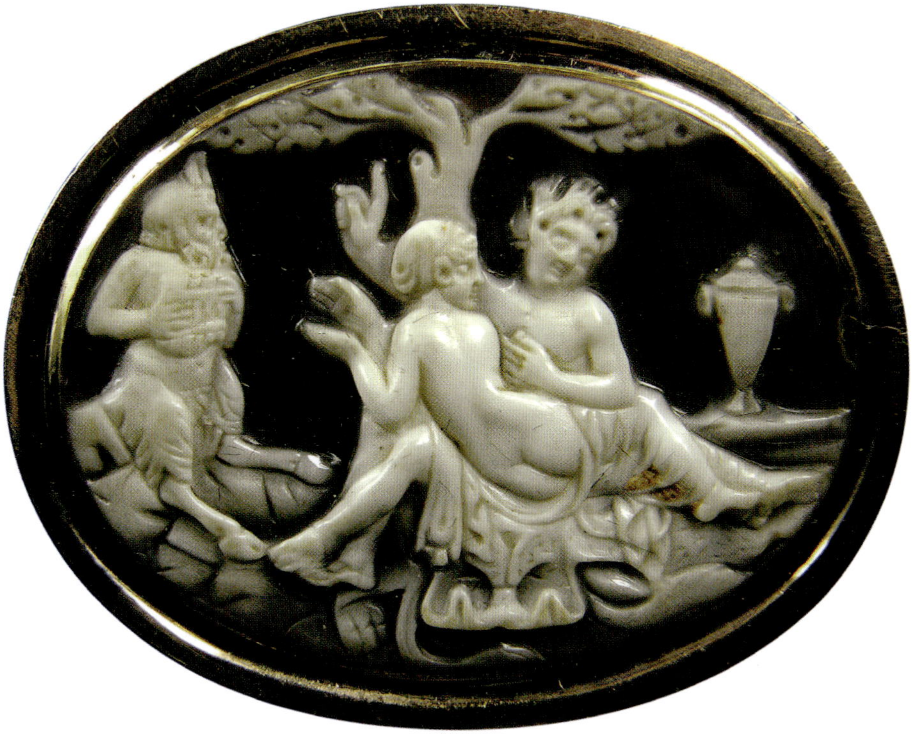

8

(10577) K39 (pl.2)
Sardonyx, white/brown, polished flat back, set in a plain gold ring
27 x 20

Once Cardinal Grimani Collection: Vico, pl. 8 (but with a Pan in the place of the pot, and the motto *Si vina tollas et Venus statim perit Nec dulca quidquam restit hinc mortalibus*);

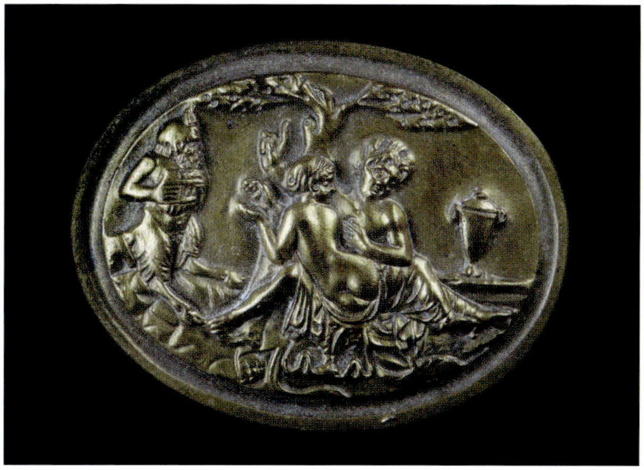

Inst.Imp. no. 7; Cades, Cent. IV, 49; Yuen 1997, 142–3, figs. 13.39, 14; SG.Imp. 131; King 1872, p. xix; King 1885, pl. 25.3; *AG* pl. 57.18; Lippold, pl. 18.4; *AGE* no. 137.

At the left Pan sits on rocks playing a syrinx. At the centre, beneath a tree, a nymph, naked but for dress around her legs and a snood, claps her hands (rather than holds a cup) and looks at a young wreathed satyr who has her on his lap and is beating time with a raised finger. They recline on dress and a lion skin. At the right is a conical lidded jar on a rocky shelf.

The subject, which derives from an ancient original (for the maenad see Bober/Rubinstein, no. 94), was often copied with various attendant figures; see the cameo in Boston, Beazley, *LHG* no. 133, and our **11**, which has part of the same scene. *AGE* no. 136 is part of a similar scene with an awning and a piping child. Weber 1992, 115, no. 99, has a corselet instead of the jar.

16th century.

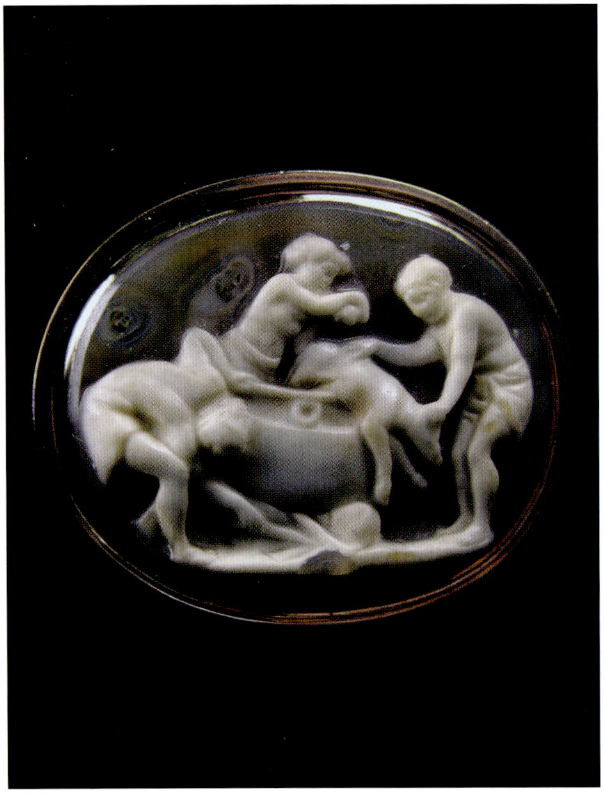

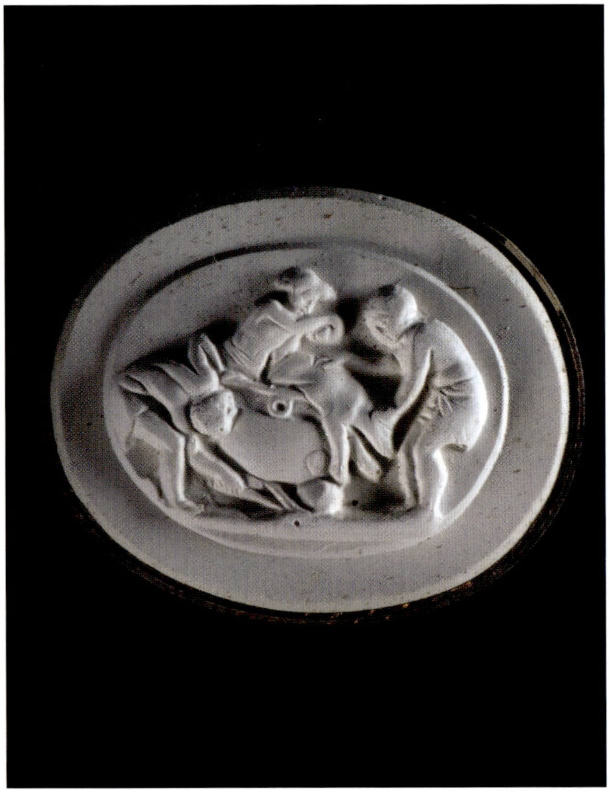

9

(10574) K36 (pl. 2)
Sardonyx, white/brown., polished flat back, set on a plain gold ring
26 x 20

Formerly Cardinal Grimani Coll.; SG.Imp. 96; *AG* pl. 50.49; Inst.Imp. no. 21; Cades, Cent. IV, 53; Yuen 1997, 142, fig. 13.36; *AGE* no. 274 W.Tassie 2894.

Three men are cooking or scalding a pig. They are dressed in loin cloths. One lifts the pig into a large cauldron, another pours on to it from a jug and the third stokes the fire. Ground line.

A popular Hellenistic/Early Roman subject, on which see *AG* II, 243–4, and S.H. Middleton, *Engraved Gems from Dalmatia* (Oxford 1991) on no. 184, for the subject and other gem versions. It appears also on a plaster cast from silver in the Begram hoard (Afghanistan): M. Menninger, *Untersuchungen zu den Gläsern und Gipsabgüssen von Begram (Afghanistan)* (Würzburg 1996) 182–4, M32. It was copied by Giulio Romano and others (see Yuen 1997, 144, 146, fig. 19). See also R. Amedick, 'Die Gruppe der Schweinsbrüher', in: *Hellenistische Gruppen. Gedenkschrift für Andreas Linfert* (1999) 187-198, the pig-scalding group indicating winter.

1st century BC/AD.

10

(10571) K33 (pl. 2)
Sardonyx, white/black., polished flat back, set on a plain gold ring
20 x 13

From the collection of Pope Paul II (Pietro Barbo); Lorenzo di Medici; acquired from James Byres (1791); Paoletti I, I.444; Lippold, pl. 12.2; L. Curtius, *Archäologische Anzeiger* 1944–5, 15–7, pl. 16.1; Dacos et al. 1972, no. 34, citing Barbo inventory 1457; Giuliano, *Cammei* p.44 (cast); Yuen 1997, 140–3, fig. 13.33; *AGE* no. 131.

Young Bacchus, wearing nebris and boots, is standing on rocks. A young satyr seated on rocks holds one of his feet, perhaps extracting a thorn or putting on his boot. Behind him a tree from which hangs a syrinx. At the right an old satyr holds a ribboned thyrsos which the young god also grasps. Incised top right .LAV.R.MED. the usual mark of the Medici Collection.

Curtius saw that the scene was a copy of a sarcophagus relief in the Capitoline Museum (his pl. 16.2). Versions of the cameo decorate the margins of two 15th-century illuminated manuscripts: Gennaioli 2010, 118–9, nos 31–2. Lord Elgin had a copy of the cameo.

15th century?

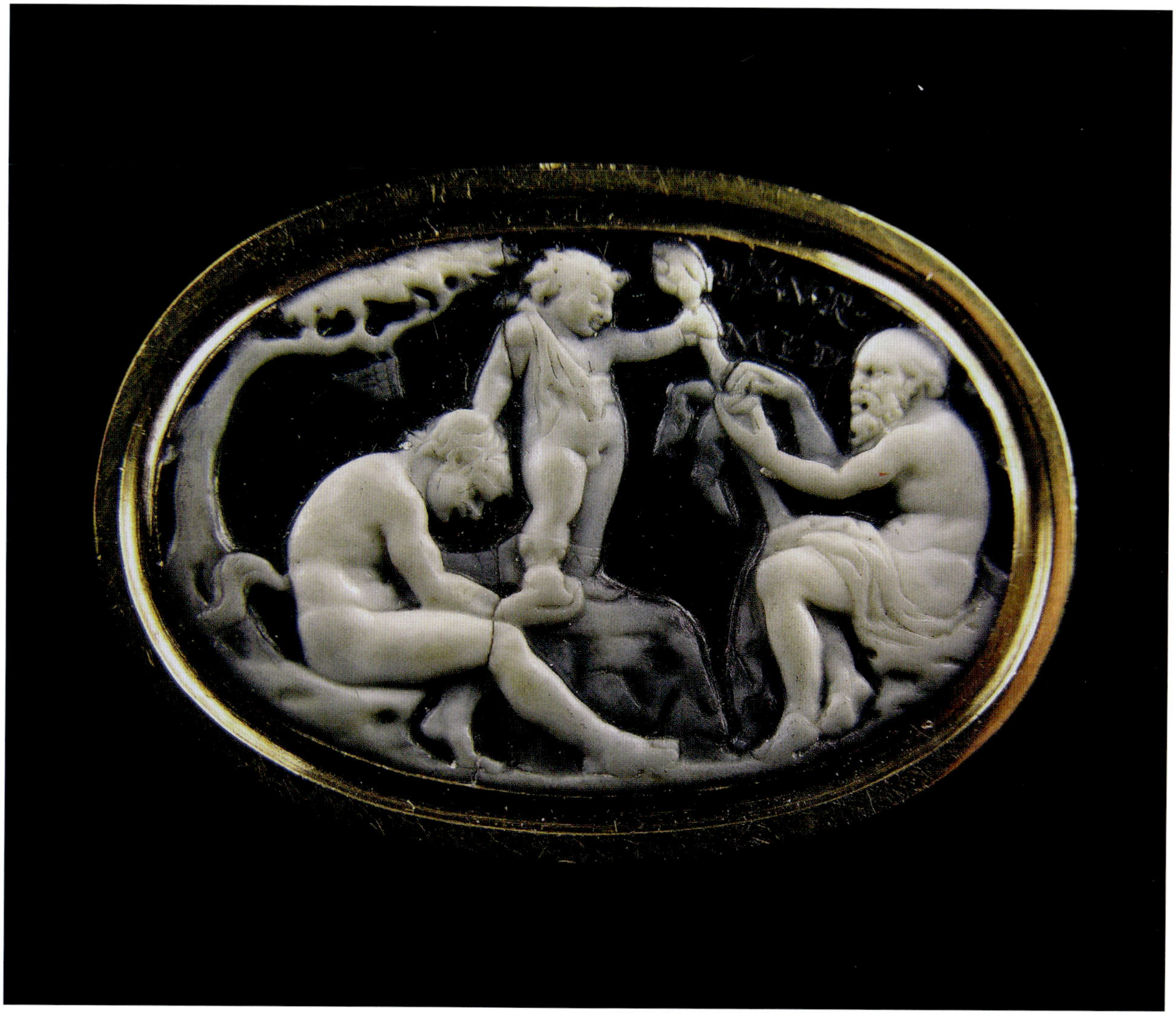

11

(10576) K38 (pl. 2)
Sardonyx fragment of a large disc, white/brown, unpolished flat back, set on a plain gold ring with hoop ends divided
33 x 23

SG.Imp. 129; Inst.Imp. no. 32; W.Tassie 1585; Beazley, *LHG* on no. 133; *AGE* no. 155.

At the left break the facing head of a young satyr (pointed ears) wearing what seems to be corn stalks in his hair. Beside him a kneeling satyr with hands raised towards the young satyr's head. It has generally been assumed that he is arranging his crown or wreath in some way, but the same clapping gesture also accompanies dancing. Above is a vine with a disc (tambourine or *oscillum*) hanging from it.

The subject is as that of the copy, our **8**, where the kneeling satyr is replaced by a jar. Beazley, *LHG* no. 133 (now in Boston) has the scene as ours and preserves the body of the nymph being held by the young satyr. A subject related to this group in Munich, *LIMC* III, pl. 447.199.

1st century BC/AD?

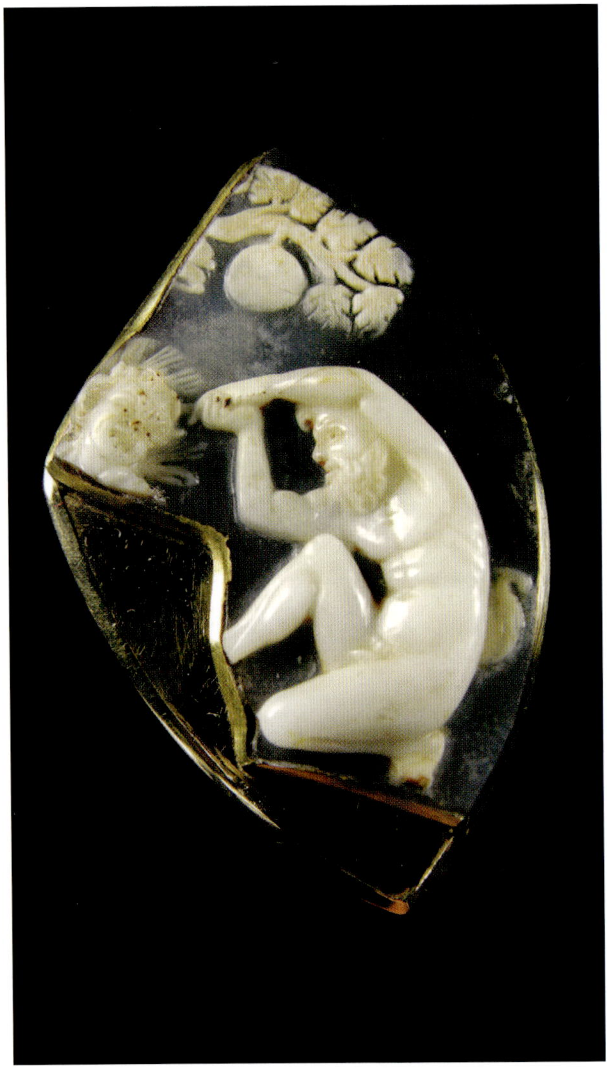

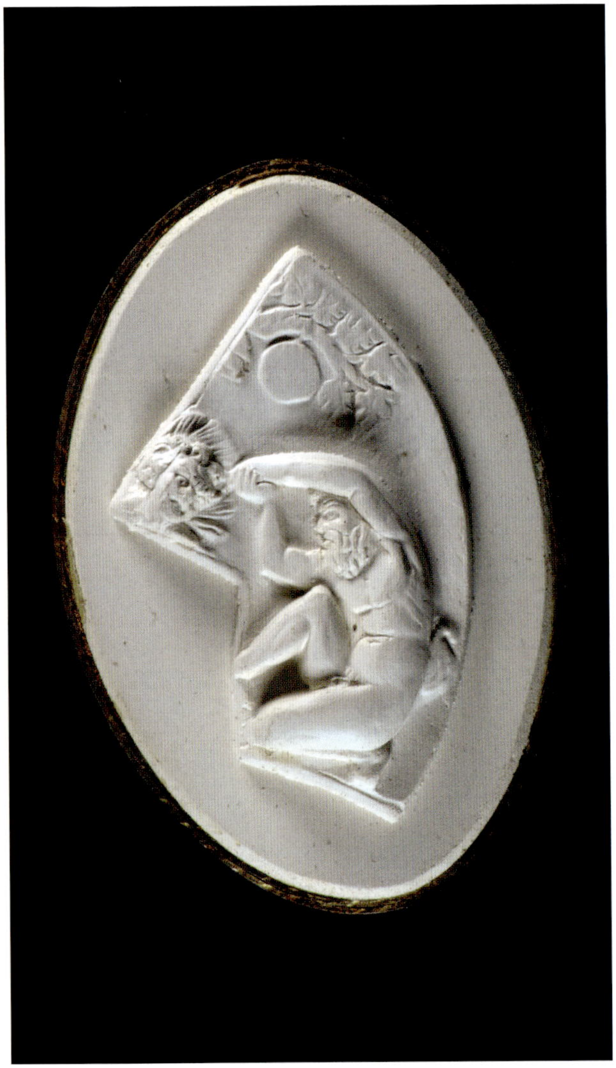

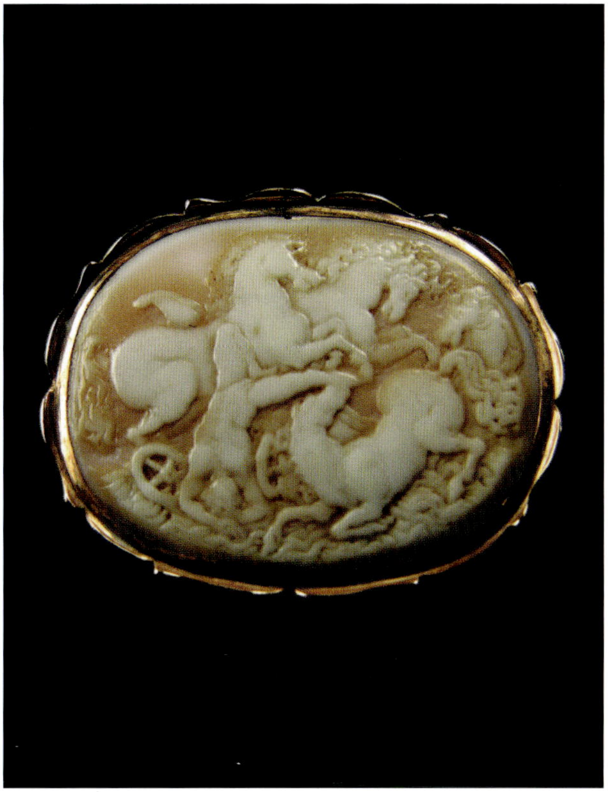

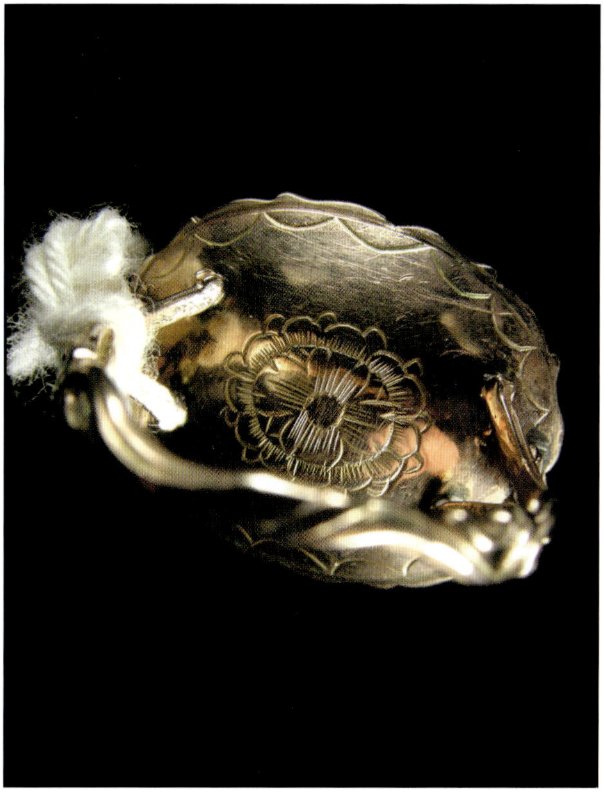

12

(10592) K54

Sardonyx, white/grey-brown, set in a gold ring with a rosette at the back and leafy ends to the hoop

19 x 15

Probably from the 1st Duchess' Collection (no. 22), since the subject is rare ('Given me by the El[ecto]r [of] Cologne'); SG.Imp. 155; Tassie 3107; Inst.Imp. no. 155; *AGE* no. 171.

The Fall of Phaethon, who had ventured too near the sun in his chariot. We see the chariot broken at the bottom of the scene and the four horses collapsing around the falling, naked body of the hero; clouds below.

The subject broadly resembles drawings by Michelangelo (one in the British Museum he gave to Tommaso Cavalieri in 1532/3), with added groups of Jupiter above and Phaethon's distraught sisters below. The drawings have a far more chaotic composition, the horses upturned, while on the cameo they are still roughly upright. It remains possible that the cameo is ancient (though not much like the only other ancient cameo with the subject except in the pose of Phaethon with crossed arms; see *AG* pl. 58.2; *LIMC* VII, 353) and helped to inspire the later scenes. Other Renaissance treatments of the subject follow the scheme on Roman sarcophagi; on our cameo and Michelangelo's drawing the group is a more compact cluster, ours with the horses upright. See Bober/Rubinstein, no. 27; L. Syson and D. Thornton, *Objects of Virtue* (Los Angeles 2001) 174–81; and E. Simon, *Ausgewählte Schriften* IV (Mainz 2012) 188–203 (191 for Michelangelo).

16th/17th century?

13

(10544) K6
Sardonyx, white/brown, polished flat back, set on a gold pendant
37 x 26

Inst.Imp. no. 50.

A naked woman, perhaps Venus, reclines on her side, her elbow on a cushion, the other hand holding dress over her head, cloth below and behind her. Cupid hovers, lifting the cloth from her body and touching her arm. A tree at the left. Ground line.

Her pose is a version of the Ariadne figures with Cupid revealing her to Bacchus (Bober/Rubinstein, no. 79).

1st century BC/AD?

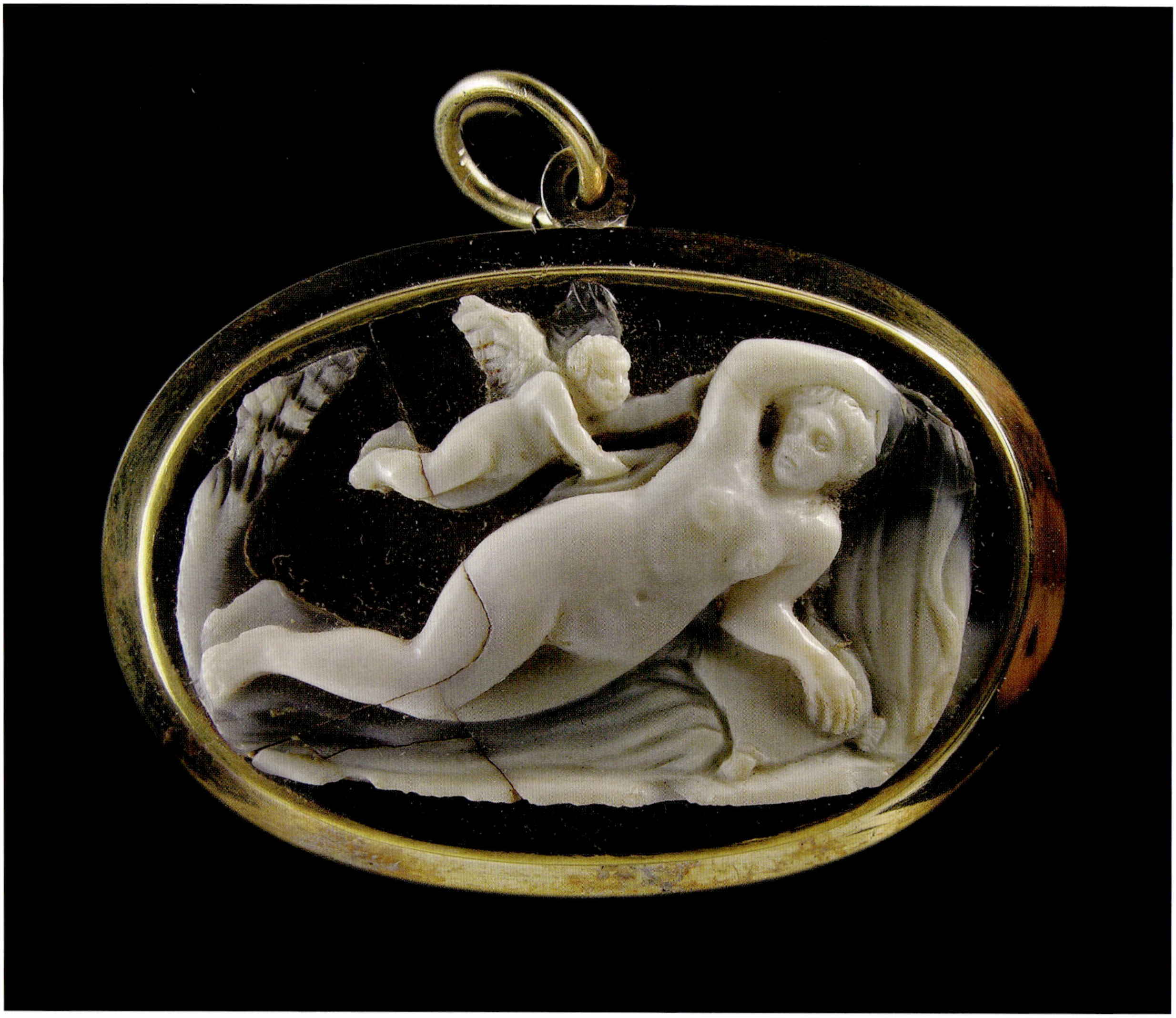

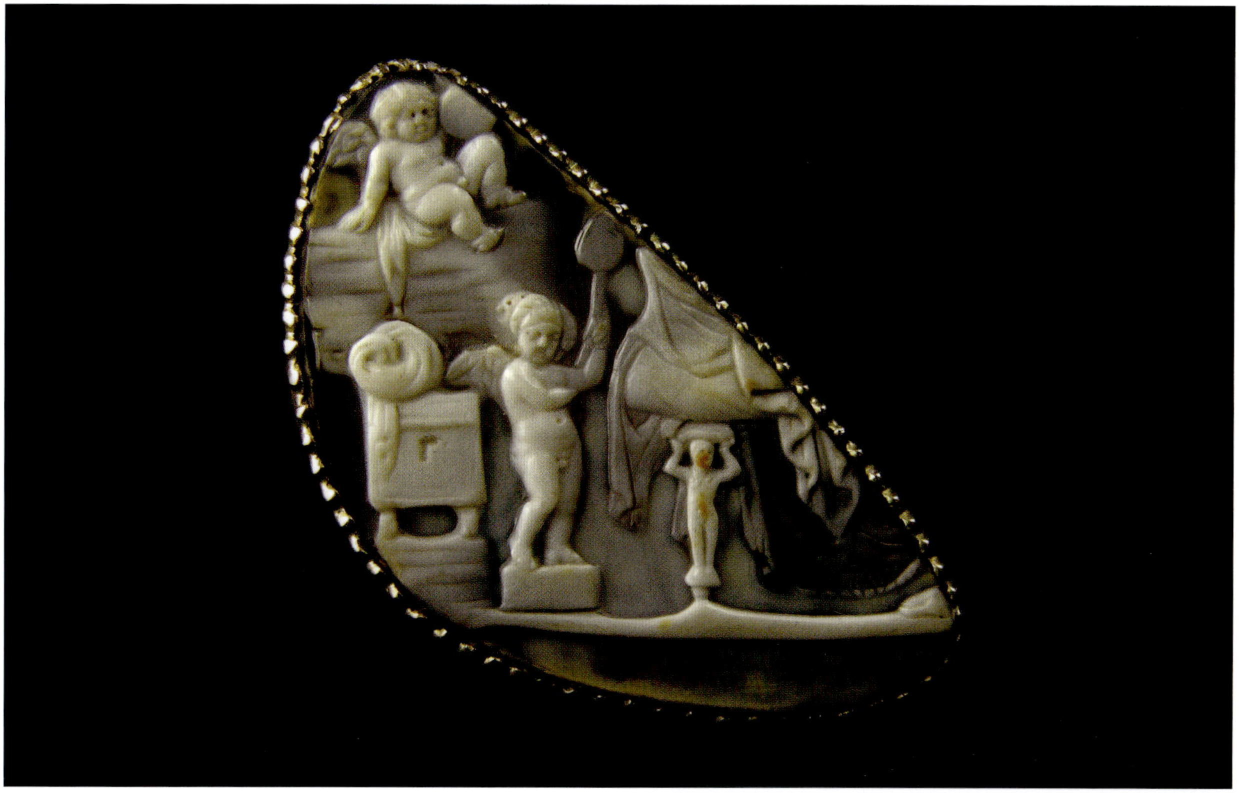

14

(10563) K25 (pl. 6)
Sardonyx fragment, brown/white/pale to dark grey/brown, polished flat back, set on a plain gold ring with beaded edge to the bezel
30 x 23

SG.Imp. 158; Inst.Imp. no. 34; Paoletti I, I.330; *AGE* no. 114.

At the centre is part of a fully dressed woman seated on a couch (?) with *atlantes* figures as legs. Behind, a Cupid standing on a block holds up a fan. Behind him is a footed coffer standing on layered rocks with a bundle of cloth with a hanging end on its lid and the letter Γ on its side. Above, another Cupid is seated on dress on rocks holding a disc (mirror?). At the right break there is part of the foot of a figure facing left. Ground line.

The couch probably carried a reclining Hermaphrodite who is sometimes shown in such a setting, as on the cameo, Walters, *London* no. 1535; *LIMC* V, pl. 198.73d.

1st century BC/AD.

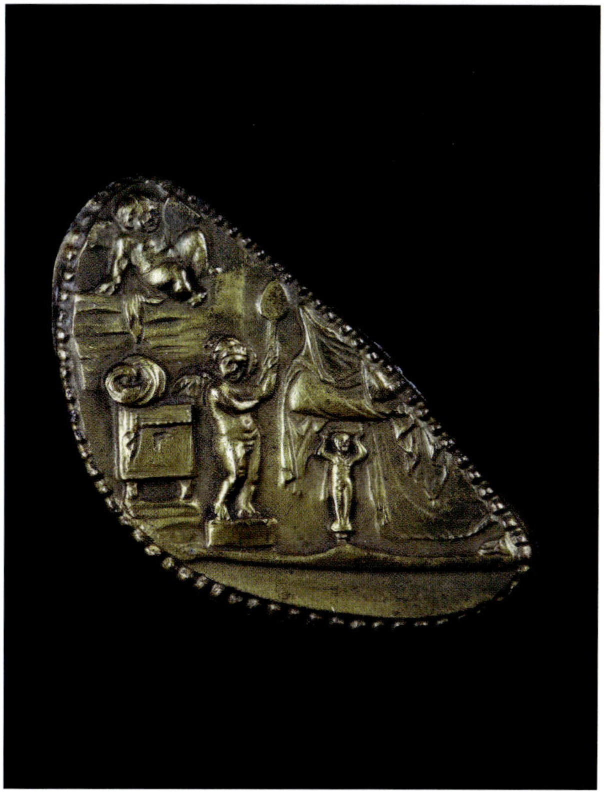

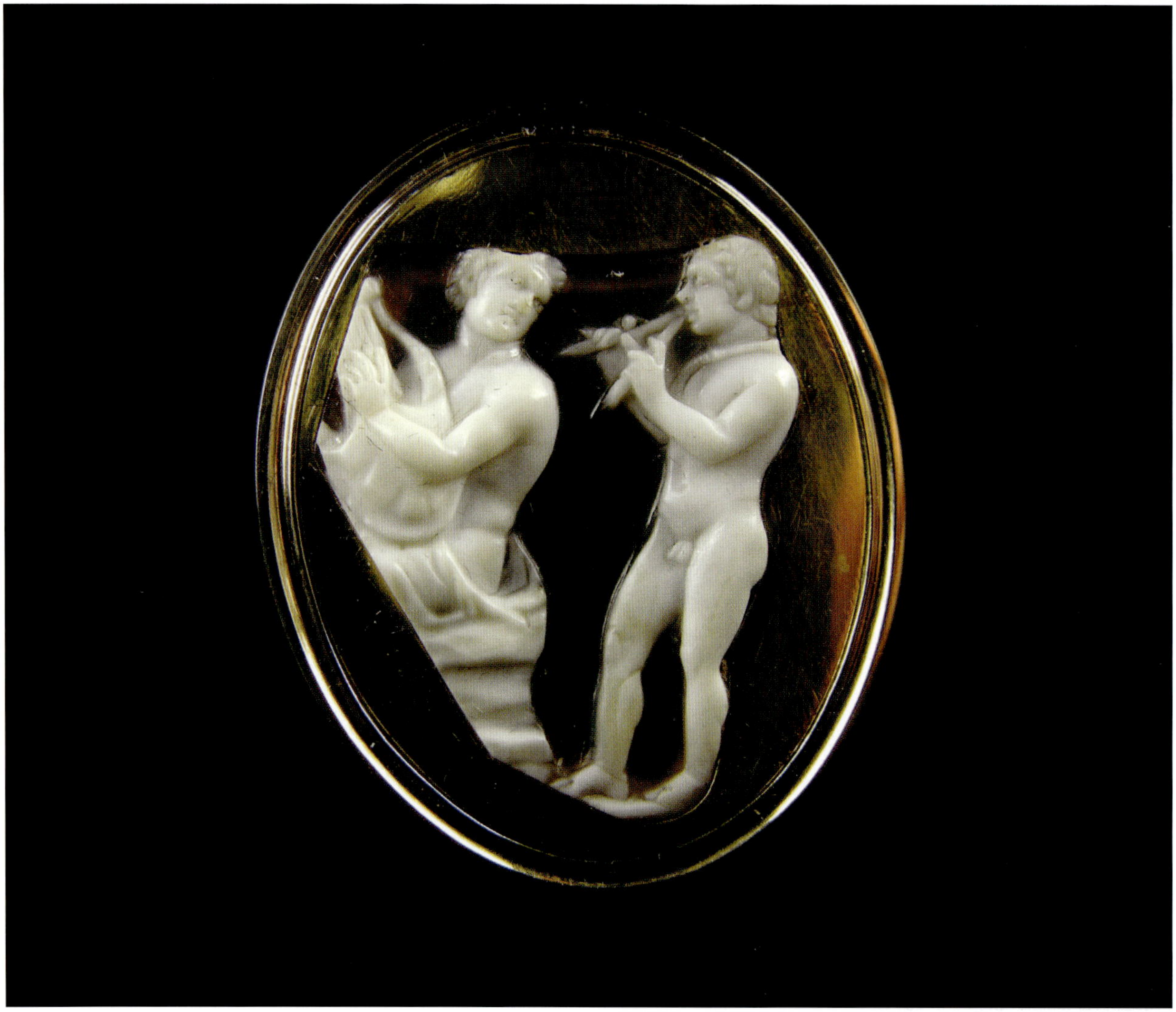

15

(10572) K34 (pl. 2)
Sardonyx fragment, white/pale brown, polished flat back, set on a plain gold ring
19 x 19

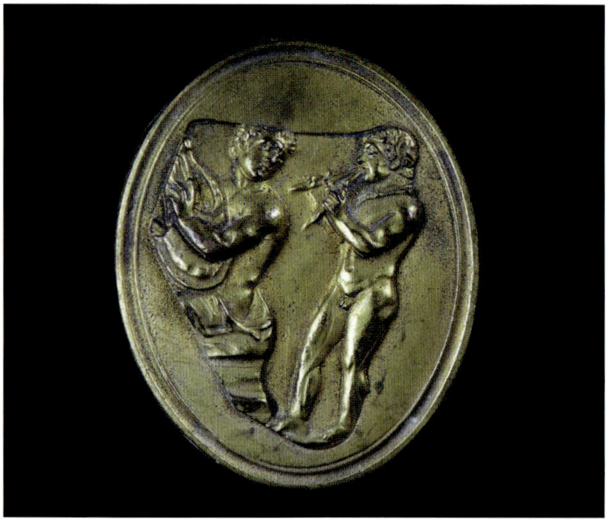

SG.Imp. 18; Tassie 4691; Inst.Imp. no. 37; Yuen 1997, 142, fig. 13.34; *AGE* no. 110.

A satyr, seated on his dress on rocks, playing a tortoise-shell lyre with goats'-horn arms, looks round at a young satyr with short curly hair wearing only a necklet and playing double pipes. Ground line.

1st century BC/AD?

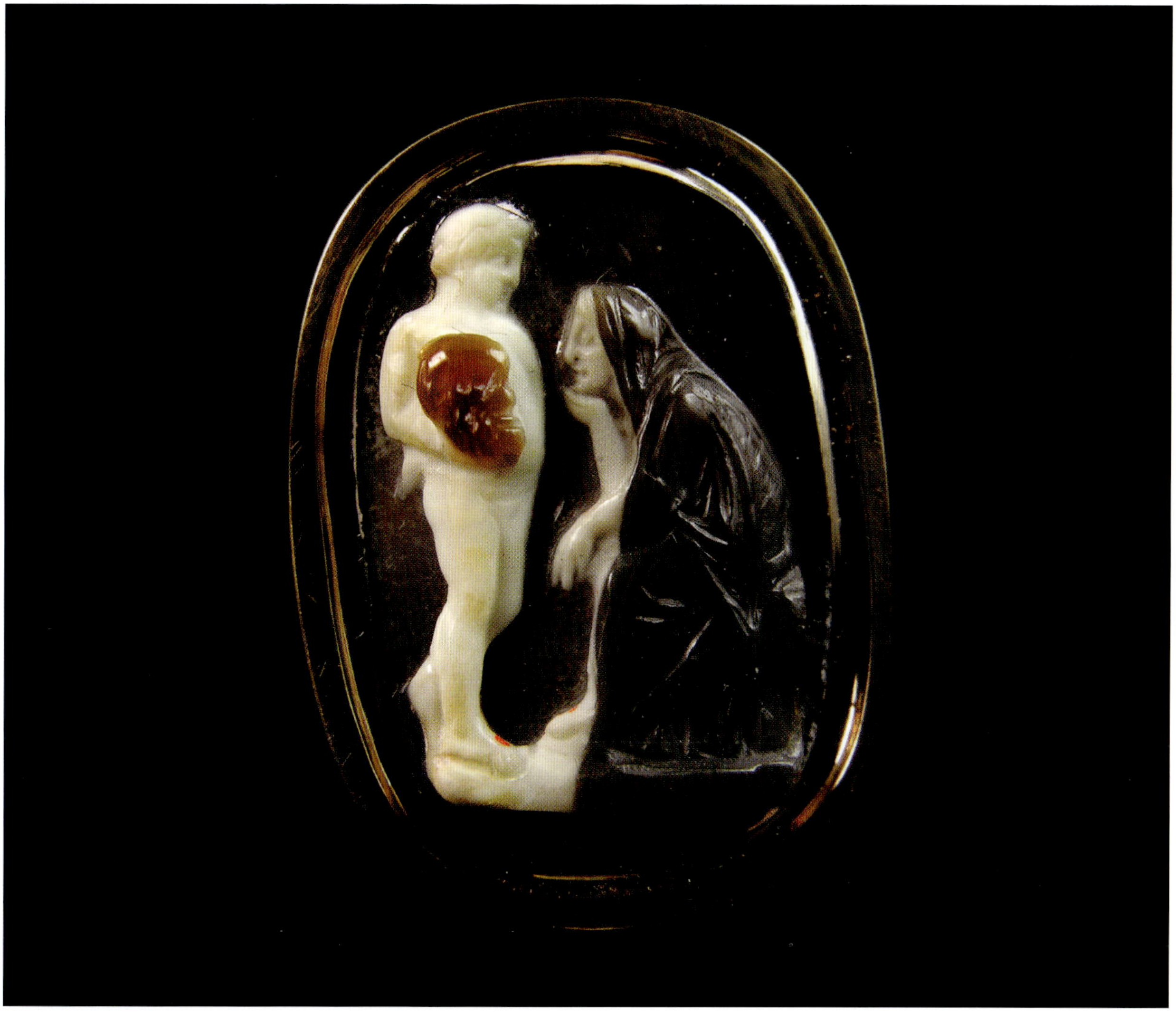

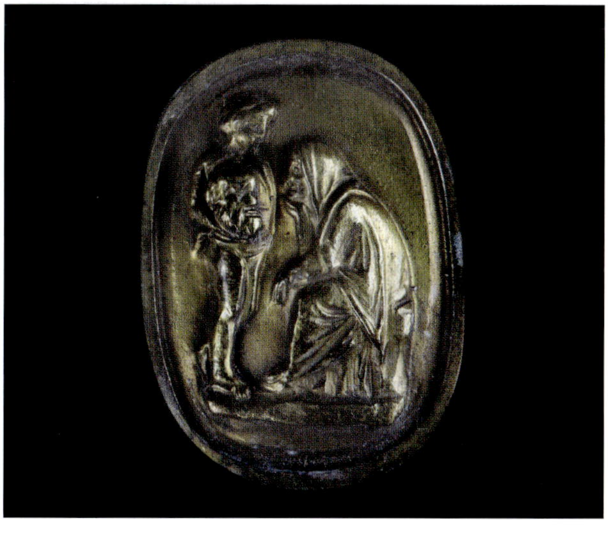

16

(10647) K109

Sardonyx, deep red: brown (mask)/white/brown-black, polished flat back, set on a plain gold ring

23 x 15

SG.Imp. 76; Inst.Imp. no 22; Cades, Cent. IV, 63 (as Orestes showing Electra the head of Aegisthus); *AGE* no. 198.

A woman (Muse or Sibyl) is seated on a stool, head on hands, heavily veiled. Before her is a young satyr holding a mask of an old satyr (Silenus). Ground line.

The identity of the woman is not clear but the mask is not an uncommon attribute of Muses.

1st century BC/AD.

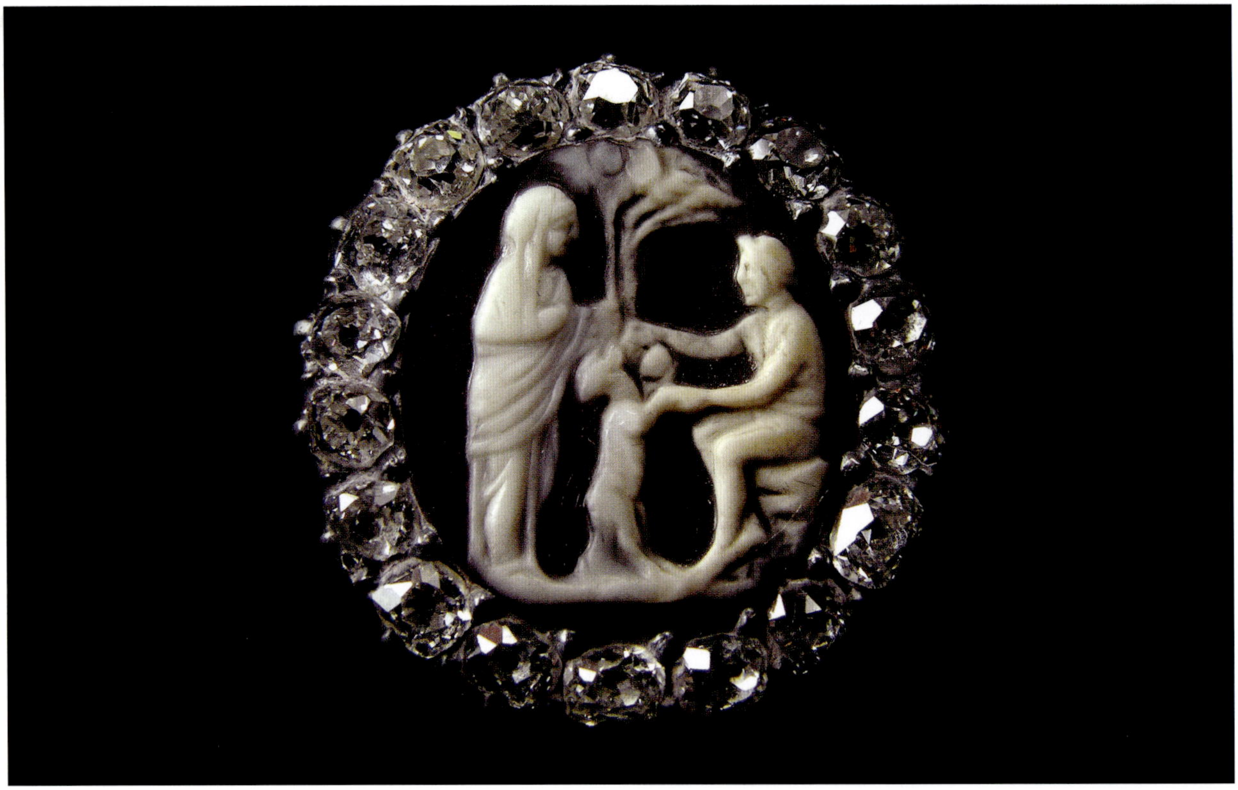

17

(10557) K19 (pl. 2)
Sardonyx, white/grey, polished flat back, set in a gold ring with diamonds mounted in silver around the bezel and floral ends to the hoop
14 x 13

SG.Imp. 78; Tassie 8429; Inst.Imp. no. 5; Yuen 1977, 142, fig.19; *AGE* no. 272.

A youth with dress around his waist seated on rocks holds a kid upright before him, and a jug. Before him stands a fully dressed and veiled woman. A tree, beyond which she touches, and ground line.

A generic rustic scene probably implying sacrifice. Compare *Content* no. 148.

1st century BC/AD.

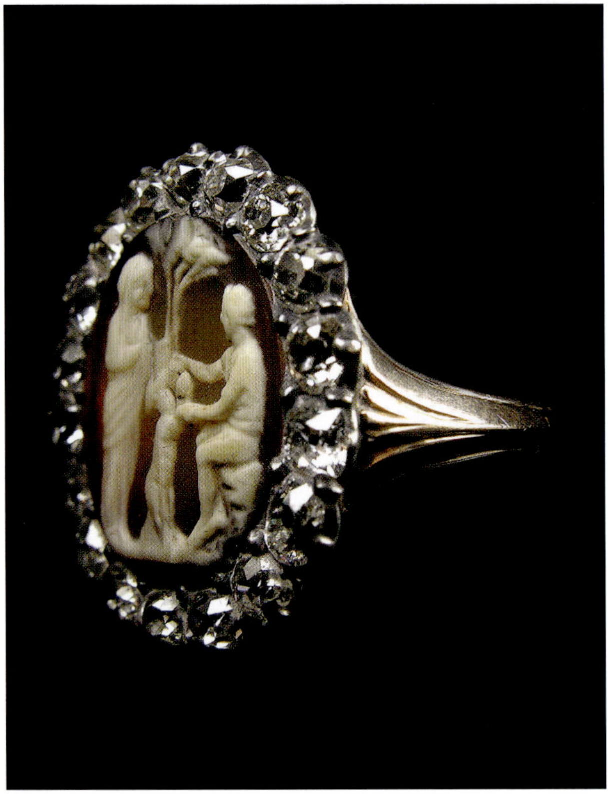

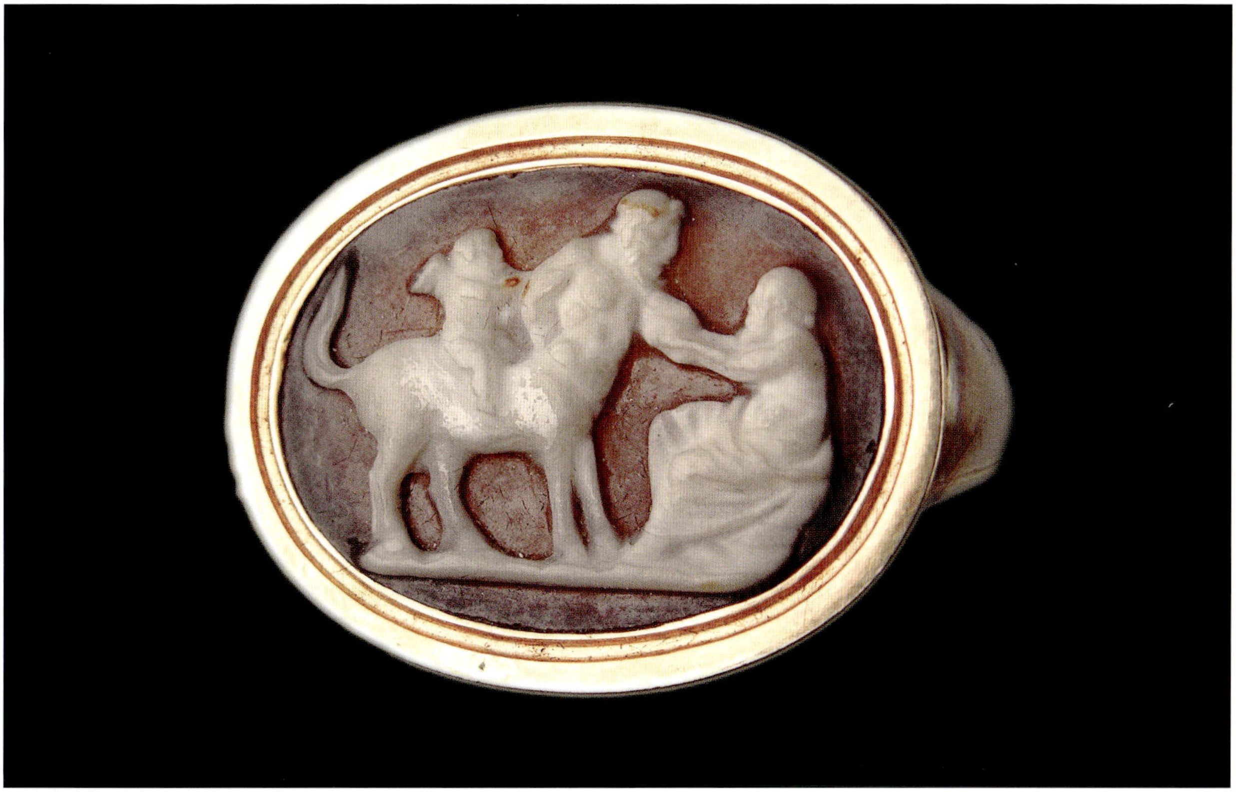

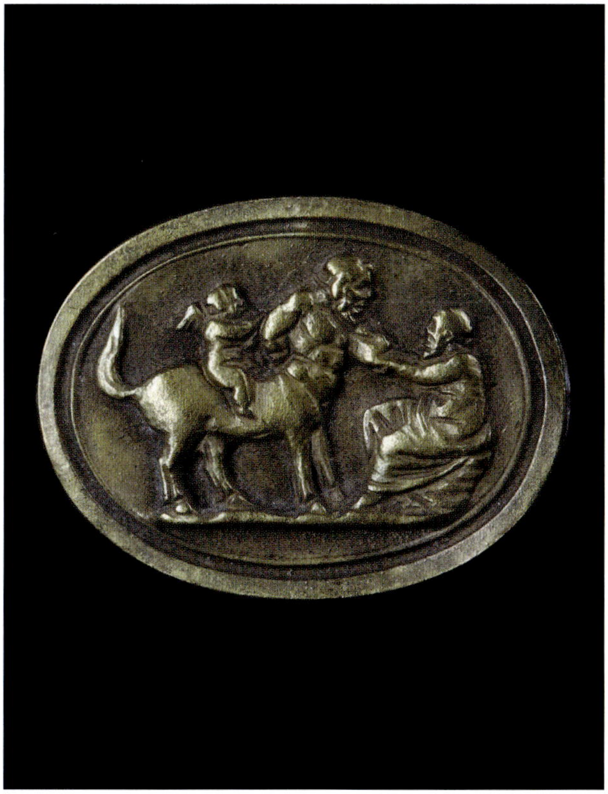

18

(10583) K45 (pl. 2)
Sardonyx, white/brown, unpolished flat back, set on a plain gold ring
18 x 12

An old man on a low seat (layered rock), dress around his legs, is offering a deep bowl to a centaur, whose hands are behind his back (bound), where a Cupid is seated. Ground line.

The unexplained subject of Cupid binding a centaur's arms appears in a statue group and on some other gems (*LIMC* VIII, Kentauroi nos 303, 305–6). Only here is an old man also involved.

1st century BC/AD.

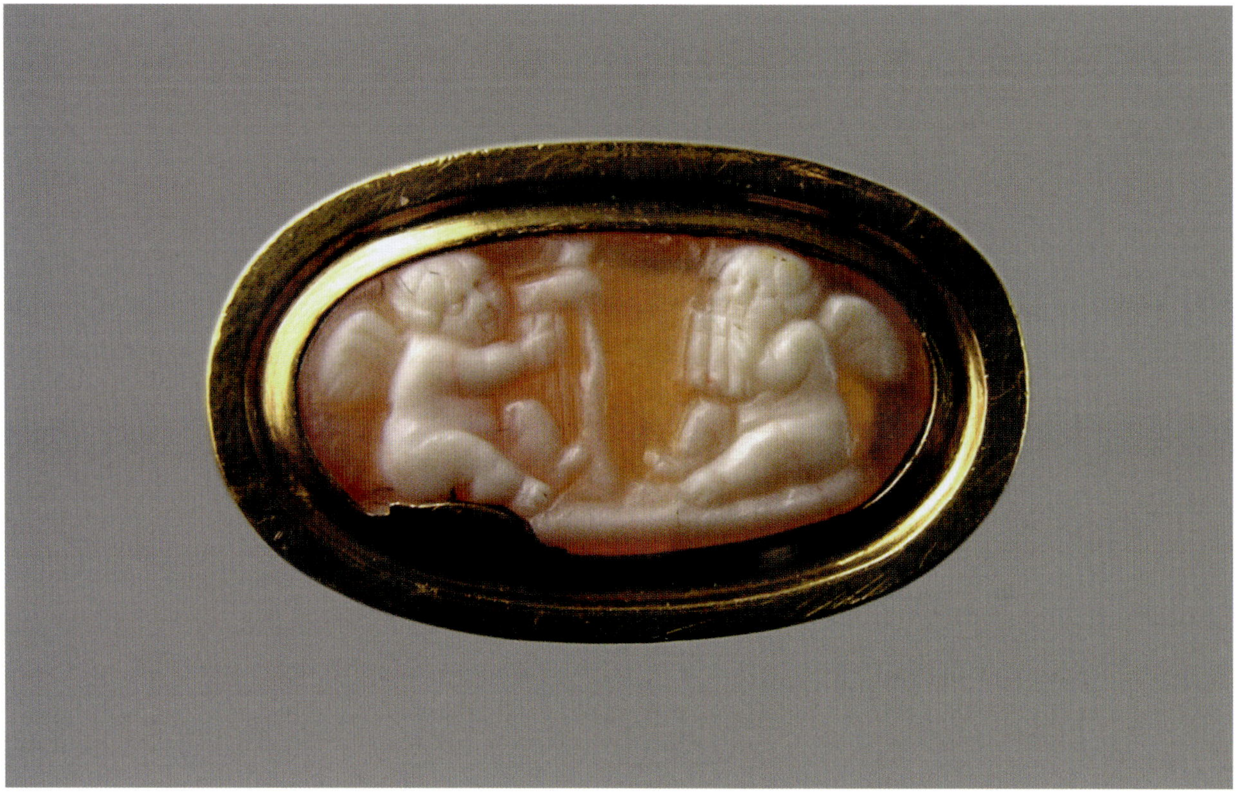

19

(10582) K44 (pl. 2)
Sardonyx, white/brown, polished flat back, set on a plain gold ring
13 x 6

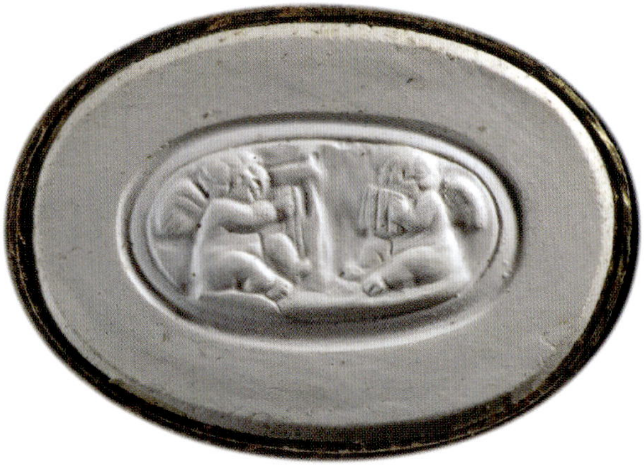

SG.Imp. 168; Inst.Imp. no. 69; W.Tassie 2233; *AGE* no. 122.

Two Cupids seated on the ground line, one playing a kithara, the other a syrinx.

Compare Giuliano, *Cammei* no. 47.

1st century AD?

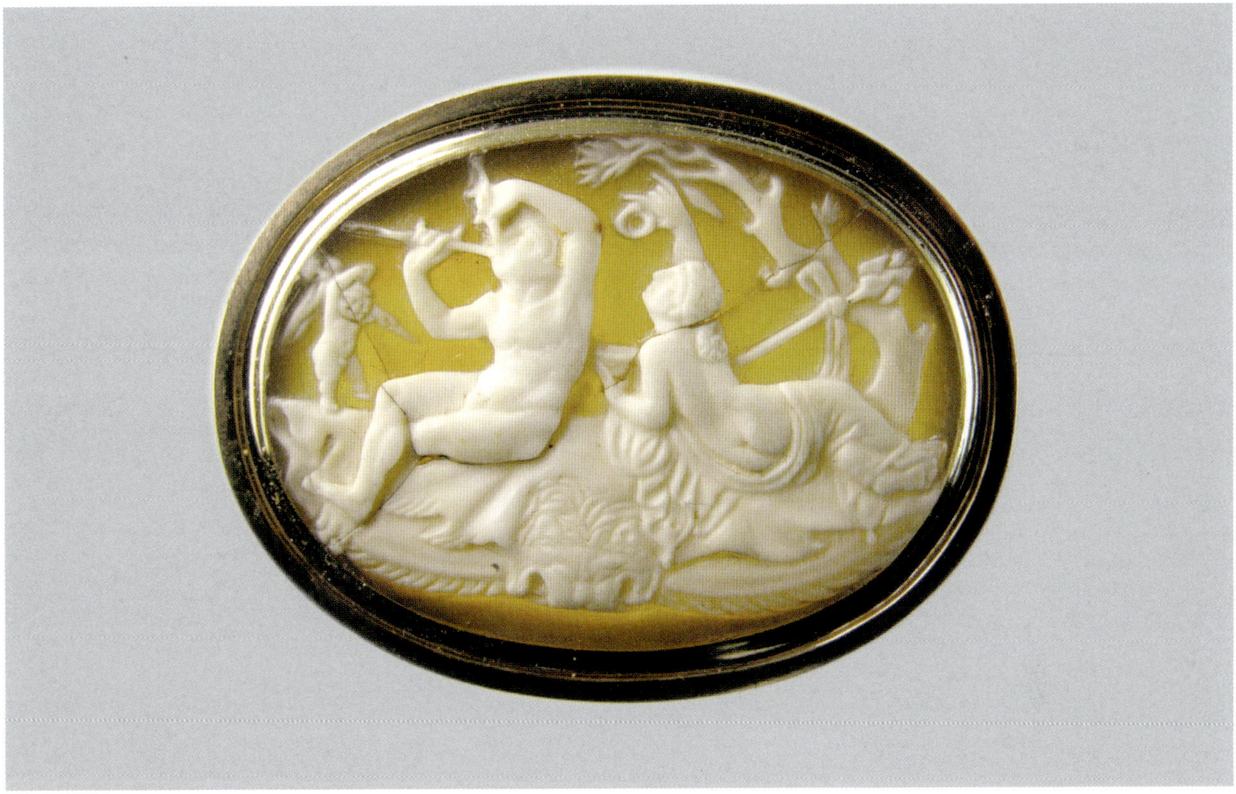

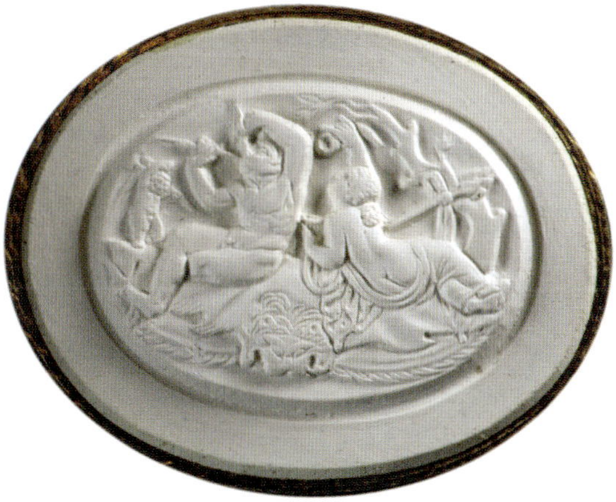

20

(10585) K47 (pl. 2)
Sardonyx, white/brown, polished flat back, set on a plain gold ring
26 x 18

Once Cardinal Grimani Collection; Vico, pl. 24 (labelled *Laetitiae Symbolum* and the verse *Dulce Melos Lasciva Venus Vinumque suave, Hec tua Laetitiam praebent curasque resolvunt*); Yuen 1997, 143, fig. 14, compare 142, fig. 13.47; SG.Imp. 127; Inst.Imp. no. 4; Cades, Cent. IV, 52; King 1872, I p. 322; King 1885, pl. 25.1; *AG* pl. 57.20; *AGE* no. 13

A young satyr plays double pipes, his head thrown back; behind him lies a maenad with dress around her legs, holding a conical cup and, upraised, a drinking horn. Beyond her is a ribboned thyrsos and a tree. At the other side stands Cupid shouldering what may be a thyrsos ('trophy' – Furtwängler). They lie on a spread lionskin, the head centre, frontal.

A much-copied subject; for the ancient models for the maenad see Bober/Rubinstein, no. 94.

16th century?

21

(10548) K10
Sardonyx, white/translucent brown, polished flat back, in a layered glass frame
51 x 33

At the centre a youth, Adonis or Paris, naked but for a Phrygian cap, sits on dress on a throne with lion legs, caressing the head of a hunting dog standing beyond him. Behind him a woman, in short sleeveless dress belted under the breasts and with hair bound up, with her hand on his shoulder, no doubt Venus. Before him is a woman, with her hand on a tree stump, dressed with one breast exposed and dress over her forearm, looking round (a rival?). At the centre back a column bearing a figure of Diana with a quiver. At either side are trees, one leafless. Ground line.

The shape suggests that it was designed for the lid of an oval snuffbox.

17th/18th century?

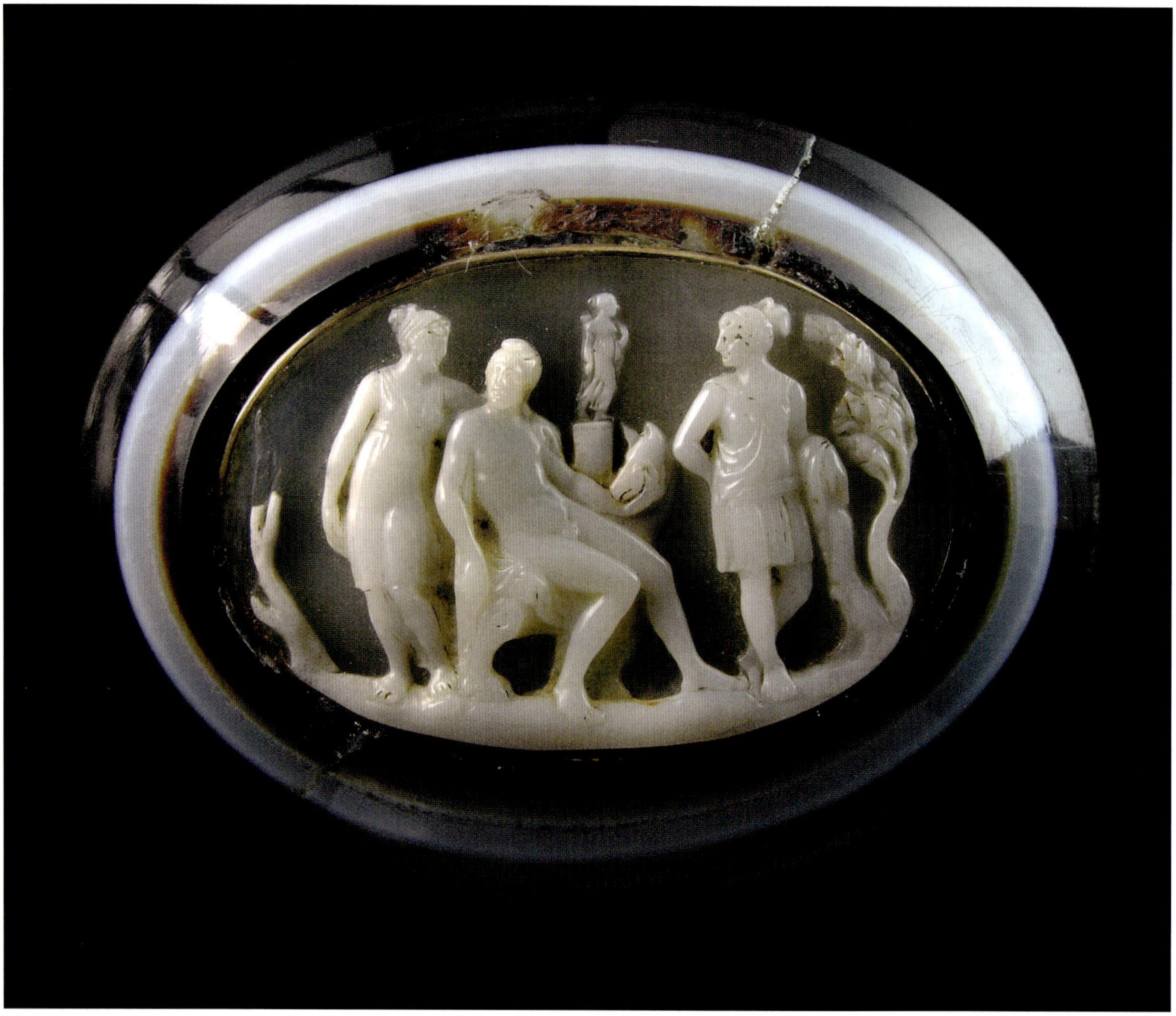

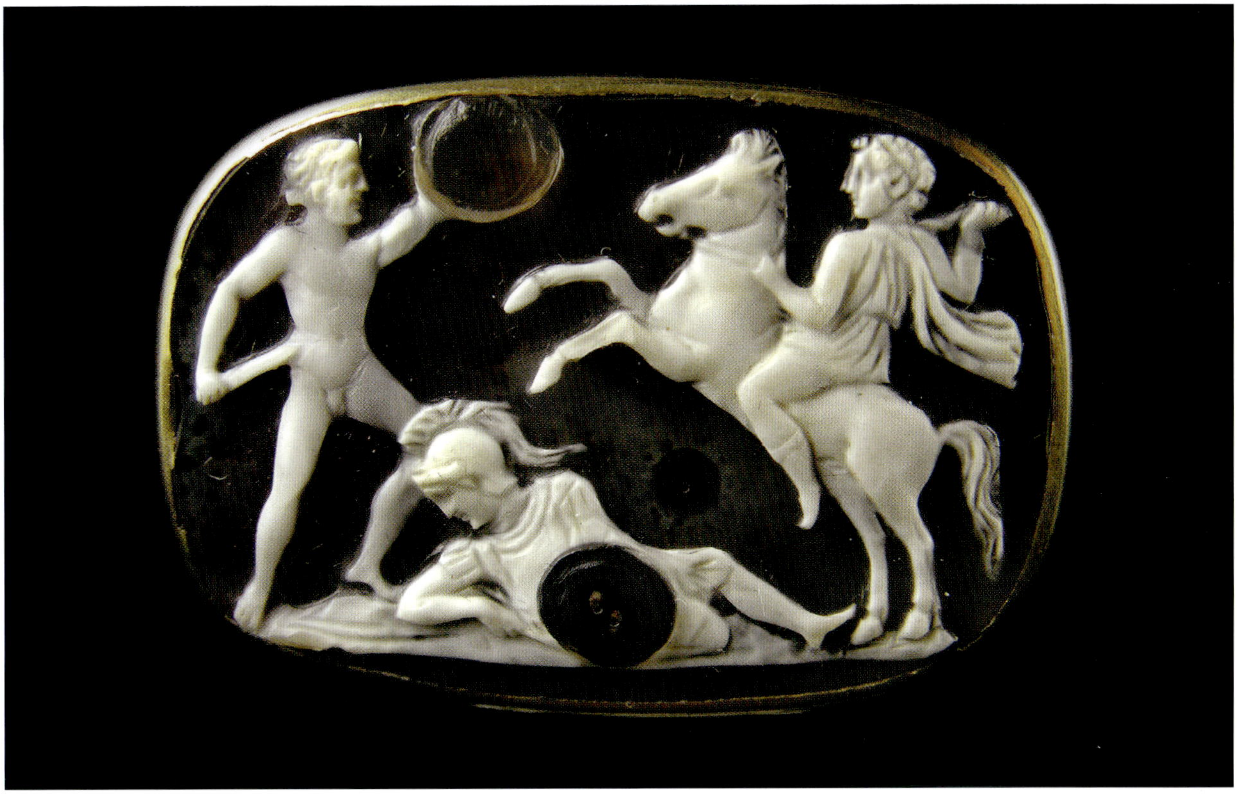

22

(10573) K35 (pl. 2)
Sardonyx, black/brown (shields)/white/black, polished flat back, set on a plain gold ring
29 x 20

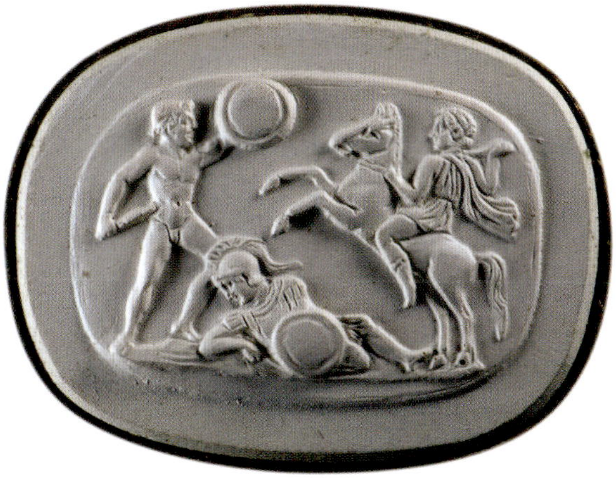

SG.Imp. 82; Inst.Imp. no. 1. Yuen 1997, 142, fig. 13.35; *AGE* no. 226.

A naked warrior with short beard and wild hair storms forward holding aloft a round shield. He appears to be stepping on another shield or rocks, on which lies a dying warrior, fully armed with helmet, corselet and shield, with two holes drilled at its centre (for a boss?). Above him a hole bored in the field for a round attachment. From the right a man in short dress and cloak, diademed and booted, on a rearing horse, advances with spear raised. Ground line.

The scheme broadly resembles ancient gems showing confrontations of warrior(s) and a rearing cavalier (as Zwierlein-Diehl, *AGN* pl. 93.424–5).

16th century.

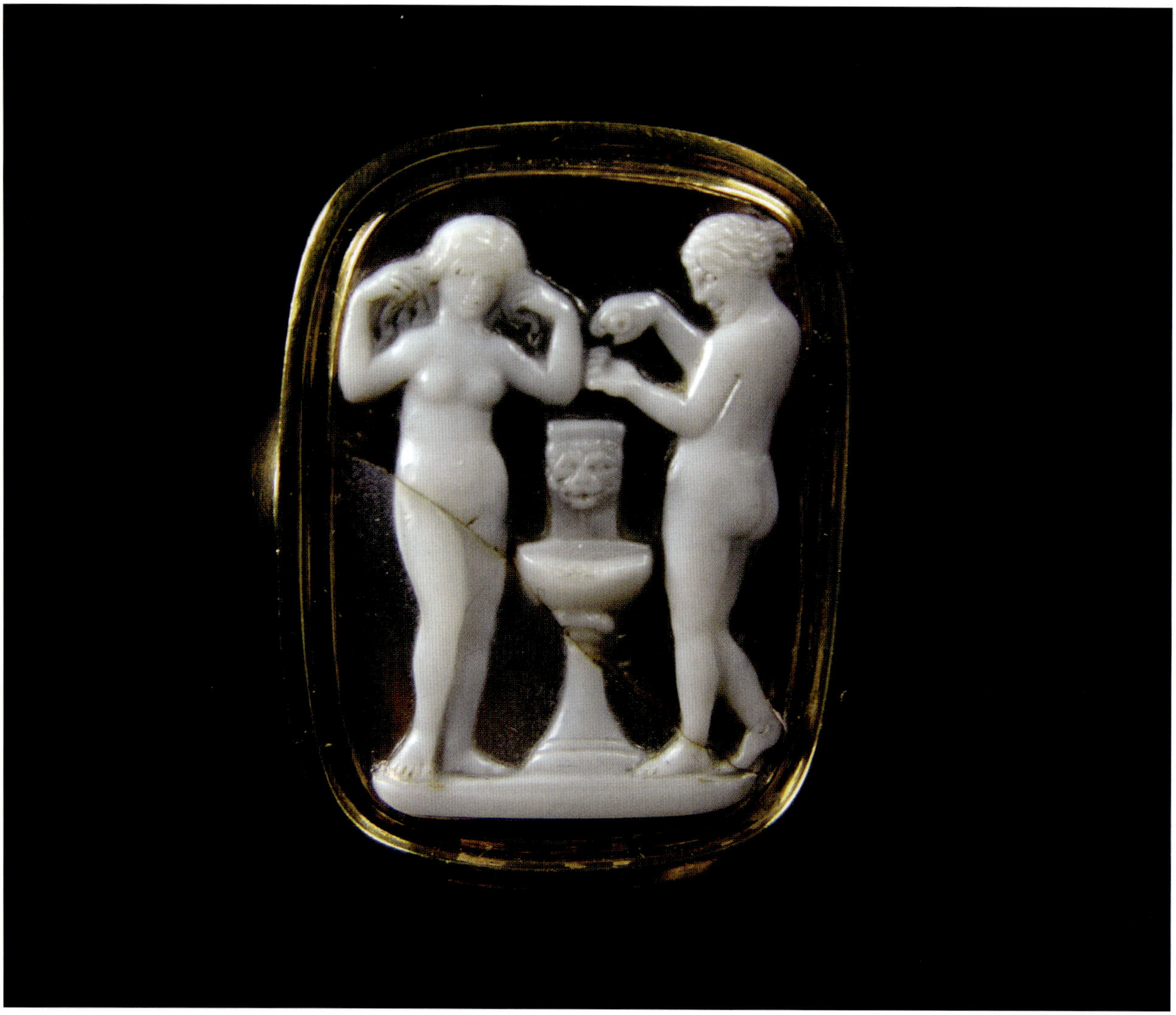

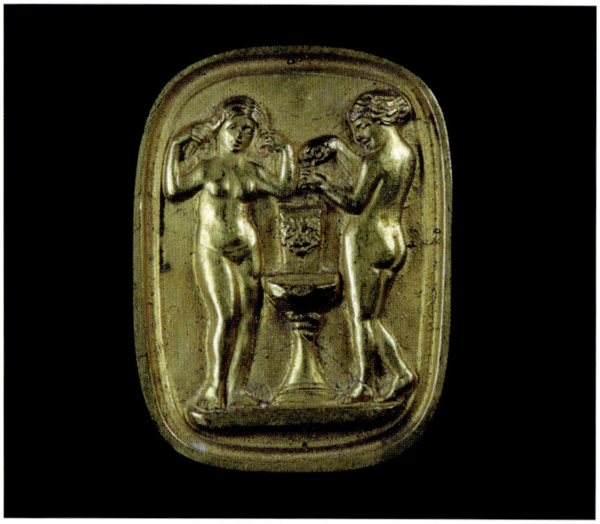

23

(10578) K40 (pl. 2)
Sardonyx, white/brown, polished flat back, set on a plain gold ring
21 x 15

Tassie 6223; Inst.Imp. no. 18; *AGE* no. 147.

Two naked nymphs bathe. One, in the frontal Venus Anadyomene pose, arranges her long hair. The other pours from an unguent vessel into a cup in her hand. Between them is a standed fountain basin with a lion-head spout above. Thick ground line.

Italian, 16th century?

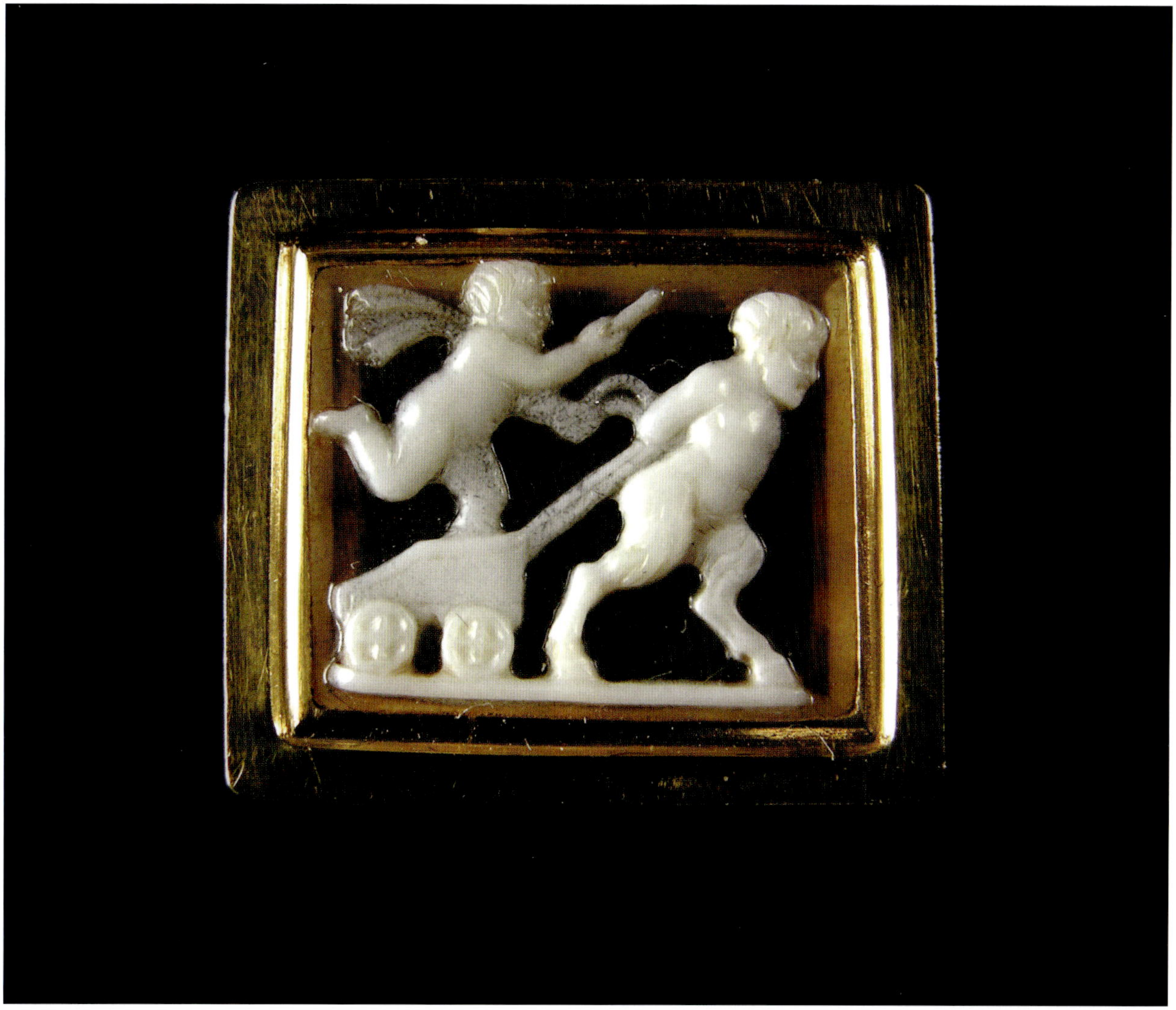

24

(10564) K26 (pl. 2)
Sardonyx, white/pale brown, rectangular, polished flat back, set on a plain gold ring
13 x 11

SG.Imp. 6; In Imp. no. 54; W.Tassie no. 2257; Lippold, pl. 114.5; *AGE* no. 26.

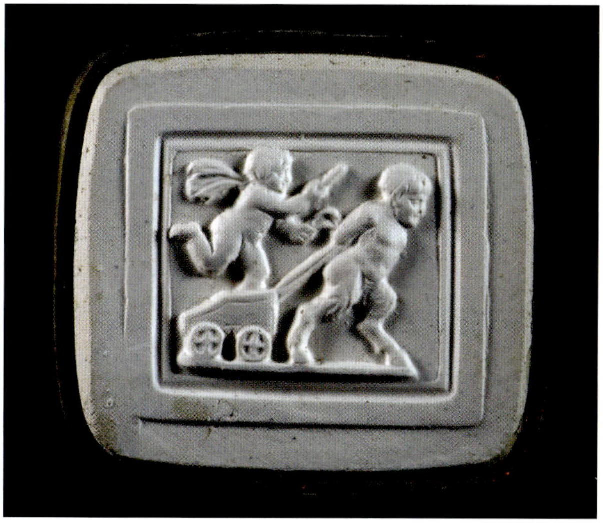

A bearded Pan pulls a four-wheeled cart driven by a child with flying cloak (not wings, though like a Cupid) holding the reins and a goad. Ground line.

18th century.

CAMEO GLASS

These fragments are in highly coloured translucent 'cameo glass', stratified, unlike other 'pastes', which are commonly monochrome. They are from decorative relief plaques or plates, rather than cameos for setting in rings or jewellery.

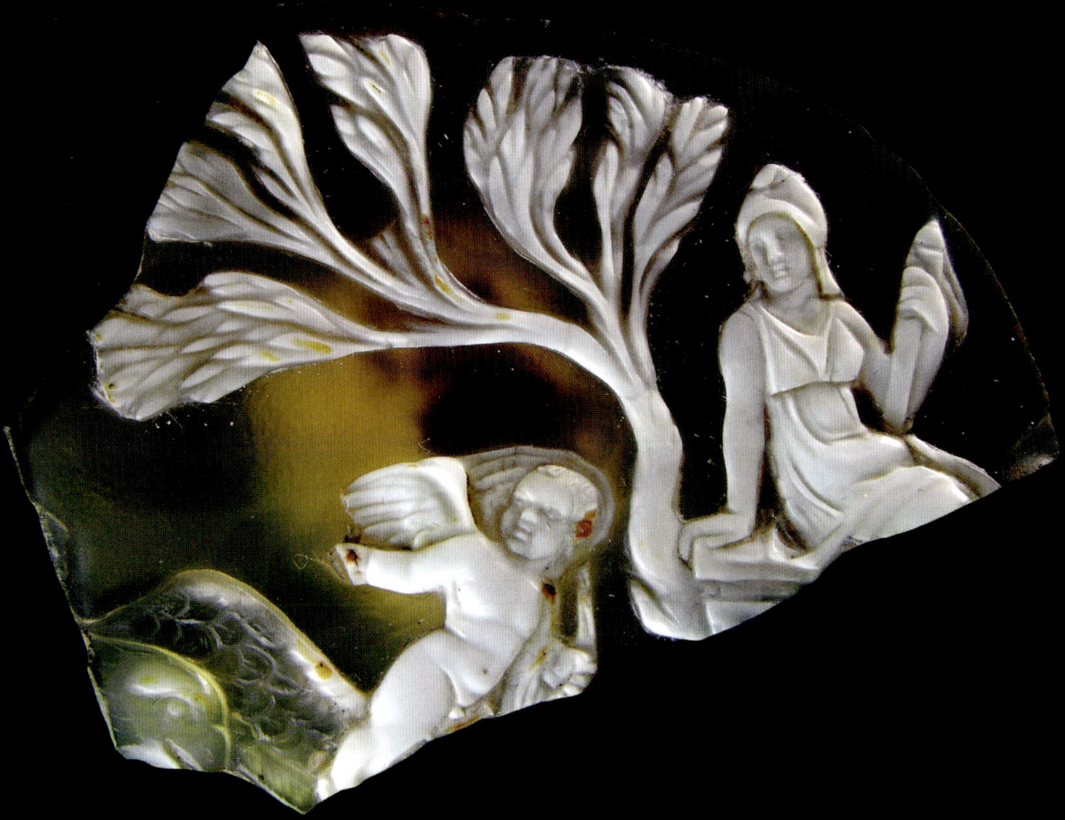

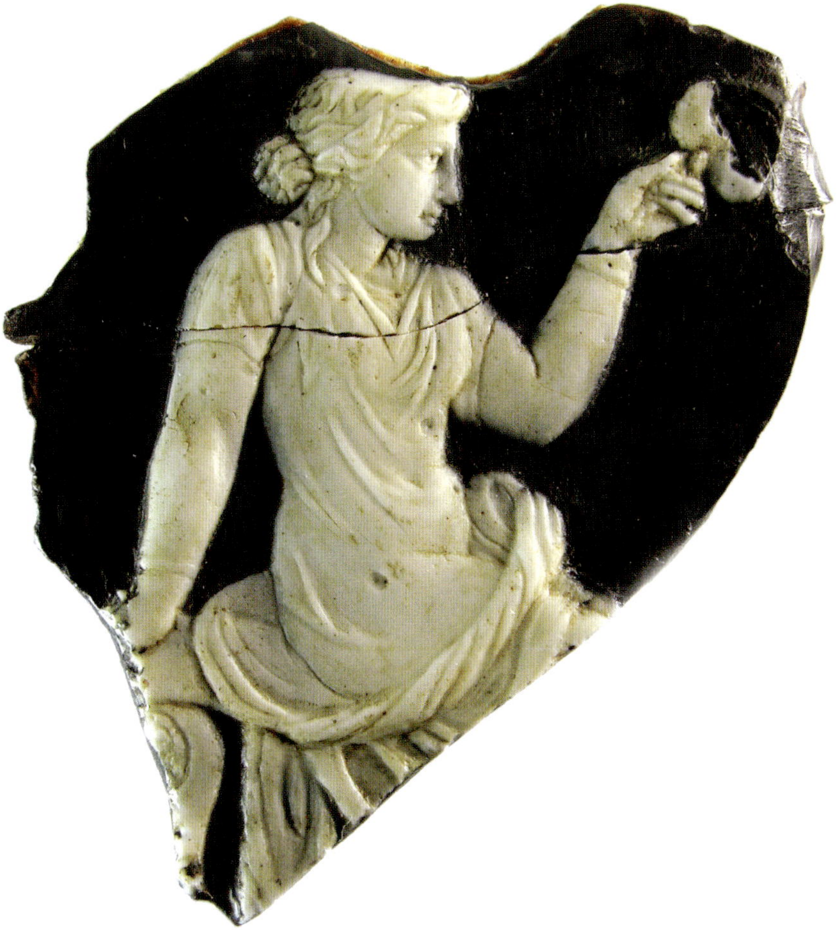

25

(10539) K1
Glass fragment, white/black
54 x 43

AGE no. 113.

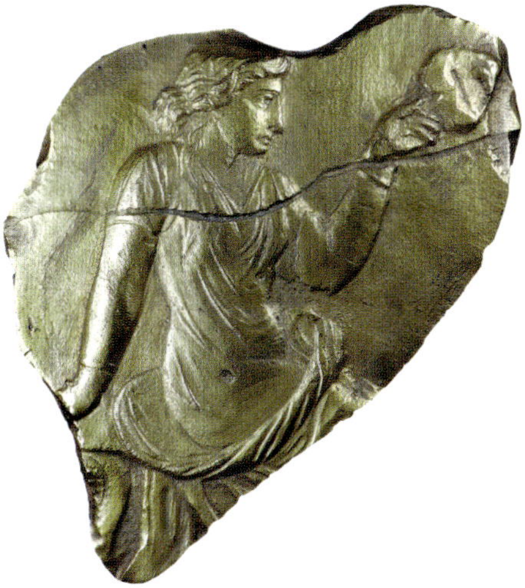

A woman seated on a stool or couch with carved baluster legs, wearing a sleeveless chiton over a short-sleeved tunic with a cloak around her legs, her hair rolled and caught in a bun, bracelets, and holding a fan (much of it broken away).

This is possibly part of a group showing the toilette of Venus but the woman's sleeves may be a hint at something more eastern – Helen (?).

1st century BC/AD.

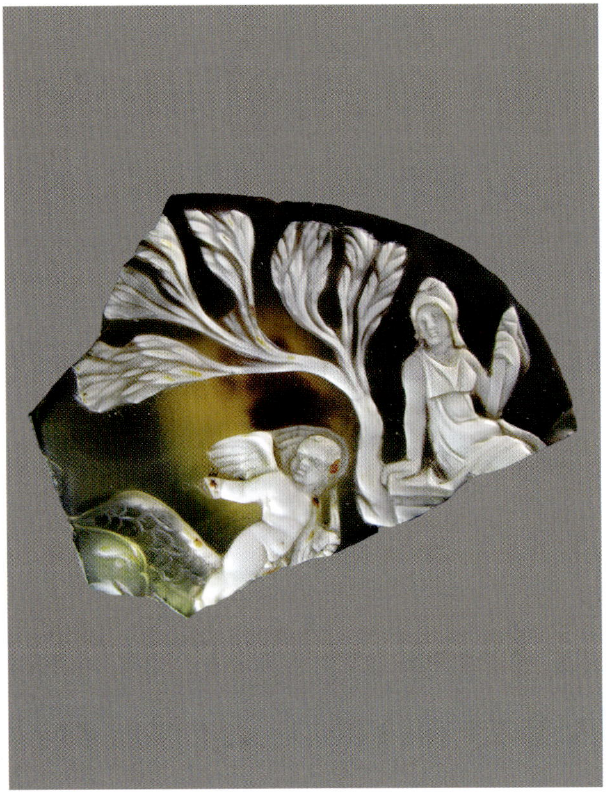

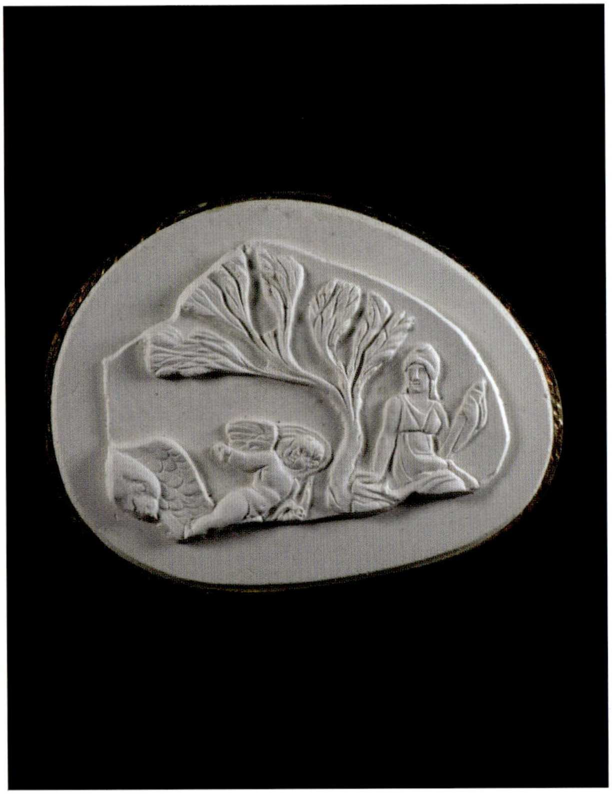

26

(10541) K3

Glass fragment of a disc plaque, white/pale brown, unpolished flat back

33 x 44

SG.Imp. 20; Inst.Imp. no. 30; *AGE* no. 120.

Flying Cupid, dress over one shoulder, is looking round, extending a hand and with the other holding the wing tip of an eagle (if not his bow) whose head and scaly base of a wing appear behind him. At the right a woman wearing a Phrygian cap, in a sleeveless chiton and holding a sheathed sword, is seated on an altar (?) beneath a tree.

The eagle, Phrygian cap and the slightly feminine dress would suit Ganymede, approached by the Jupiter eagle, but the sheathed sword is incongruous. There is nothing to recommend previous identifications as Io.

1st century BC/AD.

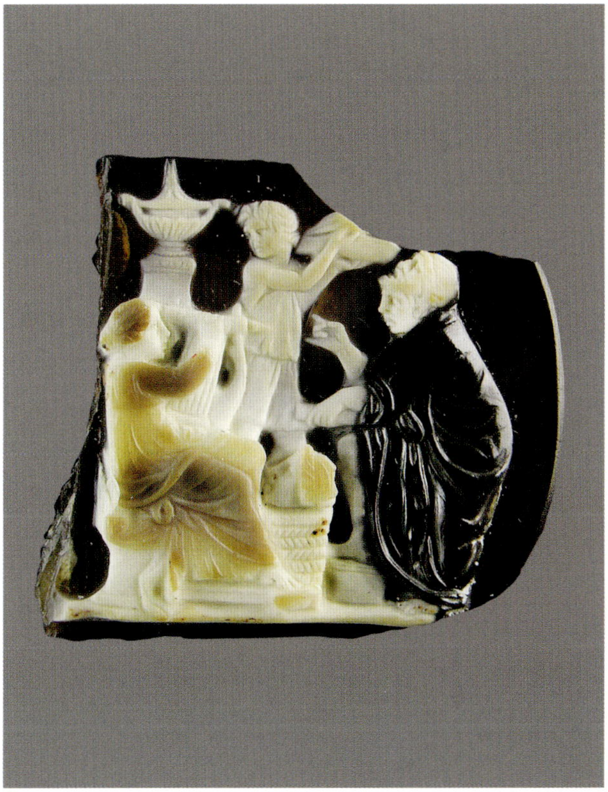

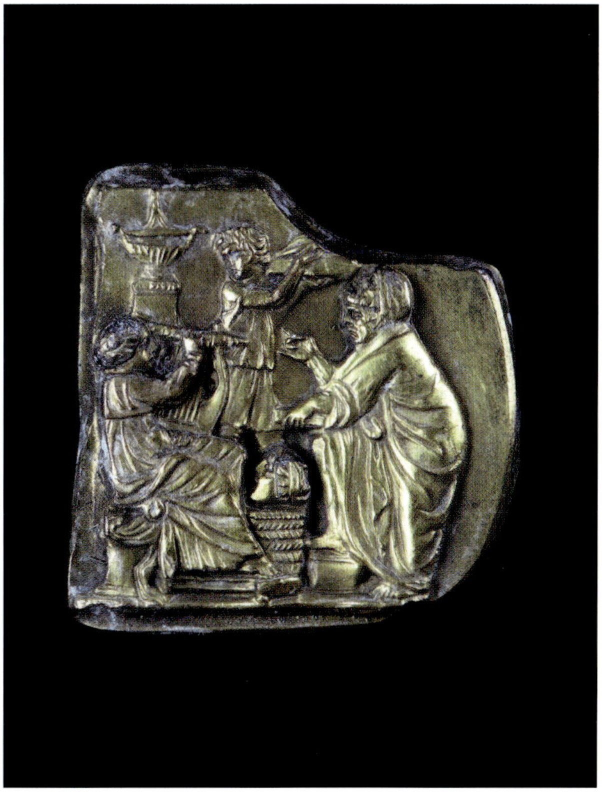

27

(10542) K4 (pl. 1)
Glass fragment of a disc plaque, mottled brown and black/white/black, unpolished flat back
23 x 23

SG.Imp. 35; Inst.Imp. no. 25; King 1872, I p. 310; Paoletti I, I.216; *AGE* no. 309.

An actor wearing a heavy cloak leans forward, one foot on a block, one hand extended making a 'horns' gesture with his fingers, the other holding a scroll, and wearing an old-man theatrical mask on the back of his head. Before him at his feet is a basket with a female mask upon it. Beyond and above stands a young satyr in short dress, looking round, and holding up a flat basket containing something veiled. Behind him is a pillar bearing a low urn, two handled and with a conical lid, in front of which is seated, on a lion-legged chair with footstool, a dressed woman playing a kithara.

The basket is the *mystica vannus Iacchi*, the winnowing fan containing sacred objects (commonly fruit or a phallos) which are veiled. This is then a Bacchic initiation scene, in which a basket also commonly appears, but containing a snake. (On initiation paraphernalia see on *Marlborough* no. 1). It is unusual for the theatrical aspect to be so prominent in such scenes. For the style and parts of the subject compare *London*, Walters no. 3496.

1st century BC/AD.

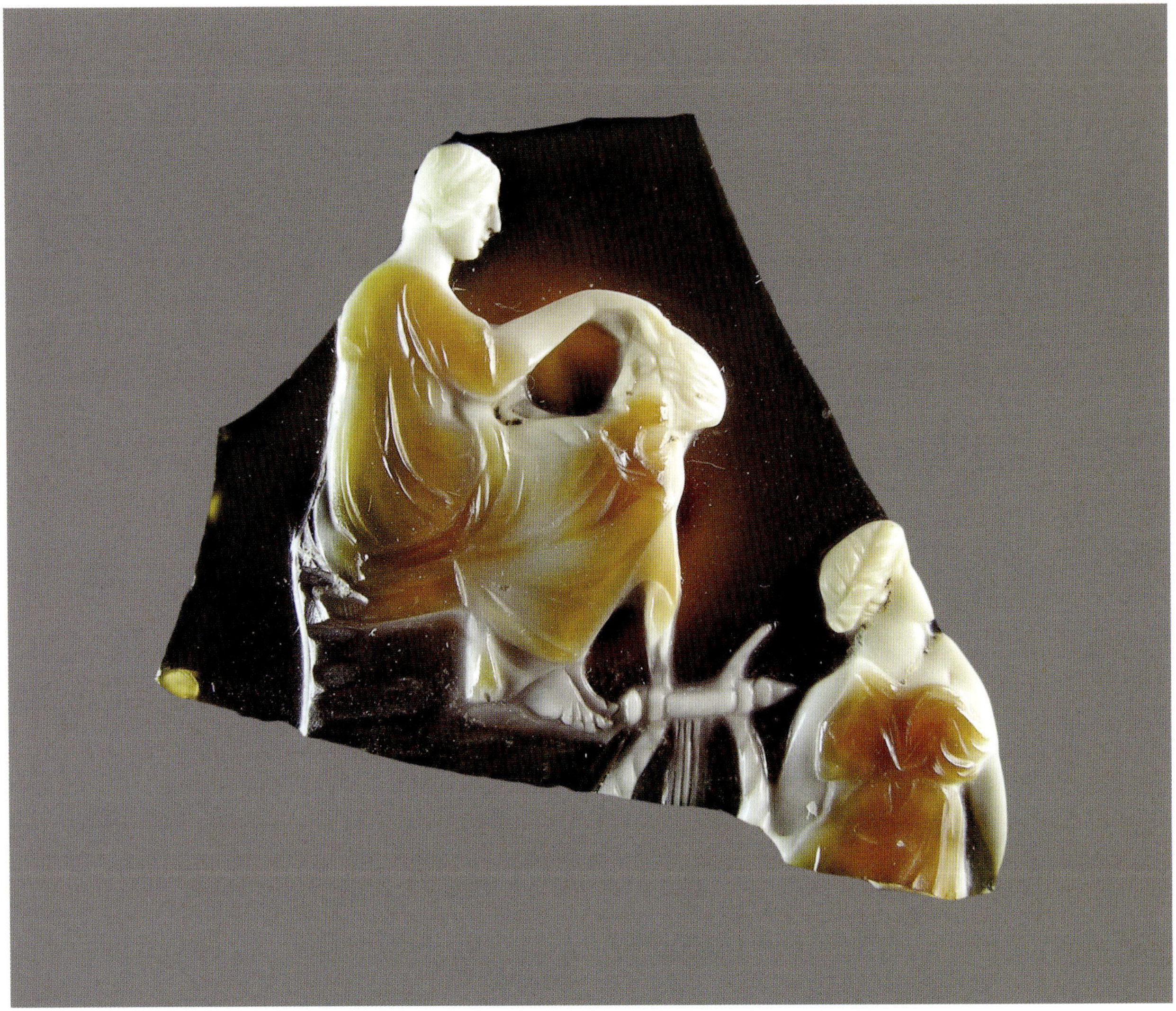

28

(10540) K2
Glass (sardonyx?) fragment of a disc plaque, brown/white/brown, polished flat back
36 x 36

SG.Imp. 114; Inst.Imp. no. 46; W.Tassie 1248; *AGE* no. 278.

Muses. Thalia, fully dressed, seated on layered rocks, holds a tragic mask in her right hand, her left on her knee. Terpsichore in sleeveless dress, with her lyre, is below, apparently seated.

1st century BC/AD.

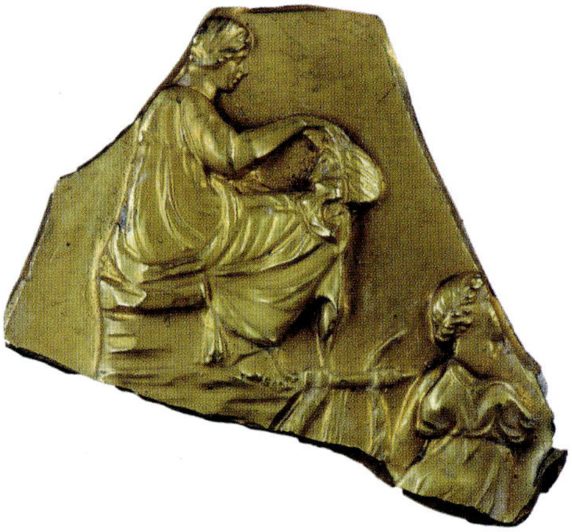

SINGLE FIGURES

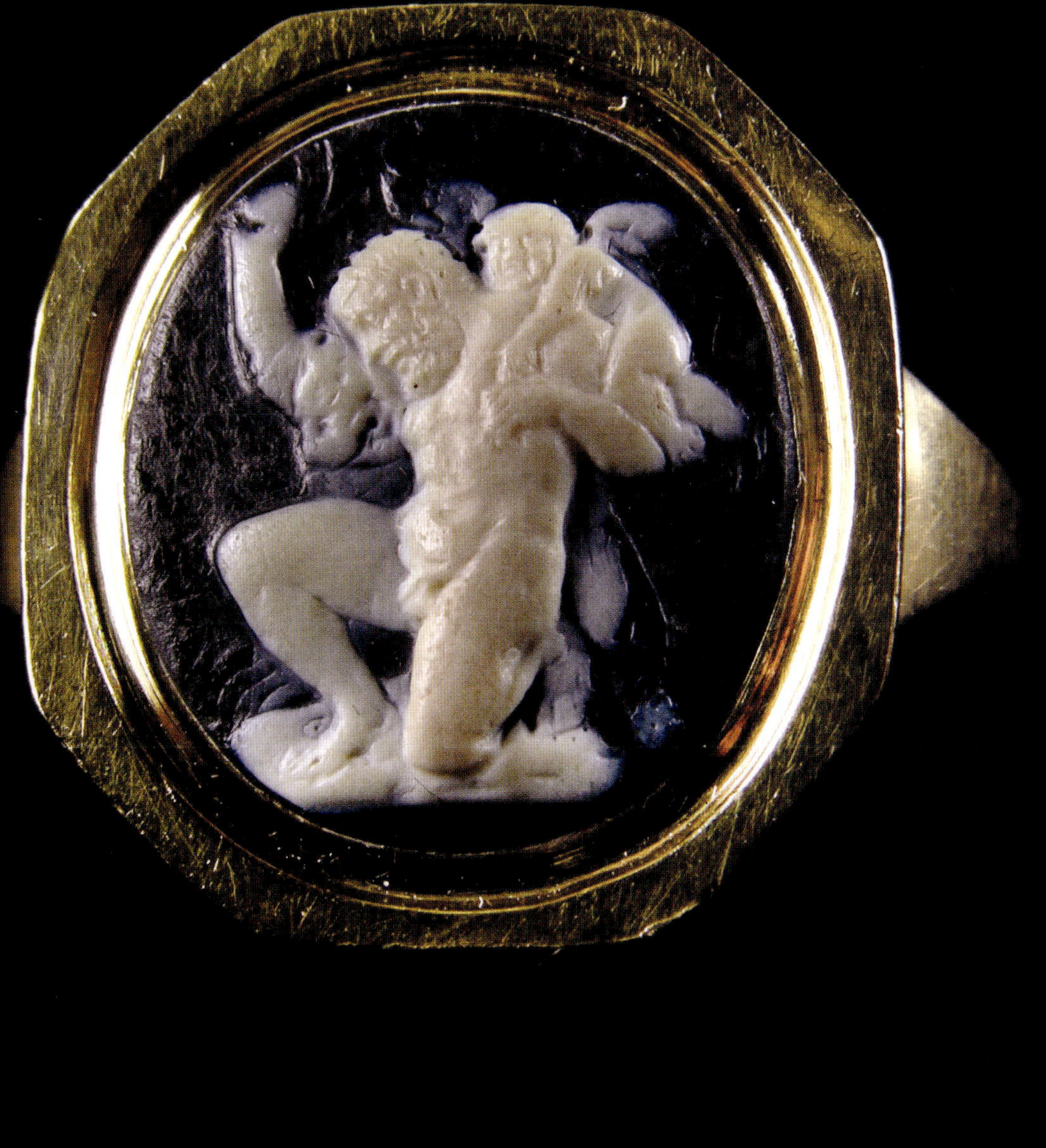

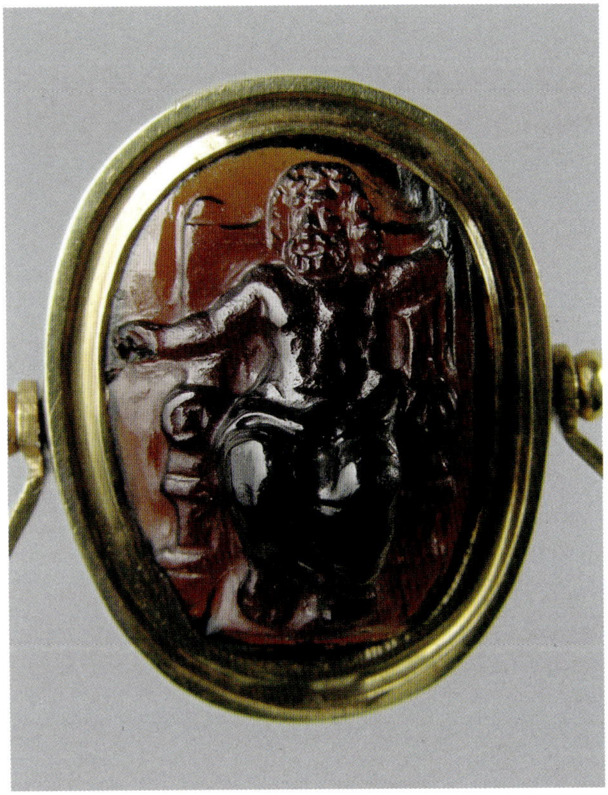

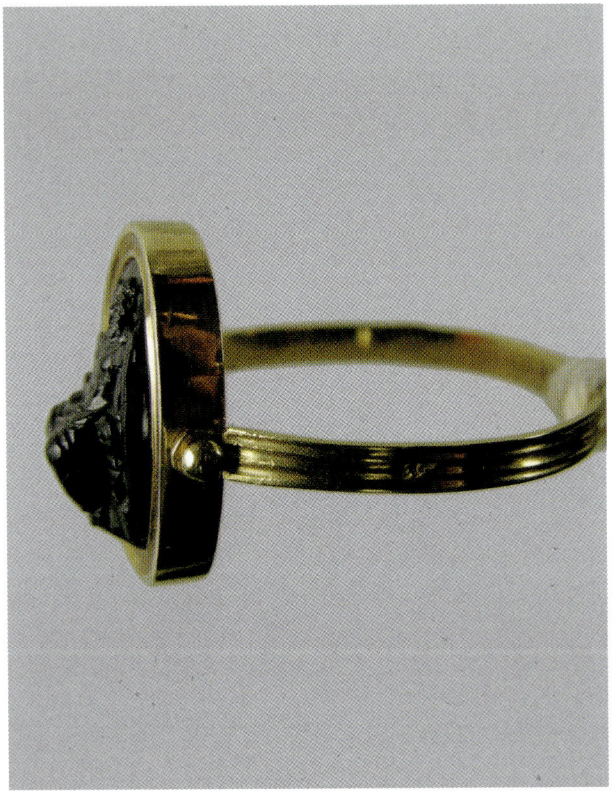

29

(10749)
Garnet, polished convex back, set on a gold swivel ring
13 x 9

Jupiter seated frontally, half-dressed, with footstool, holding a sceptre and a cup. The throne has disc ends to the arms (as *Wien* I, no. 397; *Munich* 3, no. 2269).

1st century BC/AD?

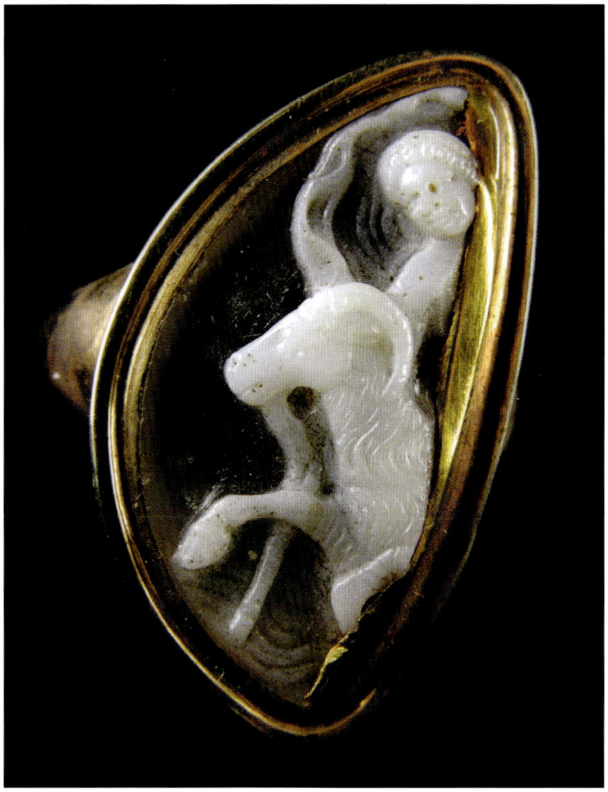

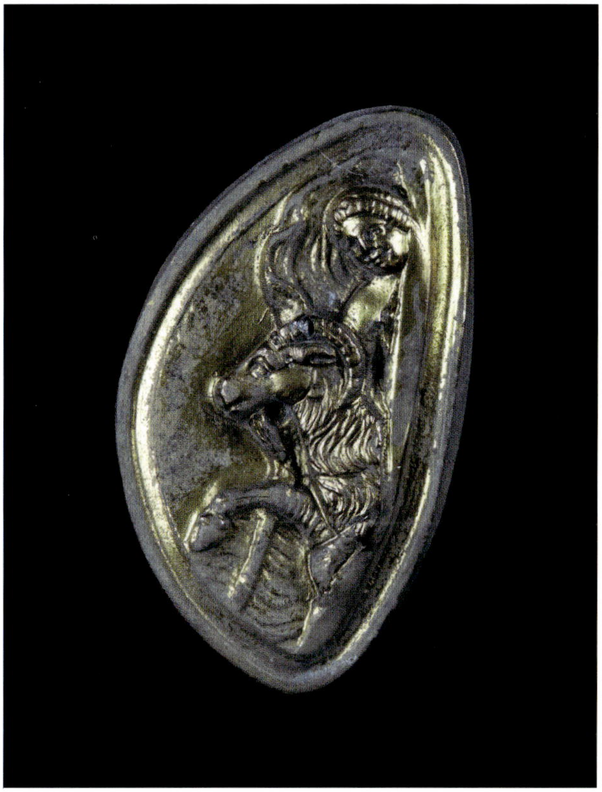

30

(10595) K57
Sardonyx fragment, white/pale brown, unpolished flat back
22 x 14

SG.Imp. 123; Inst.Imp. no. 43.

Aphrodite/Venus *(epitragia)* riding a ram over water. She is holding her dress over her head and holds a torch, as goddess of light, in her lowered left hand.

Compare *LIMC* VIII, pl. 156, 293 (cameo, Naples 25845; Paoletti I, I.282; Giuliano, *Cammei,* p. 28, below (Naples); Pannuti, *Napoli* no. 109). The torch distinguishes her from Helle; *AG* II, 261–2.

1st century BC/AD.

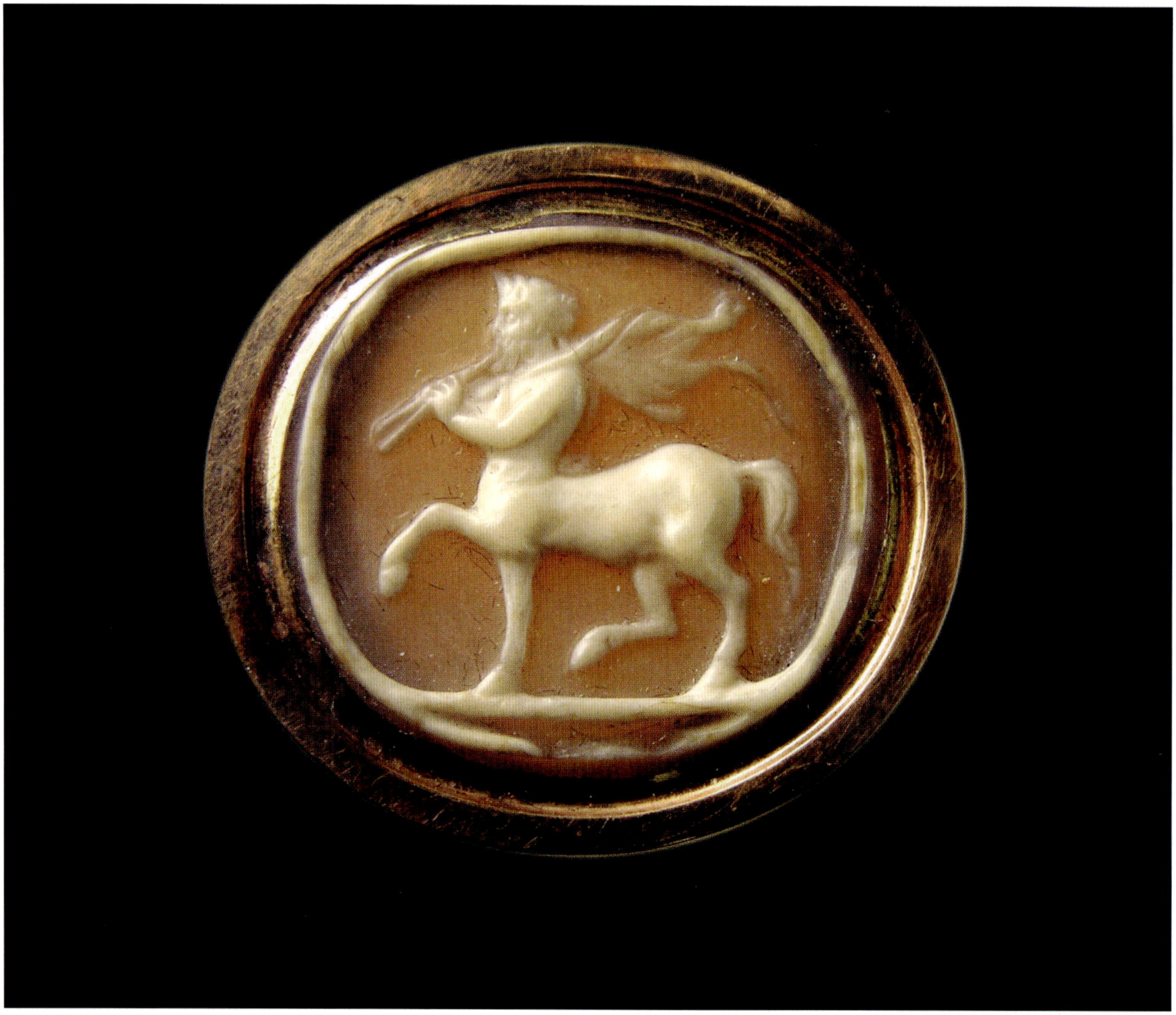

31

(10591) K53 (pl. 2)
Sardonyx, white/brown, set on a plain gold ring
17 x 15

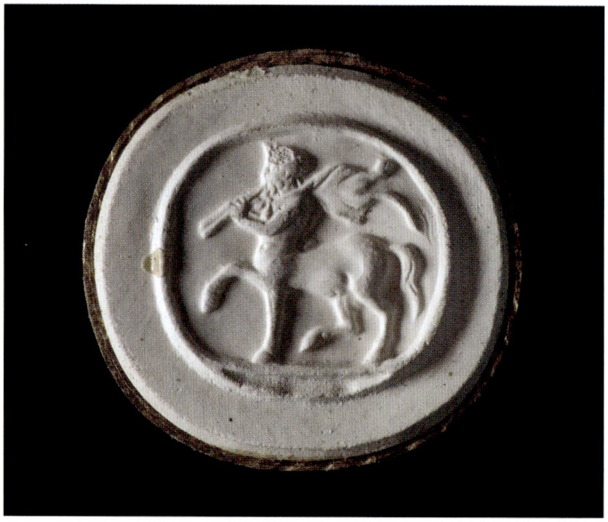

SG.Imp. 85; Inst.Imp. no. 6.

A centaur playing double pipes, his animal skin flying behind his neck. Ground line and border.

1st century BC/AD?

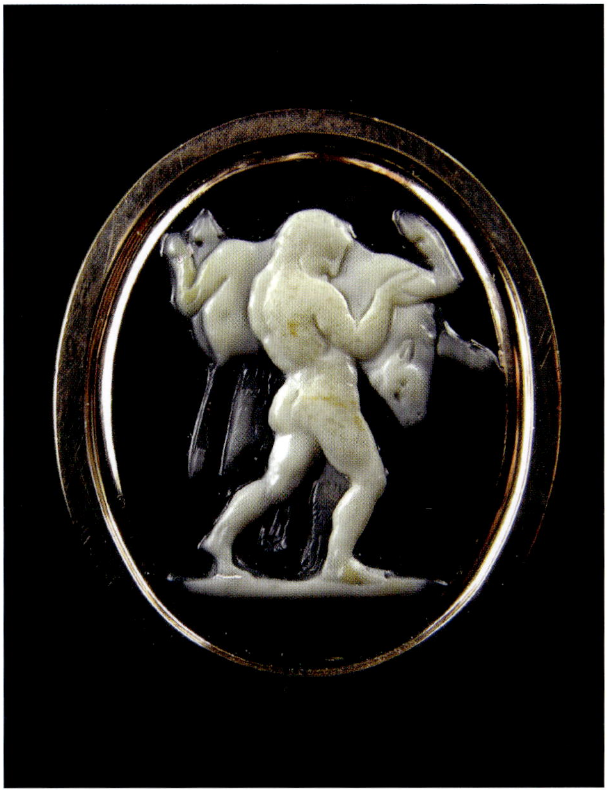

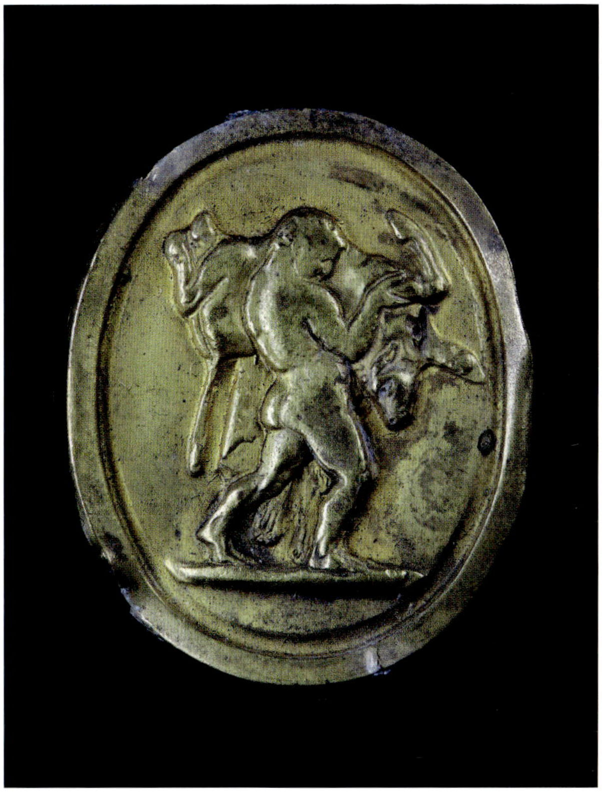

32

(10570) K32 (pl .2)
Sardonyx, white/brown, polished flat back, set on a plain gold ring
20 x 17

SG.Imp. 120; Inst.Imp. no. 11.

Hercules shouldering the Cretan Bull, his lionskin hanging beyond him by his legs. Ground line.

This is one of the conventional poses for the Labour in the Roman period, especially on gems (cf. *LIMC* V, 63). It is derived from his treatment of the boar (see our **33**).

1st century BC/AD?

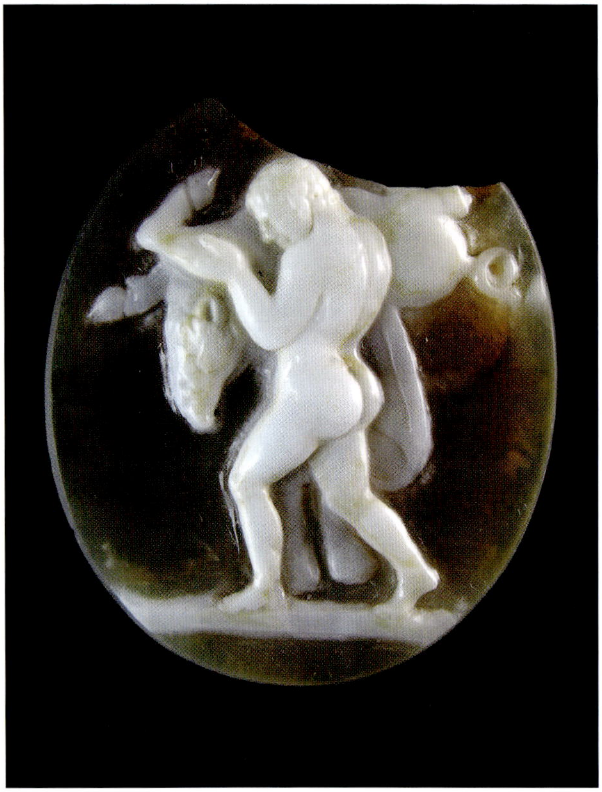

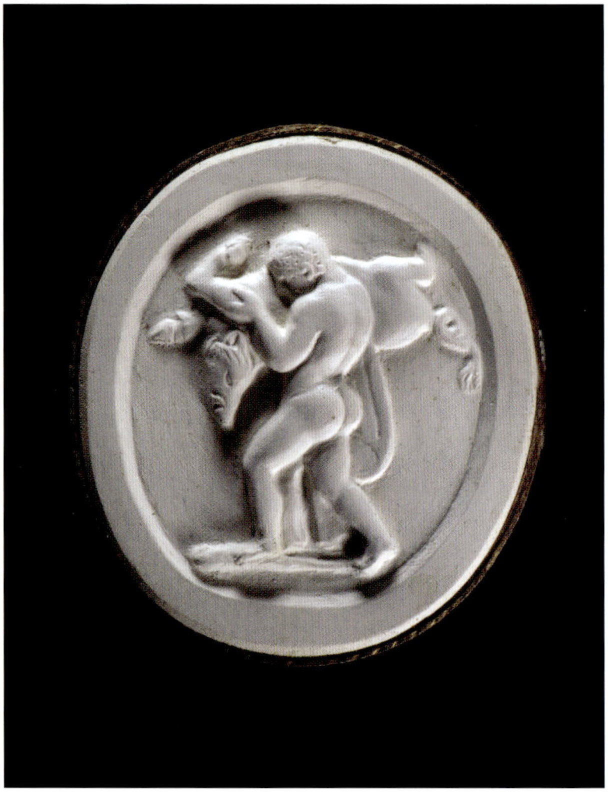

33

(10543) K5
Sardonyx, white/pale brown, unpolished flat back
38 x 35

SG.Imp. 160; AGE no. 182.

Hercules shouldering the Erymanthian Boar, his lion-skin hanging down beyond his body. Ground line.

Another of the conventional Greek poses for the Labour (cf. *LIMC* V, 46–7); he is about to deliver the Boar to King Eurystheus. Compare Giuliano, *Cammei* no. 79.

1st century BC/AD?

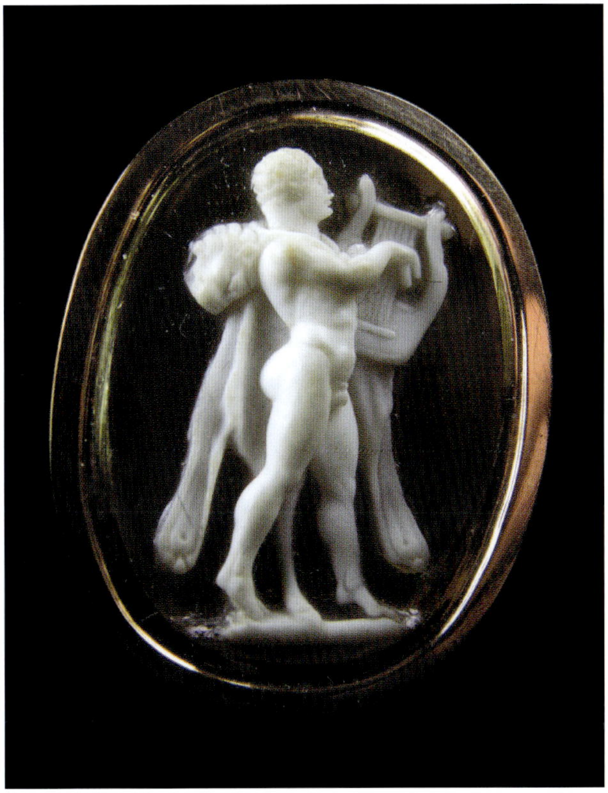

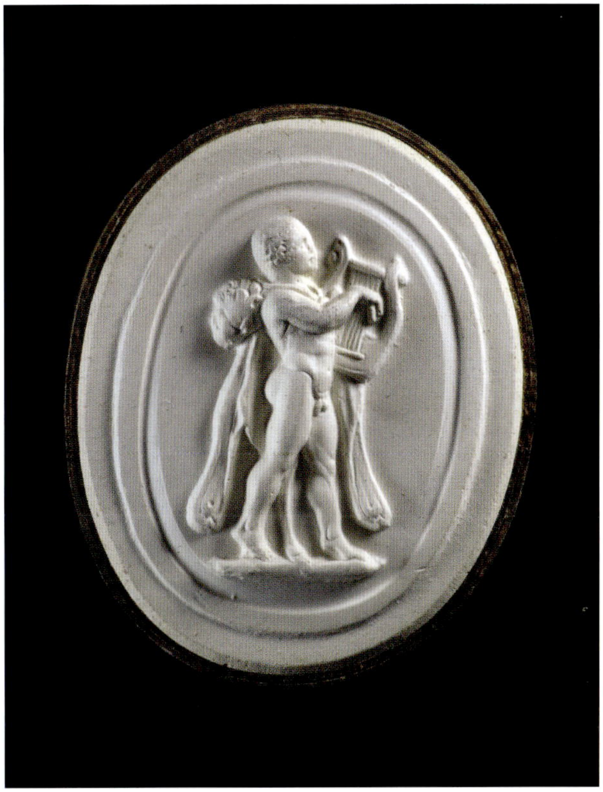

34

(10565) K27 (pl. 2)
Sardonyx, white/brown, polished flat back, set on a plain gold ring
23 x 16

From the Cardinal Grimani Collection; Vico, pl. 22 *(Hercules Musagetes ac si dicas Musarum Dux)*; SG.Imp. 73; Inst. Imp. no. 23; W.Tassie 1886; *AGE* no. 189.

Hercules Musagetes. The hero steps forward on tiptoe, playing a lyre and with his lionskin slung from his shoulder, behind him. Ground line.

Perhaps derived from the figure on a gem by Skylax (Vollenweider, pl. 92.1,3; Zwierlein-Diehl 2005, 342). See *LIMC* IV, 813. The tiptoe pose is a common one for neo-Attic deities.

1st century BC?

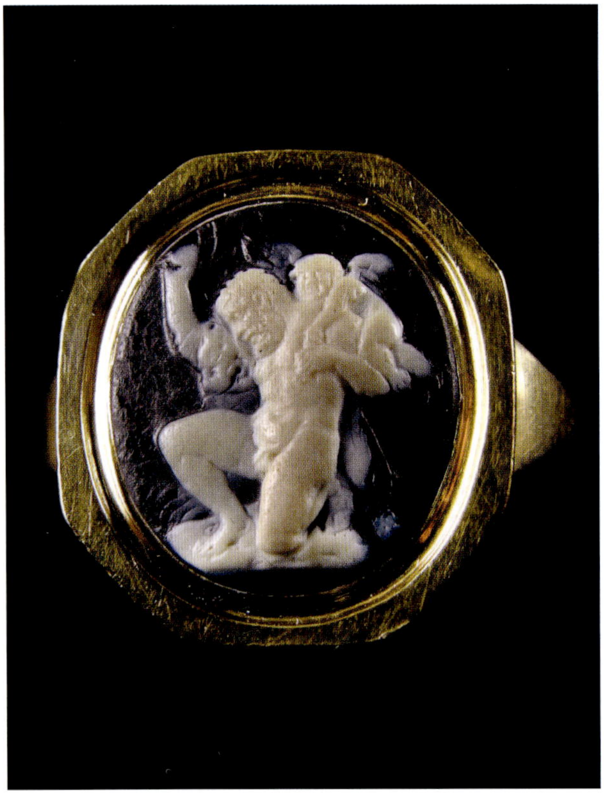

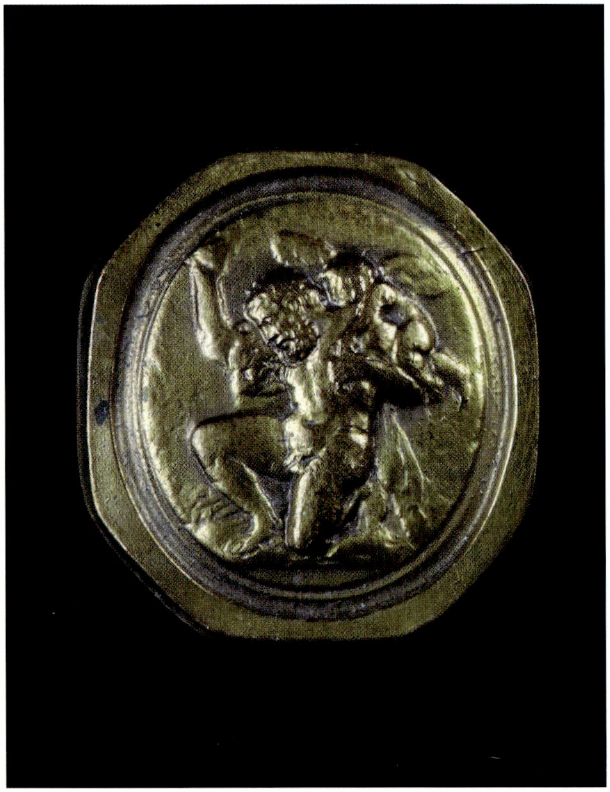

35

(10566) K28 (pl. 2)
Sardonyx, white/brown, polished flat back, set on a plain gold ring
14 x 12

SG.Imp. 101; Tassie 6007; Inst.Imp. no. 169.

Hercules kneeling, overcome by Cupid who climbs on to his shoulder, wings spread. The hero wears his lionskin, the head hanging over his arm. Ground line.

A popular subject denoting the victory of love over strength (*LIMC* V, 1740; *Oxford* on no. 382). The scheme, with Hercules' hand raised in surrender not holding the club, is that of a cameo in Naples (Vollenweider, pl. 27.6,7; compare *Würzburg* no. 385).

1st century BC.

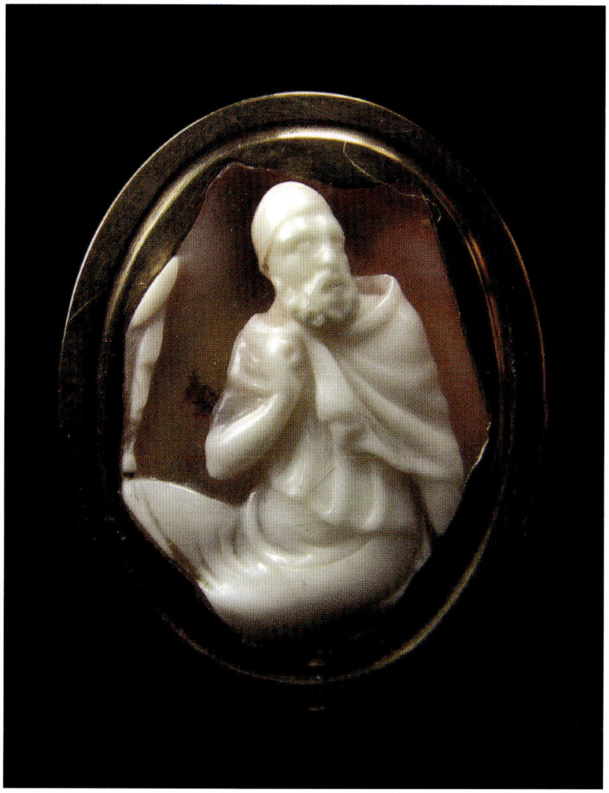

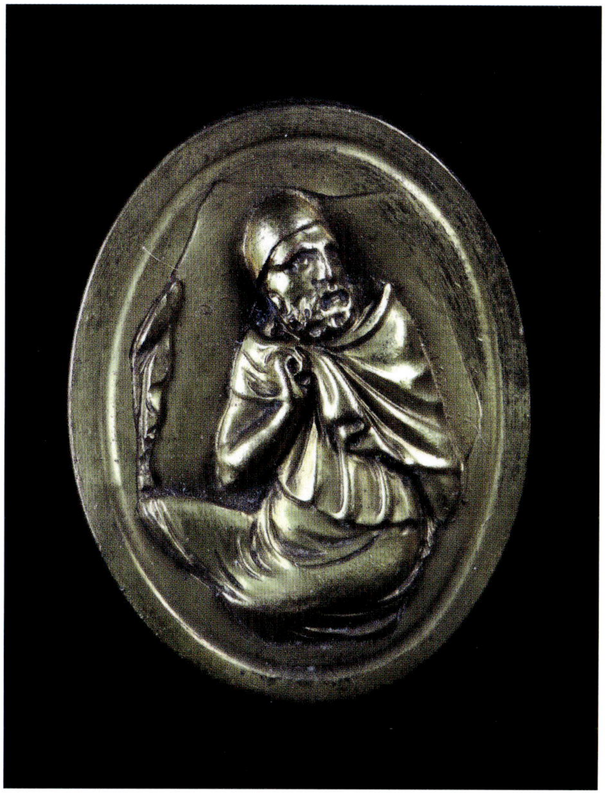

36

(10579) K41 (pl. 2)
Sardonyx fragment, white/brown, polished flat back, set on a plain gold ring
18 x 14

SG.Imp. 125; Inst.Imp. no. 42.

A seated man, probably Ulysses, wearing a cap and holding a cloak closely wrapped around his dressed body, seated. At the left the hanging dress of a second figure, standing.

1st century BC/AD.

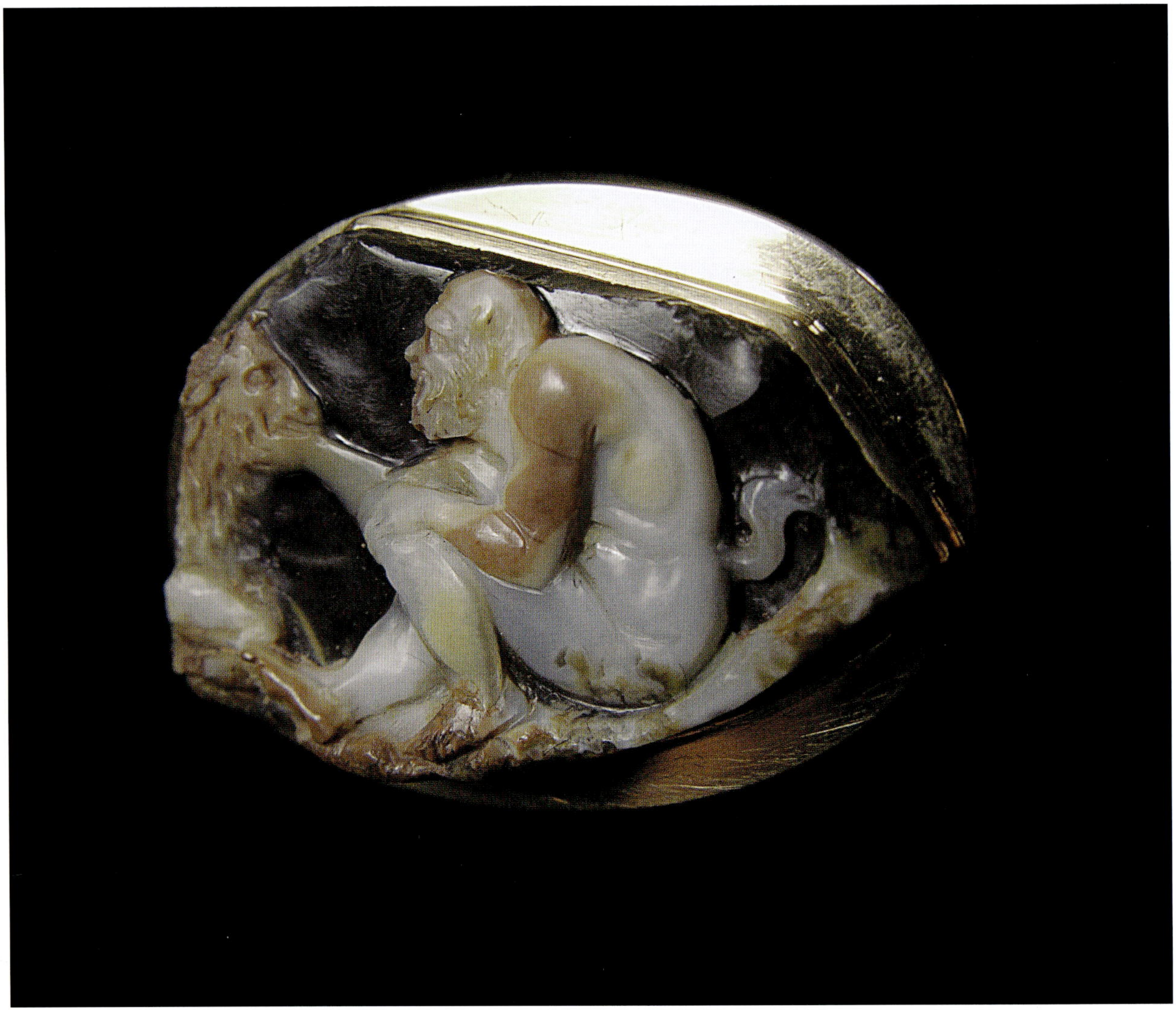

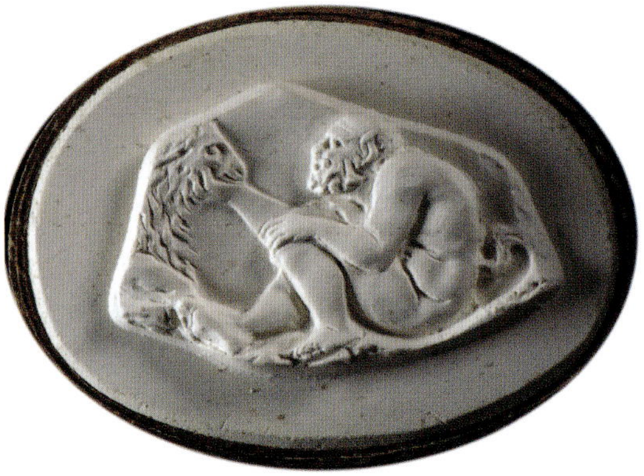

37

(10567) K29 (pl.2)
Sardonyx fragment, brown (left arm, feet)/white/dark brown, unpolished flat back, set on a plain gold ring with triple ends to the hoop
26 x 17

SG.Imp. 162; Inst.Imp. no. 35; *AGE* no. 29.

A seated satyr, his double pipes behind him on the ground, caresses the head of a kneeling goat. Ground line.

Compare *Würzburg* no. 250; *Munich* 2, no. 994; *Hanover* no. 876; Sangiorgi Coll. Satyrs, being part-goat, have an affinity with the creature.

1st century BC/AD.

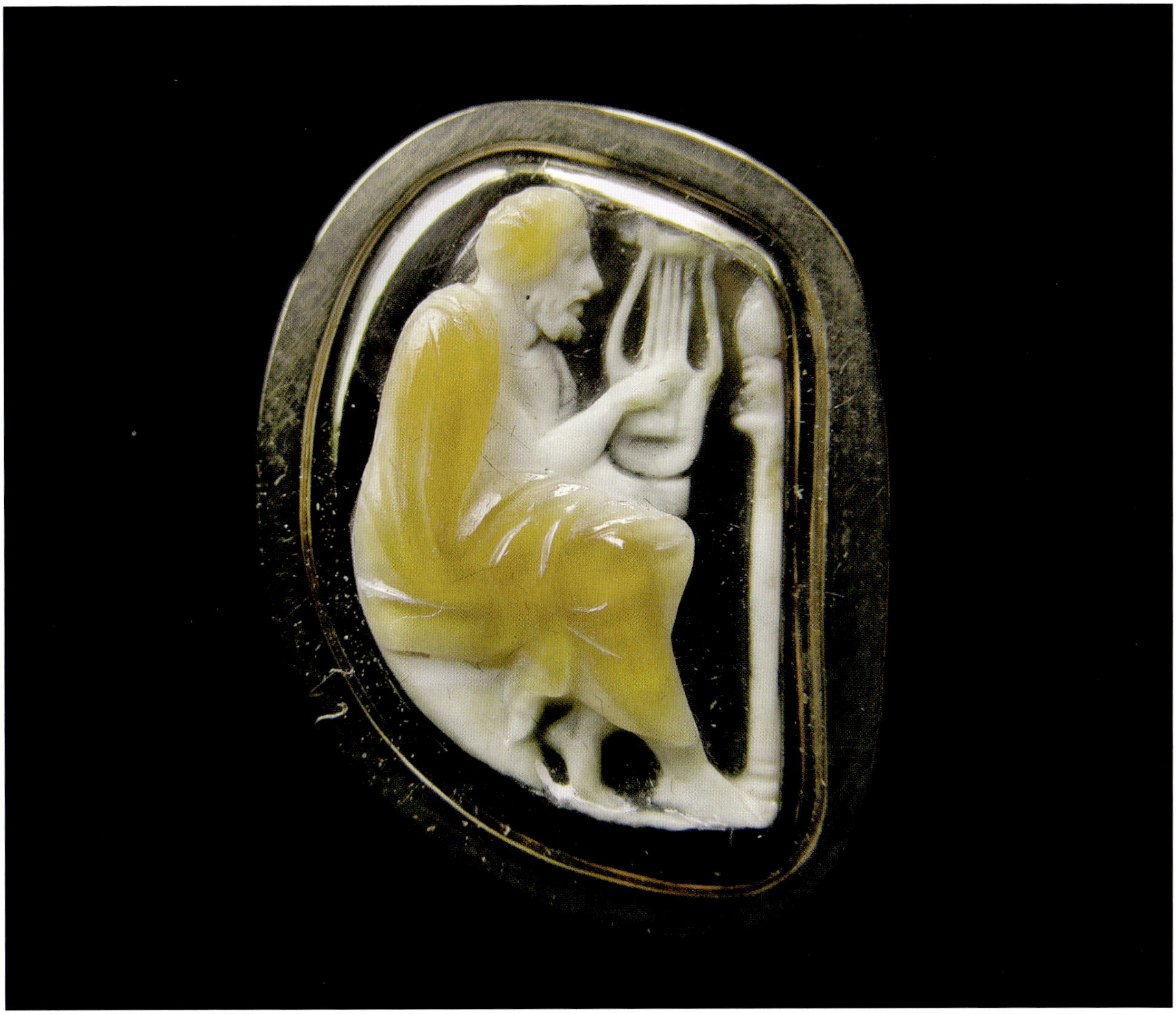

38

(10575) K37 (pl. 2)
Sardonyx, brown/white/dark brown, polished flat back, set on a plain gold ring
20 x 18

SG.Imp. 136; Inst. Imp. no. 39; Cades, Cent. IV, 80; W.Tassie 3475; King 1872, pl. 45.1; *AGE* no. 283.

An old man, heavily cloaked, seated on a block and playing a lyre before a column upon which a second figure (missing) is placing a conoid object.

Popularly taken for Homer at the tomb of Achilles.

1st century BC/AD.

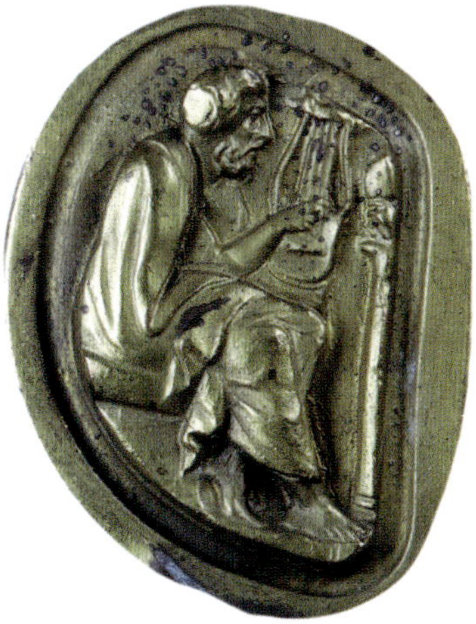

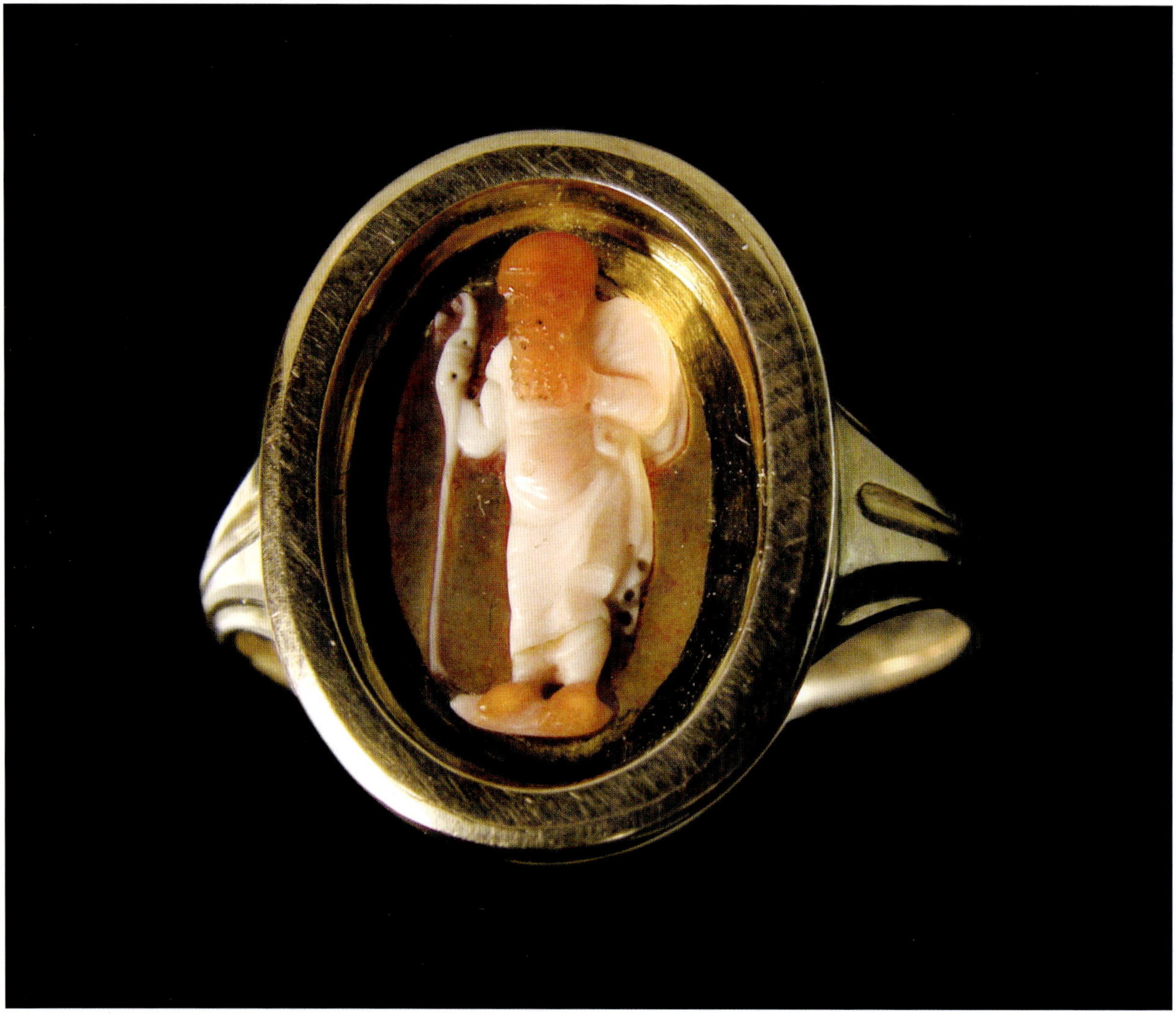

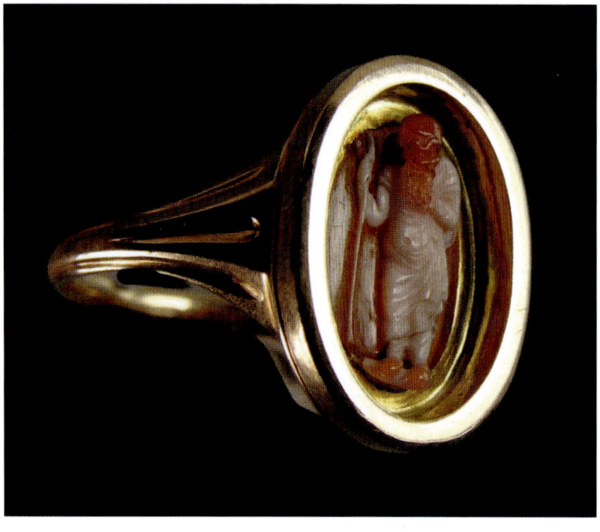

39

(10657) K119
Sardonyx, orange/white/light brown, polished flat back, set on a plain gold ring
11 x 8

AGE no. 311.

An actor wearing the pallium cloak and an old-man mask, with a staff. Ground line.

A popular subject; compare *Marlborough* no. 342; *Würzburg* no. 446; *Geneva* no. 327.

1st century BC.

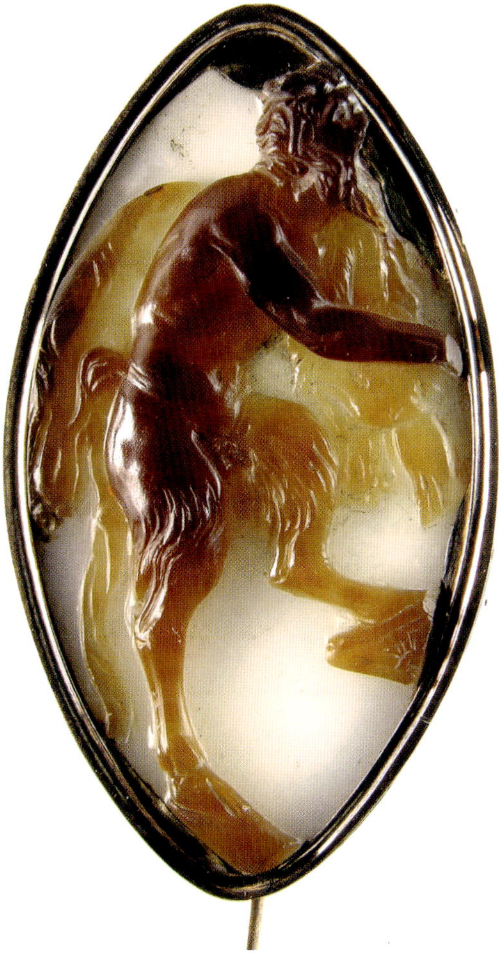

40

(10549) K11
Sardonyx, brown/white, a fragment, reshaped: the right part of the gem is heavily damaged. Unpolished flat back, mounted on a pin
38 x 22

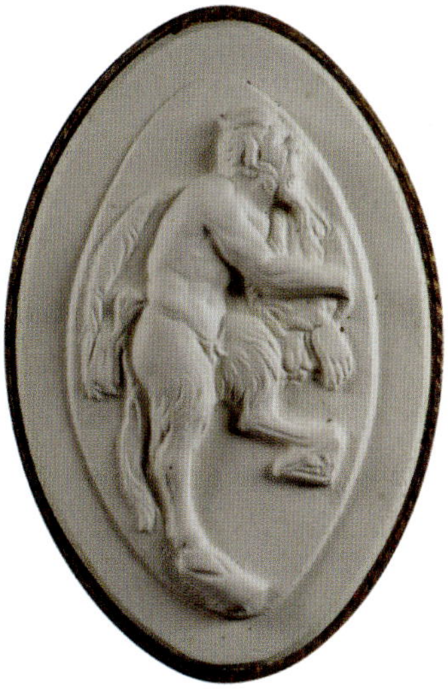

SG.Imp. 4; Inst.Imp. no. 28; Tassie 5159; *AGE* no. 157.

An elderly Pan stepping up onto a patterned ledge, possibly the step of a chariot, holding the body/skin (?) of a panther or lion over his shoulder. Thick groundline.

1st century BC/AD?

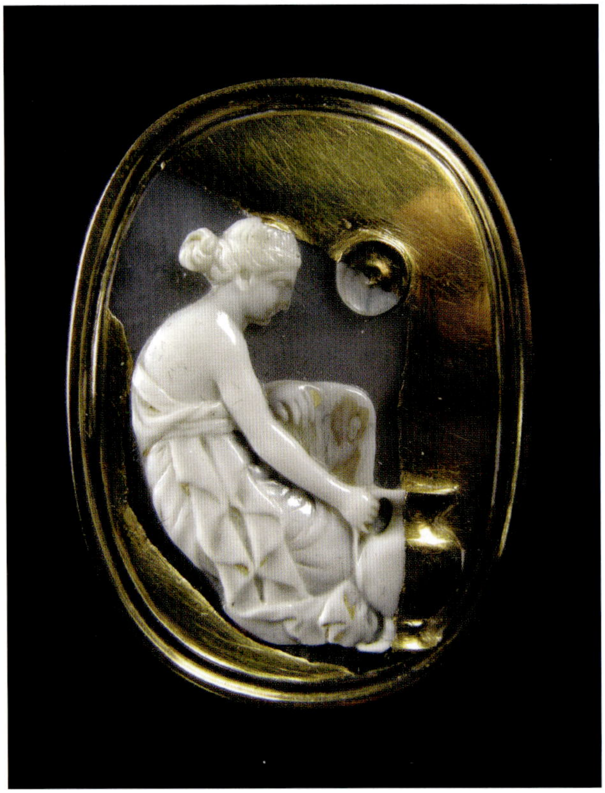

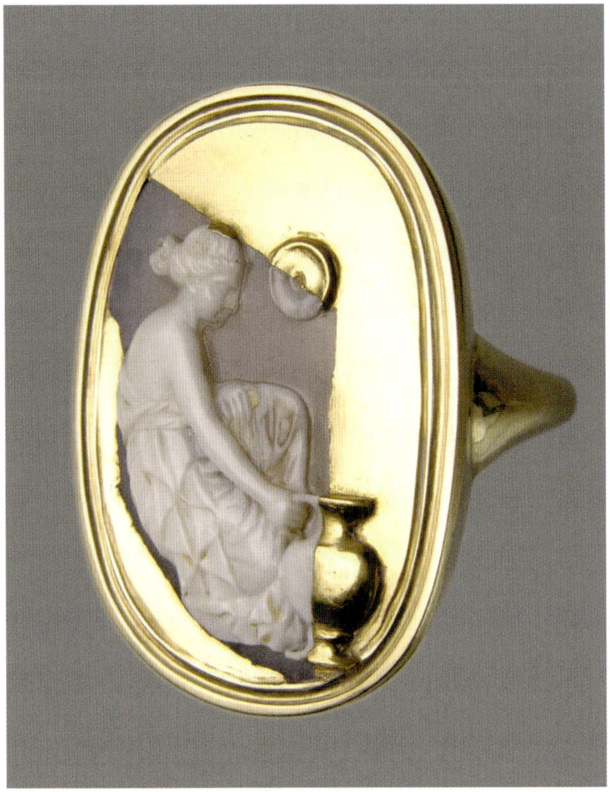

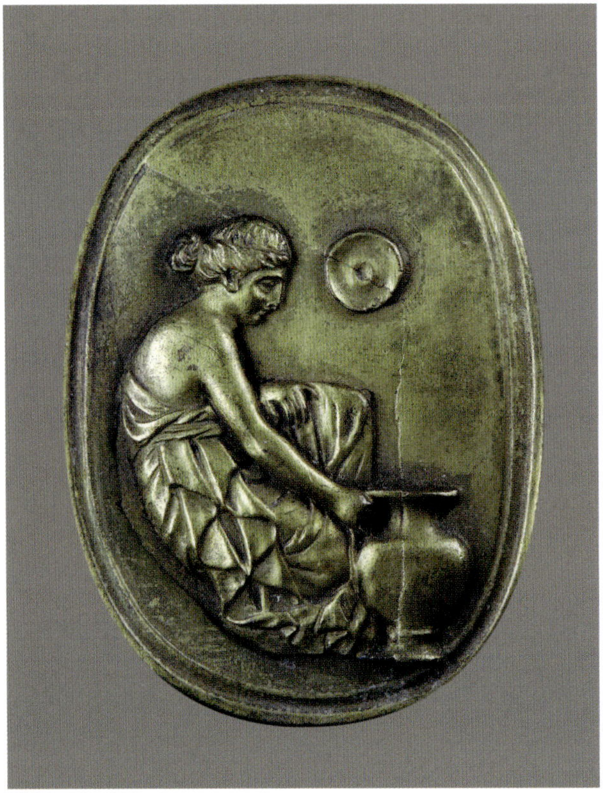

41

(10561) K23 (pl. 2)
Agate fragment restored in gold, white/grey, unpolished flat back, set on a plain gold ring
22 x 13

SG.Imp. 112; Inst.Imp. no. 49; Paoletti I, I.351; King 1872, pl. 37.7; *AGE* no. 145.

A kneeling woman, her hair tied in a bun, dressed in a peplos with one shoulder bared, holding the handle of a hydria. Part of a phiale in the field above, or the spout of a fountain.

This is Amymone at the spring, awaiting attack by a satyr or god. She appears in this pose on other gems, as *LIMC* I, 743, pls 597–8, nos 5, 7.

1st century BC/AD.

42

(10559) K21 (pl. 2)
Agate, white/brown, polished flat back, set on a plain gold ring
21 x 18

SG.Imp. 22; Inst.Imp. no. 48; *AGE* no. 115.

A naked woman, her hair tied, probably Venus, seated on dress on a couch before a pillar bearing a vase.

1st century AD.

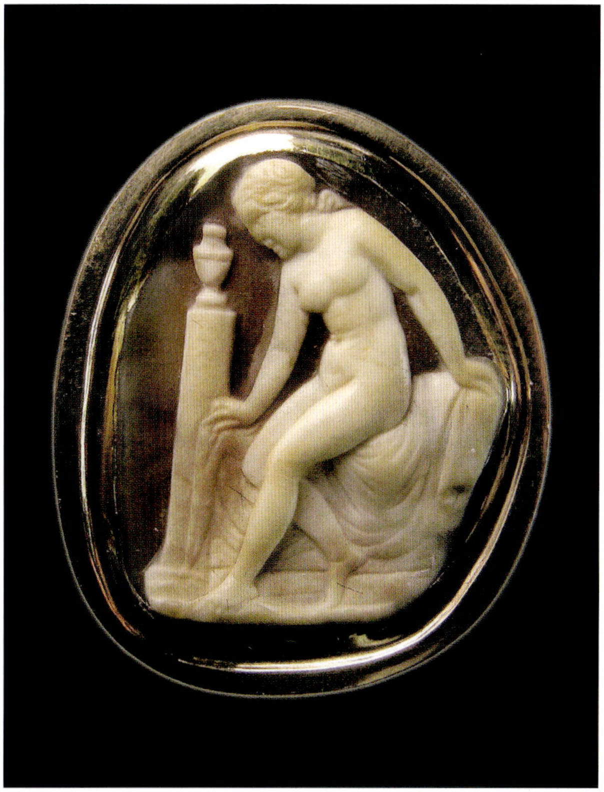

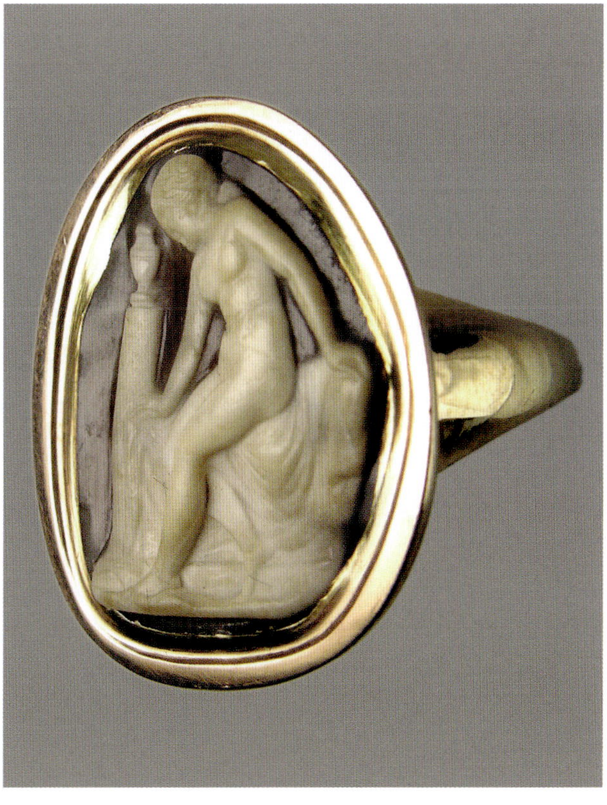

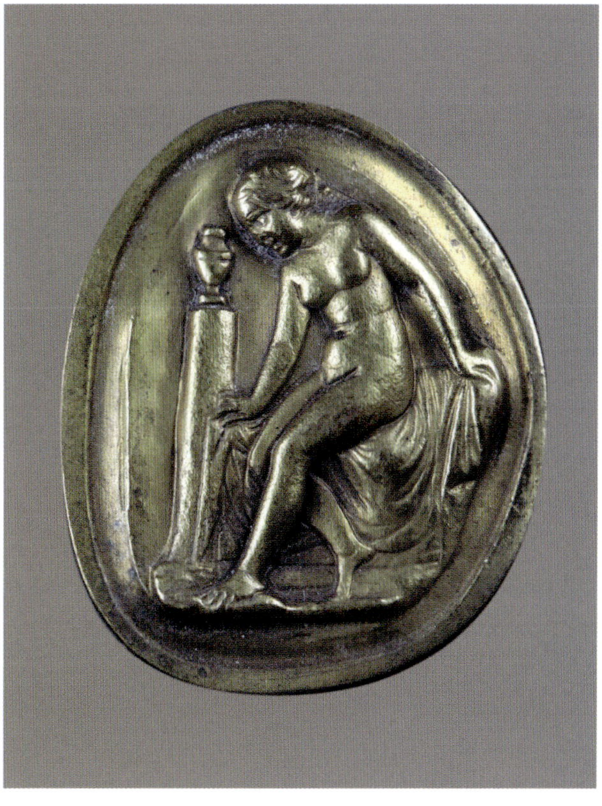

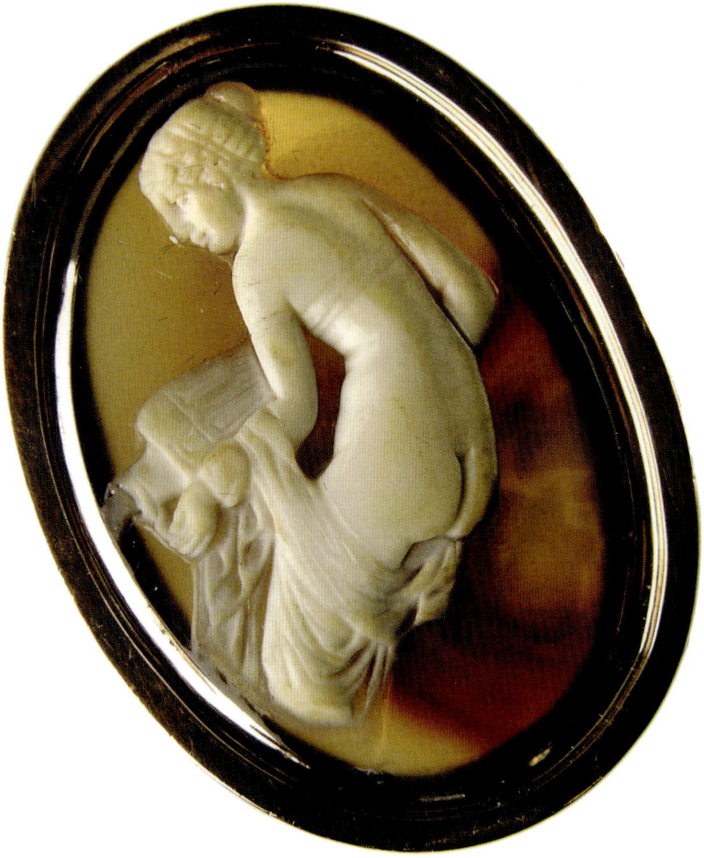

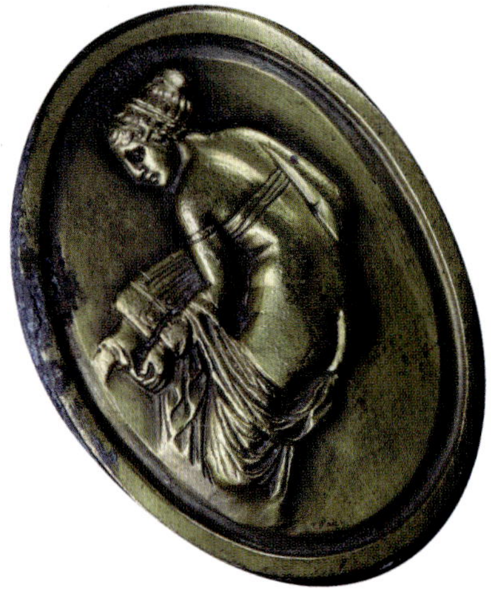

43

(10568) K30 (pl.2)
Sardonyx, white/brown, set on a plain gold ring
24 x 16

SG.Imp. 147; Inst.Imp. no. 51; King 1872, pl. 41.6; *AGE* no. 146.

A woman, her hair bound, naked but for an armlet, breastband and dress around her legs and over her forearm, is pouring water from a handled, fluted vase decorated with rosettes at the shoulder.

Perhaps a Danaid with her leaky vase. Cf. the relief, *LIMC* III, pl. 251.21.

1st century BC/AD.

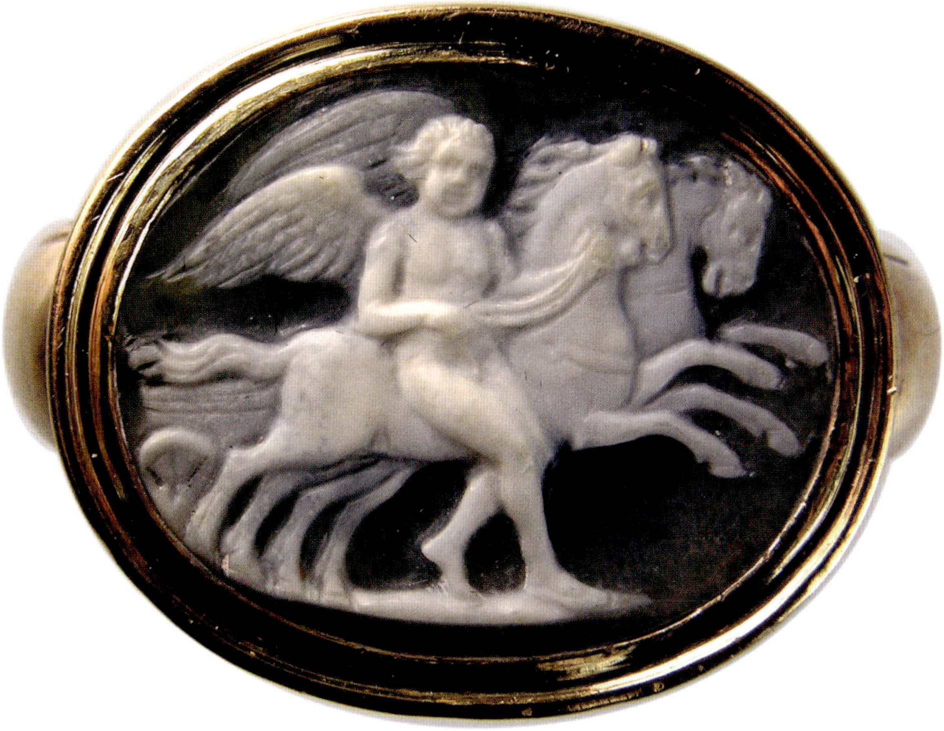

44

(10562) K24 (pl. 2)
Agate, white/mottled grey, polished flat back, set on a plain gold ring
16 x 13

SG.Imp. 150; Inst.Imp. no. 52; *AGE* no. 123.

Cupid holds the reins of a galloping biga. Ground line.

The group is part of a larger composition showing the chariot to be bearing Bacchus and Ariadne in his Triumph, and being drawn by lions. Compare our **197**. It was often excerpted in this way and the animals changed. For the lion chariot see the cameo signed by Sostratos (Vollenweider, pl. 24.1–3).

1st century BC/AD.

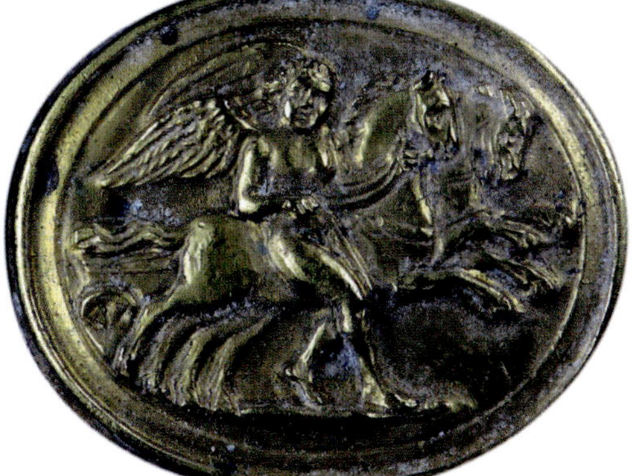

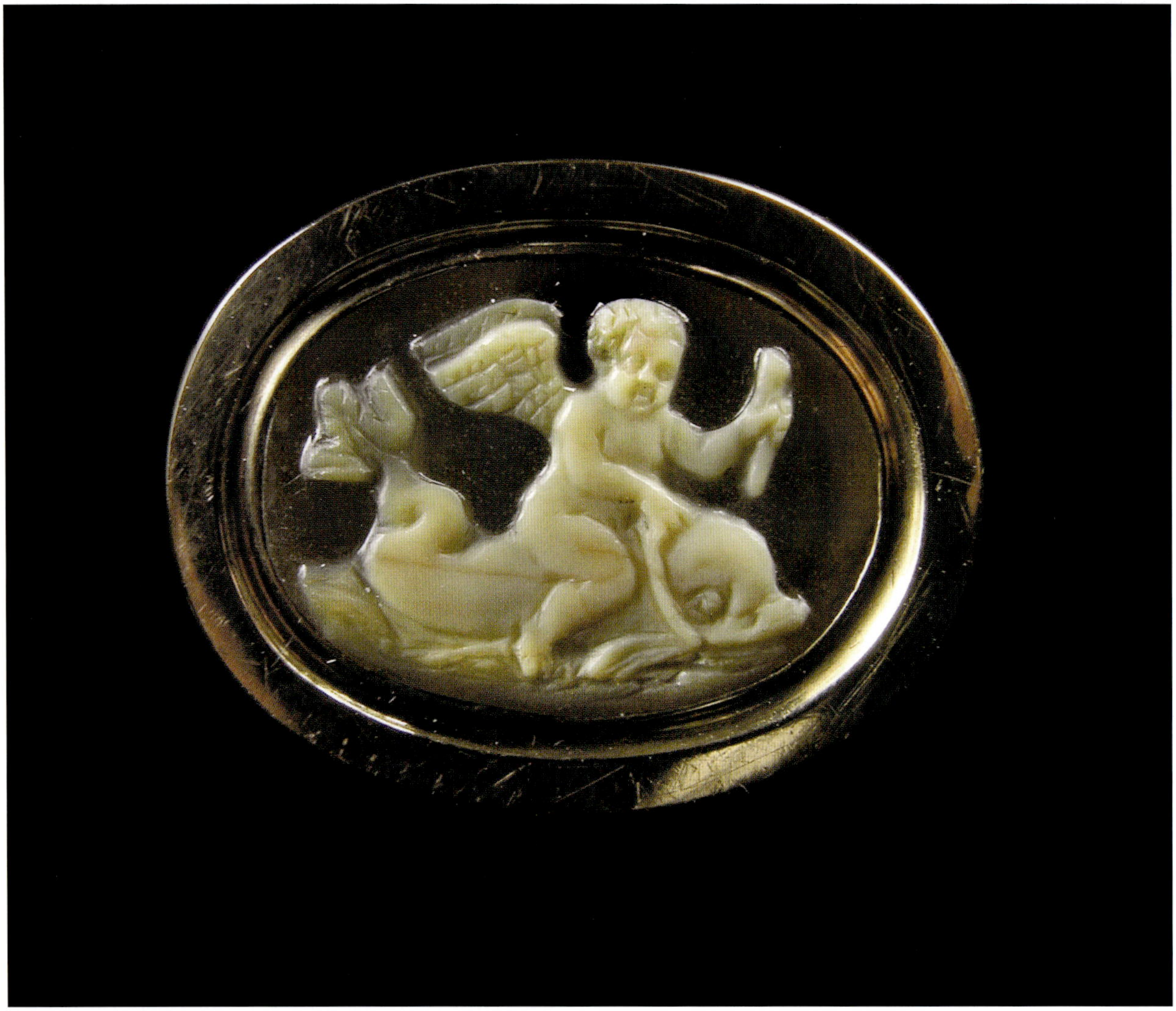

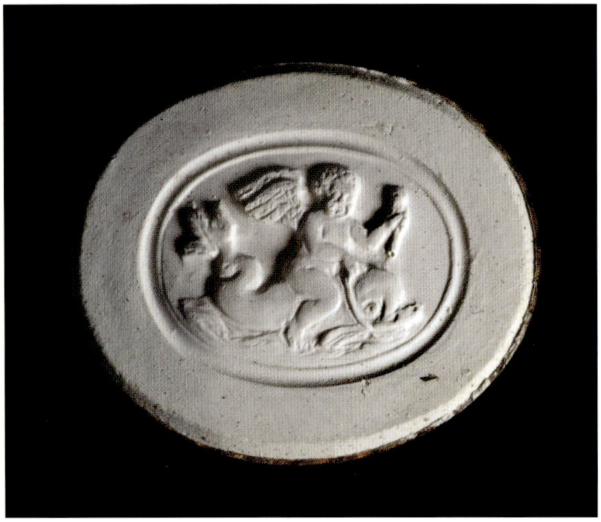

45

(10587) K49 (pl. 2)
Sardonyx, white/brown, set on a plain gold ring
13 x 10

SG.Imp. 48; Inst.Imp. no. 168.

Cupid rides a dolphin over waves, holding a torch.

For versions of the subject, *Wien* II, nos 604, 1346–9; *Munich* 3, no. 2289; *Hanover* no. 831.

1st century BC/AD.

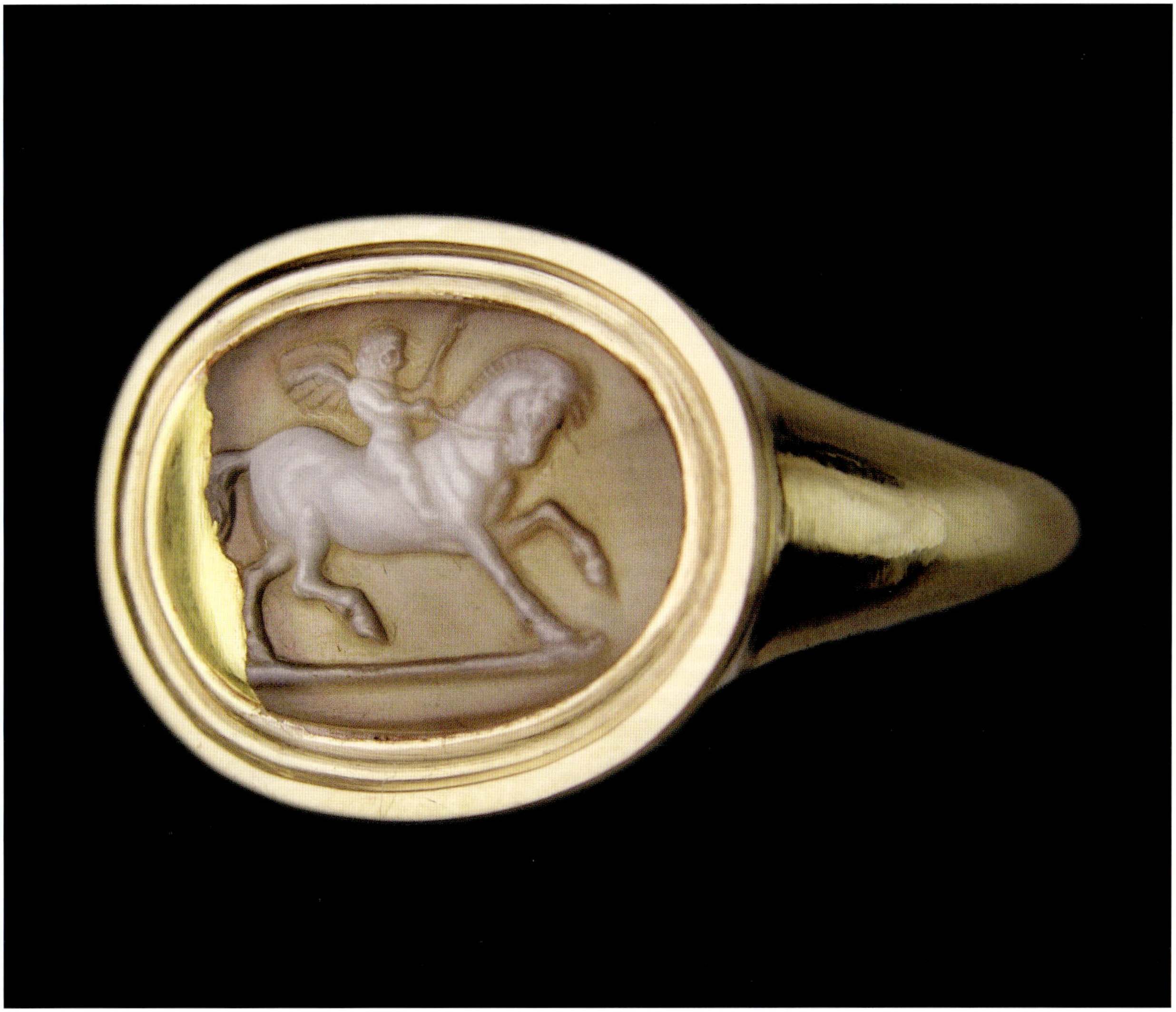

46

(10586) K48 (pl.2)
Sardonyx, white/brown, restored in gold at the left, unpolished flat back, set on a plain gold ring
12 x 8

SG.Imp. 65; Tassie 6750; Inst.Imp. no. 170.

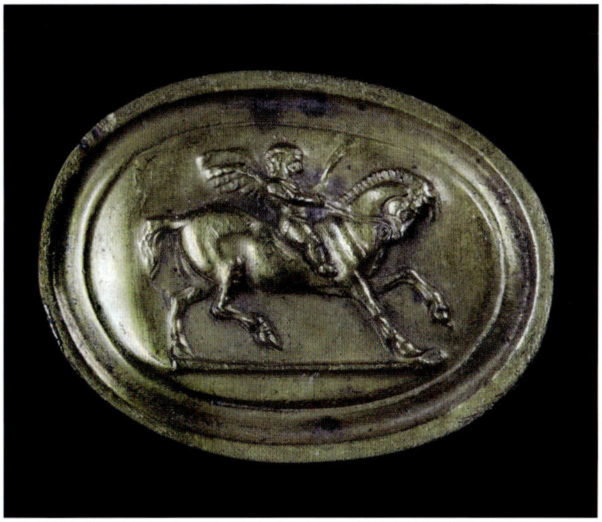

Cupid rides a horse, holding a torch. Ground line.

1st century BC/AD.

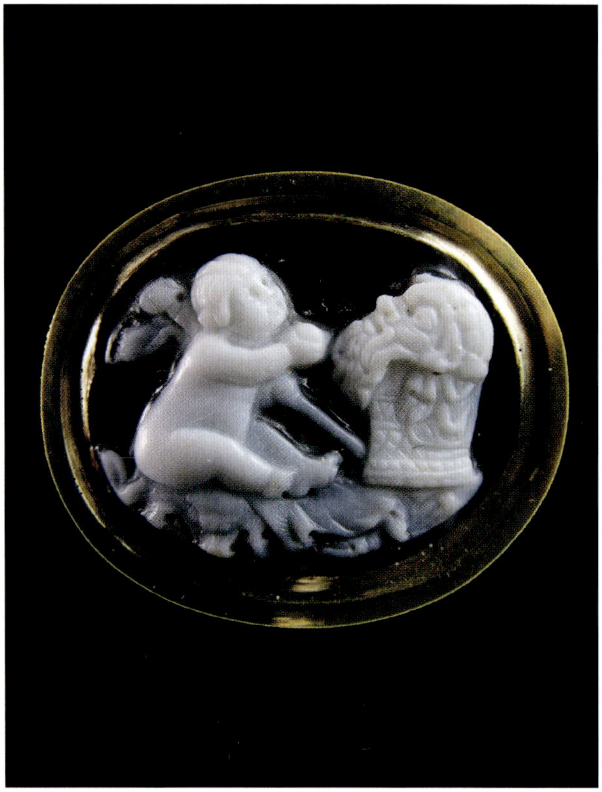

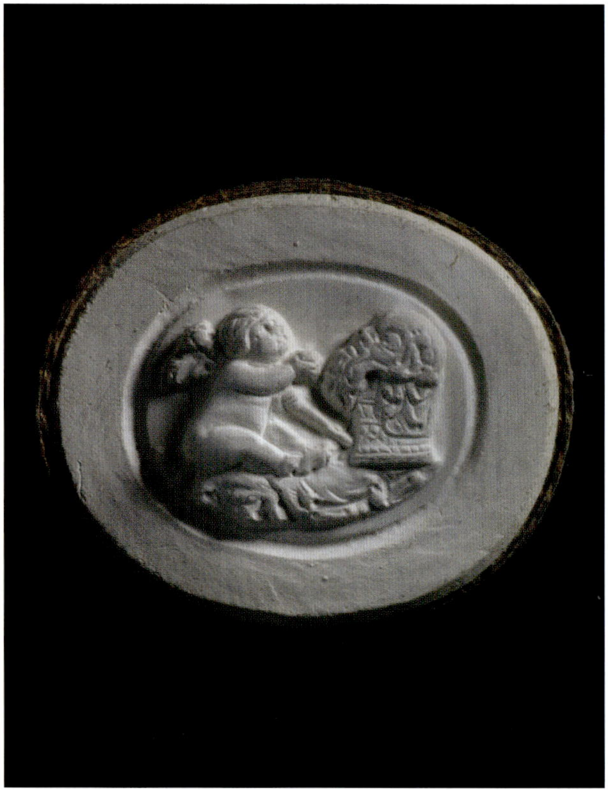

47

(10644) K106
Sardonyx, white/black, set on a plain gold ring
14 x 12

SG.Imp. 119. Inst.Imp. 40; W.Tassie 2157; *AGE* no. 150.

A Cupid with butterfly wings and shouldering a thyrsos stretches his hand, holding a fruit (?), towards a bearded satyr mask resting on a cloth over a patterned basket. Cupid is seated on a panther skin.

Compare *Würzburg* nos 192–3.

1st century BC/AD?

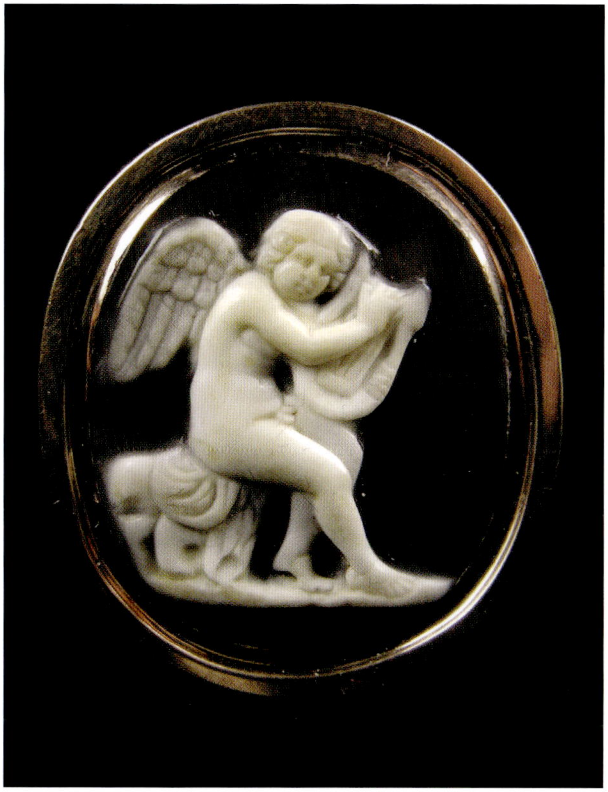

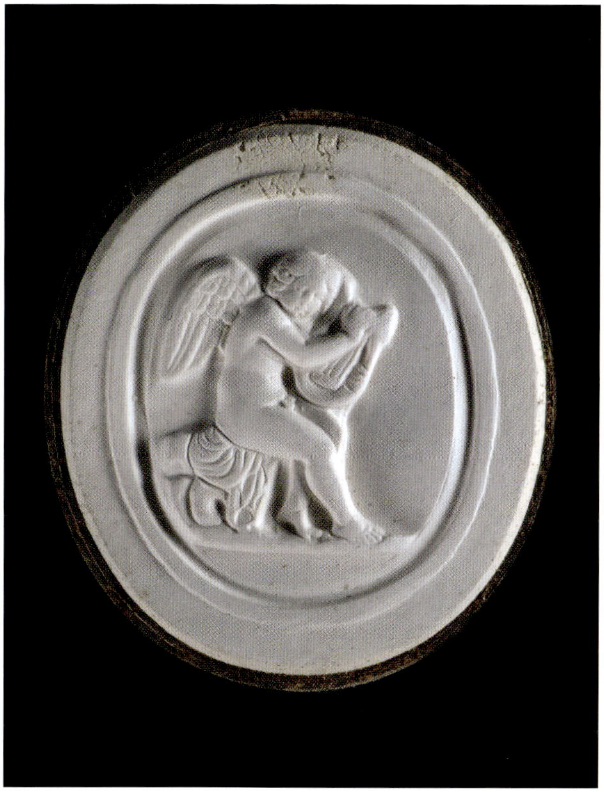

48

(10581) K43 (pl. 2)
Sardonyx, white/brown, polished flat back, pierced, set on a plain gold ring
20 x 17

SG.Imp. 57; Inst.Imp. no. 9; *AGE* no. 121.

Cupid, seated on dress on a rock, is playing a lyre. Ground line.

1st century BC/AD.

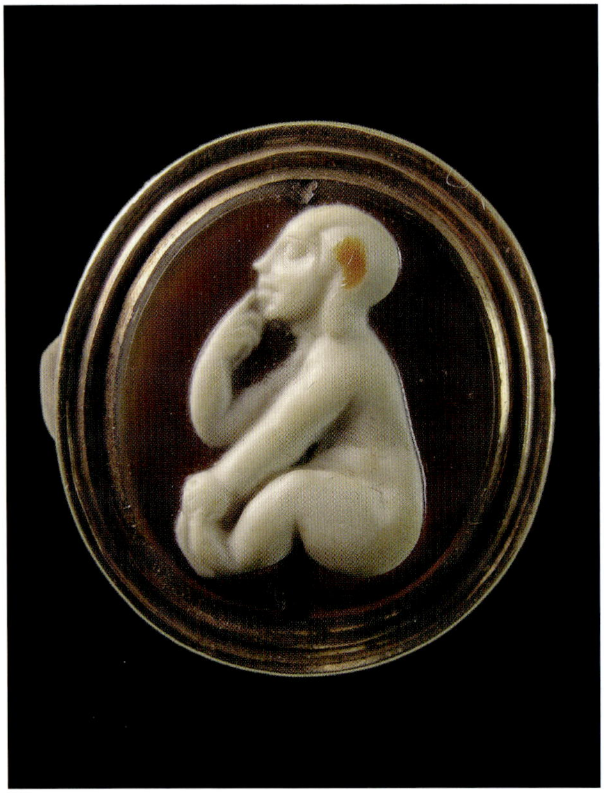

49

(10556) K18
Sardonyx, brown (the lock)/white/brown, polished flat back, pierced lengthwise, set on a plain gold ring
17 x 15

SG.Imp. 70; Inst.Imp. no. 16. Zwierlein-Diehl, op. cit. (4): pl.68.6

Harpocrates seated, a finger to his lips and the other hand holding his toes. He has the characteristic ear lock.

An Egyptian figure (Horus) much favoured in Greek Alexandria.

1st century BC.

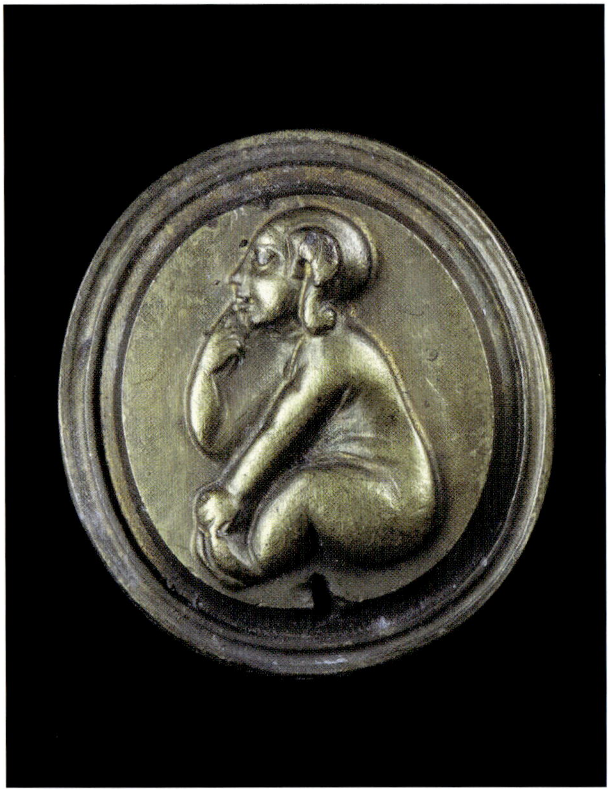

50

(10740) K202 (pl. 2)
Sardonyx, white/brown, set in an 18th-century gold ring with key pattern on the bezel border and striated triangles on the bezel side; the hoop has floral terminals
23 x 15

AGE no. 185.

Hercules, naked, his head on his hand, seated on a tree stump, a foot raised on another, contemplating his fate and fortunes. The general motif is popular in the 17th/18th century, usually with more paraphernalia. Ground line.

Compare *Marlborough* nos 669, 670; Lippold, pl. 136.1. He also appears on a 16th-century cameo owned by Fulvio Orsini (1529–1600), copied by Annibale Caracci on the frescoed ceiling of the Palazzo Farnese (Kagan/Neverov 2000, 59, no. 8/6). In antiquity it probably derived from Lysippus' famous group of the weary Hercules, of which variants are found with the head on hand: *LIMC* IV, 772–4.

18th century?

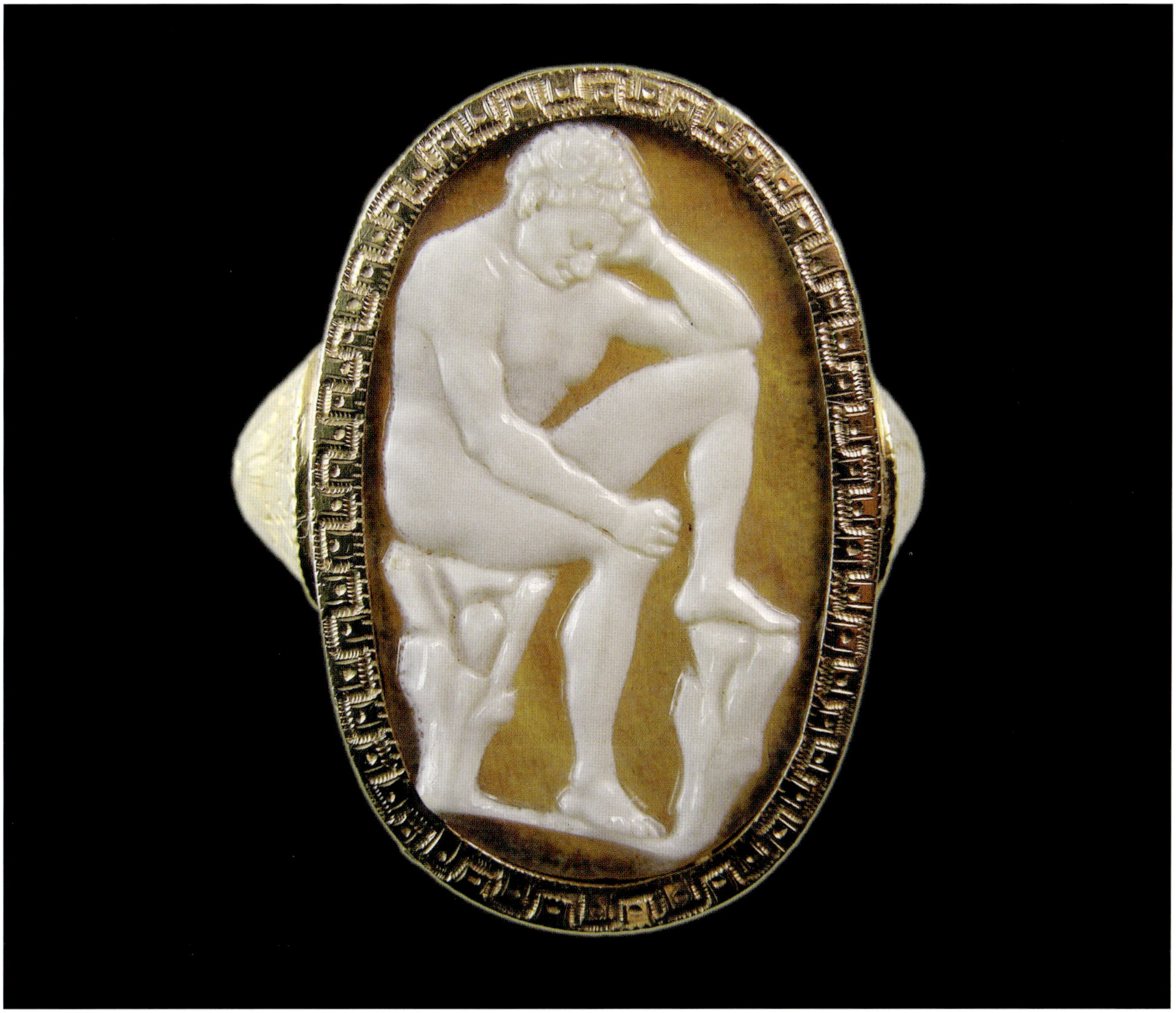

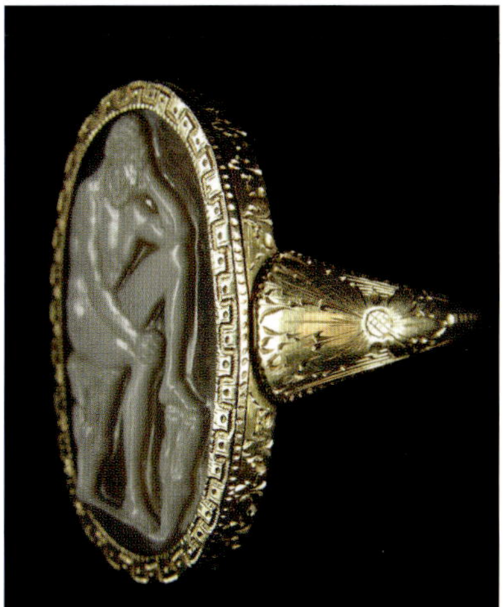

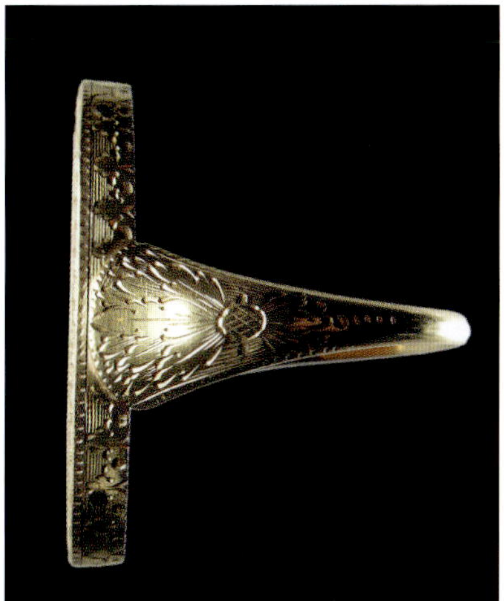

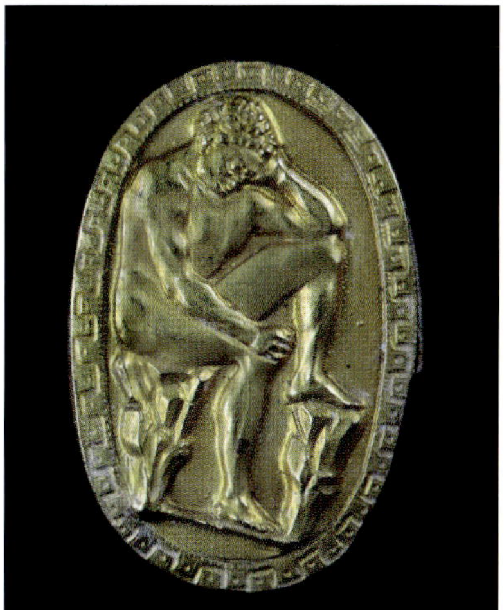

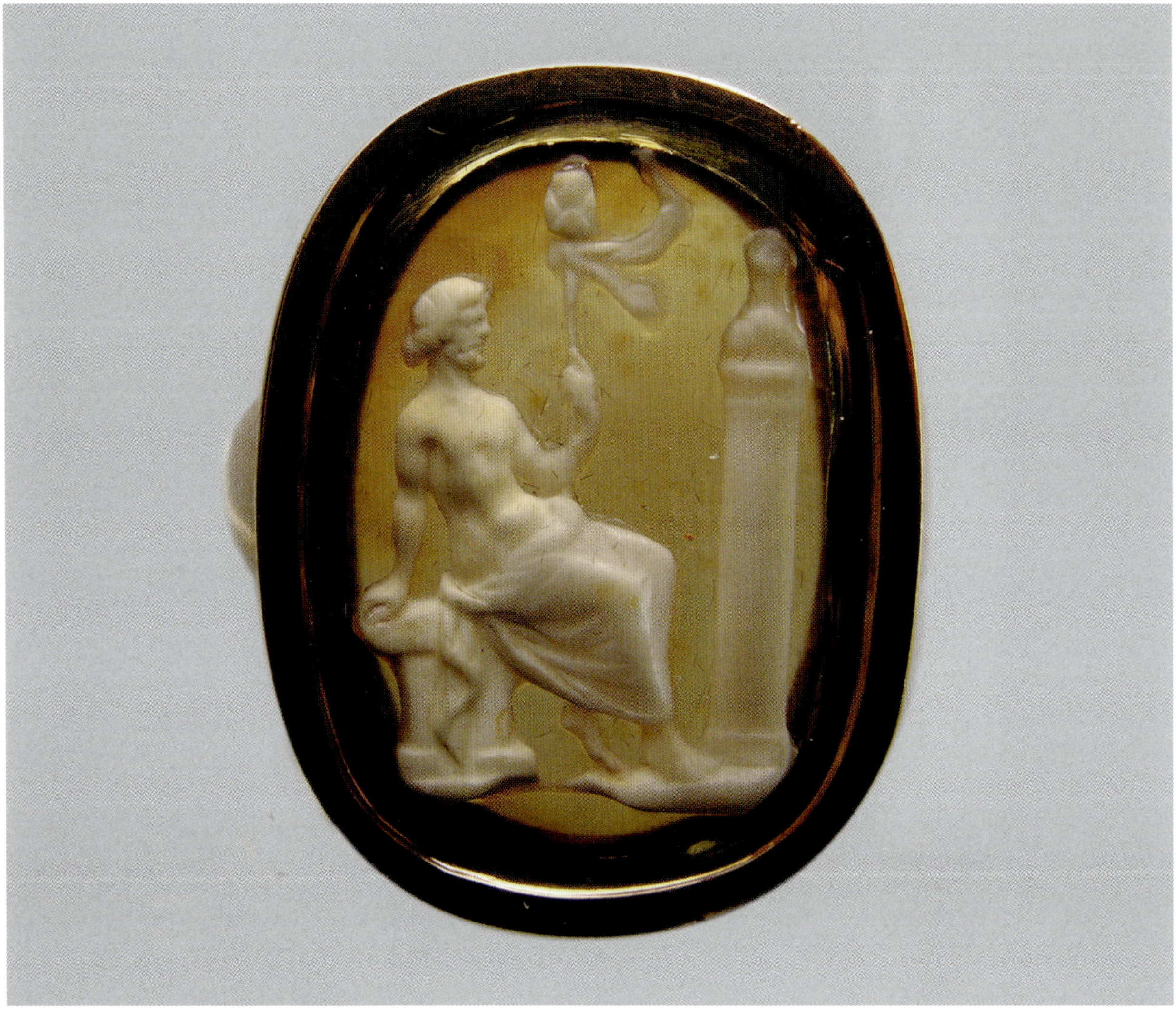

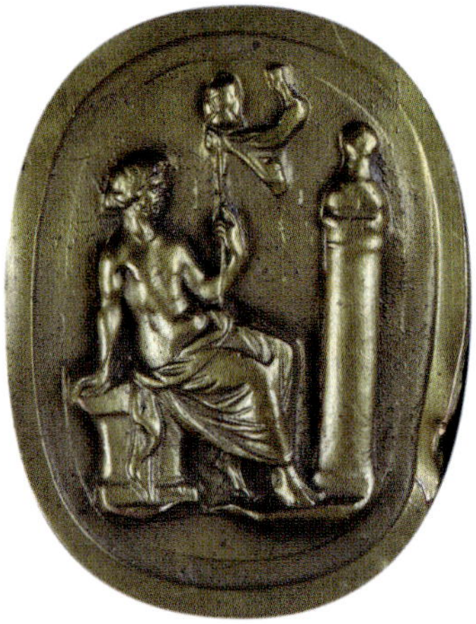

51

(10569) K31 (pl. 2)
Sardonyx, white/brown, polished flat back, set on a plain gold ring
18 x 13

SG.Imp. 64; Inst.Imp. no. 27; W.Tassie 1680; *AGE* no. 140.

A bearded man with rolled hair, dress around his legs, seated on an altar and holding a ribboned thyrsos before a column bearing a sphere. Broken ground line.

Probably meant for Bacchus (taken for a woman by King and in *AGE*).

17th/18th century?

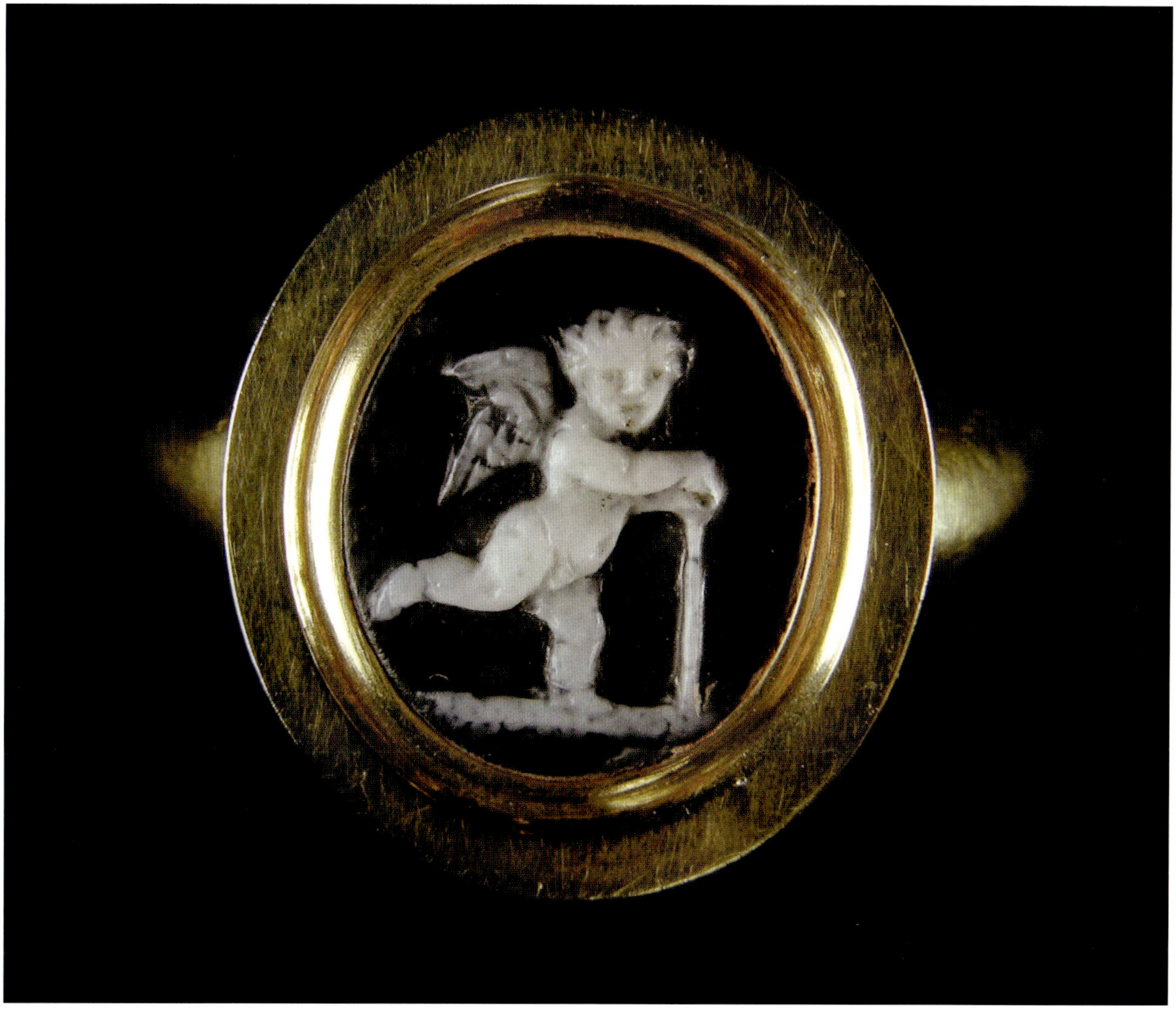

52

(10584) K46 (pl. 1)
Sardonyx, white/brown, unpolished flat back, set on a plain gold ring
9 x 6

SG.Imp. 28; Inst.Imp. no. 75; W.Tassie 2120; *AGE* no. 125.

Cupid running, facing the viewer, holding a staff with a circular handle (?); just possibly this is an upturned torch. Wavy ground line.

When Cupid holds a torch, he is not usually so active (compare Spier, *Gulbenkian* no. 43; *LIMC* III pls 689–90).

18th century.

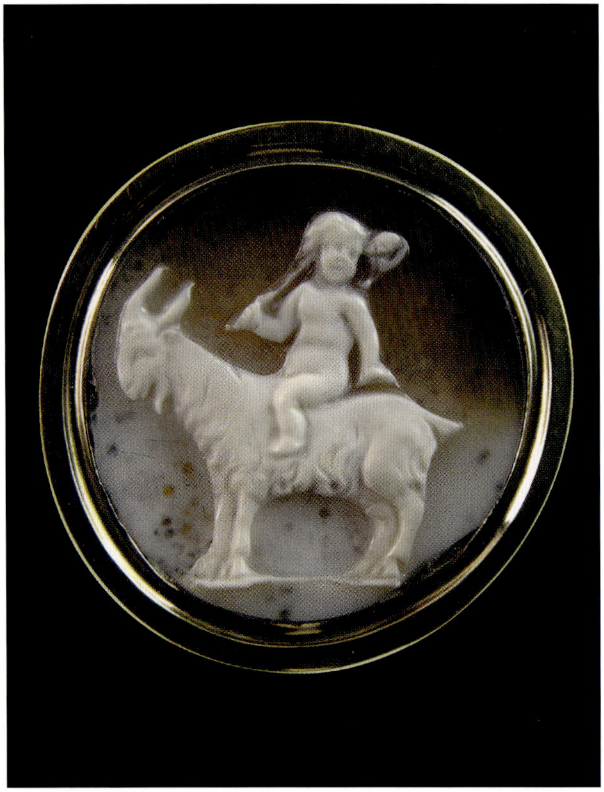

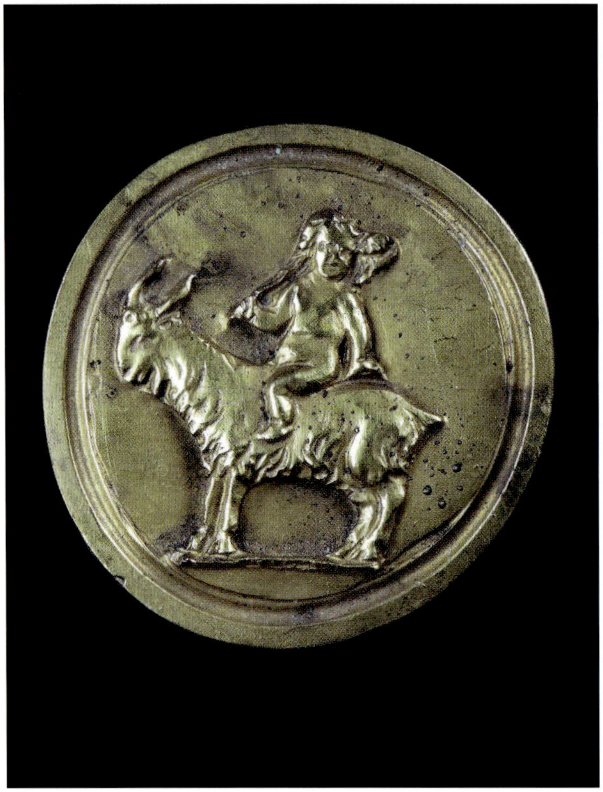

53

(10645) K107
Sardonyx, white/brown-mottled white, unpolished flat back, set on a plain gold ring
16 x 16

SG.Imp. 61; Lippold, pl. 107.1; *AGE* no. 148.

The child Bacchus shouldering a ribboned thyrsus (?), riding a goat. Ground line.

A late classical example on an ivory box, *LIMC* III, pl. 445.176.

18th century?

54

(10810)
Sardonyx, white/pale brown, flat polished back, set in a plain gold ring
22 x 14

AGE no. 251.

A dressed woman, breast bared, her hair tied and falling onto her shoulder, stands, legs crossed, grieving, clasping the top of an altar-like monument decorated with a wreath enclosing the letters AB. Ground line.

The initials AB could commemorate Amy Burrell, grandmother of the 2nd Duchess and of Lady Beverley (see our **55**), but if not, either their sister Amelia Bennett (died 1837) or else Lord (Algernon) Beverley (died 1830).

19th century.

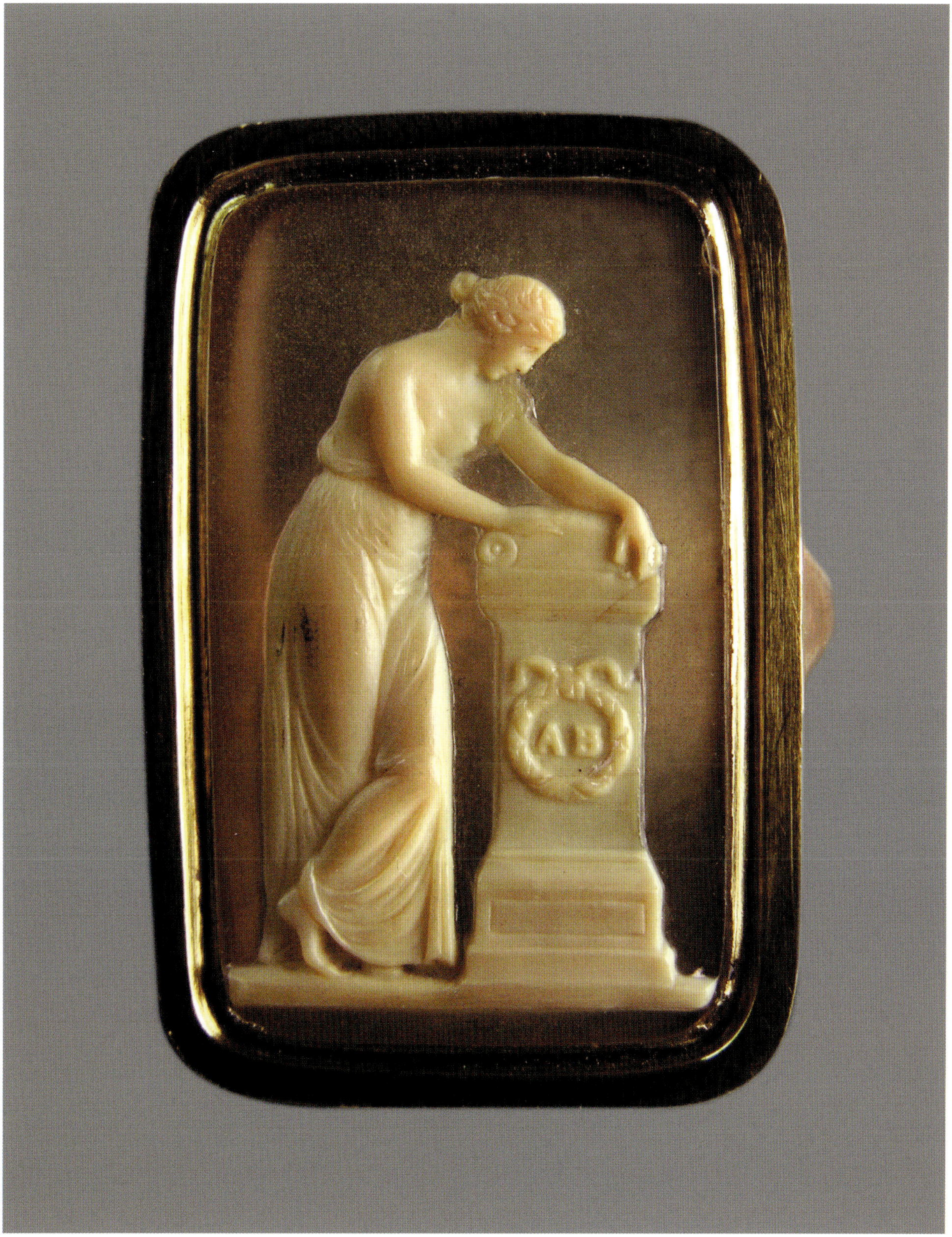
AB

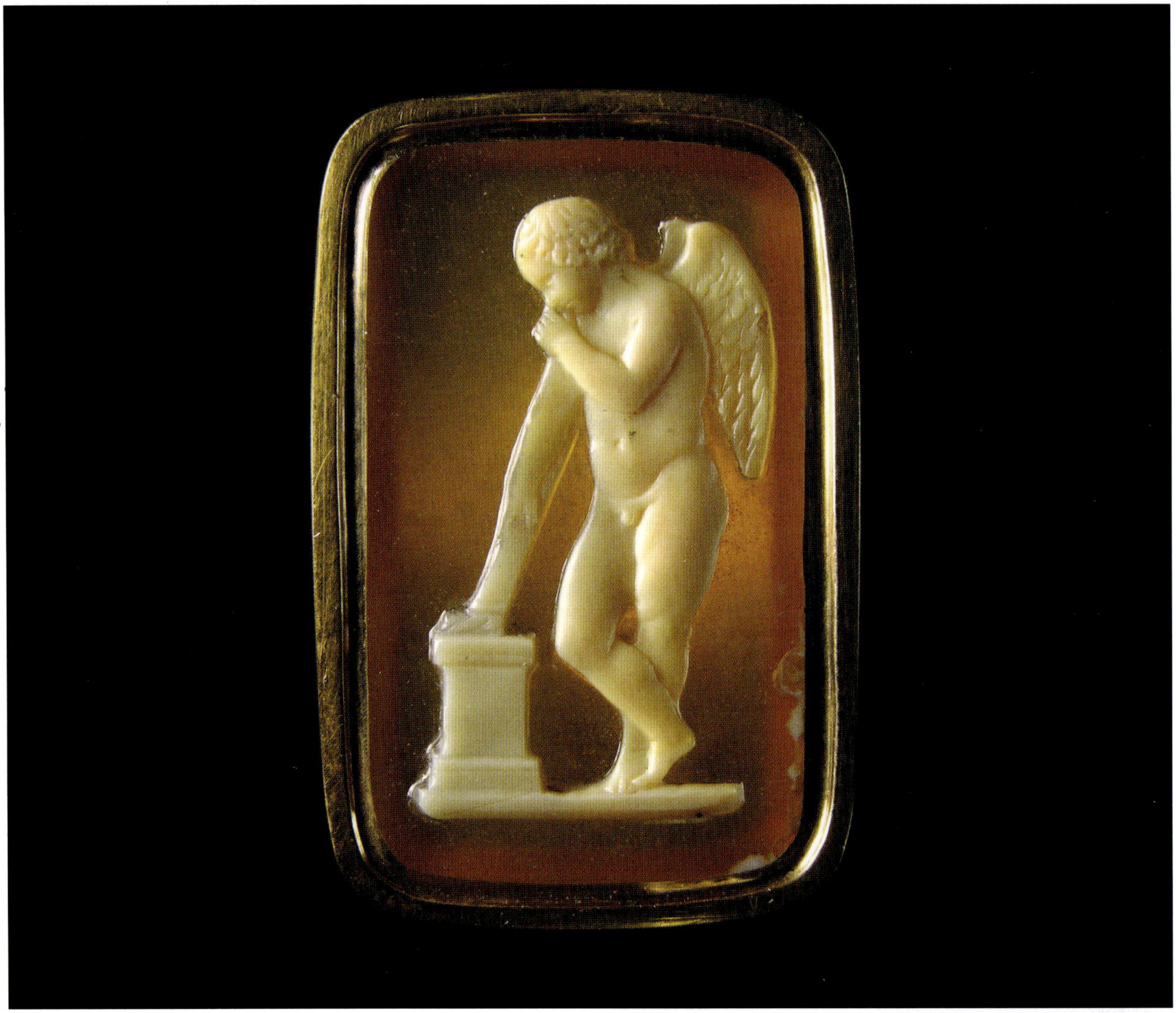

55

(10811)
Sardonyx, white/pale brown, set in a plain gold ring
24 x 14

AGE no. 250.

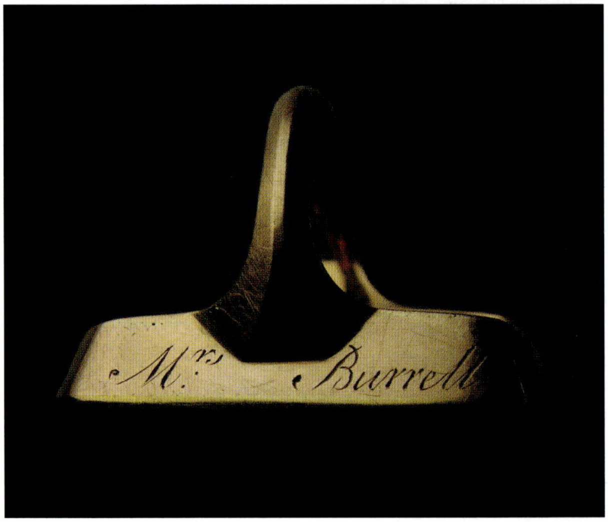

Cupid grieving, legs crossed, leaning on his upturned torch, set on an altar. Ground line. The edges of the bezel are inscribed: Mrs Burrell. Aet. 89. Ob:16. Aug.1789.

This commemorates the death of Mrs Peter Burrell (Amy), grandmother of the Duchess of Northumberland and of Lady Algernon Percy.

19th century.

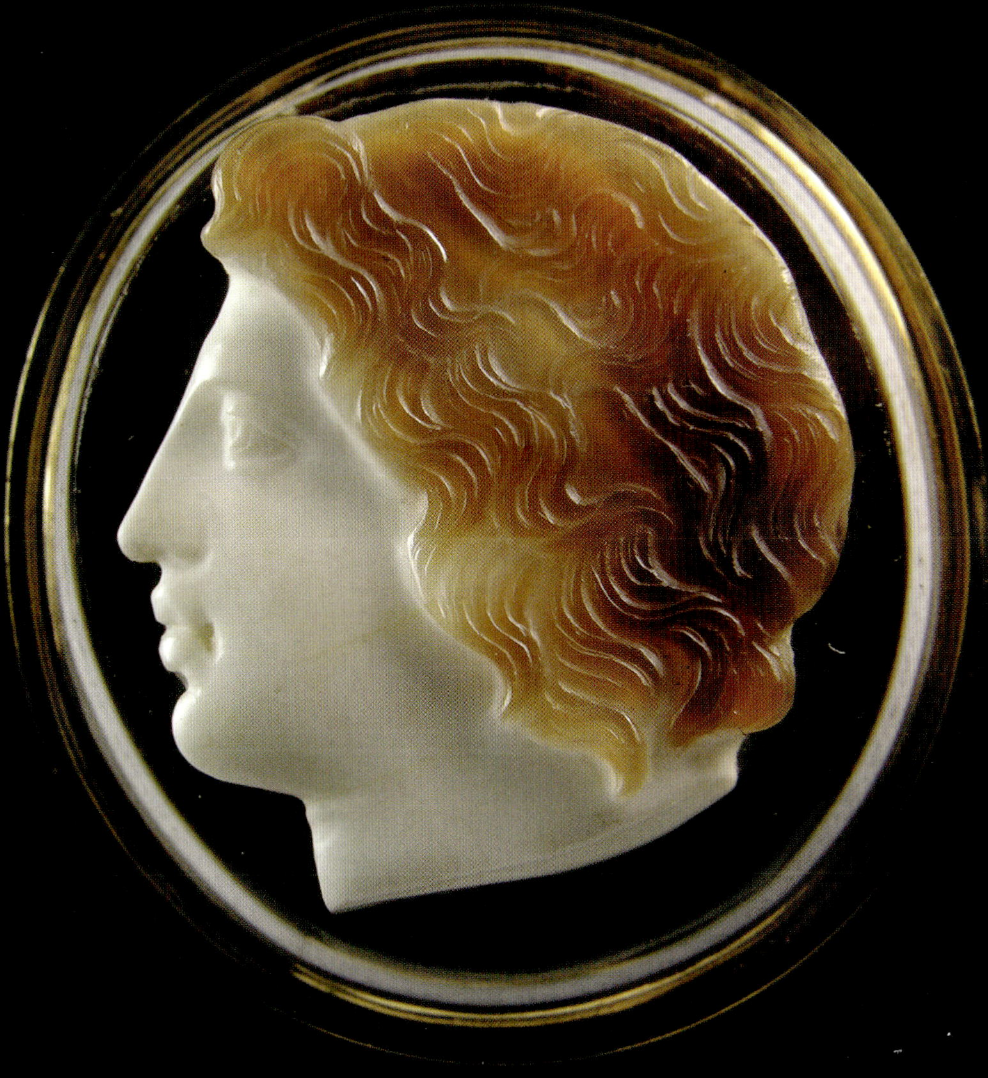

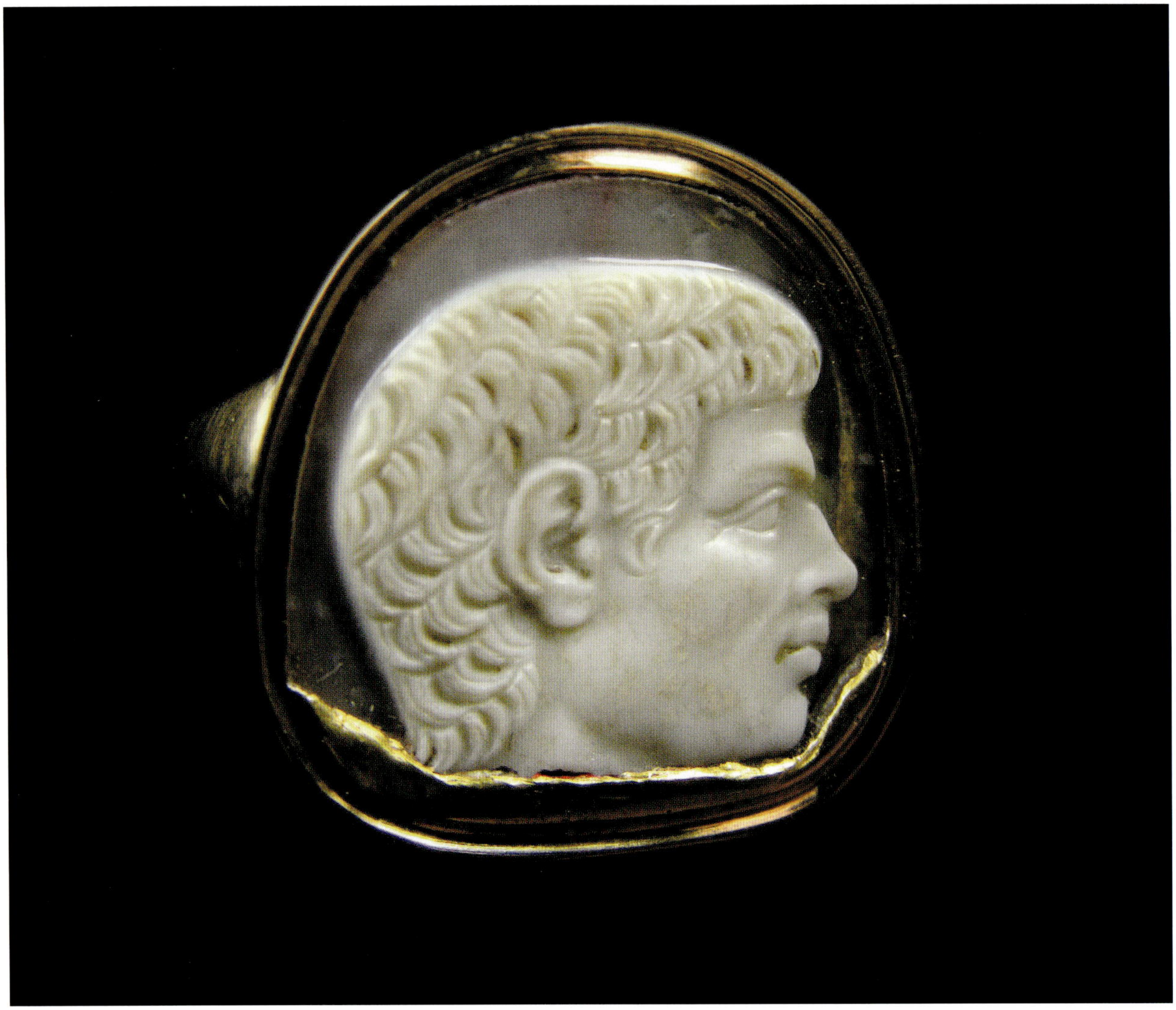

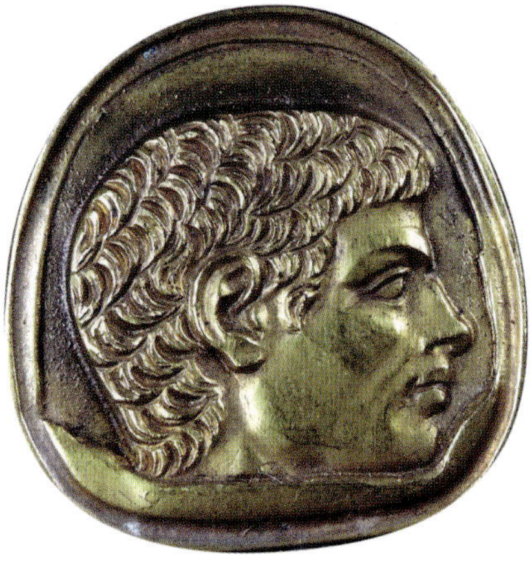

56

(10589) K52 (pl. 1)
Sardonyx, white/brown, the lower part missing.
Unpolished flat back, set on a plain gold ring
17 x 17

SG.Imp. 29; Inst.Imp. no. 47; *AGE* no. 38.

Portrait head of Marcus Junius Brutus, assassin of Julius Caesar.

Mid-1st century BC.

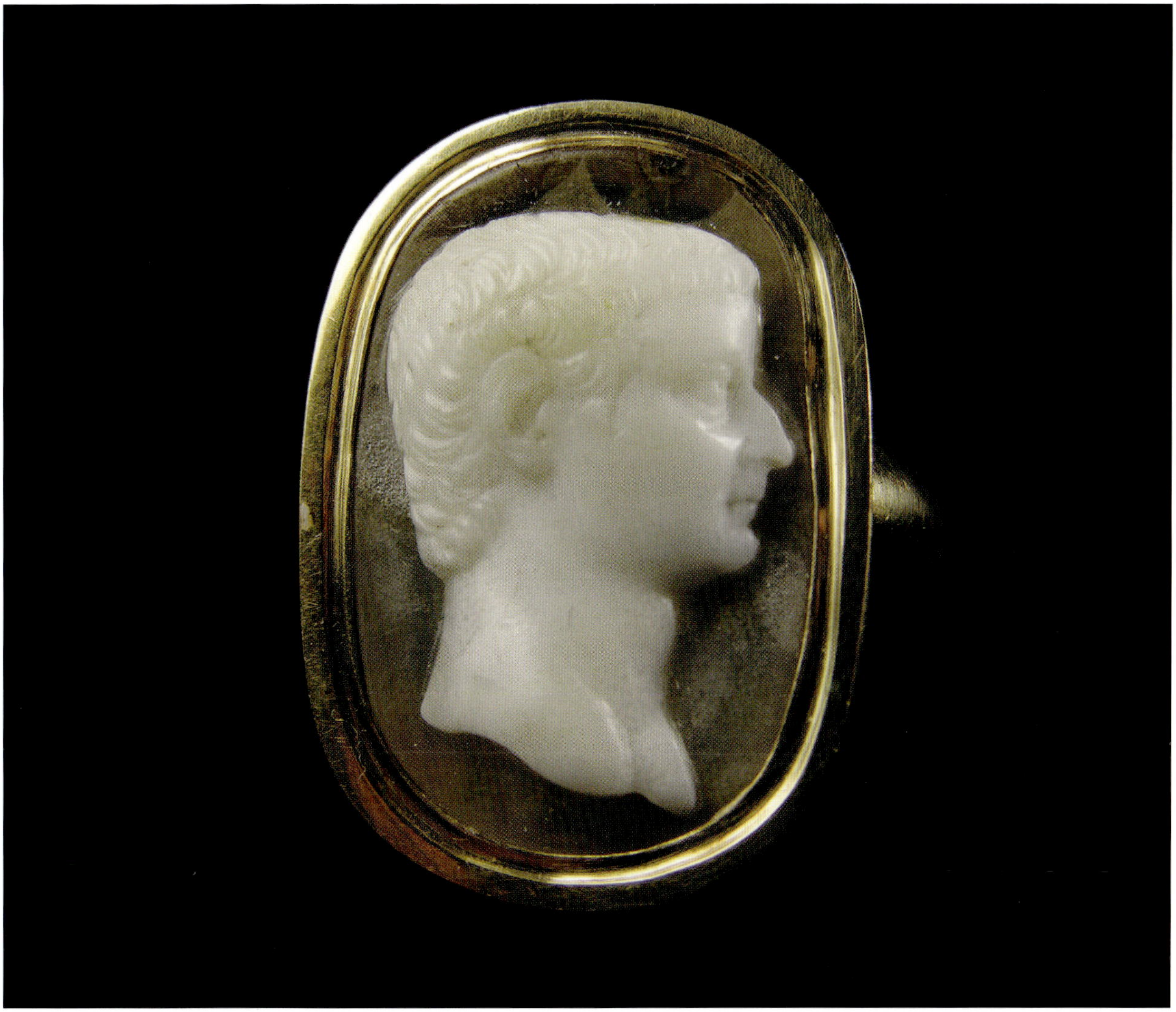

57

(10596) K58 (pl. 1)
Sardonyx, white/brown, unpolished flat back, set on a plain gold ring
22 x 15

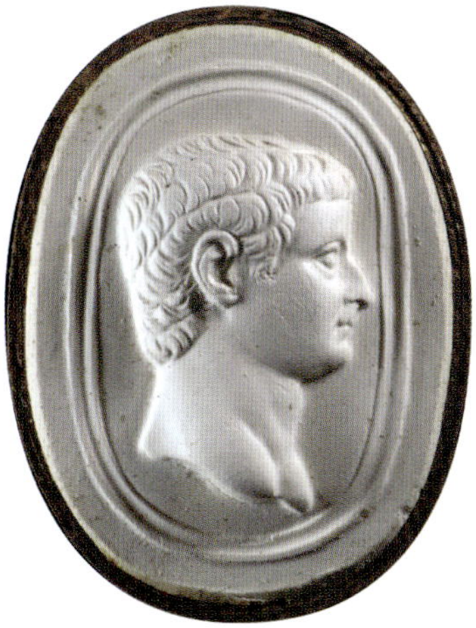

SG.Imp. 178; Inst.Imp. no. 8; *AGE* no. 34.

Portrait head of Drusus the Elder (38–9 BC).

Late 1st century BC?

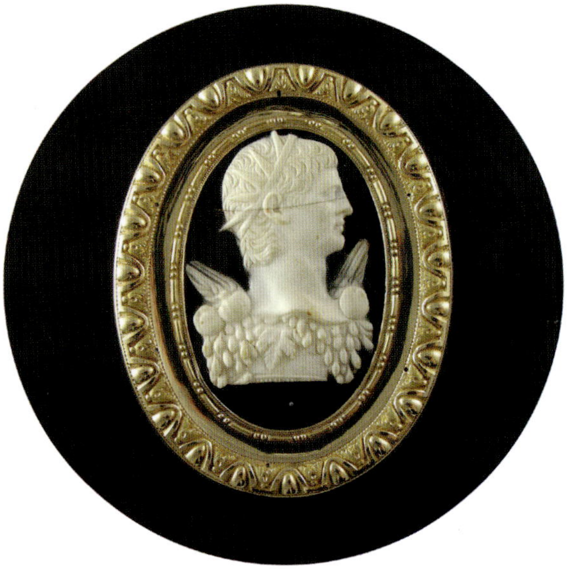

58

(10736) K198

Mottled sardonyx, white/black, broken across the head, polished convex back, set in the lid of a tortoiseshell and gold snuffbox

43 x 29

SG.Imp. 67; Inst.Imp. no. 2; Tassie 11119; Cades, Cent. IV, 94; King 1872, I, p. 304; Lippold, pl. 72.3; *AGE* no. 11.

Head of radiate Claudius, set over a cornucopia containing a vine (grapes and a leaf), fruit (apple, pomegranate and poppy?) and ears of corn.

Cf. E. Zwierlein-Diehl, 'Der Divus-Augustus-Kameo in Köln' *KölnJb* 17 (1980) 44f, pl. 13.78.

1st century AD?

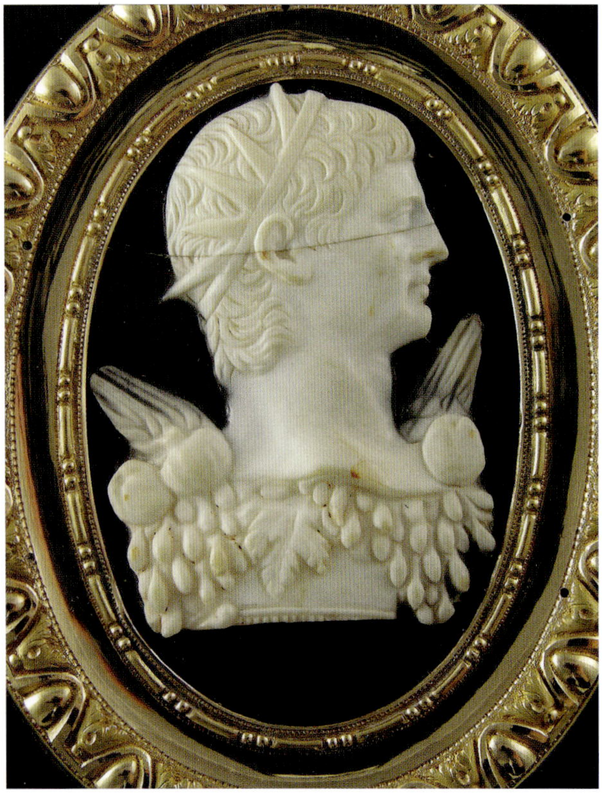

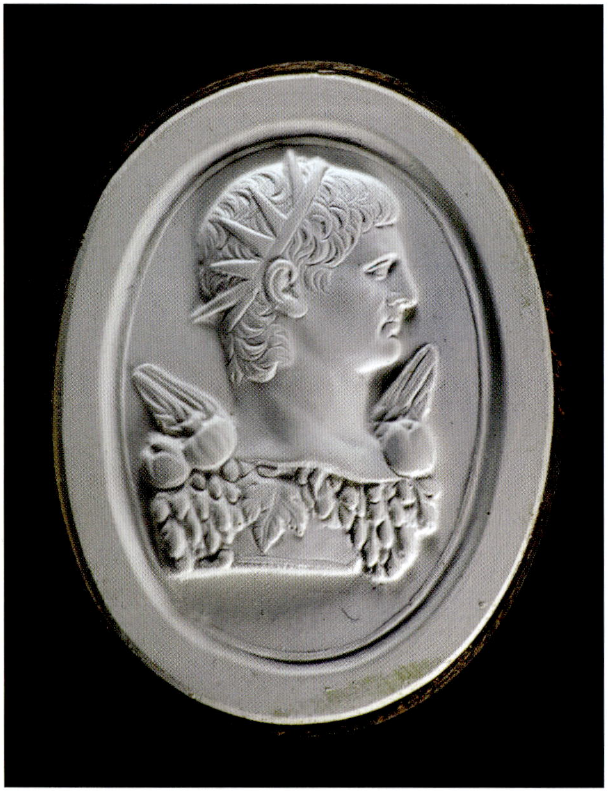

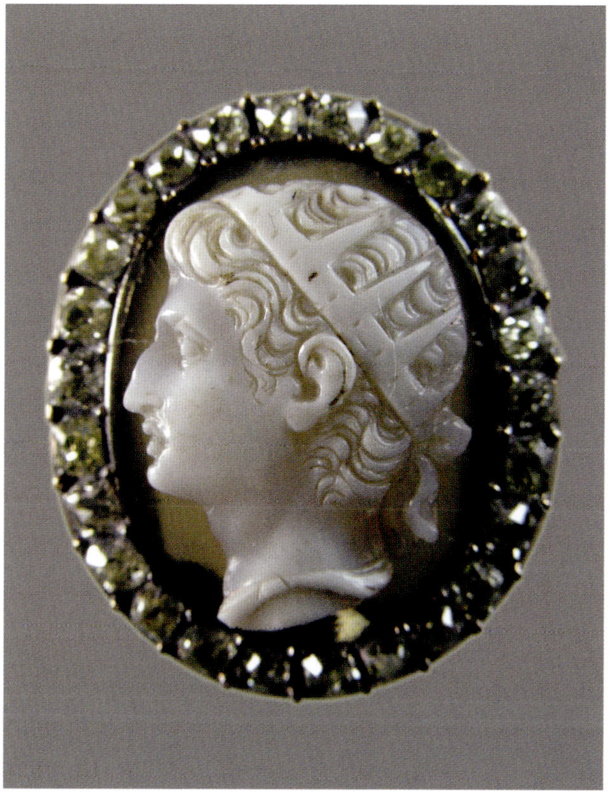

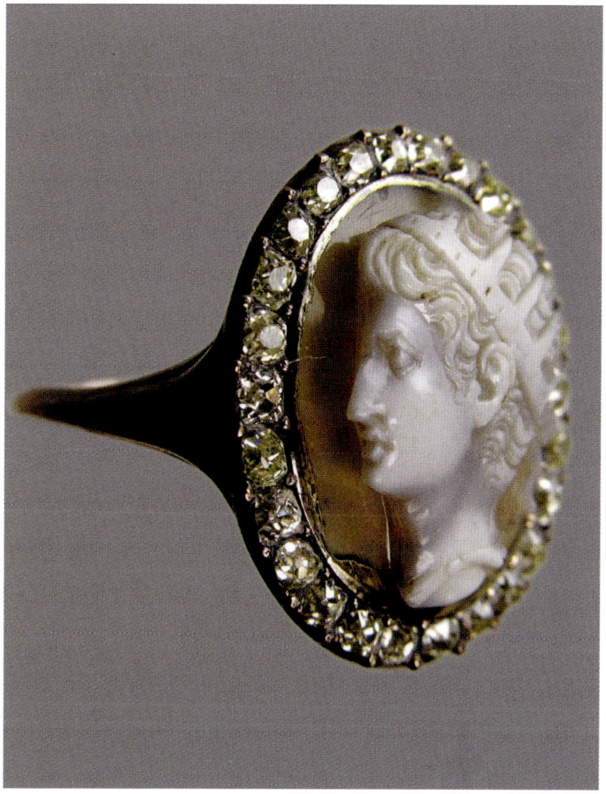

59

(10649) K111 (pl. 1)
Sardonyx, pale grey/brown, set in a gold ring, with border of diamonds and forked ends to the hoop
16 x 13

AGE no. 13.

Head of radiate Augustus (?), dress at his neck.

18th century.

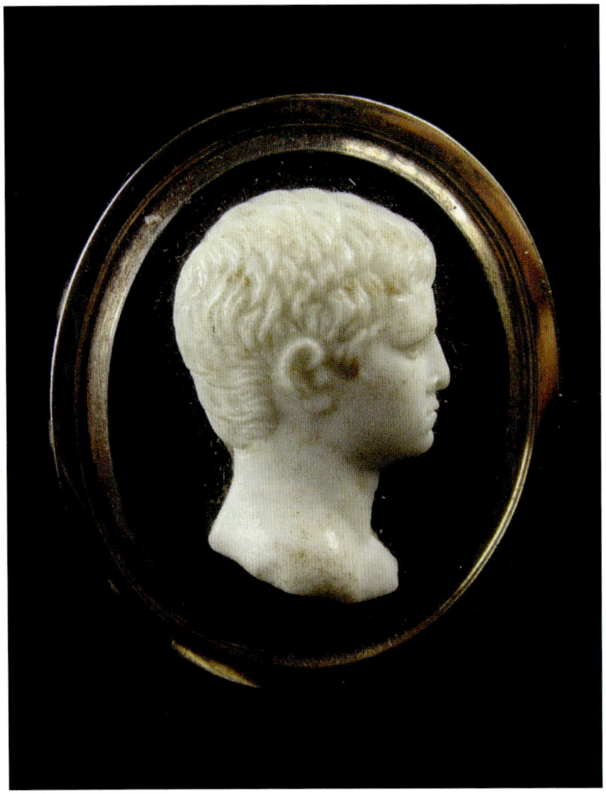

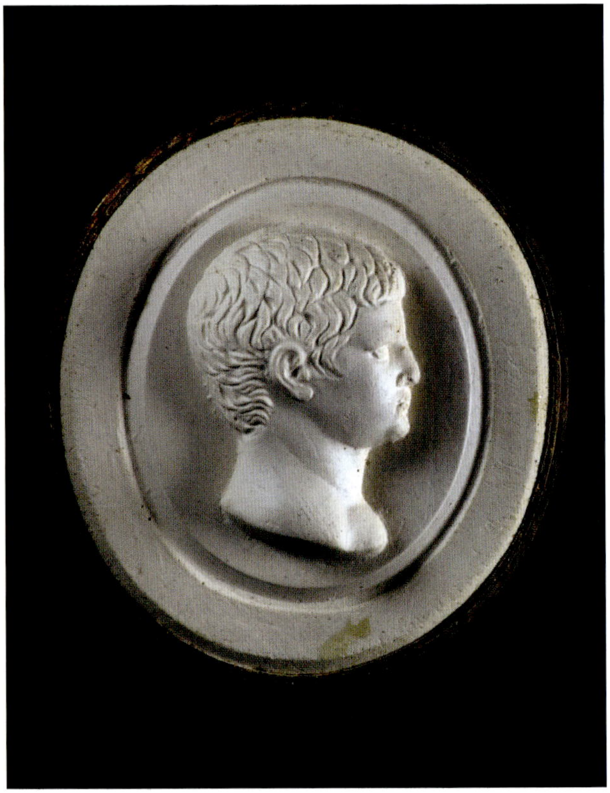

60

(10593) K55 (pl. 1)
White onyx head mounted on black agate, polished flat back, set on a plain gold ring
21 x 17

SG.Imp. 33; Inst.Imp. no. 13; Tassie 11049?

Head of a Roman, possibly Caius Caesar; cf. Megow, pl. 2.1.

1st century BC/AD.

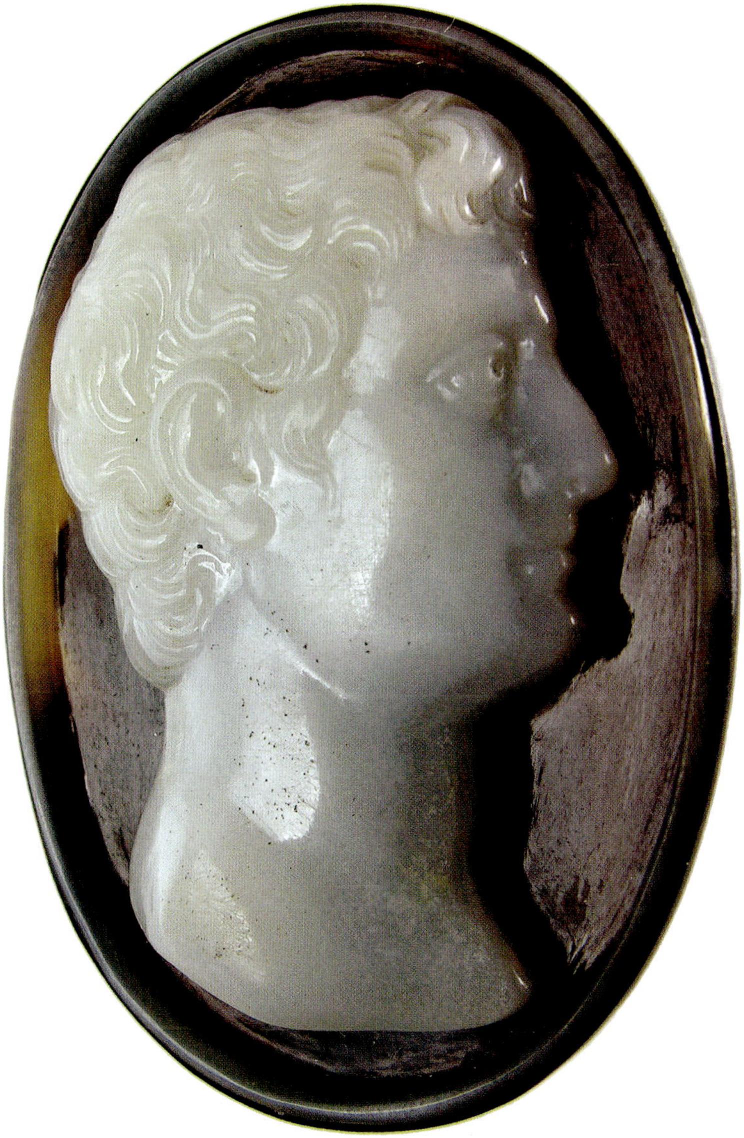

61

(10545) K7 (pl. 1)
Sardonyx, white/brown, polished convex back, set on a plain gold ring
48 x 35

Tassic 11044; *AGE* no. 12.

Portrait head of the Emperor Augustus.

16th century.

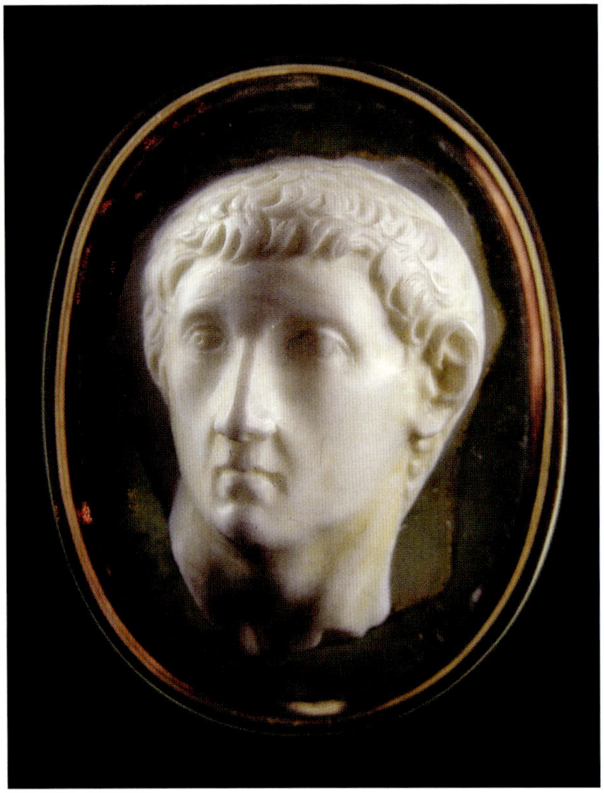 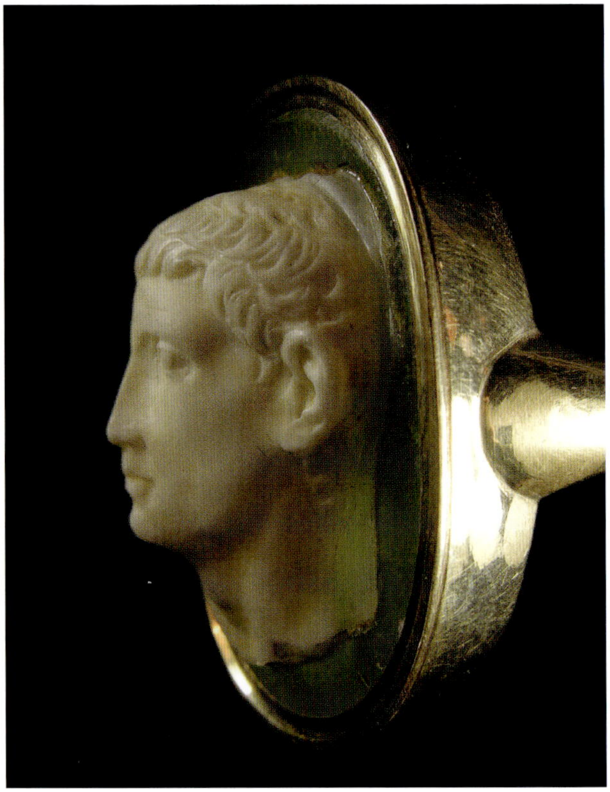

62

(10741) K203 (pl. 1)
Sardonyx, white/translucent green, ground largely missing, set on a plain gold ring
25 x 18

AGE no. 33.

Facing head, perhaps of Drusus the Elder (38–9 BC).
Cf. Megow, pl. 10.8.

Late 1st century BC.

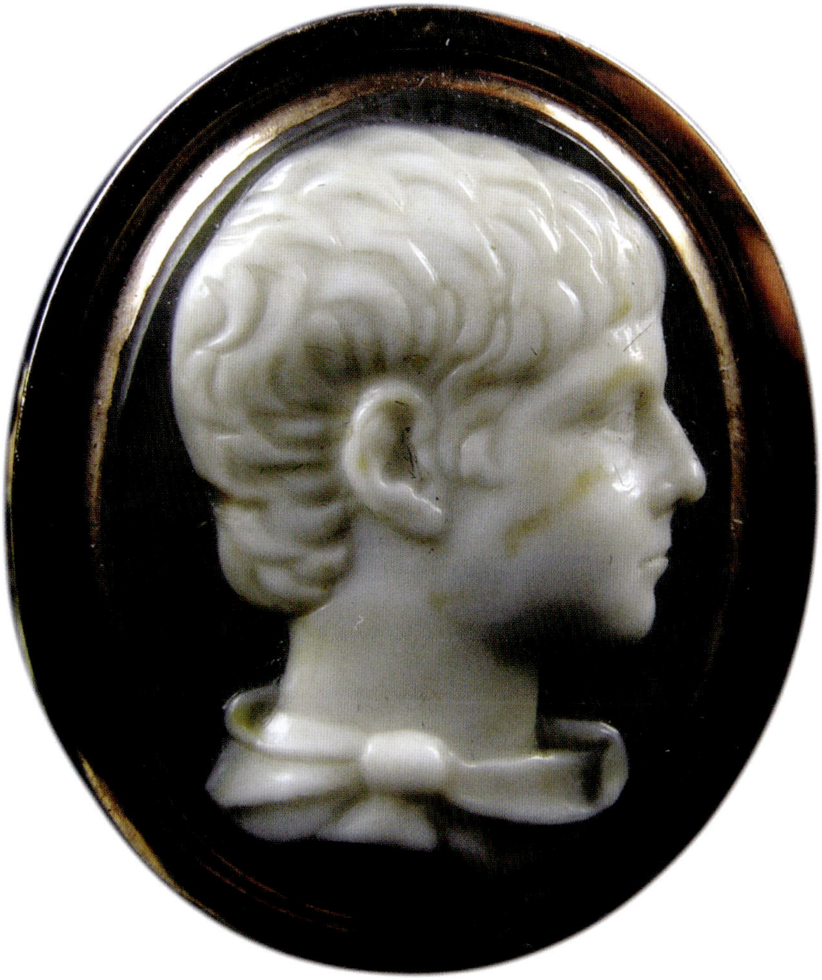

63

(10598) K60 (pl. 1)
Sardonyx, white/brown, polished flat back, set on a plain gold ring
20 x 16

SG.Imp. 154.

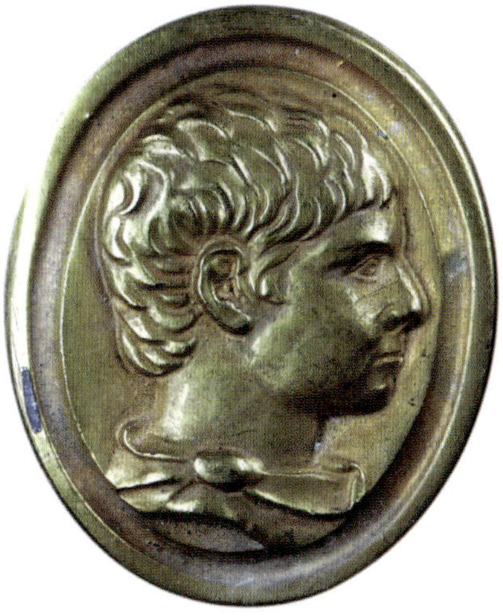

Head of a Roman prince, dress fastened at his neck.

Probably Germanicus, slightly younger than on the portrait gem by Epitynchanos (Vollenweider, pl. 88.4).

Early 1st century AD.

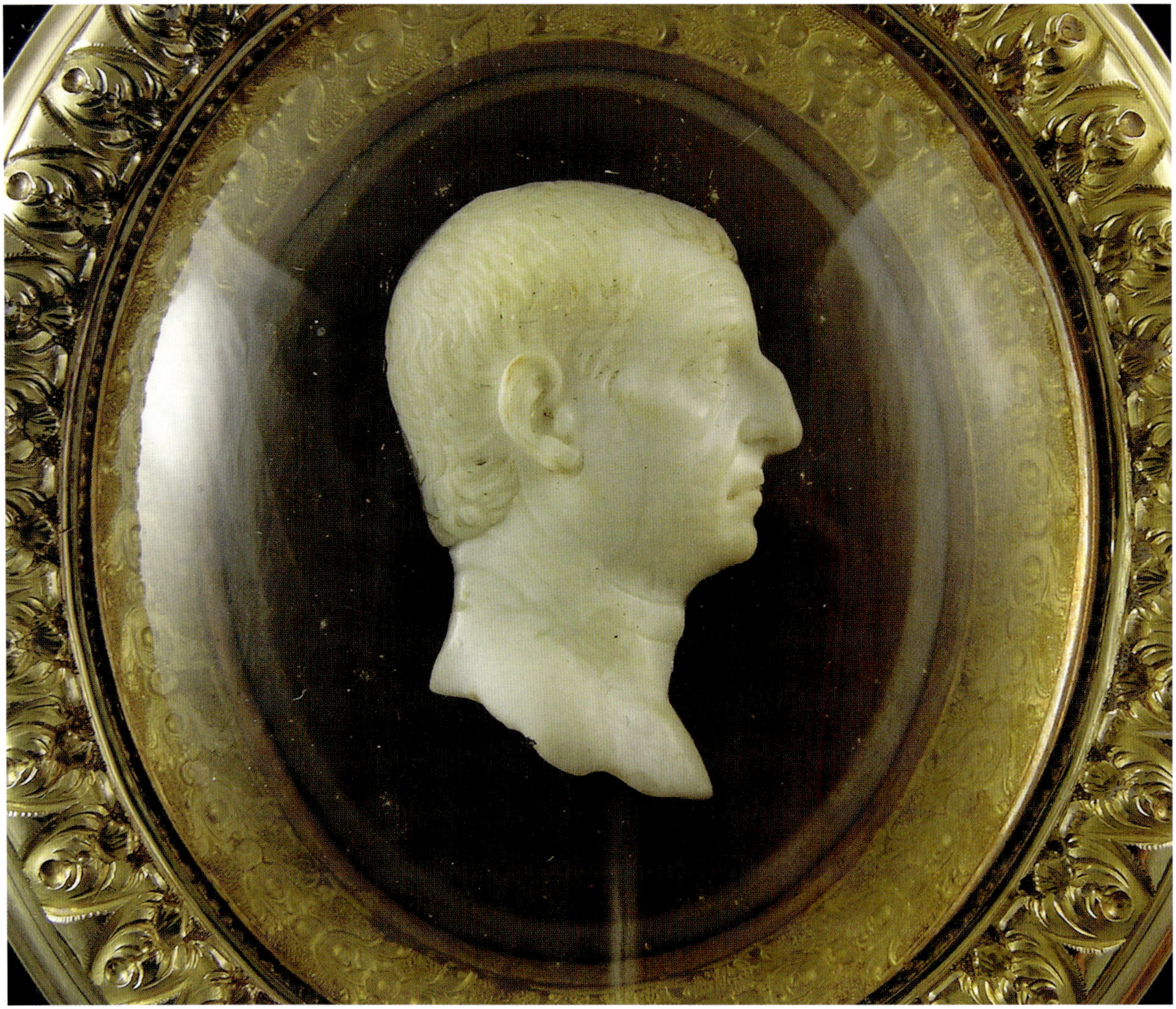

64

(10737) K199
White agate set on a sardonyx ground (brown/grey), bevelled edge, set on a tortoiseshell snuffbox
Height of head 23

AGE no. 15; Vollenweider, 79, pl. 91.3–4.

Head of a man.

1st century AD

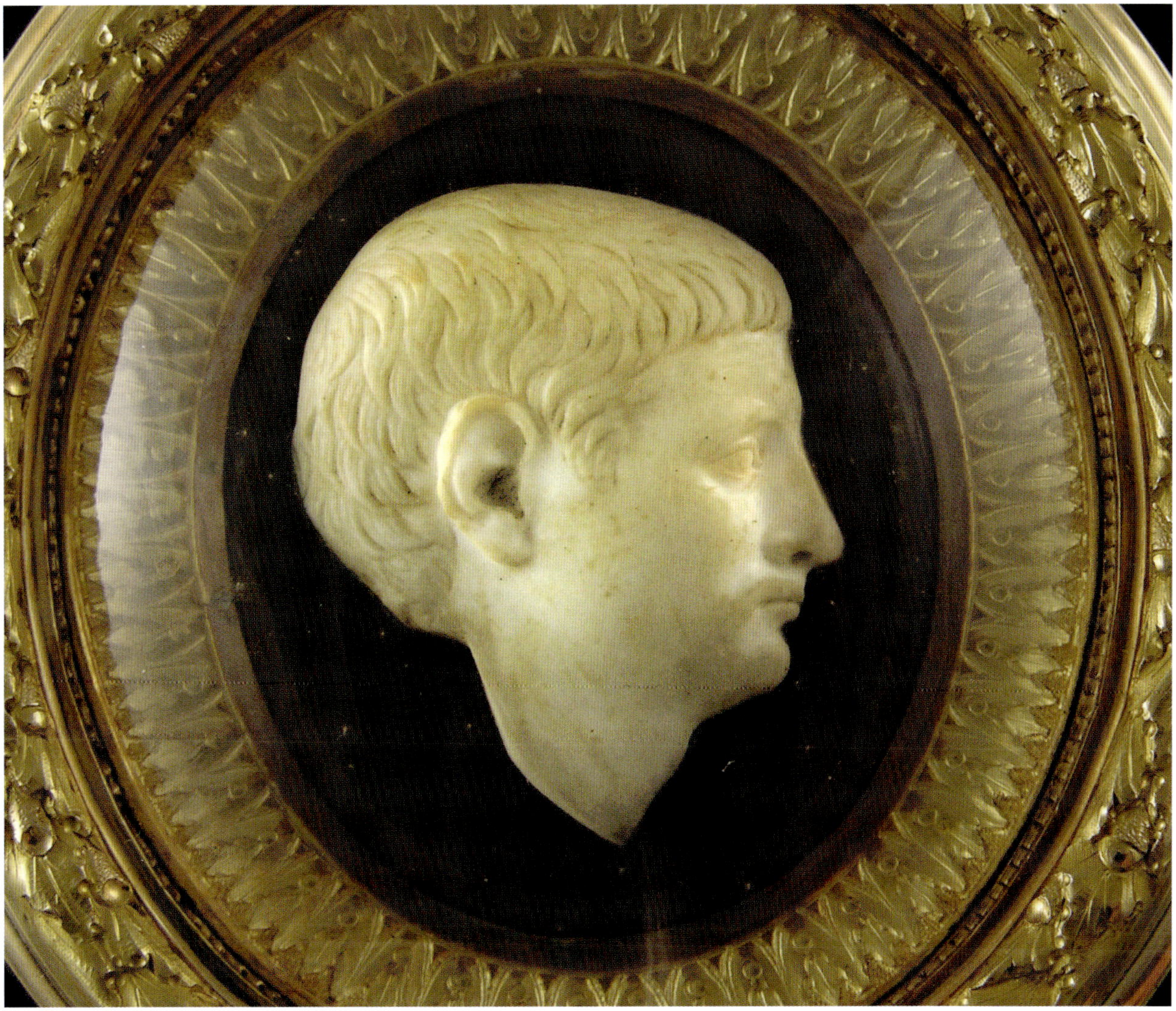

65

(10738) K200

Onyx head set on red glass, set in the lid of a tortoiseshell and gold snuffbox

Height of head 23

AGE no. 200; Vollenweider, 78, pl. 91.1–2; Megow, 272 (as 18th century).

Identified by Vollenweider as Tiberius Gemellus (AD 19–37), murdered by the Emperor Caligula.

Possibly ancient.

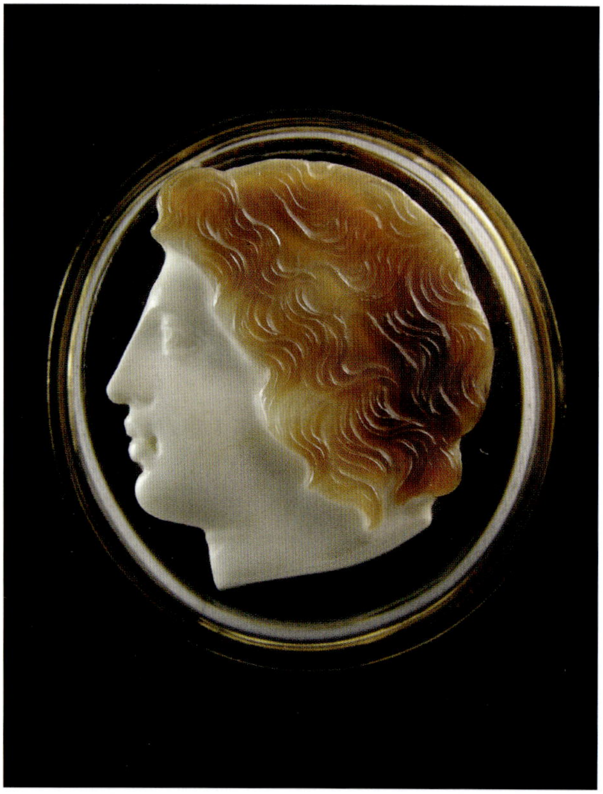

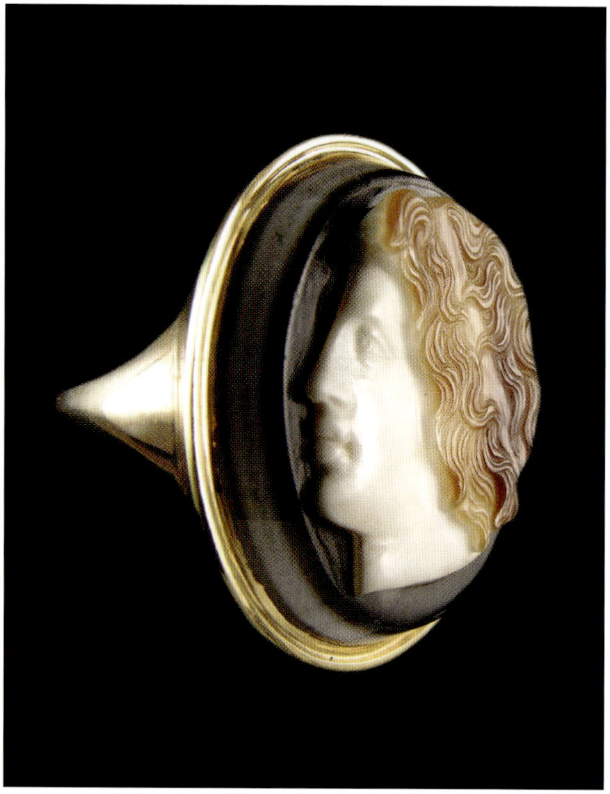

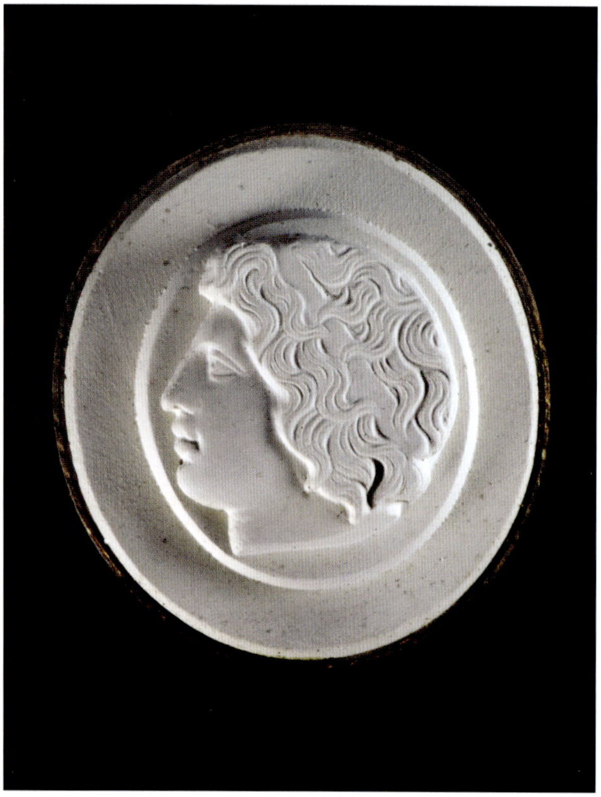

66

(10743) K205 (pl. 1)
Sardonyx, mottled orange/white/black, set on a plain gold ring
23 x 21

SG.Imp. 145; Inst.Imp. no. 10; W.Tassie 3344; *AGE* no. 109.

Head of a Hellenistic ruler wearing a diadem.

W.Tassie suggests 'Demetrius II King of Syria'. The profile shows similarities to those found on coins of Demetrios I Soter (185–150 BC).

2nd/1st century BC.

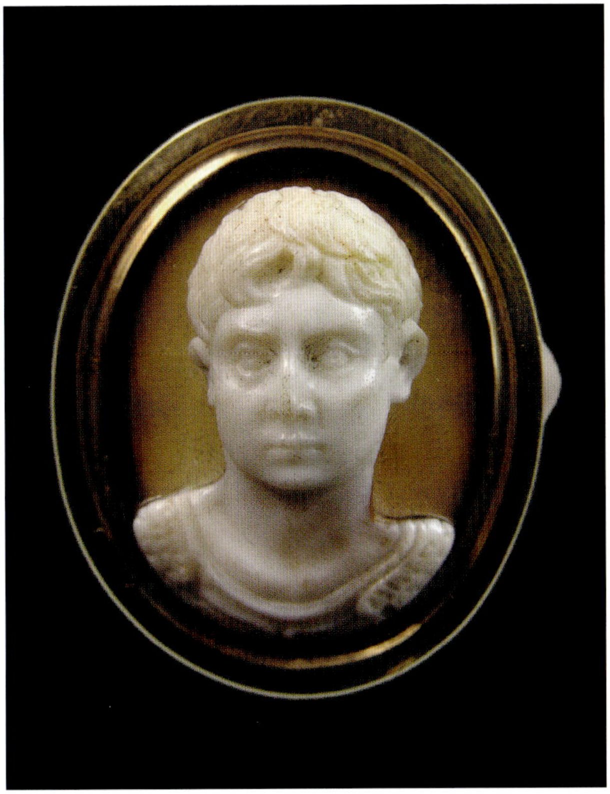

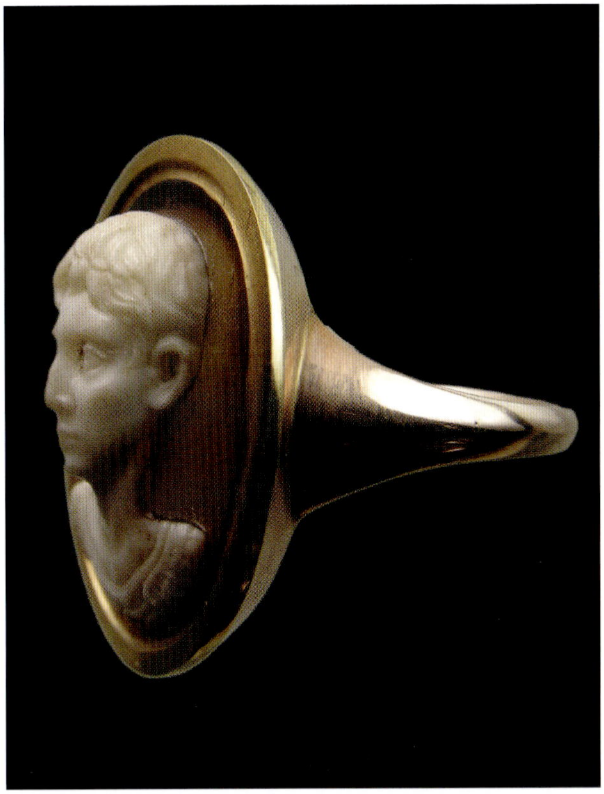

67

(10651) K113 (pl. 1)
Sardonyx, white/brown, unpolished flat back, set on a plain gold ring
18 x 14

SG.Imp. 80; Inst.Imp. no. 59.

Facing head of a man wearing a corselet.

18th century.

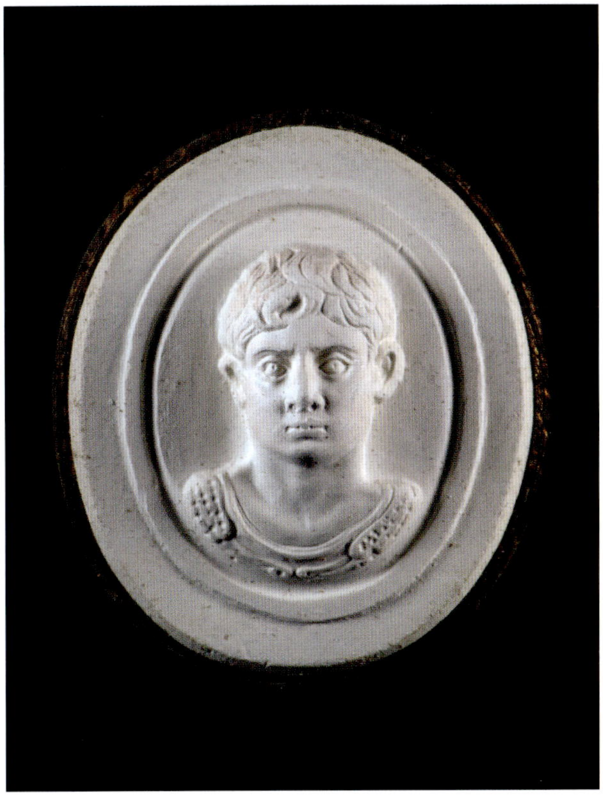

68

(10788)
Jasper stoneware white/dark blue, set on a plain gold ring
18 x 15

Head of M. Atilius Regulus. A small dagger represented behind his neck. Cf. Würzburg no. 927; C. Weiss, *Archäologischer Anzeiger* (1995), 557–559.

18th century.

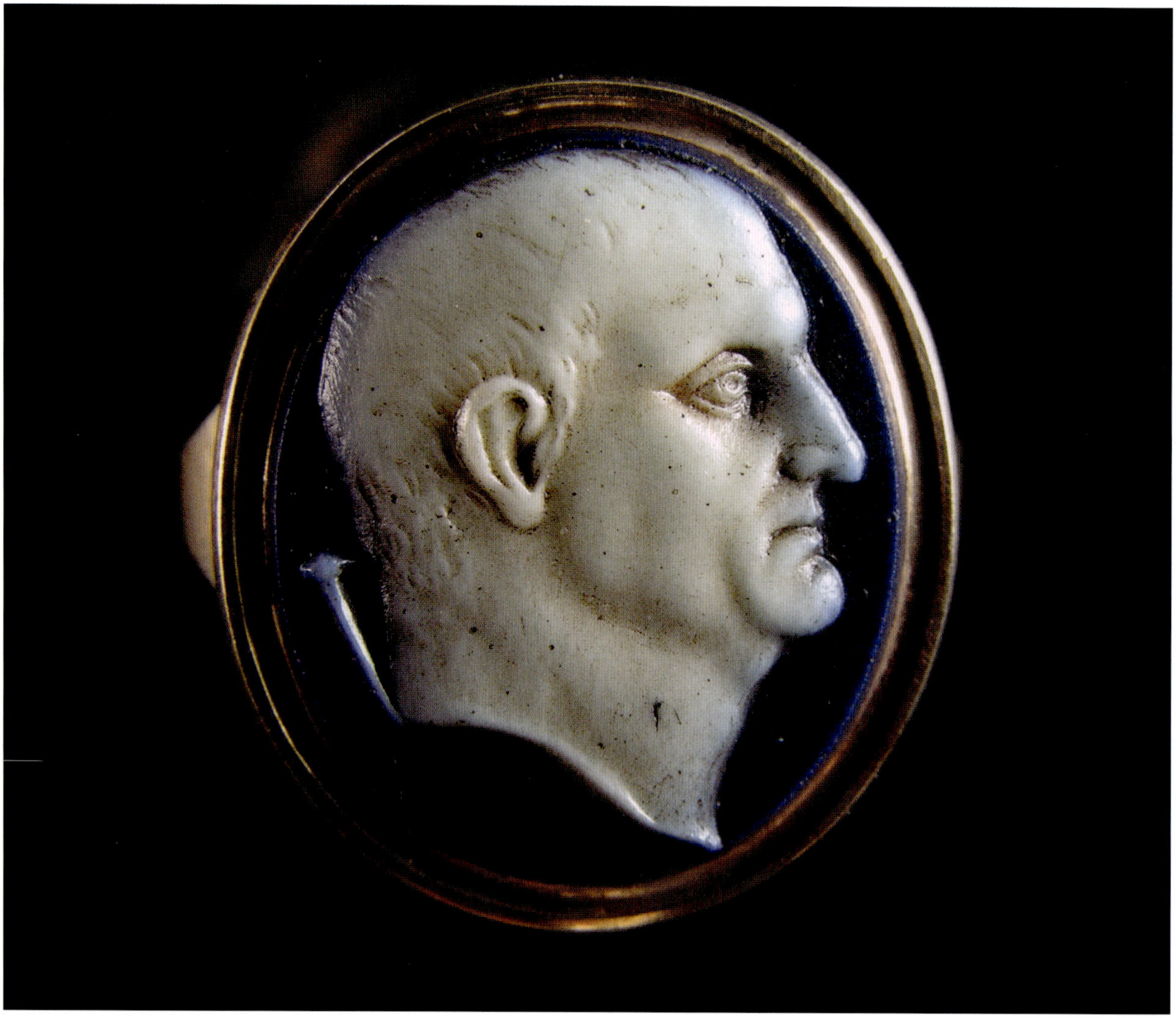

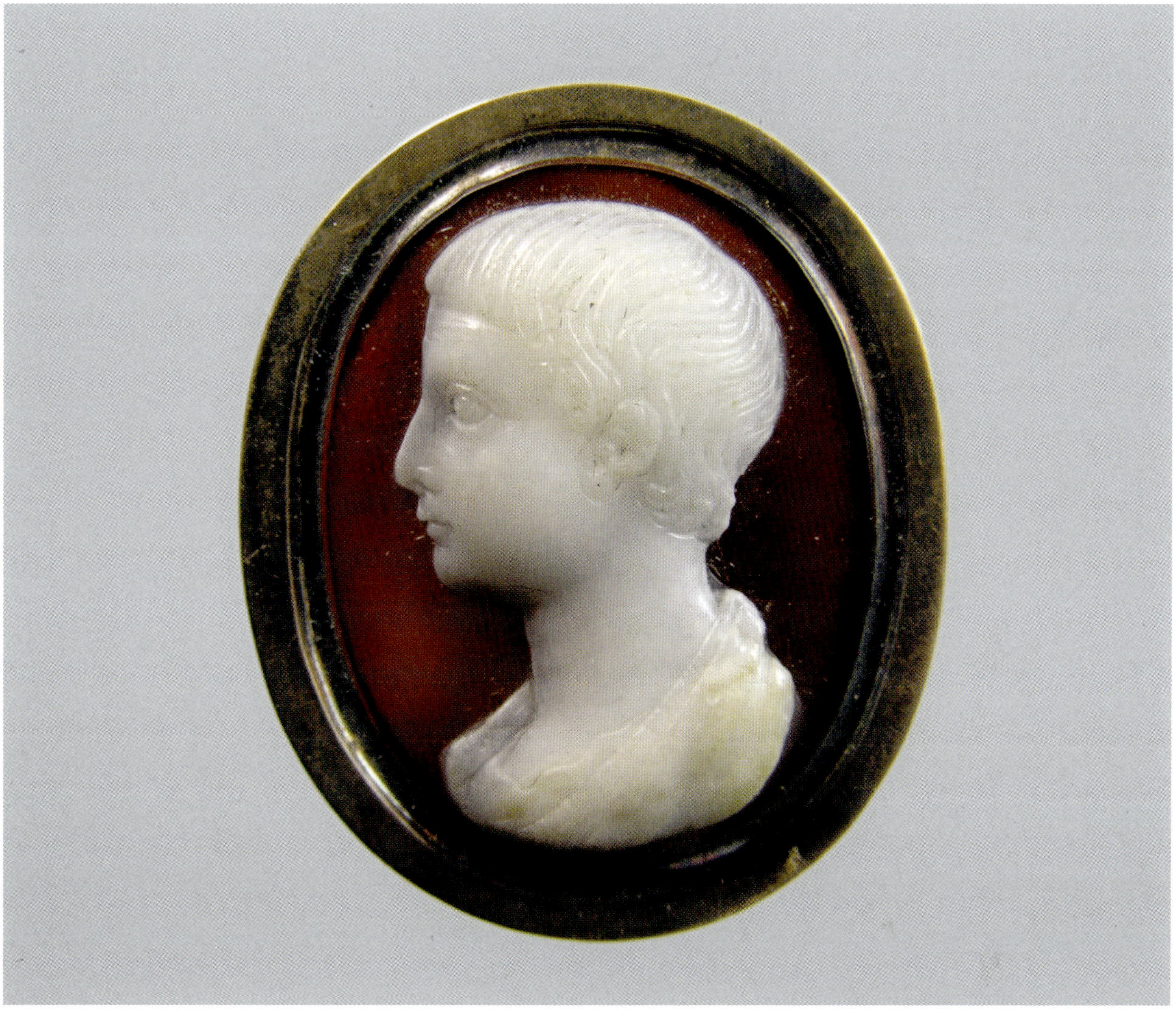

69

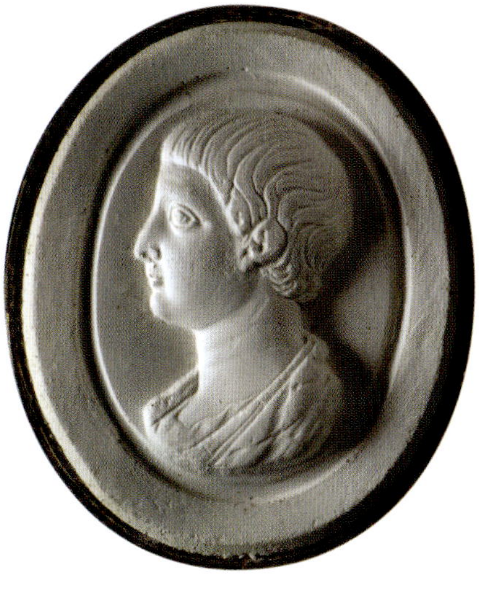

(10648) K110 (pl. 1)
Sardonyx, white/black, polished flat back, set on a plain gold ring
21 x 16

Probably in the 1st Duchess' Collection (no. 2; 'Gift of my Lord'); SG.Imp. 84; Inst.Imp. no. 12.

Bust of a Roman prince, dressed, perhaps Caius Caesar.

16th century?

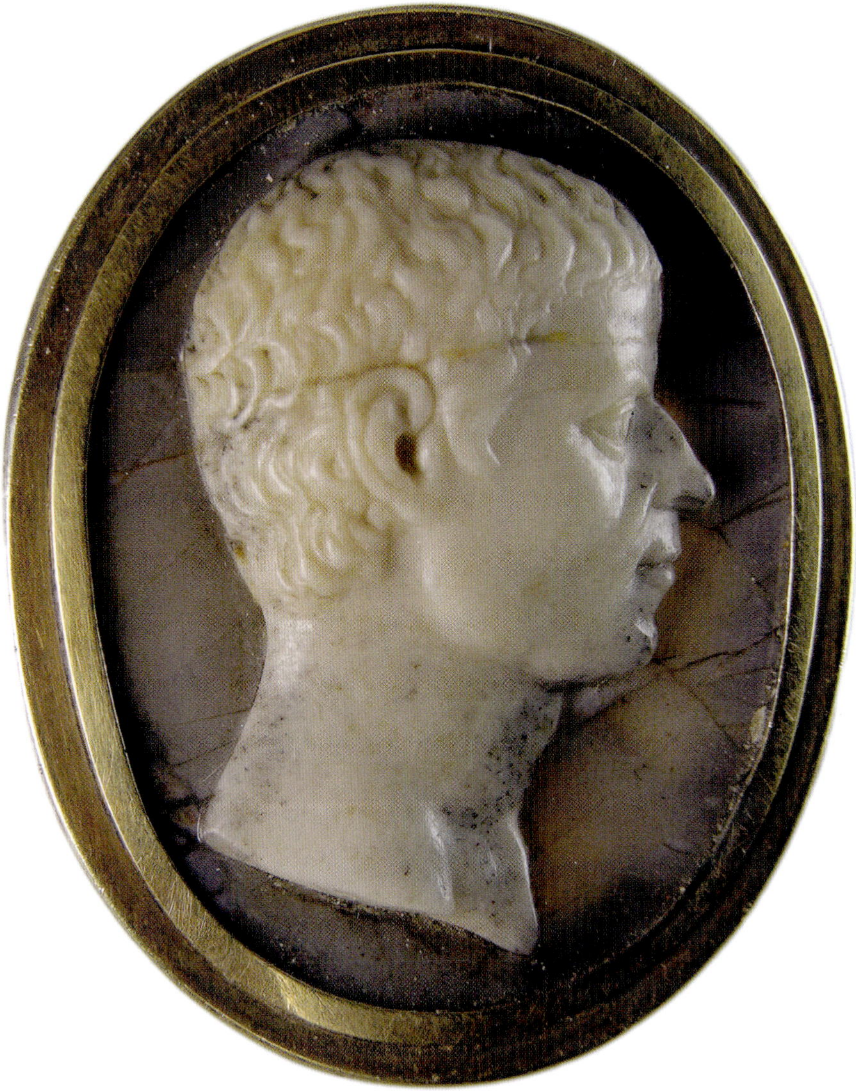

70

(10787)

Sardonyx, white/grey mottled-white, polished flat back, set on a plain gold ring

26 x 20

Head of Brutus.

18th century?

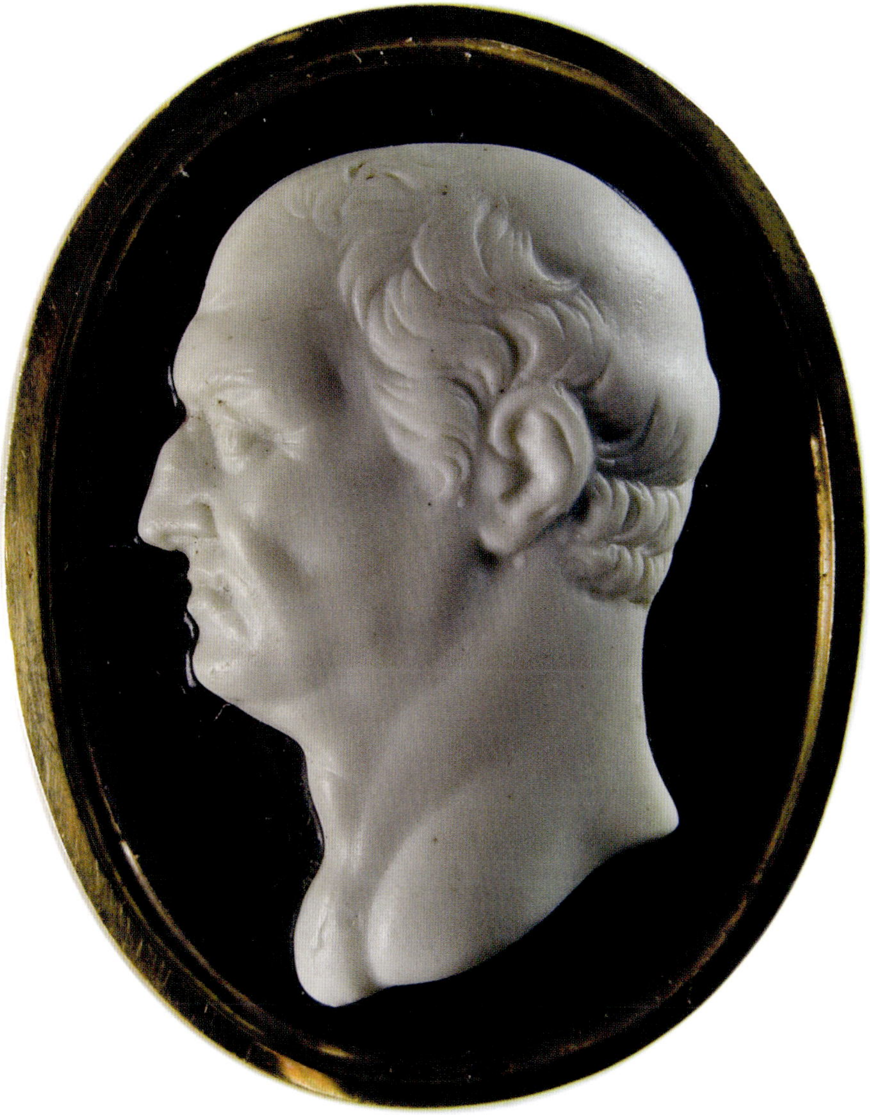

71

(10786)
Sardonyx, white/black, polished flat back, set on a plain gold ring
14 x 10

Head of a balding man. Variously identified as Solon (Fulvio Orsini), Maecenas (after the suggestion of the Duc D'Orleans) and Cicero; cf. *Würzburg* no. 859

17th/ 18th century.

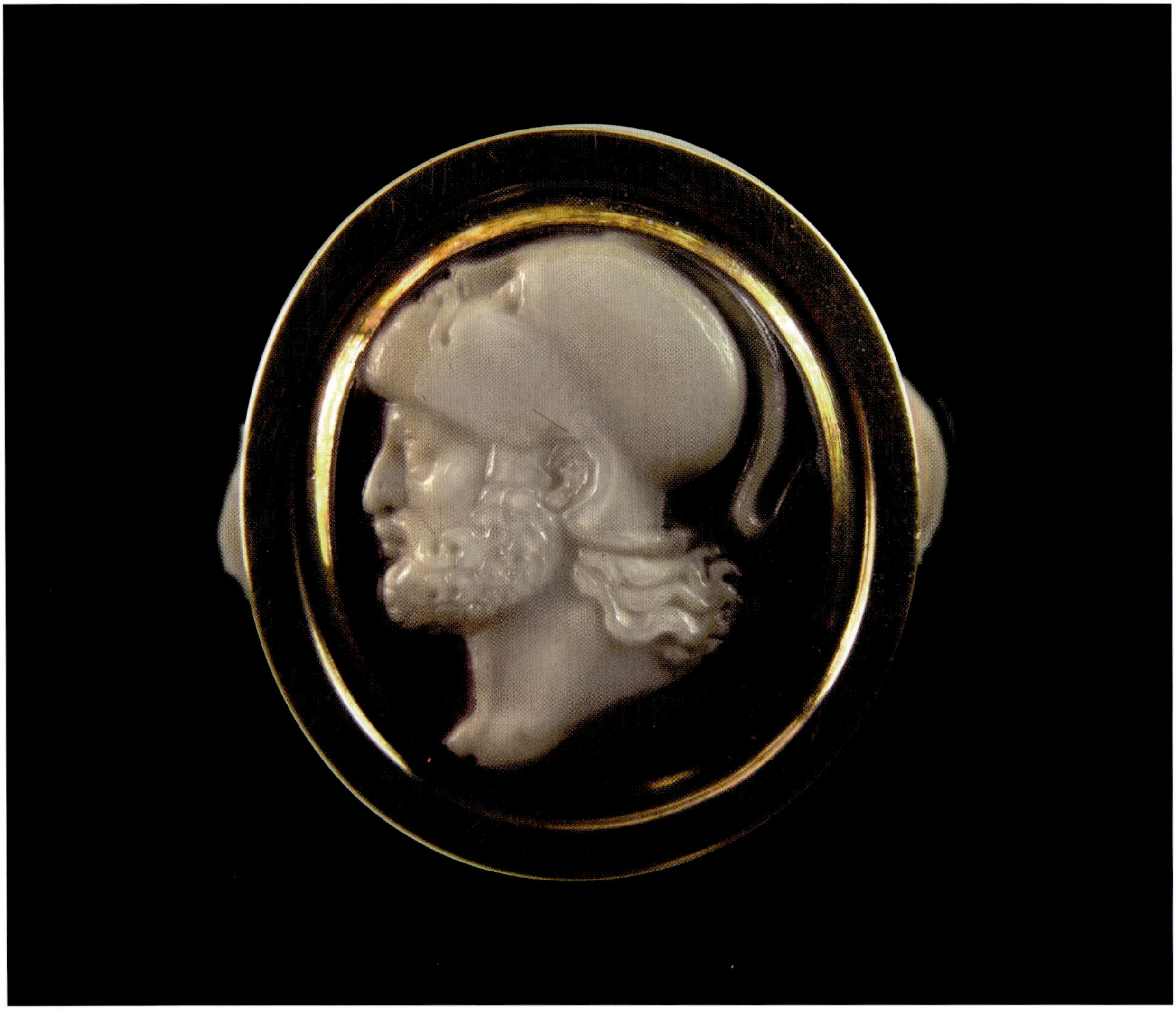

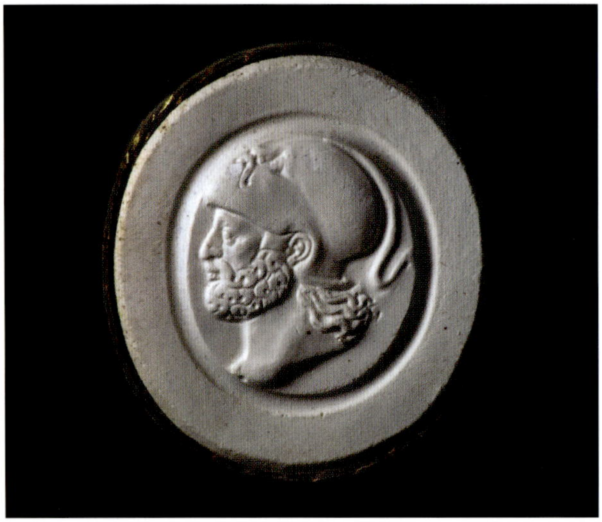

72

(10646) K108 (pl. 1)
Sardonyx, brown (beard on helmet)/white/black, polished flat back, set on a plain gold ring
13 x 12

SG.Imp. 31; Inst.Imp. no. 31.

Head of a bearded man wearing a helmet, the crest of which is outlined in white, with the crown and visor in the form of a bearded head.

17th/18th century?

73

(10652) K114 (pl. 1)
Sardonyx, black/red/white/black, unpolished flat back, set on a plain gold ring with triple branches at end of hoop
10 x 9

Head of Hercules wearing the lionskin.

The neat beard might indicate a portrait 'as Hercules', but see Spier, *Gulbenkian* no. 51.

16th/17th century?

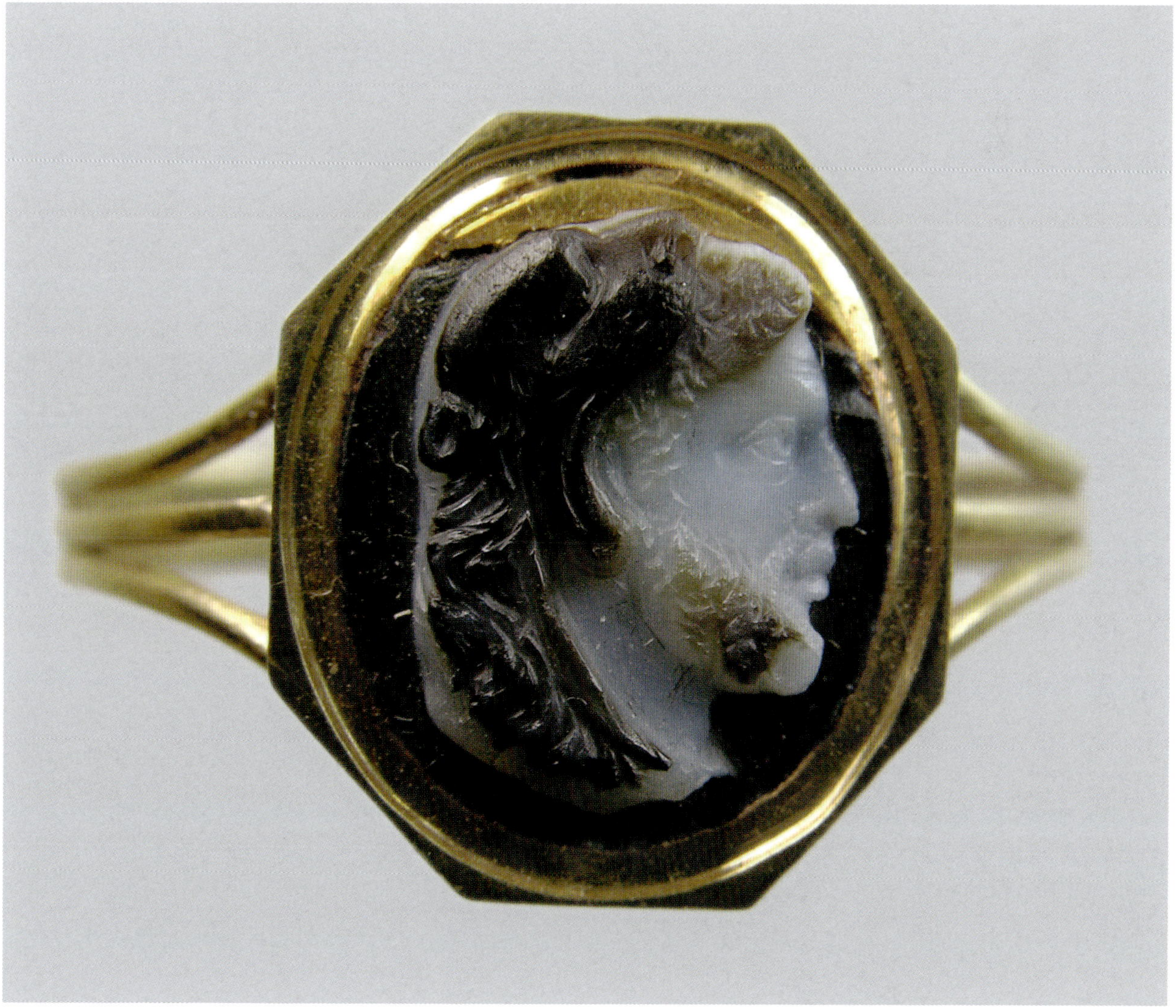

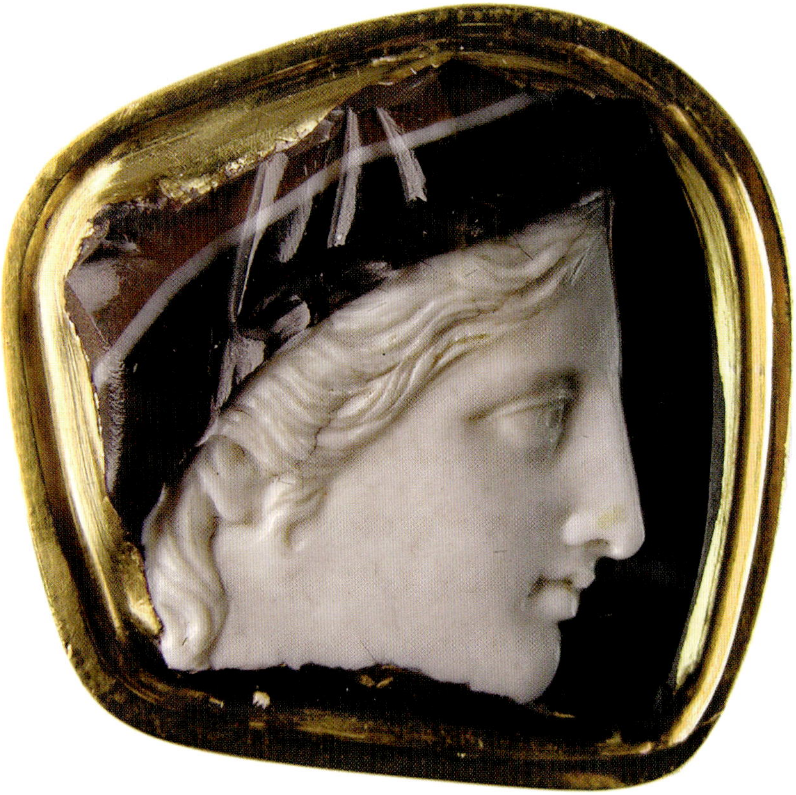

74

(10594) K56 (pl. 1)
Sardonyx fragment, black with a white stripe/white/ black, unpolished flat back, set on a plain gold ring
16 x 16

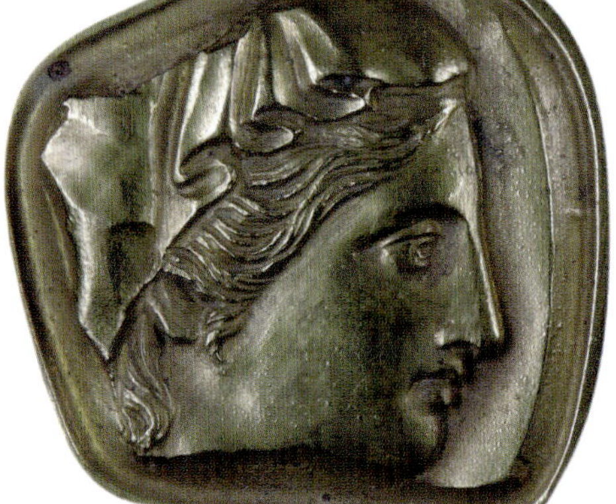

Bought from Sir William Hamilton by the Earl of Beverley for £350 in 1801. SG.Imp. 179; Inst.Imp. no. 45; *AGE* no. 29.

Head of Livia (58 BC–AD 29) or Antonia Minor (36 BC–AD 37; thus, *AGE*), her hair veiled.

18th century?

75

(10597) K59 (pl. 1)
Sardonyx, creamy white/brown, repaired in gold left and below, unpolished flat back, set on a plain gold ring
21 x 15

SG.Imp. 151; Inst.Imp. no. 44; *AGE* no. 30.

Head of Antonia Minor (compare our **74**) wearing a veil and diadem.

1st century AD.

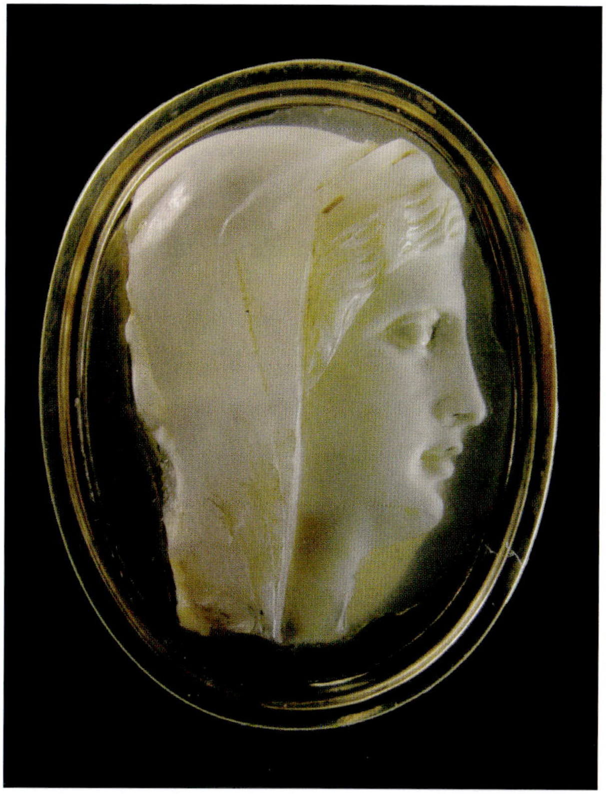

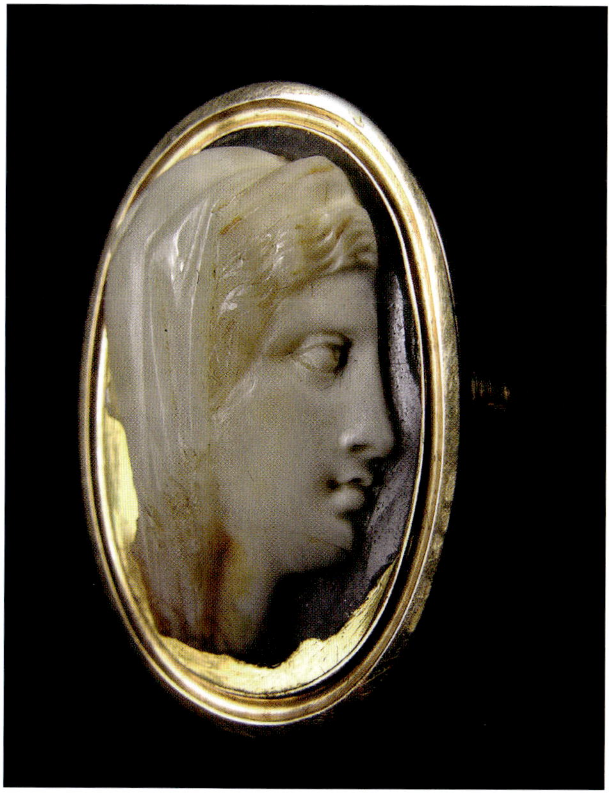

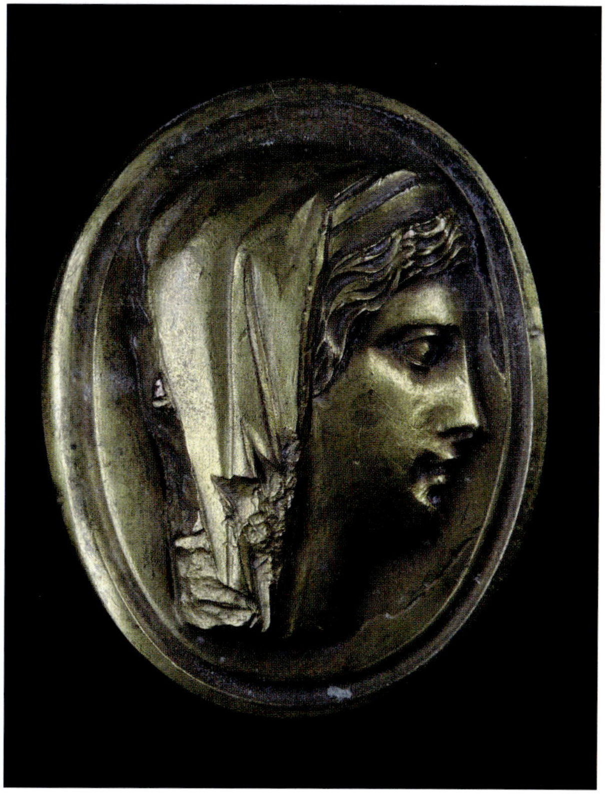

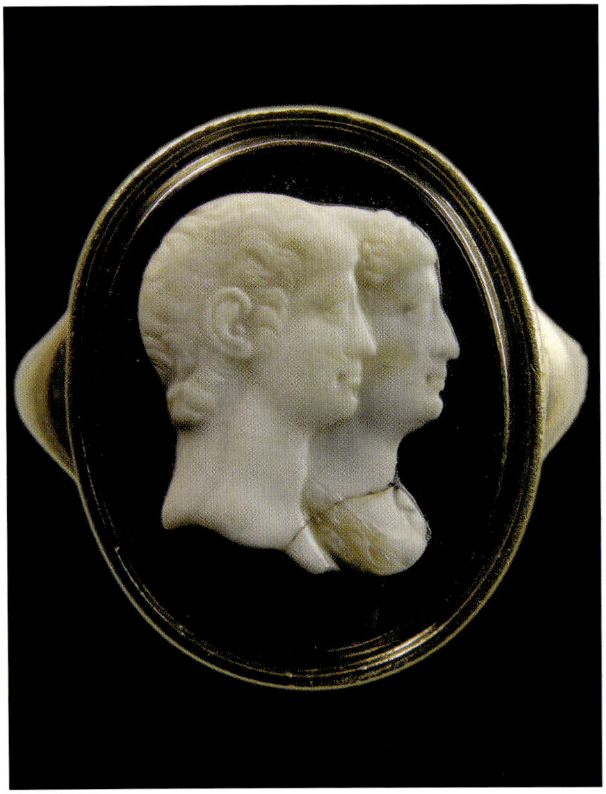

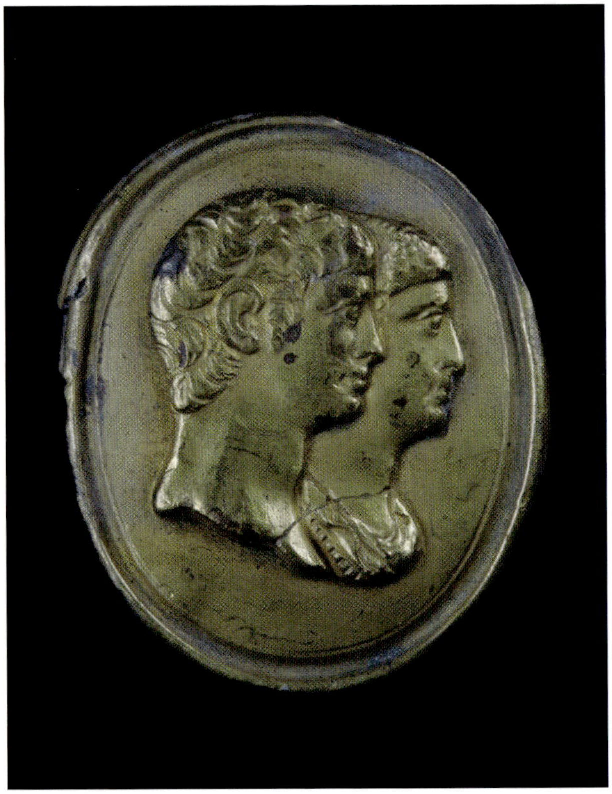

76

(10650) K112 (pl. 1)
Sardonyx, white/black, polished flat back, set on a plain gold ring
16 x 13

SG.Imp. 50; Inst.Imp. no. 124; W.Tassie 3636; *AGE* no. 245.

Heads of a royal couple.

Possibly Claudius (died AD 54) and Agrippina Minor (or Messalina) with hair bound. The female portrait is close to that of the woman depicted with Claudius on the 'Gemma Claudia' (compare Megow, pl. 31). The exact identification, however, is also unclear here (another contender is Drusilla). The emperor is closer to being an idealised portrait of Caligula. Formerly taken for Jupiter and Juno.

1st century AD.

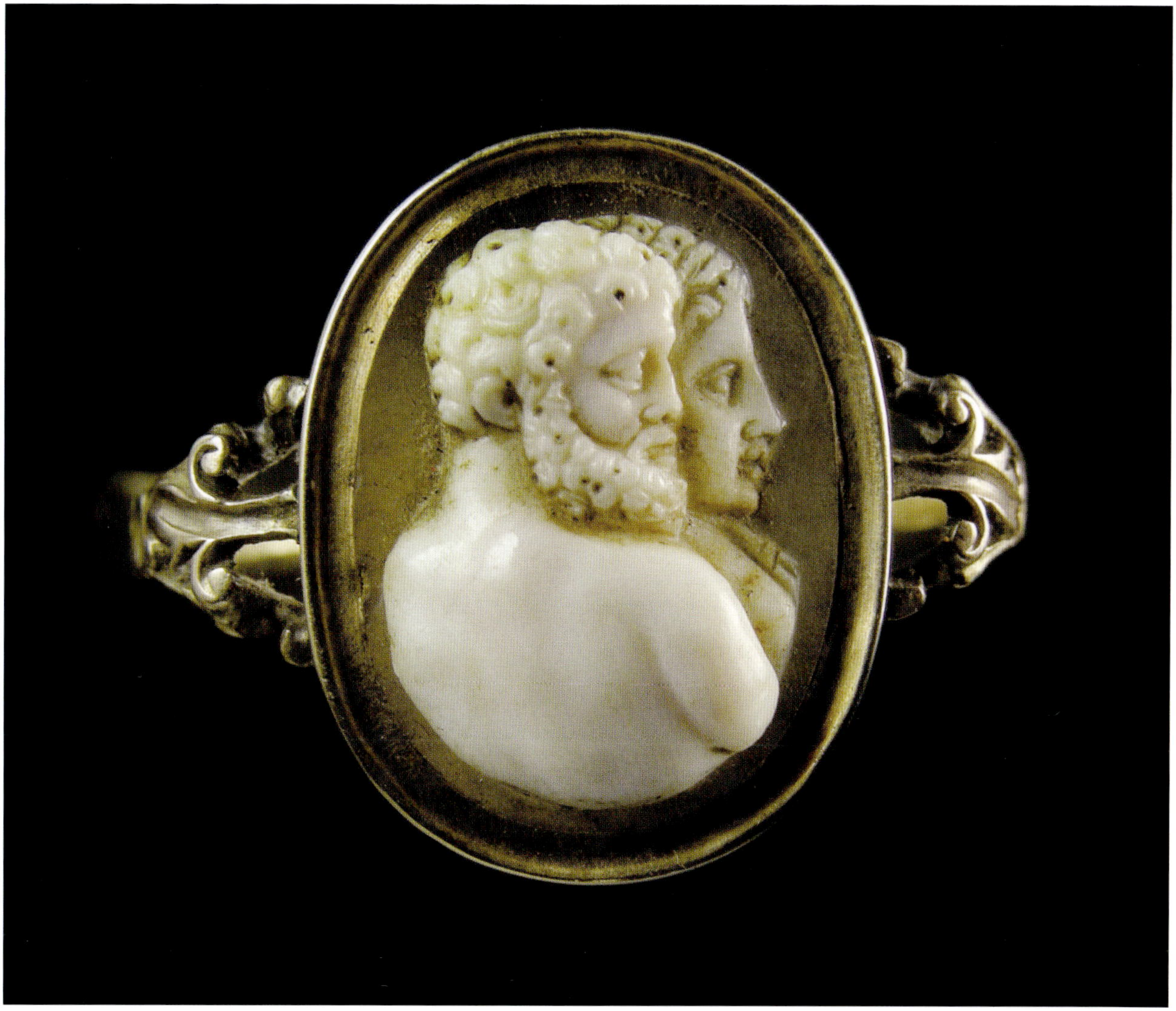

77

(10809)
Sardonyx, white/pink/red/grey, polished flat back, set on a gold ring with floral terminals
15 x 10

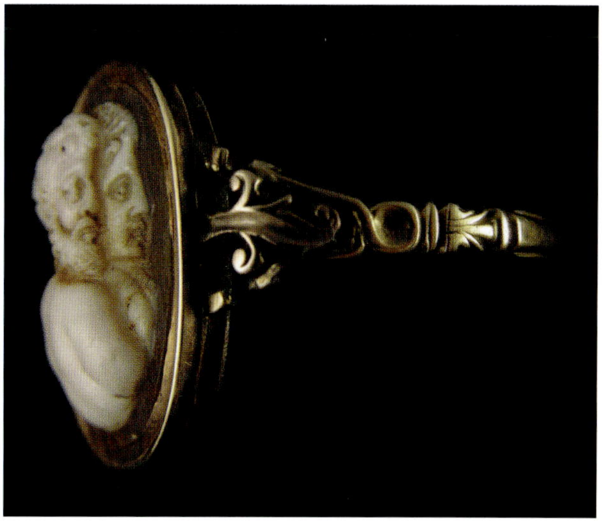

Slade Collection; Spilsbury no. 33 (as 'Hercules and Omphale').

Three-quarter back view of a bearded man and of a youth with curly hair, laureate (?) with a ribbon end at his shoulder.

See Weber 1995, no. 350, for a glass version signed ΚΑΡΠΟΥ, deriving from a Hercules and Iole attributed to Sirletti (d. 1737).

1st century BC?

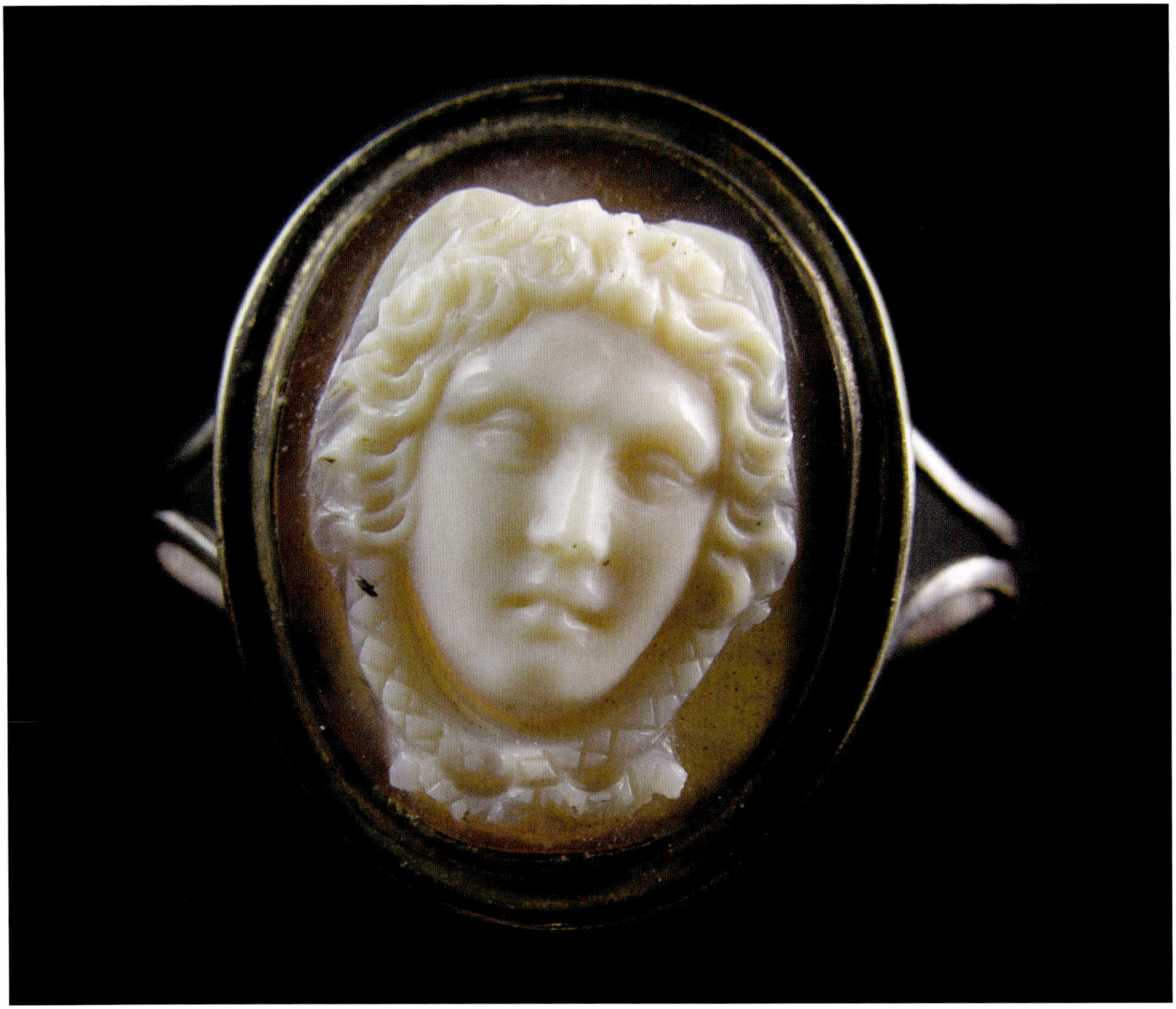

78

(10770)

Sardonyx, white/grey, unpolished convex back, set on a modern gold ring with forked terminals to the hoop
16 x 13

Medusa head with wings in the hair, snakes at the neck.

17th/18th century?

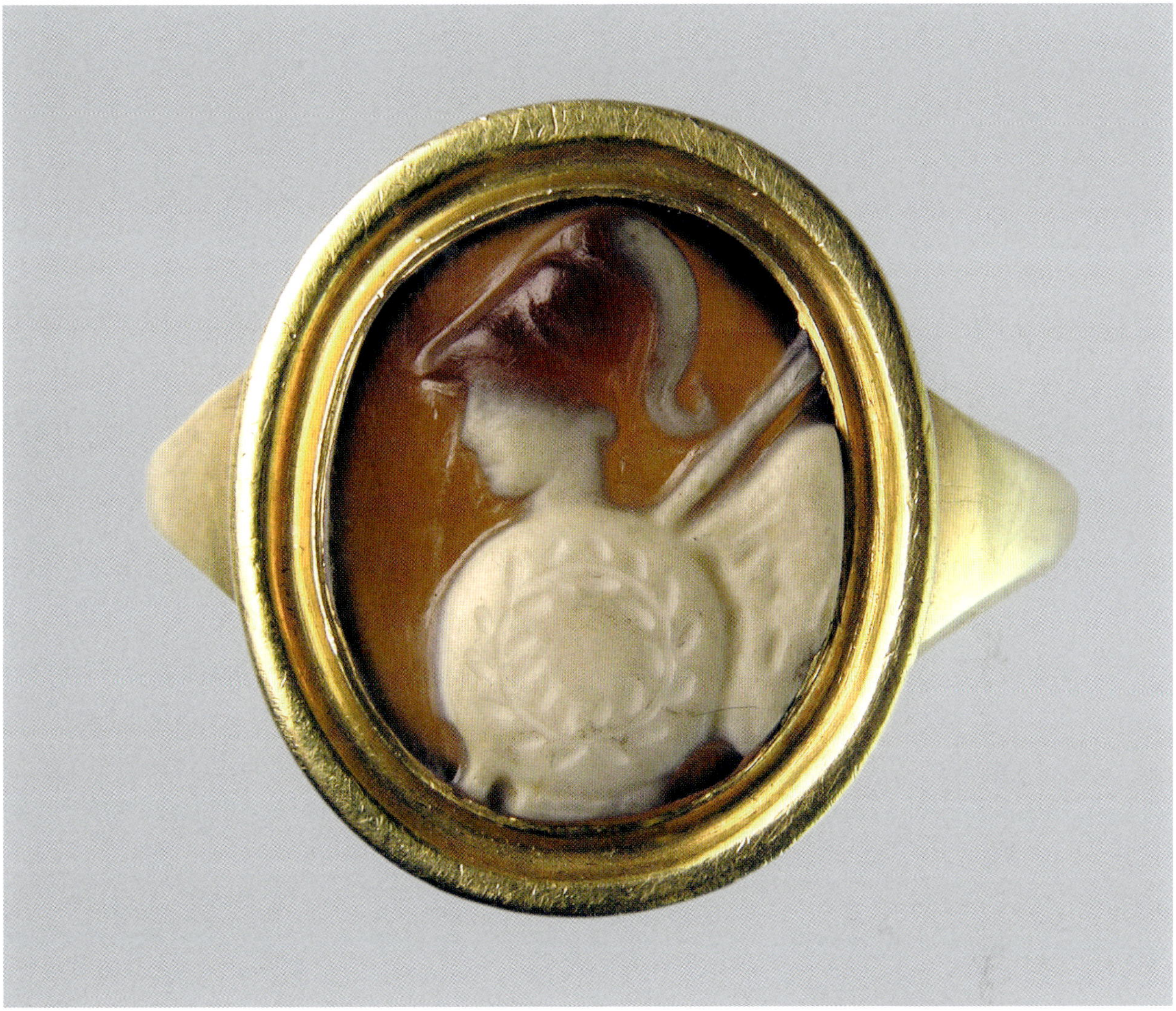

79

(10560) K22 (pl. 1)
Sardonyx, black/grey (helmet crest)/white/brown, polished flat back, set on a plain gold ring
12 x 10

Upper half of a figure of a youth (or Athena, but the head is short-haired), wearing a helmet with long curling crest, holding a round shield decorated with a wreath, holding a spear over the shoulder and, below it, what may be meant for an aegis (if Athena) draped on another spear (?), if not a wing.

18th century?

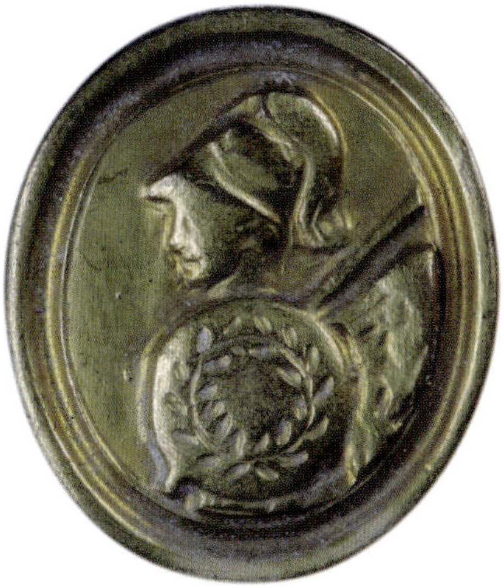

ANIMALS AND OBJECTS

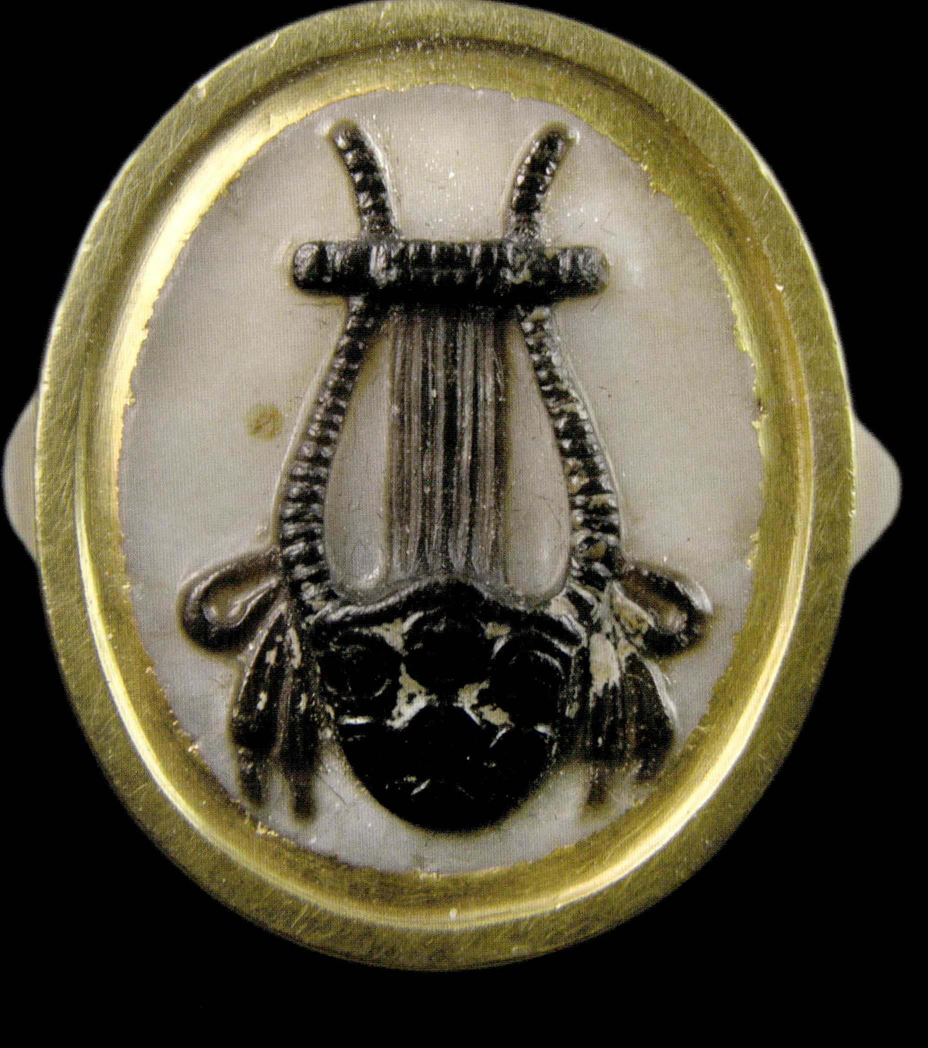

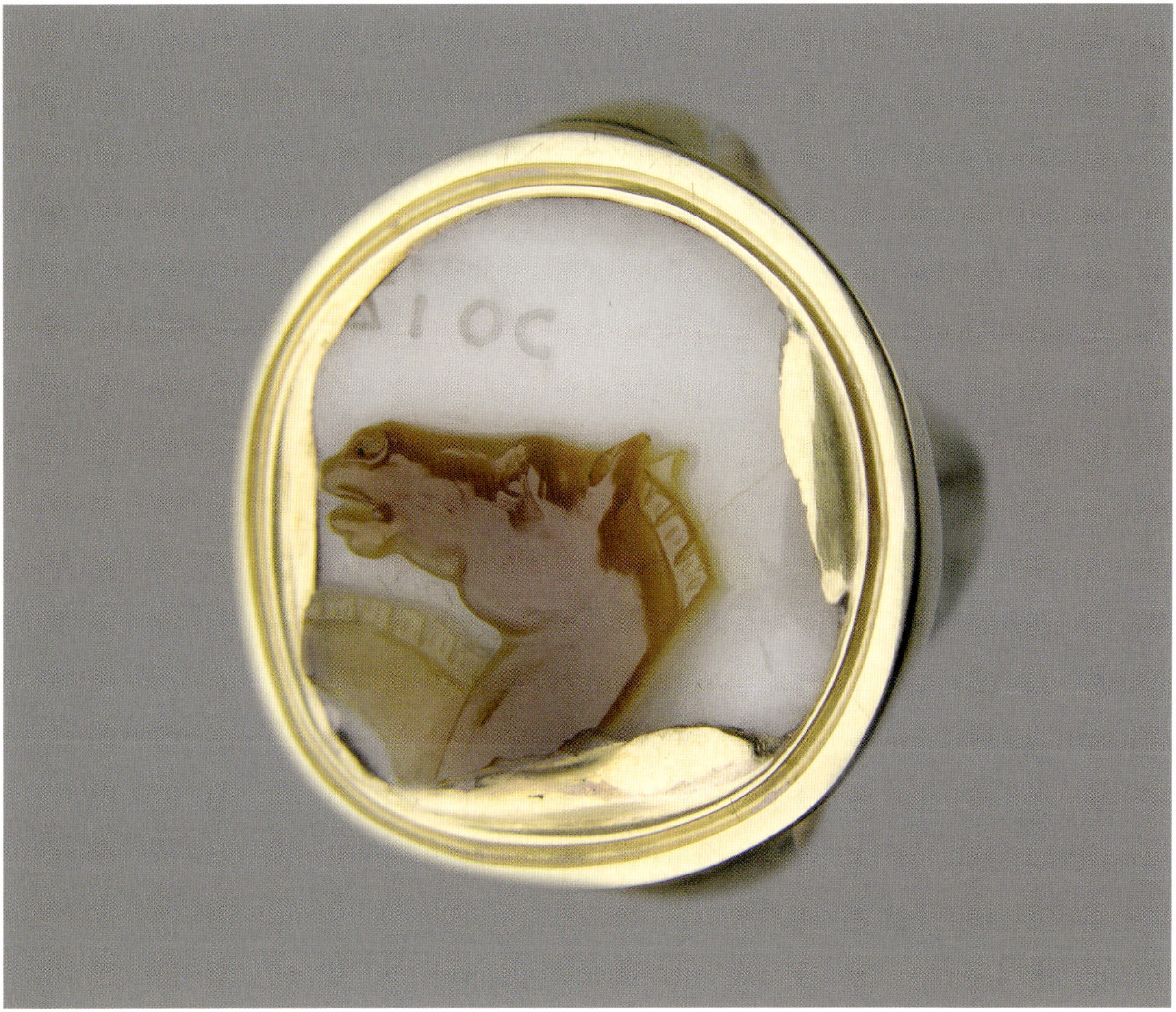

80

(10655) K117 (pl. 1)
Sardonyx fragment, unpolished flat back, set on a plain gold ring
Width 10

SG.Imp. 124; Inst.Imp. no 38; *AGE* no. 263.

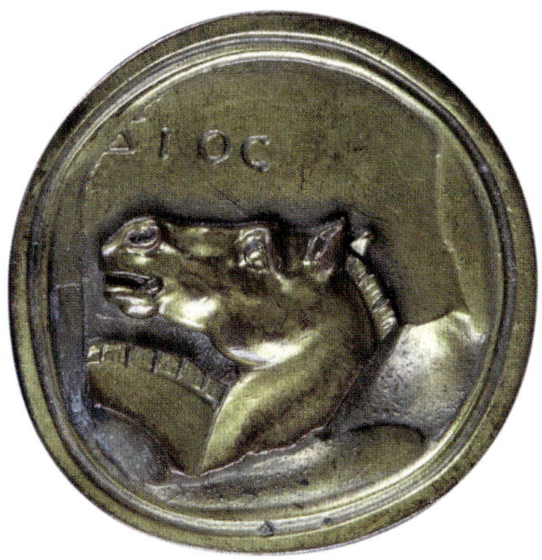

The head of a horse and part of the mane of a second; before them the end of an inscription]ΔIOC.

From a large cameo perhaps showing a chariot team. The inscription may be the end of the artist's name (*AGE* took it for an abbreviation of 'Dioskourides').

1st century BC/AD.

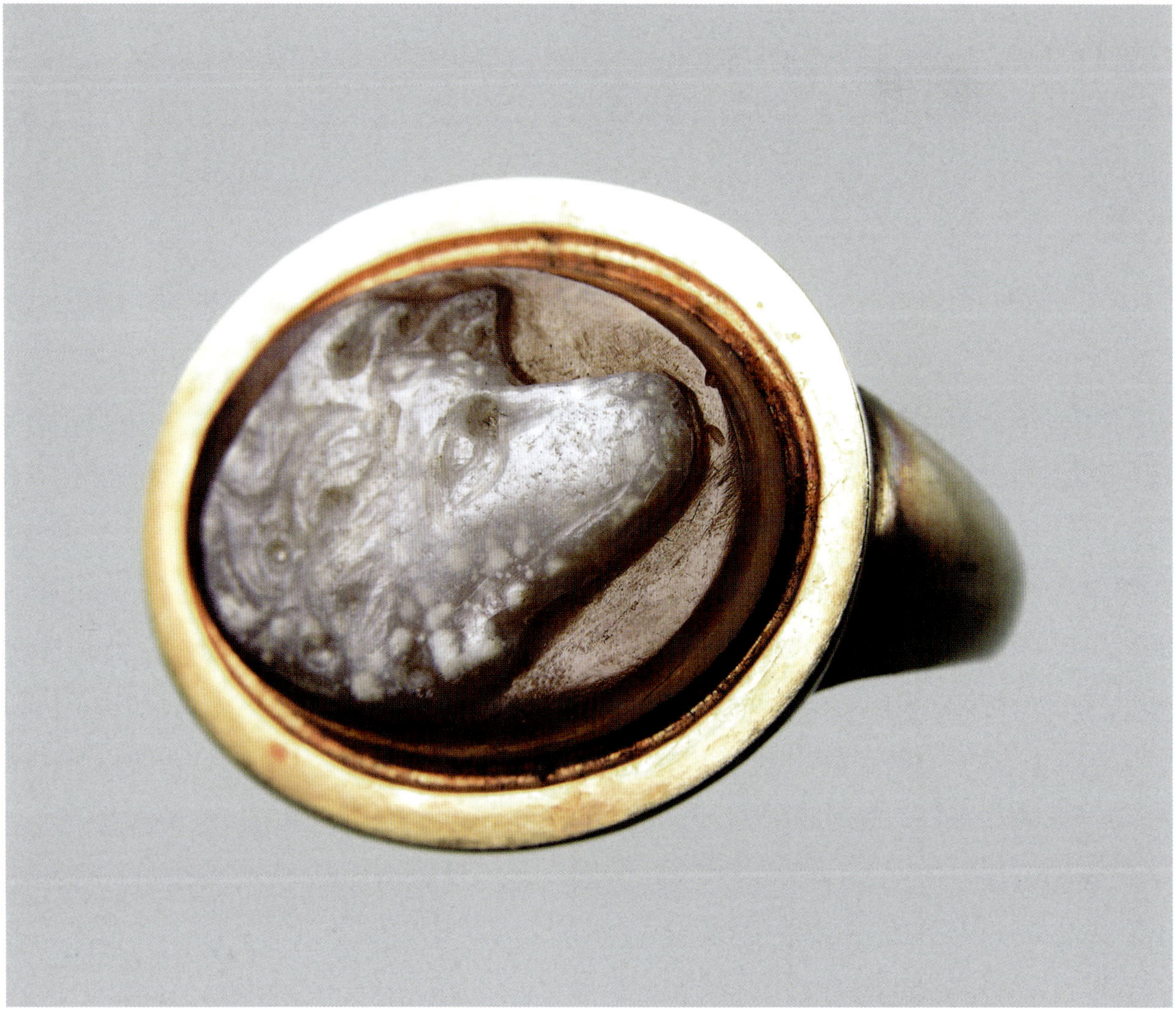

81

(10653) K115
Sardonyx, white/red/white, polished flat back, set on a plain gold ring
16 x 13

SG.Imp. 32; Inst.Imp. no. 36.

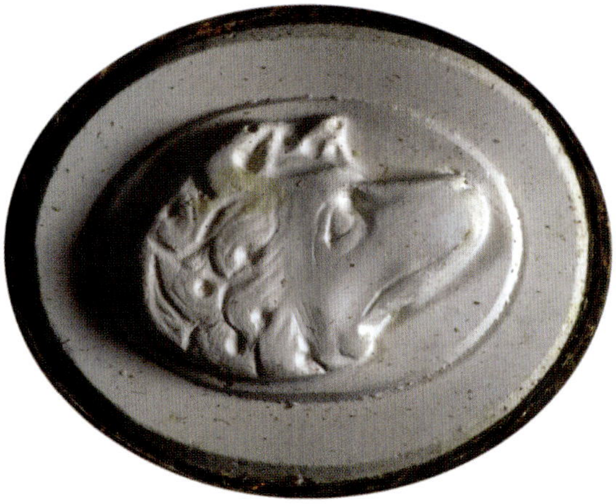

The head of a dog, perhaps Cerberus.
Compare *Wien* I, no. 387.

1st century BC?

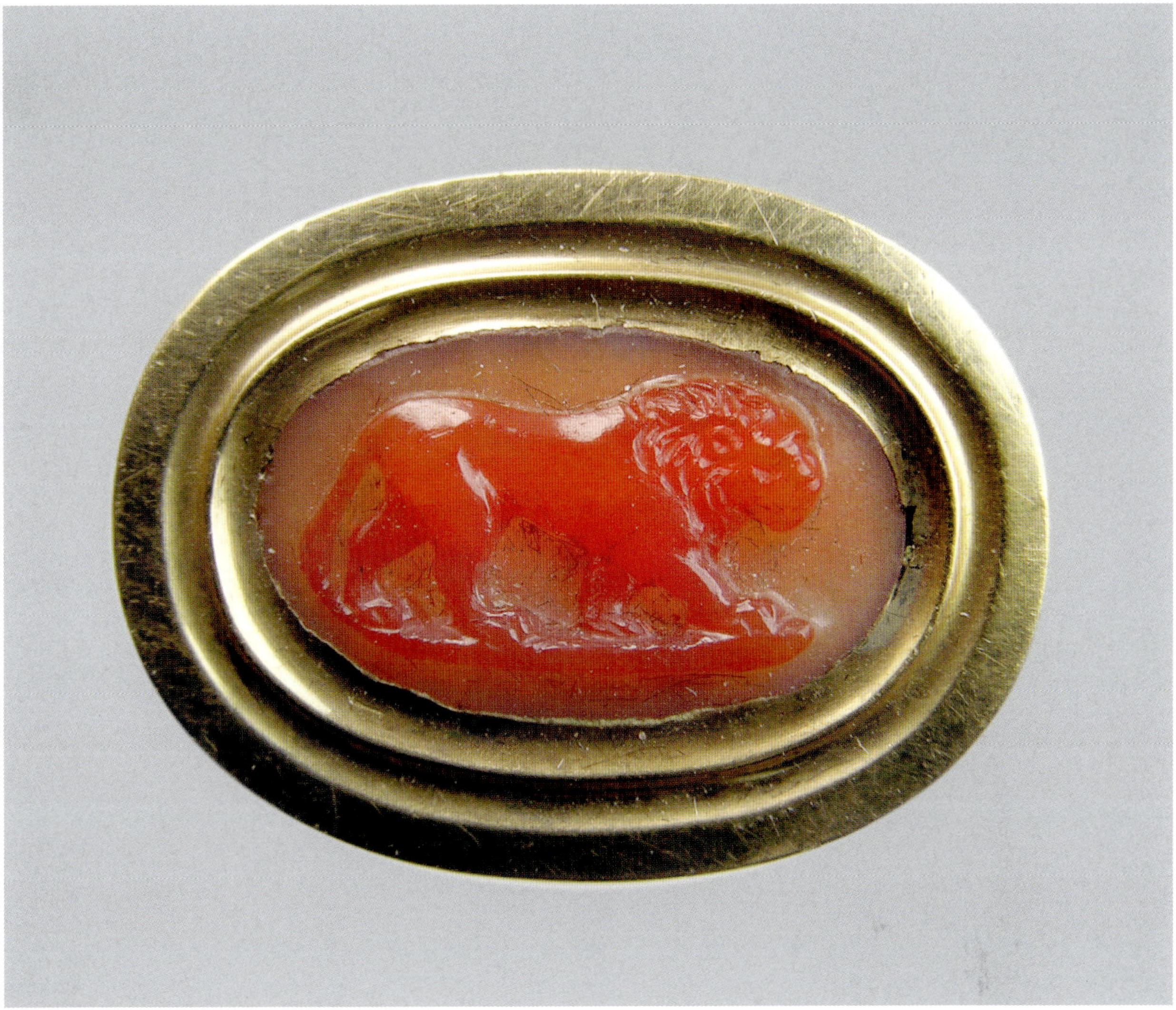

82

(10656) K118
Sardonyx, red/white, unpolished flat back,
set on a plain gold ring
11 x 7

A lion walking. Ground line.

1st century AD?

83

(10654) K116 (pl. 6)
Agate, the pale brown layers used to distinguish the wing feathers, unpolished flat back, set on a plain gold ring
13 x 12

AGE no. 256.

A partridge. Ground line. On the bird type see Spier, *Getty* no. 442.

2nd/3rd century AD.

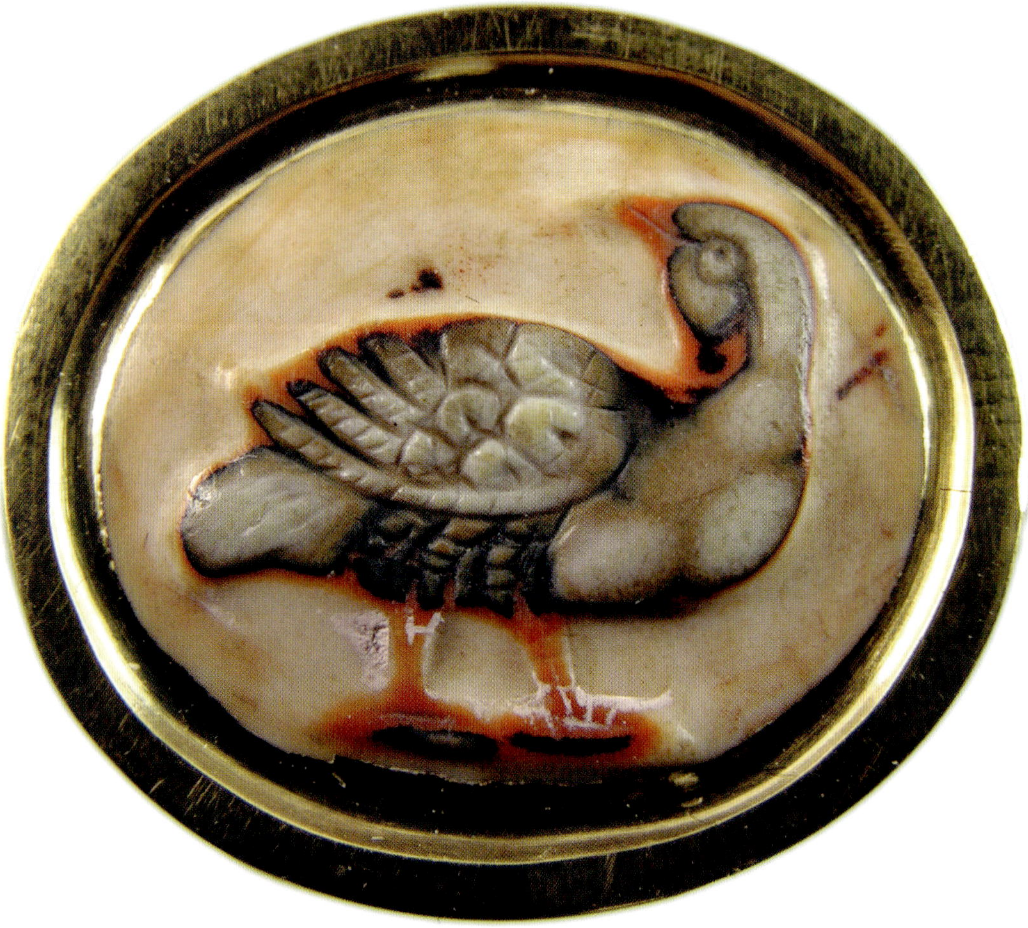

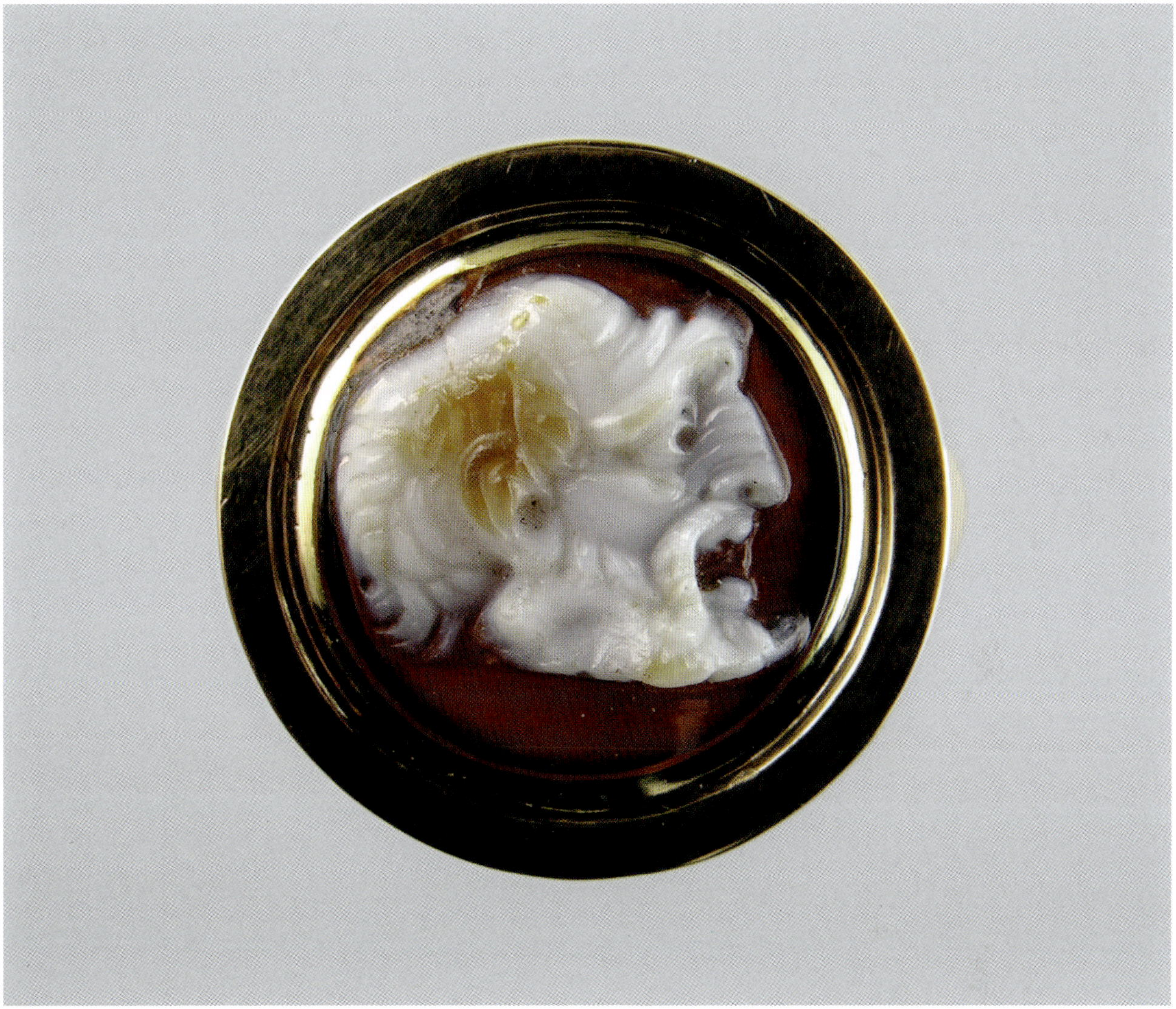

84

(10590) K51 (pl. 1)
Sardonyx, brown (hair and ear)/white/dark brown, polished flat back, set on a plain gold ring
13 x 13

Inst.Imp. no. 84; SG.Imp. 128; *AGE* no. 313.

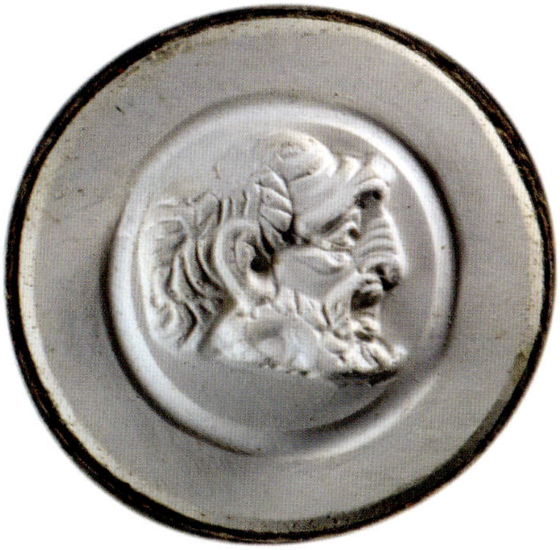

The comic mask of an old man.
Compare *Würzburg* no. 612.

1st century BC/AD.

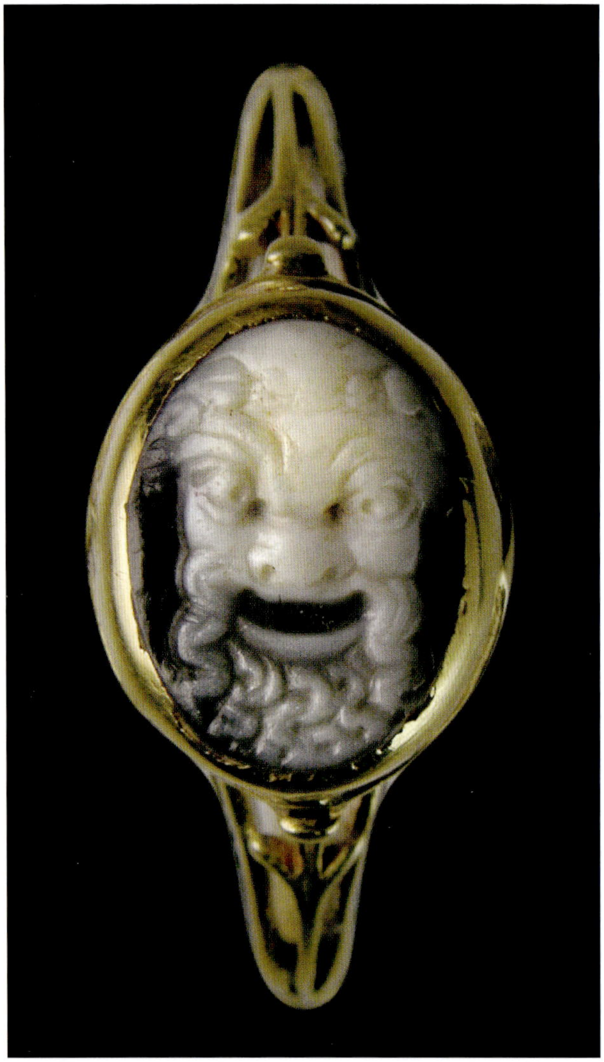

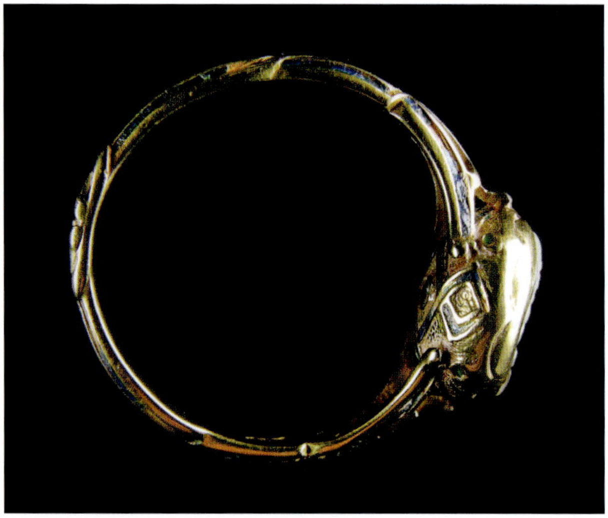

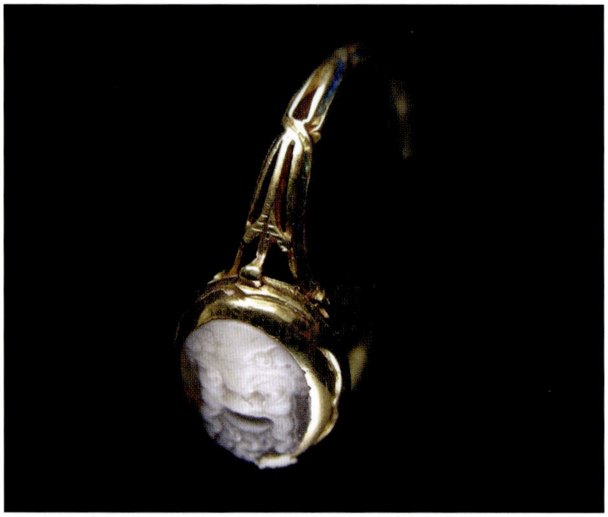

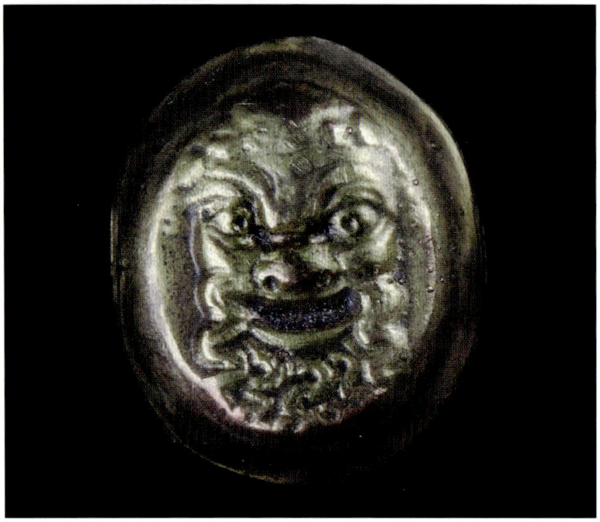

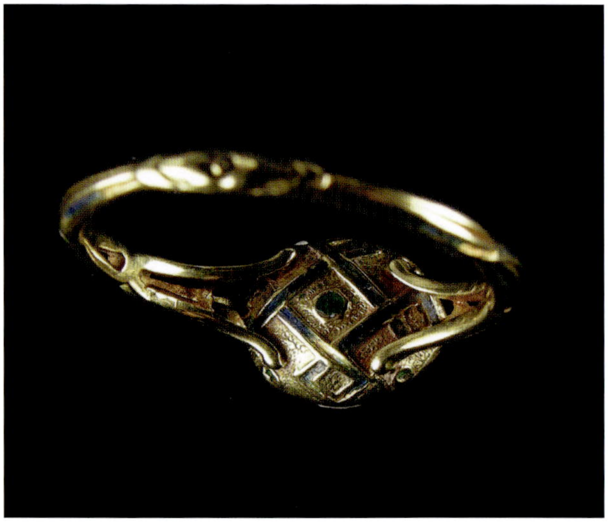

85

(10588) K50 (pl. 1)
Sardonyx, white/black, set on a 17th-century enamelled gold ring with a knot on the hoop, blue-enamelled cross straps on the bezel back, floral terminals
11 x 7

SG.Imp. 141; Inst.Imp. no. 92; *AGE* no. 314.

Comic mask of a garlanded old man or Silenus.

Cf. SG.Imp. 141 (the same or another(?); Inst.Imp. 29 seems to be the same but with a pelleted border).

1st century BC/AD.

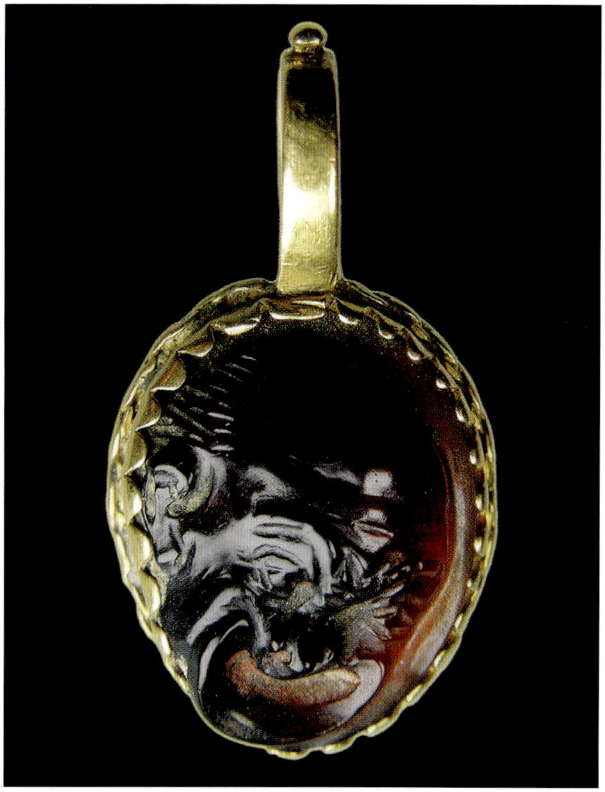

86

(10739) K201
Sard, set on a gold hoop as pendant
12 x 7, pendant height 20

Comic mask in high relief.

A common subject, as Giuliano, *Cammei* no. 252; Pannuti, *Napoli* no. 252.

1st century BC/AD.

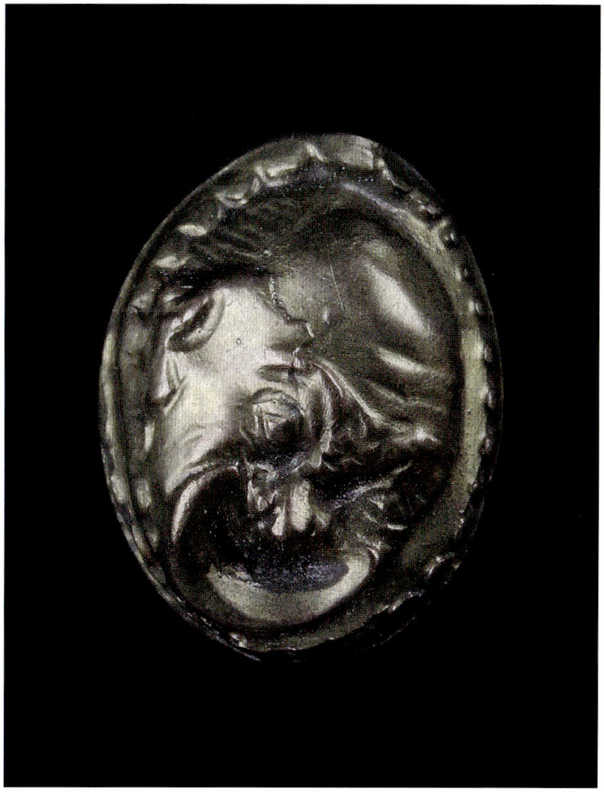

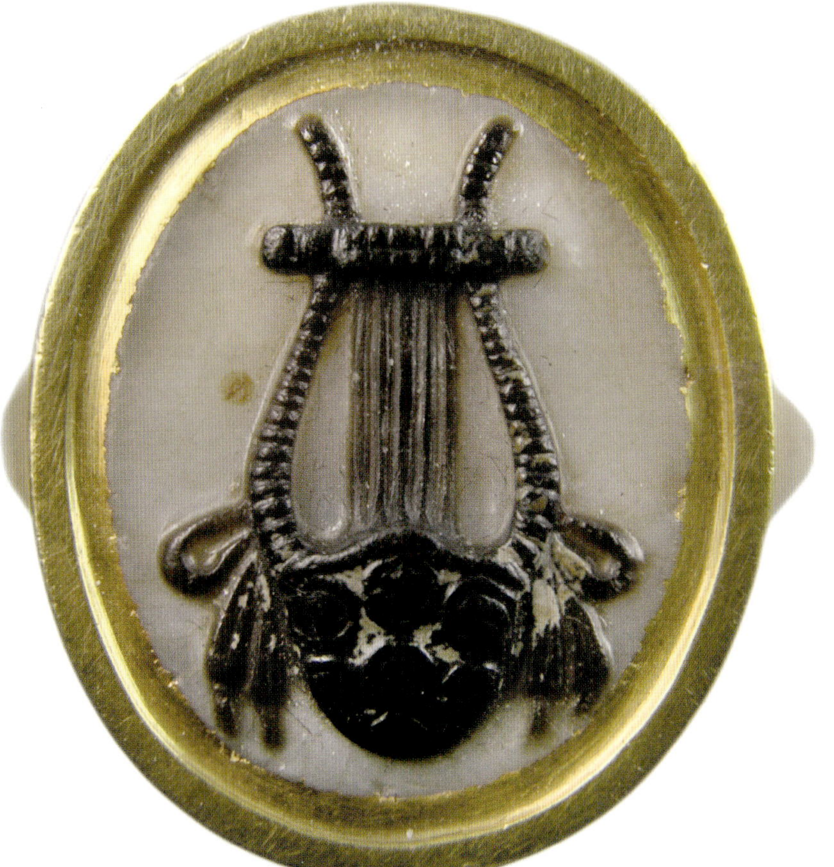

87

(10659) K121
Sardonyx, blue/blue-white/grey, unpolished flat back, set on a plain gold ring
18 x 14

Inst.Imp. no. 26.

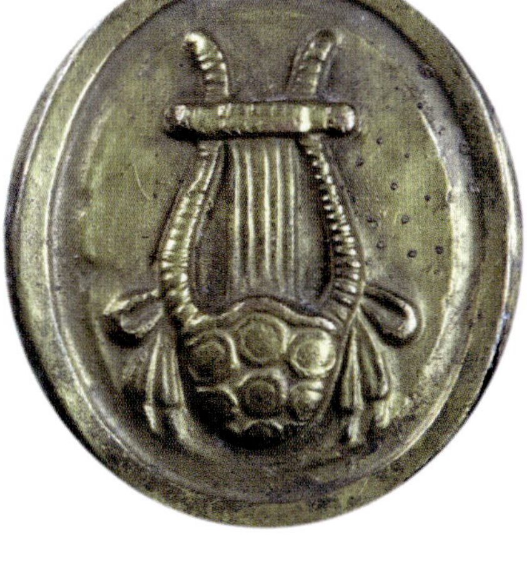

A lyre, ribboned, a tortoiseshell sound box.

Perhaps commissioned by a poet; compare the popularity of the Orpheus theme in art of the late 16th/17th century, and the Farnese cameo, Paoletti I, I.199.

16th century?

88

(10660) K122 (pl. 1)
Sardonyx, black/white, set on a plain gold ring
16 x 12

SG.Imp. 25; Inst.Imp. no. 24.

A lyre, a slightly smaller version of the last, and probably a later copy.

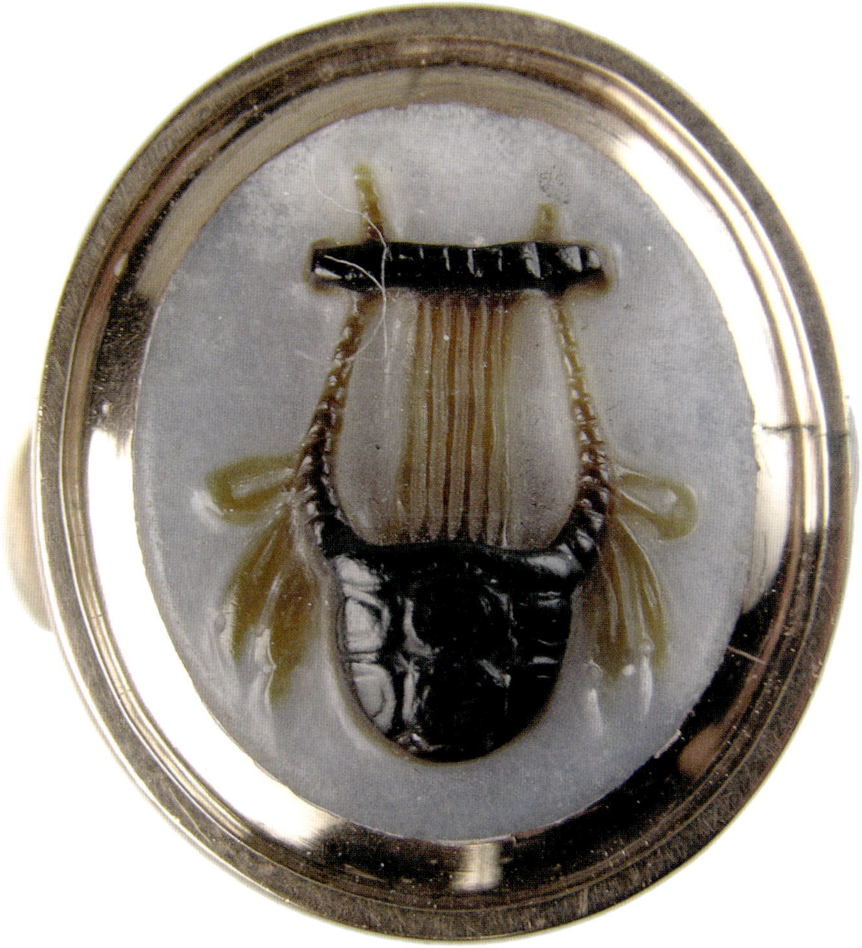

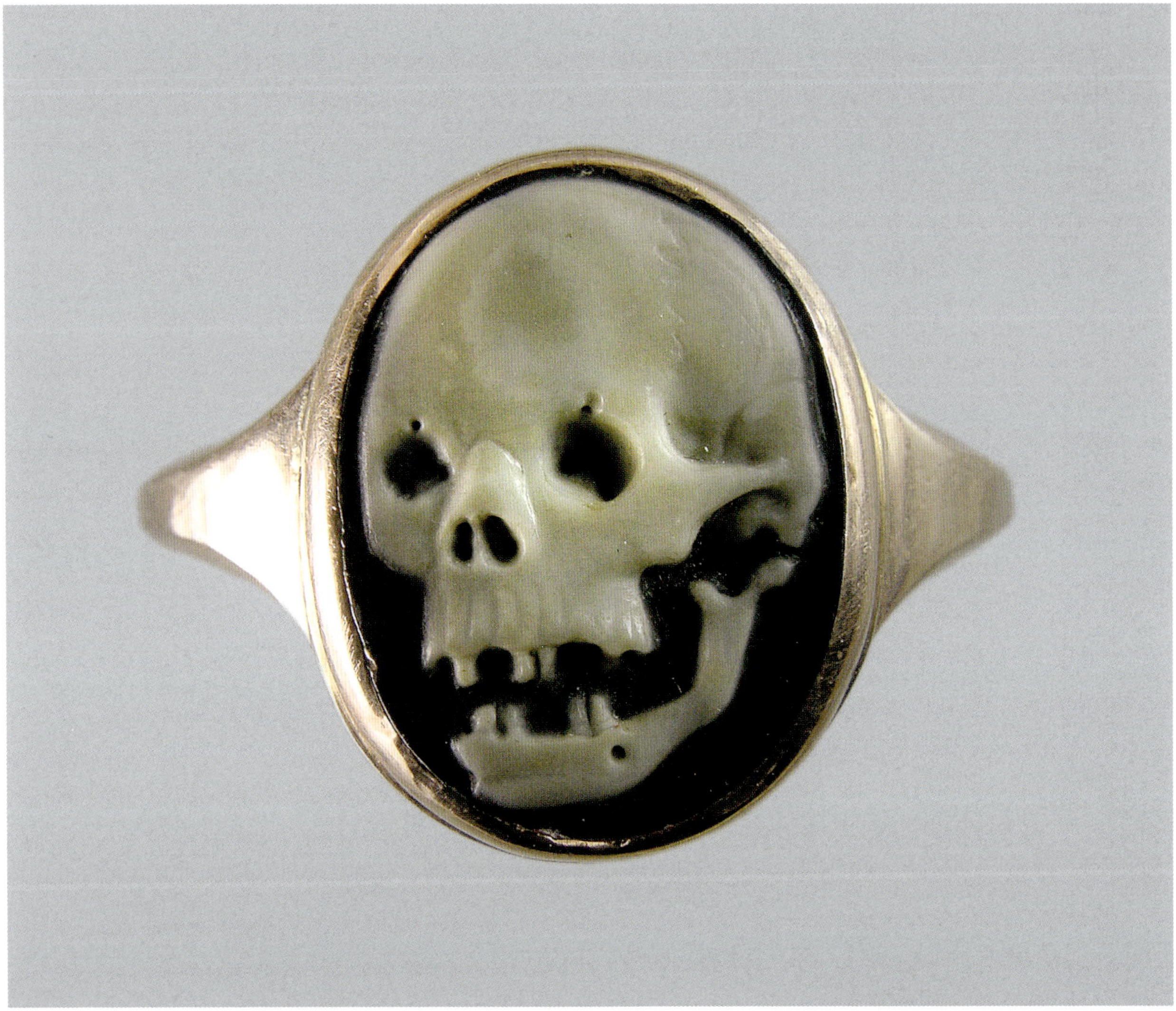

89

(10658) K120 (pl. 1)
Sardonyx, white/black, set on a plain gold ring
10 x 13

SG.Imp. 130; Tassie 8221; Inst.Imp. no. 93; *AGE* no. 253.

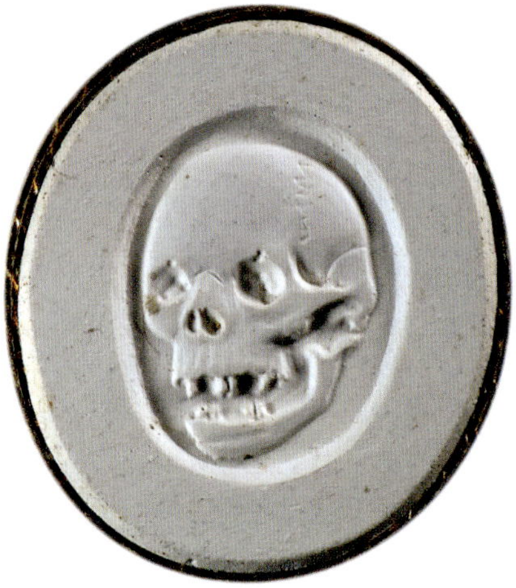

A skull. *Memento mori*.

In Fletcher's play *The Chances*: 'And keep it as they keep deaths heads in rings. To cry memento to me.'

16th/17th century.

INTAGLIOS

SIGNATURES WITH ANCIENT NAMES

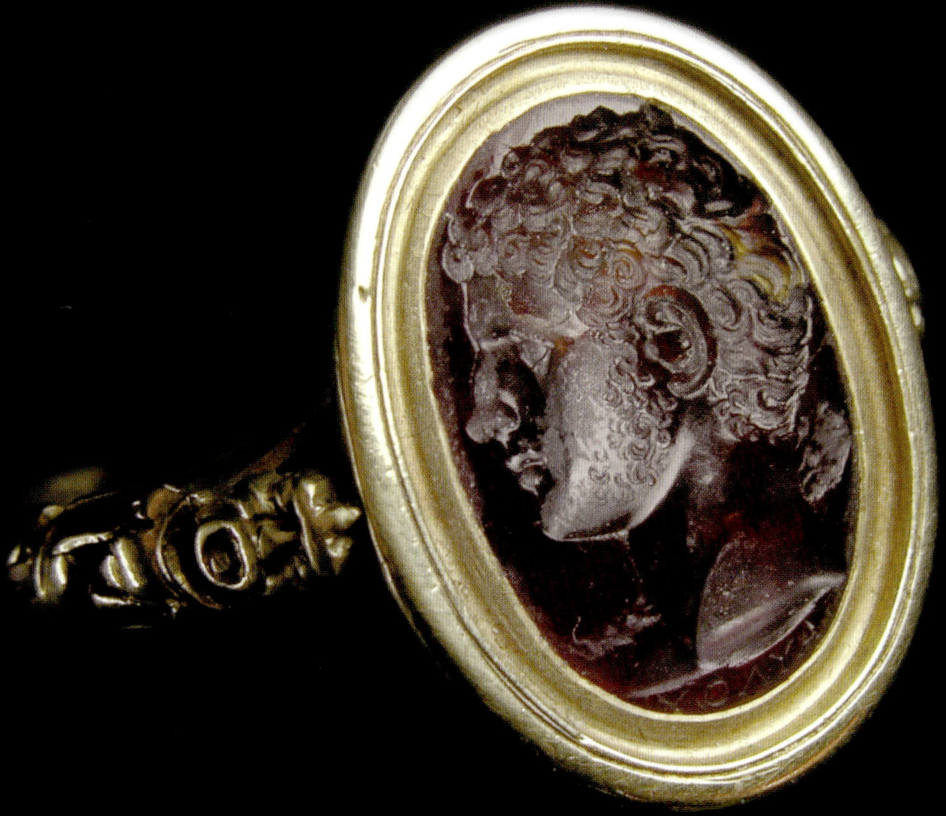

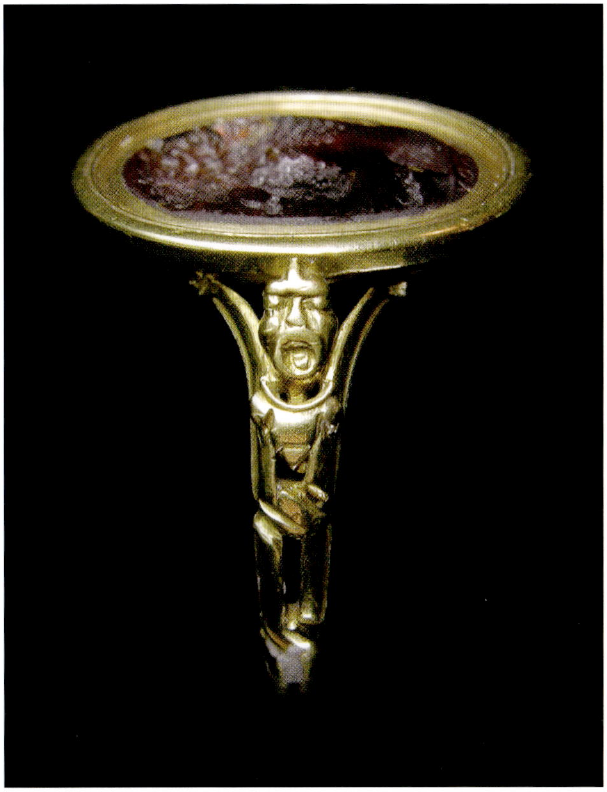

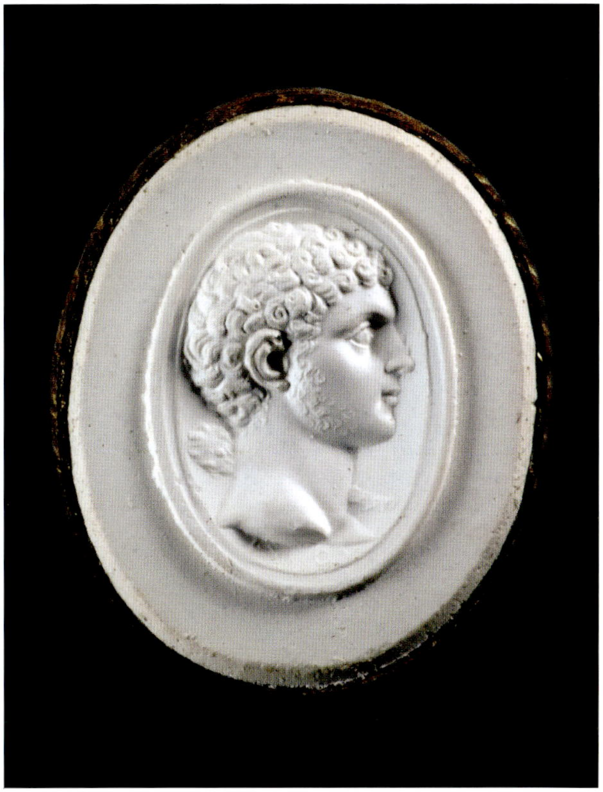

90

(10673) K135 (pl. 6)
Sard fragment, break in stone (part of hair), polished flat back, set on a gold ring with grotesque heads at the hoop ends
12 x 8

SG.Imp. 121; Tassie 5467; Inst.Imp. no. 60; Bracci 1784; Vollenweider, pl. 33.8,10

Bust of the young Hercules shouldering his club. Signed AVΛOV.

Aulos was a freely signing artist of the second half of the 1st century BC; see Vollenweider, 40–3.

1st century BC.

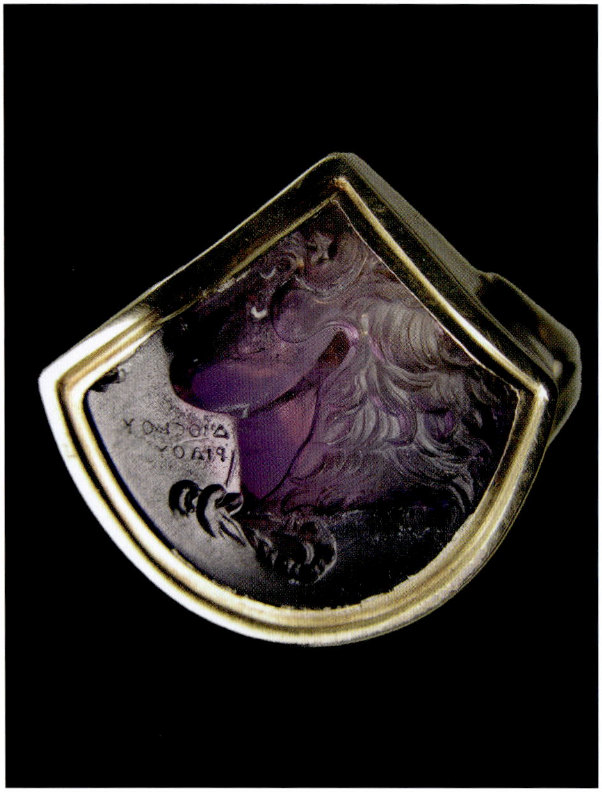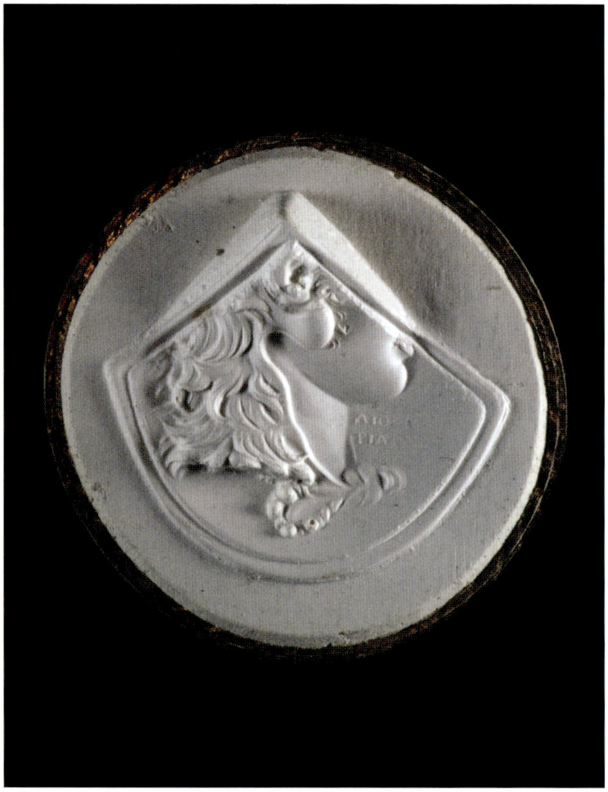

91

(10728) K190 (pl. 6)
Amethyst fragment, polished flat back, set on a plain gold ring
Width 18

'Lord Beverley notes that he bought the gem of a Neapolitan courier for 30 guineas' (Knight, 40). SG.Imp. 26; Inst.Imp. no. 88; W.Tassie 1915 ('cornelian'); Plantzos no. 397; Spier, 'Two Hellenistic Gems Rediscovered', *AntK* 34 (1991), 91, and n. 2. ; Zwierlein-Diehl 2005, 340(classicising).

Head of young Hercules or Omphale wearing the lion skin, knotted at the neck. Inscribed in two lines ΔΙΟCΚΟΥ ΡΙΔΟΥ, 'by Dioskourides', a distinguished engraver of the 1st century BC.

King thought this was by T. Pichler. Knight took this for 18th century, broken to look more ancient, and refers to a communication by L. Forrer, who attributes the gem to Antonio Berini (1770–1861).. Some other gems by the master Dioskourides are known only in later copies. This may be part of another, although the lettering style could easily pass as ancient (compare *Würzburg* no. 417). Spier, followed by Plantzos, believes this to be by Dioskourides himself. For works signed by him see *Würzburg*, pp. 100–2. Our **235** is a copy.

Late 1st century BC or 18th century.

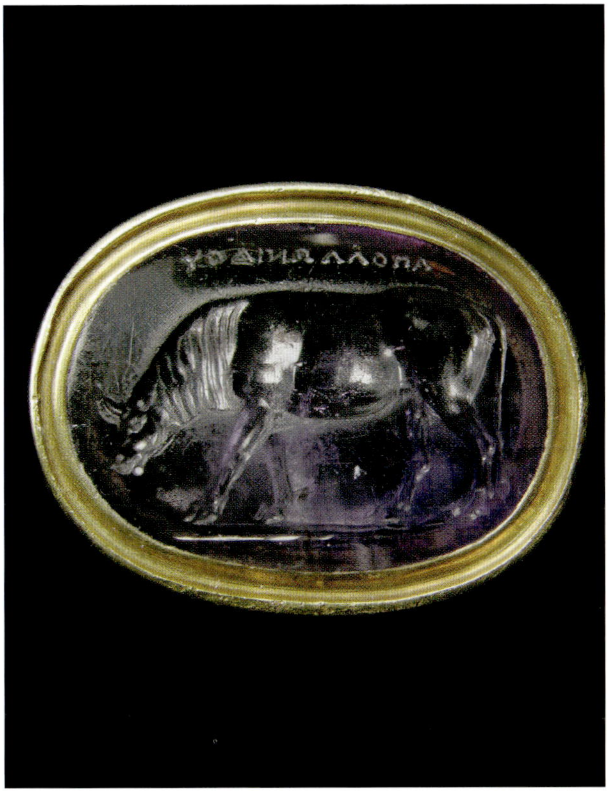

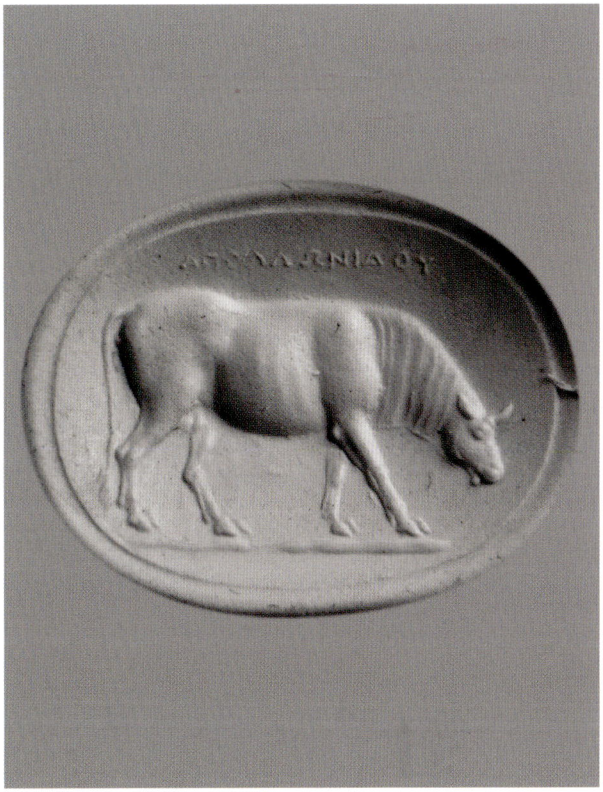

92

(10783)
Amethyst. polished convex back, set on a plain gold ring
17 x 12

Tassie 13127 ('Mr Poggi')?

A cow grazing. Ground line. Signed ΑΠΟΛΛΩΝΙΔΟΥ.

The artist Apollonides is well attested but it is not clear whether this is an original work, or if the inscription alone is modern. It seems to have been first known in the early 18th century. See Zwierlein-Diehl 2005, 338; *Würzburg*, 96–7.

1st century BC?

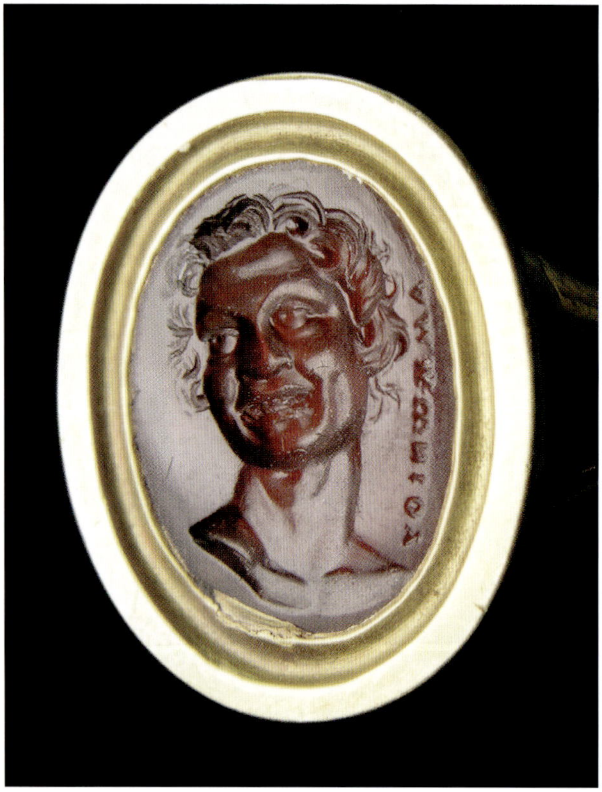

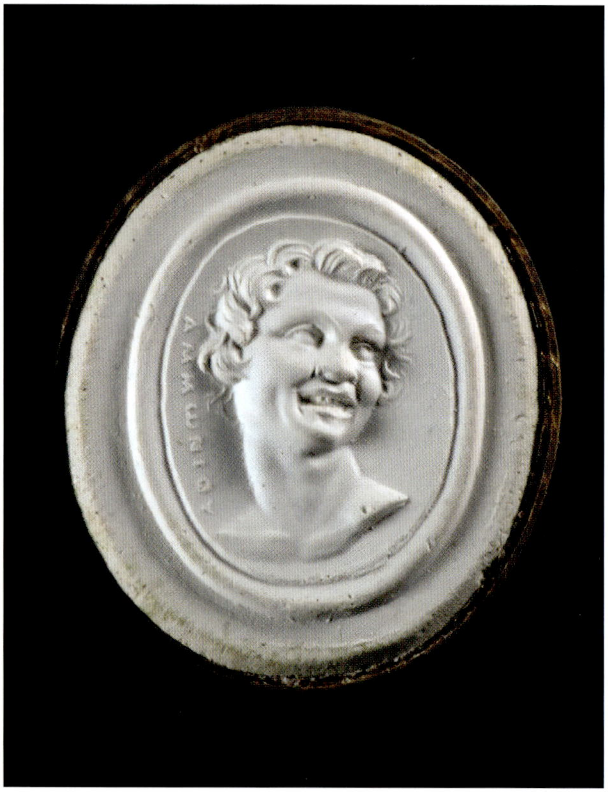

93

(10730) K192 (pl. 6)
Sard, polished flat back, set on a plain gold ring
10 x 8

Tassie 4510 ('Lord Louvain'), pl. 39; SG.Imp. 122; Inst. Imp. no. 82; Paoletti I, IV.265; A. Furtwängler, *JdI* 3 (1888) pl. 10.21; H. Rambach, *Jewellery History Today*, 1 (2008) 12.

Facing head of a young laughing satyr. Inscribed ΑΜΜΩΝΙΟΥ, 'by Ammonios', which is the name of several ancient artists, none a gem-engraver.

Compare Zazoff 1983, pl. 80.7 (signed Aulos); *London*, Dalton no. 732.

18th century.

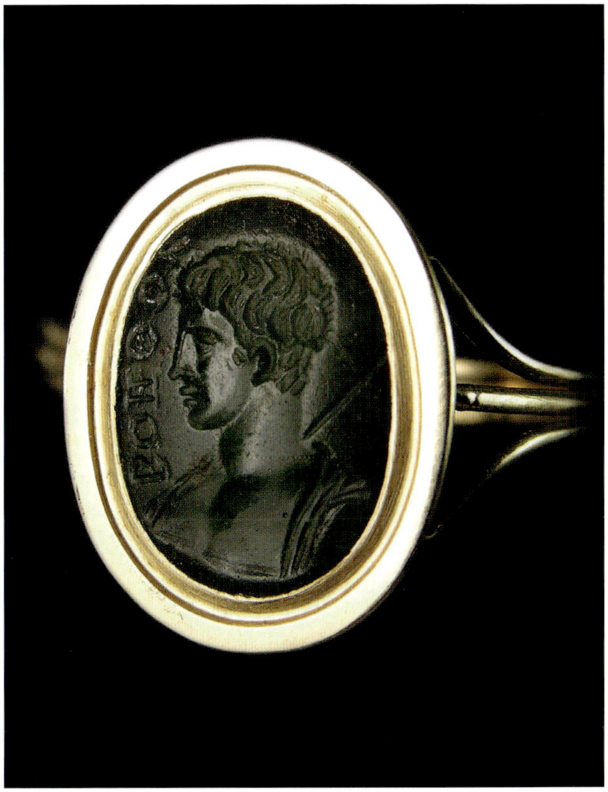

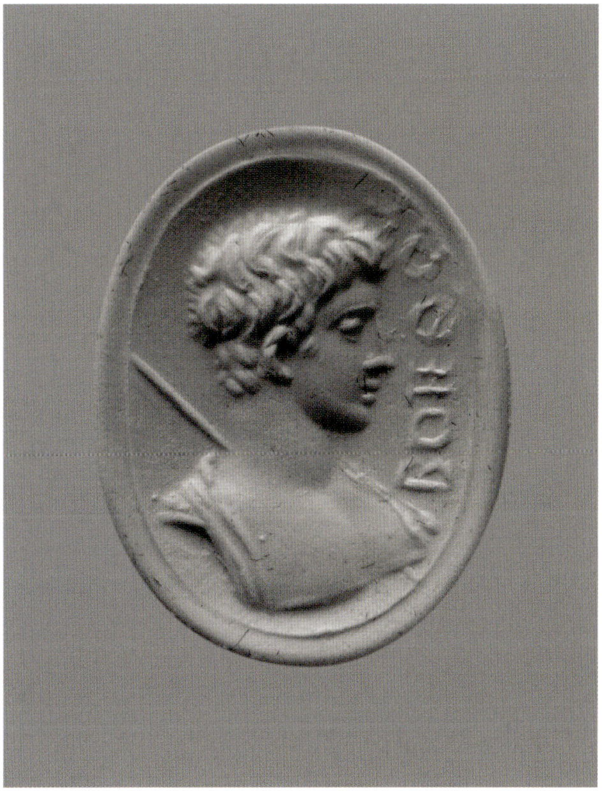

94

(10692) K154 (pl. 5)
Plasma, set in a plain gold ring
13 x 9

Bust of a youth with a cloak, shouldering a spear. Inscribed ΒΟΗΘΟΥ, 'by Boethos.'

Boethos was a 1st-century BC engraver (see our **3**), but the signature was often copied.

18th century.

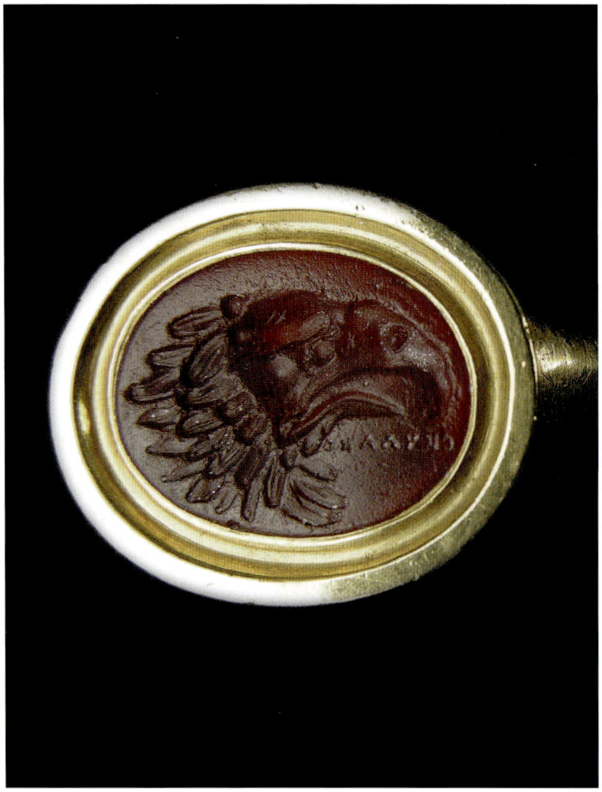

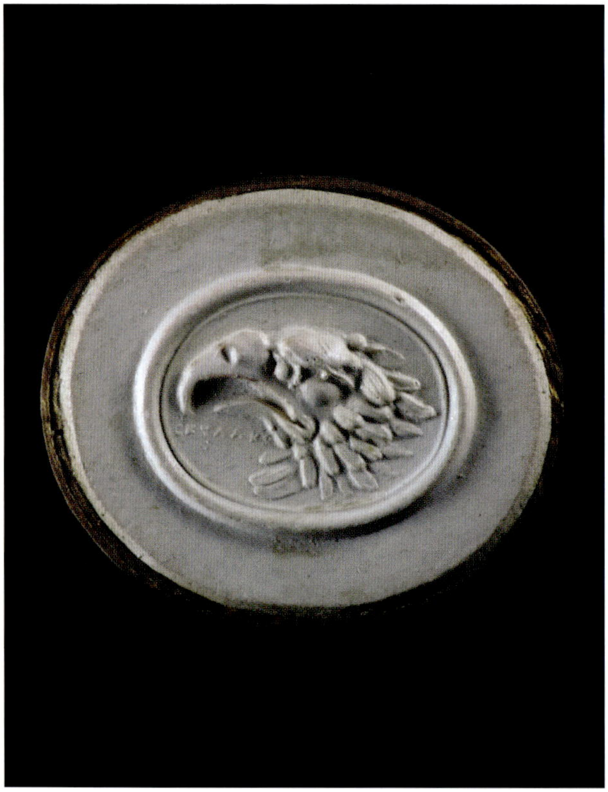

95

(10600) K62 (pl. 3)
Orange sard, polished flat back, set on a plain gold ring
11 x 8

SG.Imp. 91; Tassie 1017; Inst.Imp. no. 71; Paoletti I, IV.246; King 1872, pl. 54.6; King 1885, pl. 86.

The head of an eagle. Inscribed ΣΚΥΛΑΚΟ.

Skylax was an engraver of the 1st century AD (Vollenweider, 79, n. 78). This, together with our **96**, is a slightly reduced copy of the 18th-century original, also once in the Beverley Collection, now in St Petersburg (A.XII.41; *Würzburg* no. 875; cf. Lippold, pl. 164.5). For ancient examples of the subject, *Munich* 1, no. 912; 3, 2440; *Hanover* nos 1116, 1272, 1274–6; *Cambridge* no. 228.

18th century.

96

(10751)
Red glass (?), polished flat back, set on a plain gold ring
13 x 10

The head of an eagle. Inscribed ΣΚΥΛΑΚΟ.
A copy of our **95**.

18th century.

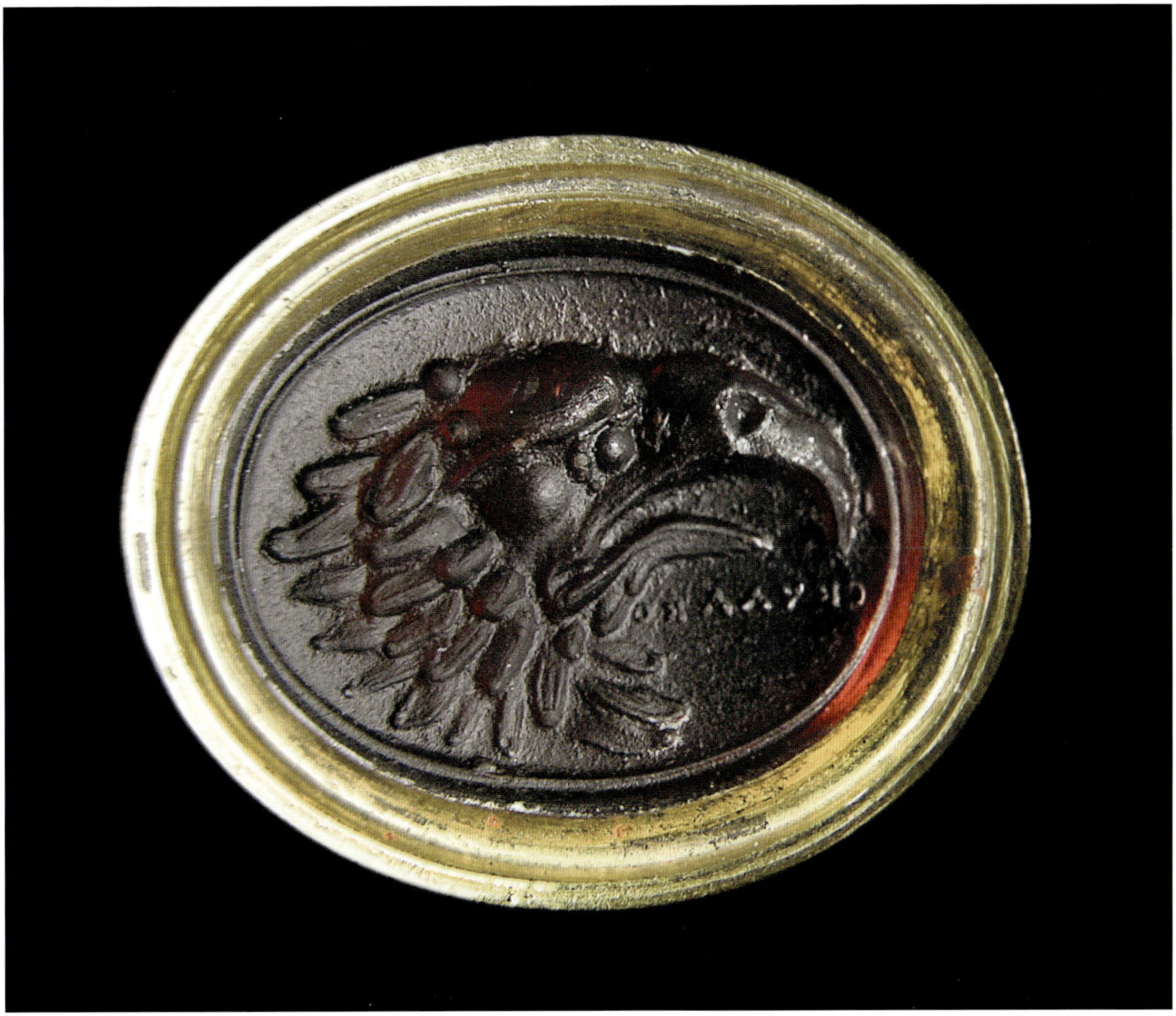

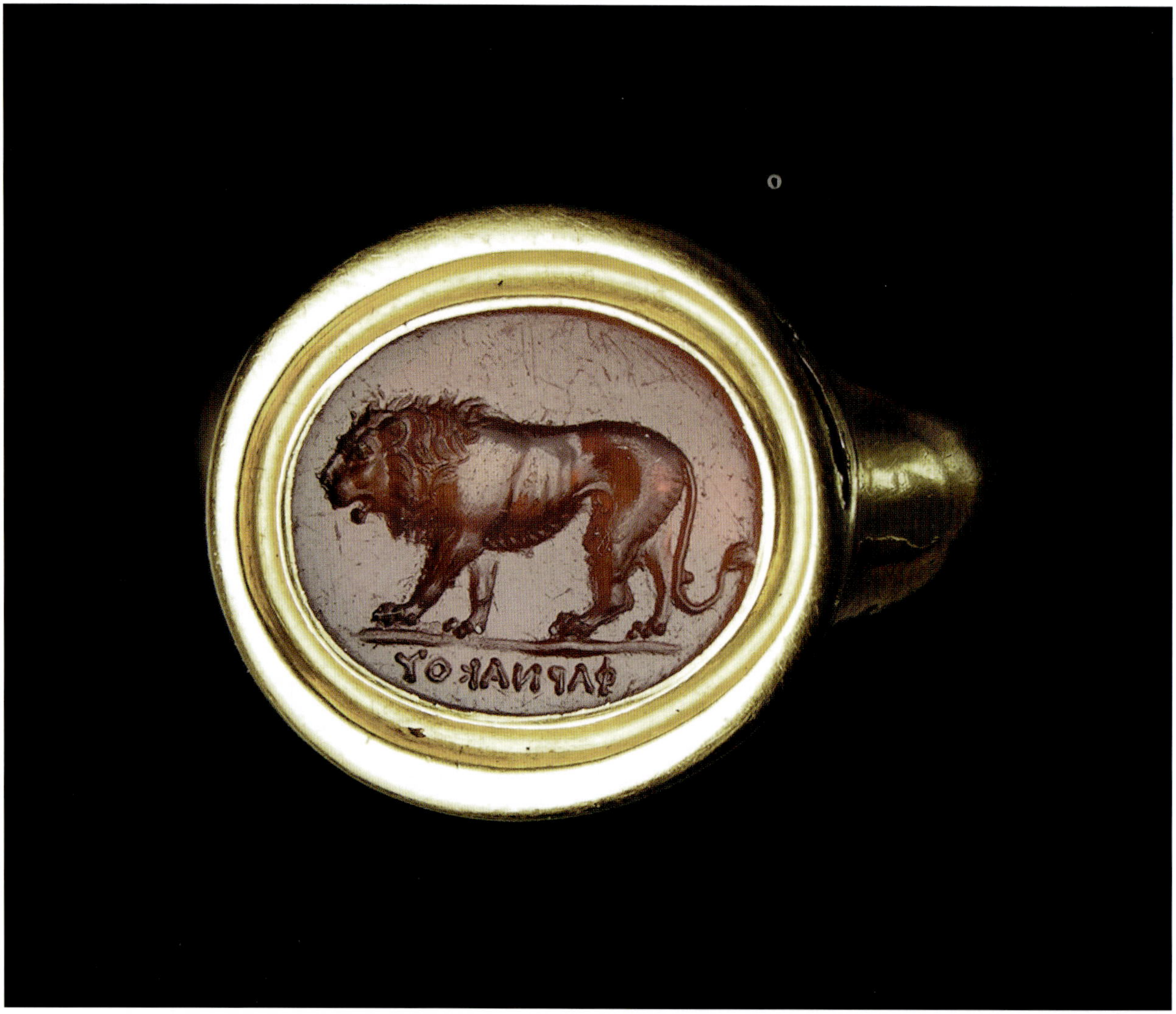

97

(10745)
Carnelian, polished flat back, set on a plain gold ring
11 x 8

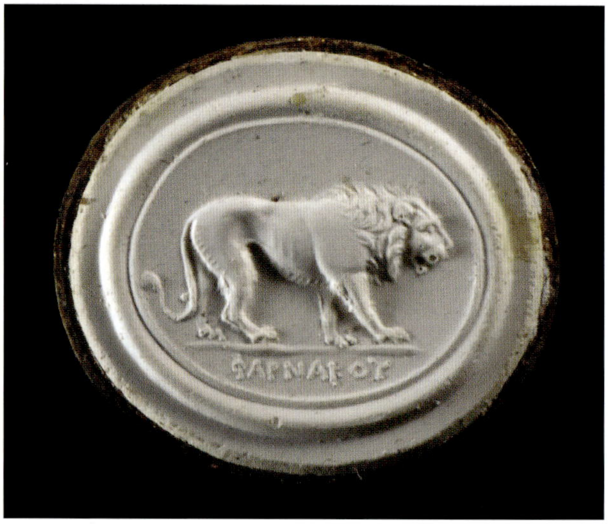

SG.Imp. 170; Lippert III, no. 434; Spilsbury, no. 11 (Greville coll.); Tassie 12836.

A lion standing. Ground line. Inscribed ΦΑΡΝΑΚΟΥ.

Apparently a close copy of a banded sardonyx once in the Beverley Collection (SG.Imp. 170): R. Perry in *Tainia* (Festschrift Roland Hampe, Mainz, 1980) 343, pl. 68.1–2, in an essay on the engraver Pharnakes; *Würzburg* p. 109. Another carnelian copy (?), Sotheby, New York, 13 June 2000, lot 427.

18th century.

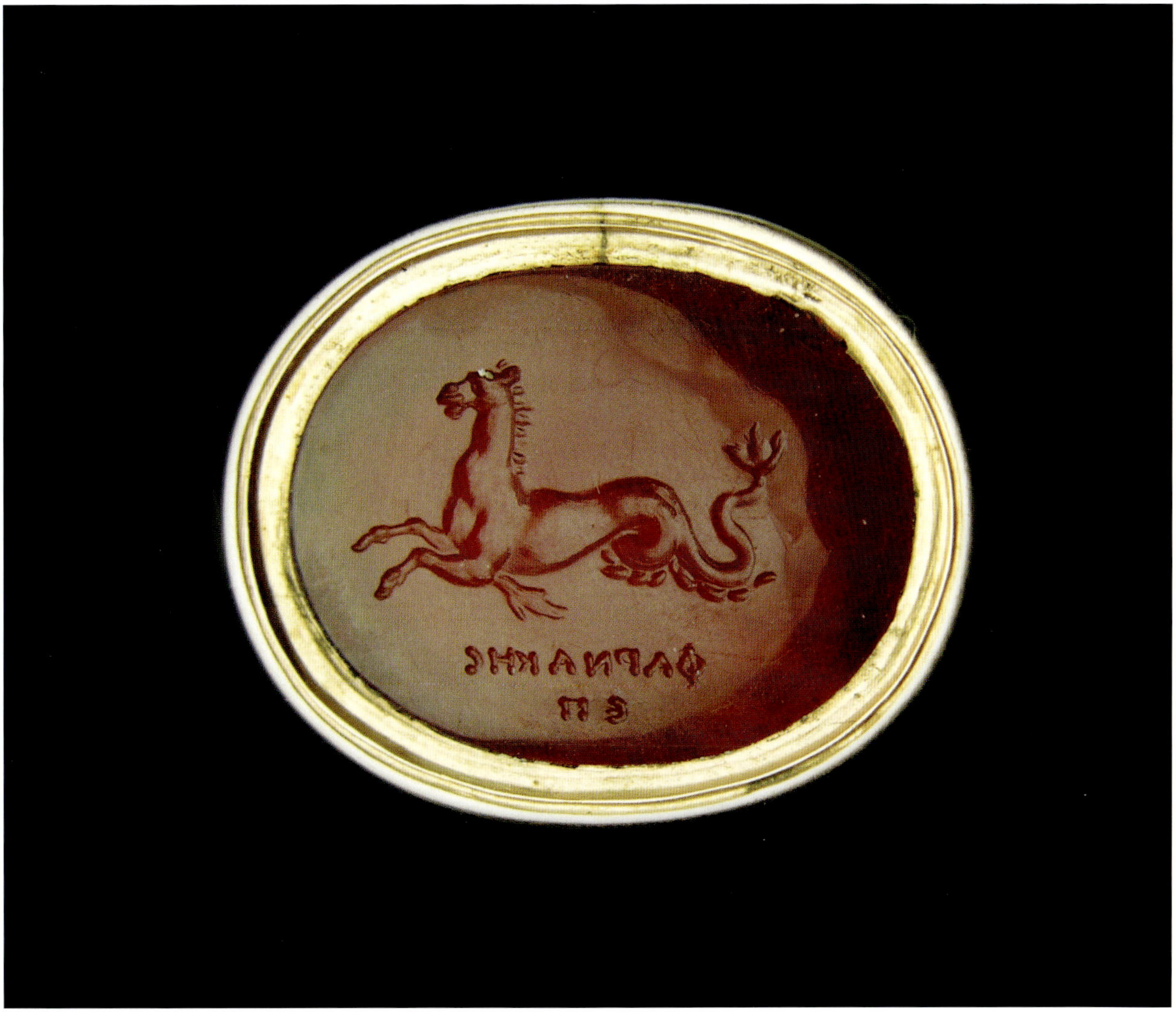

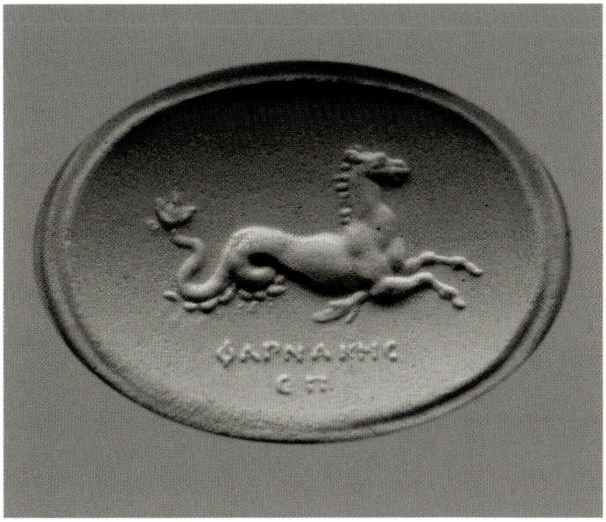

98

(10784)
Carnelian, polished convex back, set on a plain gold ring
14 x 10

A sea horse. Signed ΦΑΡΝΑΚΗϹ ΕΠ – 'Pharnakes made me.'

Apparently a copy of an original once in the Orsini and Farnese collections (Paoletti I, III.526). See Perry, op. cit., 345–6, pl. 68.7; Zwierlein-Diehl 2005, 338; *Würzburg* no. 151.

18th century.

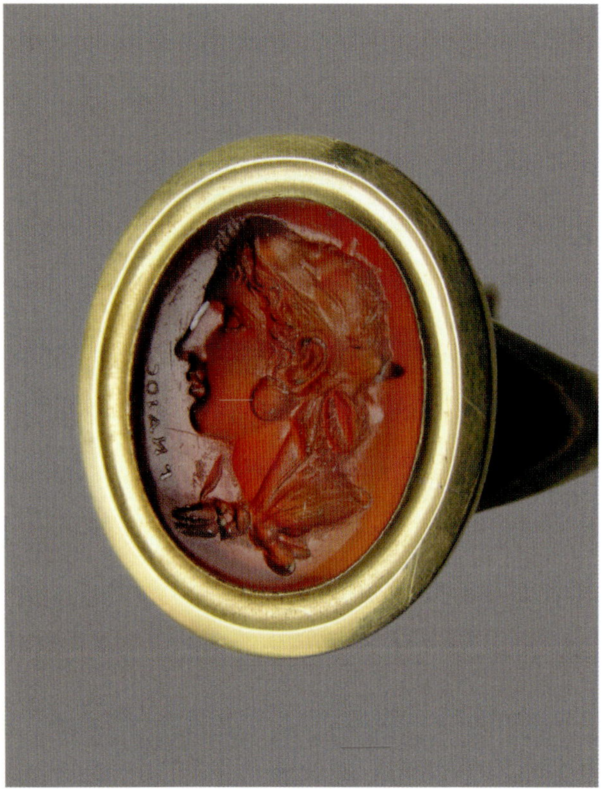

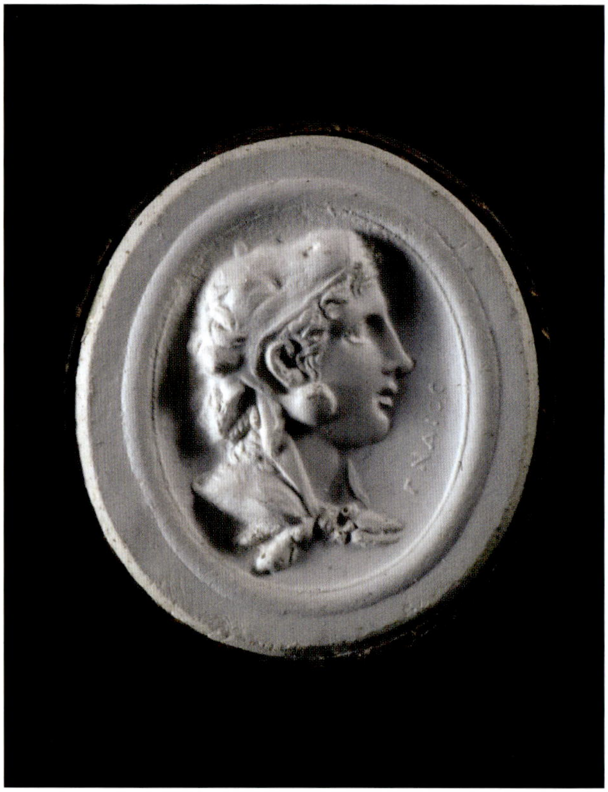

99

(10686)K148(pl.4)
Sard, polished flat back, set in a plain gold ring
14 x 13

SG.Imp. 83; *AG* pl. 40,44.

Taken to be the head of young Hercules or Omphale wearing the lionskin, but the 'paws' knotted at the neck look like cloven hoofs, and the headdress is bovine. Signed ΓΝΑΙΟC.

A very similar headdress was designed by Calandrelli for a Poniatowski gem showing Theseus (wearing the Minotaur head), also inscribed ΓΝΑΙΟC, 'by Gnaios' (J. Prendeville, *Photographic Facsimiles of the Antique Gems formerly possessed by the Late Prince Poniatowski* (London 1857–9) no. 624), and this should be the same subject from the same source.

Early 19th century.

SIGNATURES WITH MODERN NAMES

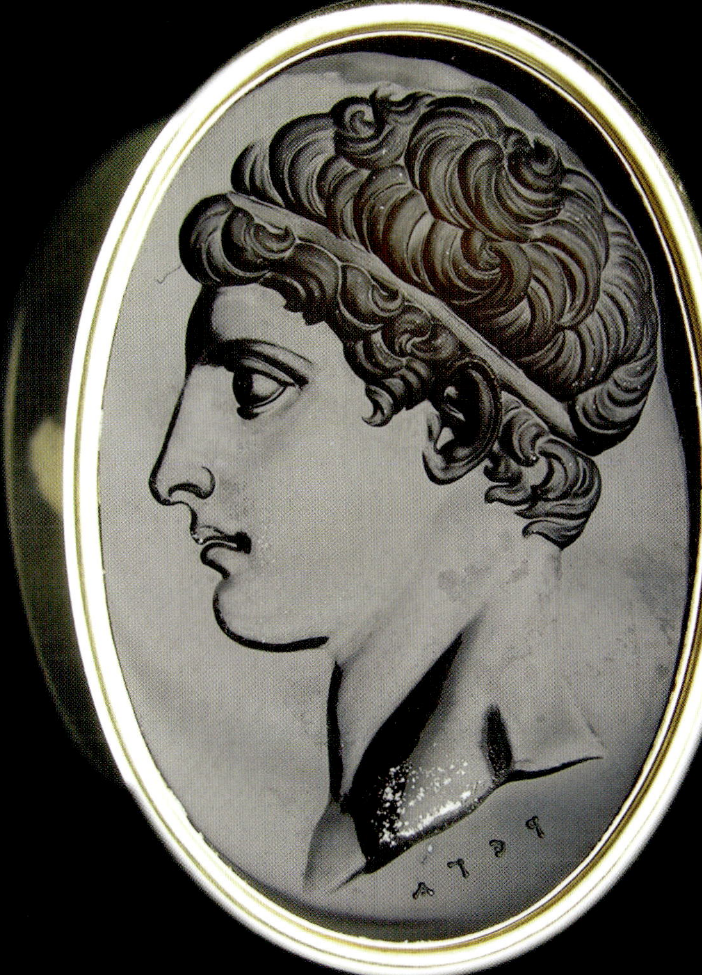

100

(10796)
Carnelian, polished flat back, set on a plain gold ring
32 x 22

AGE no. 7.

Head of a youth, his hair in a fillet in the Hellenistic manner. Signed ΡΕΓΑ.

Filippo Rega was a distinguished Italian neo-classical engraver who counted Sir William Hamilton and Emma among his subjects. This is probably a classicising study rather than a true portrait.

By Filippo Rega (Naples, 1761–1833).

101

(10795)
Carnelian, polished flat back, set on a plain gold ring
22 x 18

Tassie 11732 (? as sardonyx); *AGE* no. 43; see under Seidmann 1987, no. 10.

Head of Antinous. Signed MARCHANT F[ECIT].

This head of the Emperor Hadrian's favourite derives from a portrait of him on a marble relief in the Villa Albani, Rome. Marchant made another copy for the Duke of Marlborough, signed MARCHANT F.ROMAE (*Marlborough* no. 756). On Nathaniel Marchant see also now Kagan 2010, esp. 202–6, as well as Seidmann's exhaustive study of the artist, the leading British engraver of his day.

By Nathaniel Marchant (1739–1818).

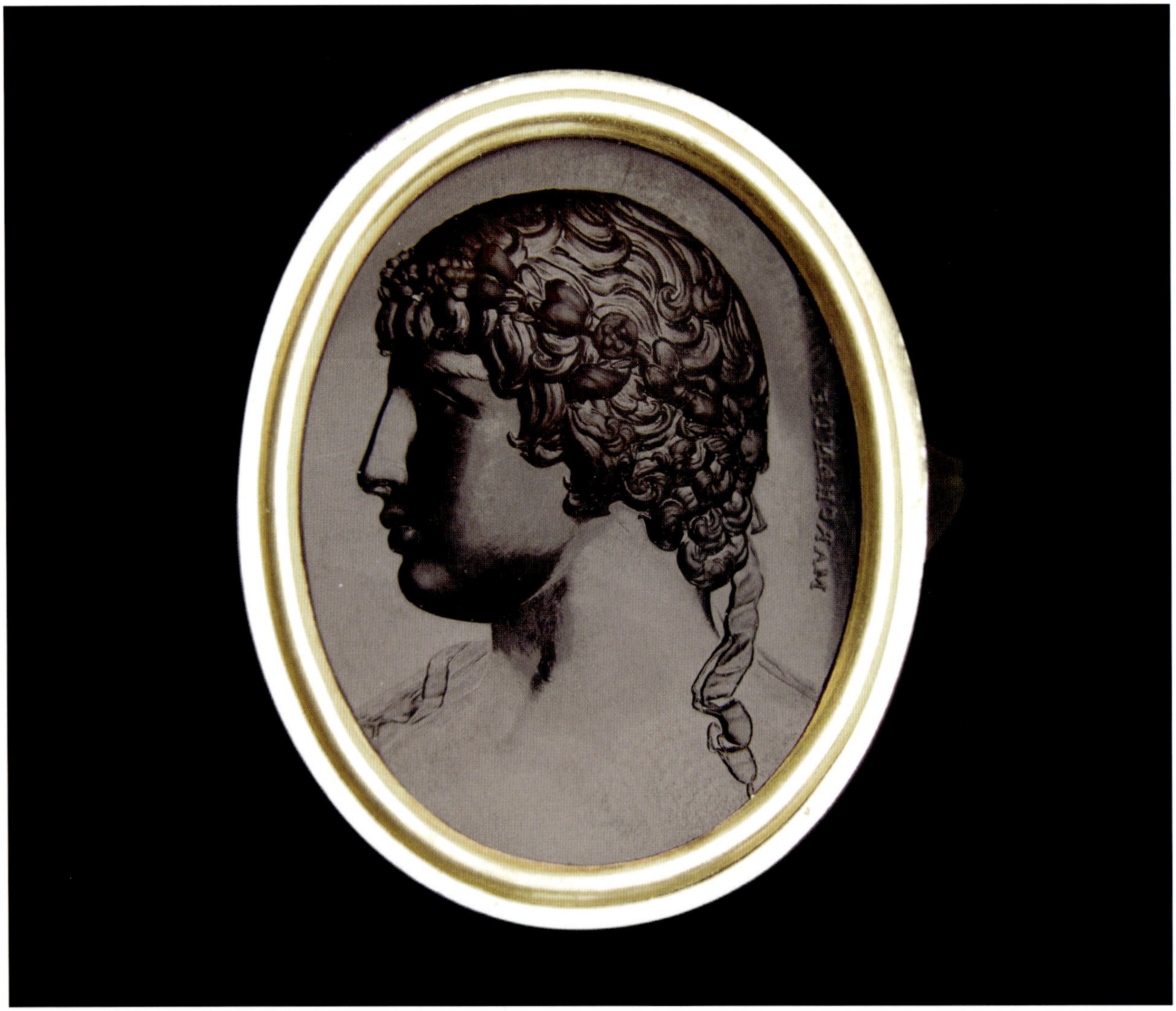

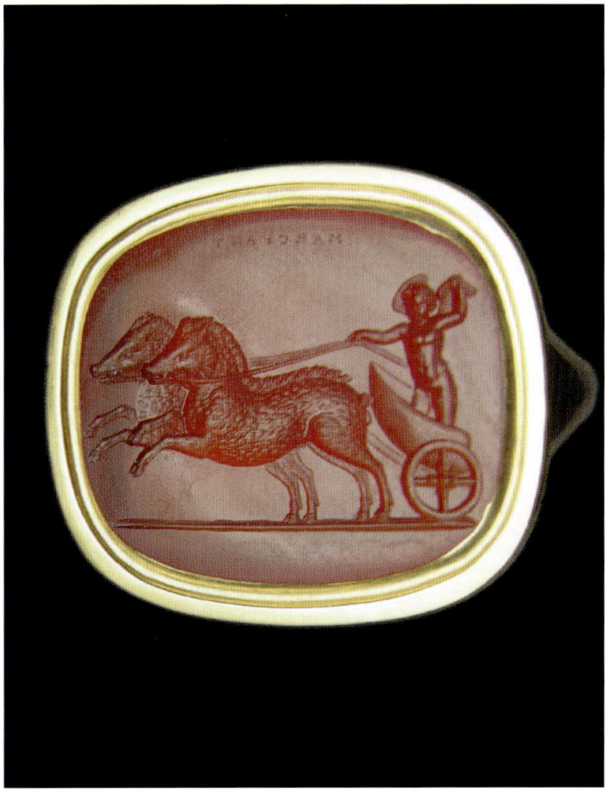

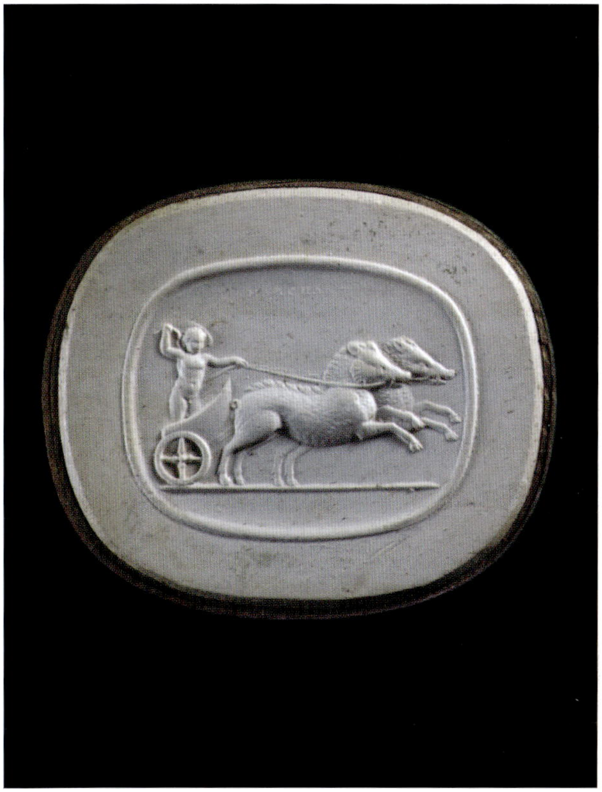

102

(10755)
Carnelian in a modern ring, polished convex back, set on a plain gold ring
21 x 16

SG.Imp. 184; Inst.Imp. no. 144; W.Tassie 2272; Lippold, pl. 125.1; *AGE* no. 130; Seidmann 1987, no. 38.

Cupid, one arm raised, standing in a shell-like chariot holding the reins of two running boars. Ground line. Inscribed MARCHANT (see the last).

This copies a relief in the Museo Pio-Clementino, Vatican, Rome (W. Amelung, *Die Sculpturen des Vatikanischen Museum* II (1908) pl. 38, no. 158 – the Cupid largely restored, probably Hadrianic; two reliefs with a similar subject are in the Louvre, from Rome), apparently the only ancient version of Cupid with a boar-chariot.

By Nathaniel Marchant (1739–1818).

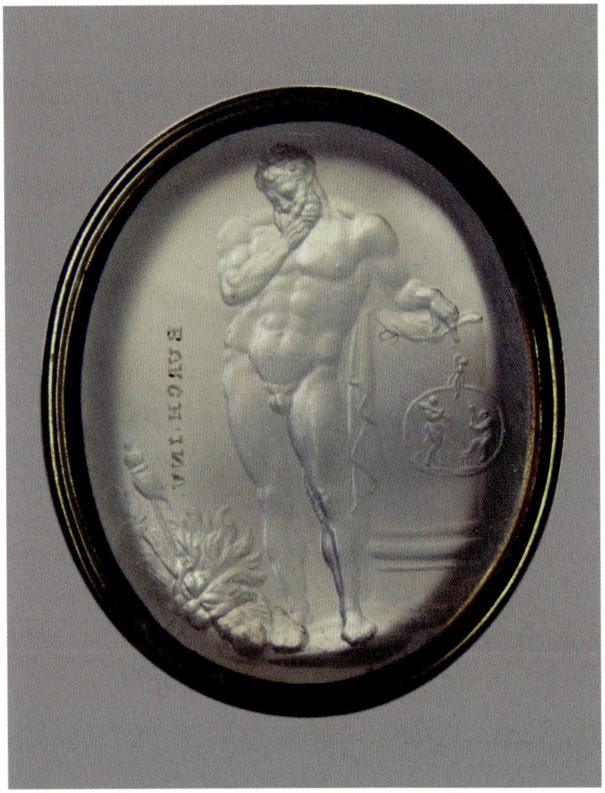

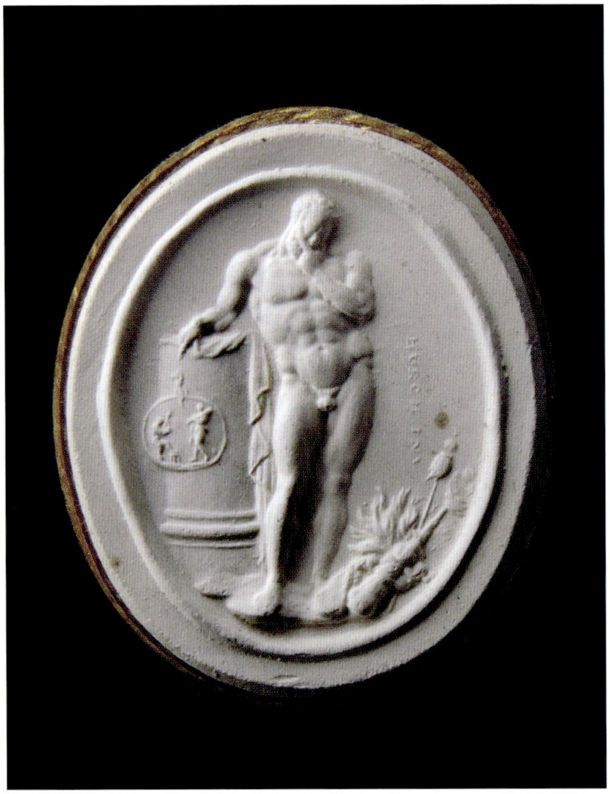

103

(10775)
Pale blue chalcedony, polished convex back, set on a plain gold ring
24 x 20

SG.Imp. 187; Tassie 5950; Inst.Imp. no. 146; G. Seidmann in *Engraved Gems* (ed. C.M. Brown, 1997) 270–1, fig. 16; Paoletti II, V.76.

Naked Hercules leaning on a draped altar decorated with a hanging oval plaque depicting Hercules and Omphale, where she is naked but wearing his lionskin and holding his club, he seated, with a footstool, holding her distaff. The hero looks down pensively at objects reflecting on his condition – lionskin, club and distaff (reference to Omphale). Signed BURCH.INV.

The 'inv(enit)' implies that Burch had invented the scheme. Edward Burch (1730–1814), on whom see Kagan, esp. 198–202, was a notably inventive British engraver. In the 1975 catalogue of his works, 15f., LV, Lord Fortrose remarks, 'from a large model in clay, done at the artist's subscription Academy St. Martin's Lane' (cited, Seidmann, loc. cit.).

18th/ early 19th century.

104

(10776)
Carnelian, flat polished back, set on a plain gold ring
21 x 16

Inst.Imp. no. 150; *AGE* no. 184.

Hercules, holding his club, supports the limp body of an Amazon, Hippolyta, holding her pelta shield. She is naked but for light dress around her body and with elaborately dressed hair, her axe before her. Ground line; below it the signature ΑΡΡΙΣ.

William Harris was exhibiting in the 1780s and 1790s: see Kagan, 180, 212, 292. The subject was a popular one in the 18th century; this is copy of our **142**, q.v.; a copy by Pichler, Lippold, pl. 134.7; by Burch, Hull Grundy, no. 830; by Marchant, Paoletti II, V.9; and on the type and copies, Paoletti II, V.227.

Late 18th/early 19th century.

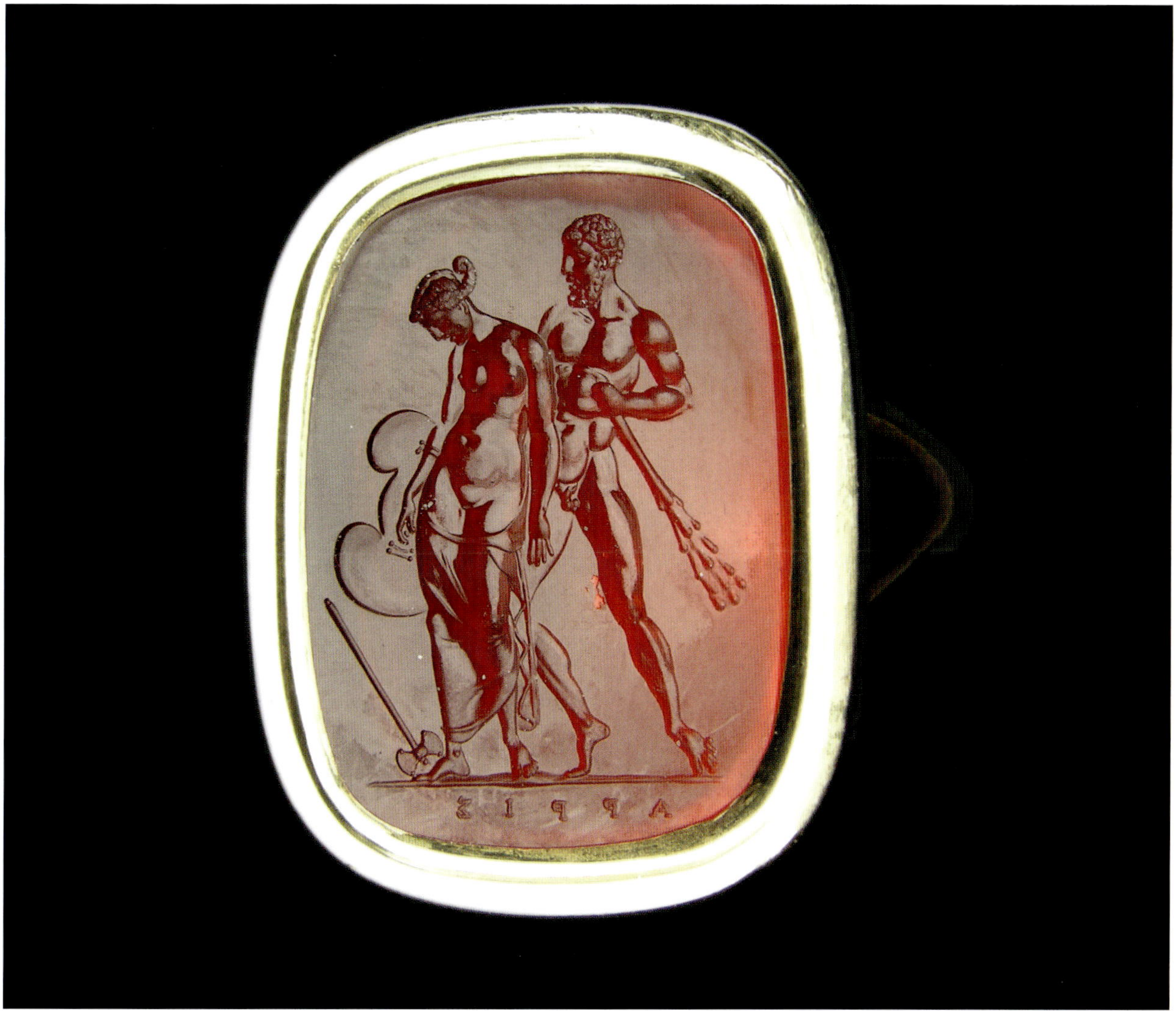

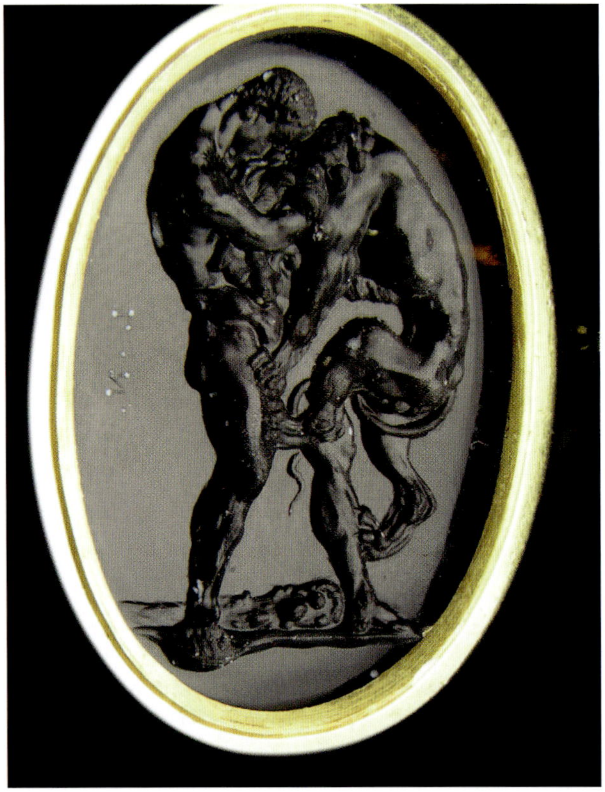

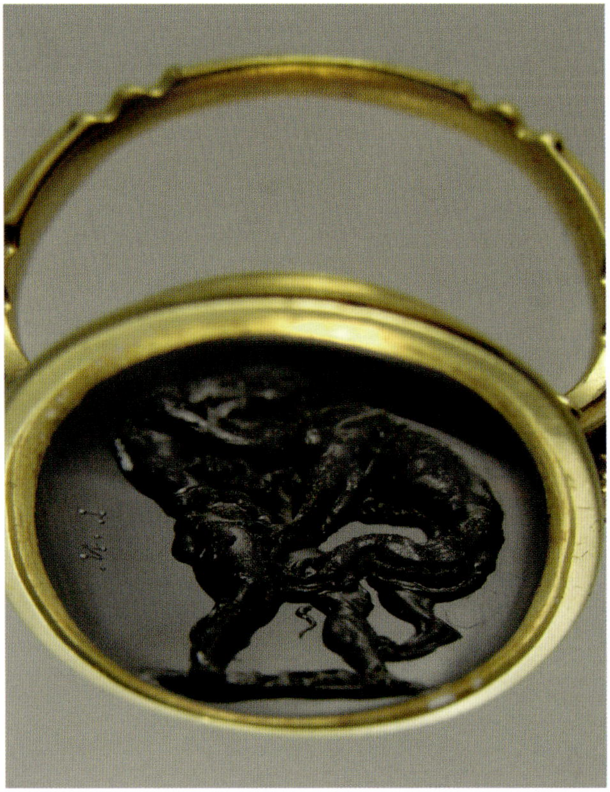

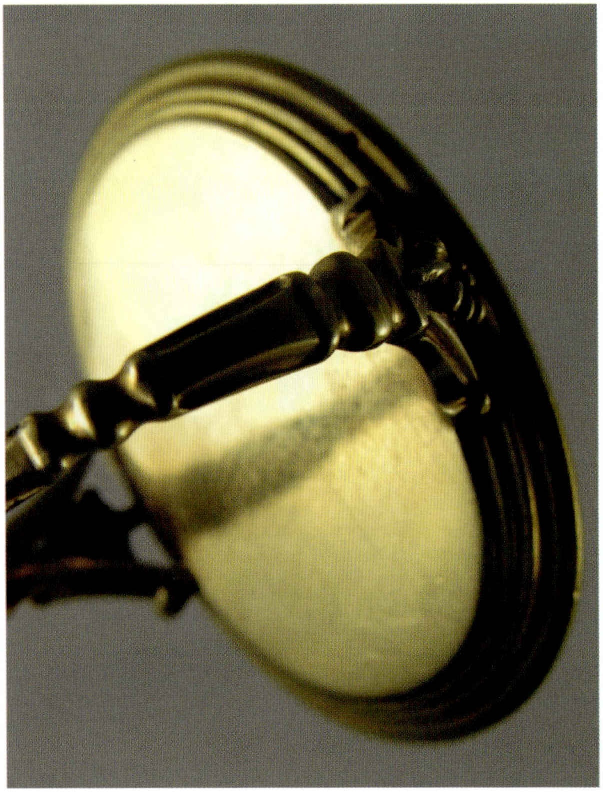

105

(10774)
Sard, set on a ring with forked ends to the hoop
22 x 15

Tassie 5696.

Young Hercules lifting and strangling the Nemean Lion, his club at his feet. Ground line. Signed L.N.

Lorenz Natter visited England in the mid-18th century intending to publish a *Museum Britannicum* of gems in British collections, but also making gems for collectors. He drew this one (his page F30-1, in the Hermitage), without the signature, as belonging to the collector Thomas Hollis (1720–74), much of whose collection was sold in 1821. This, or more likely a duplicate, was in the Alnwick collection and, allegedly, sold to Catherine of Russia in 1786, but it cannot be located in the Hermitage, where there is a cast: see E. Nau, *Lorenz Natter* (Biberach 1966) Kat. 20, fig. 53 (which is not of our stone: note the lion's tail tip). Natter probably made several versions. On the ancient, 4th-century BC type, see *Würzburg* no. 54.

By Lorenz Natter (1705–63).

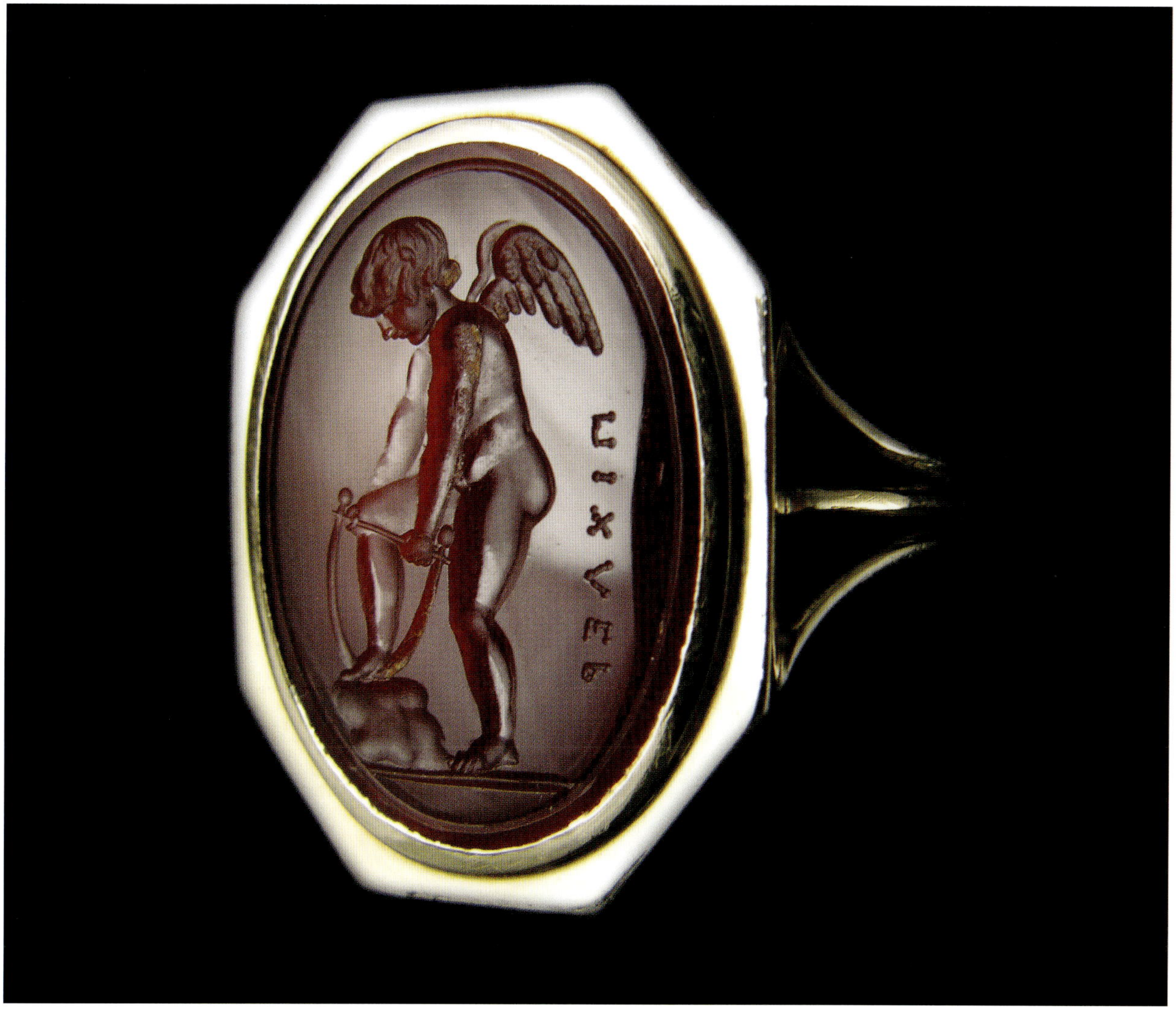

106

(10757)
Carnelian in an 18th-century gold ring with hexagonal bezel, with polished convex back, set on a plain gold ring with triple-forked ends to the hoop
18 x 13

Paoletti II, VIII.287; *AGE* no. 129.

Cupid attending to his bow, his foot raised on a rock. Ground line. Signed ΠΙΧΛΕΡ.

The strokes of the letters of the signature are mainly lines of dots instead of the usual dot terminals only. This is a simplified, perhaps misunderstood, copy of the painting by Parmigianino in Vienna, where Cupid is carving his bow. The engraver has omitted the vertical bow and made Cupid appear to be stringing a complete bow, but in an unlikely pose for the action. However, Cupid adopts this pose on ancient gems where he is fixing a greave; compare *Munich* no. 591. By Giovanni Pichler (see Rollett 1874, 29, no. 19), of the famous Austrian family of gem-engravers.

By Giovanni Pichler (1734–91).

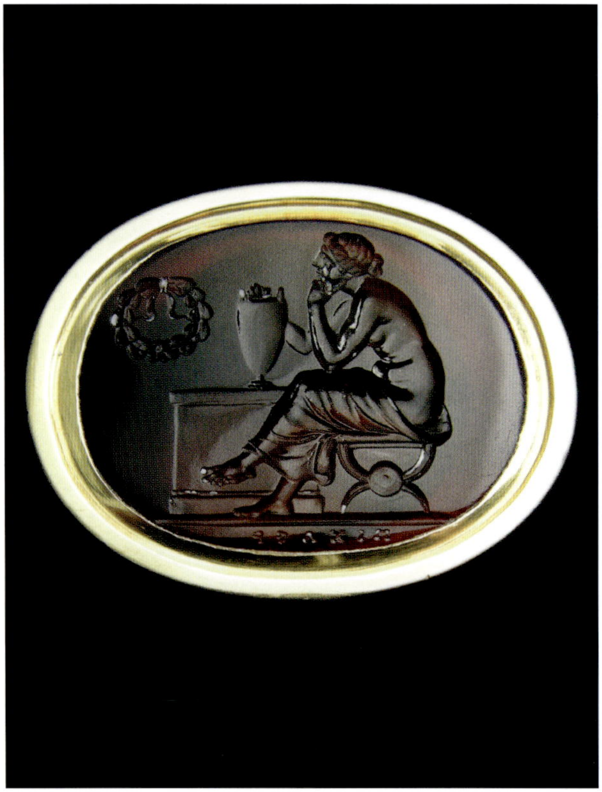

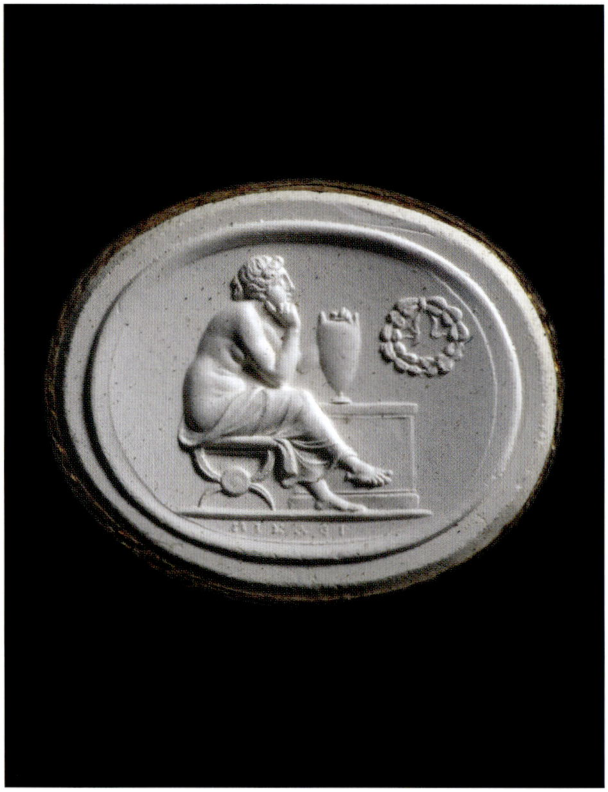

107

(10812)
Carnelian, polished concave back, set in a plain gold ring
18 x 15

SG.Imp. 181; Tassie 11277 (as Agrippina mourning Germanicus); Inst.Imp. no. 153; Paoletti II, V.338; Lippold, pl. 57.2; *AGE* no. 240.

A woman, dress around her legs, seated on a folding stool, before a base on which stands an urn, a wreath beyond. Ground line. Signed ΠΙΧΛΕΡ.

Again, a work by Giovanni Pichler (see the last; Rollett 1874, 30, no. 40). Taken to be Queen Artemisia mourning the death of Mausolus, and contemplating drinking a potion containing his ashes; or Agrippina mourning Germanicus. This was a subject for painters from the 17th century on, including Rembrandt. Rollett says that Pichler's version is after a gem (not identified). Both this and our **106** are extremely unusual and original choices of subject for any Pichler. With a reversed image, see R. Nicholls, *The Wellcome Gems* (Cambridge 1983) no. 236.

By Giovanni Pichler (1734–91).

108

(10806)
Carnelian, polished convex back,
set in a plain gold ring
14 x 10

Bust of a woman, dressed, wearing a mitra, Sappho. Signed ΠΙΧΛΕΡ.

Copy of our **245**.

By Giovanni Pichler (1734–1791)?

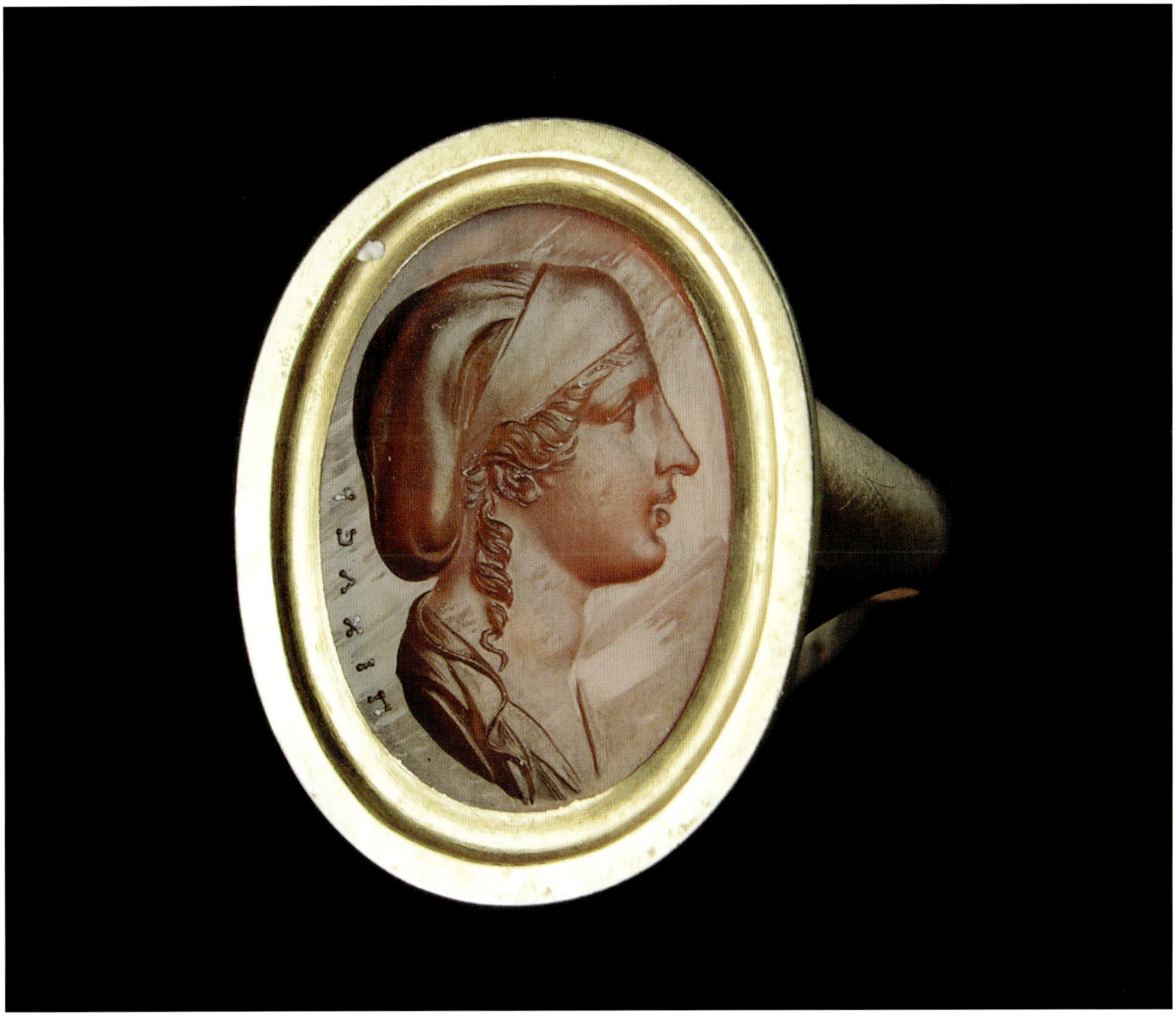

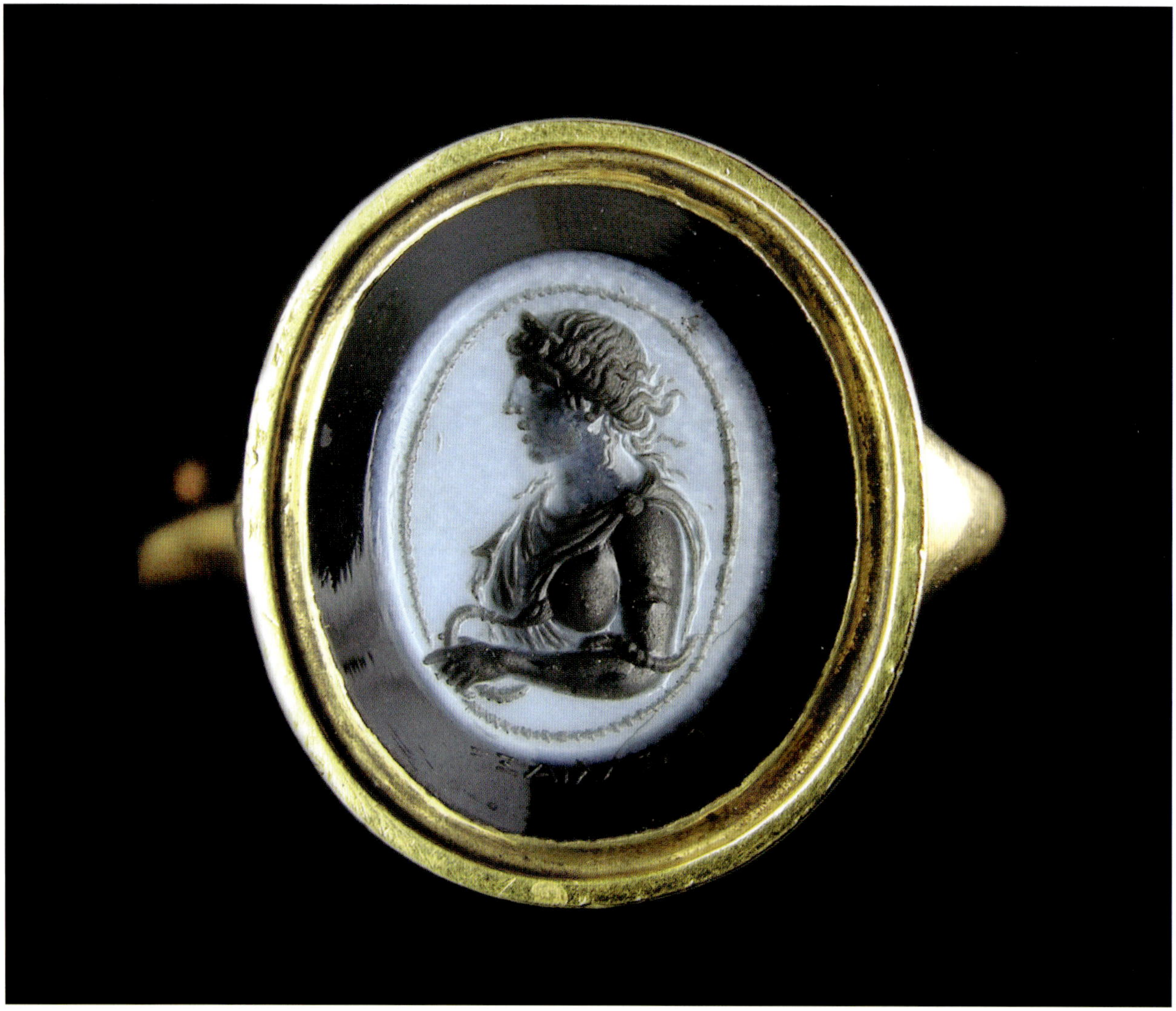

109

(10554) K16 (pl. 3)
Nicolo with a broad bevelled edge to the face, polished flat back, set on a plain gold ring
16 x 13

Cleopatra. Bust of a dressed woman who holds a snake, which bites her bared breast. Dotted border. Signed on the bevelled border below the figure ΠΑΣΑΛΙΑΣ =.

The signature is that of A. Passaglia. Compare Paoletti I, II.159; Lippold, pl. 160.5; C.W. King, *Antique Gems and Rings* (London 1872) 438. For the subject compare Spilsbury, no. 32.

By A. Passaglia (1736–1815).

110

(10780)
Carnelian, polished flat back, set on a plain gold ring
23 x 17

SG.Imp. 183; Tassie 6498; Inst.Imp. no. 142; Paoletti II, VIII.111; *AGE* no. 266.

A young hunter ('Adonis'), his dress draped behind him over both arms, holds a spear, testing its tip with a finger. Ground line. Signed in the exergue CADES.

By Alessandro Cades (1734–1809).

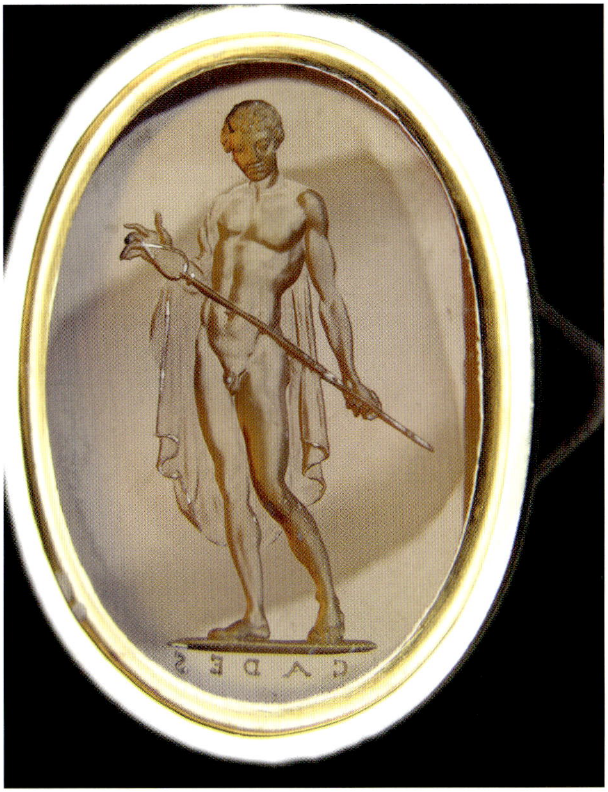

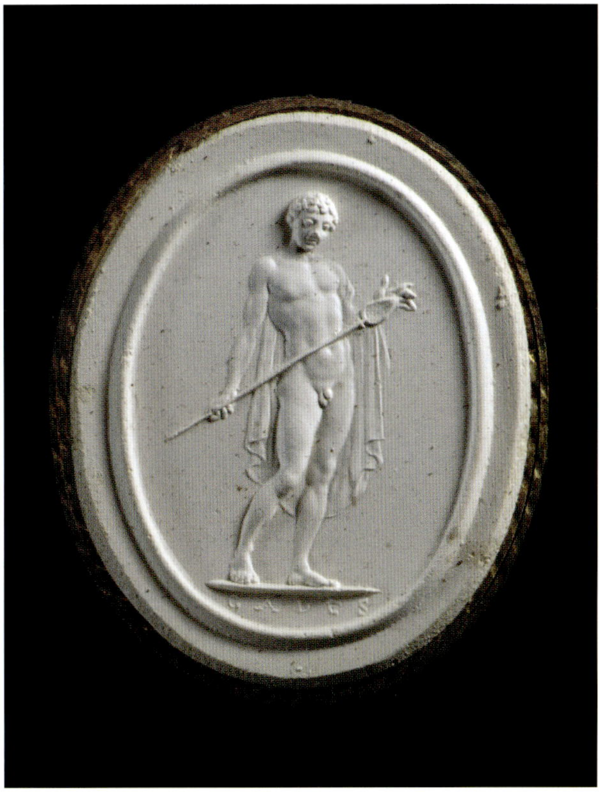

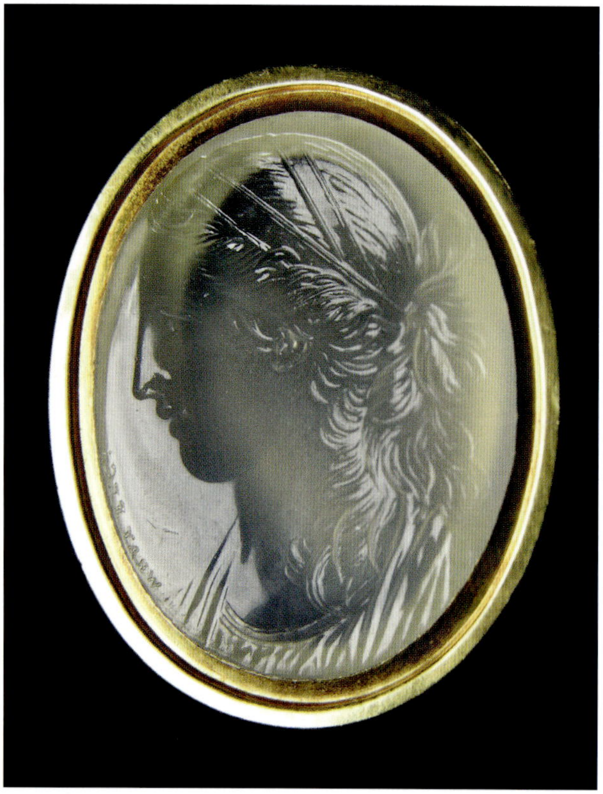

111

(10808)
Pale blue chalcedony, polished flat back, set on a plain gold ring
20 x 16

From the 1st Duchess' Collection (no. 46); SG.Imp. 182; Tassie 14701; Inst.Imp. 148; Paoletti II, VIII.551.

Head of a dressed woman with bound hair. Signed WRAY FEC:. This is a version of 'The Fair Laundress' by Robert Wray, after a drawing by Giles Hussey (1710–88), a keen Jacobite patronised by the 1st Duke. On the engraver Robert Bateman Wray and his inspiration for such heads in prints, see Kagan, 196–7.

By Robert Bateman Wray (1715–79).

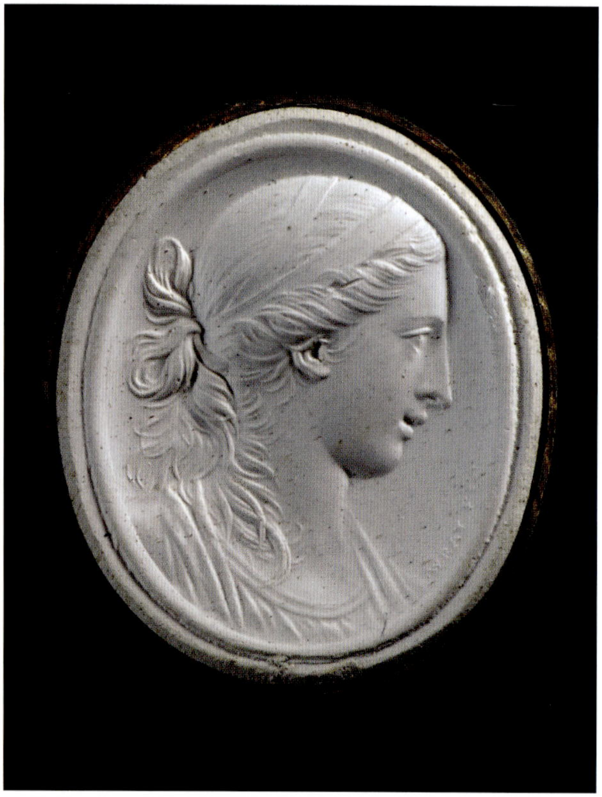

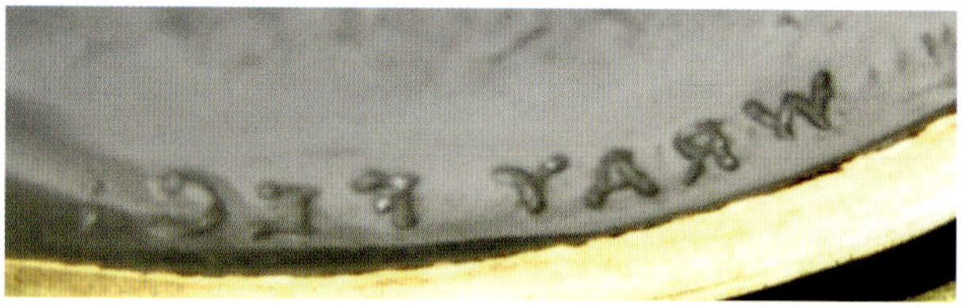

ETRUSCAN, ETRUSCANISING AND ITALIC

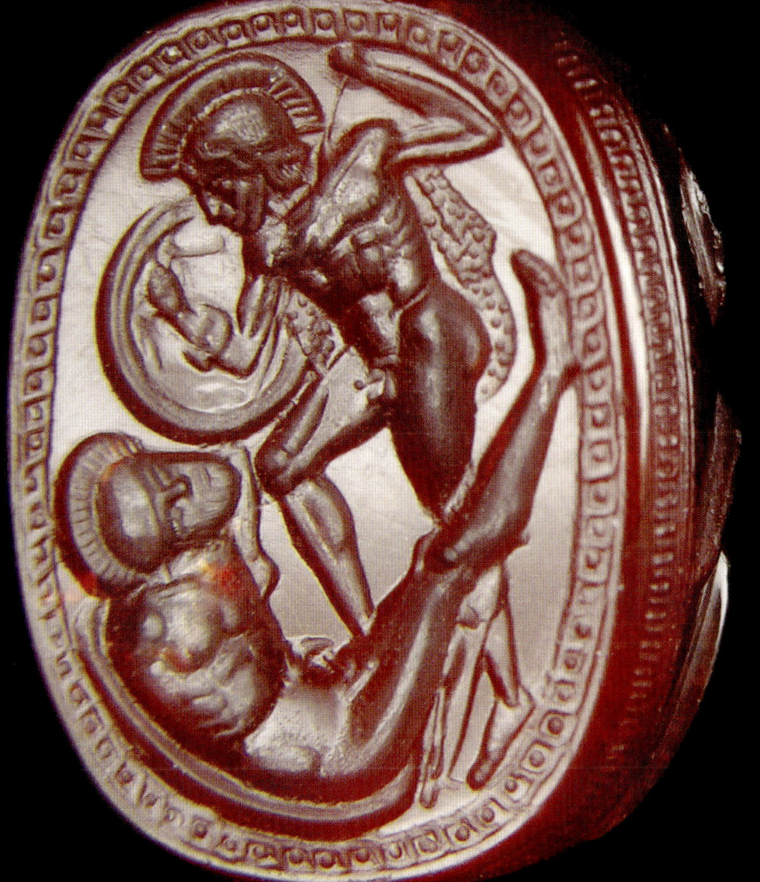

There are only two Etruscan scarabs, others are intaglios for mounting in finger rings.

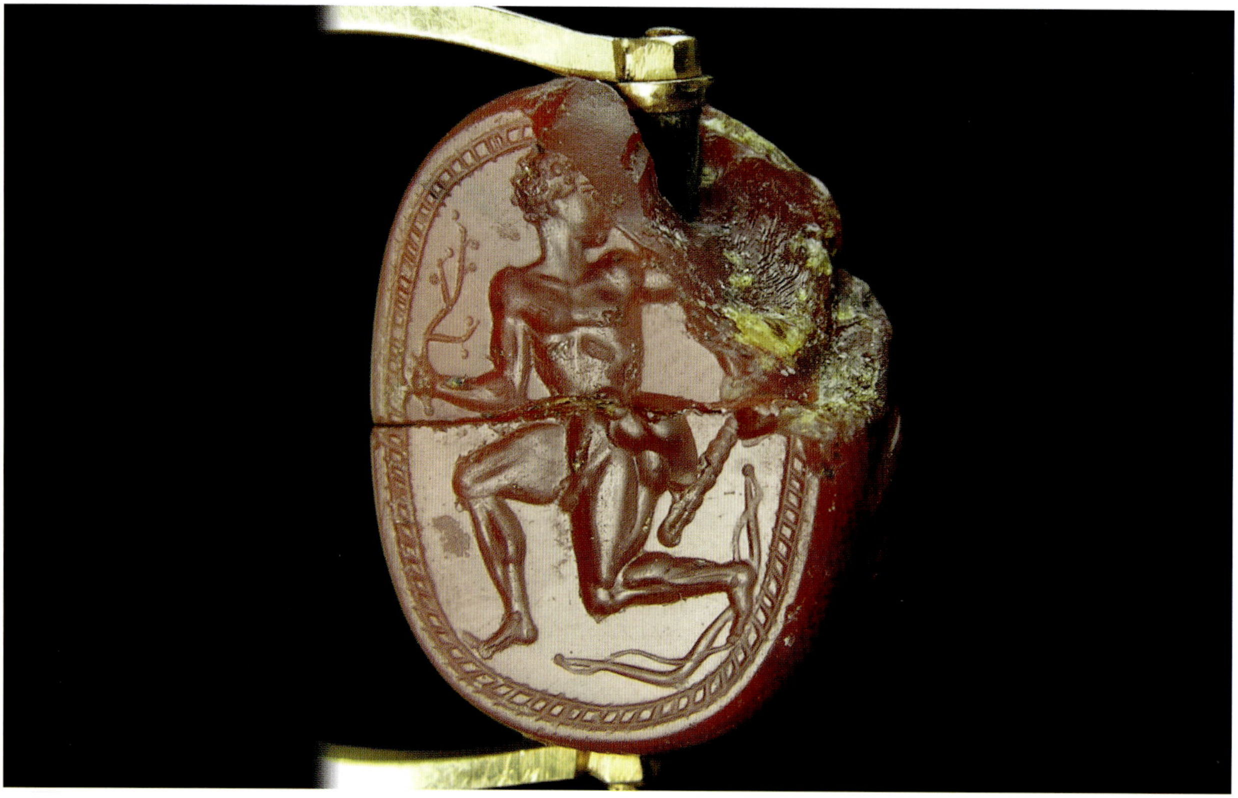

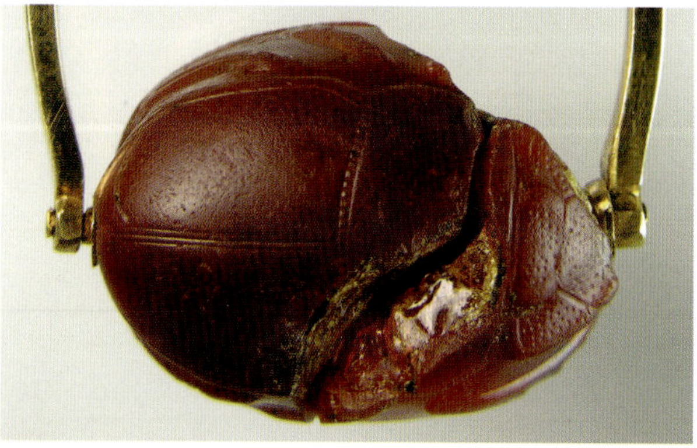

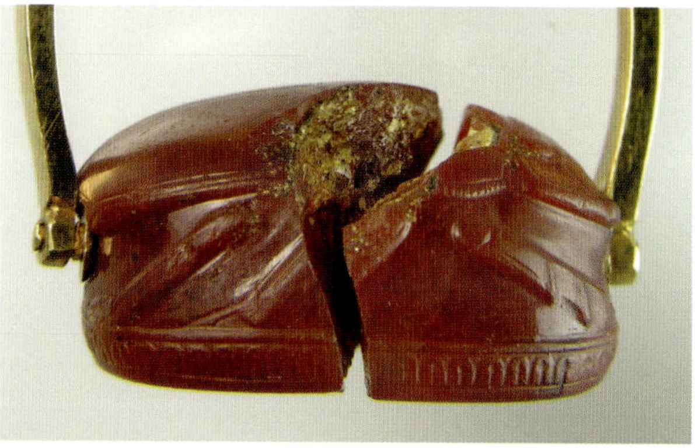

112

(10816)
Carnelian broken scarab with an ovolo edge to the plinth, dotted head
17 x 12 x 8

Young Hercules (?) running, looking back, naked, holding his club and a small branch, his bow on the ground with slack string. Hatched border.

The branch is unexpected unless it relates to his meeting with the Hesperides.

Late 5th/4th century BC.

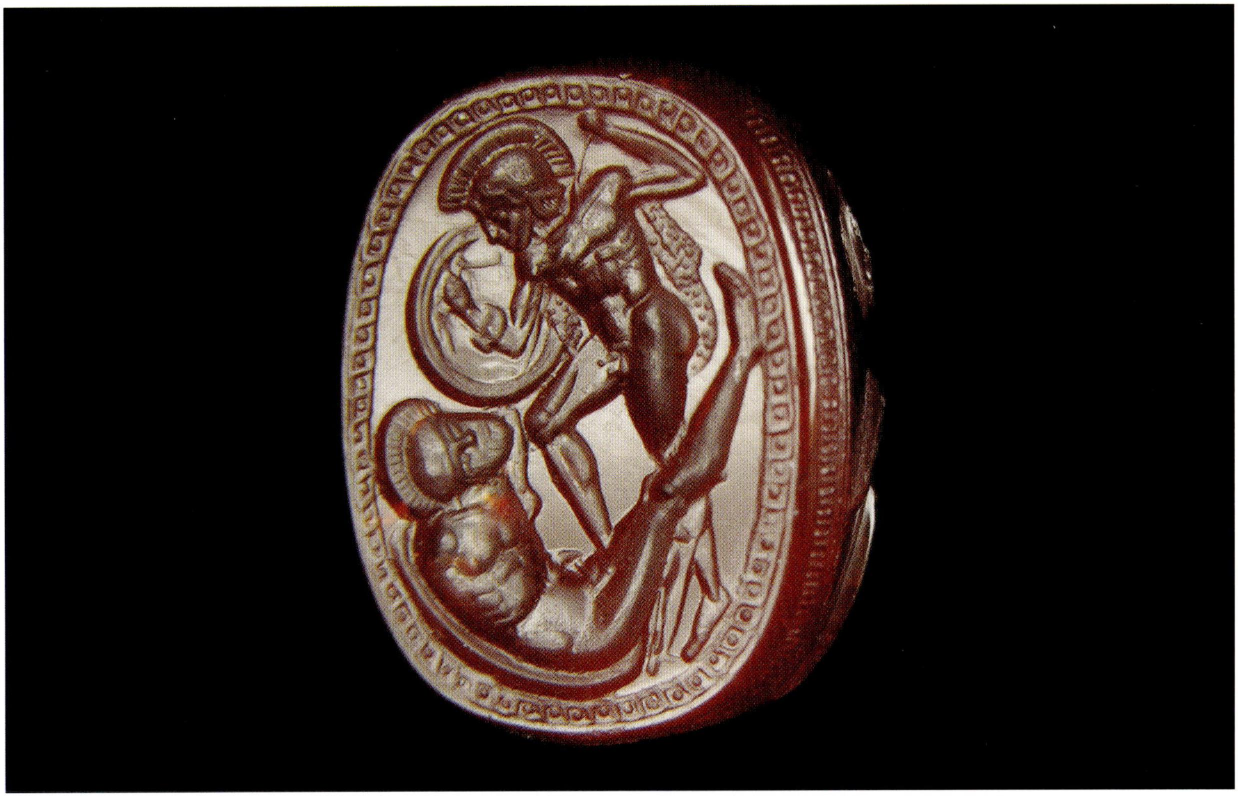

113

(10748) K210
Carnelian scarab with with an ovolo and dotted border to the plinth
14 x 11 x 8

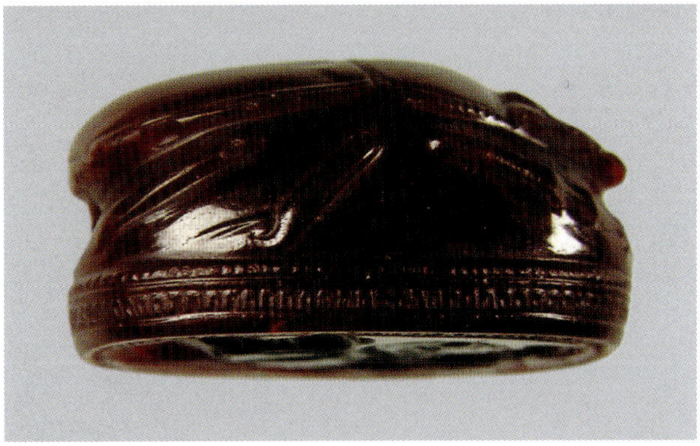

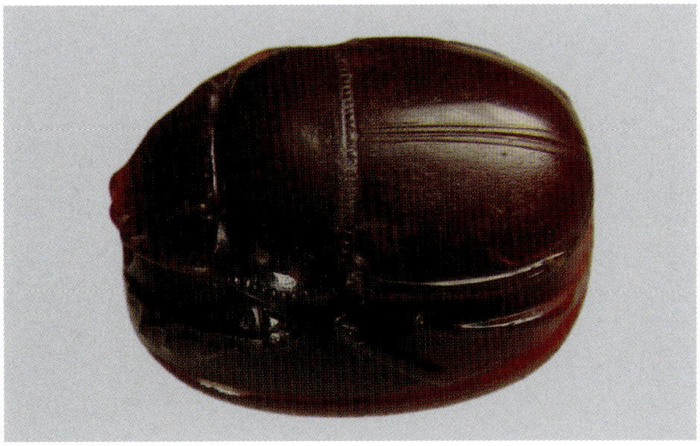

Tassie 7451.

Two warriors fight. The attacker is bearded, wearing a helmet and dotted cloak, carrying a shield and striking his adversary with a spear. The second figure wears a helmet, the crest seen frontally; he has fallen on his shield, one arm behind him holding the shield, the other bent up towards his attacker, one leg outstretched, the other bent. Cable border.

Knight took the figures for Achilles and Hector. The general group with the fallen figure is met on other Etruscan scarabs but not generally so anatomically detailed.

Etruscan, around 400 BC.

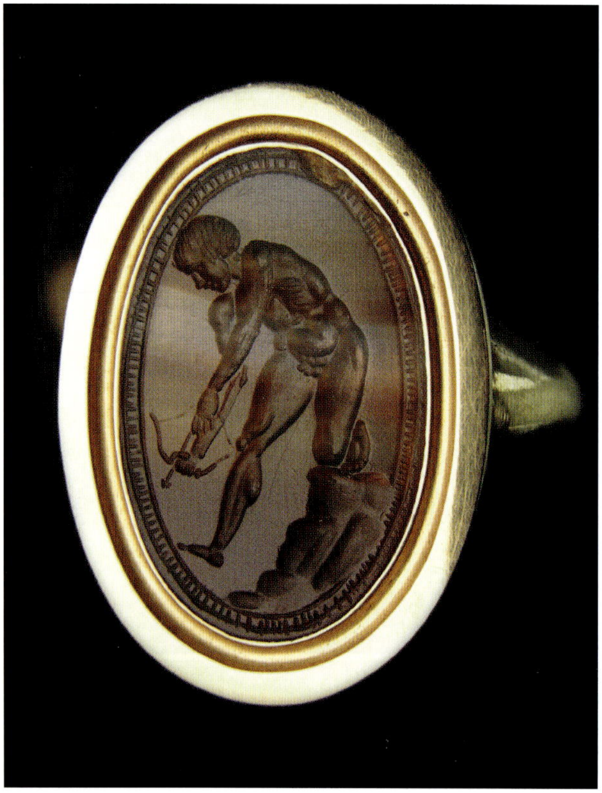

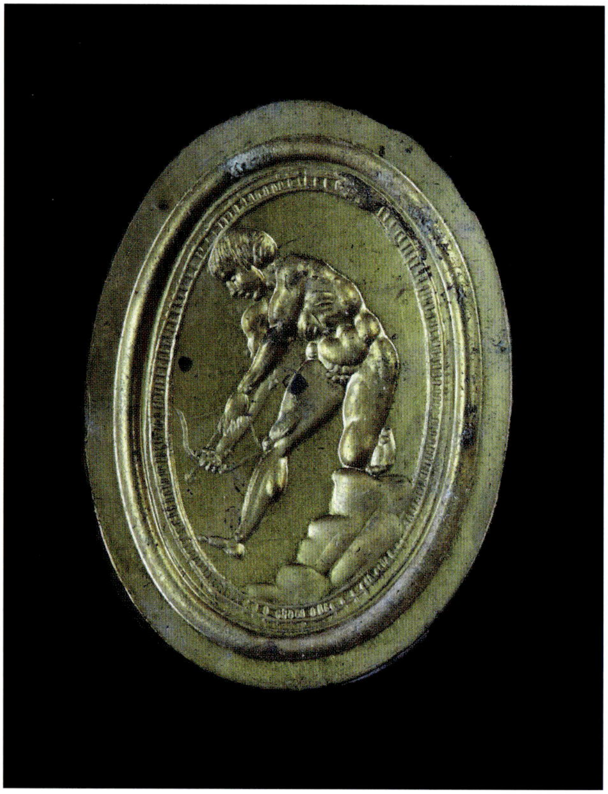

114

(10721) K183 (pl. 5)
Agate, polished flat back, set in a plain ring
17 x 12

A youth kneels on rocks and draws his bow, pointing down. Hatched border.

Commonly identified as Paris (or Hercules, by Knight), for no good reason; see Martini, pl. 2.2–3.

3rd century BC.

115

(10711) K173 (pl. 5)
Sard, polished flat back, set in a plain gold ring
16 x 13

A naked youth is scraping his shin with a strigil. Ground line. Hatched border.

A popular classical subject seen also on late Etruscan scarabs and their early Roman copies, as Zazoff, *ES*, pl. 55.297.

3rd/2nd century BC.

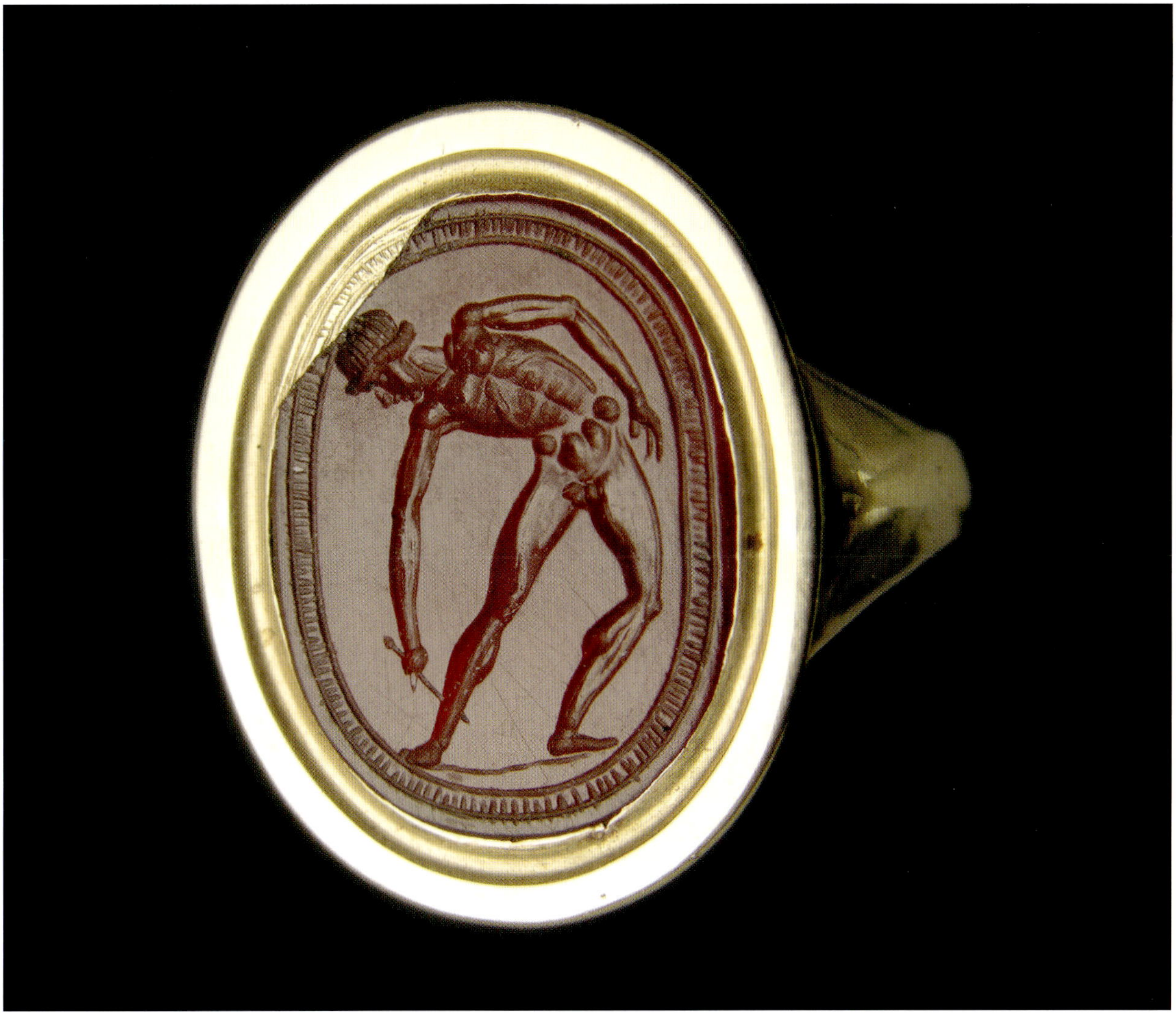

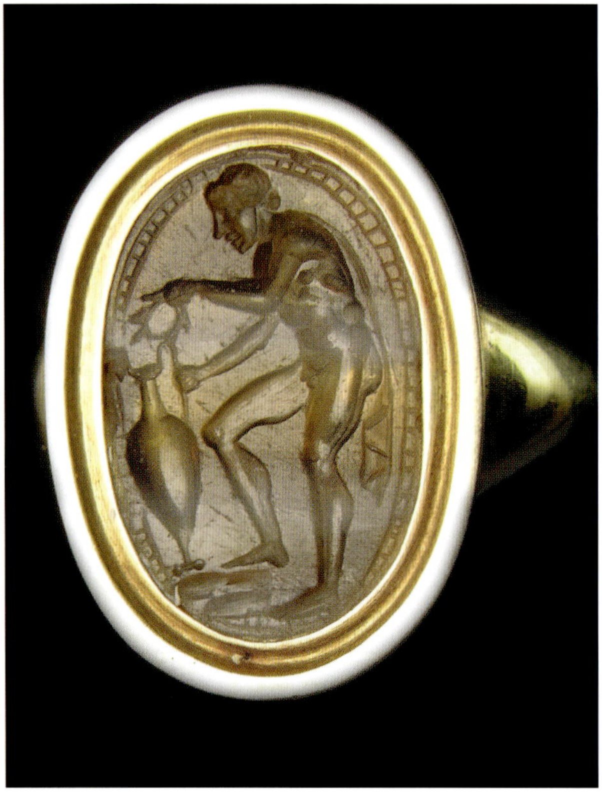

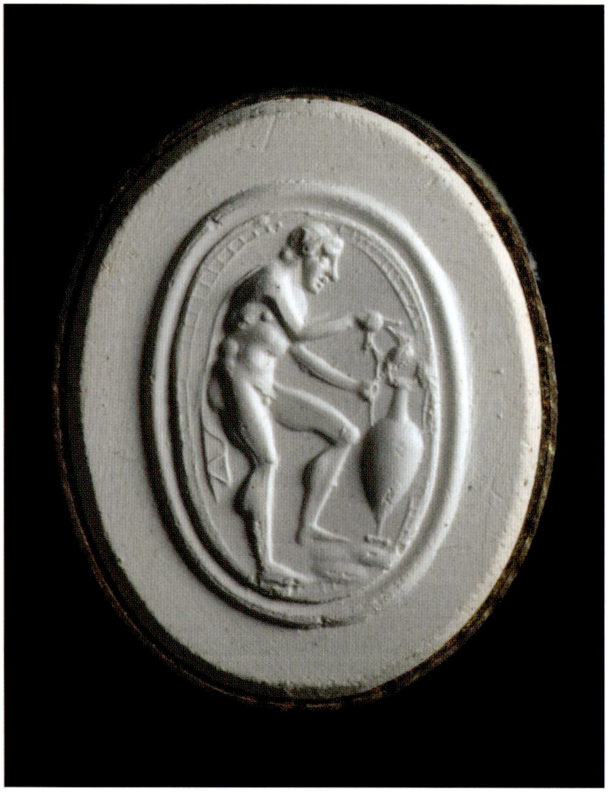

116

(10708) K170 (pl. 5)
Agate, set in a gold ring, polished flat back
14 x 9

SG.Imp. 9; Tassie 7994; Inst.Imp. no. 118.

A youth with a cloak over his shoulder, one foot on rocks, over which he holds a wreath and a wine amphora. Hatched border. Compare Martini, pl. 8.3 (man with fillet or crown, rather than Cadmus with the snake).

The scene commonly represents Hercules getting water.

3rd century BC.

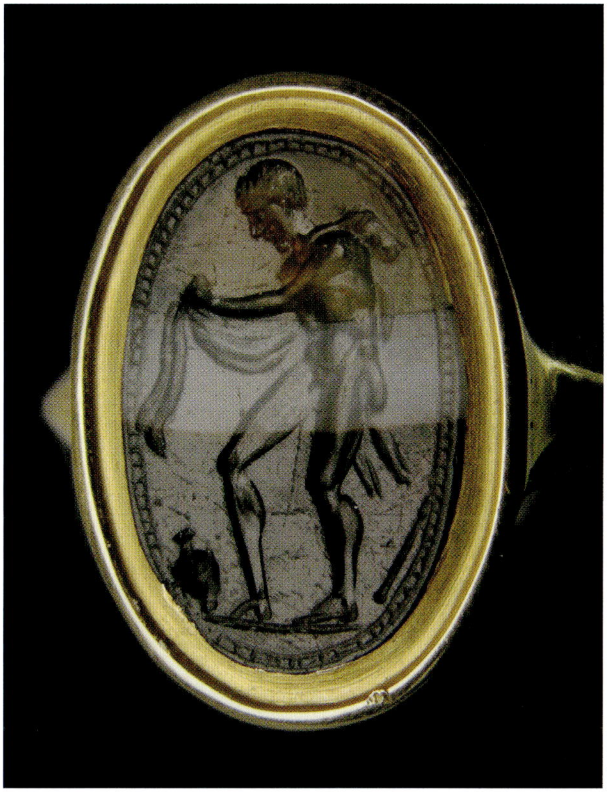

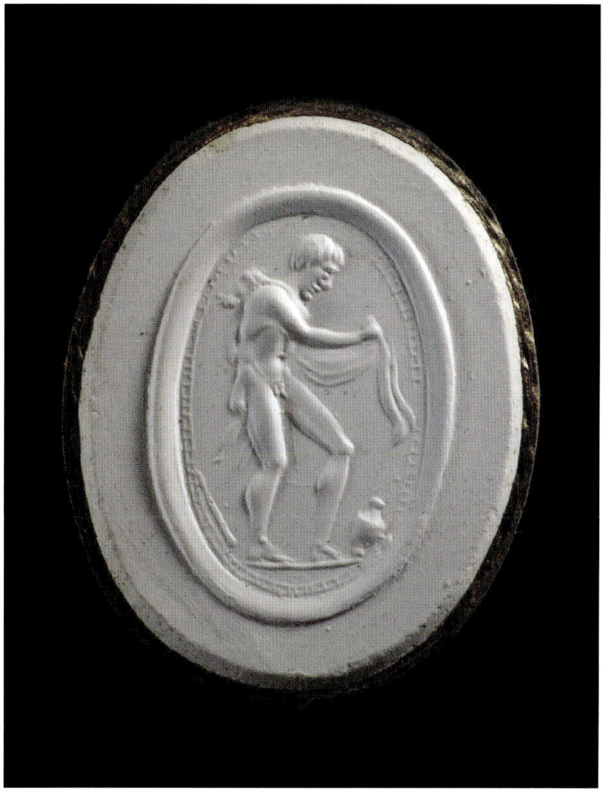

117

(10712) K174 (pl. 6)
Onyx with central white band, the upper part restored in gold, polished flat back, set in a plain gold ring
15 x 9

SG.Imp. 167; Tassie 4637; Inst.Imp. no. 115.

Young Hercules wearing a skin at his back (paws?) and holding out dress over an amphora, implying activity at a fountain, a common motif for the hero. Behind him in the field, his club. Ground line.

3rd century BC.

118

(10714) K176 (pl. 5)
Pale agate, with strong central red stripe, cracked across the body, polished flat back, set on a plain gold ring
15 x 10

A youth, wearing spotted cloak, stoops over a sheathed sword he is holding, before a pillar (incense-burner?). Hatched ground line and hatched border.

Very like the device on a scarab, *AG* pl. 20.8; Zazoff, *ES* no. 807; Martini, pl. 4.1; *Galerie Nefer* Exh.Cat. 1996, no. 13. On a similar ringstone, *Cambridge* no. 124.

3rd century BC.

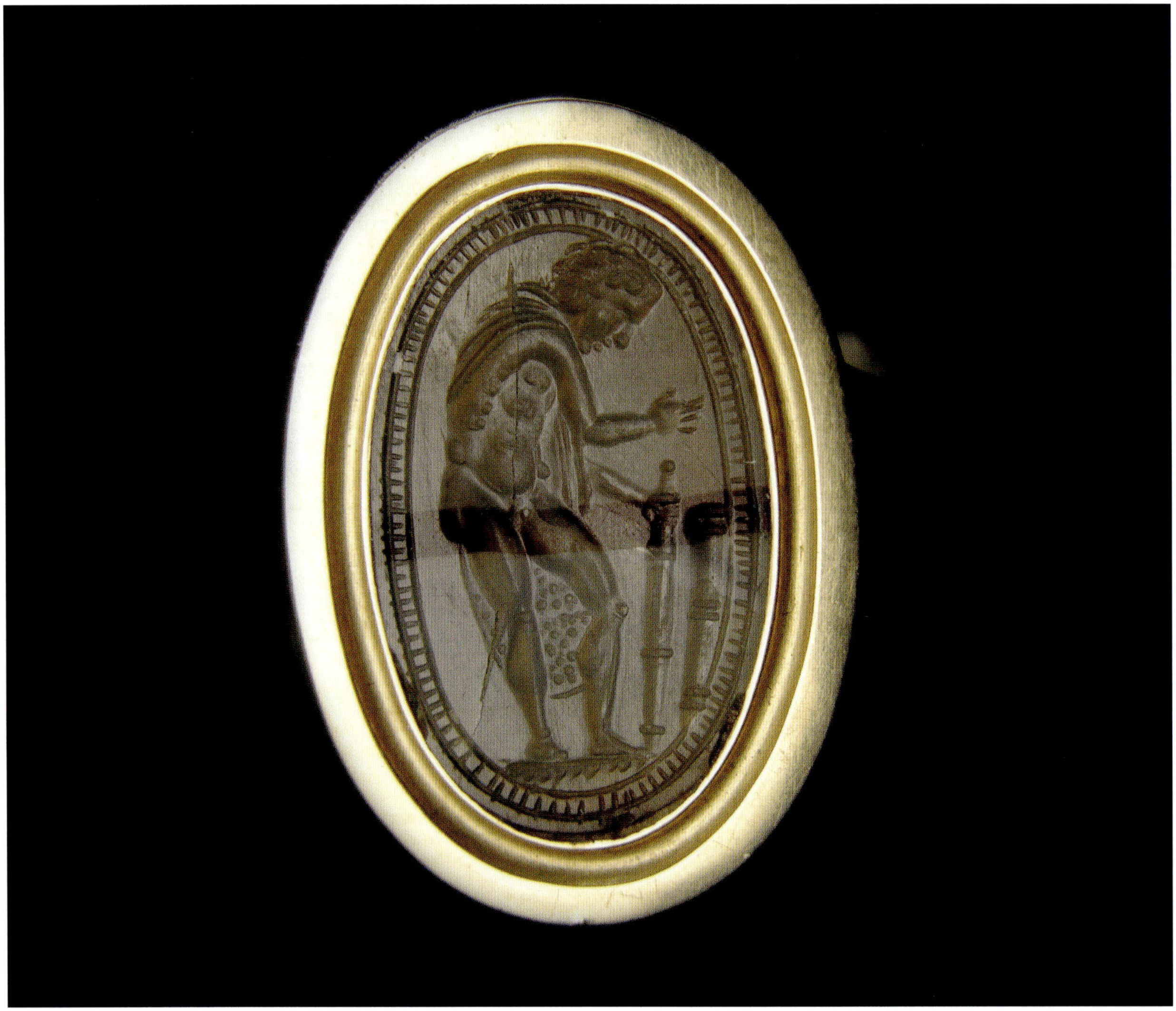

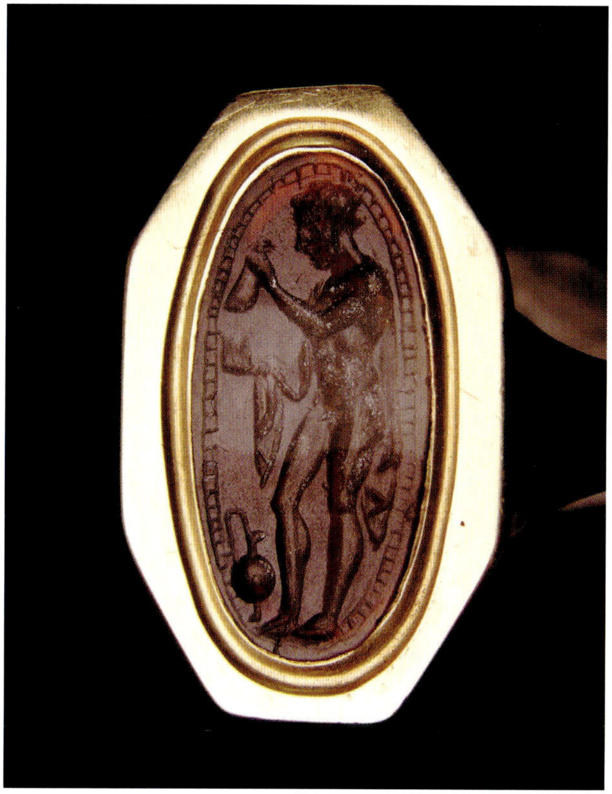 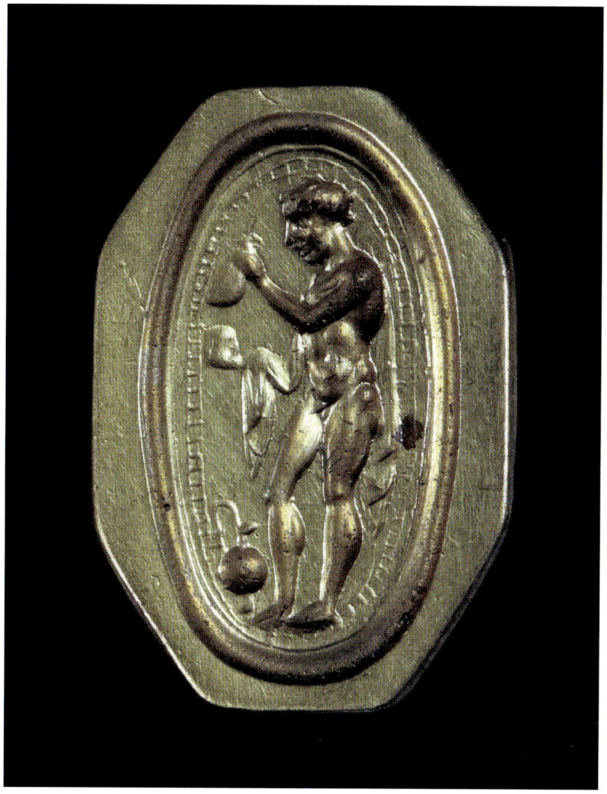

119

(10715) K177 (pl. 5)
Banded onyx, red/white/red, polished flat back, set on a plain gold ring
15 x 7

A youth with cloak over one shoulder is holding what appears to be a small skin flask which he is emptying into a cup. A jug on the ground. Hatched border.

3rd/2nd century BC.

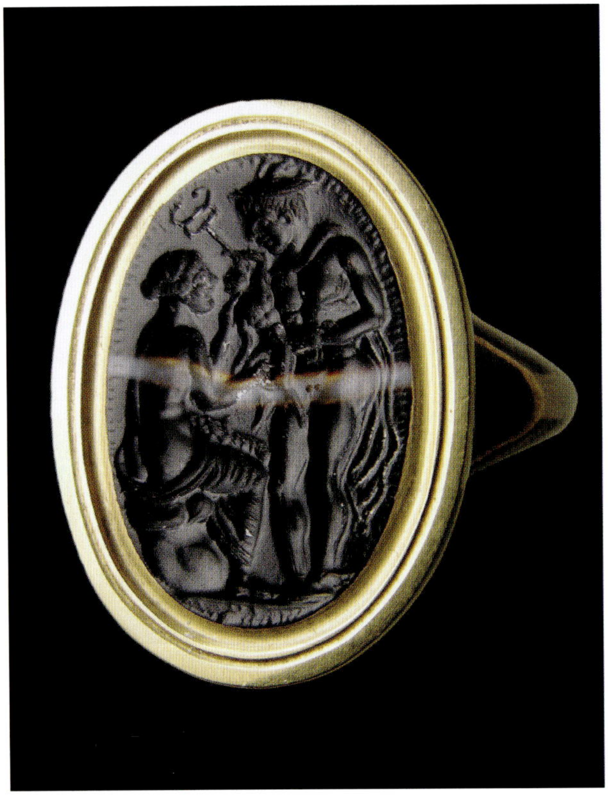

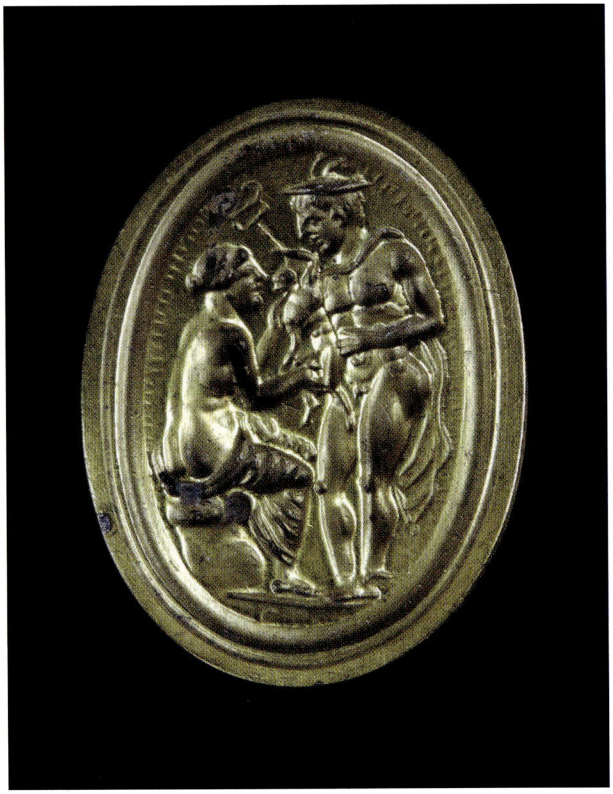

120

(10672) K134 (pl. 5)
Banded onyx, red/white/red, polished convex back, set on a plain gold ring
18 x 12

SG.Imp. 138; Inst.Imp. no. 161; Paoletti I, I.442.

Mercury/Hermes, with winged petasos, cloak, caduceus and winged sandals, is handing a baby to a half-dressed woman seated on rocks. Hatched border and cross-hatched exergue.

The baby is Bacchus, being delivered to a nymph. The subject is not uncommon although not exactly in this form, compare *LIMC* III, 479–80.

3rd century BC.

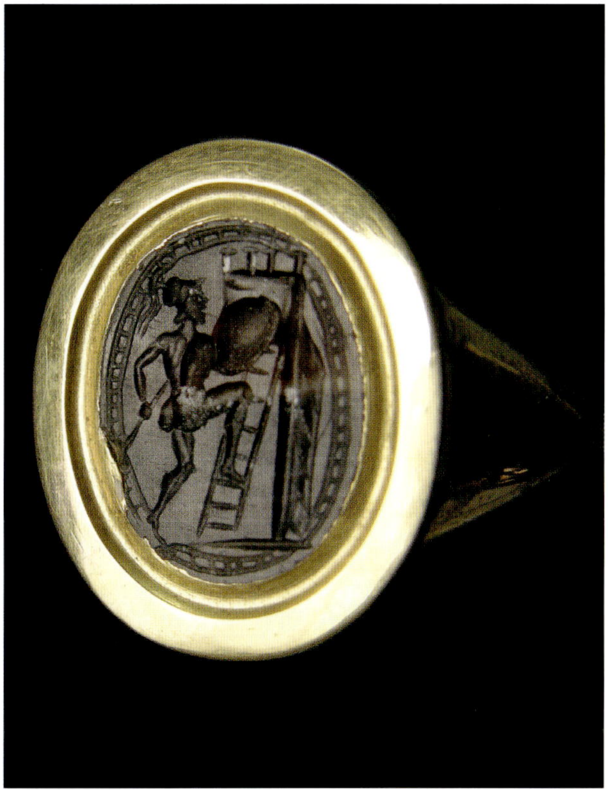

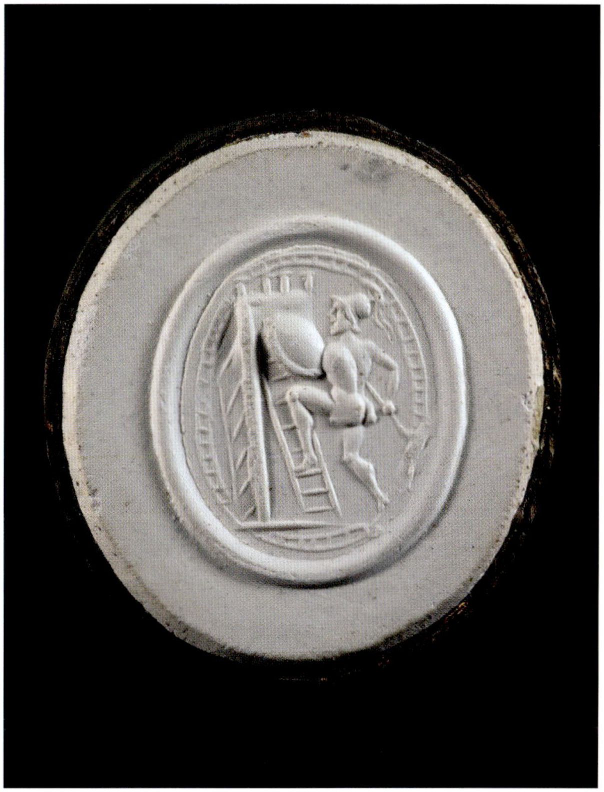

121

(10717) K179 (pl. 6)
Banded agate, red/white/deep red, polished flat back, set on a plain gold ring
11 x 9

SG.Imp. 21; Inst.Imp. no. 121.

A warrior with helmet, shield and spear, mounts a ladder set against a tower with battlements and a gate beside it. Ground line. Hatched border.

Probably Capaneus at Troy, usually shown with his ladder breaking.

2nd century BC.

122

(10718) K180 (pl. 6)
Carnelian, polished flat back, set on a plain gold ring
11 x 9

SG.Imp. 157; Inst.Imp. no. 128.

A stricken warrior fallen to his knees, with helmet, shield and sword. Hatched border.

Probably Capaneus is intended; compare Martini, pl. 28.4–6; *Würzburg* no. 131.

2nd century BC.

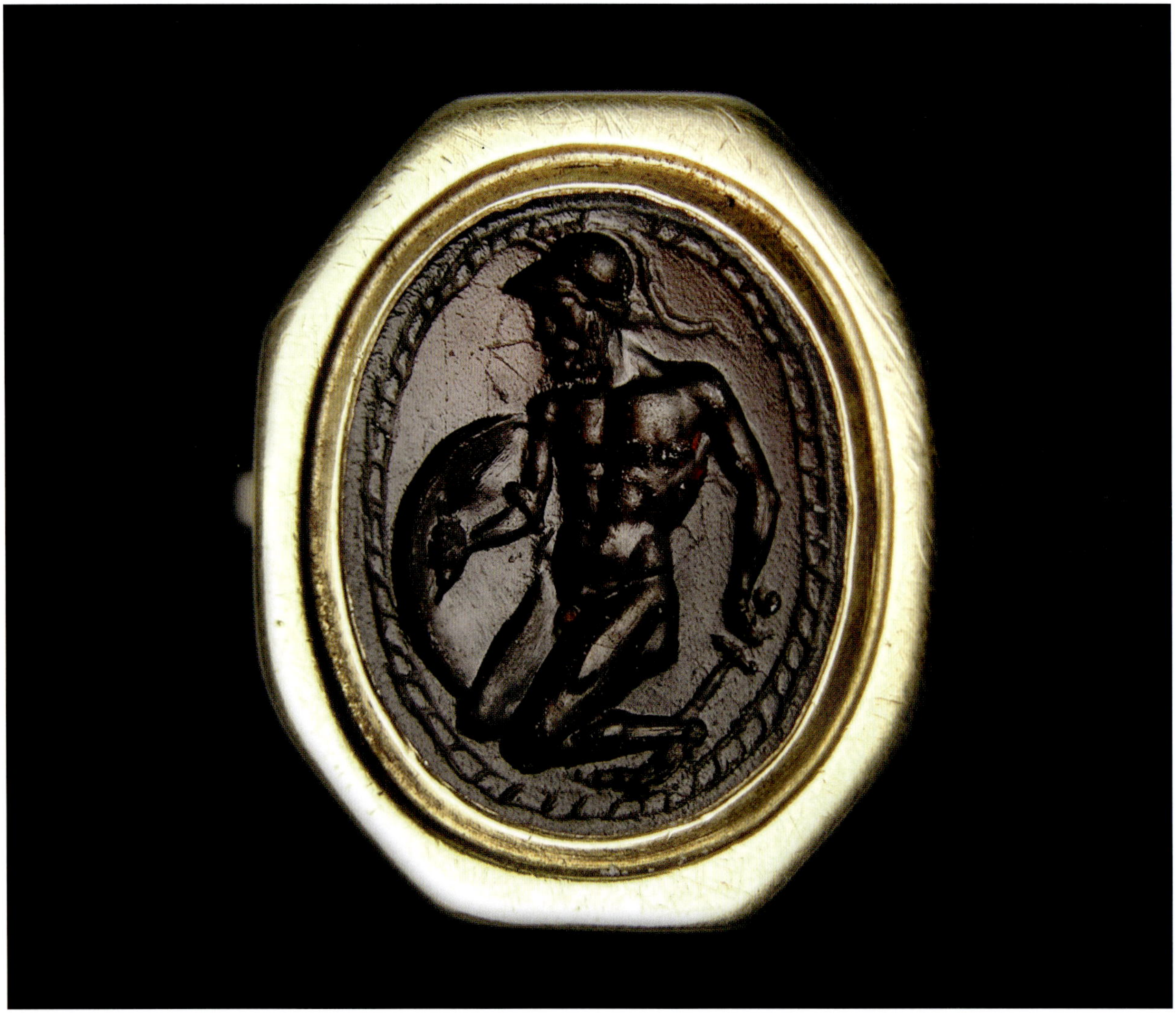

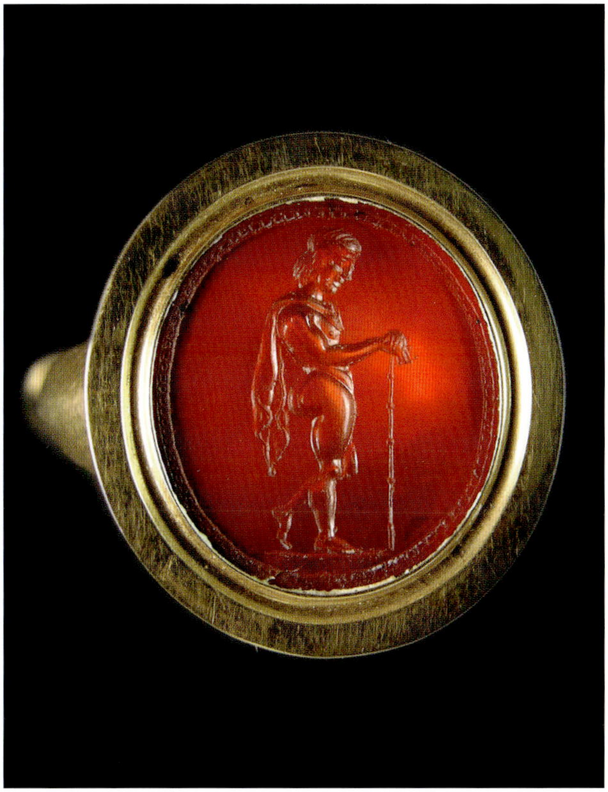

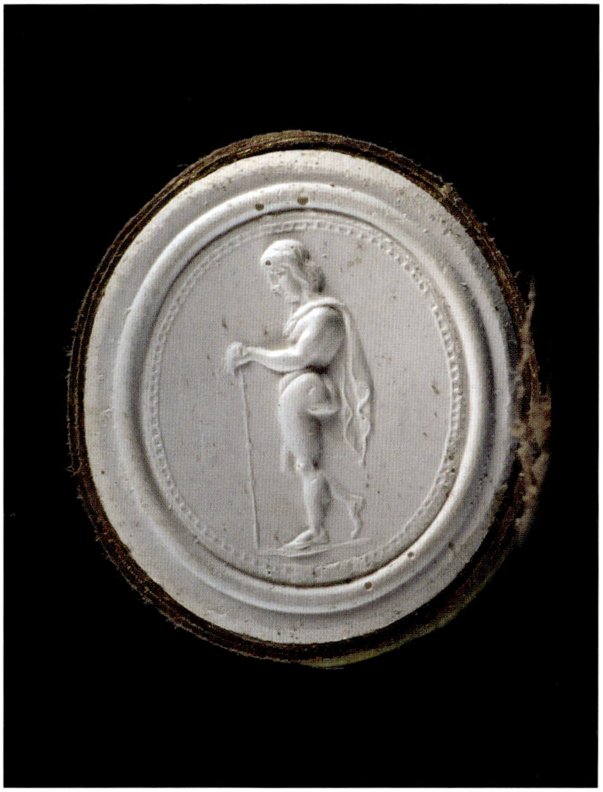

123

(10703) K165
Sard, polished flat back, set on a plain gold ring
12 x 10

SG.Imp. 63; Inst.Imp. no. 135.

A youth with a cloak stands holding a knobbed stick. Ground line. Hatched border.

2nd century BC.

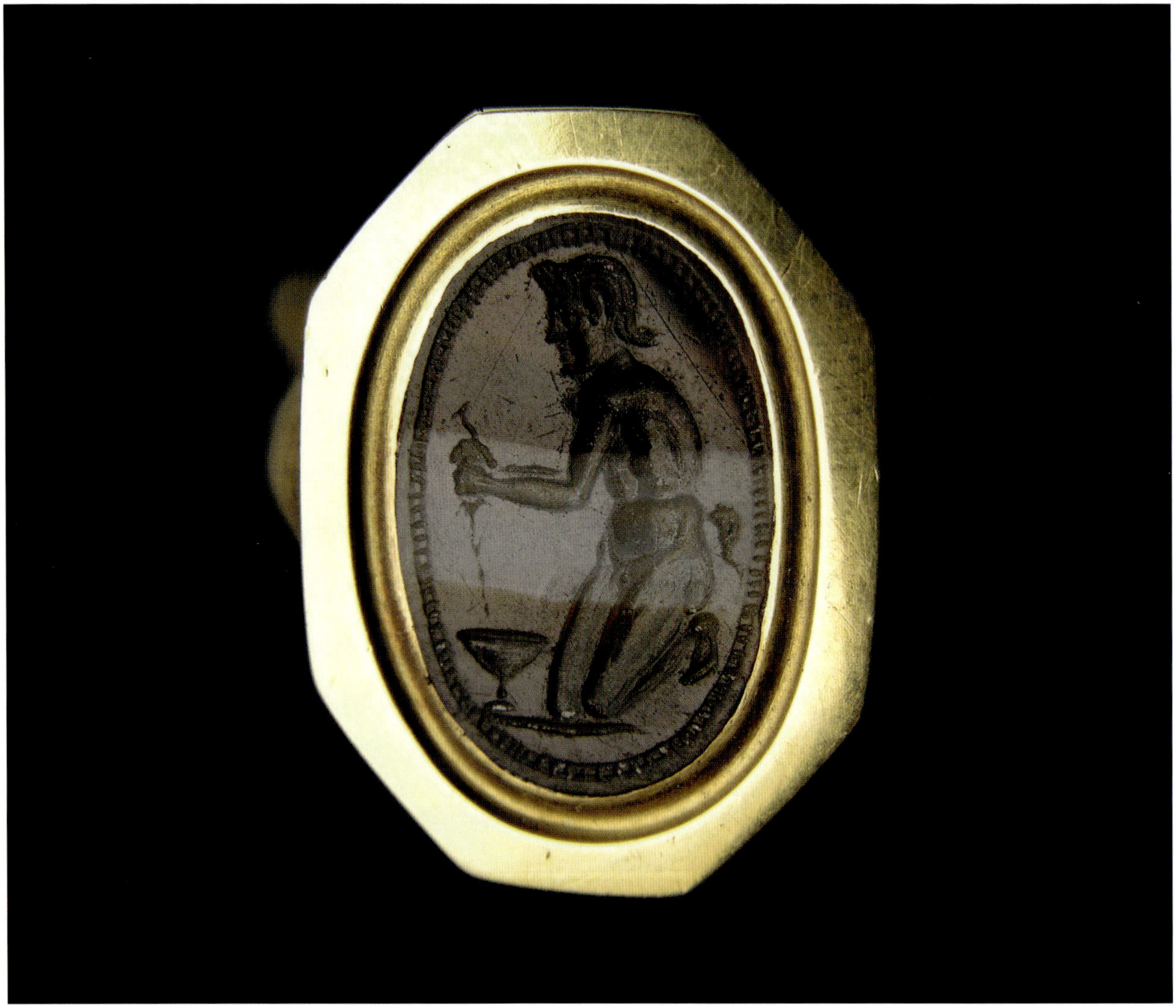

124

(10722) K184
Banded agate, red/white/brown, polished flat back, set on a plain gold ring
13 x 8

Spilsbury, no. 16 (Greville Coll.).

A kneeling satyr squeezes a bunch of grapes into a stemmed bowl. Ground line. Hatched border.

For the type cf. *AG* pl.21.30 and on a stone in Newcastle City Museum (Shefton Collection).

3rd century BC.

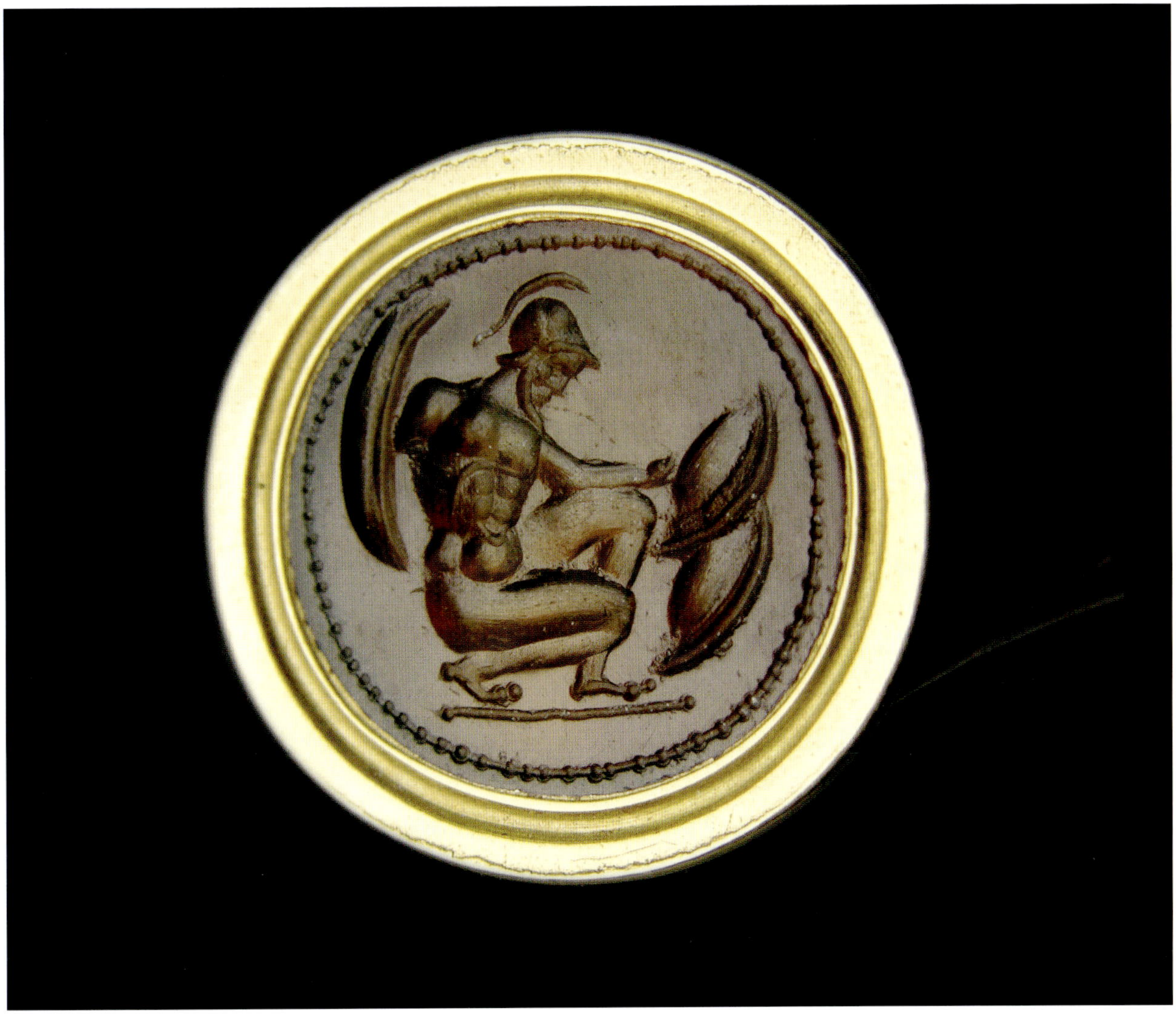

125

(10719)K181 (pl. 6)
Pale sard, polished flat back, set on a plain gold ring
11 x 10

SG.Imp. 14; Inst.Imp. no. 126.

Othryades, a kneeling warrior with helmet and shield, before two shields, one of which he is inscribing. Short ground line. Linked-dot border.

For this less common version of the subject see Spier, *Getty* no. 146.

1st century BC?

126

(10814)
Black glass, set in a gold ring with forked ends to the terminals of the hoop
12 x 4

A man with dress over his shoulder is stooping to write on a tablet the oracle being uttered by the small bearded head before him.

A popular subject on Italic gems, the head sometimes being taken for that of Orpheus. Compare Martini, pl. 27.2–3.

3rd/2nd century BC.

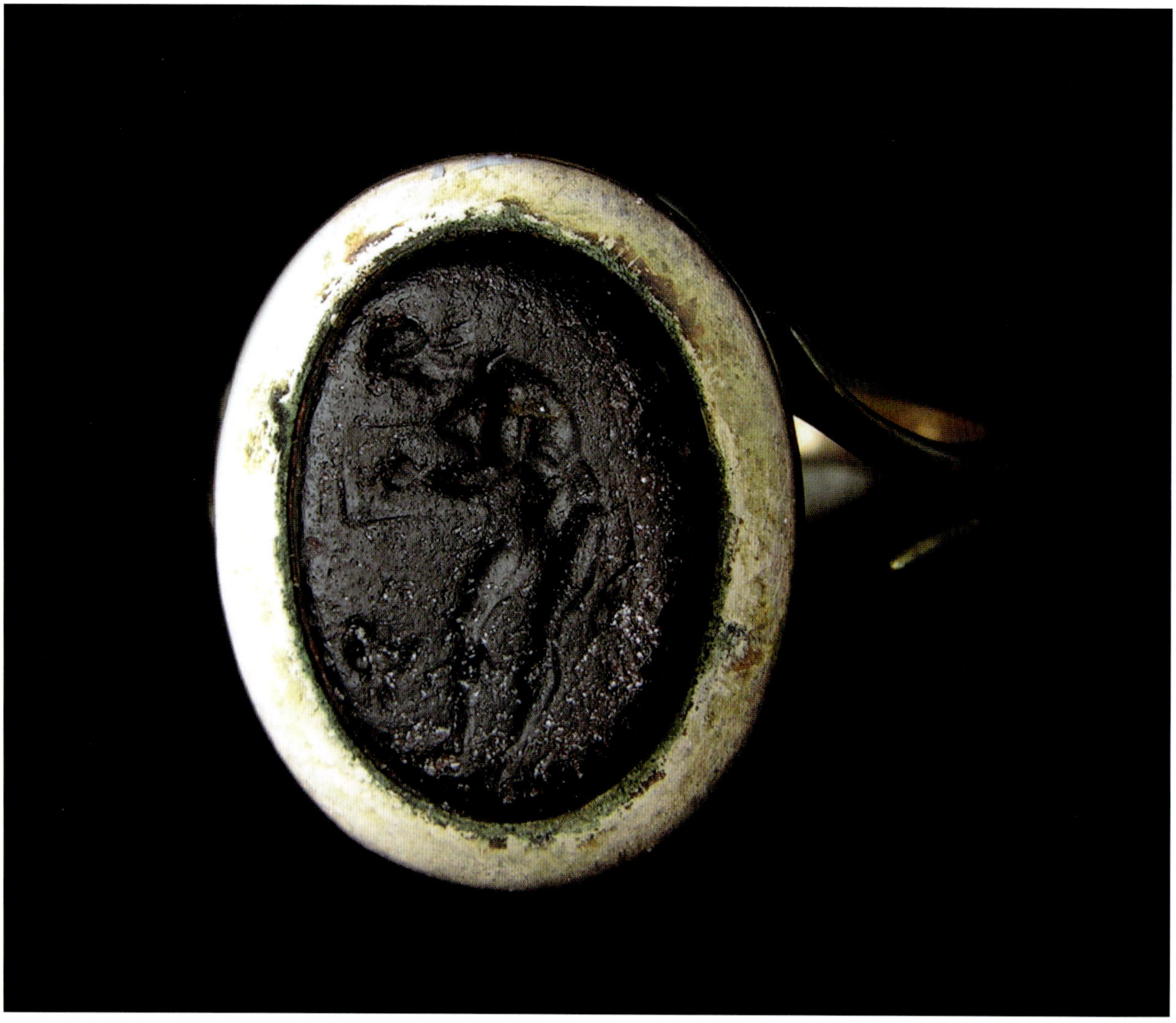

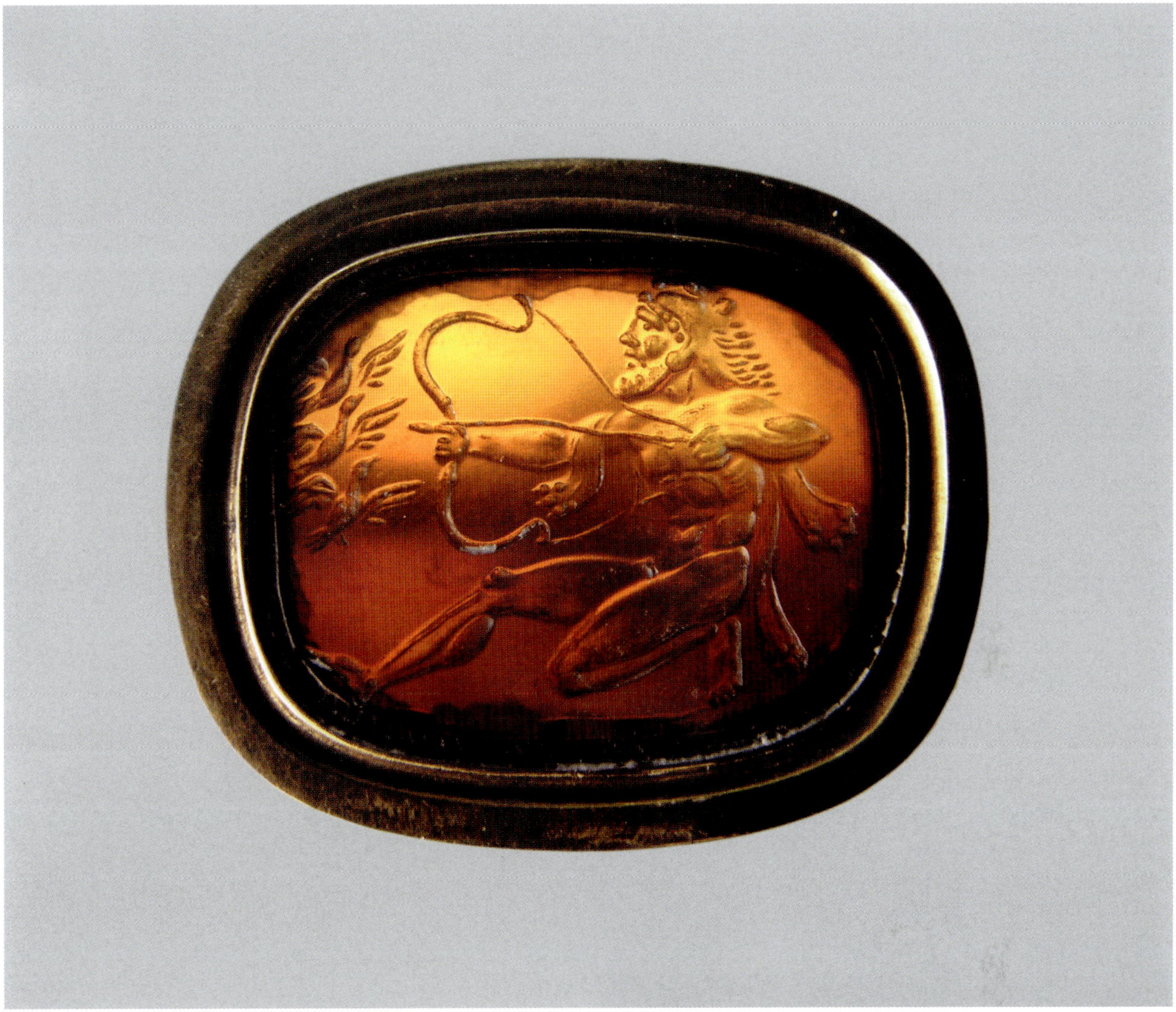

127

(10676) K138 (pl. 5)
Sard, unpolished flat back, set on a plain gold ring
17 x 13

SG.Imp. 135; Inst.Imp. no. 159; Lippold, pl. 37.12.

Hercules wearing his lionskin, crouching to shoot at three Stymphalian birds. Hatched border.

See *Würzburg* nos 111–2. See also the next, and for late copies, Paoletti II, V.141, VIII.320.

Italic, 3rd/2nd century BC.

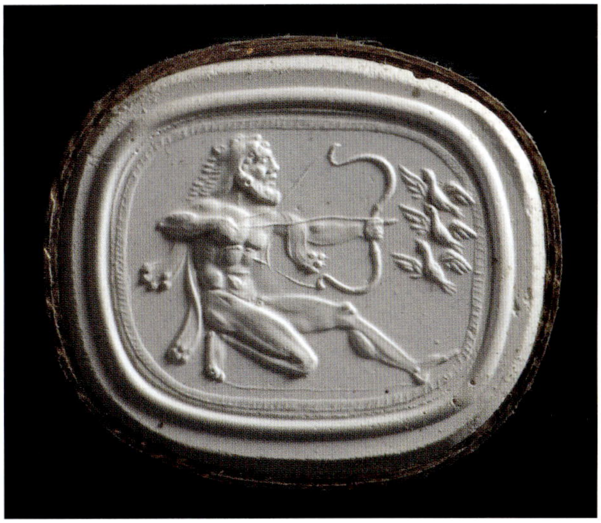

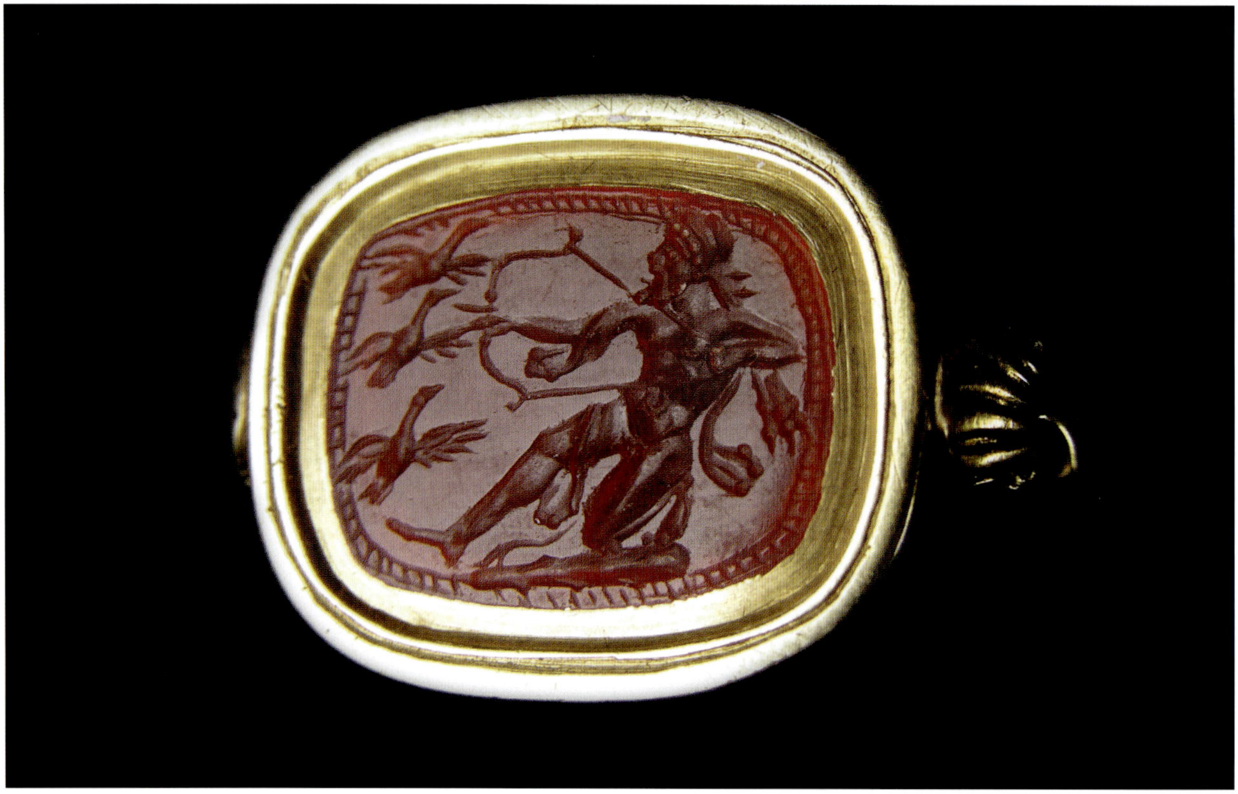

128

(10687) K149 (pl. 5)
Sard, polished flat back, set on a gold ring with arrow and palmette ends to the hoop
12 x 9

SG.Imp. 166; Inst.Imp. no. 164.

The subject as the last, but Hercules has his club on the ground beside him.

A copy on a scarab, *Hamburg* no. 43–4.

Italic, 1st century BC.

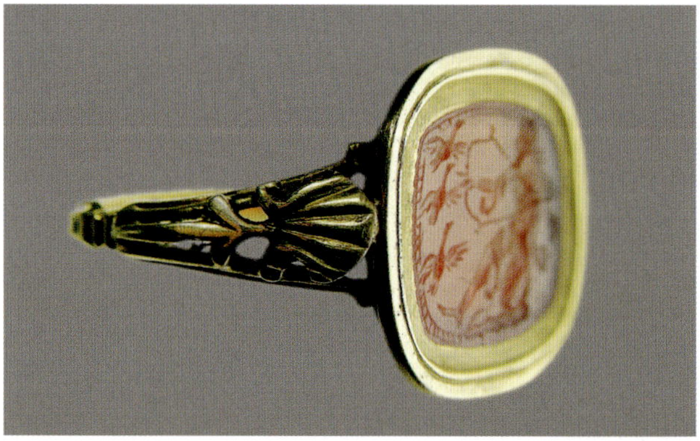

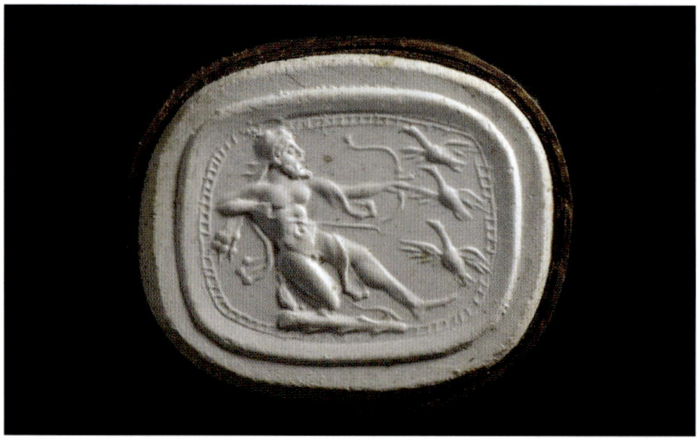

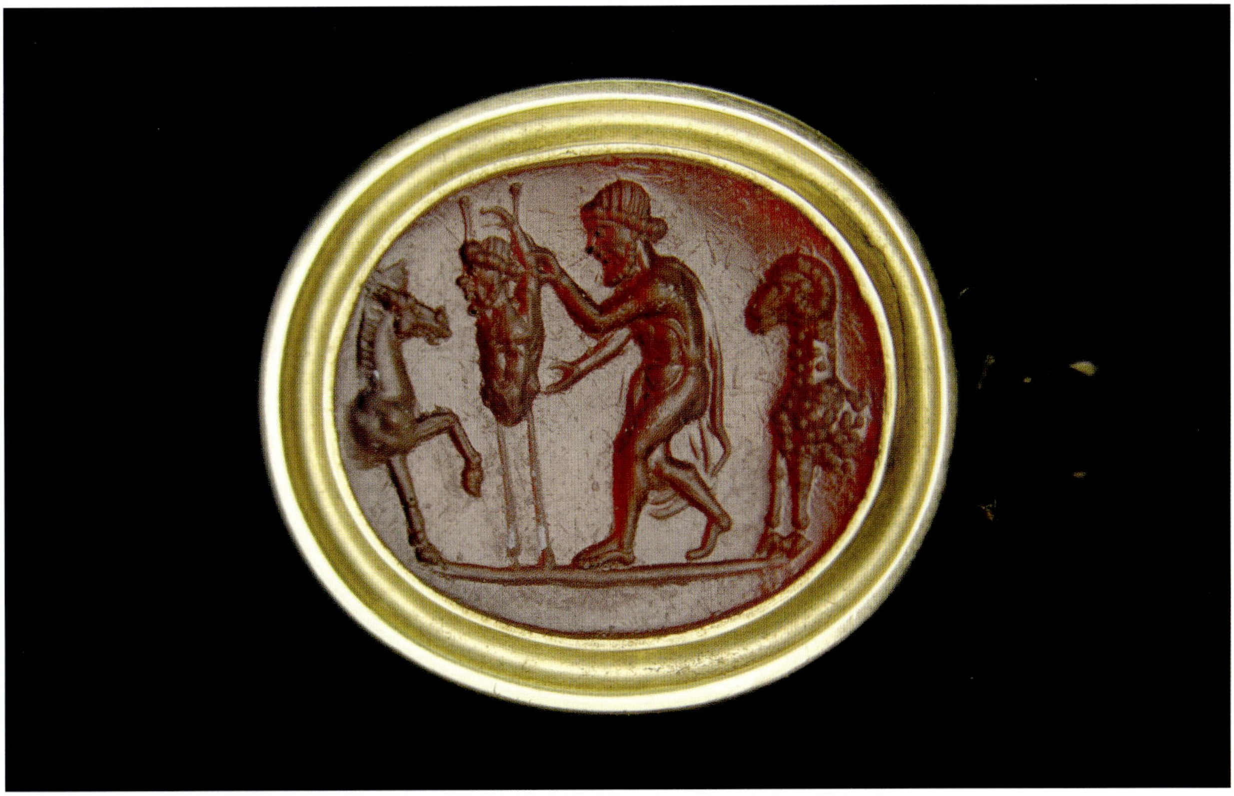

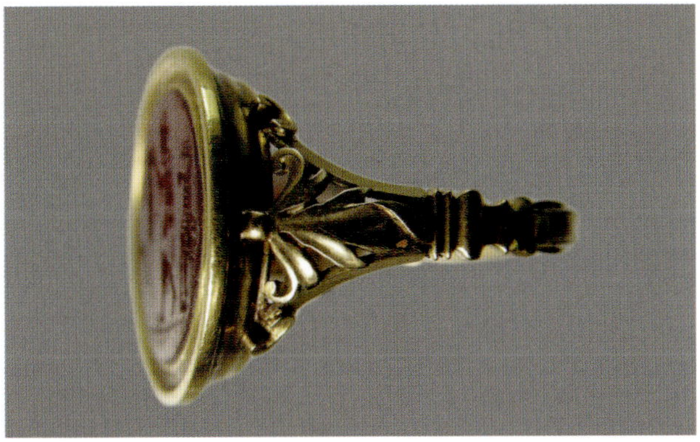

129

(10726) K188 (pl. 6)
Sard, polished flat back, set on a gold ring with palmettes at the forked ends of the hoop
13 x 11

Once Duke Carafa Noia (Naples); Ficoroni 1757, T.4; SG.Imp. 139; Tassie 8575; Inst.Imp. no. 62; Paoletti I, II.114; King 1872, I p. 351; King 1885, pl. 28.7; *AG* pl. 21.61; Lippold, pl. 46.7; G. Tassinari in *Xenia antiqua* 1, 1992, 101–2, fig. 33 (on Prometheus).

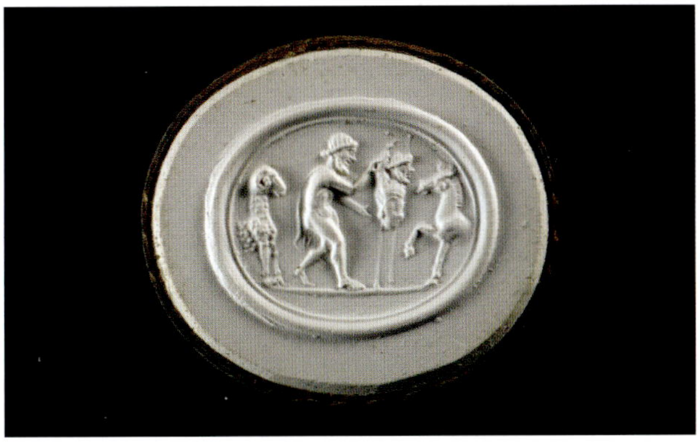

Prometheus, in a cloak, works on the modelling of the upper part of a bearded man, supported on two poles. Before and behind him the foreparts of a horse and a ram. Ground line.

Compare *LIMC* VII, pl. 428, but the animals here are unexpected.

Italic, 2nd century BC.

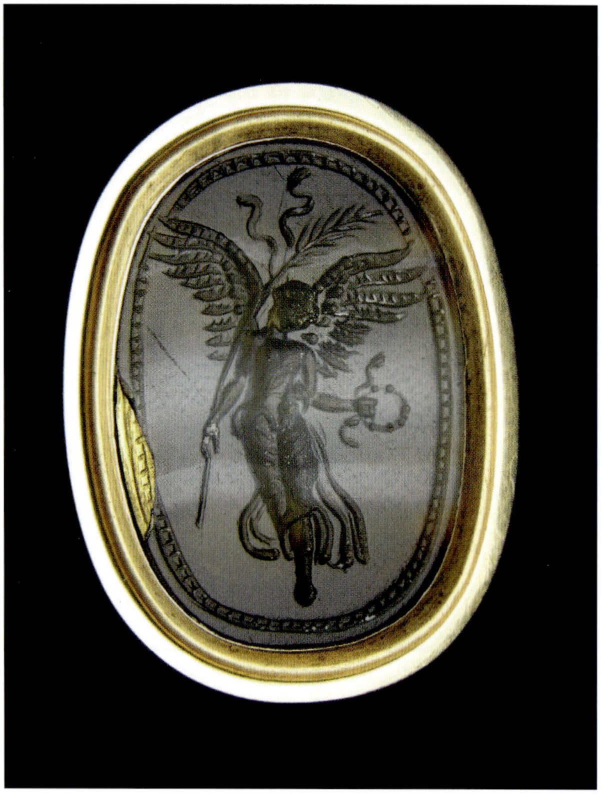

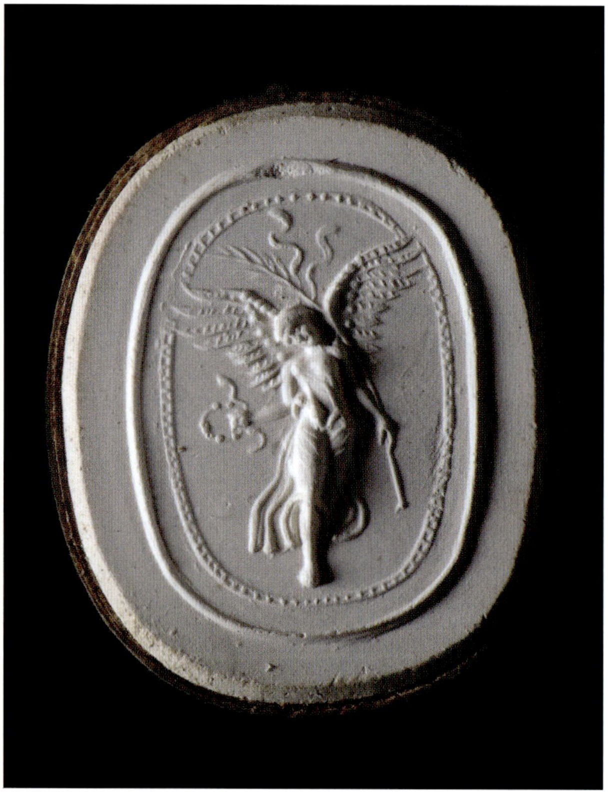

130

(10716) K178 (pl. 5)
Banded agate, multiple white/brown, border repaired with gold at the left, unpolished flat back, set on a plain gold ring
16 x 11

SG.Imp. 30; Inst.Imp. no. 120; W.Tassie 2699; Paoletti I, I.311; *AG* pl. 42.3; Lippold, pl. 32.10.

Nike/Victoria flies holding a ribboned wreath and ribboned palm branch. Hatched border.

The type is that of the statue of Victory in the Curia. Compare *AGN* 421, no. 510 with earlier bibliography.

Last quarter of the 1st century BC.

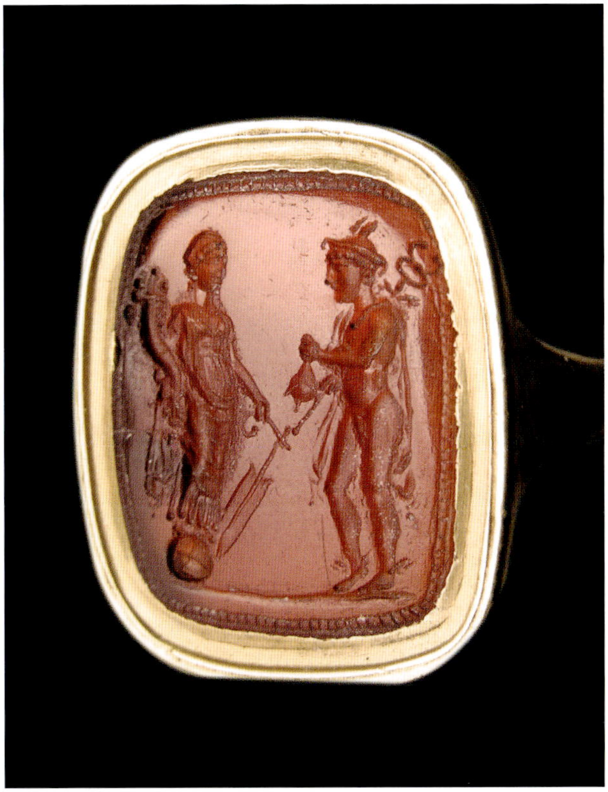

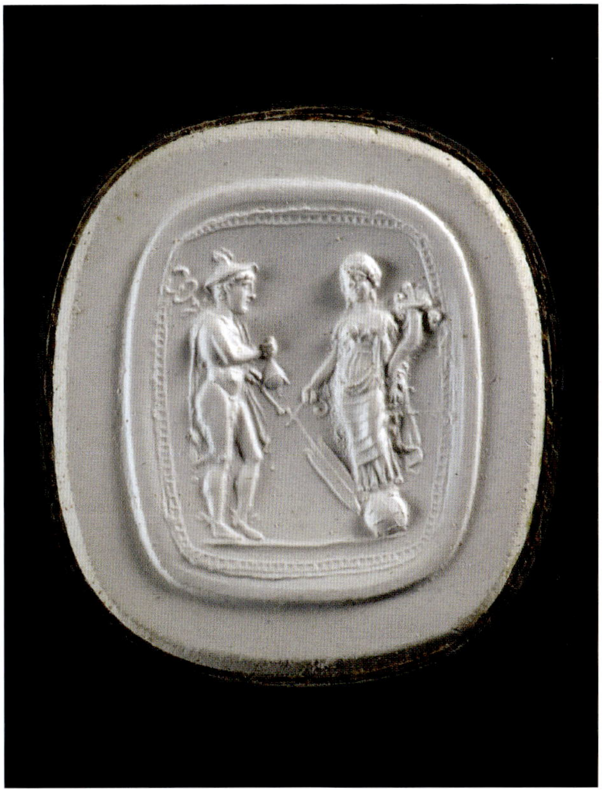

131

(10662) K124 (pl. 4)
Sard, polished flat back, set on a plain gold ring
15 x 12

SG.Imp. 66; Tassie 2443; Inst.Imp. no. 116; Cades, Cent. IV, 14; King 1872, pl. 22.1.

Mercury, with winged petasos, cloak, winged sandals and caduceus, is offering a purse to Fortuna, fully dressed, standing on a globe and holding a rudder and cornucopia. Ground line. Hatched border.

For the subject, *LIMC* VIII, 134.

1st century BC.

132

(10617) K79 (pl. 3)
Sard, polished flat back, set on a plain gold ring
11 x 7

SG.Imp. 15; Tassie 9312.

Probably three of the Seven Heroes drawing lots for which Theban gate they will attack. One warrior is fully armed, the others with helmets only, casting lots into a one-handled vase. Above and behind the central figure is the top of a pillar with an animal on it, and an oval outline (shield?), probably indicating a shrine or even gate.

The subject was formerly taken to be the three Herakleidai (*LIMC* IV, 726). For the interpretation see E. Zwierlein-Diehl in *Wien* I on nos 284–5; *Würzburg* no. 110; and E. Simon, *Ausgewählte Schriften* IV (Mainz 2012) 149–50. A popular Italic subject.

1st century BC.

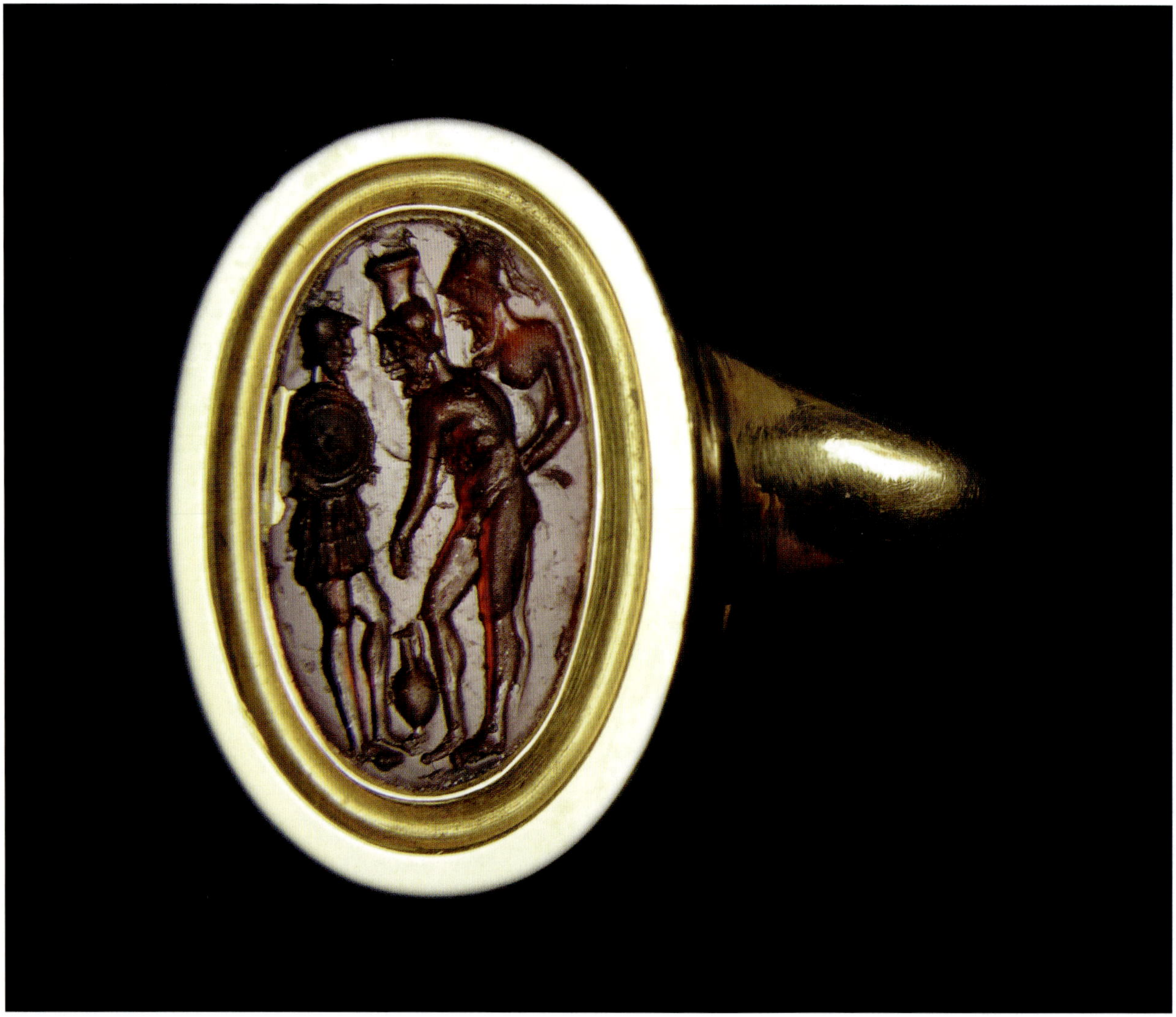

MULTIFIGURE GROUPS

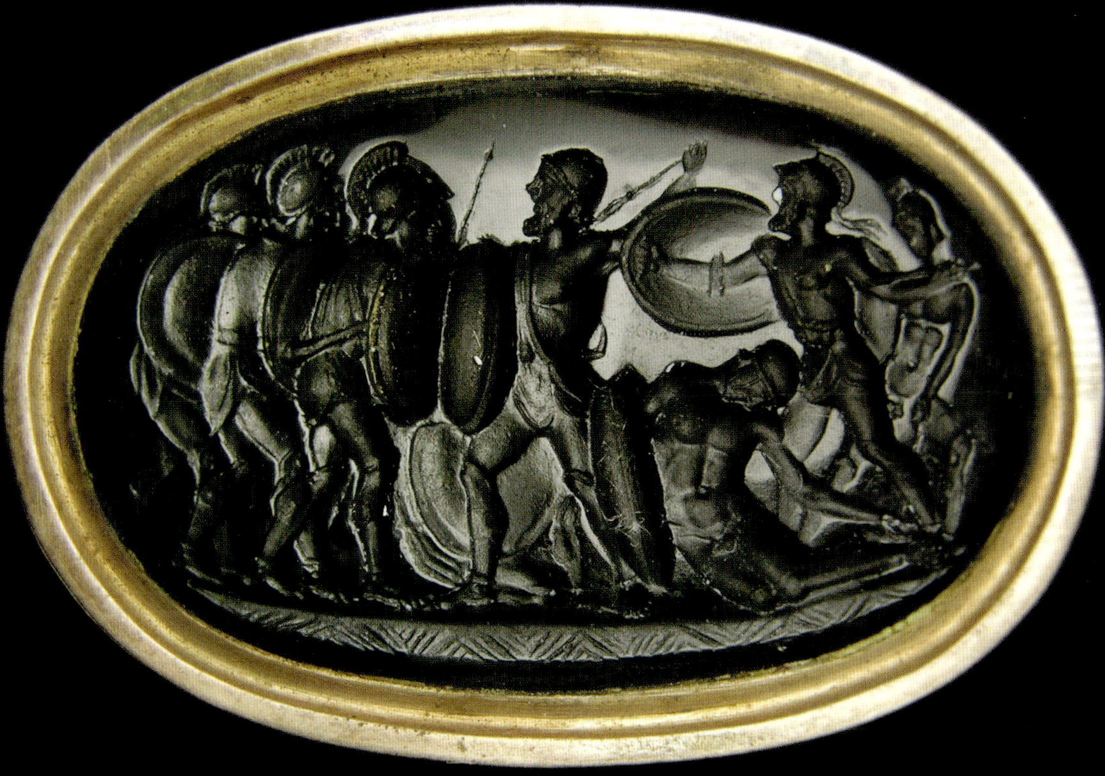

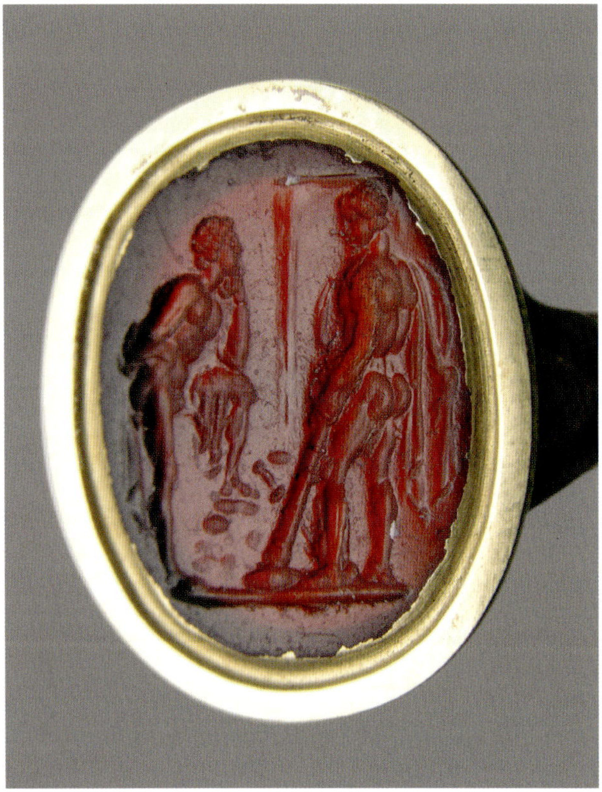

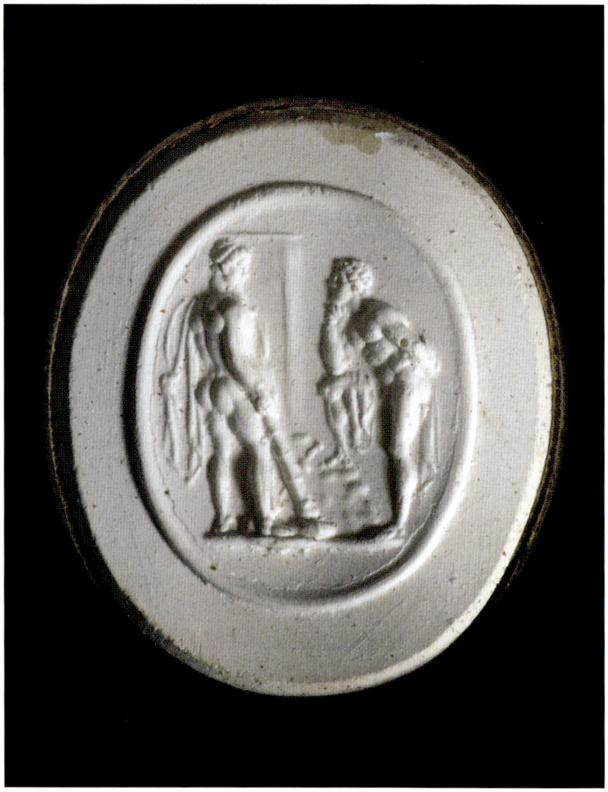

133

(10681) K143 (pl. 5)
Sard, polished flat back, set on a plain gold ring
15 x 11

SG.Imp. 24; Inst.Imp. no. 147; Cades Cent.III, 65 (as Hercules and Eurystheus); W.Tassie 1879.

This is probably Ulysses, a cloak around his body with his foot raised on rocks and hand to his chin, pensively, standing before Theseus, his club lowered and with a cloak over his shoulder, at the doorway to Hades. Ground line.

See *Würzburg* no. 361, for the subject. The Ulysses has neither pilos nor beard.

1st century BC.

134

(10781)
Agate, polished convex back, set on a plain gold ring
23 x 17

Troy. It shows a fully armed Achilles, distressed at being thwarted, with his arm over his head, before him Apollo with his bow, remonstrating, and behind Apollo the back view of a Trojan warrior escaping into the walls of Troy. Ground line.

A copy of the Marlborough gem (*Marlborough* no. 339), which is known in other copies and cameos. The image illustrates Homer, *Iliad* 22, 8–10. The Marlborough gem is taken as 1st century BC and this could be of the same date or a good 18th-century copy.

1st century BC/18th century?

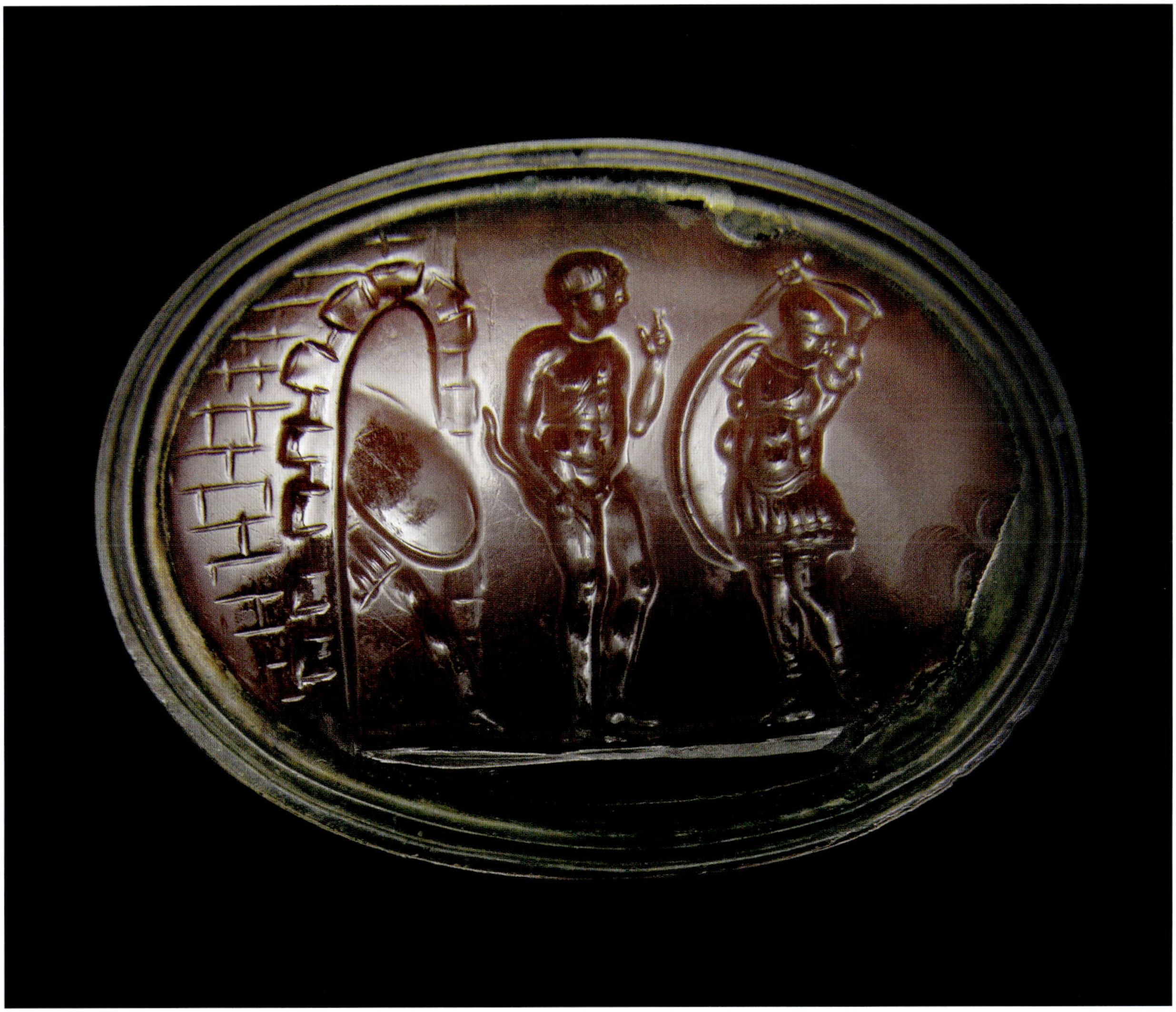

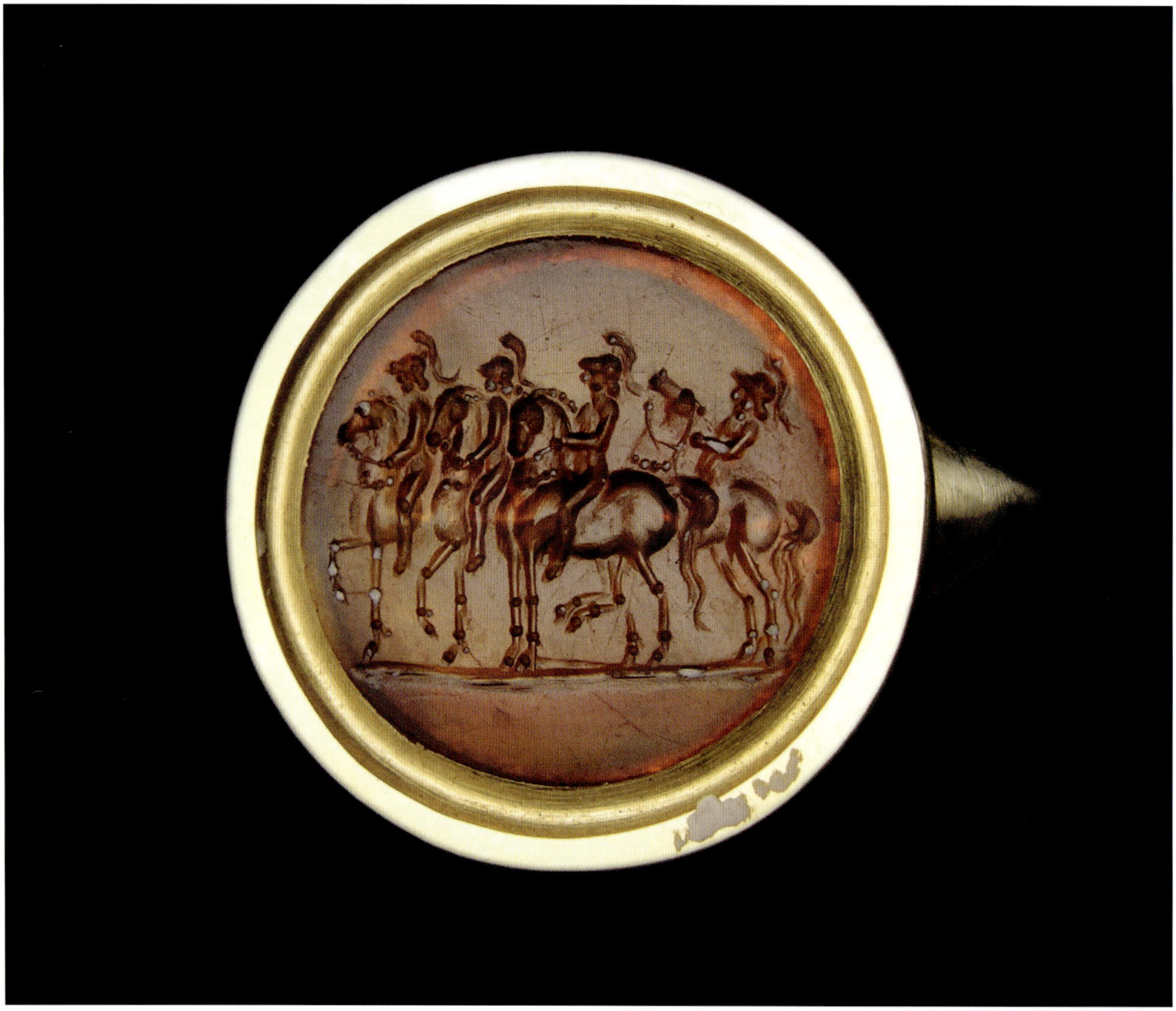

135

(10707) K169 (pl. 5)
Sard, polished flat back, set on a plain gold ring
13 x 13

SG.Imp. 87; Tassie 7604; Inst.Imp. no. 160.

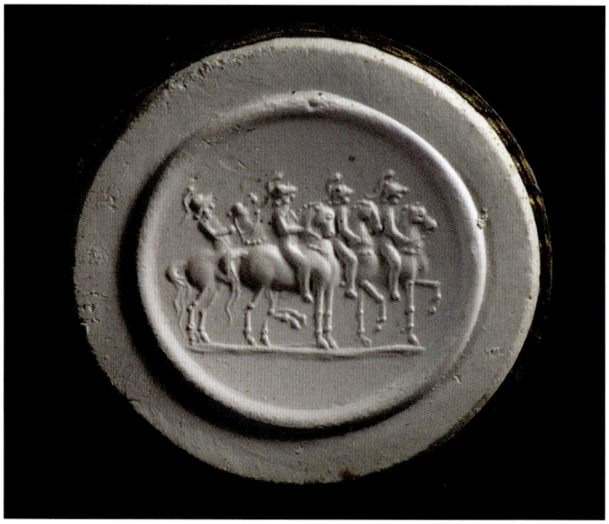

Four helmeted horsemen, the last on a restive horse. Ground line.

Compare *Cambridge* no. 81.

2nd century BC?

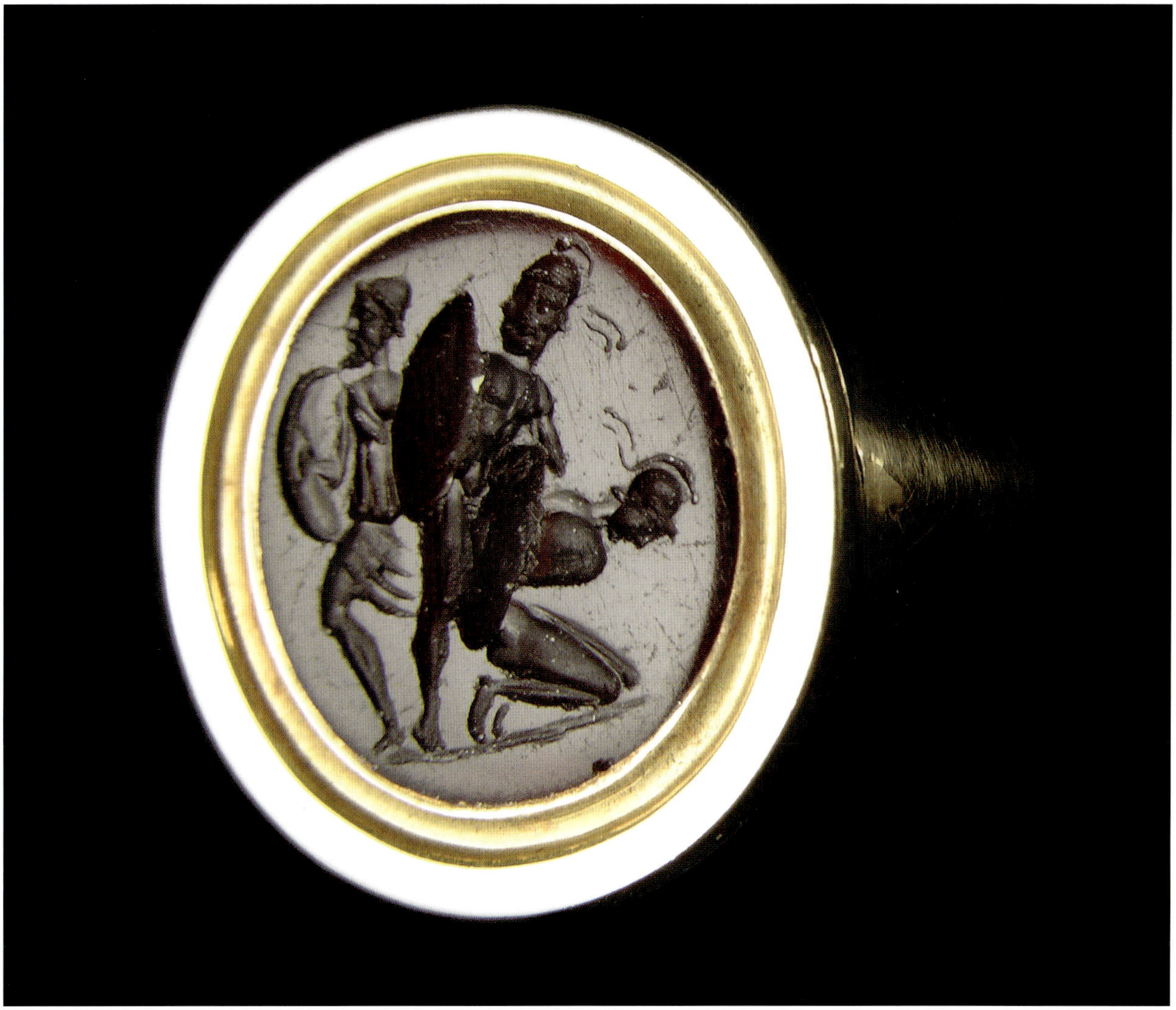

136

(10622) K84 (pl. 3)
Sard, polished flat back, set on a plain gold ring
12 x 10

SG.Imp. 95; Spilsbury, no. 38.

Three warriors. Ulysses, fully armed, wearing a pilos and exomis, moves right as to protect the other two – one with helmet and with shield stooping over the falling body of another, also with helmet and shield. Ground line.

This is probably meant for Ajax and Ulysses protecting the falling Achilles. Compare *Würzburg* no. 359; *Hanover* no. 96; *Wien* II, no. 676; Tassie 9334 (Devonshire Coll.).

1st century BC/AD.

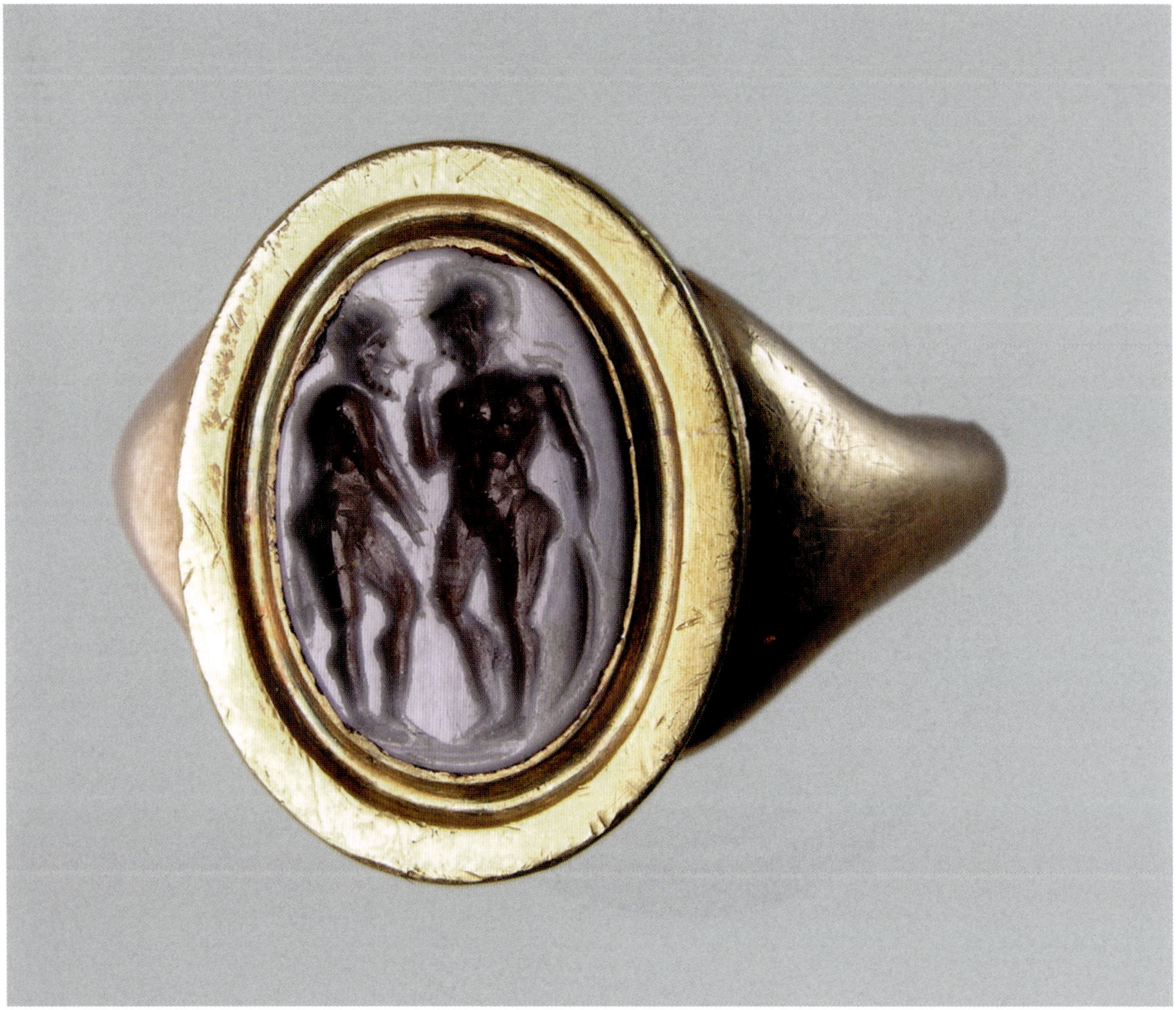

137

(10699) K161
Nicolo, polished flat back, set on a plain gold ring
12 x 9

A young warrior, naked but for helmet and shield, converses with a naked bearded man, cloak over his shoulder. Ground line.

1st century BC/AD.

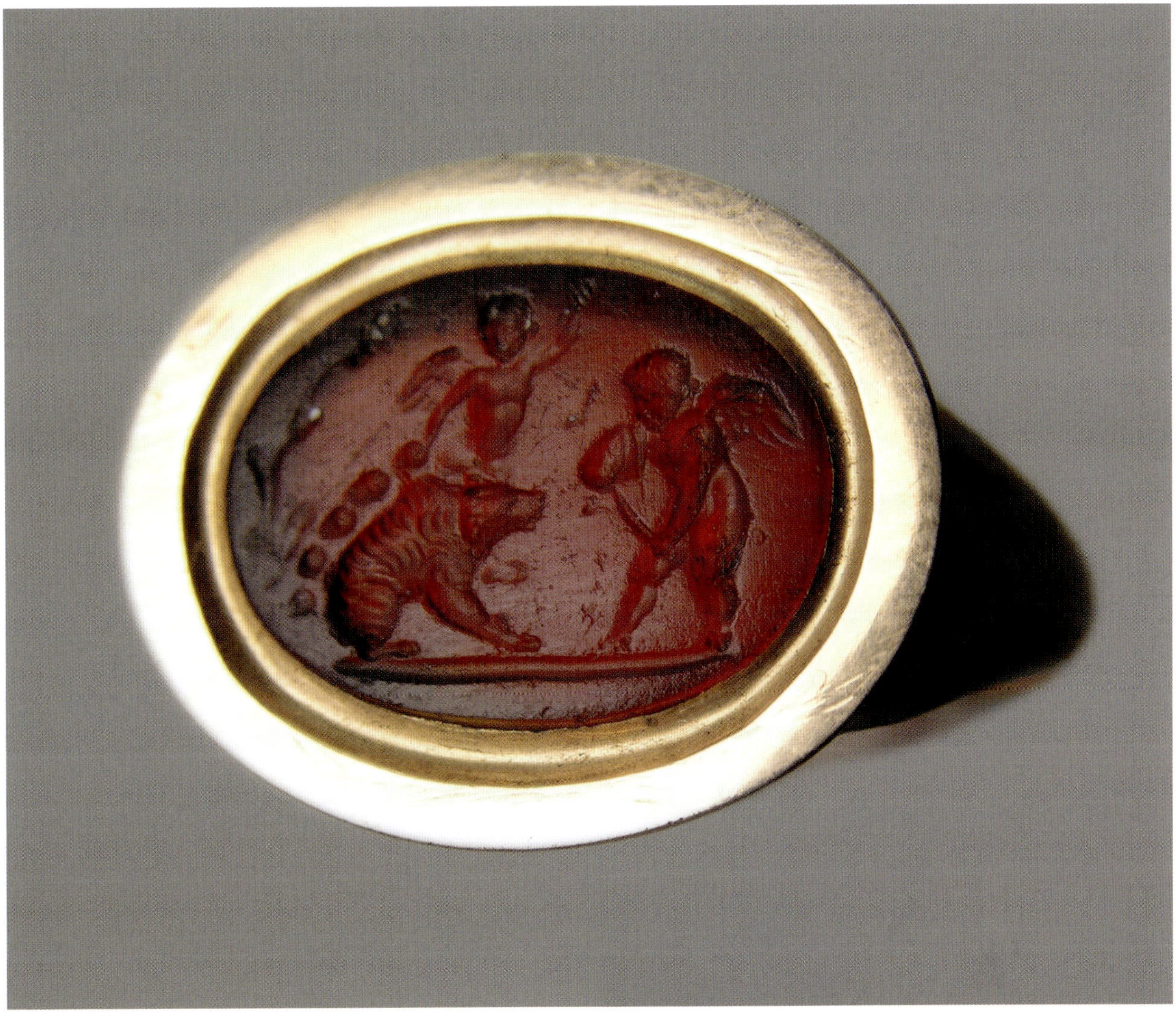

138

(10678) K140 (pl. 4)
Sard, polished flat back, set on a plain gold ring
12 x 9

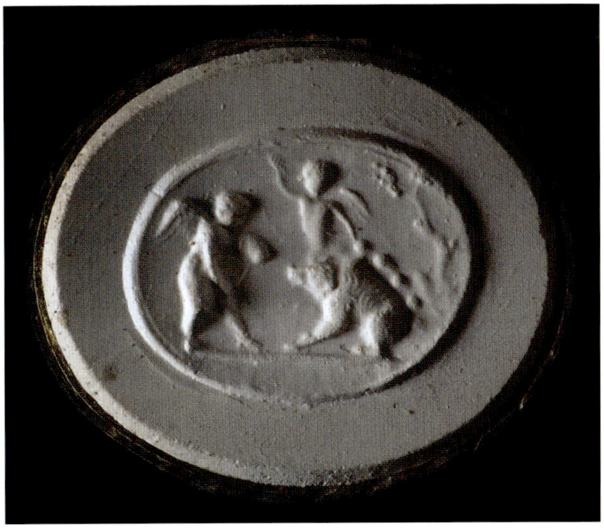

SG.Imp. 93; Inst.Imp. no. 70.

Two Cupids tease a bear. One holds a knife and has a cloak wrapped around one arm, the other holds a spear (?). The bear emerges from a cave shown by a row of blobs, behind which is a vine with grapes. Ground line.

This is a popular ancient subject with various treatments of the Cupids' behaviour; see on *Marlborough* no. 619.

1st/2nd century AD.

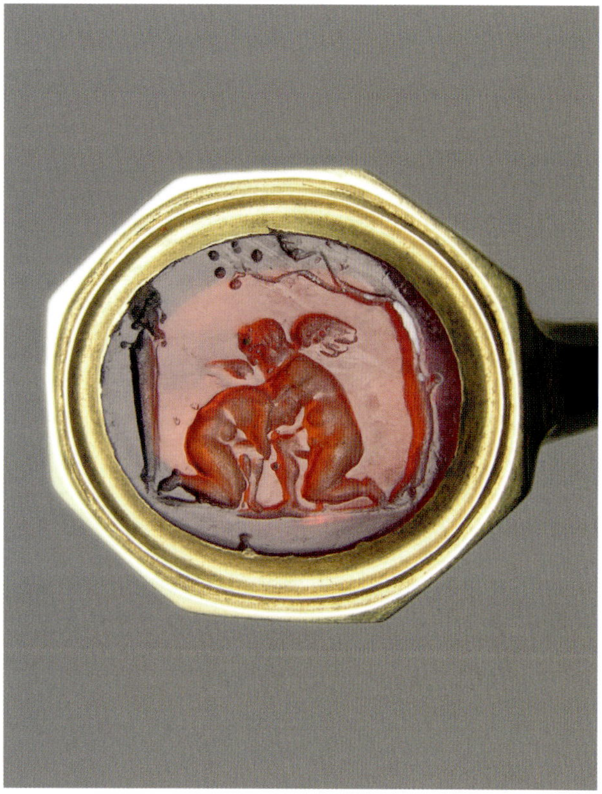

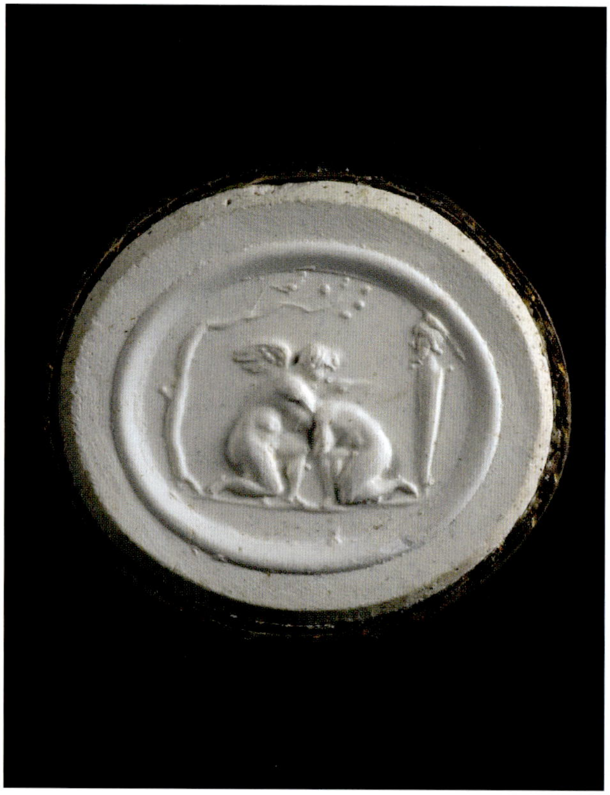

139

(10688) K150 (pl. 5)
Sard, polished flat back, set on a plain gold ring
12 x 9

SG.Imp. 10; Tassie 6947; Inst.Imp. no. 68.

Two Cupids wrestle under a tree and before a bearded herm.

For the subject, *LIMC* III, 985. Ground line.

1st century BC/AD.

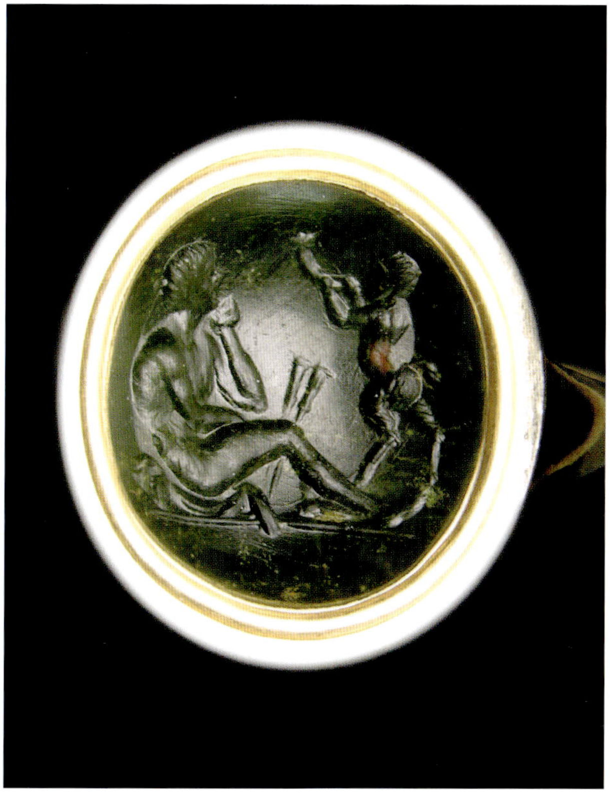

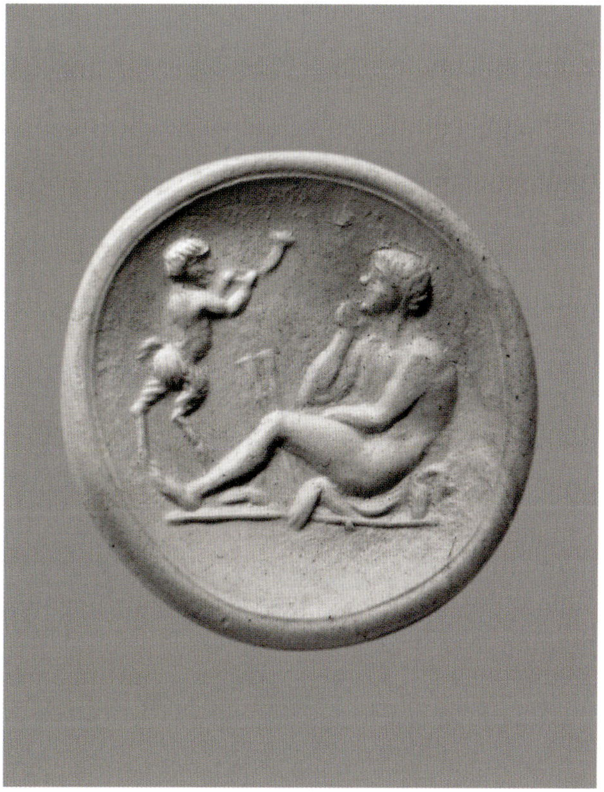

140

(10764)
Plasma, polished concave back, set on a plain gold ring
13 x 13

A young satyr seated on dress on the ground line, with a pair of pipes propped against his legs. Before him a small Pan blowing a horn.

1st century BC/AD?

141

('40915')
Carnelian fragment, polished flat back, set in a plain gold ring
7 x 7

A young boxer; behind him an elaborate lidded amphora (prize vase?) decorated with ribbons, and in relief on its body a bust (?) over tongues. Ground line, linked-dot border.

1st/2nd century AD.

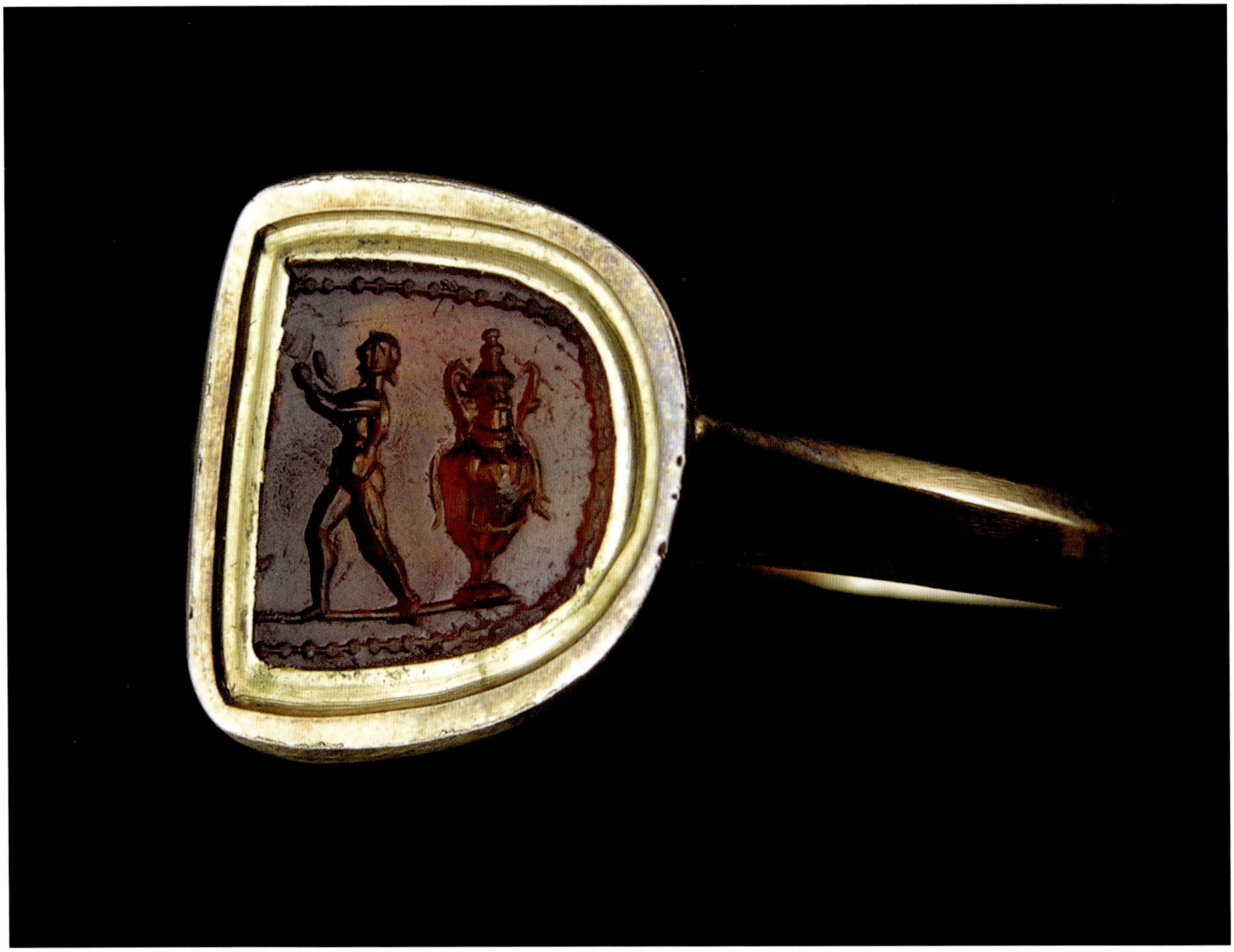

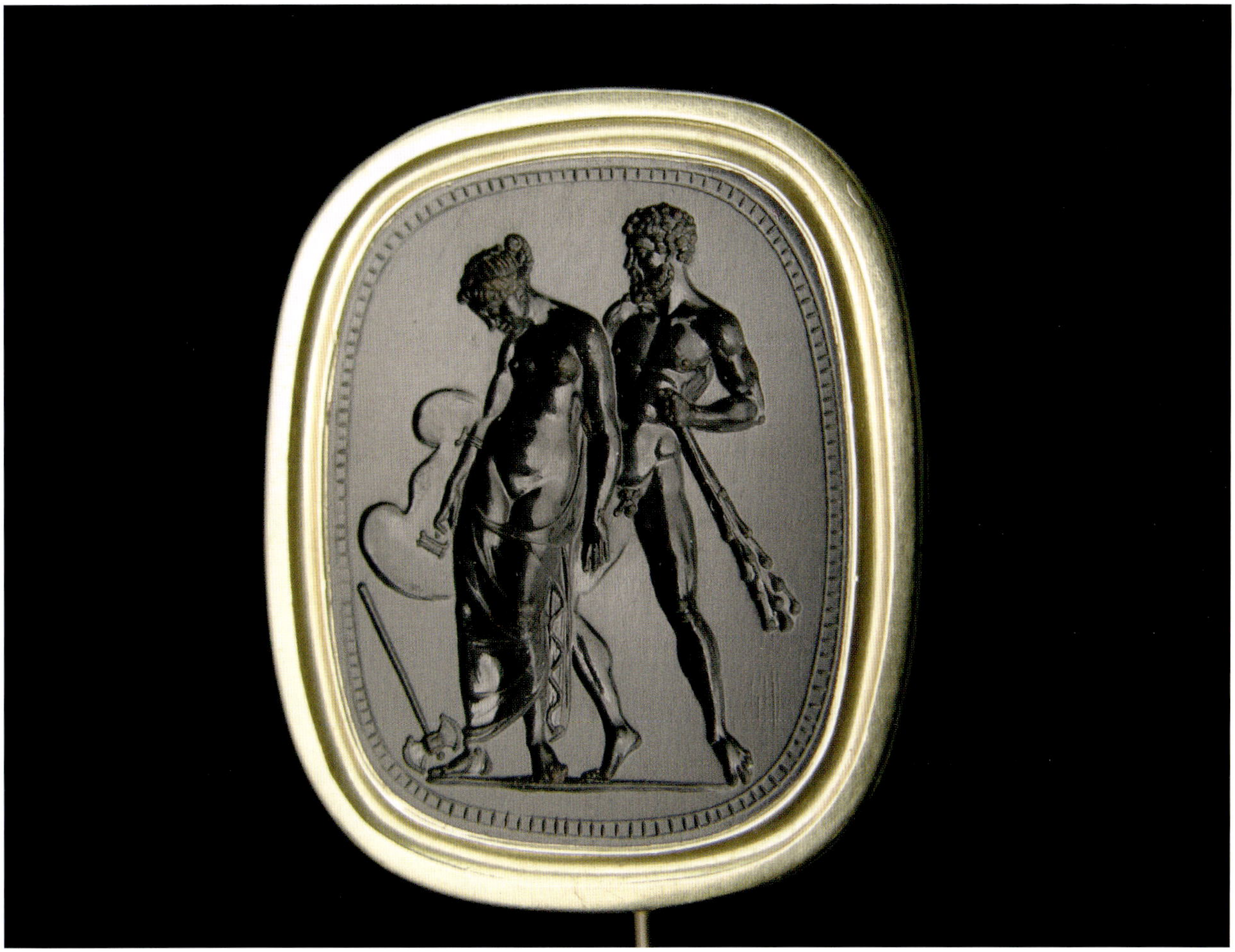

142

(10555) K17
Sard, polished convex back set on a gold pin
20 x 15

SG.Imp. 186.

Hercules and Hippolyta. The hero, holding his club, supports the collapsing figure of the Amazon queen, dress around her legs, holding her pelta shield, having dropped her battle axe. Hatched border. Ground line.

The queen is never so gently handled in ancient art and the group derives from depictions of Achilles supporting the dying Amazon Penthesilea. See on *Marlborough* no. 671 for the motif and copies.

Knight writes: 'It was purchased out of the Barberini Collection at Rome by a Mr. Paul Binfield for £300, who presented it to the then Duke of Northumberland. Sixty years later, Sir William (then Mr.) Hamilton, the famous connoisseur and collector, showed the work to Pistrucci, who recollected its history and valued it at a very high figure.' In the manuscript note (at Alnwick) on which this is based, the Amazon is called Melanippe, Hippolyta's sister. The Hamilton referred to was not Sir William (d. 1803) but W.R. Hamilton (1777–1859), ex-secretary of Lord Elgin and friend of Pistrucci, and of Mr Heber Percy who had inherited the Beverley gems. Pistrucci did not value it at more than £150 and said it would be difficult to find a buyer. The stone was copied by Marchant and by Burch; a copy by Harris is our **104**, and see *Hanover* no. 1752; Tassie 5775–80; Paoletti II, VIII.347.

17th/18th century.

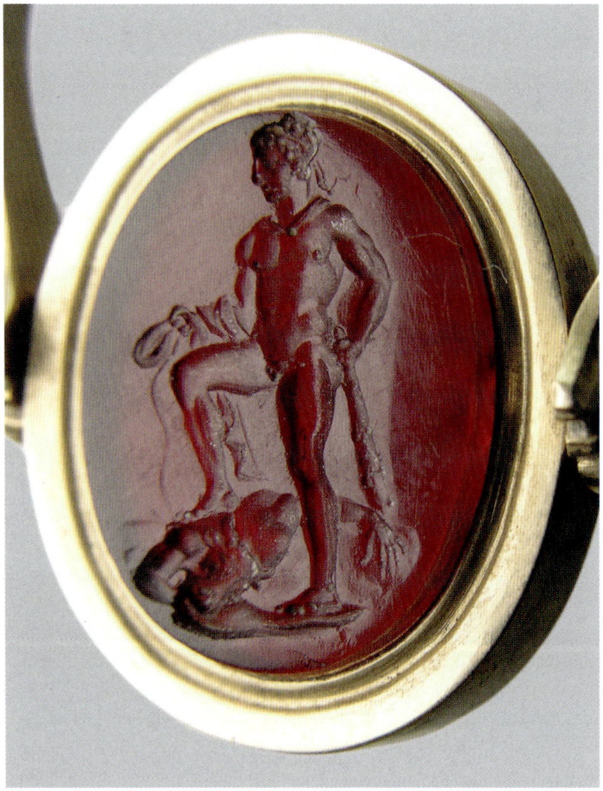

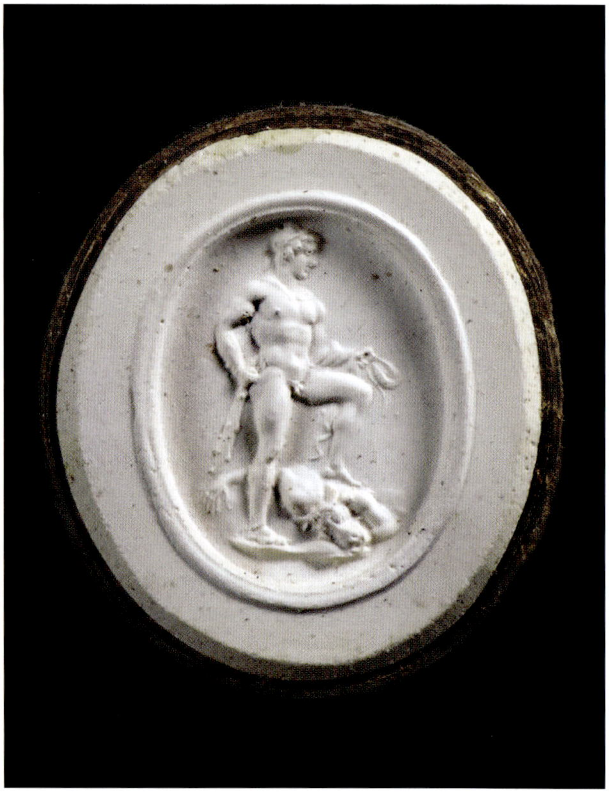

143

(10682) K144 (pl. 6)
Sard, polished flat back, set on a gold swivel ring
12 x 9

SG.Imp. 176; Inst.Imp. no. 151.

Theseus, ribboned and with a cloak, stands with one foot on the dead Minotaur. He also holds the thread by which he was able to find his way through the Labyrinth. Ground line.

18th century?

144

(10779)
Brown glass, unpolished flat back
25 x 15

Three fully armed warriors with spears (Trojans) storm forward against a warrior (Ulysses) wearing a pilos helmet and with shield and raised spear. Behind him is a kneeling figure of whom we see just the back, legs and shield; then the body of a warrior (Achilles) collapsing onto his shield with one hand to his pierced heel. A warrior stands over him to protect him and another leans away, one hand lowered apparently holding a cord to drag the body away. Ground line and in the exergue a zigzag pattern with alternately hatched triangles.

The device is taken as ancient by Furtwängler (*AG* 112, pl. 23.4) and to represent the death of Achilles, and the dress of the foremost Greek perhaps better suits Ulysses (pilos and no armour). The original gem (a sardonyx), formerly in the Boncompagni and Boncompagni Ludovisi collections, is now in Boston, Museum of Fine Arts, coll. Warren, inv. 10.174. J.J. Winckelmann published the gem in an engraving (*Monumenti antichi inediti* (Rome 1767) 170–1, no. 128) and interpreted the scene as the fight over the body of Patroklos. For a comprehensive list of impressions see Paoletti II, VII.97. As in Cades 29, III E, 115, the impressions of the Piombino gem show the damage on the side, repaired in the gold mount. It was much copied in the 18th and 19th centuries, twice by Giovanni Calandrelli: Cades 74, 969 (attributed by Cades) and Paoletti II, VII.97 (signed). Other copies are known (e.g. Paoletti I, II.43, *Hanover* no. 1756; Weber 1995, no. 251). This glass impression is probably taken from the attributed Calandrelli copy rather than the Boston original. Furtwängler most likely confused the Calandrelli copy with the original when he believed it to be 'ex-Poniatowski collection'.

Late 18th/early 19th century.

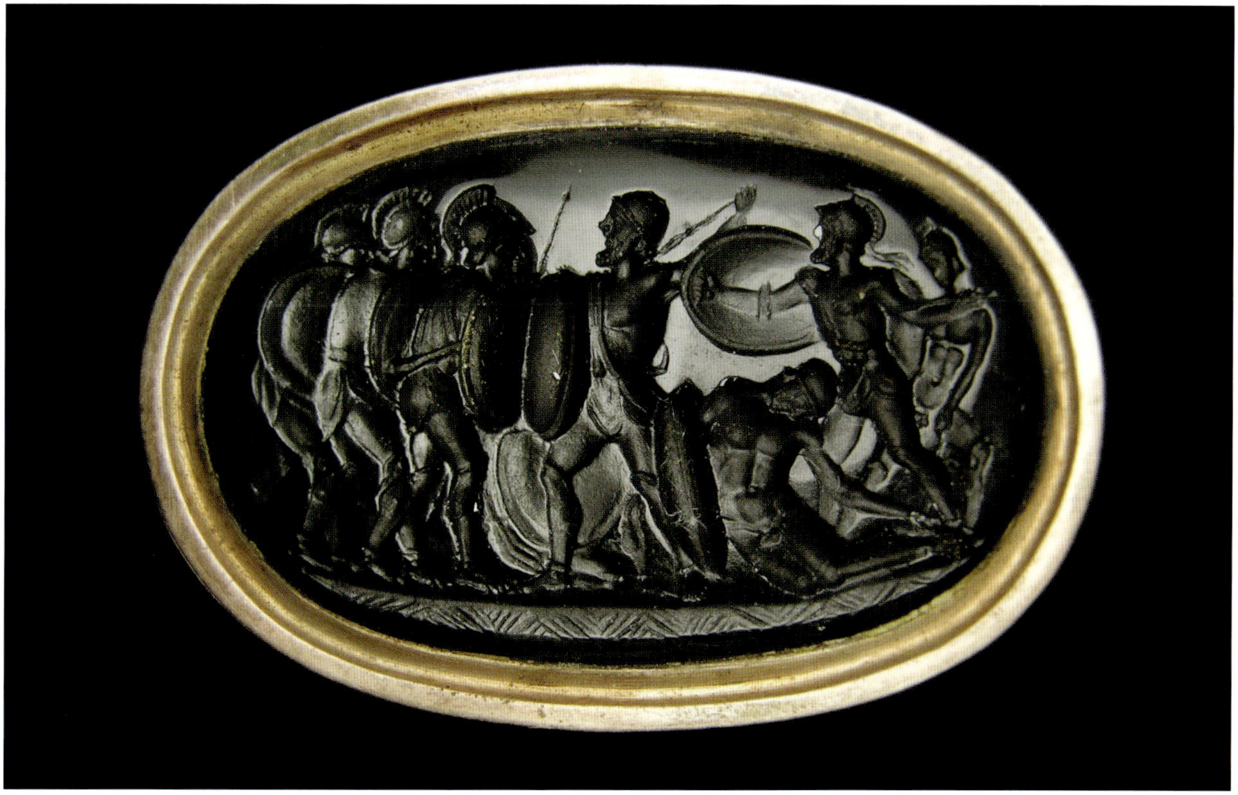

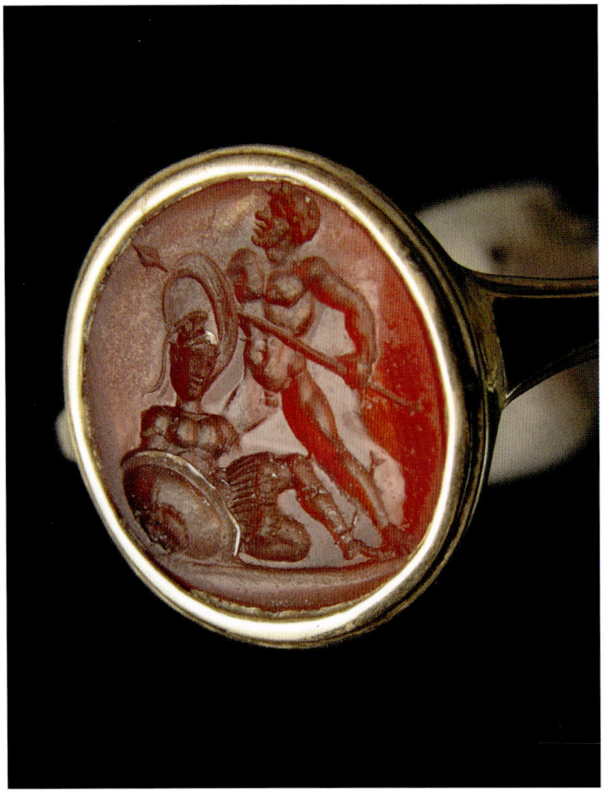

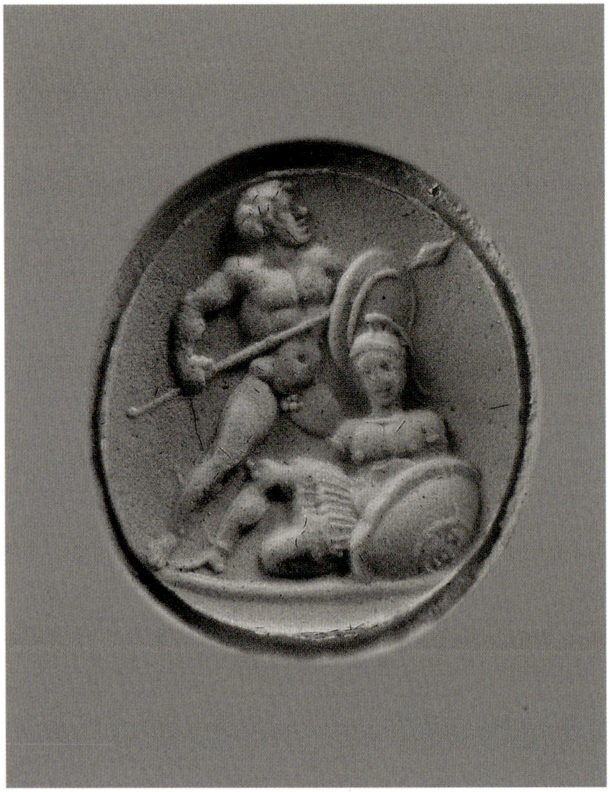

145

(10713) K175 (pl. 5)
Sard, polished convex back, set on a plain gold ring
11 x 9

Inst.Imp. no. 132.

Ajax protecting the fallen Achilles. A naked warrior with spear and shield stands over another warrior falling onto his shield (shield device: gorgoneion), fully armed with helmet, corselet and an arrow in his ankle. Ground line.

18th century.

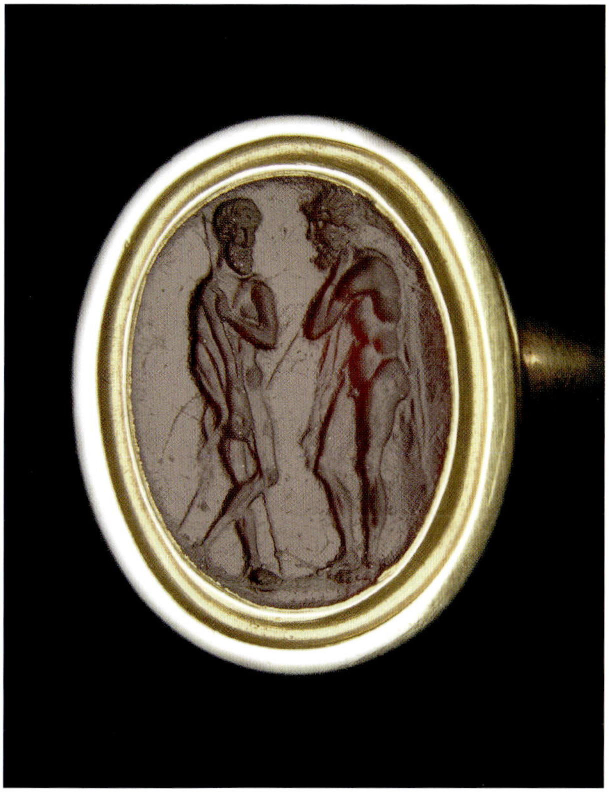

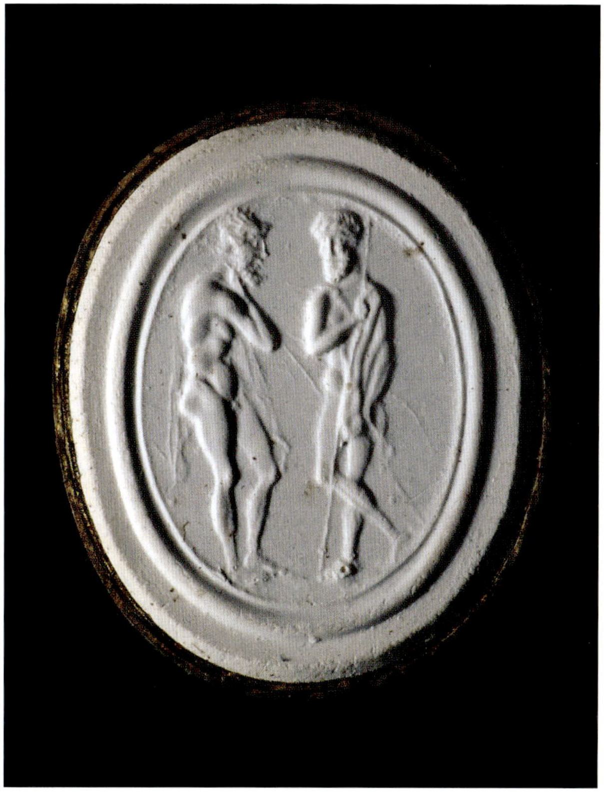

146

(10616) K78 (pl. 3)

Sard, polished flat back, set on a plain gold ring

13 x 11

SG.Imp. 132; Inst.Imp. no. 112; Paoletti I, II.33.

Two old men, both with cloaks and spears and wreathed (?), converse. 'Menelaus and Agamemnon.' Ground line.

18th century?

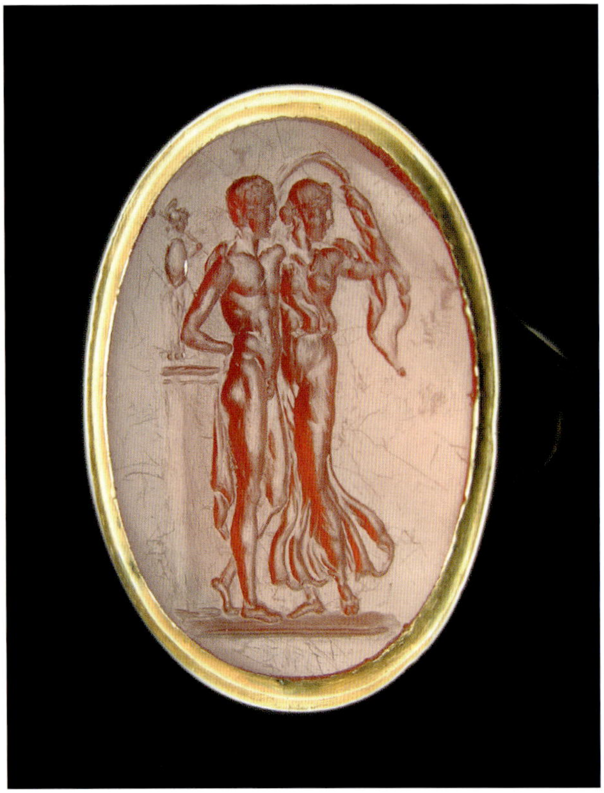

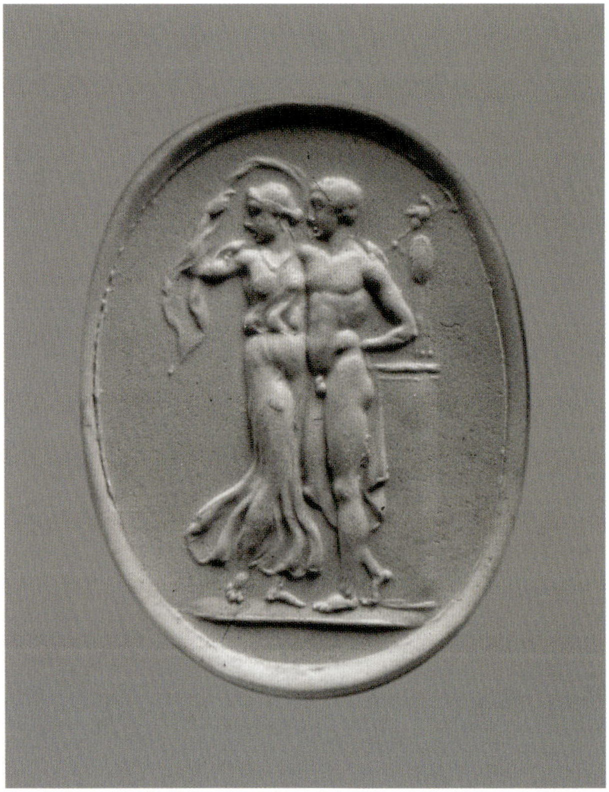

147

(10754)
Carnelian, polished flat back, set on a plain gold ring
22 x 15

A youth naked but for dress held behind his back, against a pillar bearing a statue of the armed Minerva, has his arm around a woman, dressed, with one hand holding a veil over her head.

The figures are possibly the Aurora and Cephalus also copied by Wedgwood (Catalogue 1787, no. 253).

18th century.

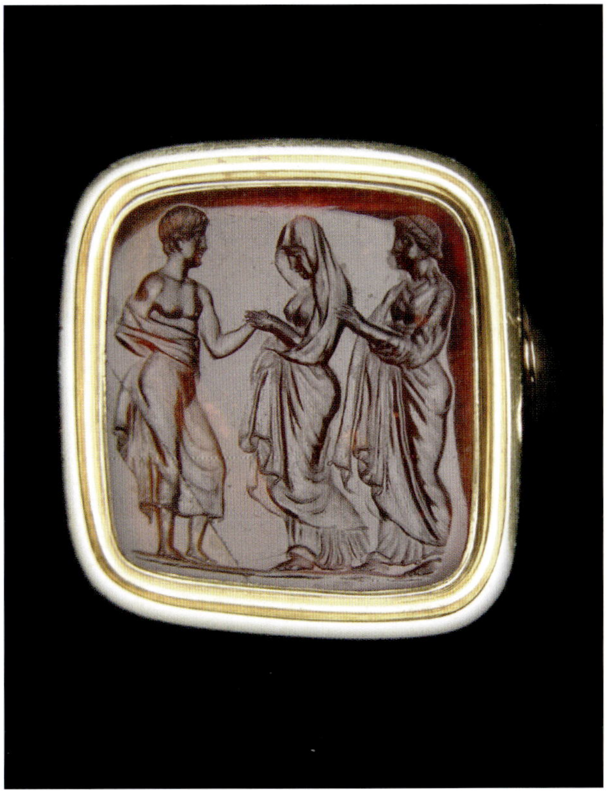

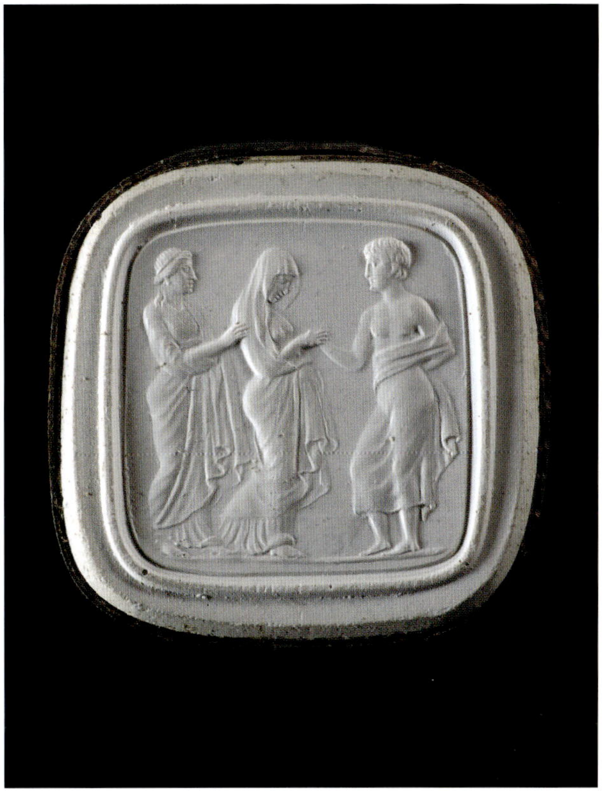

148

(10601) K63 (pl. 3)
Orange sard, polished flat back, set on a plain gold ring
16 x 16

SG.Imp. 68; Lippert IIIB, 394; Tassie 7231; Inst.Imp. no. 154; Paoletti II, VIII.417; *AGE* no. 243.

A woman presents a veiled bride to her husband. All dressed. Ground line.

The scene derives from a Roman terracotta relief said to show the marriage of Peleus and Thetis, also copied by Luigi Baccani: Santarelli 1981, no. 314.

18th century.

SINGLE FIGURES

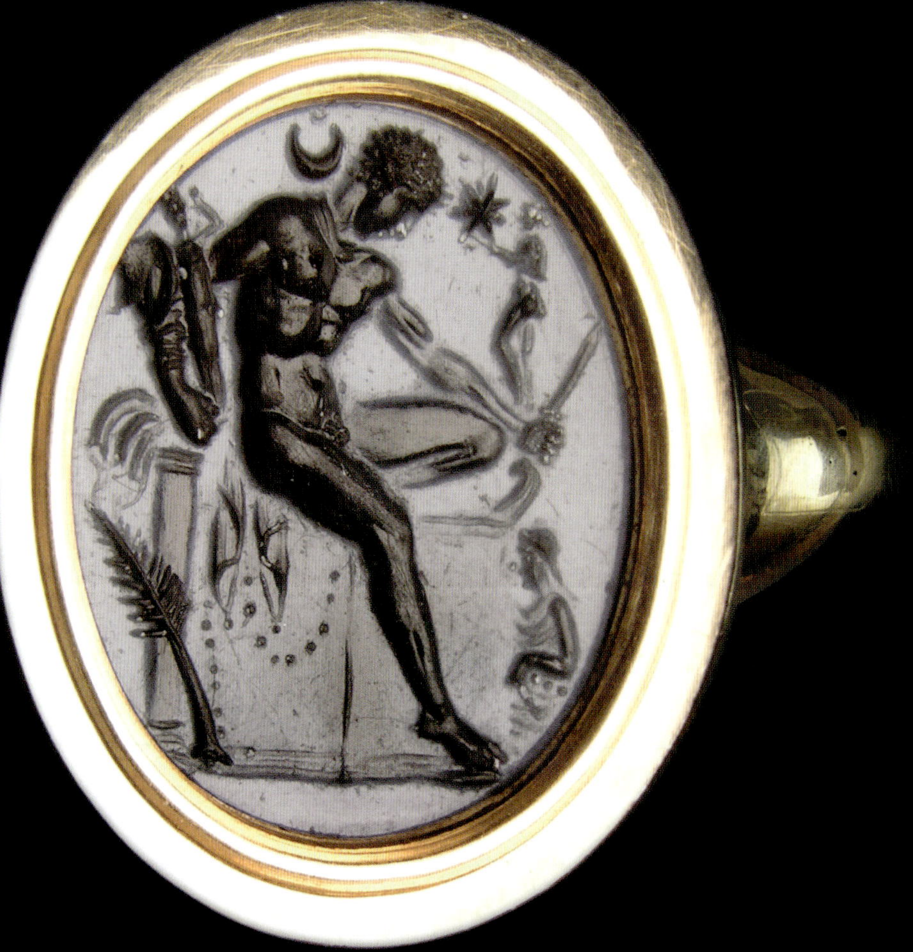

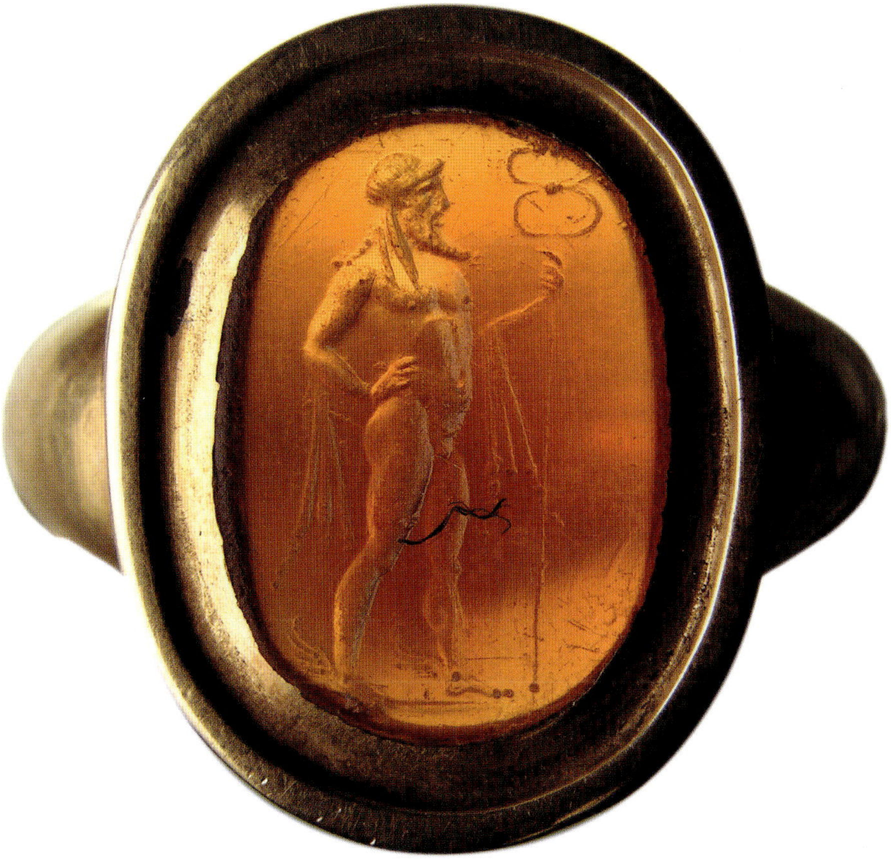

149

(10675) K137 (pl. 4)
Sard, polished convex back, set on a plain gold ring
12 x 8

SG.Imp. 60; Tassie 2397, pl. 30; Paoletti I, I.256; Inst.Imp. no. 133; King 1872, pl. 21.3; King 1885, pl. 52.3; *AG* pl. 39.12.

Hermes/Mercury, cloak over his shoulder, holding a long caduceus, with winged sandals, steps forward. Ground line.

The stance is typically archaising, neo-Attic; as Lippold, pl. 5.1; Wagner-Boardman, no. 68.

1st century BC.

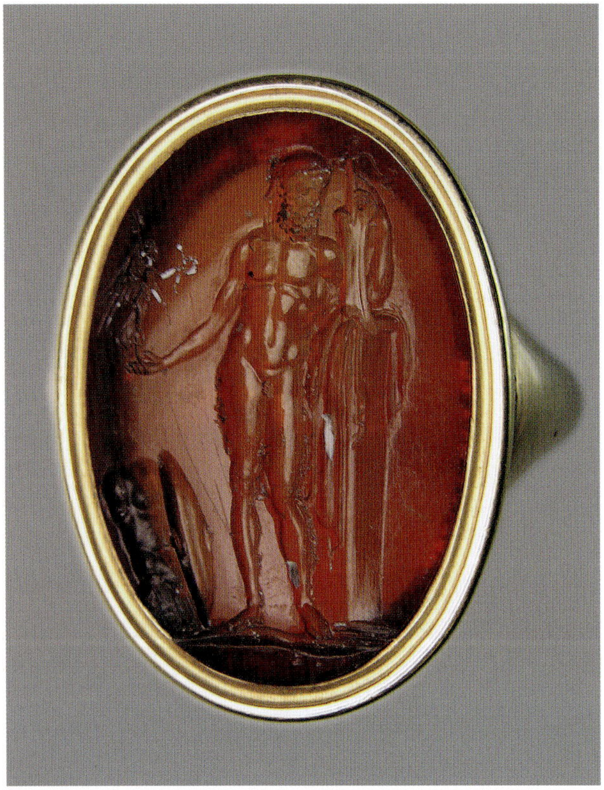

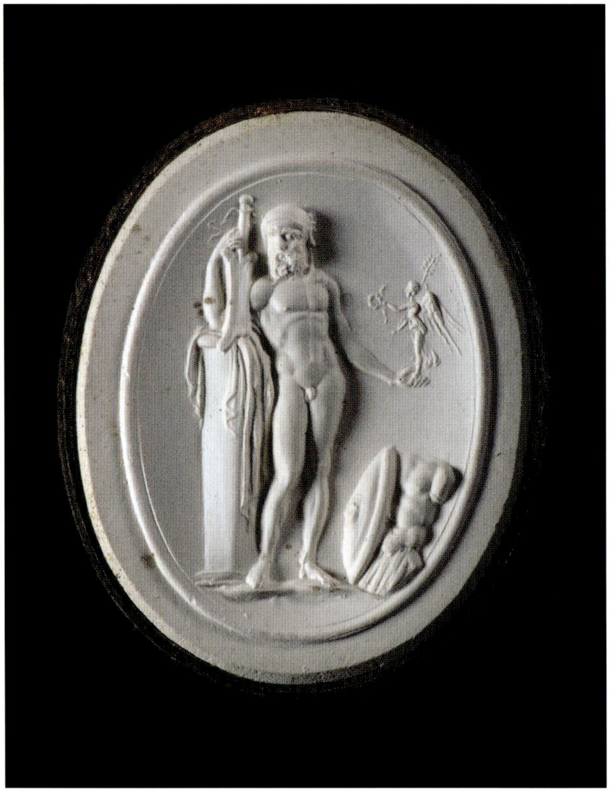

150

(10705) K167 (pl.5)
Sard, polished flat back, set on a plain gold ring
25 x 18

SG.Imp. 116; Tassie 15453; Inst.Imp. no. 167; King 1872, pl. 26.2; King 1885, pl. 53.1.

A bearded man, naked, wearing a helmet, stands holding a rudder on a pillar, which is draped. On his other hand is a Nike/Victory with a wreath and palm branch, and below are his shield and corselet. Ground line.

The implication is a naval victory.

1st century AD?

151

(10704) K166
Sard, break at the left border filled with gold, polished flat back, set on a plain gold ring
16 x 12

Inst.Imp. no. 134.

A Roman in full armour but bareheaded (a cross beside his head) holds an inverted spear and pours a libation over a burning altar from a phiale. One foot rests on a globe. Ground line, cut so as to run up into the altar base.

This is an emperor, possibly Caracalla; compare the cameo on which such a figure is lacking the globe, *Content* no. 60, and the central figure on groups such as that with Caracalla (Megow, pl. 49.1).

2nd/3rd century AD?

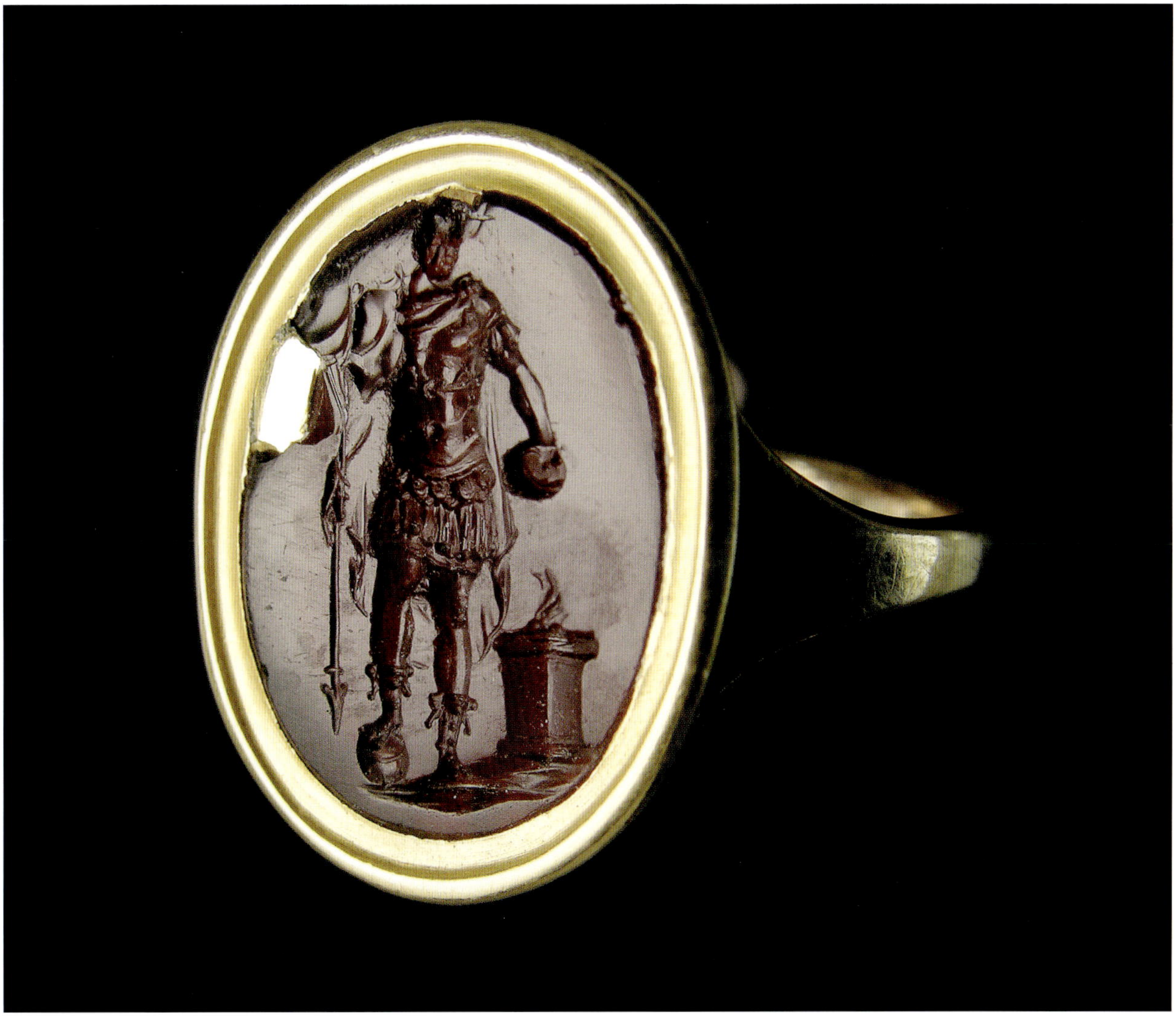

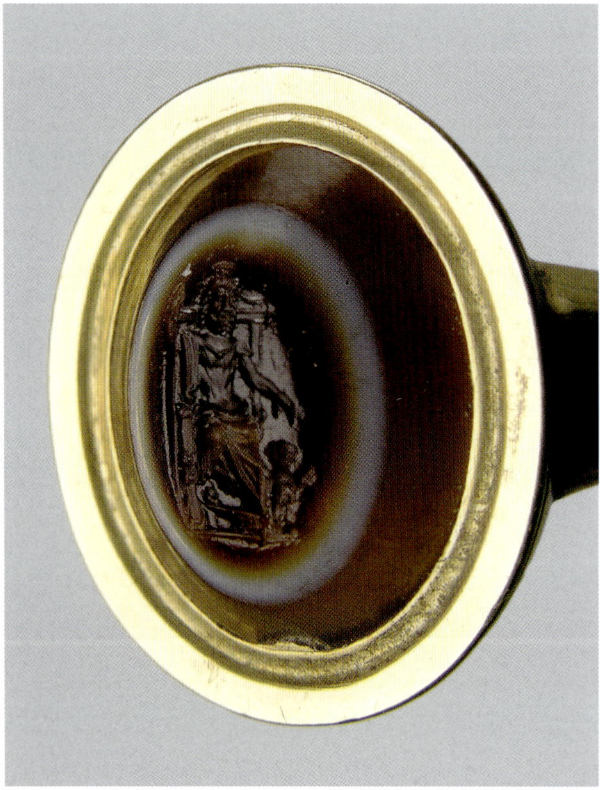

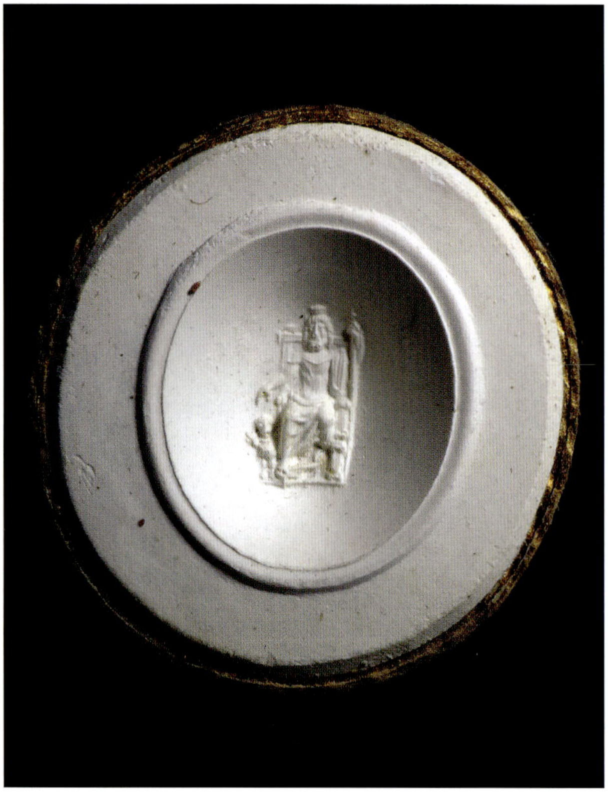

152

(10664) K126 (pl. 4)
Sardonyx with bevelled edge to the face, brown/white/brown, unpolished flat back, set on a plain gold ring
12 x 9

SG.Imp. 111; Inst.Imp. no. 119.

Jupiter Serapis enthroned, with sceptre, and with eagle or Cerberus seated on the ground beside him.

Compare R. Veymiers, *Ἵλεως τῷ φοροῦντι. Sérapis sur les gemmes et les bijoux antiques* (Brussels, 2009), type II.AA1–26; in particular *Marlborough* no. 595 and *Würzburg* no. 324.

1st–2nd century AD.

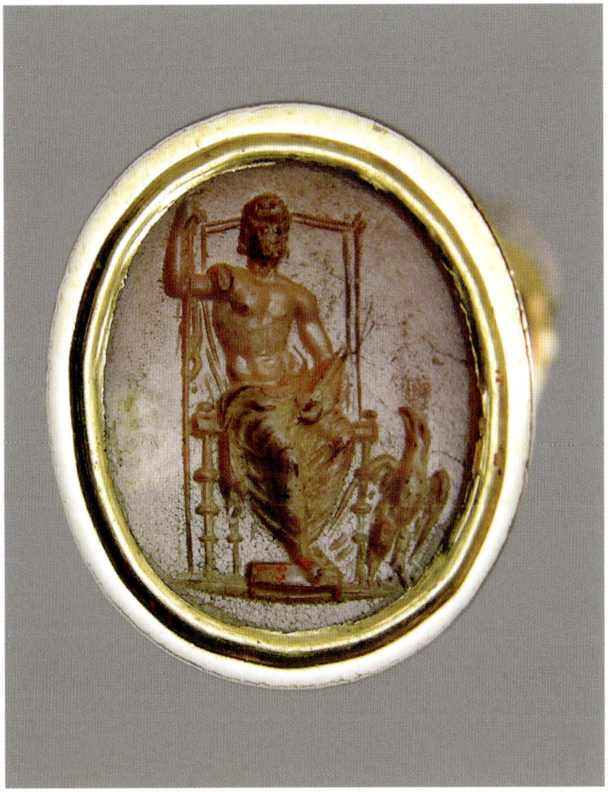

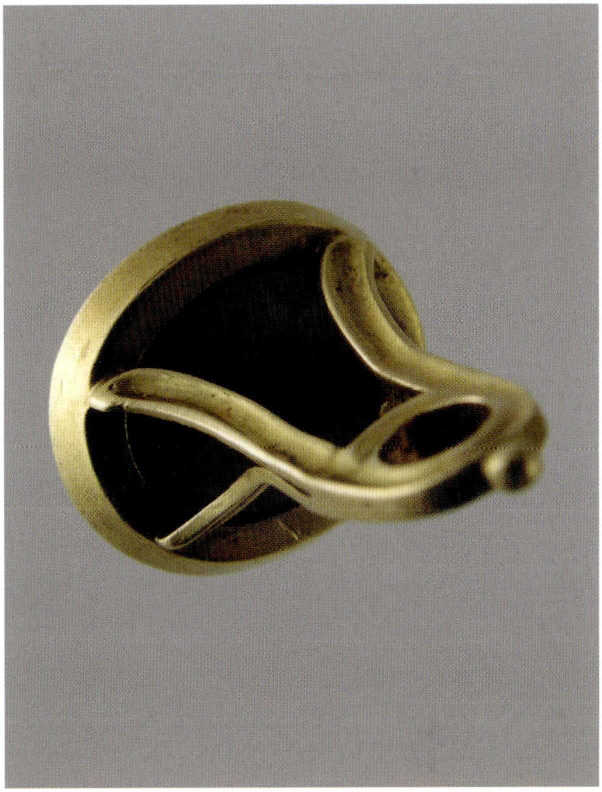

153

(10750)
Pale red jasper, burned, unpolished flat back, set in a gold stamp
17 x 10

Jupiter with naked torso seated frontally on a high-backed throne with footstool. He holds a ribboned sceptre and his thunderbolt; at his feet his eagle.

1st/2nd century AD?

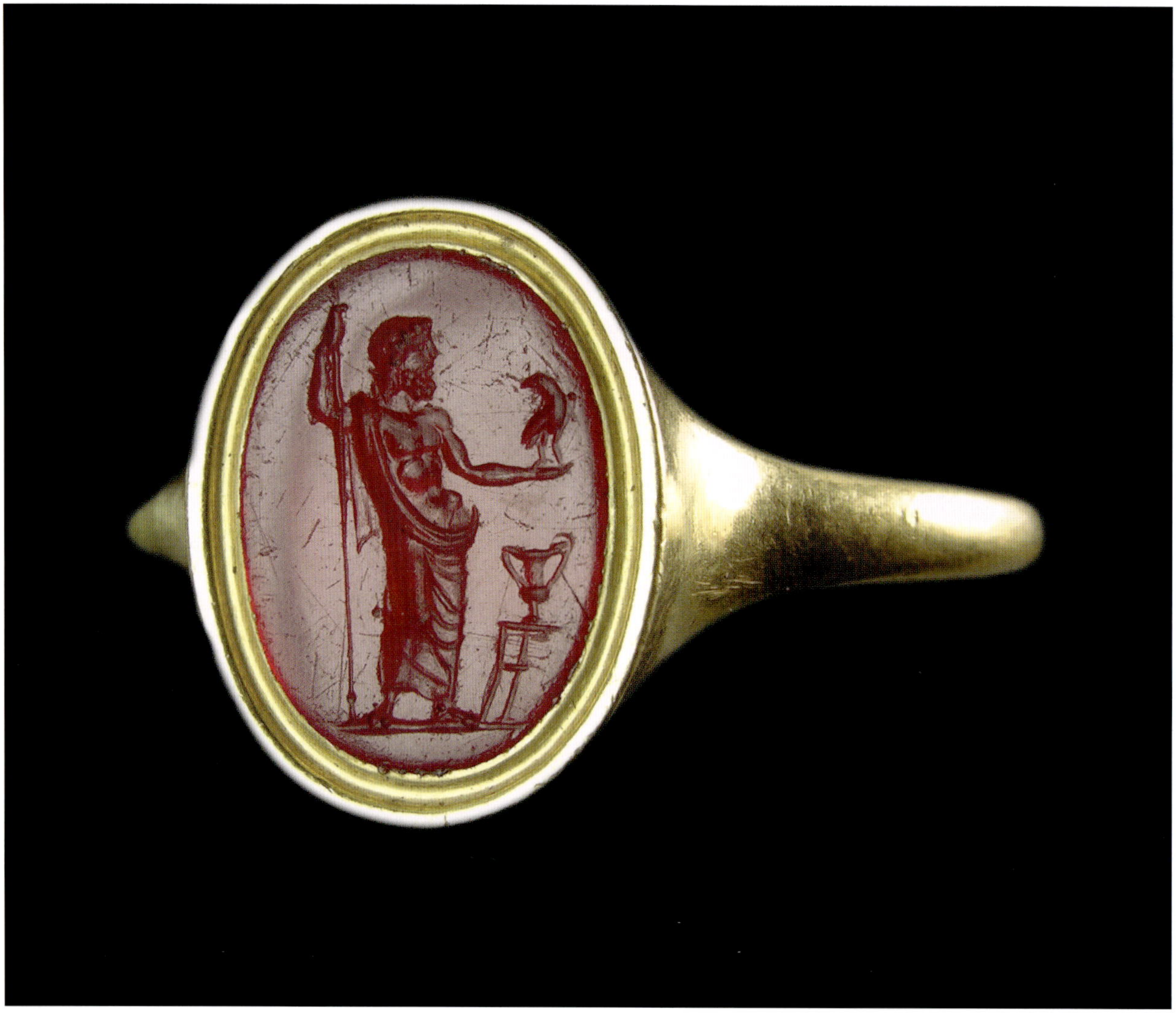

154

(10551) K13 (pl. 3)
Sard, polished flat back, set on a plain gold ring
13 x 9

SG.Imp. 11.

Jupiter standing, dressed, holding a sceptre and an eagle, before him a table with a kantharos upon it. Ground line.

1st century AD?

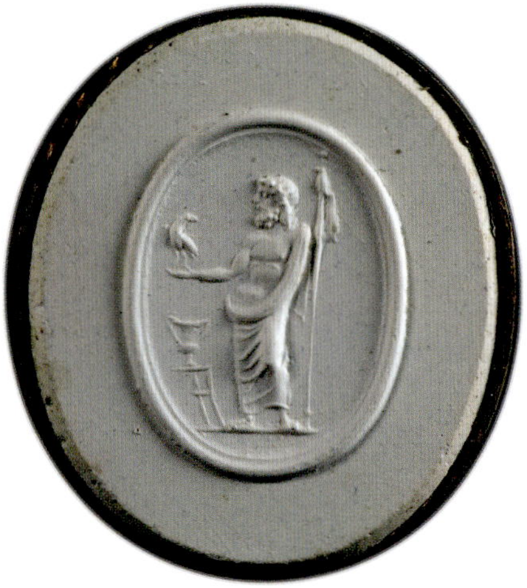

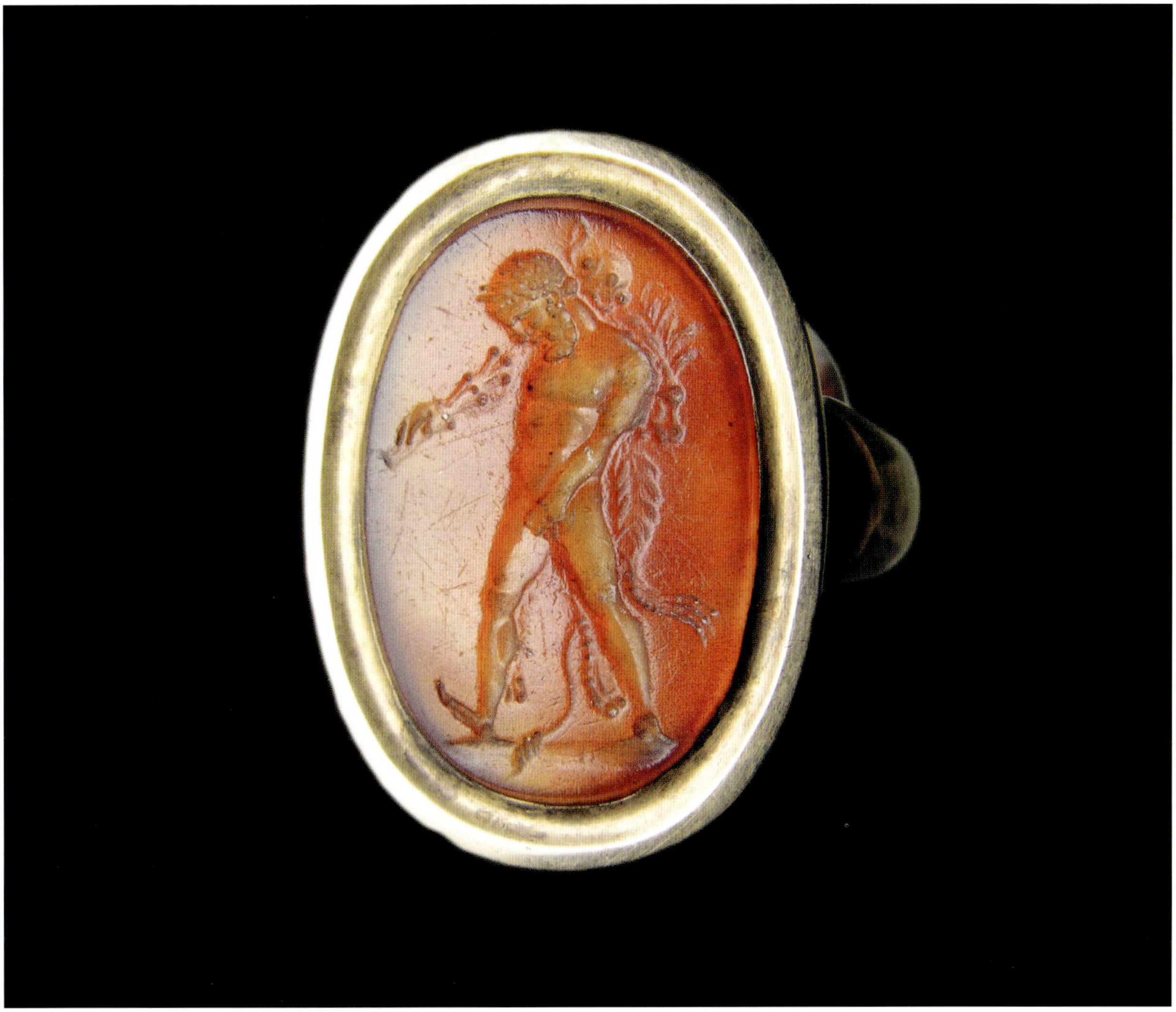

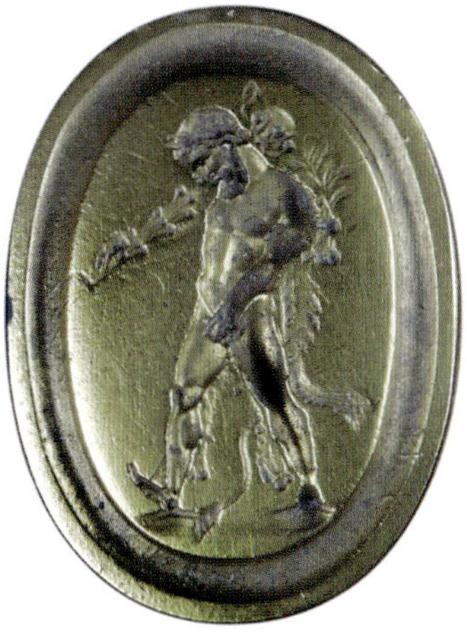

155

(10671) K133 (pl. 6)
Sard, unpolished flat back, set on a plain gold ring
18 x 13

SG.Imp. 108; Tassie 5931; Inst.Imp. no. 157; Paoletti I, IV.12.

Hercules, wreathed and shouldering his club, with his lionskin over one shoulder, steps forward, peeing. Ground line.

This reflects on the results of his bucolic behaviour, often illustrated in this way on gems. See *LIMC* IV, 771.

1st century BC/AD.

156

(10782)
Carnelian, polished convex back
17 x 12

Tassie 8819; SG.Imp. 134; Inst.Imp. no. 152.

Meleager, naked but for a cloak at one shoulder, holding two spears, before a rock altar with a small dressed figure atop on a base, holding two torches. On the rock a boar's head, a stalk of corn, a frontal stag's skull with horns and three rosettes; beside it, Meleager's two dogs. Wavy ground line.

The subject is as *Wien* I, no. 494; *London,* Dalton no. 809 (late copy). Attributed to Carlo 'Gobbo' Costanzi. Just possibly from the 1st Duchess' collection, no. 43.

17th/18th century.

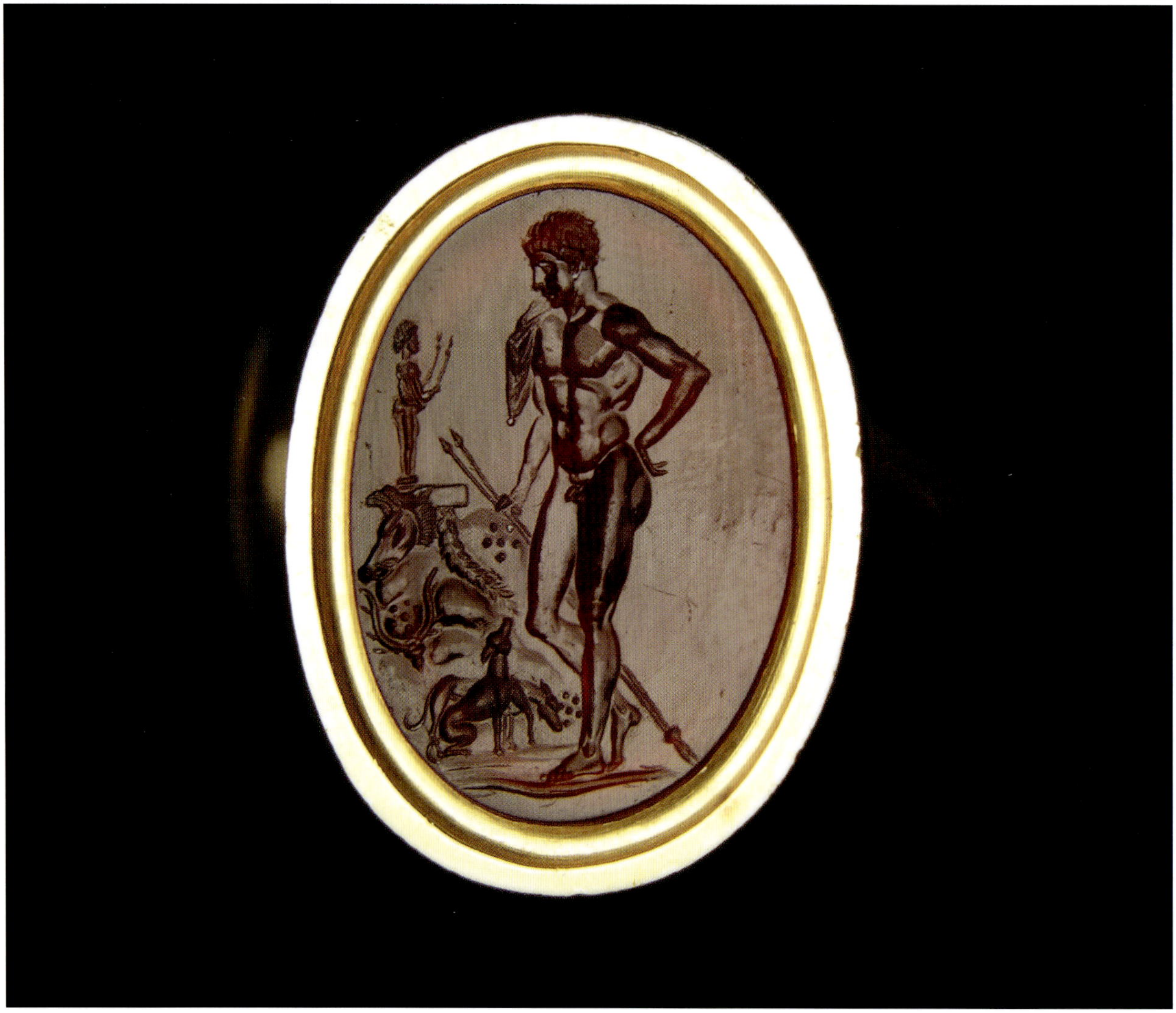

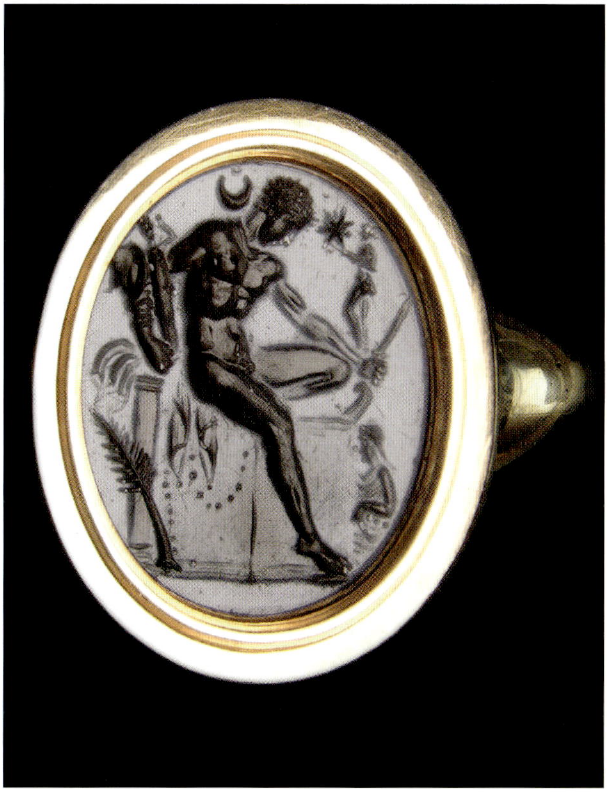

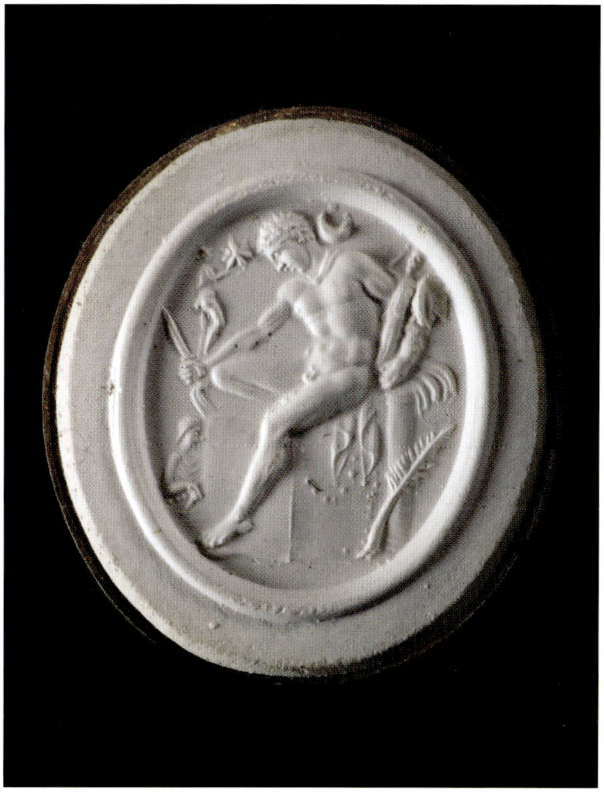

157

(10706) K168 (pl. 5)
Nicolo with a pale blue stratum above, polished flat back, set on a plain gold ring
17 x 14

Natter, *Mus.Brit.* F28-2 (as Robert Dingly collection); SG.Imp. 140; Tassie 9429 (Dingly, as onyx); Inst.Imp. no. 156; Cades E280; King 1872, pl. 44.7; King 1885, pl. 45.4 (as onyx); *AG* pl. 43.21; Vollenweider, pl. 47.5,6,8 (as by Solon); *Würzburg* no. 367; Moret, *Palladion* no. 223, pl. 44.

Diomedes stealing the *palladion* statue of Athena from Troy. The hero has a cloak at his back, holds a sword and the *palladion* on his forearm. He is leaping over a wreathed altar, beyond which, above, is the statue of a naked god (on a pillar), and below, the upper part of a dressed guard or attendant. Behind the altar, a pillar with a palm branch against it. In the field, a crescent and star. Ground line.

There is a very similar version in garnet in a private collection (Sangiorgi; Moret, *Palladion* no. 287, pl. 57). This is one of the finer representations of a popular scene – see Moret. It is variously described as in nicolo or onyx and a copy might be involved here, though the 'onyx' is not located.

1st century BC.

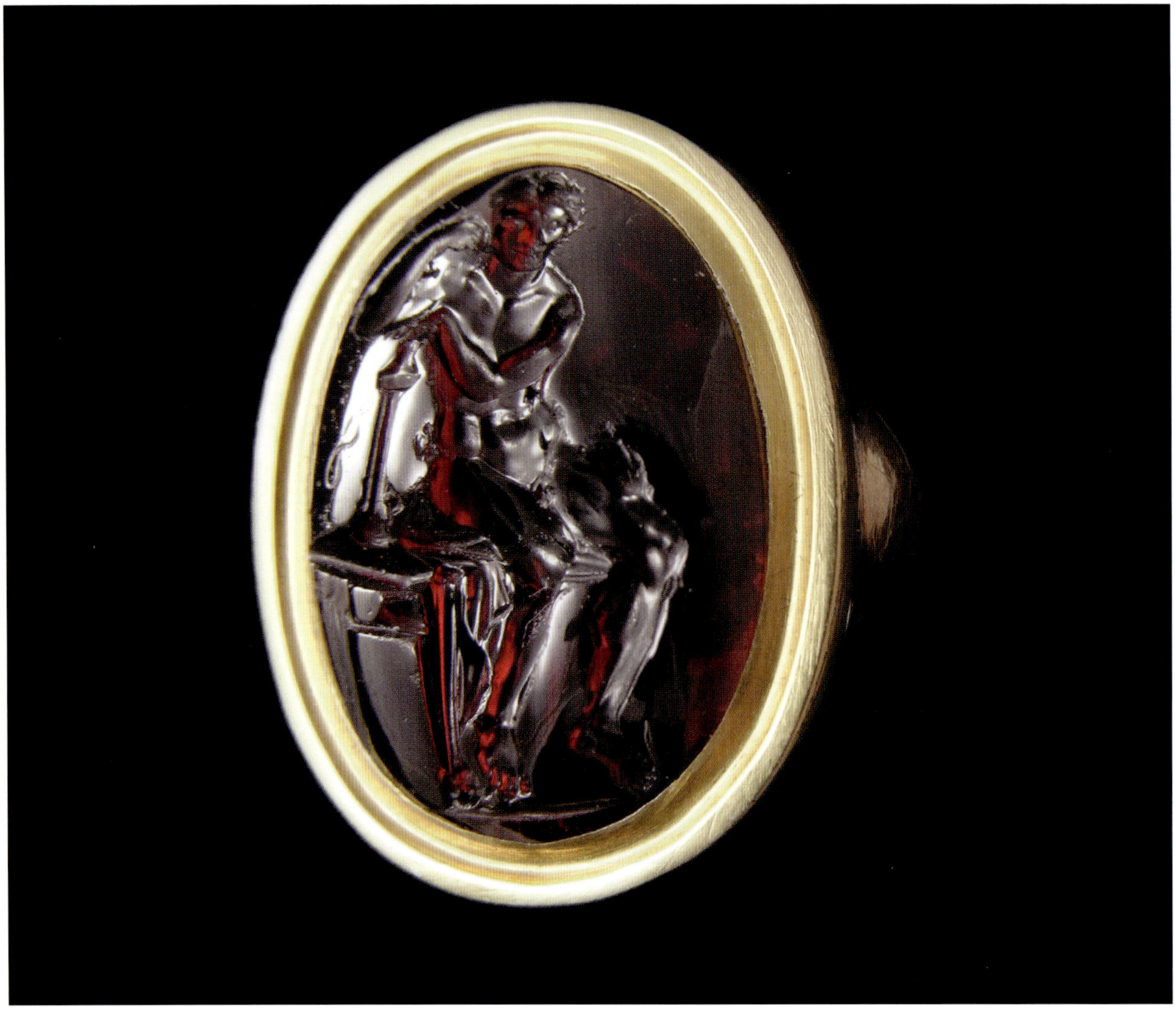

158

(10629) K91 (pl. 4)
Jacinth, polished concave back, set on a plain gold ring
19 x 13

Paoletti I, III.542; King 1872, pl. 43.3, 1885, pl. 68.2; *AG* pl. 43.18; M.-L. Vollenweider, *Die Porträtgemmen* (1972–4) 111–3, pl. 69.1–3.

A naked youth seated on dress on a four-legged table, resting one hand on a sheathed sword and with the other hand to his head, pensively. Ground line.

He is perhaps meant for Achilles mourning Patroclus, or sulking; compare *Würzburg* no. 366, *Munich* I, no. 551. Vollenweider surmises a reference to Pompey. Knight saw a Hermaphrodite here, for the 'androgynous' physique. Moret (*Palladion* 123) compares gems where the subject suggests an emperor as the hero.

Mid-1st century AD.

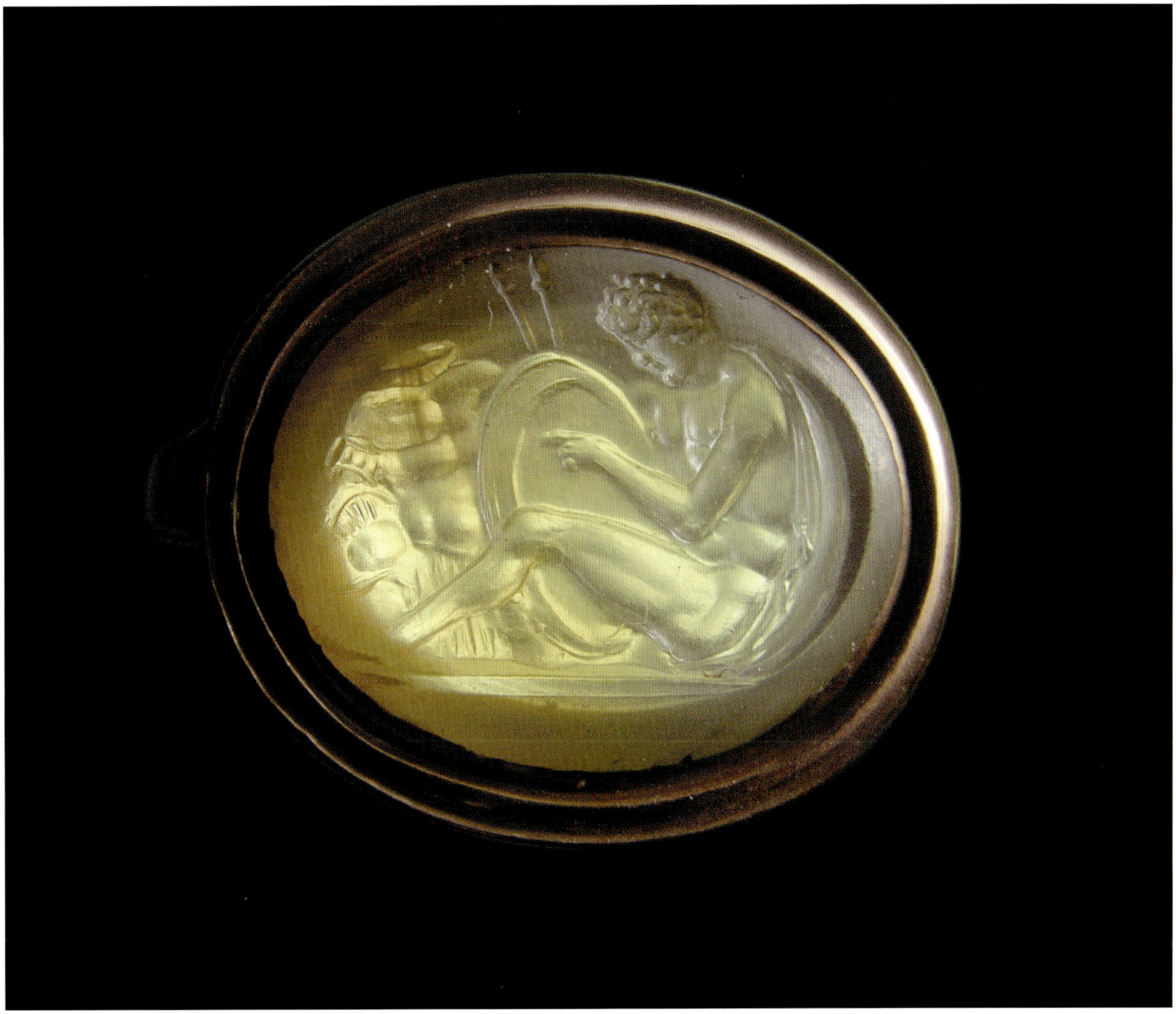

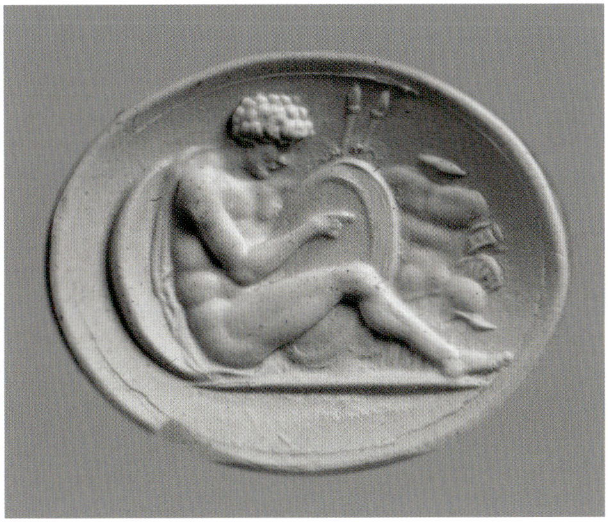

159

(10778)

Yellowish green chalcedony, polished convex back, set in a plain gold ring

15 x 11

Tassie 7510.

Othryades seated on the ground, cloak at his back, inscribing his shield; before him his corselet, scabbard, helmet and two spears. He rests against a shield (?). Ground line.

Compare *Würzburg* nos 115–9; *London*, Walters no. 1346.

2nd/1st century BC?

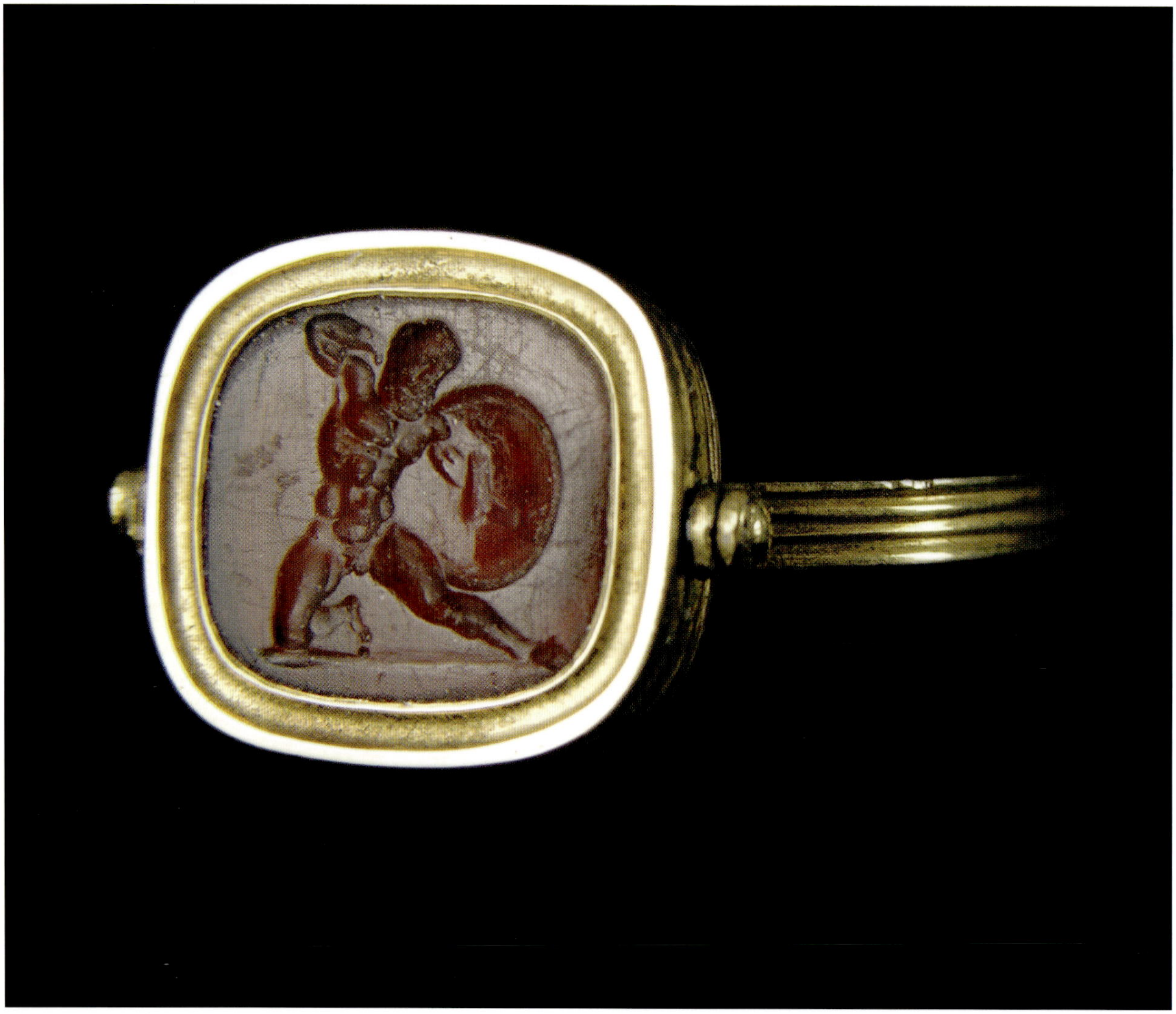

160

(10631) K93 (pl. 4)
Sard, polished flat back, set on a gold swivel ring
8 x 7

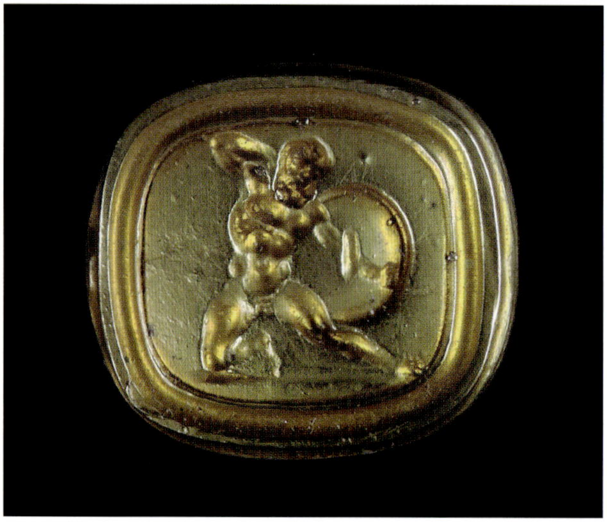

Capaneus struck in the back by Jupiter's thunderbolt. He is naked but for his shield. Ground line.

Cf. Paoletti II, V.514 ('Epaminondas').

1st century AD.

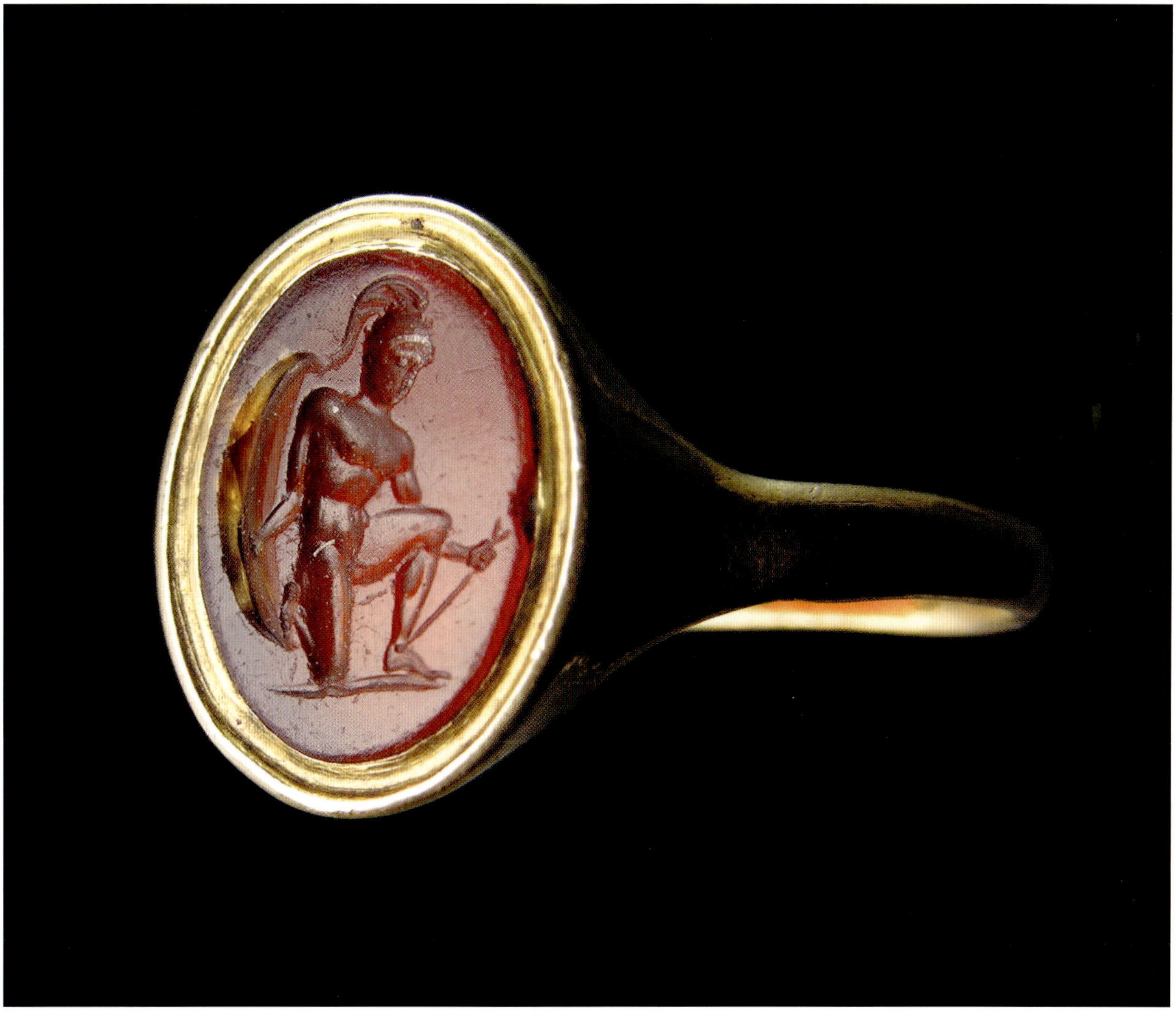

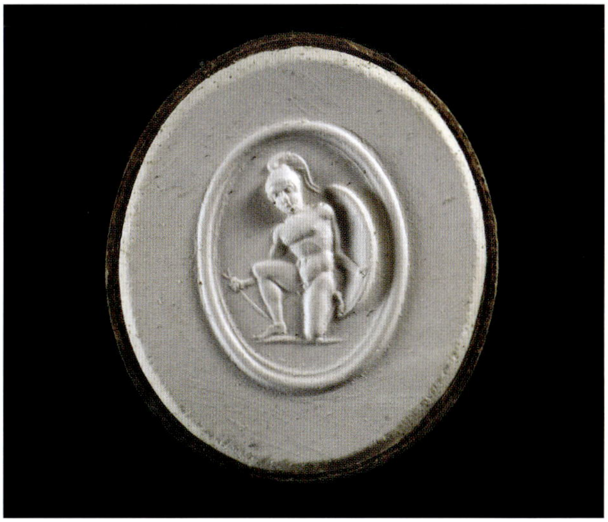

161

(10550) K12 (pl. 3)
Sard, unpolished flat back, set on a plain gold ring
10 x 7

SG.Imp. 177; Cades, Cent. I, 90.

A hero with helmet and shield kneels to extract an arrow from his ankle. Ground line.

This is a subject for Etruscan gems, but not with the hero in this pose (*LIMC* VIII, pl. 110, Tydeus 3, 4).

2nd/1st century BC.

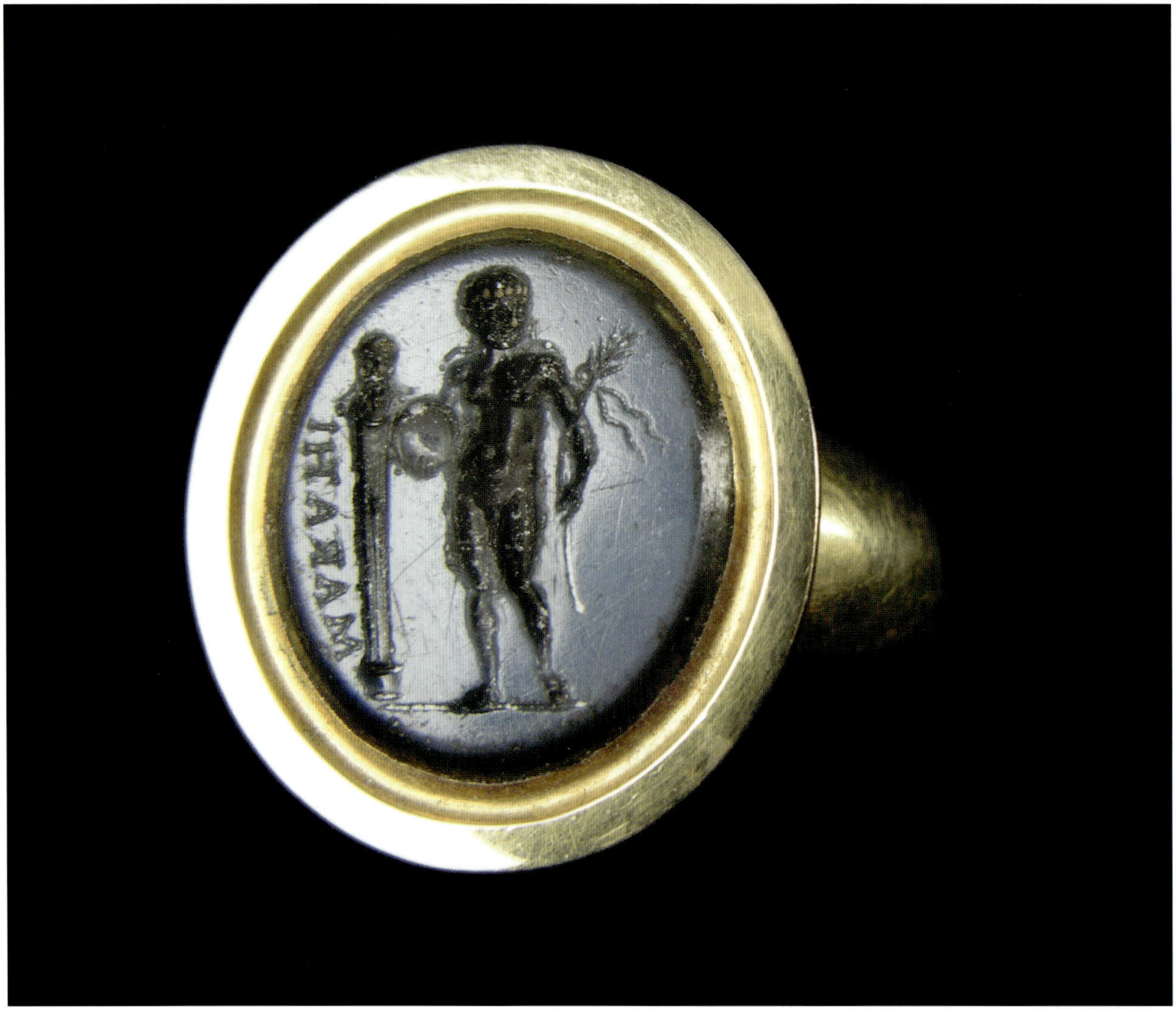

162

(10624) K86 (pl. 3)
Nicolo, unpolished flat back, set on a plain gold ring
13 x 10

SG.Imp. 118; Cades, Cent. IV, 72; *AG* pl.44.22.

A naked athlete holding a victor's palm and discus, beside a bearded herm (mask?). Inscribed MARATHI.

He is possibly meant for the hero founder of Marathon.

1st century BC.

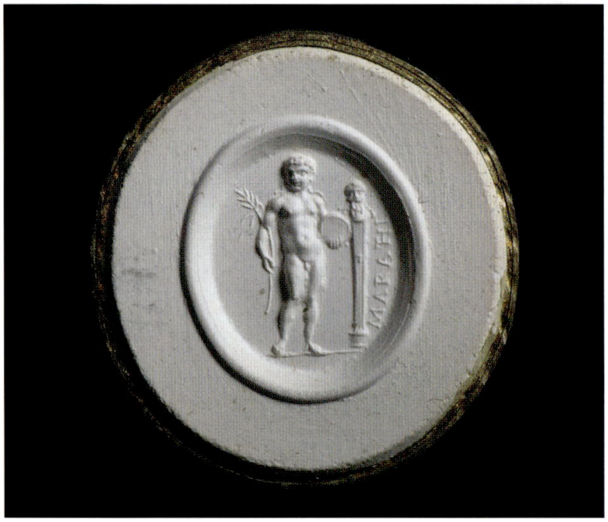

163

(10623) K85 (pl. 3)
Sard, polished flat back, set on a plain gold ring
10 x 8

A naked man rides a galloping horse over a palm branch, signifying victory.

1st century BC/AD?

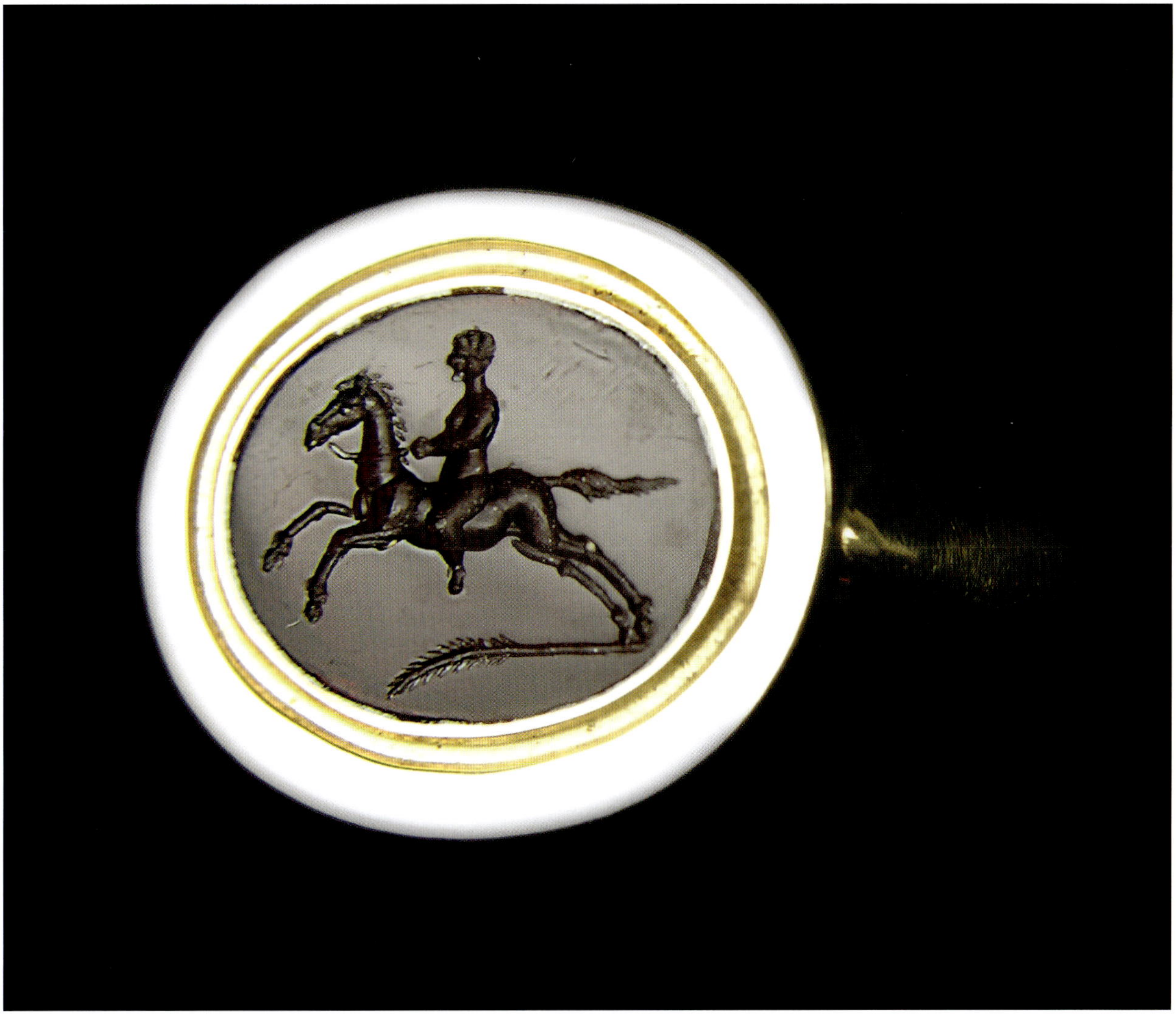

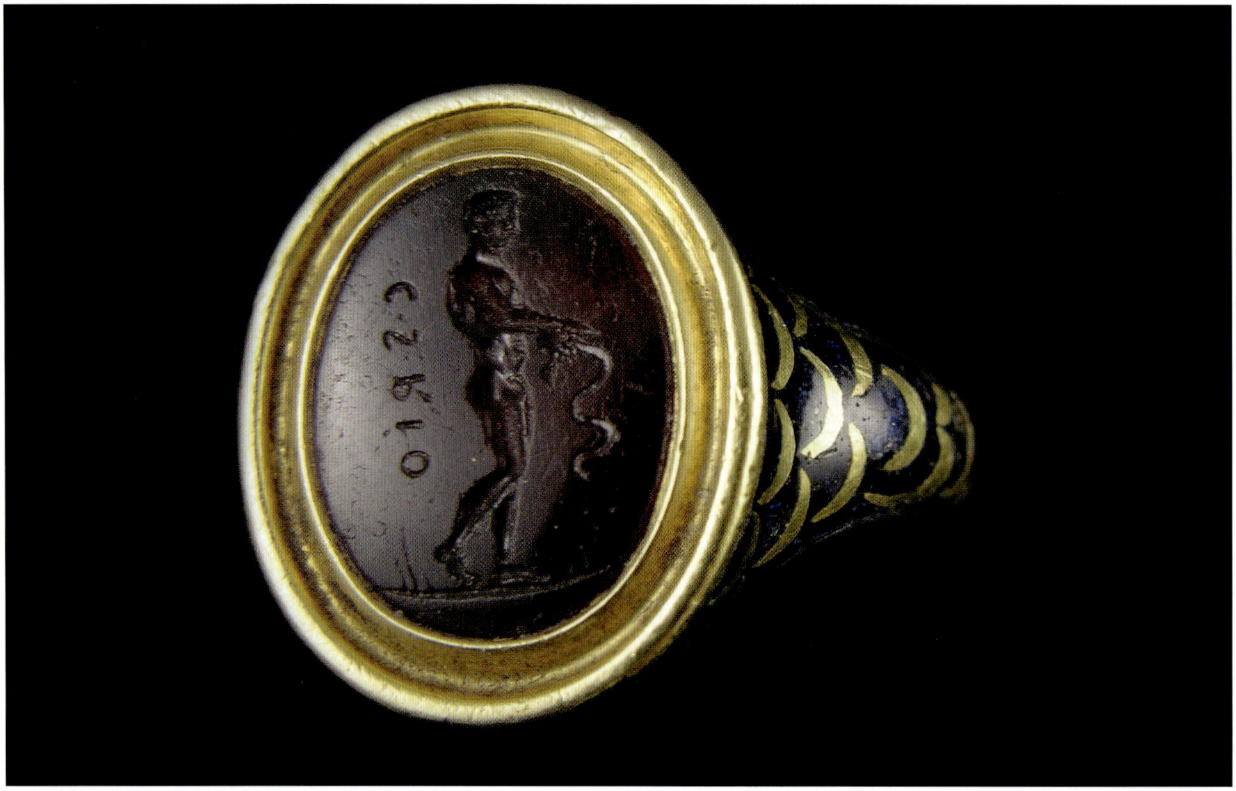

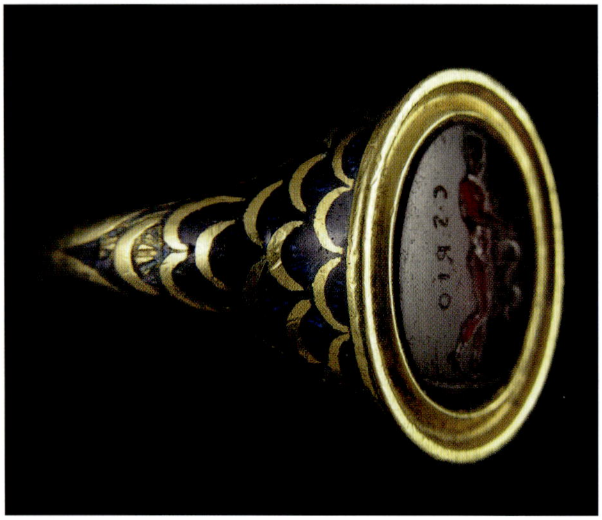

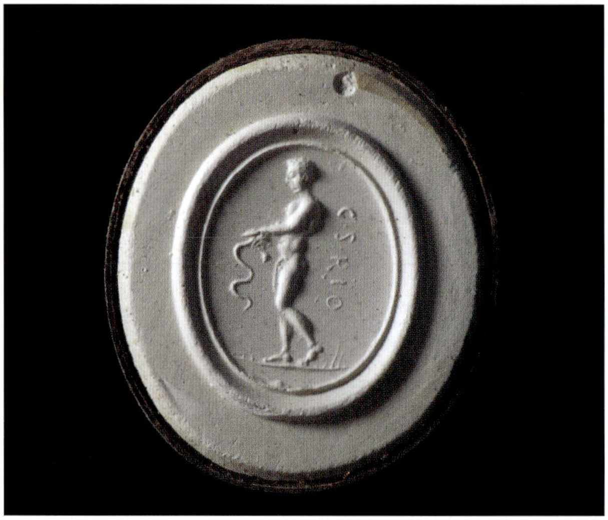

164

(10638) K100 (pl. 4)

Sard, polished convex back, set in a gold ring with blue-enamelled shoulders, with crescents reserved

11 x 8

SG.Imp. 23; Tassie 7105; Inst.Imp. no. 140; King 1872, pl. 38.9 (as Telegonus).

A naked youth holds a snake. Inscribed C·S·RIO. Ground line with stalks.

1st century AD?

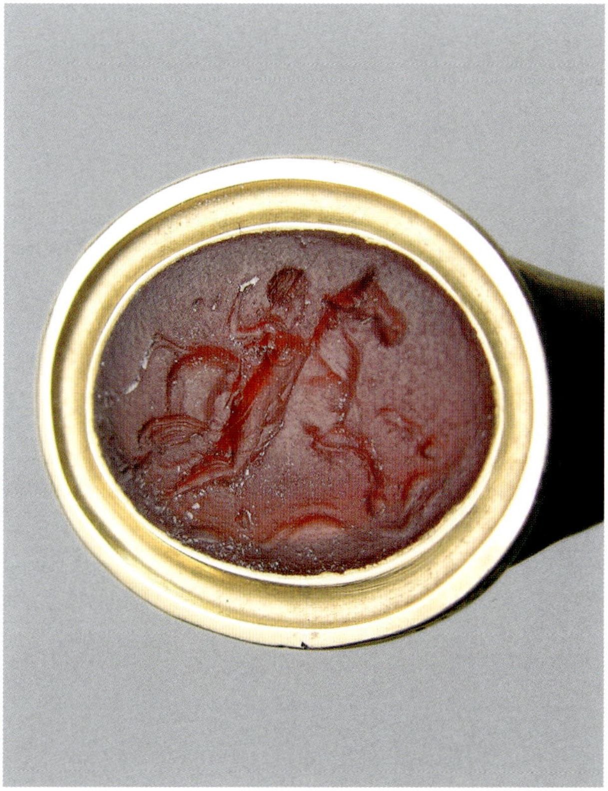

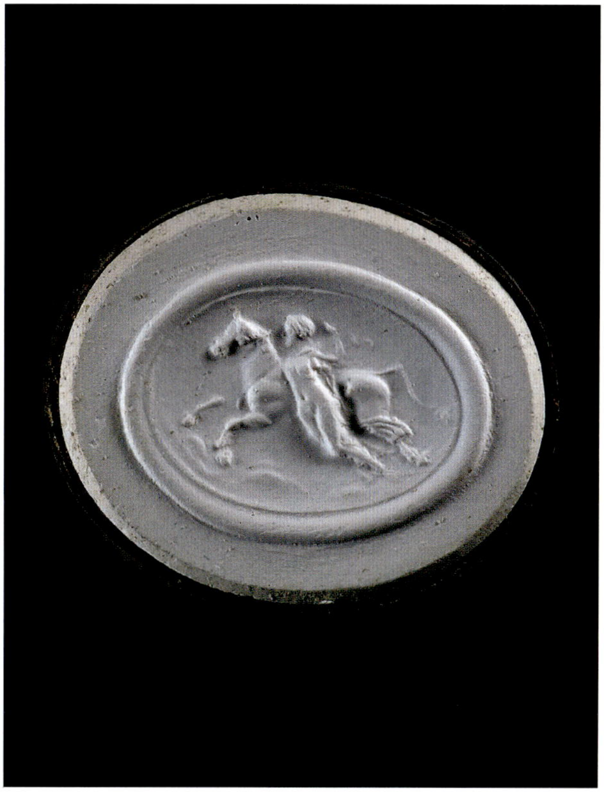

165

(10663) K125 (pl. 4)
Cornelian, polished convex back, set on a plain gold ring
12 x 8

SG.Imp. 75; Tassie 1169; Inst.Imp. no. 125; Paoletti I, IV.242.

Europa, mainly naked but with dress flying, clasps the flank of the Jupiter bull carrying her over waves.

This is a common subject in this form for the Roman period, compare *LIMC* IV, pl. 41.

1st century BC/AD.

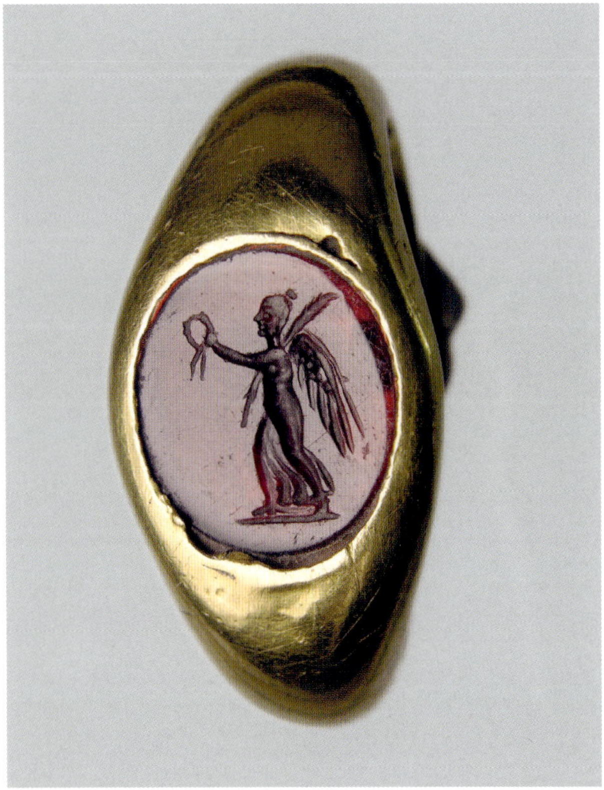

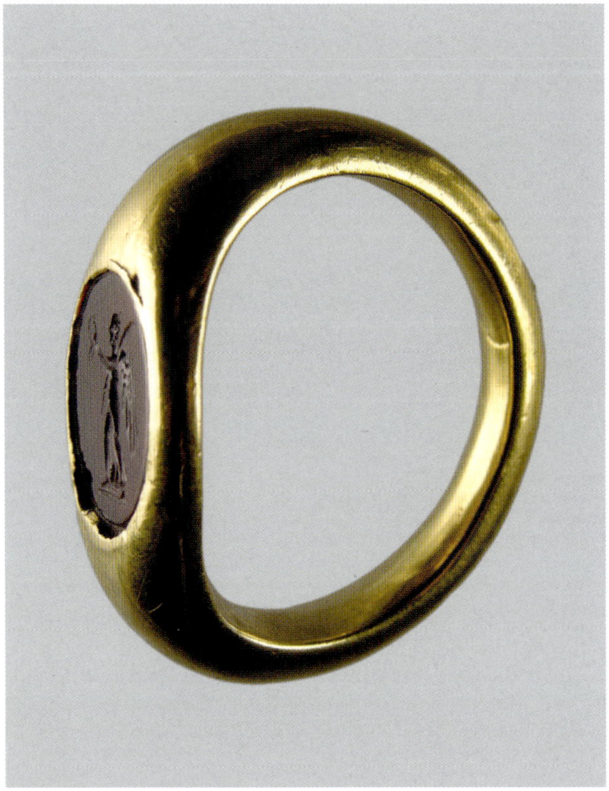

166

(10747) K209 (pl. 3)
Sard, set in an ancient gold ring
11 x 9, ring 25 x 20

AGE no. 228.

Nike/Victoria with palm branch and wreath. Ground line.

This is 'The Scipio Ring'. Knight recounts the history of the ring: 'discovered within the great *peperino* sarcophagus of a member of the Scipio family in 1780, and presented by the then Pope, Pius VI, to M. Dutens, tutor to Lord Beverley, the founder of the present collection, during his second visit to Rome [i.e. in 1790]. On this occasion Dutens had two long political conferences with the Pope after presenting a genealogy of the Scipios. A manuscript note in the archives of the Duke of Northumberland gives the link with the present cabinet: 'The Pope presented it (the ring) to Monsieur "Du Temps" [= Dutens] who gave it to Lord Algernon Percy, with whom he was travelling.' Visconti, in his description of the tomb of the Scipios (Op.Var. I, p.5) says: 'La superba cassa di Scipione Barbato – vi si rinvennero ancora alcuni frammenti di scultura ed un'anello nella cui gemma incisa una Vittoria, che fu donato del Santo Padre al coltissimo Sig. Durens.'

Lucius Cornelius Scipio Barbatus defeated the Etruscans in 298BC and died in 280. His sarcophagus is now in the Vatican Museum. But the ring and its gem cannot be earlier than the 1st century AD, and so is likely to have belonged to one of the later members of the family buried in the tomb, which was erected in the early 1st century AD (if indeed it has anything at all to do with the Scipios).

The 6th Duke had copies made: one is in the Fitzwilliam Museum, Cambridge (*Cambridge* no. 837), another was sent to Visconti's grandson, who acknowledges the gift in a letter in the Alnwick Archives.

1st/2nd century AD.

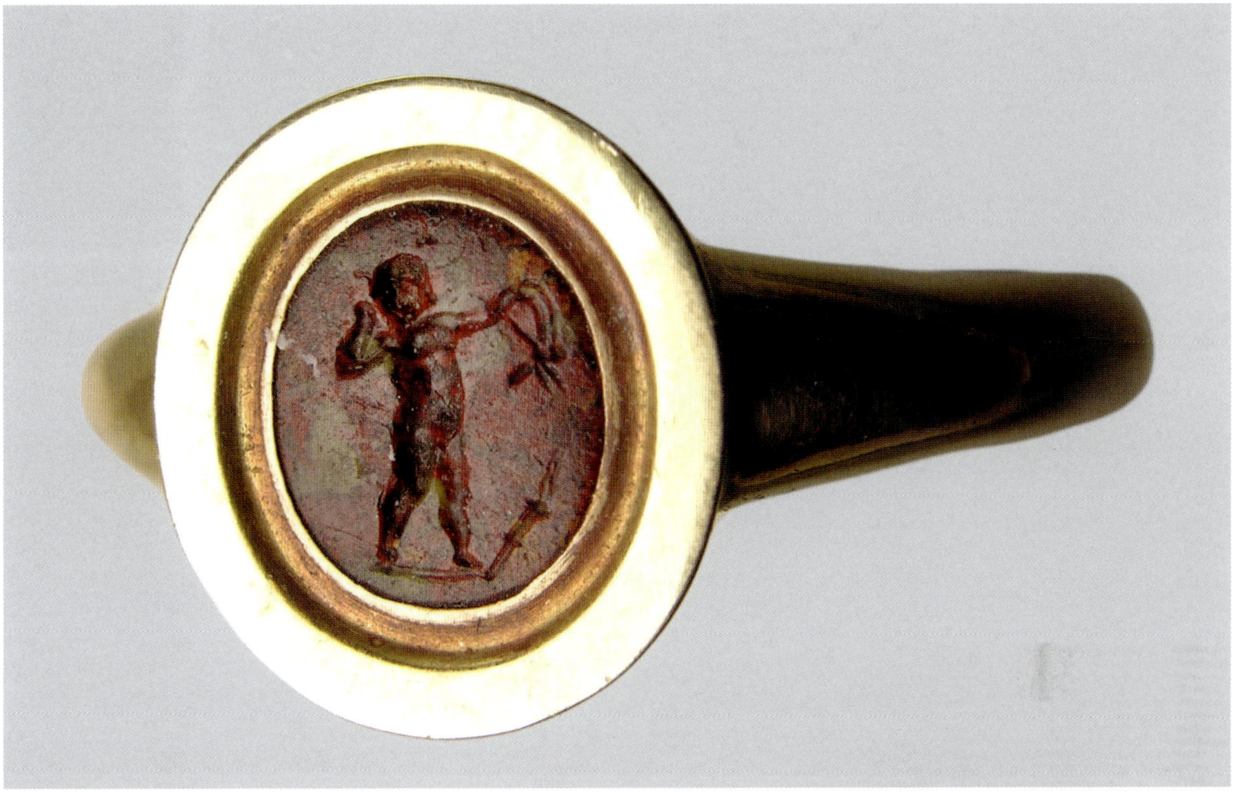

167

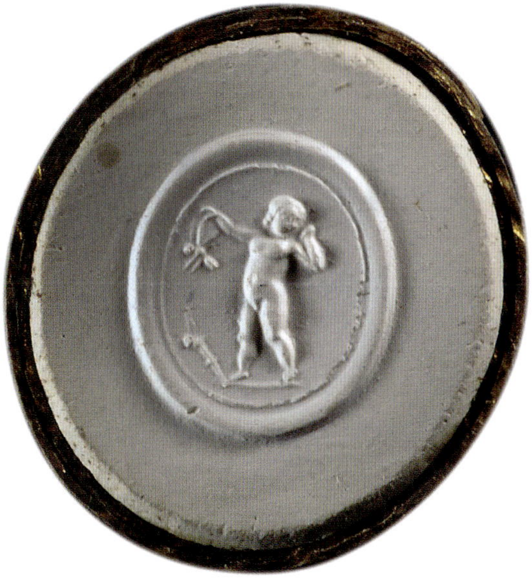

(10667) K129 (pl. 4)
Mottled red/yellow jasper, unpolished flat back, set on a plain gold ring
6 x 5

SG.Imp. 90; Inst.Imp. no. 145.

Wingless Cupid holding a butterfly (Psyche) over a blazing torch. Ground line.

Compare *Würzburg* nos 208–9; *Cambridge* no. 296; *Marlborough* no. 396.

1st century BC/AD.

168

(10759)
Carnelian, polished convex back, set in a plain gold ring
13 x 11

Cupid stands burning a butterfly (Psyche) with a torch. Ground line.

Cf. *LIMC* III, 970. For a Pichler copy, Paoletti II, V.157.

1st/2nd century AD?

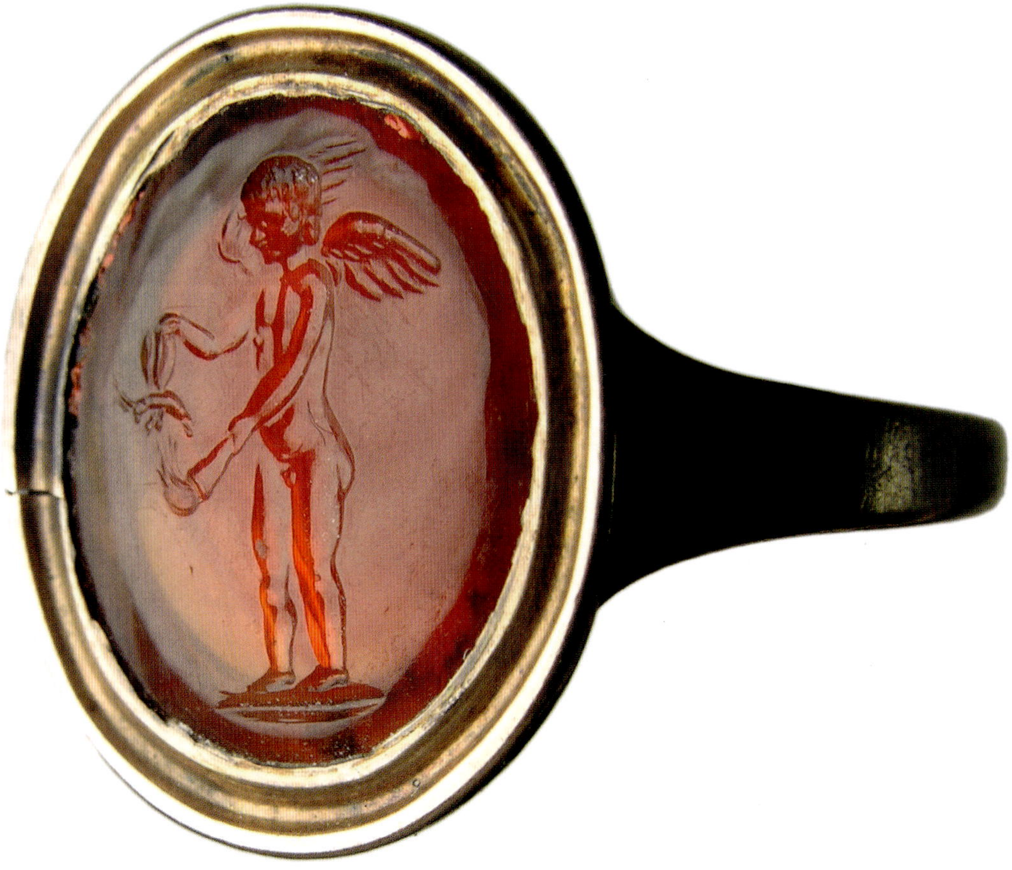

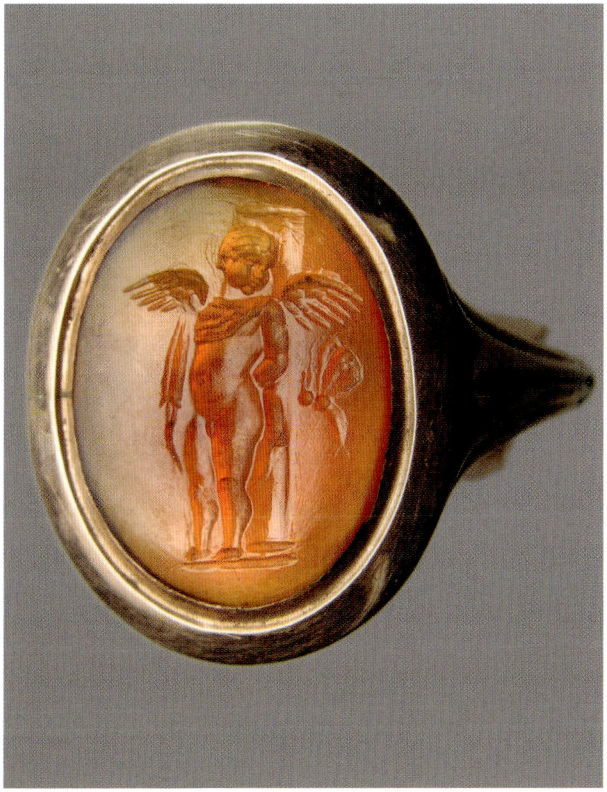

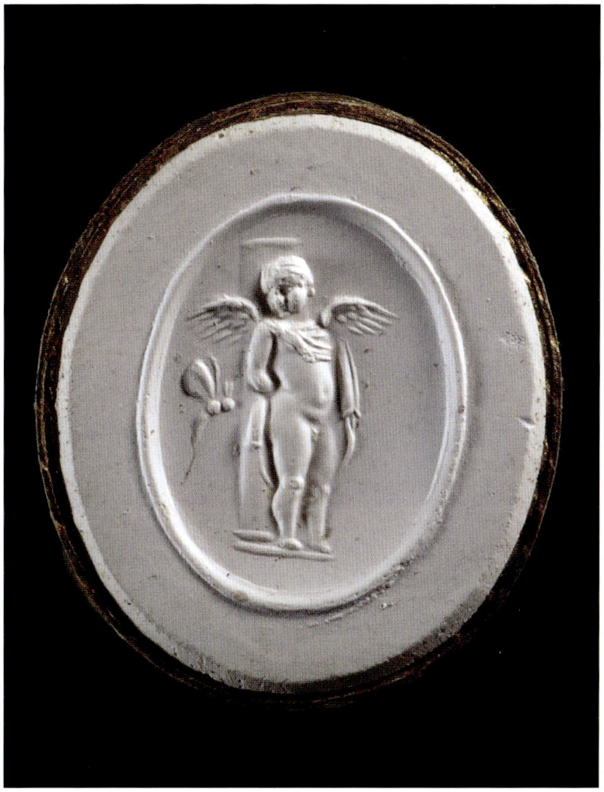

169

(10674) K136 (pl. 4)
Sard, polished convex back, set on a plain gold ring
18 x 19

SG.Imp. 169; Tassie 7099; Inst.Imp. no. 63; Paoletti I, I.347.

Cupid, dressed with a cloak, is tied to a column by a butterfly (Psyche). Ground line.

Compare *LIMC* III, pl. 683.70; Paoletti II, V.543.

1st century BC/AD.

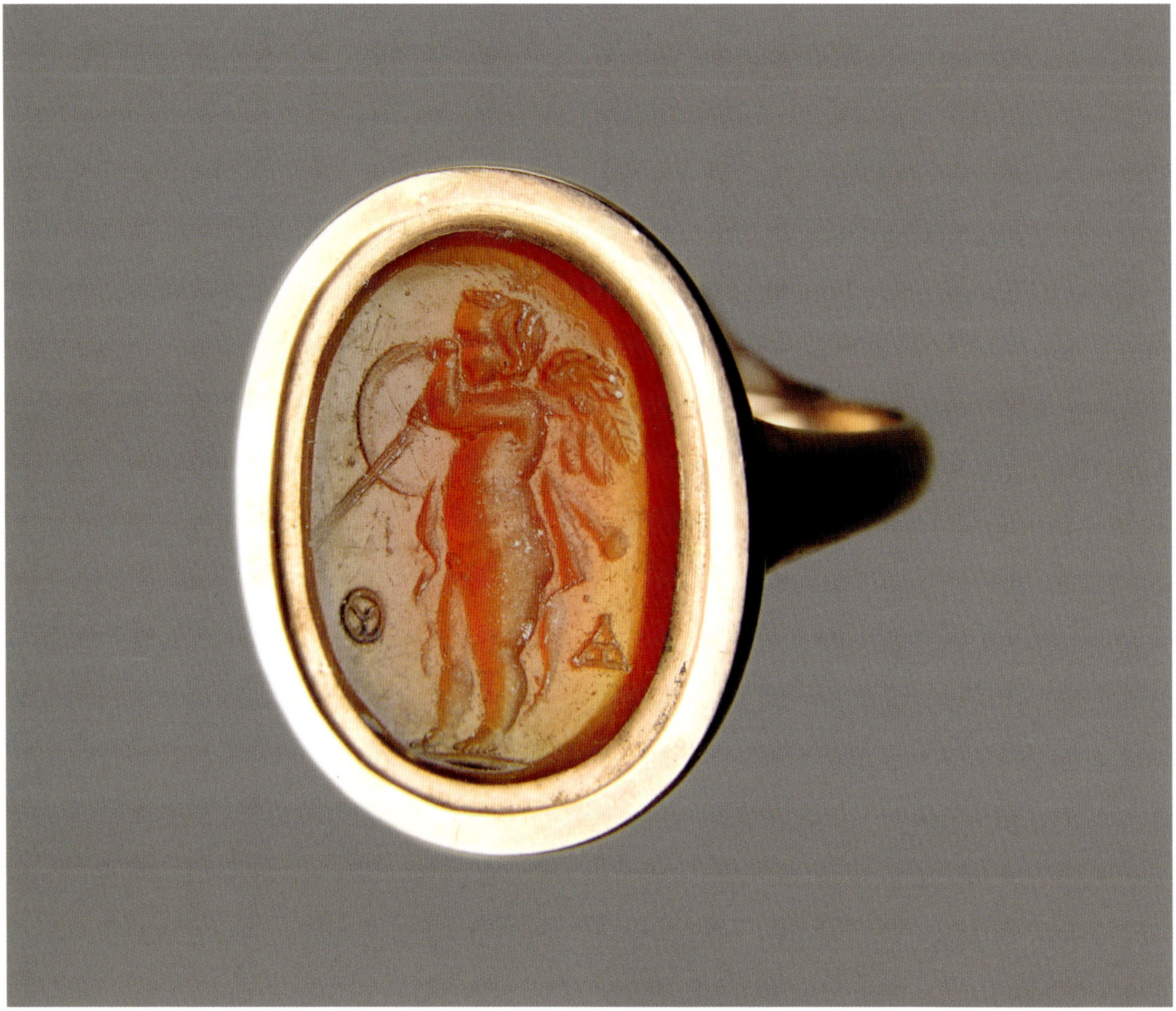

170

(10670) K132 (pl. 4)
Sard, polished convex back, set on a plain gold ring
15 x 13

SG.Imp. 126; Tassie 15398; Inst.Imp. no. 77.

Cupid holding spears and a shield (Knight has a hoop and stick), hand to head, with scabbard and dress behind him. In the field monograms of Δ and T, and O and Y. Ground line.

1st century BC/AD.

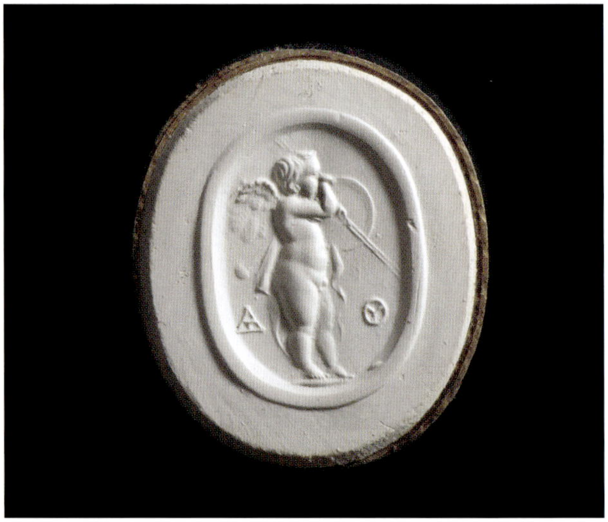

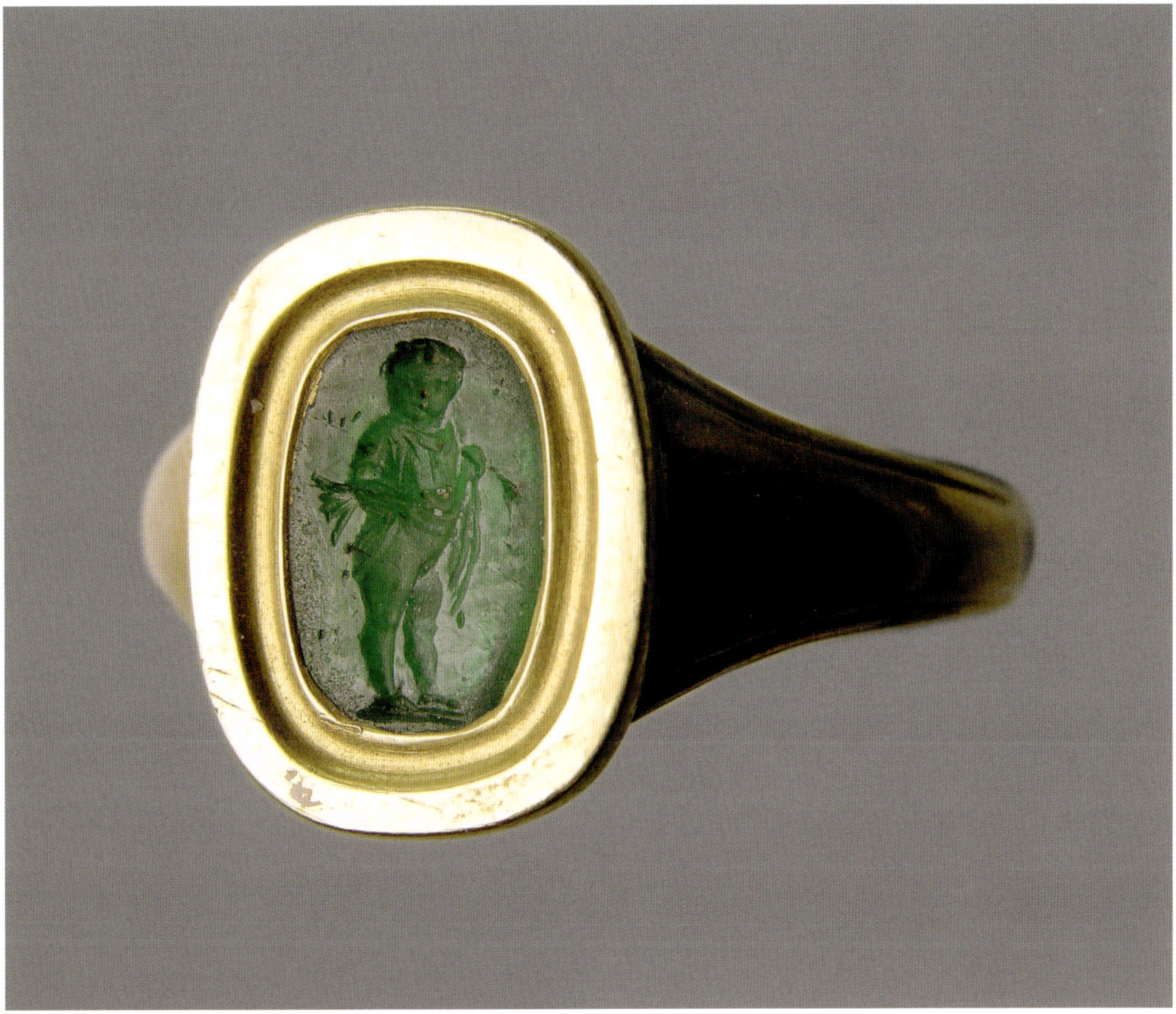

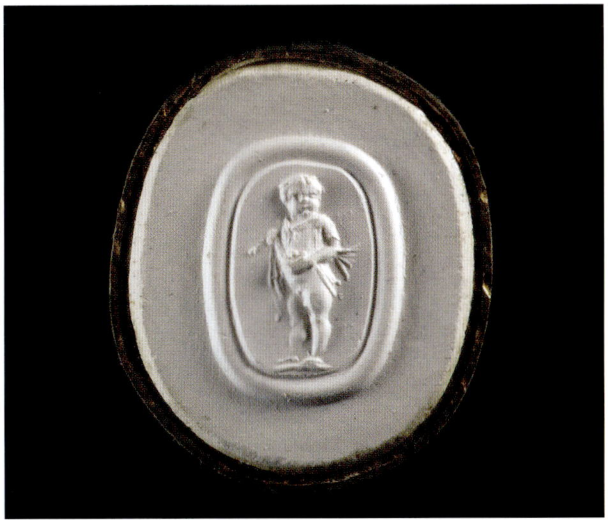

171

(10683) K145 (pl. 6)
Emerald, polished convex back, set on a plain gold ring
7 x 4

SG.Imp. 137; Tassie 6915; Inst.Imp. no. 143.

A boy child, lifting his dress to carry fruit? Ground line.

Probably 18th century.

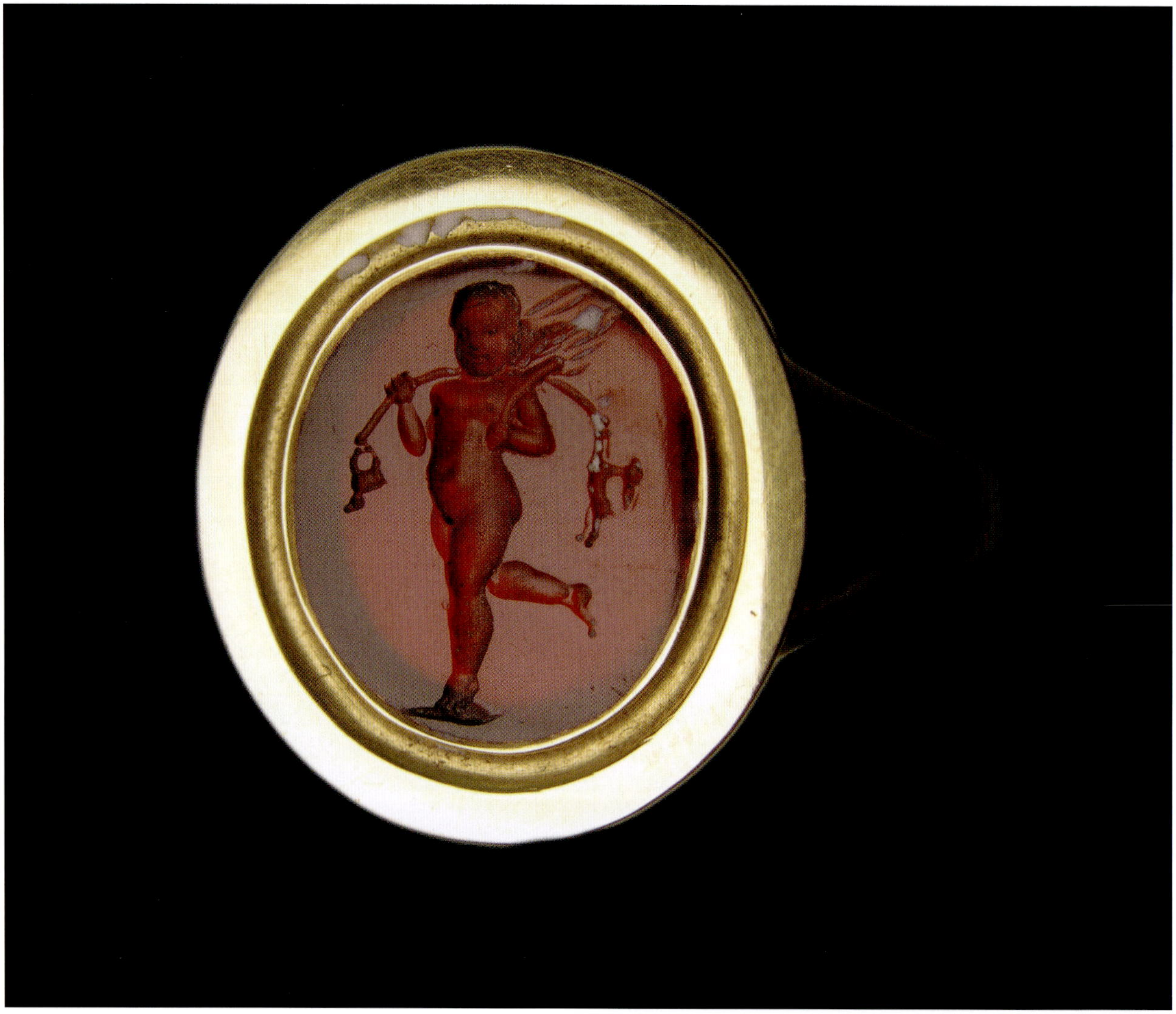

172

(10668) K130 (pl. 6)
Sard, polished flat back, set on a plain gold ring
11 x 9

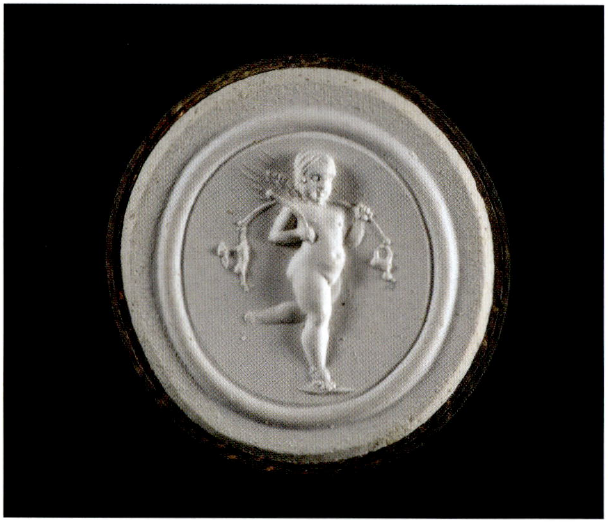

SG.Imp. 34; Tassie 7026; Inst.Imp. no. 73; Paoletti I, I.368.

Cupid skips forward holding a stick over his shoulder from which hang two dead hares, one earless. He holds a throwing stick *(pedum)*. Ground line.

For Cupid as a hunter see *LIMC* III, 991–4.

1st century BC/AD.

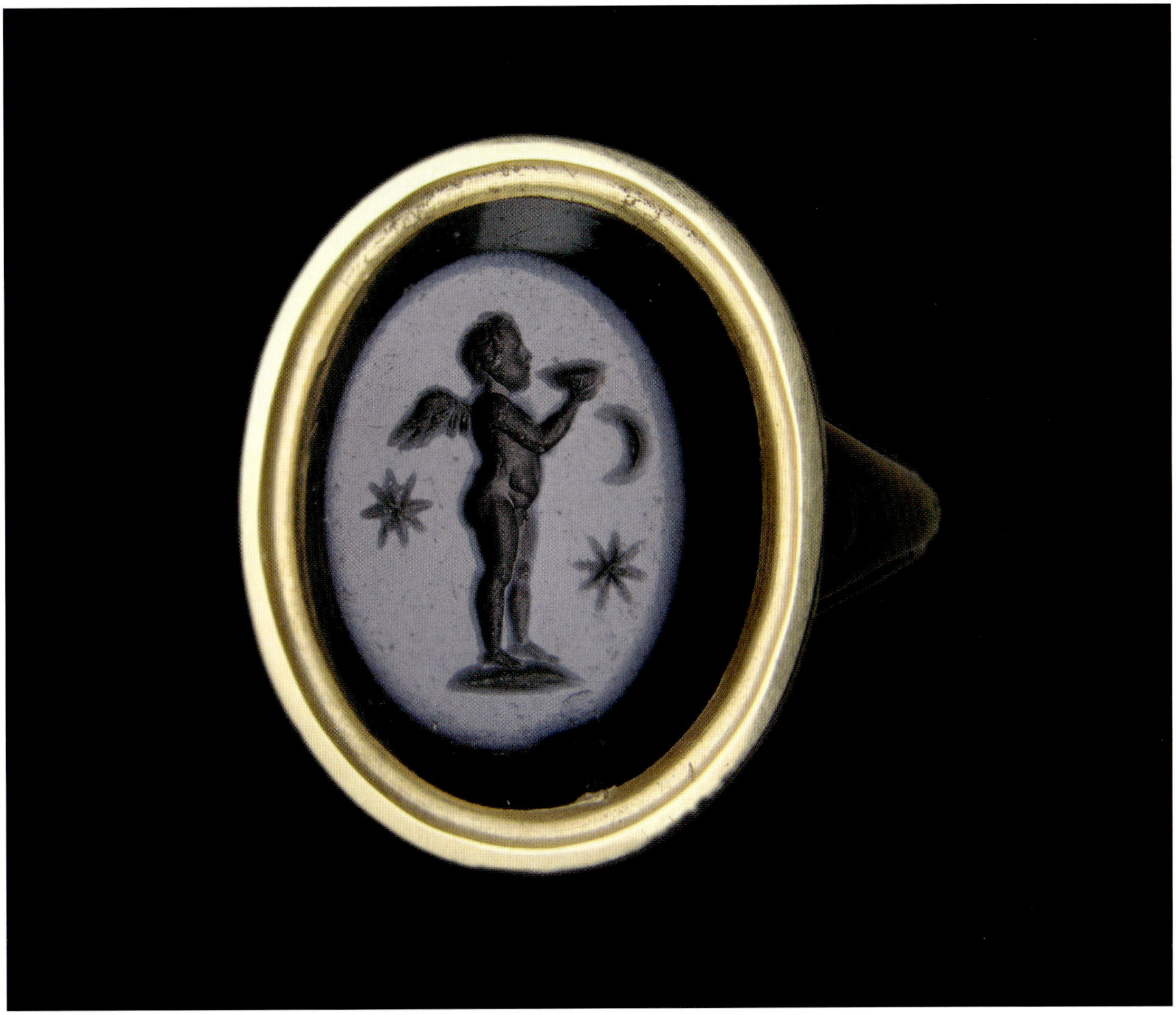

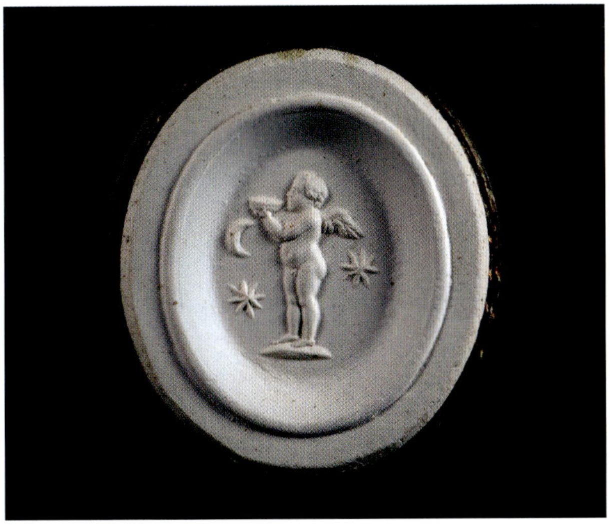

173

(10665) K127 (pl. 4)
Nicolo, polished flat back, set on a plain gold ring
17 x 14

SG.Imp. 13; Tassie 6862; Inst.Imp. no. 81.

Cupid lifts a cup to his lips. In the field a crescent and two stars. Ground line.

1st century BC/AD.

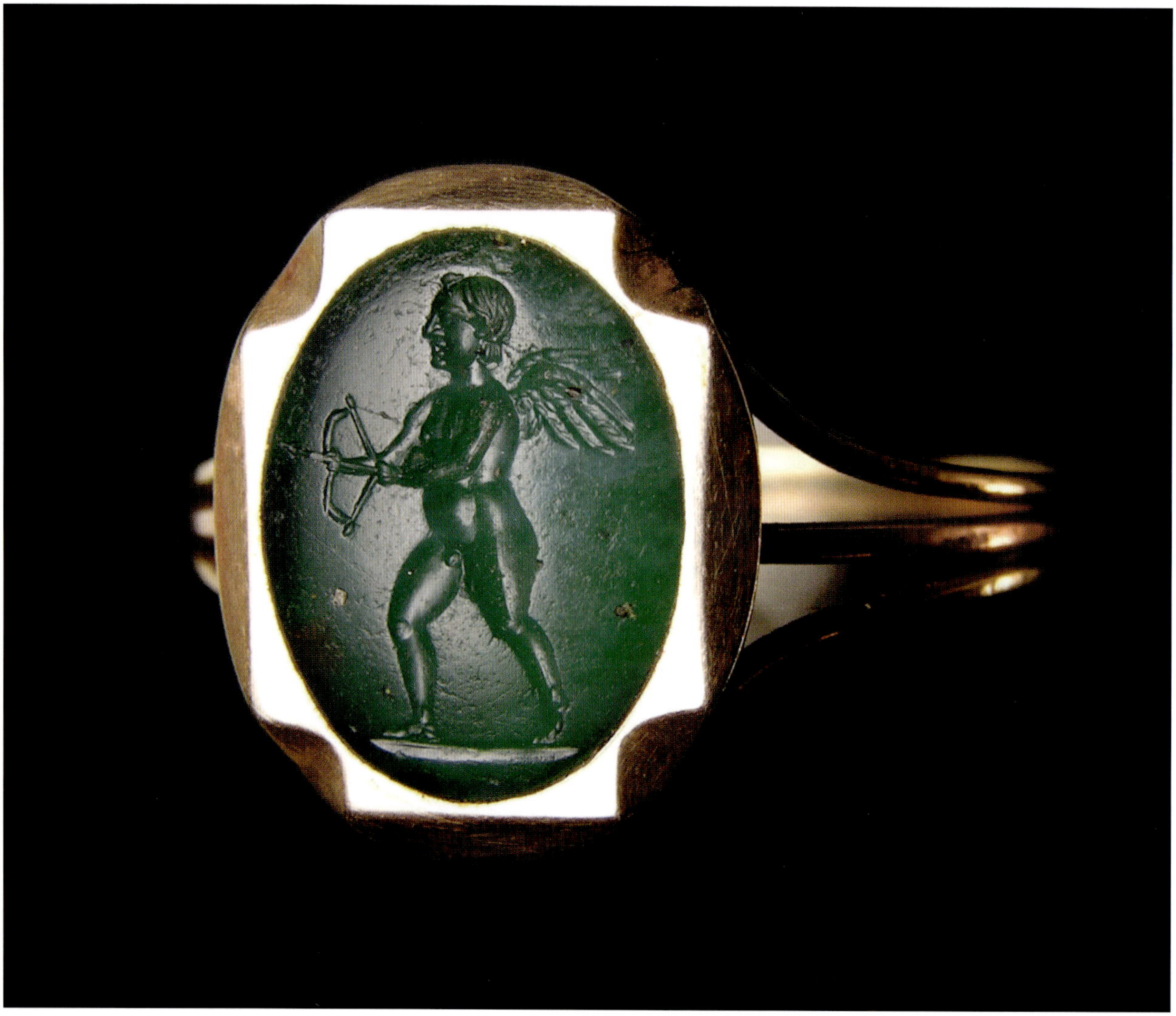

174

(10758)
Green translucent chalcedony, deep flat back with faceted edge, set in a modern gold ring with rectangular bezel and faceted corners on an oval base
11 x 8

Cupid stepping forward with a bow. Ground line.

1st century AD.

175

(10669) K131 (pl. 4)
Sard, polished flat back, set on a plain gold ring with ribboned edge to the bezel
10 x 10

SG.Imp. 36; Tassie 6931; Inst.Imp. no. 53.

Wingless Cupid seated on a draped couch, holding a comic mask over his head. A shoe (?) and a pedum (?) behind him.

The subject is as Paoletti I, I.220; *Munich* 3, no. 2346, and compare the cameo, Vollenweider, pl. 24.4, with Cupid on a couch holding a mask, and our **47**. For Roman Cupids wearing masks (not on gems), B.P. Venetucci, *Studi Miscellani* 28 (1991) 221–36; on sarcophagi, W. Deonna in *Rev. Arch.* (1916) 74–97; their appearance in the Renaissance, L. Hadermann-Misguich in L. Hadermann-Misguich and G. Raepsaet (eds), *Rayonnement grec: hommages à Ch. Delvoye* (Brussels 1982) 513–23. Our **176** is an exact copy.

1st century BC.

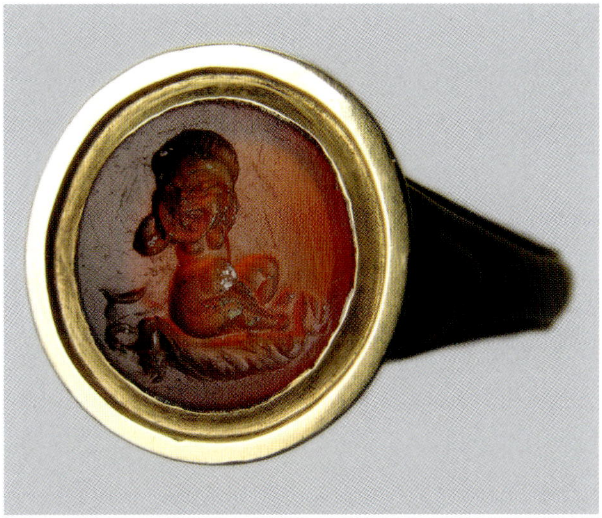

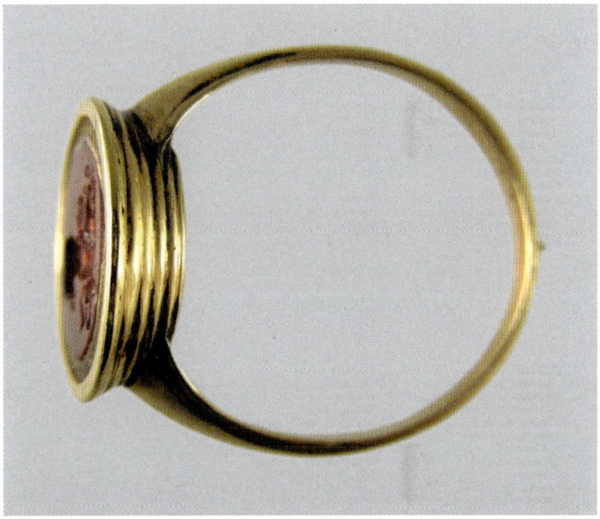

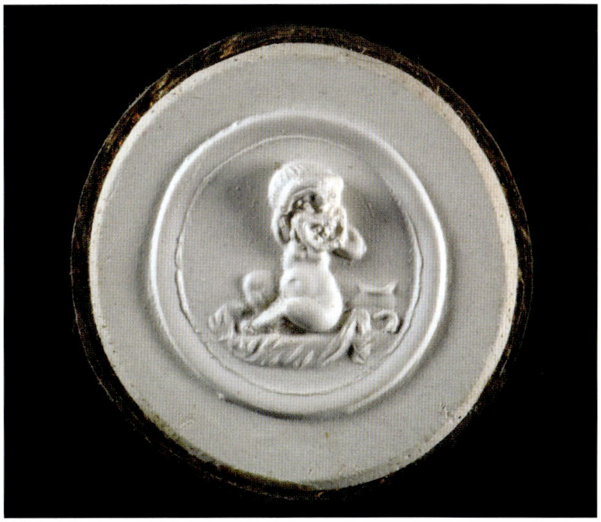

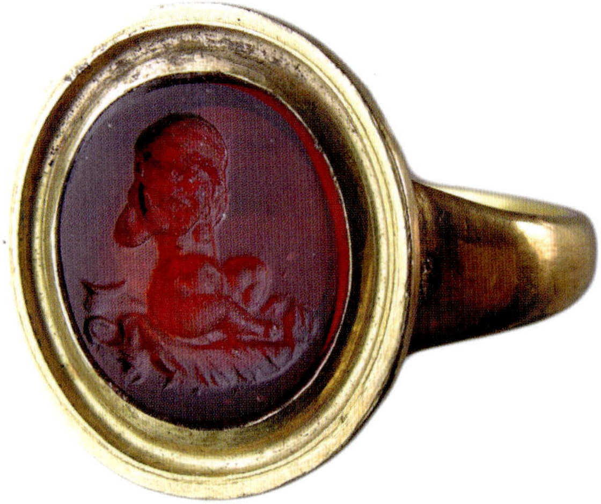

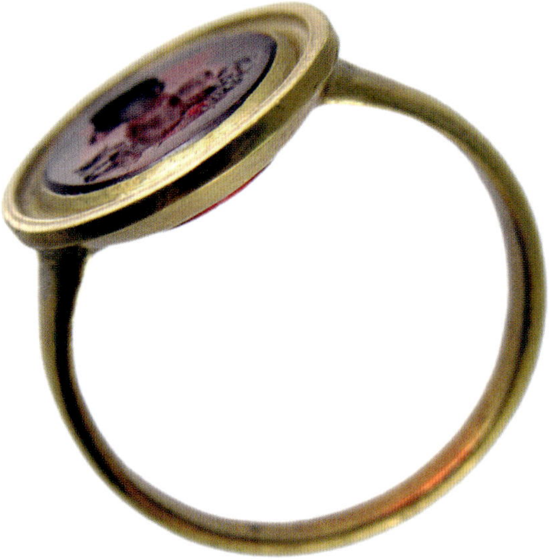

176

(10761)
Sard,polished flat back, set on a plain gold ring.
10 x 10

An exact copy of the last.

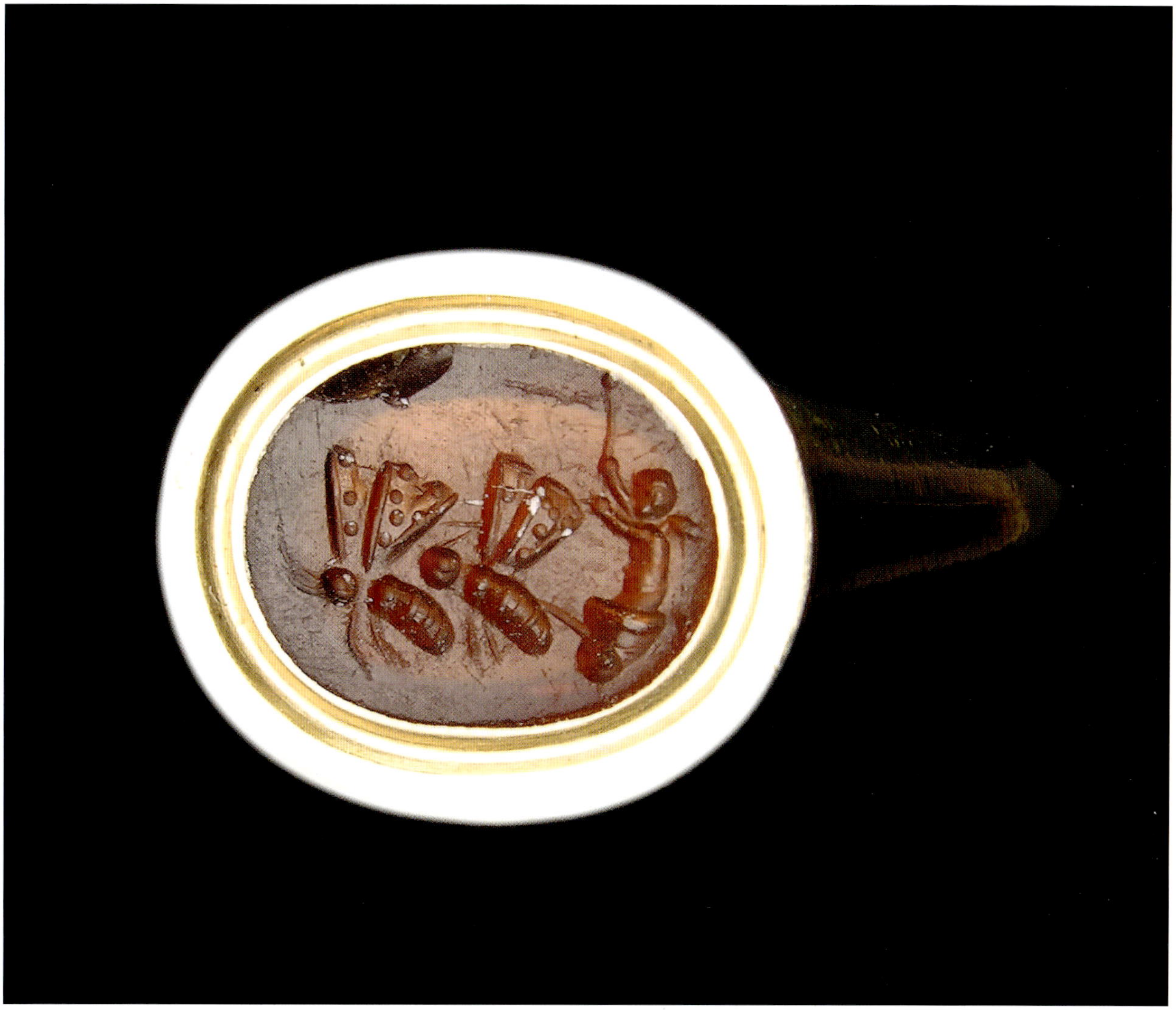

177

(10756)
Carnelian, polished flat back, set in a plain gold ring
8 x 7

Cupid holding a whip in a chariot in the shape of a shell drawn by two bees or butterflies.

The subject is as *Wien* I, no. 441 (in a nutshell chariot), and a late copy, Paoletti II, V.144.

1st century AD.

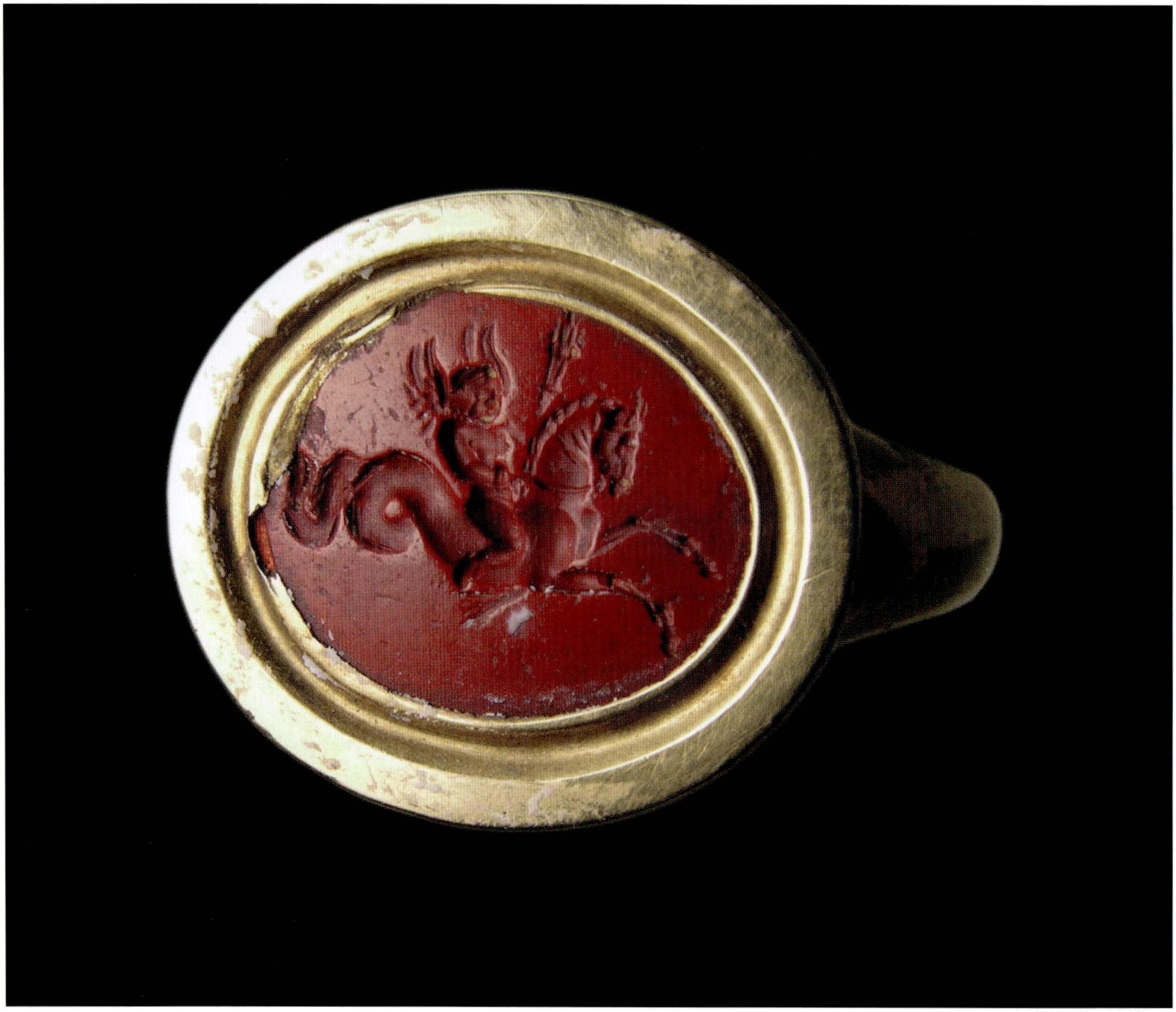

178

(10677) K139 (pl. 4)
Red jasper, polished flat back, set on a plain gold ring
9 x 8

SG.Imp. 12; Tassie 6805; Inst.Imp. no. 123.

Cupid holding a torch rides a sea-horse.

For the subject compare *Würzburg* nos 178–80; *Wien* II, no. 603; *Marlborough* no. 335.

1st century BC.

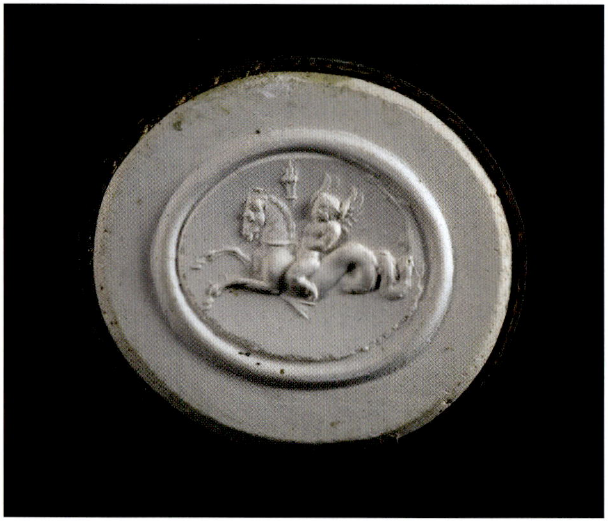

179

(10762)
Cornelian, polished convex back, set in a plain gold ring
15 x 11

A woman wearing a diadem and seated on dress (Ariadne?) holds out a kantharos, on a cart pulled by a pantheress and a goat. Ground line.

This must be an excerpt from a Triumph of Bacchus which Ariadne often attends.

1st/2nd century AD.

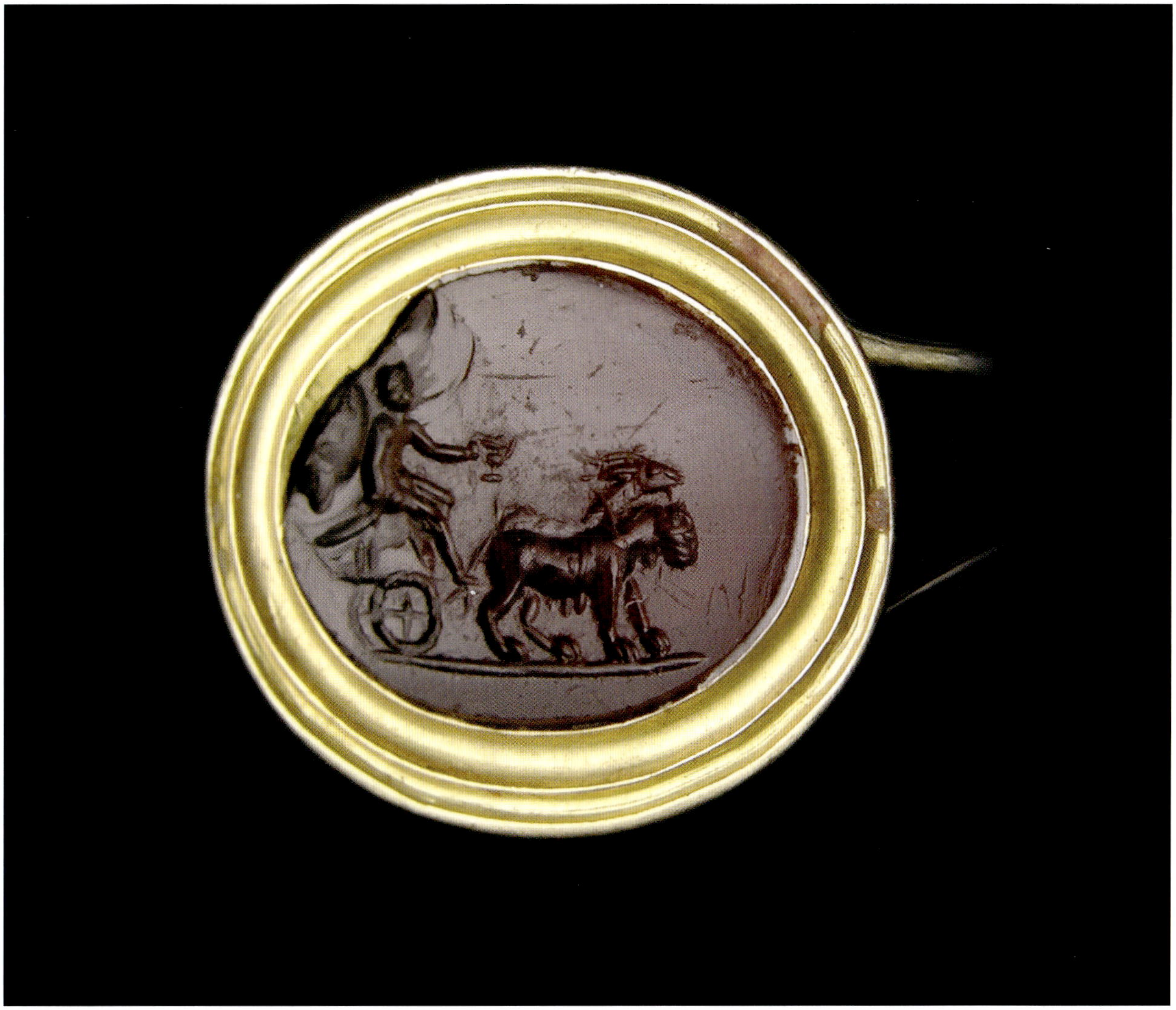

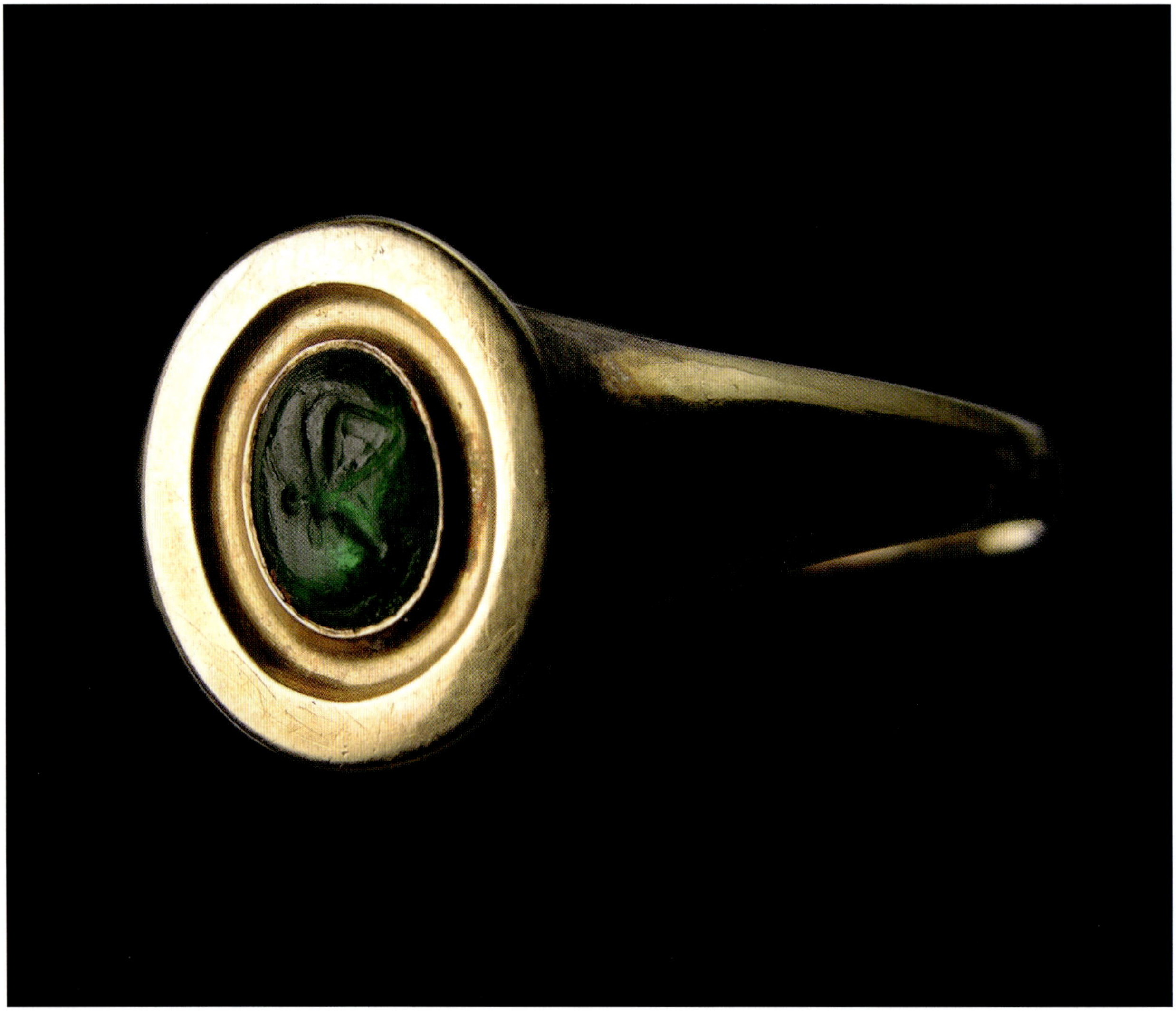

180

(10760)
Emerald, polished hemispherical back, set in a plain gold ring
3 x 4

A butterfly.

1st century BC/AD.

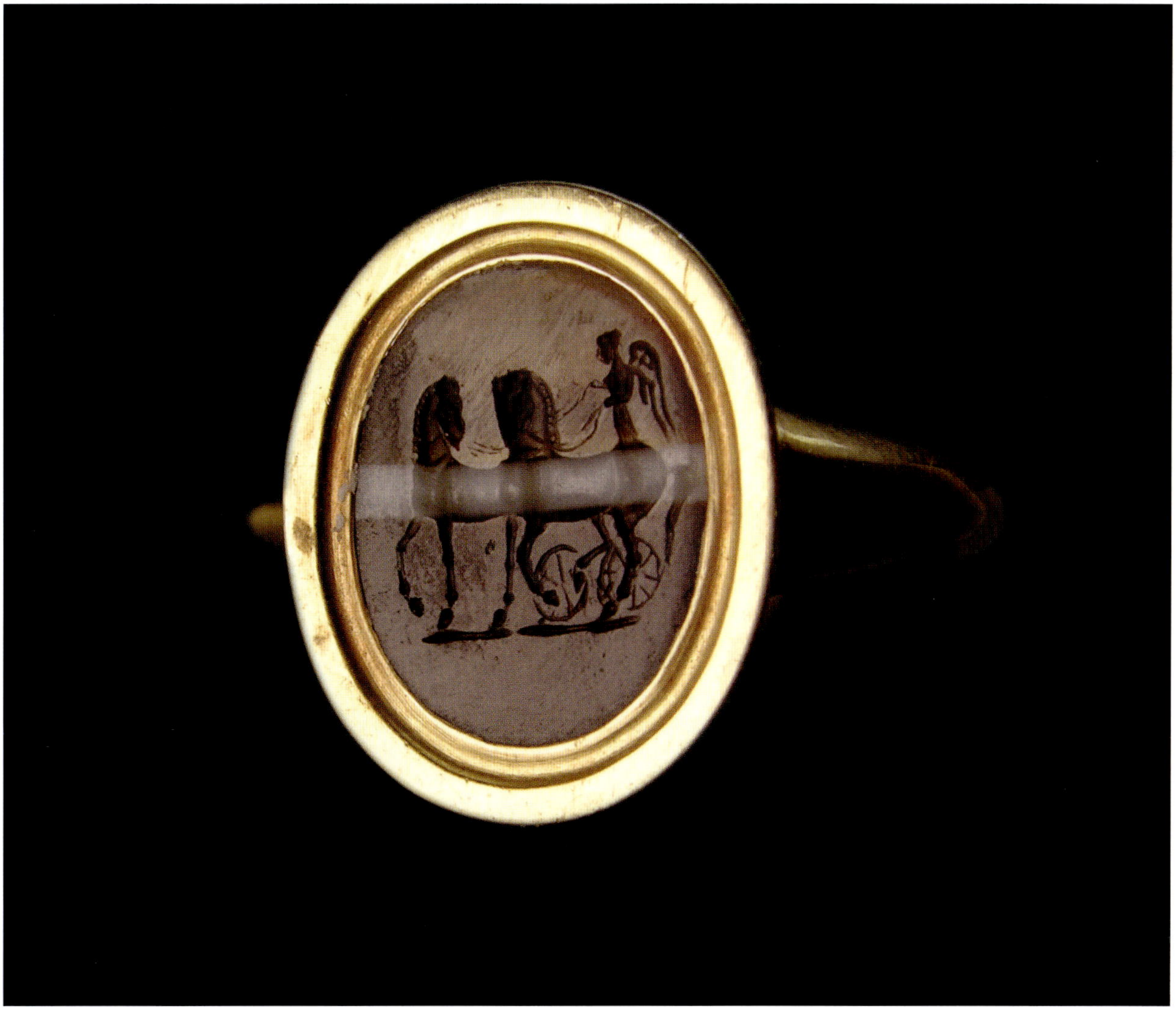

181

(10768)
Sardonyx, brown with white stripe, polished flat back, set in a plain gold ring
11 x 9

Victory drives a biga shown in three-quarter view, the body of the chariot not shown. Ground line.

For the subject compare U. Pannuti, *Catalogo della collezione glittica del Museo Nazionale di Napoli* (Rome 1983) no. 100.

1st/2nd century AD.

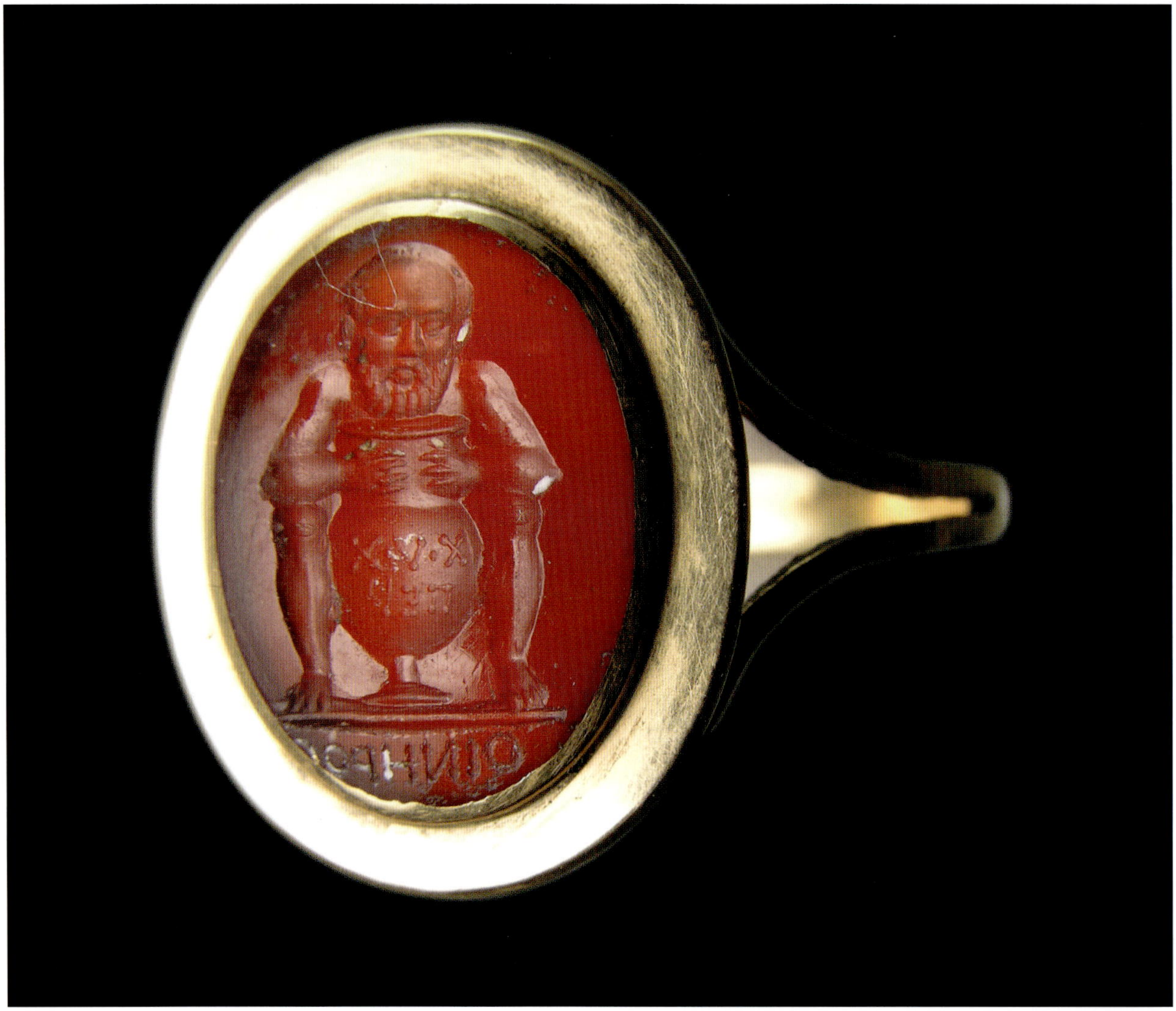

182

(10679) K141 (pl. 6)
Sard, polished convex back, set on a gold ring with forked ends to the hoop
13 x 10

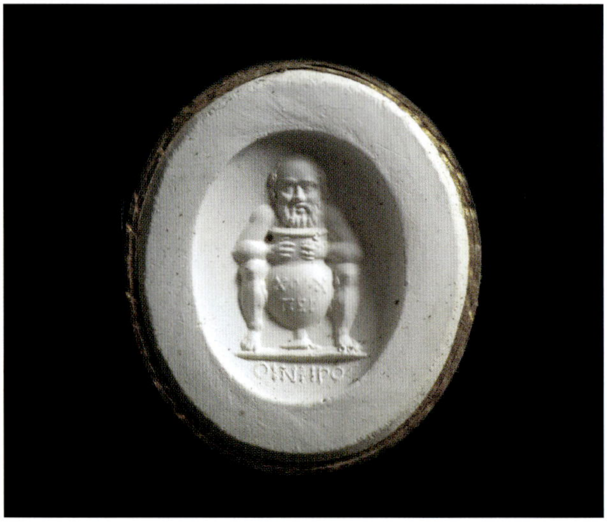

SG.Imp. 164; Inst.Imp. no. 129.

An old satyr squats holding the neck of a large, footed wine jar. On the jar is inscribed X·V·X and ΠΕΙ (ΠΙΕΙ = 'drink'). In the exergue ΟΙΝΗΡΟϹ. (*oineros* = 'containing wine').

2nd century BC?

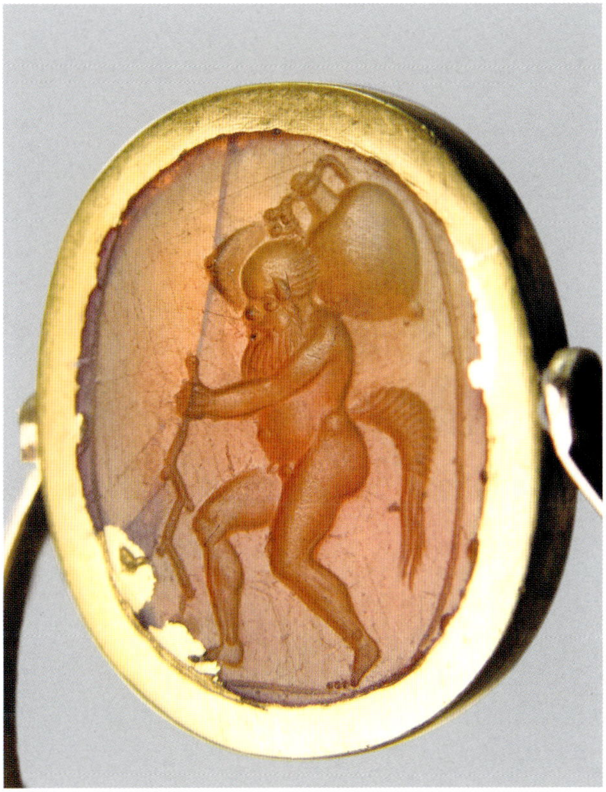

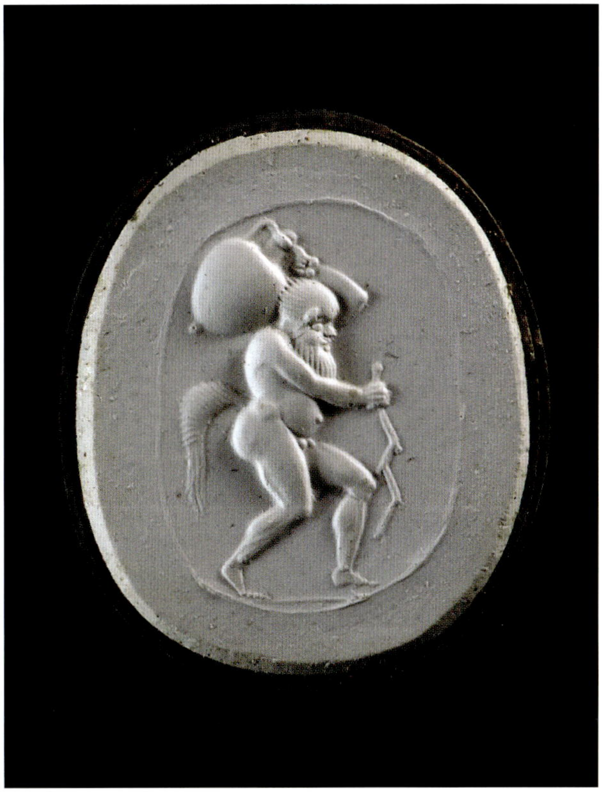

183

(10680) K142 (pl. 4)
Sard, polished convex back, set on a gold swivel ring
12 x 11

SG.Imp. 159; Inst.Imp. no. 136.

An old satyr shoulders a wine amphora, leaning on a bent stick. Ground line and close-stippled border.

Probably 2nd/1st century BC.

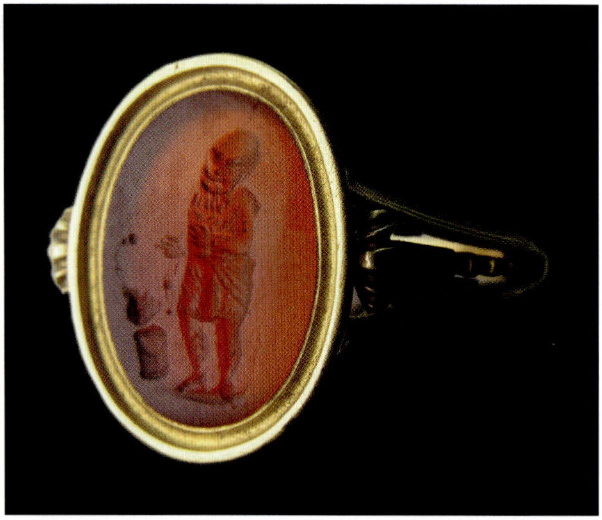

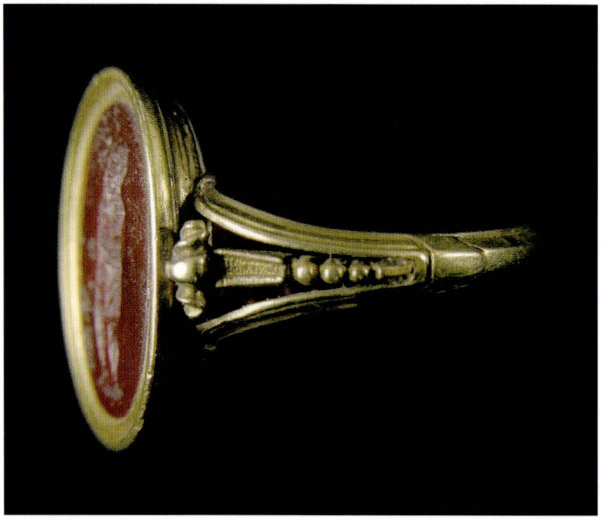

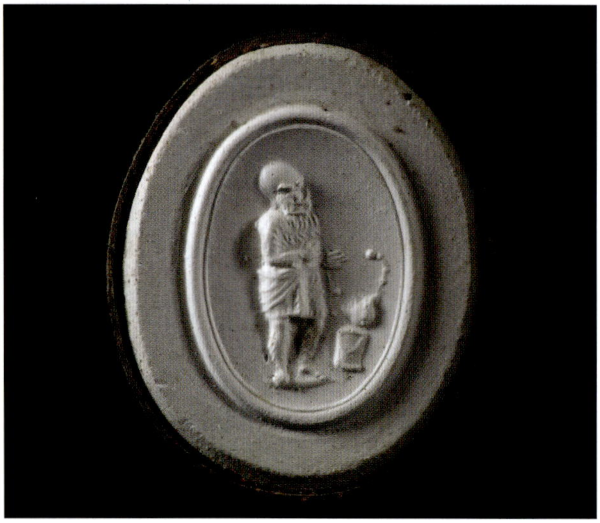

184

(10607) K69 (pl. 3)
Sard, polished flat back, set on a plain gold ring with forked, floral shoulders
12 x 8

SG.Imp. 46; Tassie 3587; Inst.Imp. no. 113.

A masked comic actor in short dress and trousers, holding a cloak around his waist, stands before a wreathed altar on which is a tragic mask, a *pedum* throwing stick behind it. Ground line.

1st century BC?

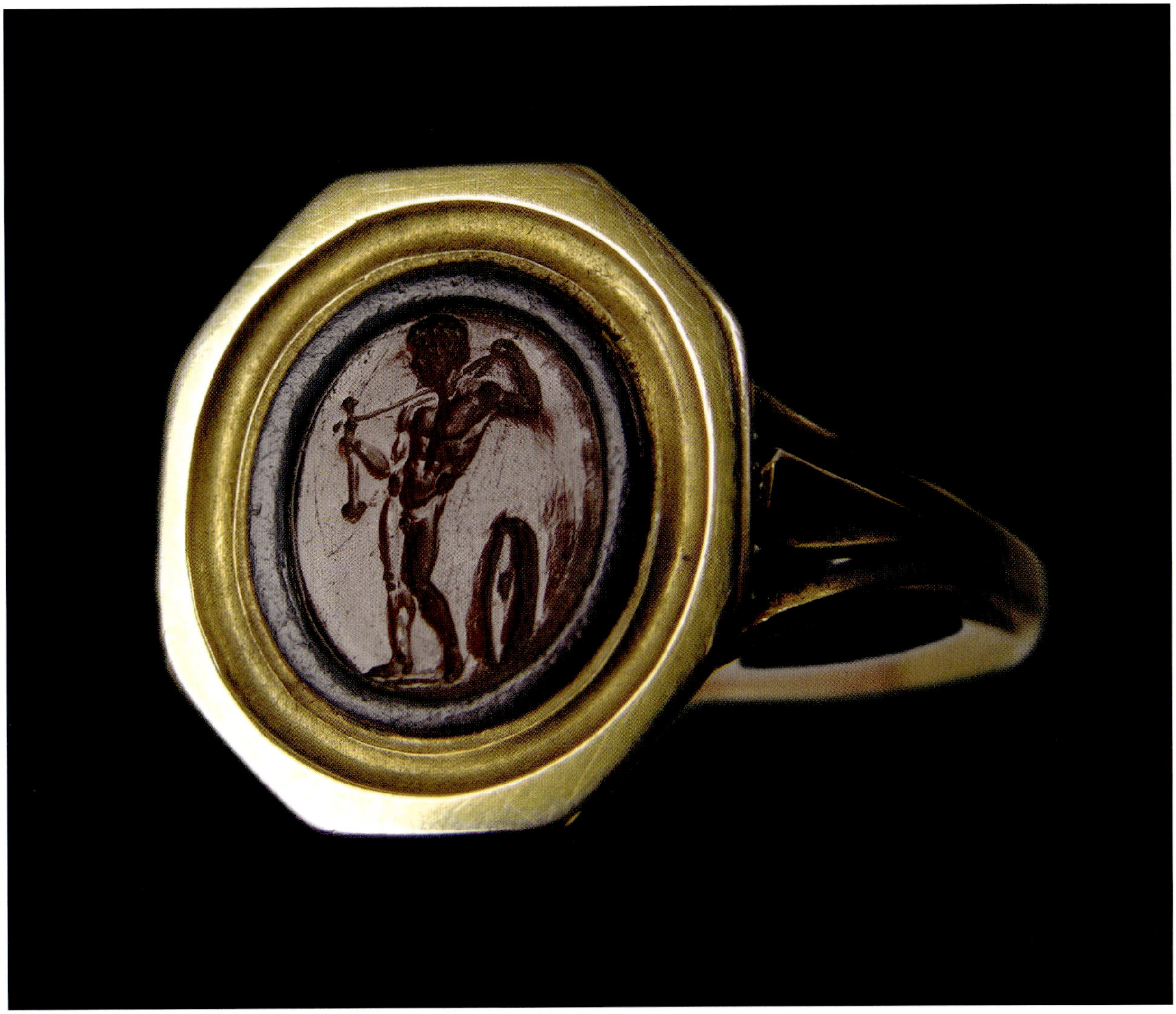

185

(10618) K80 (pl. 3)
Red and blue opaque glass, polished flat back, set on a plain gold ring
10 x 8

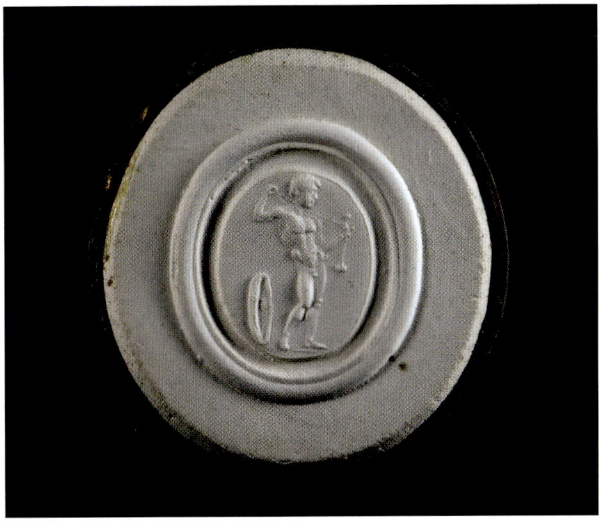

SG.Imp. 19; Inst.Imp. no. 127.

A naked warrior is slinging his sword around his neck, his shield behind him. Ground line. The stone has a flat raised border.

1st century BC/AD.

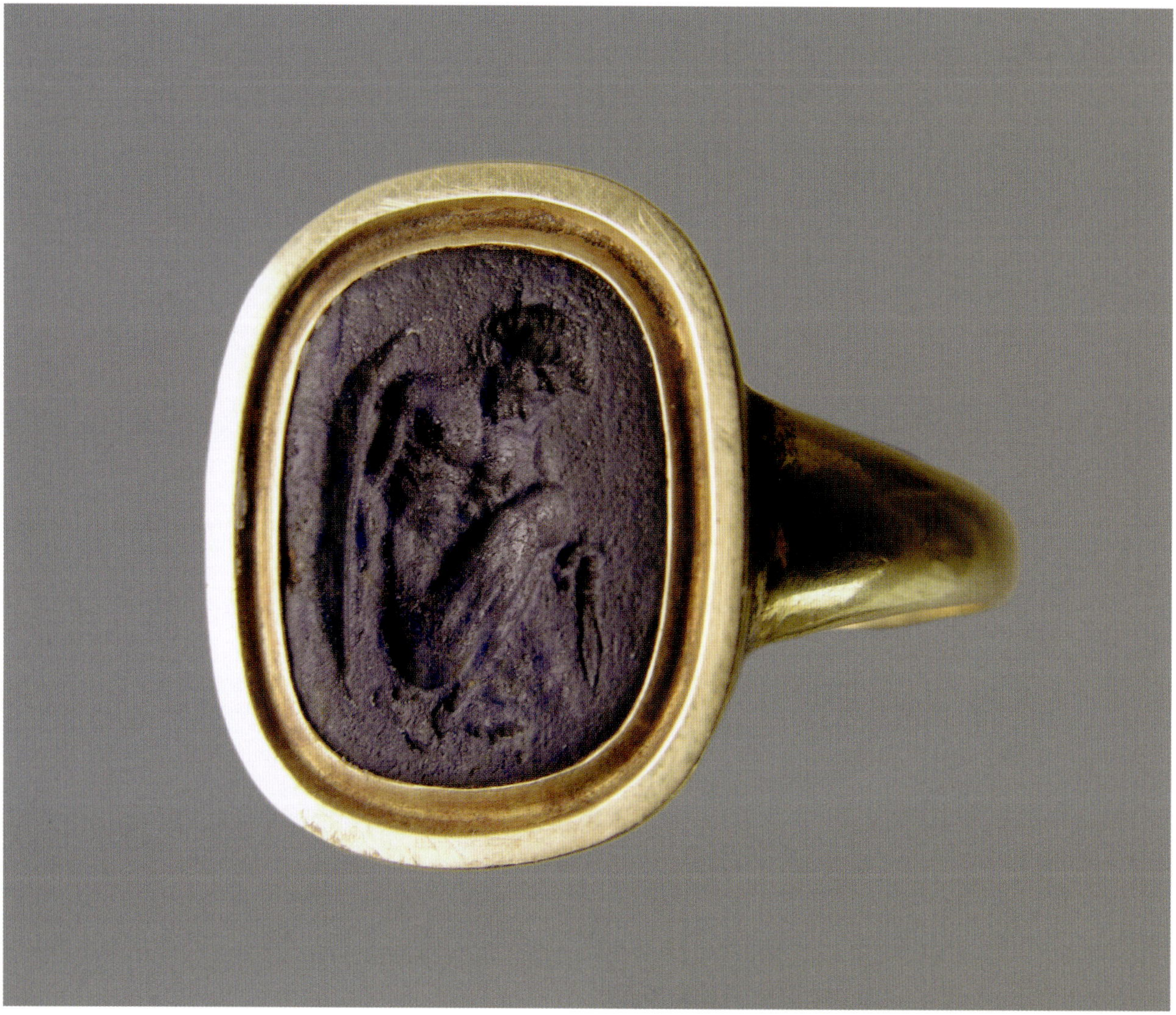

186

(10628) K90 (pl. 4)
Lapis lazuli, unpolished flat back, set on a plain gold ring
12 x 8

SG.Imp. 47; Tassie 7481; Inst.Imp. no. 122.

A naked youth with a shield crouches, holding a dagger.
Both the material and the subject here are unusual.

2nd/1st century BC?

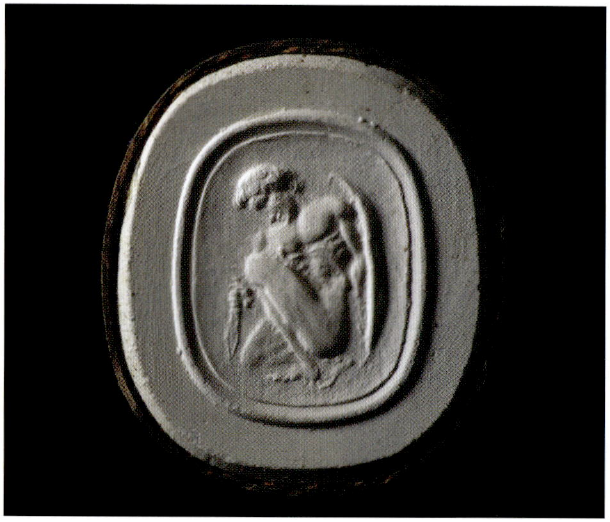

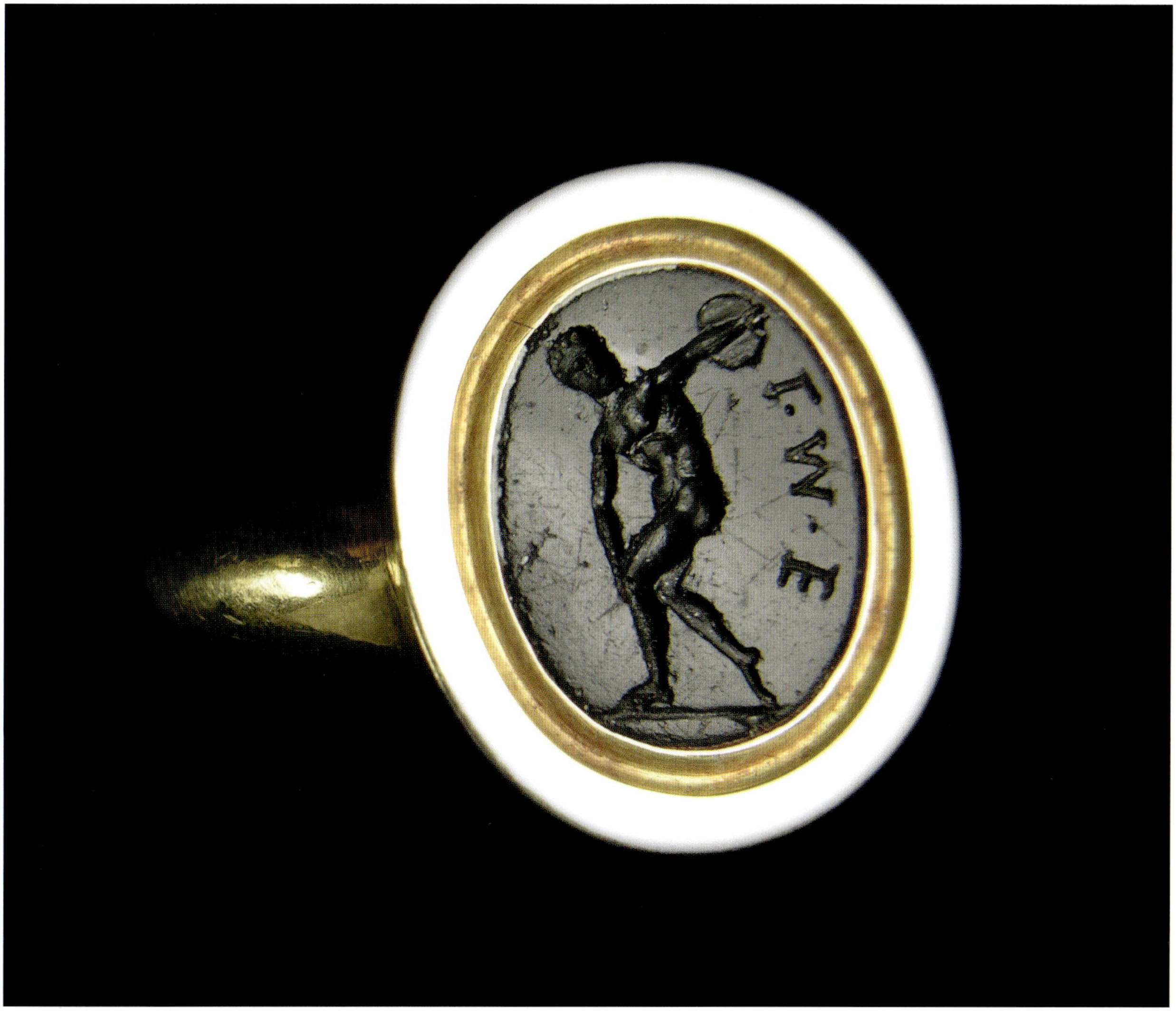

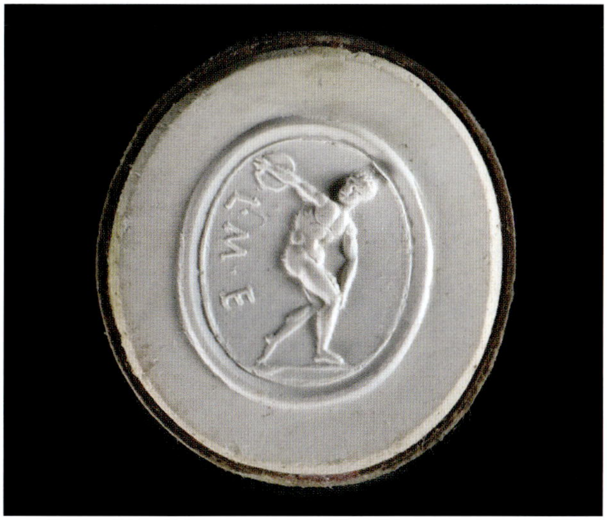

187

(10625) K87 (pl. 3)
Sard, polished flat back, set on a plain gold ring
10 x 8

SG.Imp. 58; Inst.Imp. no. 117; Paoletti I, II.565; *AG* pl. 44.26.

An athlete preparing to throw the discus, in the pose of Myron's statue. Ground line. Inscribed L.M.E.

For this popular subject see *Munich* 3, no. 2389; *Marlborough* no. 341.

1st century AD.

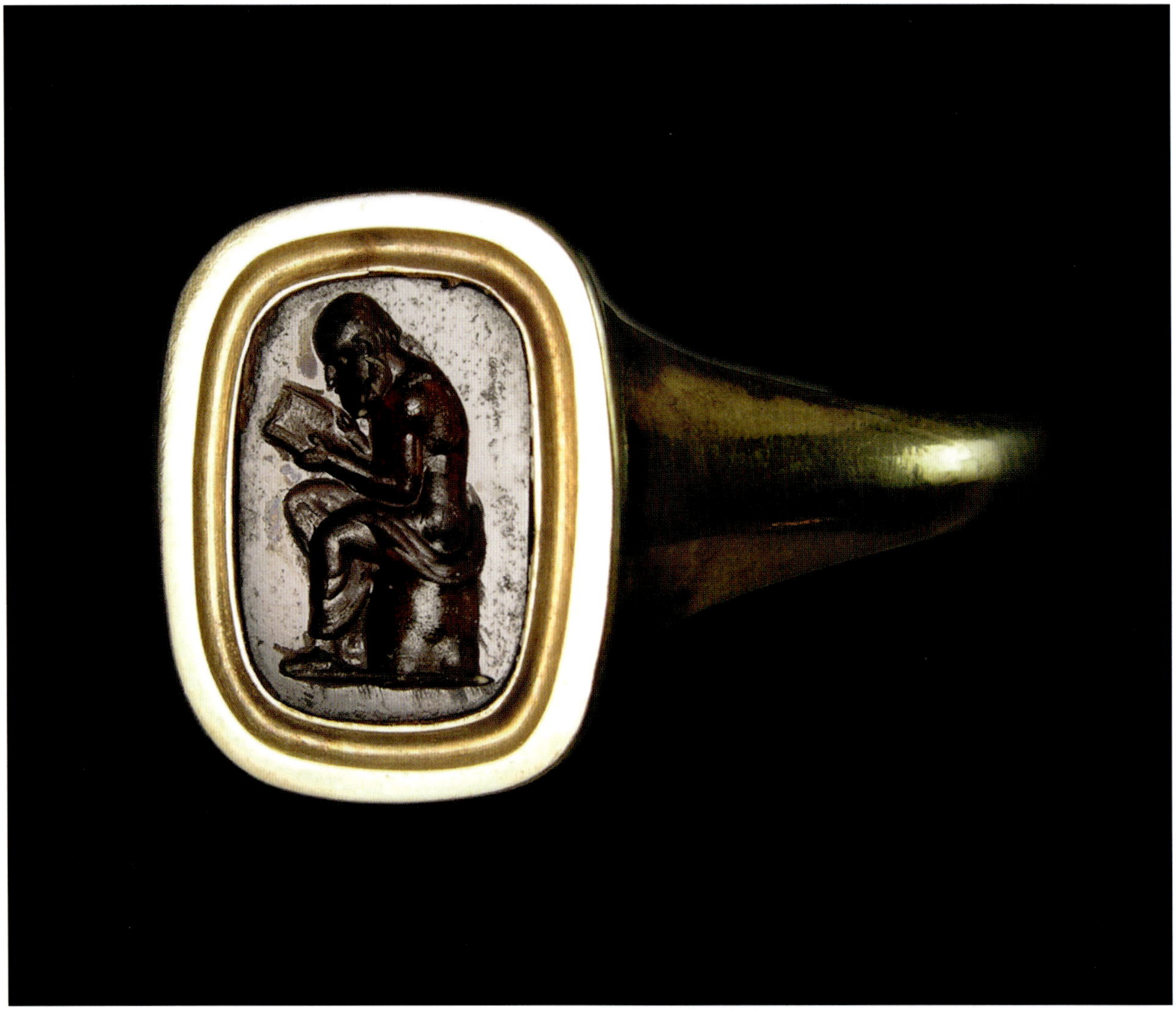

188

(10702) K164
Jacynth, convex back, set on a plain gold ring
9 x 6

SG.Imp. 55; Inst.Imp. no. 80.

An old man in a cloak sits on a block reading a scroll. Ground line.

For the subject compare *Würzburg* no. 443 and Lang, *Wissen,* 81–85, 167–172 (G TypA1-102).

2nd/1st century BC.

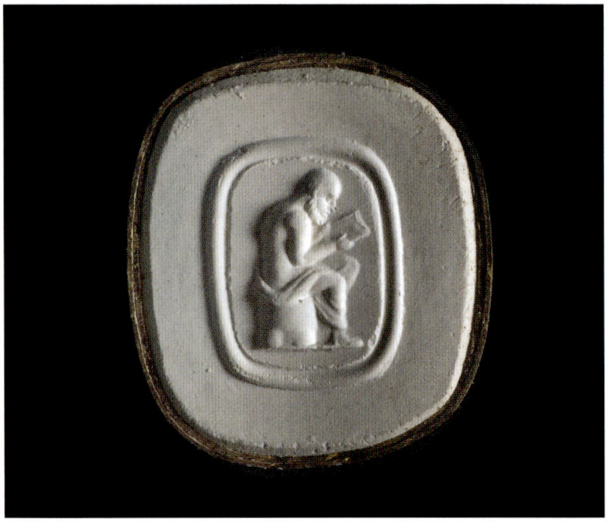

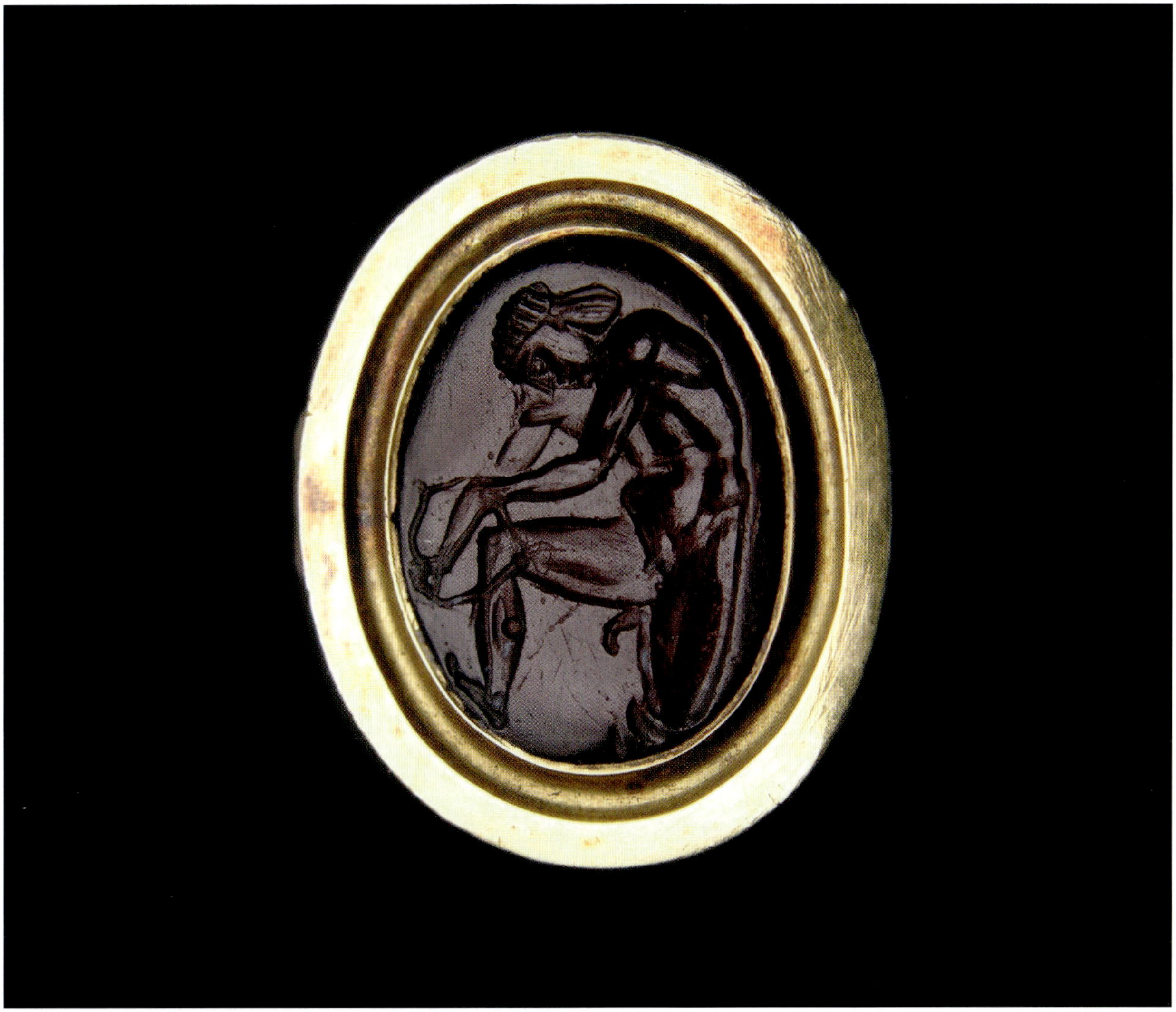

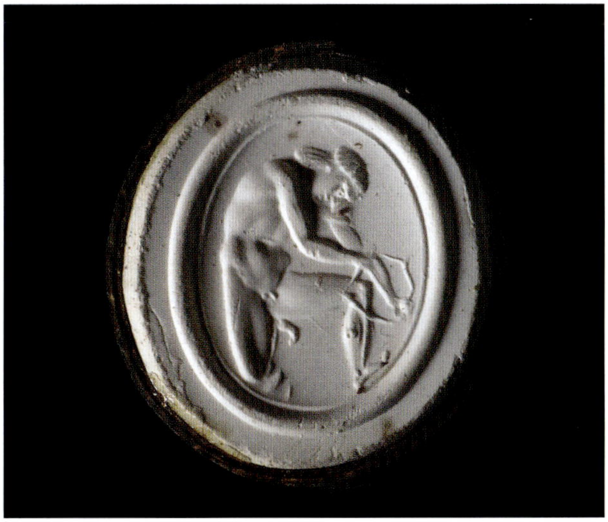

189

(10720) K182 (pl. 5)
Sard, polished flat back, set on a plain gold ring
9 x 7

SG.Imp. 94; Tassie 9368; Inst.Imp. no. 130; *AG* pl. 20.55.

A naked youth kneels to shoot an arrow. Furtwängler suggests Apollo.

2nd century BC.

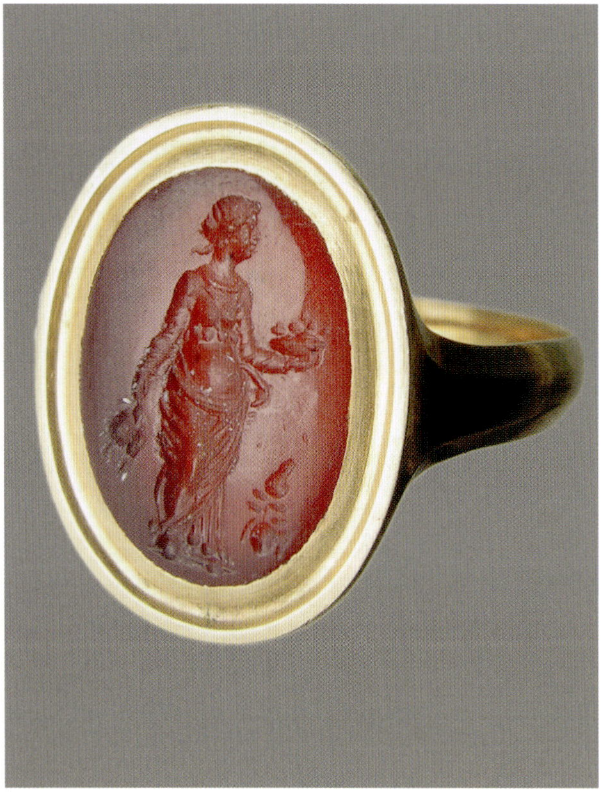

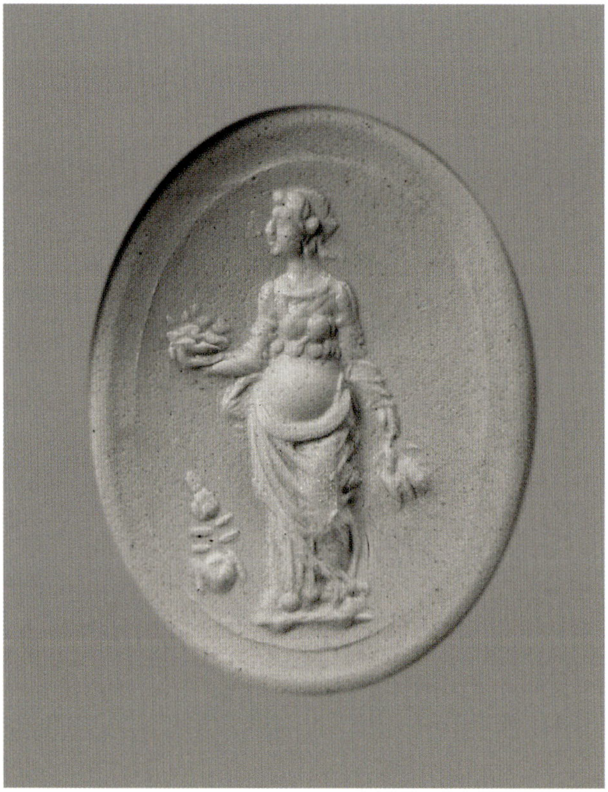

190

(10767)
Carnelian, polished flat back, set in a plain gold ring
13 x 10

Ceres, fully dressed, holding ears of corn and a basket of fruit. An ant in the field before her. Short ground line.

For a discussion of the type and earlier bibliography see M. Henig, *A Corpus of Roman Engraved Gemstones from British Sites*, BAR Brit.ser.8 (Oxford 1974), 30–40, no. 259.

1st century BC/AD.

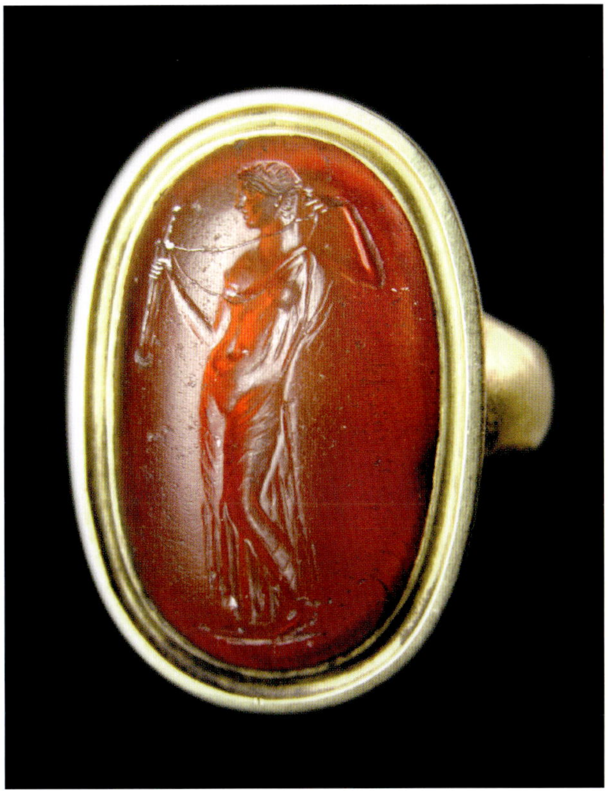

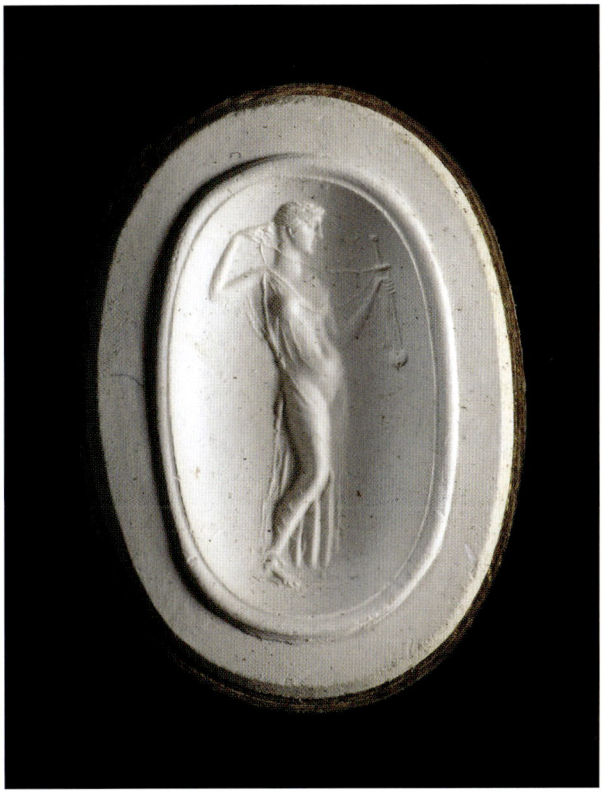

191

(10725) K187 (pl. 5)
Sard, polished flat back, set on a plain gold ring
22 x 12

SG.Imp. 173; Tassie 12673; Inst.Imp. no. 163.

A woman in light dress is slinging a sword around her neck. Ground line.

Venus is equipping herself with the arms of Ares. The same subject on a cameo in Florence, *LIMC* I, pl. 52.531.

2nd/1st century BC.

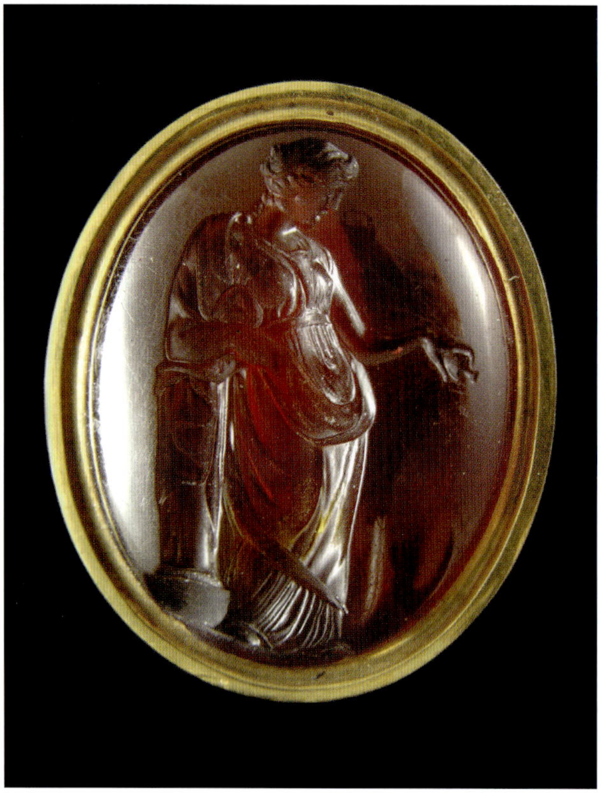
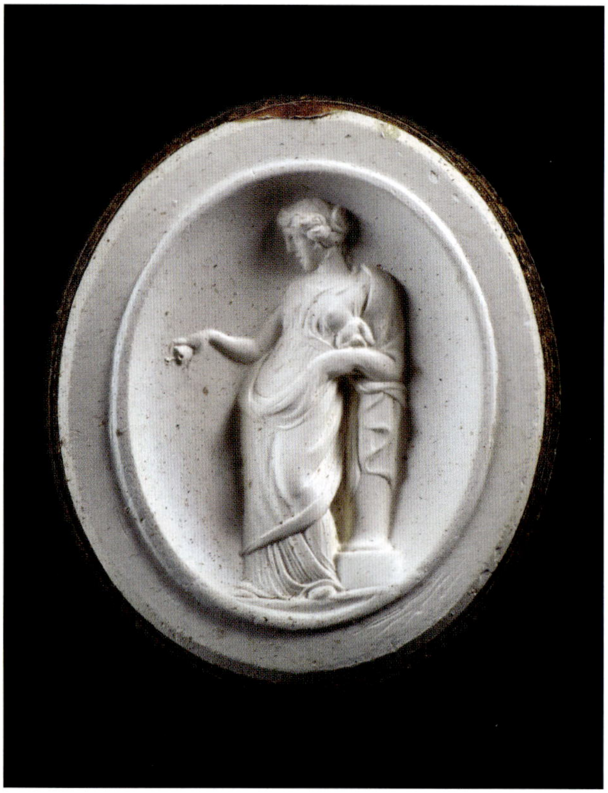

192

(10619) K81 (pl. 3)
Sard, Polished flat back. Set on a plain gold ring.
25 x 19

SG.Imp. 185; Inst.Imp. no. 171; W.Tassie 1954; King 1872, pl. 23.3; King 1885, pl. 55.1.

A woman, fully dressed and immaculately coiffed, leans on a low column and pours from a small flask. Ground line.

The pose with the column is a popular Hellenistic one for goddesses and others.

2nd century BC.

193

(10765)

Green glass with the reversed intaglio figure gilt, set in a silver ring with hatched sides to the bezel

15 x 11

A naked maenad dancing but holding her dress behind her and a staff with balls at each end. Short ground line.

For the unusual technique compare an early example, *GGFR* pl. 822, and a gold ring showing a panther from a tomb at Mentana, G. Bordenache Battaglia, *Corredi funerari di età imperiale e barbarica nel Museo nazionale romano* (Rome 1983), 44–48, no. 3, with a discussion of others. The technique was revived in the Renaissance. Valerio Belli produced a gilded reverse intaglio carving of Mars, Minerva, Venus, and Cupid, in rock crystal, now in the Cleveland Museum of Art.

1st century AD.

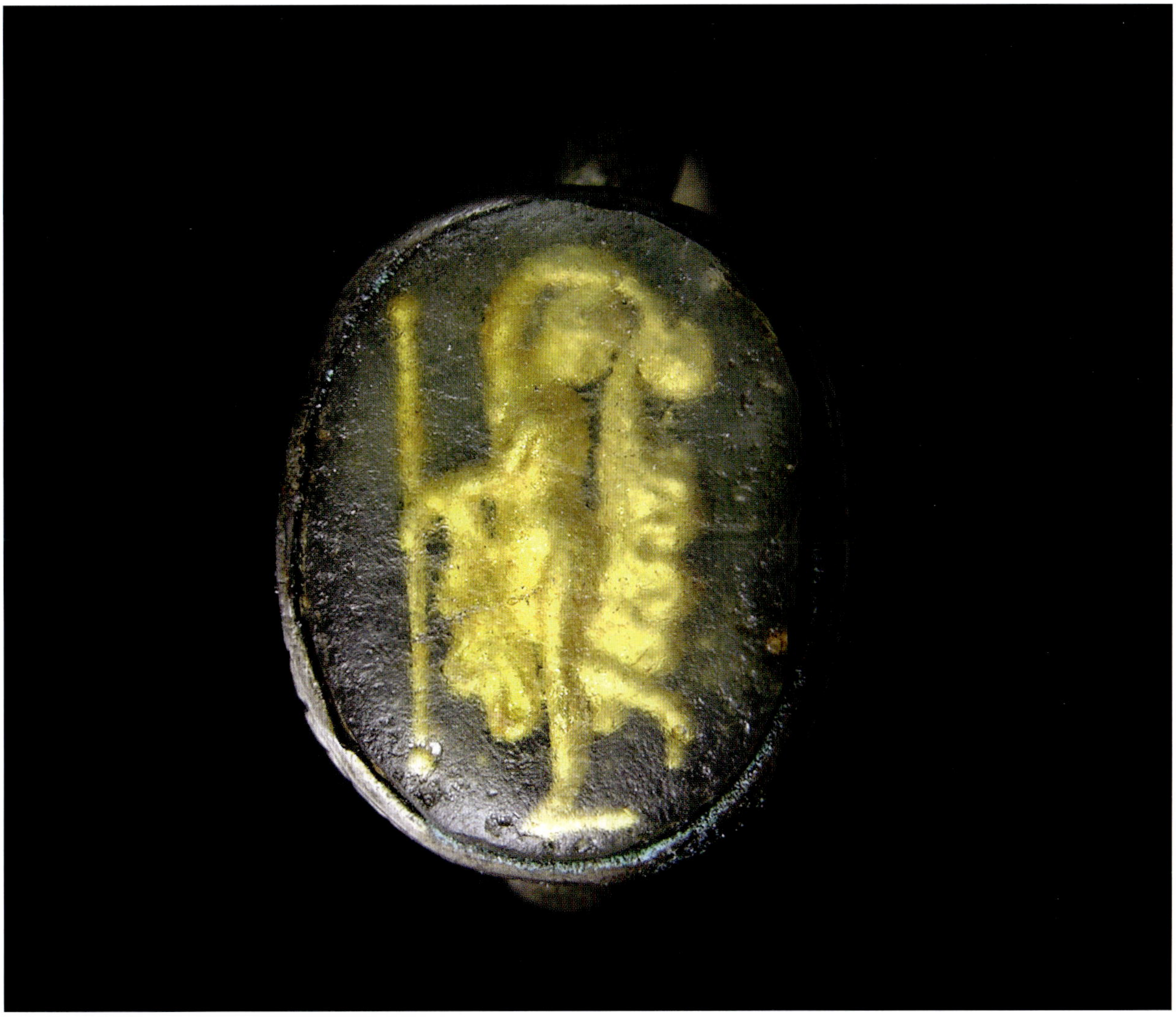

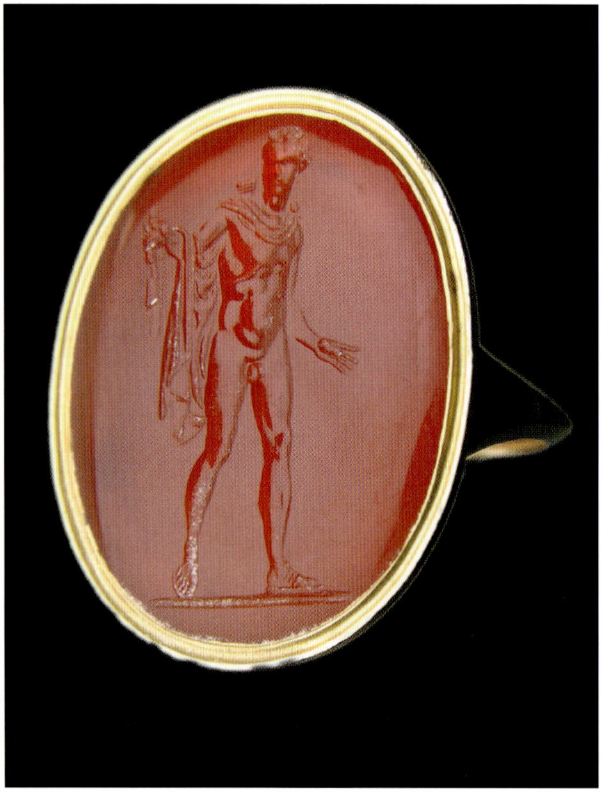

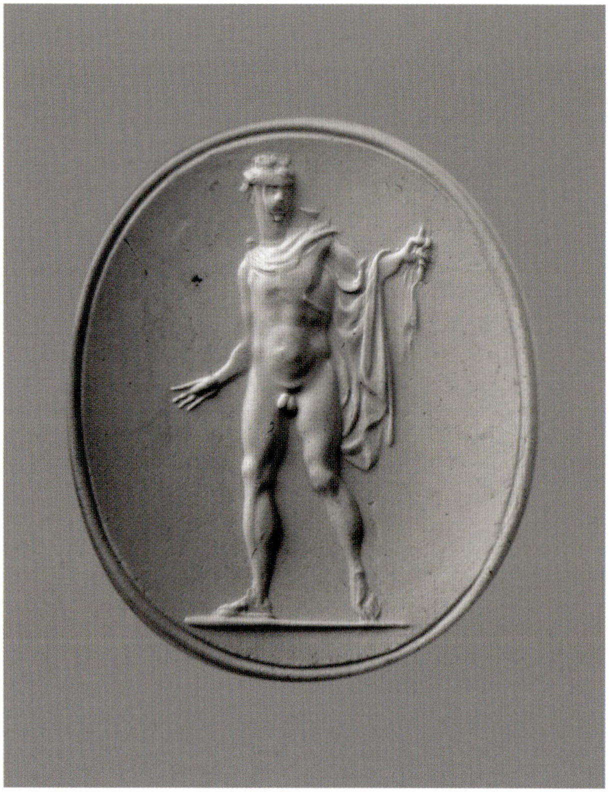

194

(10753)
Carnelian, polished convex back, set in a plain gold ring
23 x 19

Apollo Belvedere, a copy of the statue in the Vatican. The god, with dressed hair, wears a quiver, stepping forward with dress around his neck and over one arm holding what appears to be a short stick (originally a bow). Ground line.

Compare the figure on *Marlborough* no. 605 (where he holds a scroll); Paoletti II, VIII.298.

18th century.

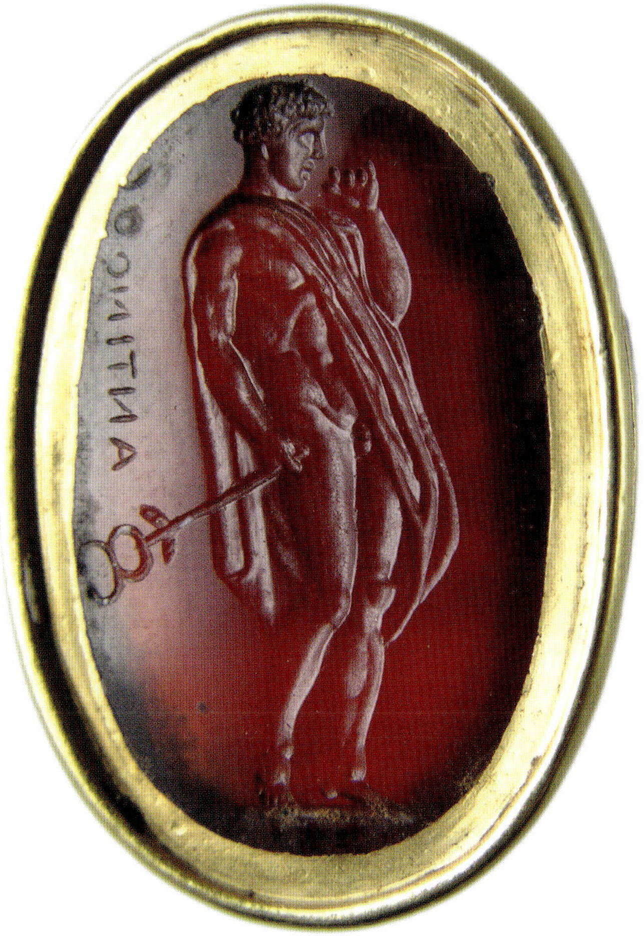

195

(10769)
Carnelian, polished convex back, set on a gold ring with enamelled floral terminals and a black enamel lump at the back of the hoop
17 x 11

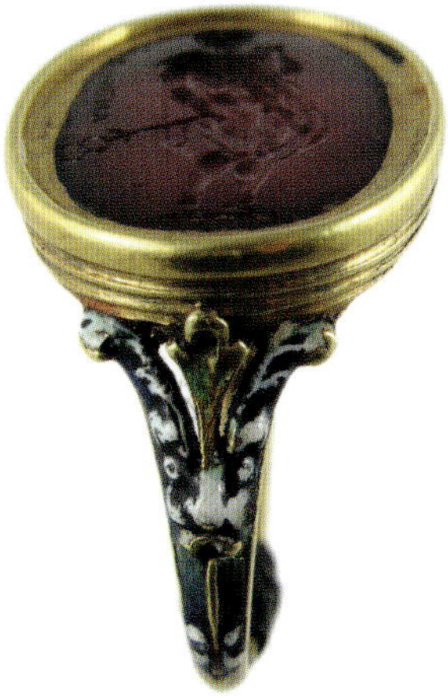

Hermes/Mercury standing, dress around one shoulder, holding a winged caduceus, with his other hand raised towards his head. Ground line.

Inscribed ANTINOOC, as if Hadrian's favourite posing as a god, a possible conceit for antiquity but this is probably 18th century.

18th century?

196

(10666) K128 (pl. 6)
Nicolo, polished flat back, set on a plain gold ring
13 x 10

Tassie 7063; Inst.Imp. no. 55.

Wingless Cupid raises a butterfly (Psyche) in his arms, seated on what Knight perhaps rightly judged to be the chrysalis from which the insect had emerged.

18th century?

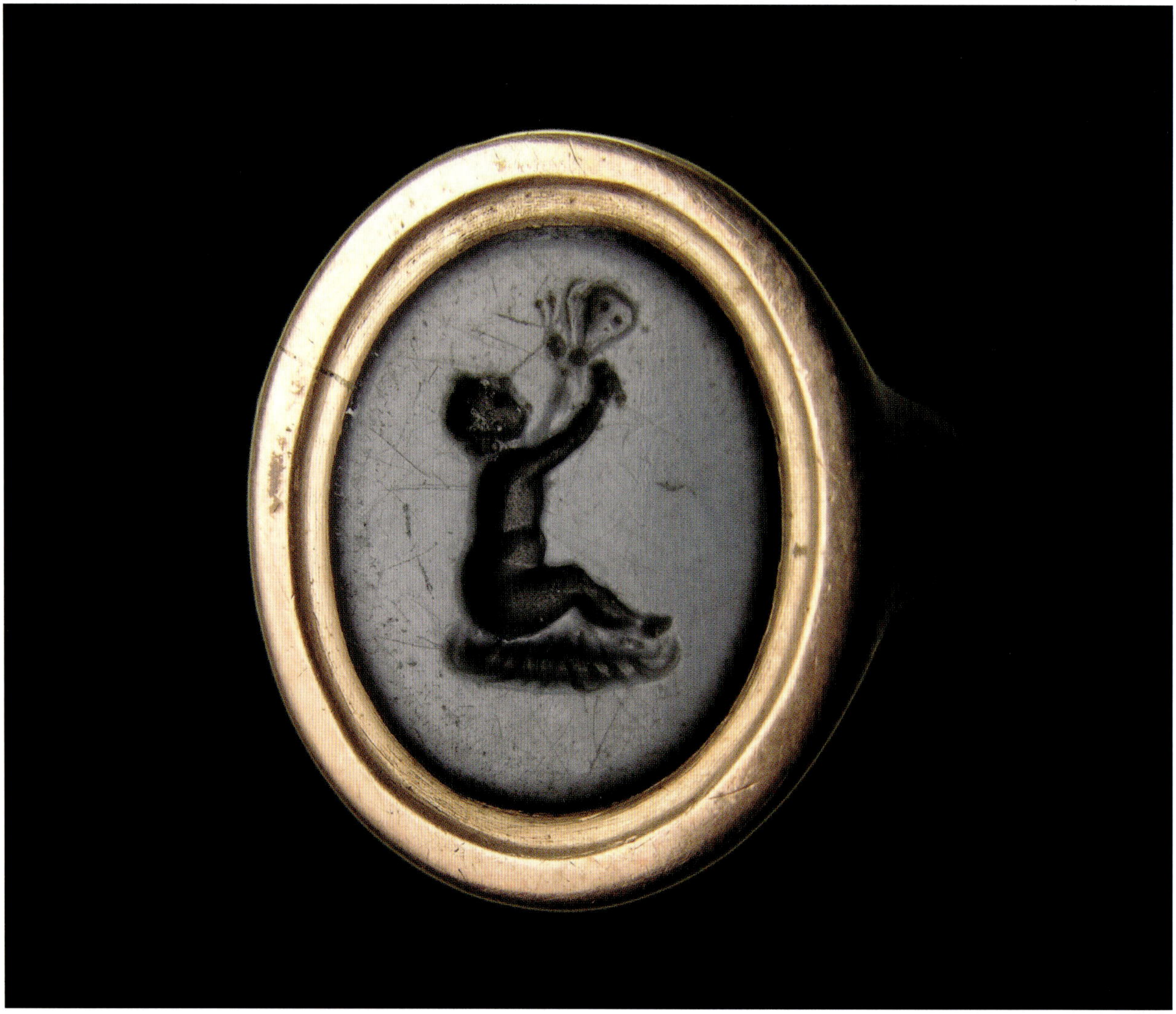

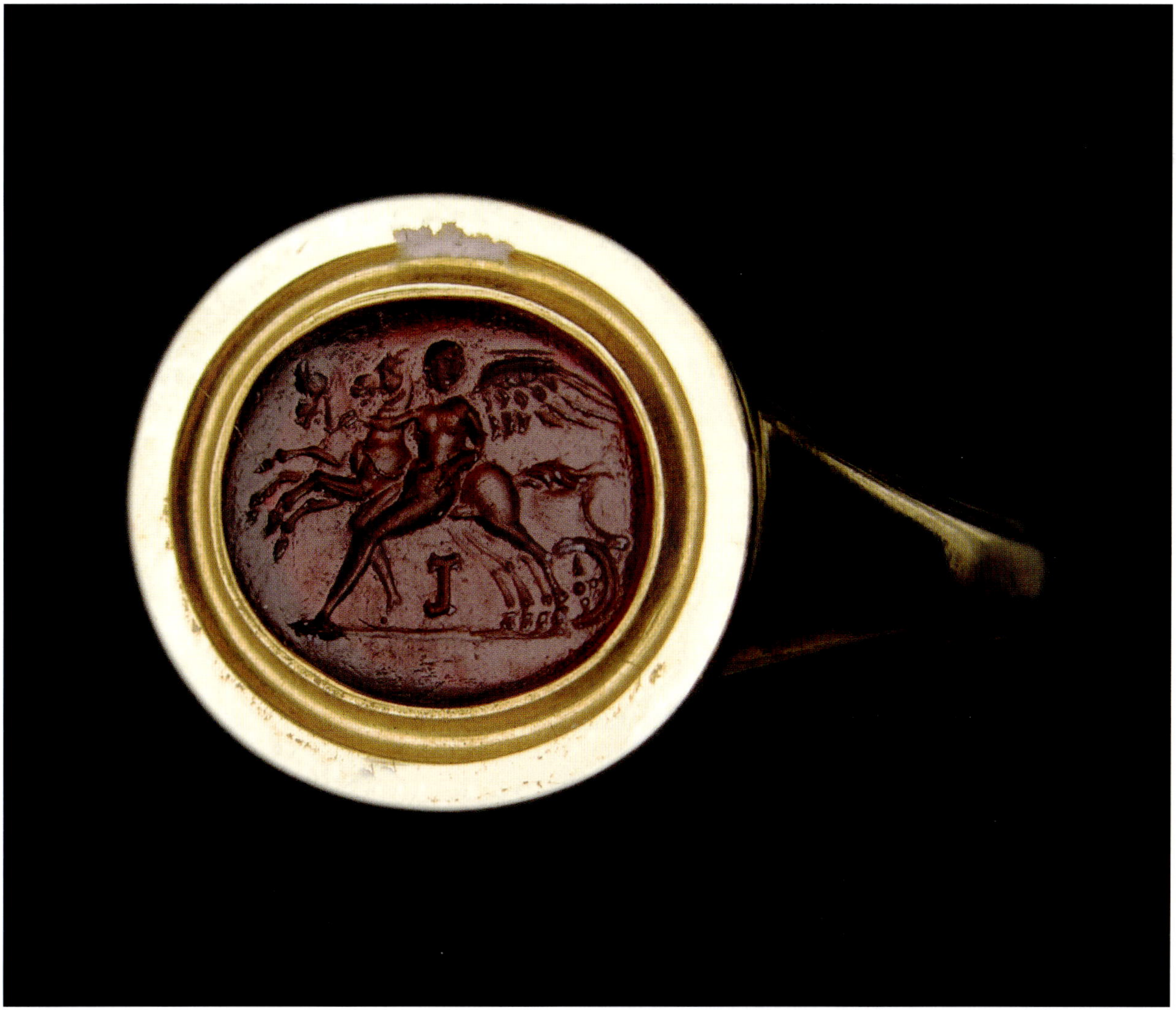

197

(10709) K171 (pl. 6)
Sard, polished flat back, set on a plain gold ring
9 x 7

SG.Imp. 74; Inst.Imp. no. 131; Paoletti I, I.400.

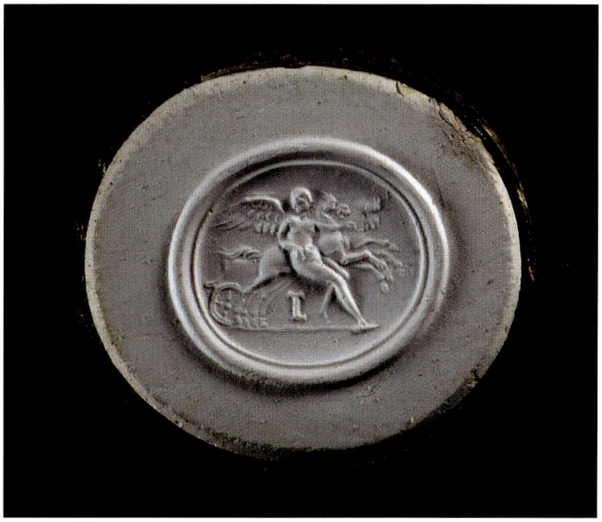

Cupid holds two horses drawing a chariot of which we see the wheels and car. Inscribed I.

This is a popular excerpt, found also in antiquity, from a fuller scene where we see that the chariot was that of Bacchus, in his Triumph, and drawn by two lions not horses. Compare our **44**. See Vollenweider, 33, pl. 24.1–2, by Sostratos.

Probably 18th century.

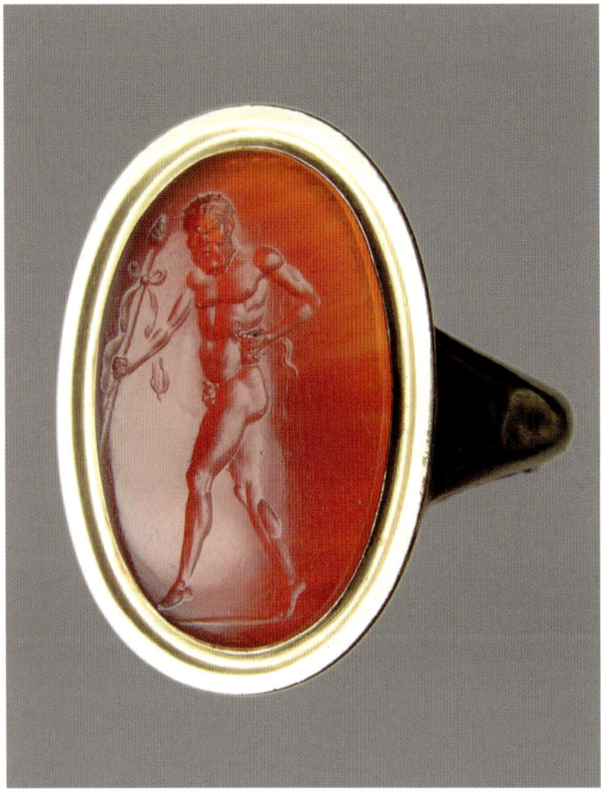

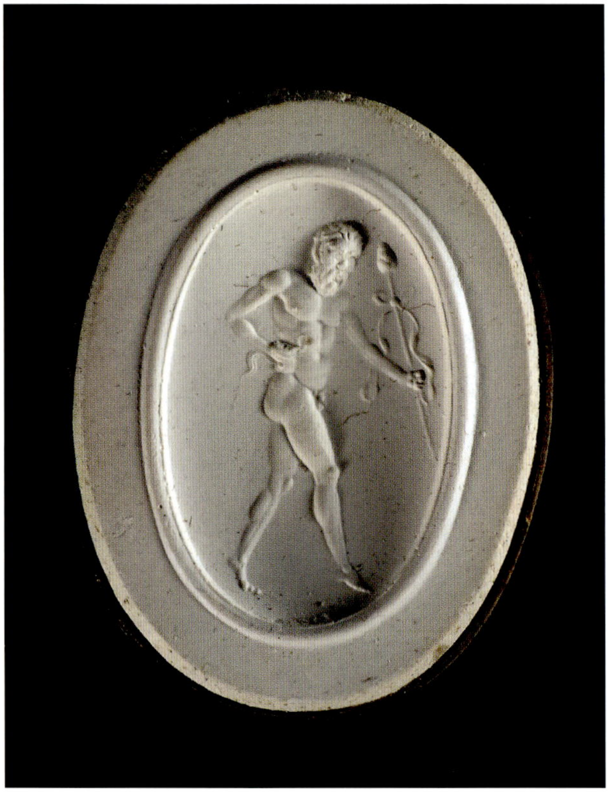

198

(10763)
Carnelian, polished flat back, set in a plain gold ring
18 x 11

SG.Imp. 104; Inst.Imp. no. 165; Paoletti II, VIII.262; Lippold, pl. 109.4.

A bearded satyr walking on tiptoe holding a ribboned thyrsos and a bunch of grapes. Ground line.

18th century.

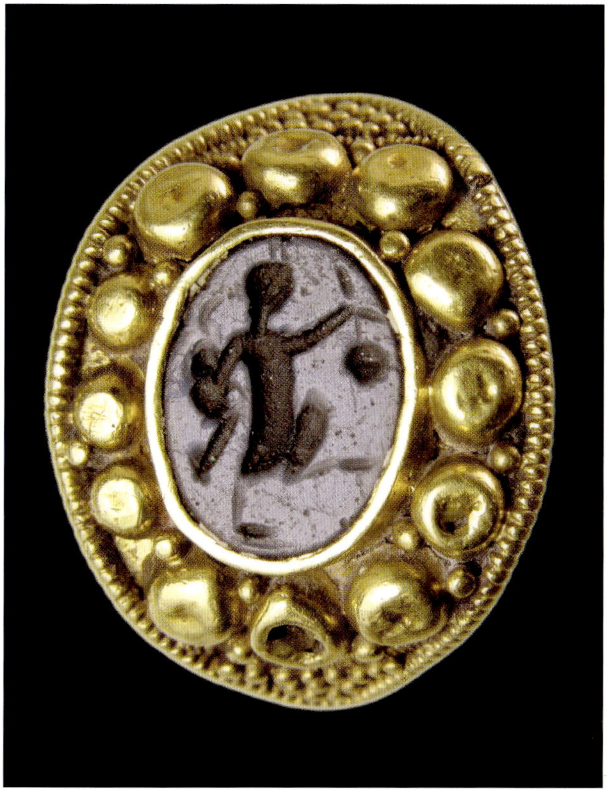 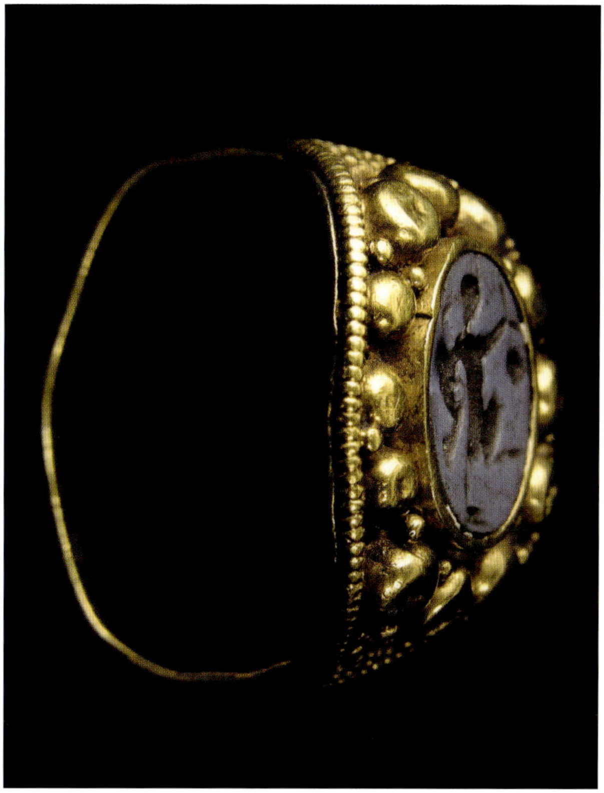

199

(10552)
Nicolo, set in a gold ring with a broad edge to the bezel, decorated with studs
11 x 9, bezel 22 x 23

A young Pan dancing, holding a wineskin and a bunch of grapes.

The ring is perhaps Merovingian. Hadjadj 2007, no. 448, illustrates a ring with a similar circular bezel with the centre stone surrounded by cabochon gems and pearls (gold globules here) in a beaded border, found in north France.

Intaglio: 1st/2nd century AD; ring: either AD 400–450 or AD 600–650.

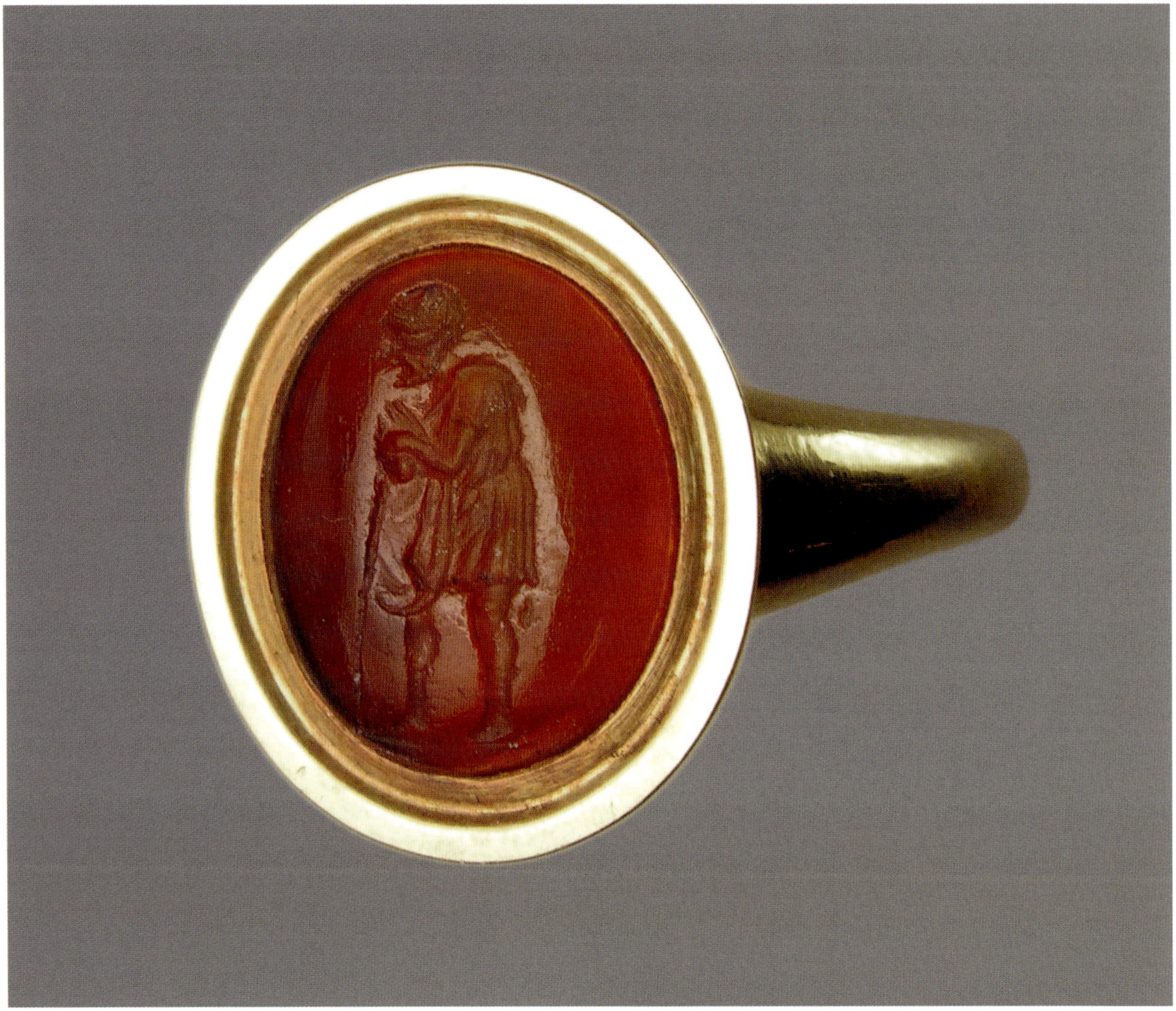

200

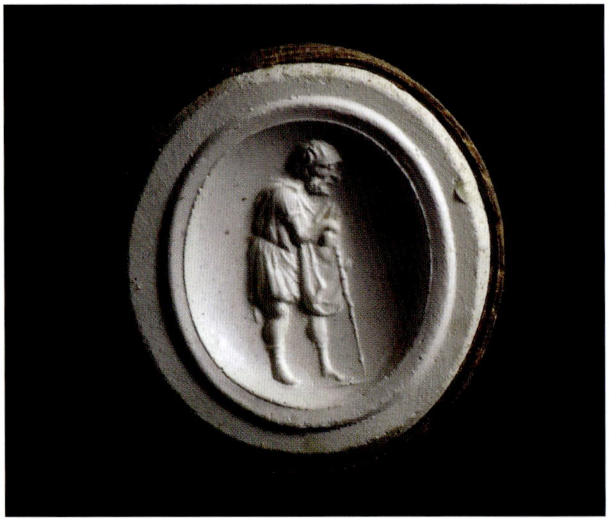

(10701) K163 (pl. 6)
Sard, polished flat back, set on a plain gold ring
12 x 10

SG.Imp. 86; Inst.Imp. no. 138.

An old man in short dress, a voluminous cloak covering his front and back, and boots is leaning on a knobbed staff, holding a purse (?). Ground line.

Compare *Geneva* no. 496, 497

1st century BC.

201

(10620) K82 (pl. 3)
Sard, polished flat back, set on a gold ring with forked ends to the hoop
12 x 11

A bearded and bald poet or actor in a cloak seated on a wicker chair (with a back rest) before a mask of a youth on a column. He is holding a scroll and raising a finger, as if declaiming. Ground line.

For a detailed discussion of the type see Lang, *Wissen*, 81–85, with comparanda.

1st century BC/AD.

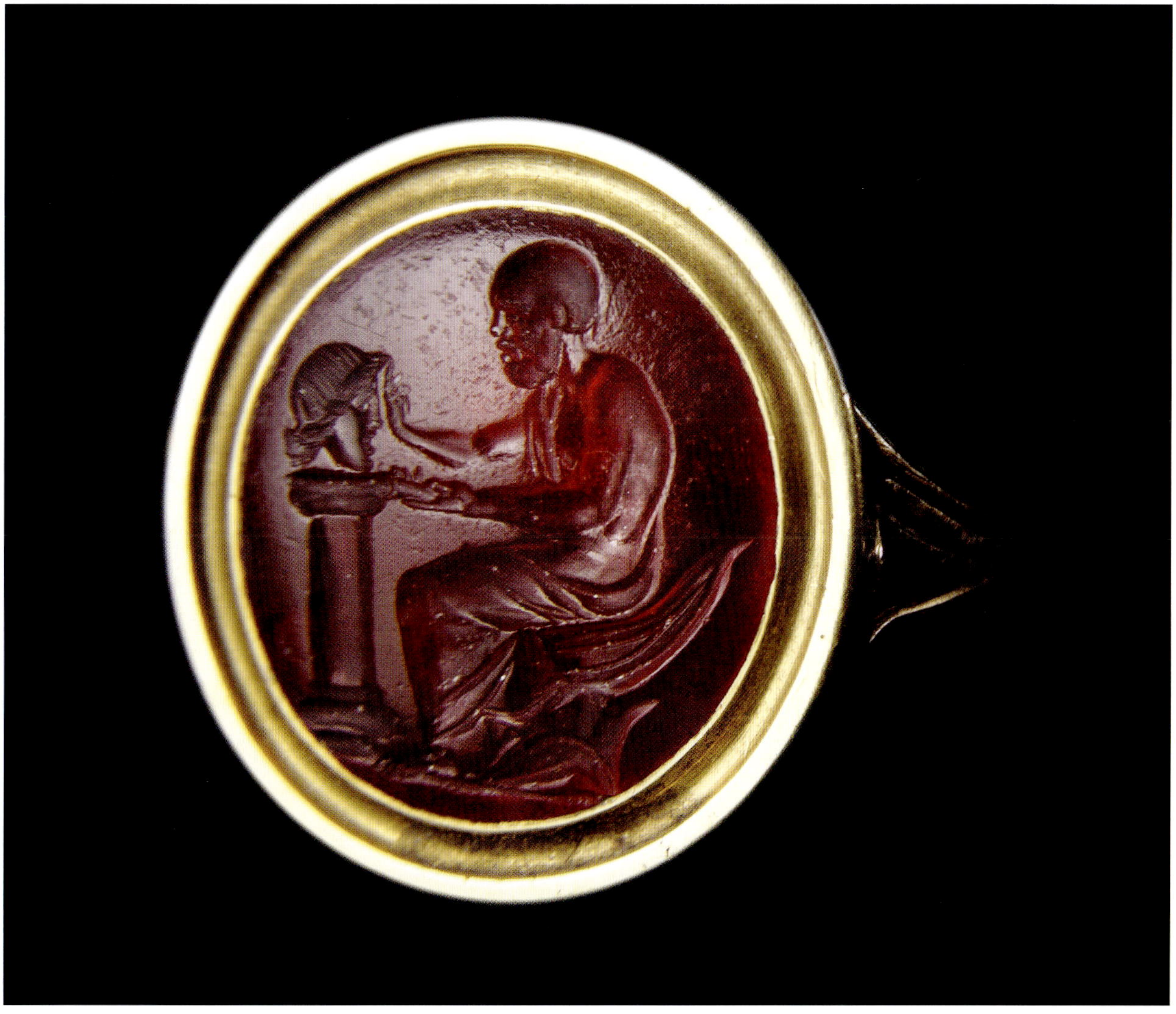

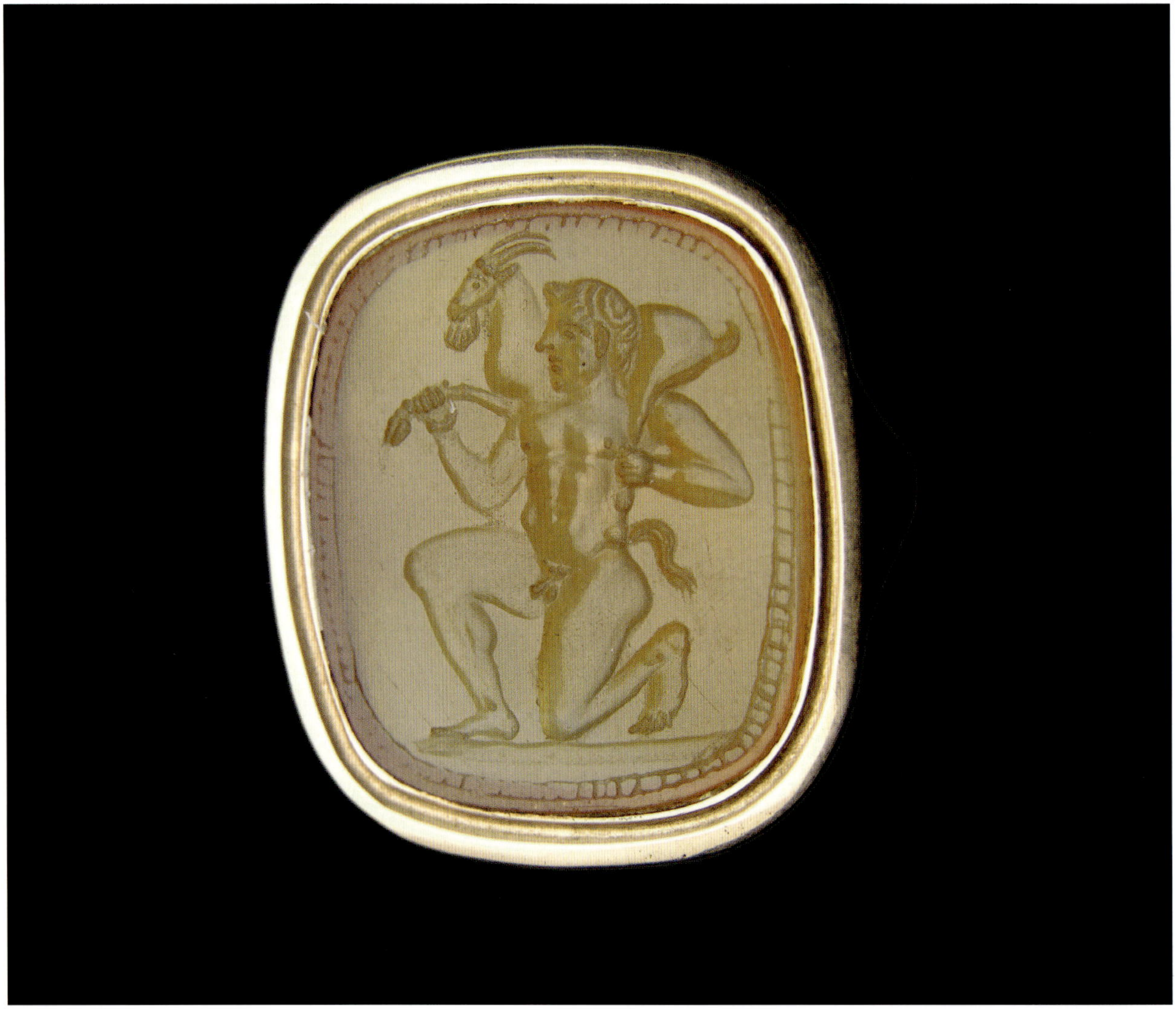

202

(10723) K185 (pl. 5)
Pale sard, polished flat back, set on a plain gold ring
21 x 18

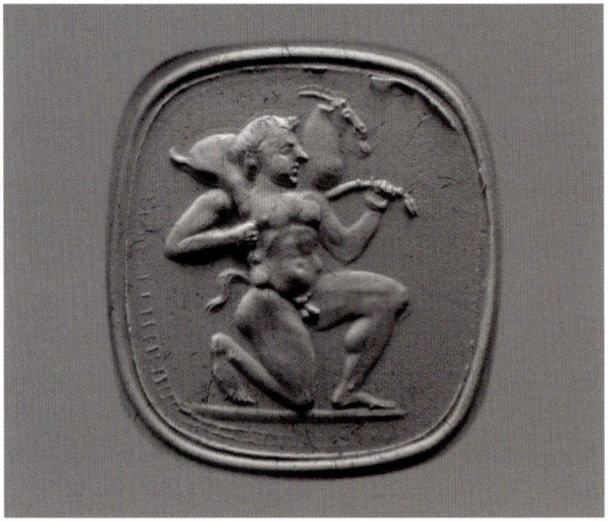

Paoletti II, V.134; Lippold, pl. 109.1.

A naked young satyr kneels, shouldering a billy goat. Ground line. Hatched border.

Possibly Italic. 1st century BC.

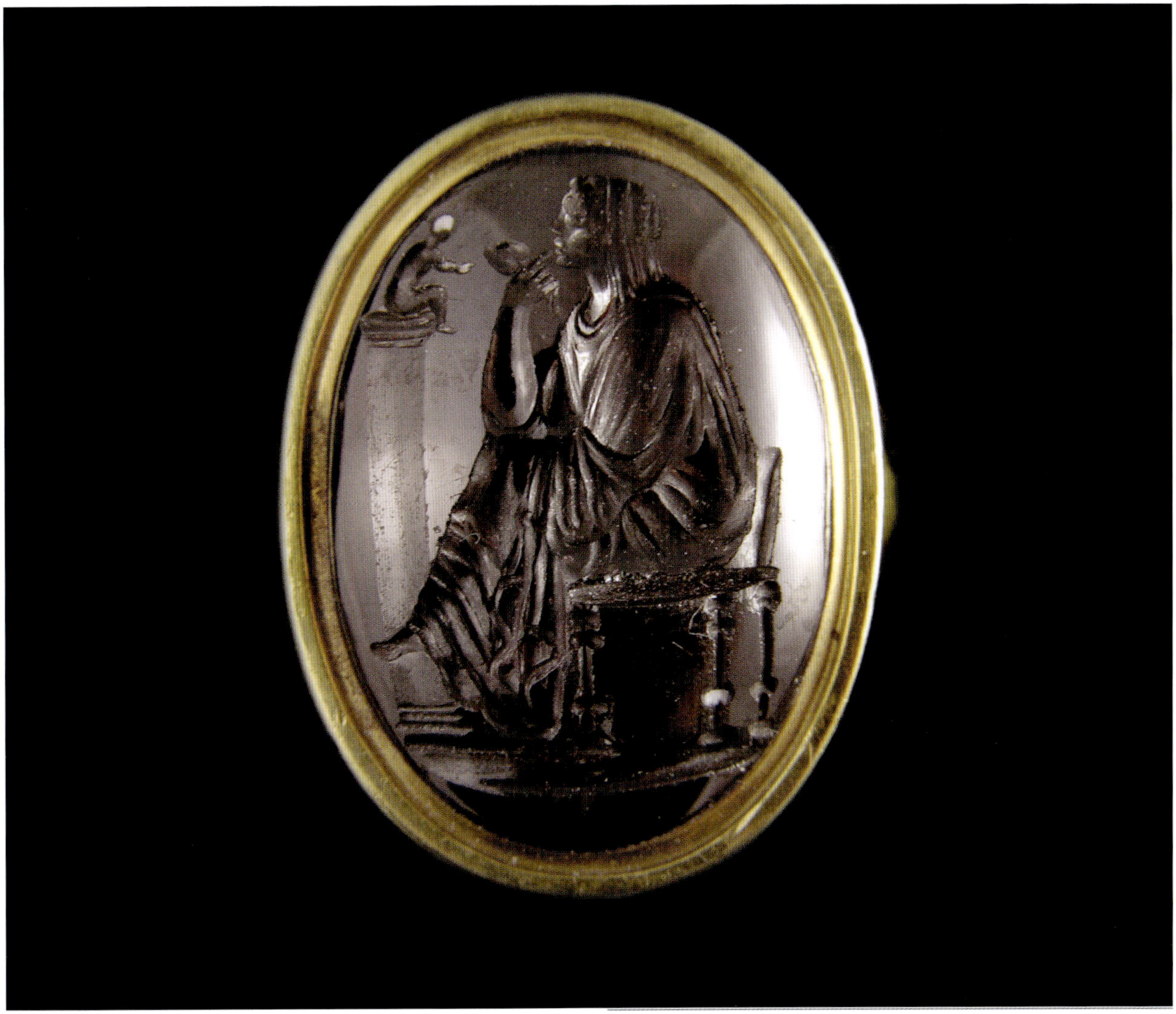

203

(10636) K98 (pl. 4)
Almandine, polished flat back, set on a plain gold ring
20 x 14

King 1872, pl. 17.8 (as Polymnia, once Calpurnia).

A fully dressed and veiled woman, seated on a chair with turned legs, and holding an ivy leaf up to her face, pensively, contemplates a column on which is seated a boy stretching his arms to her. Footstool and ground line.

She is probably a version of a figure of a Muse, after the garnet in the Cabinet des Médailles ('Calpurnie inquiète sur le sort de César', Mariette 1750, pl. 104) which Vollenweider takes to be a portrait of Arsinoe III with an infant Cupid or Bacchus (*Camées et Intailles* I (1995) no. 74). Otherwise taken for Juno and the infant Mars (Paoletti I, I.156; II, V.478). A shell cameo copy in the British Museum, Hull Grundy, no. 884.

18th century.

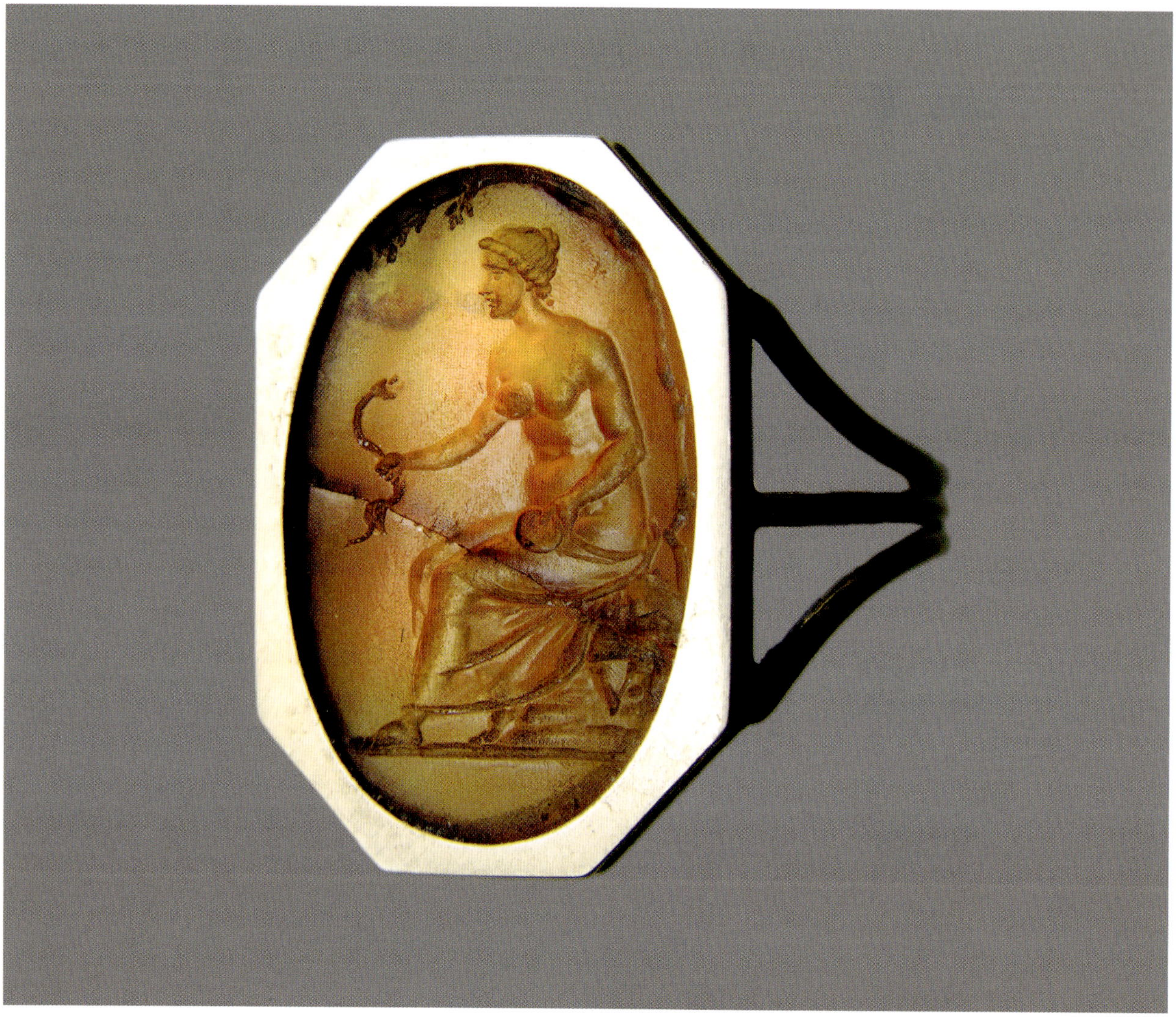

204

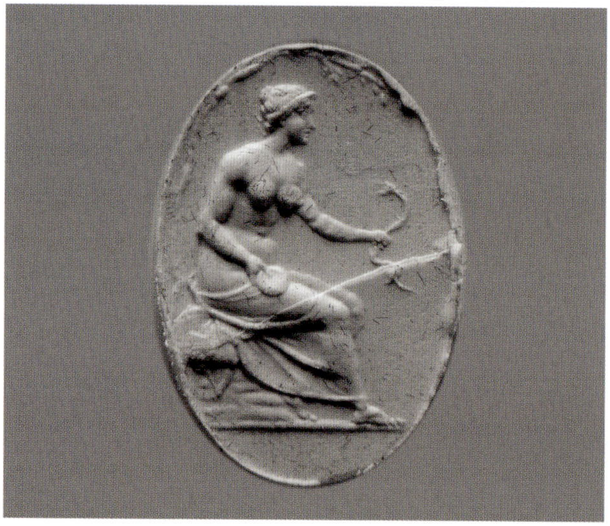

(10731) K193 (pl. 5)

Sard, polished flat back, set on a gold ring with triple forks at the hoop ends.

18 x 12

Hygieia, dress around her legs, seated on a rock, holding a phiale and a snake, beneath a tree.

Ancient figures of this goddess are always more fully dressed.

18th century.

205

(10553) K15 (pl. 3)
Carnelian, polished flat back, set on a plain gold ring
21 x 12

A young wreathed satyr, wearing an animal skin at one shoulder, is playing double pipes. Ground line.

18th century?

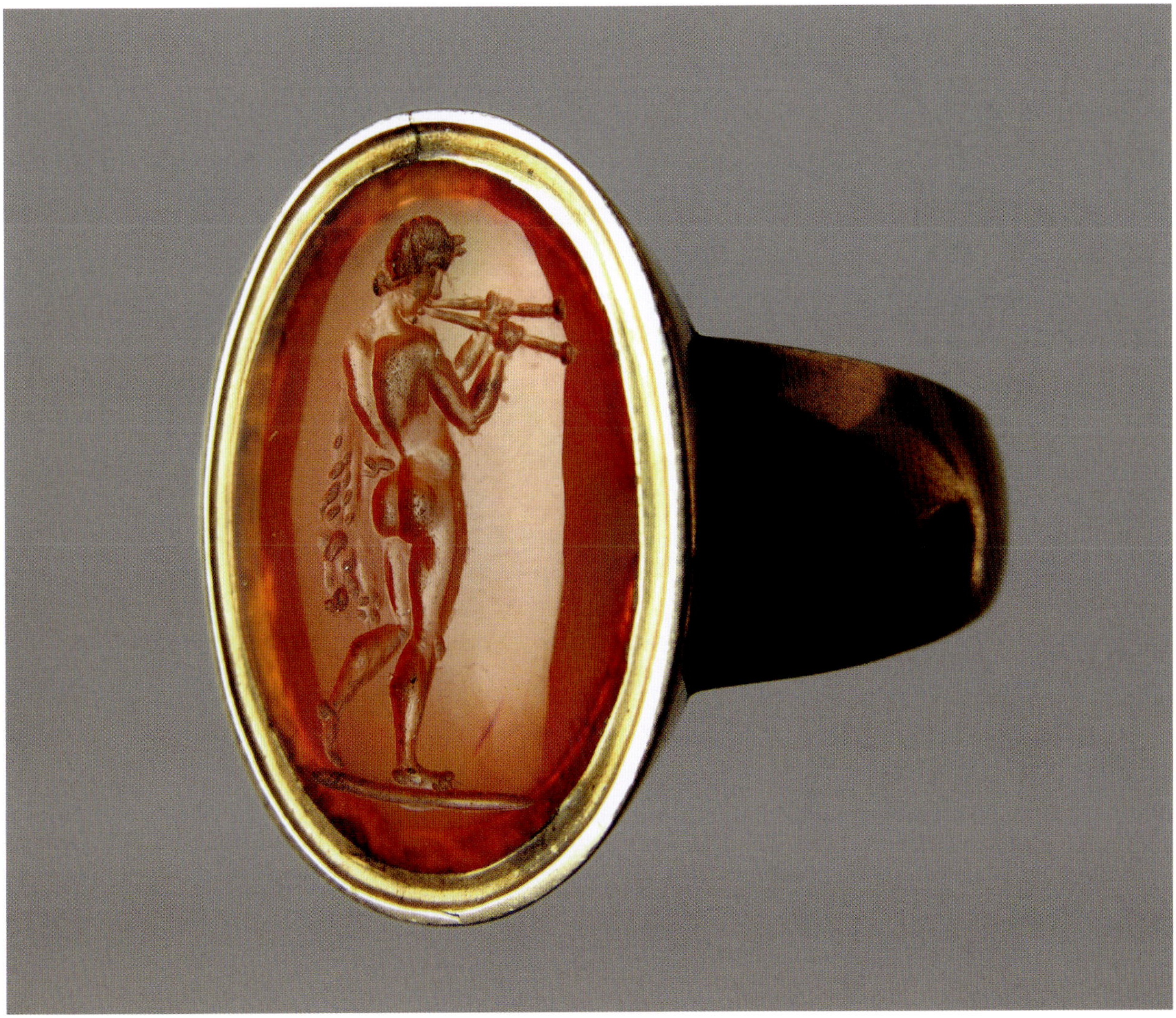

HEADS AND BUSTS, MALE

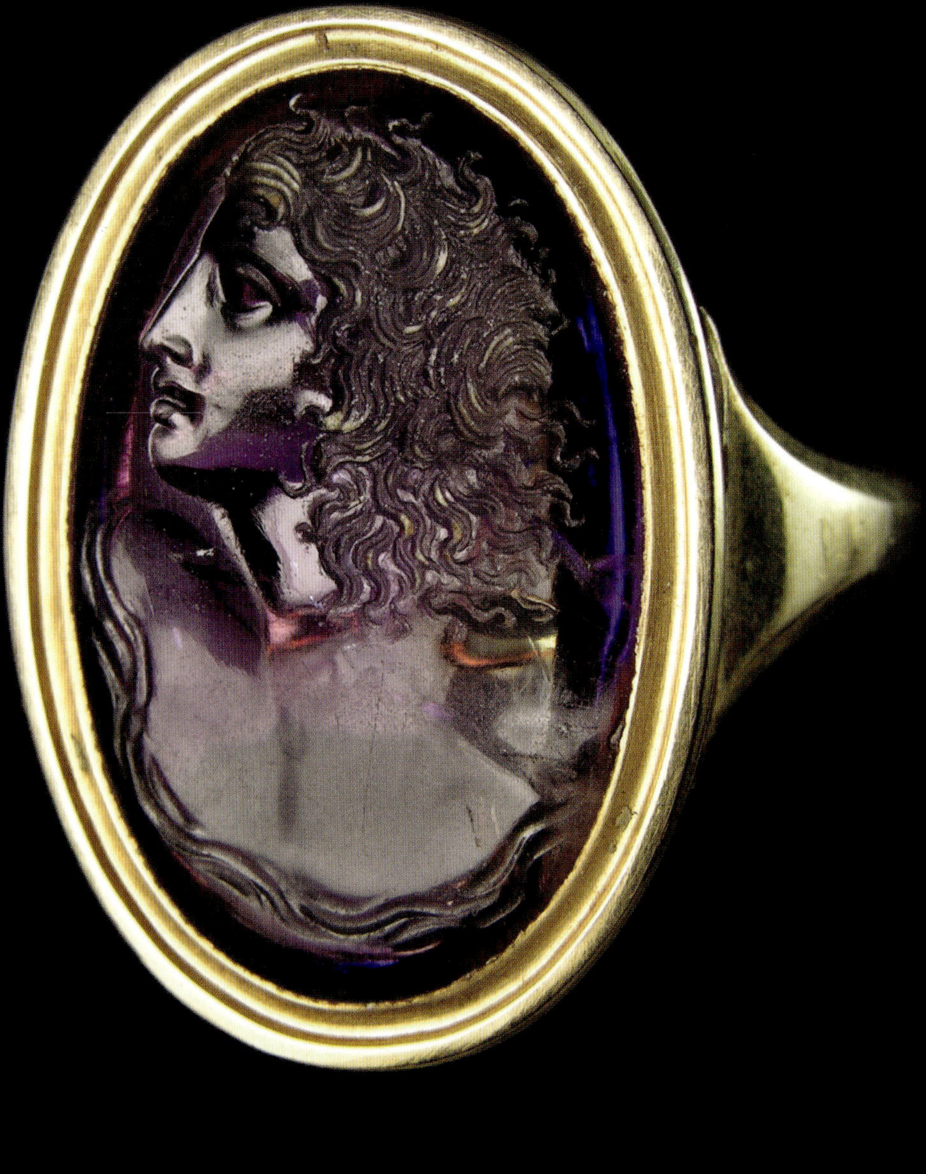

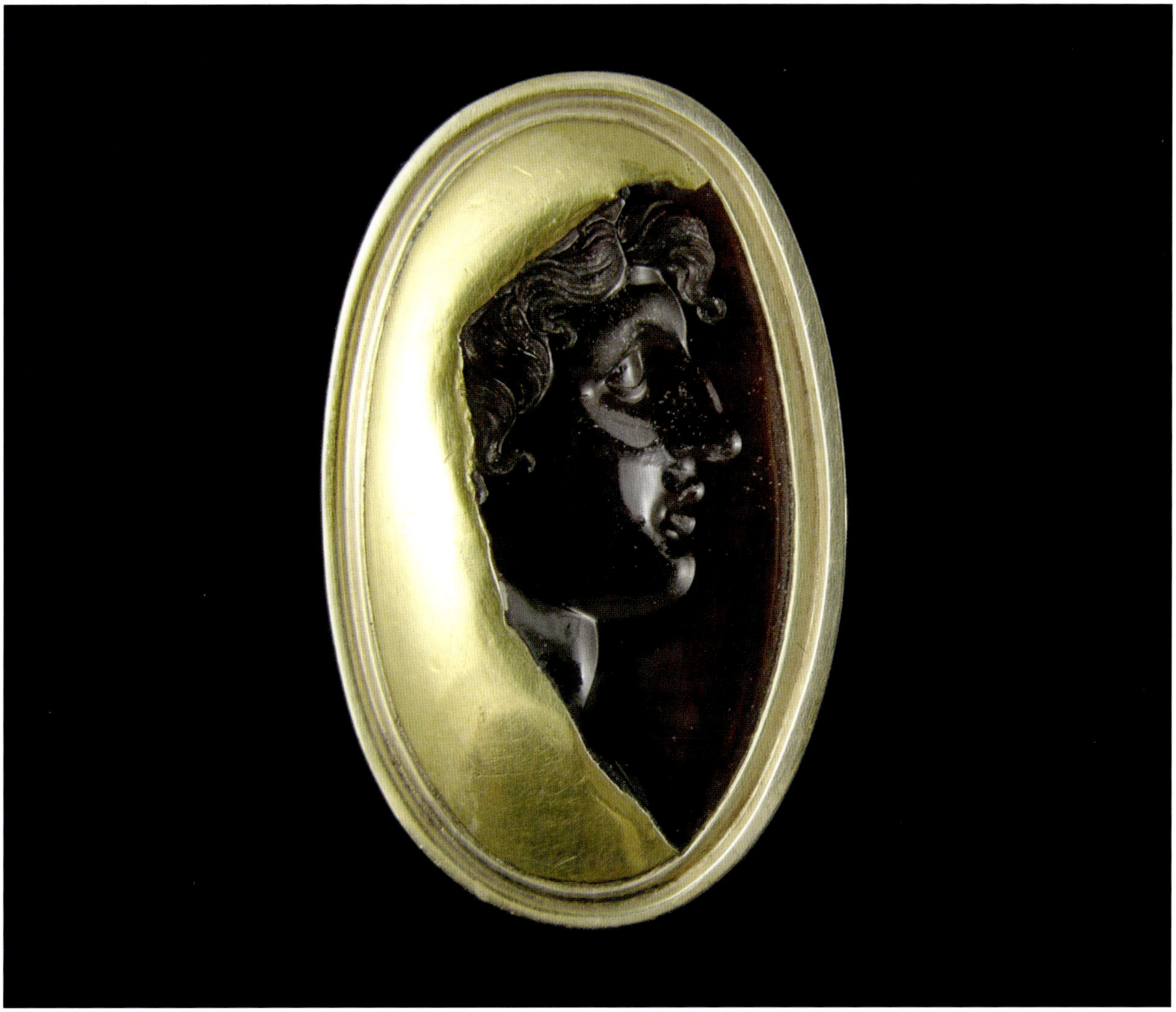

206

(10635) K97 (pl. 4)
Sard fragment, polished flat back, set on a plain gold ring
23 x 10

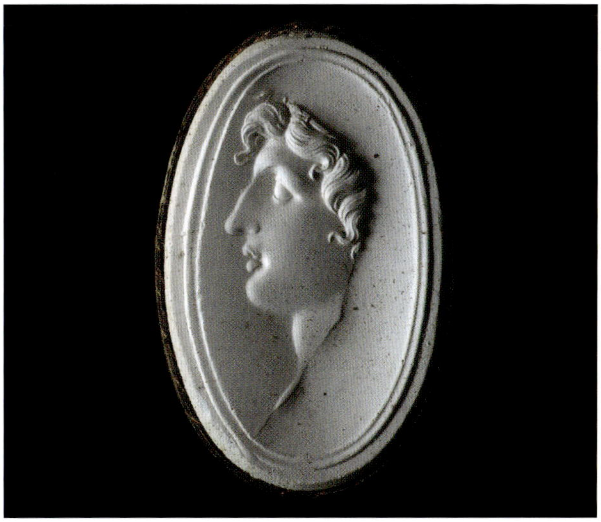

SG.Imp. 180; Inst.Imp. no. 94; Paoletti I, II.477; Kagan 2010, 295, fig. 48.

Head of Alexander the Great (?).

The head was copied by Marchant for a gem also once in the Beverley Collection, but now in the Hermitage, St Petersburg (see Seidmann 1987, 41, no.7; Kagan 2010, 294–5). Compare *Würzburg* pl. 15 for the type.

3rd/2nd century BC?

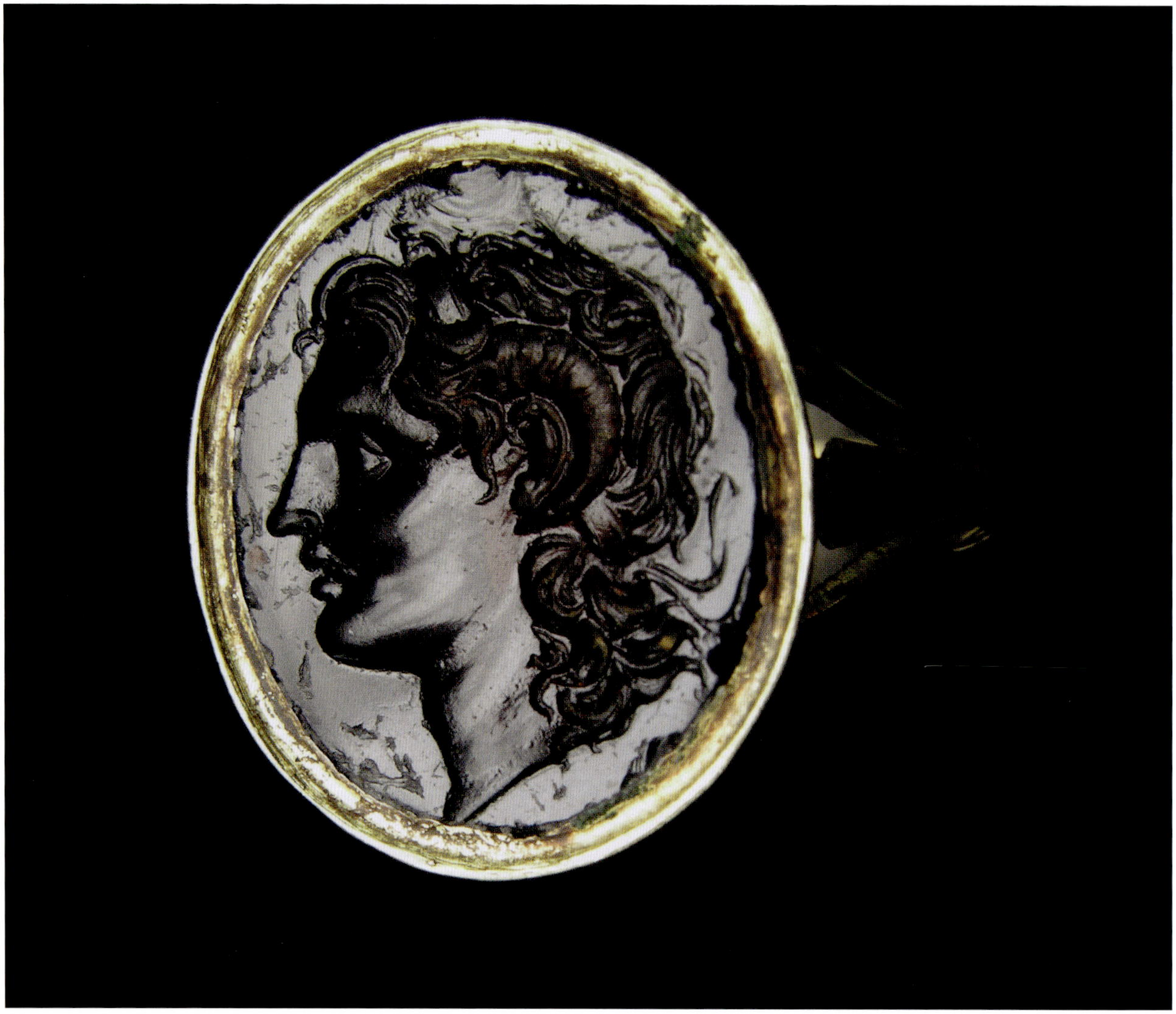

207

(10789)
Garnet, polished convex back, set on a gold ring with triple-forked terminals to the hoop
15 x 13

Head of Alexander the Great wearing the horns of Ammon.

This is probably Hellenistic, 2nd/1st century BC.

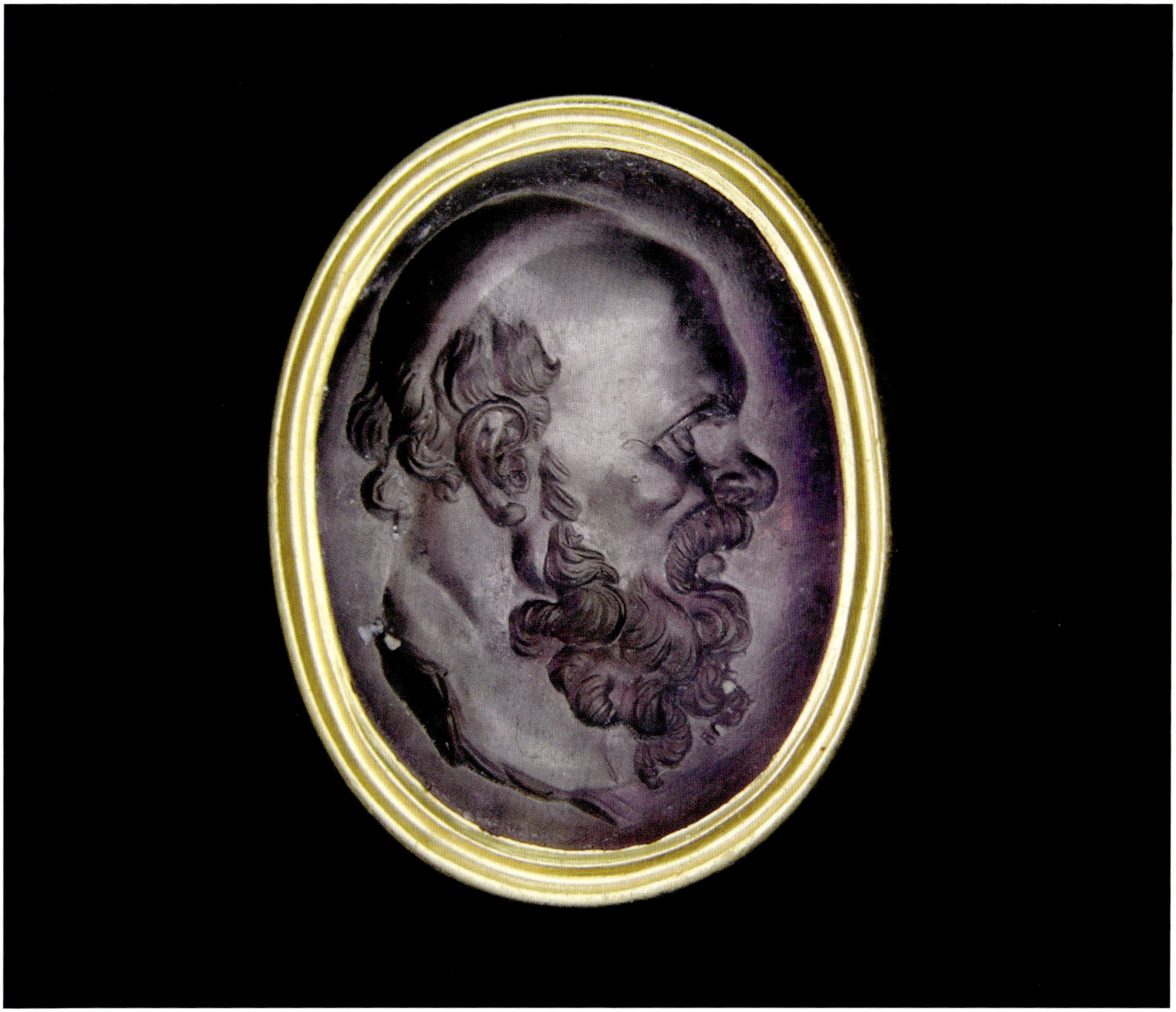

208

(10797)
Amethyst, polished flat back, set on a plain gold ring
16 x 13

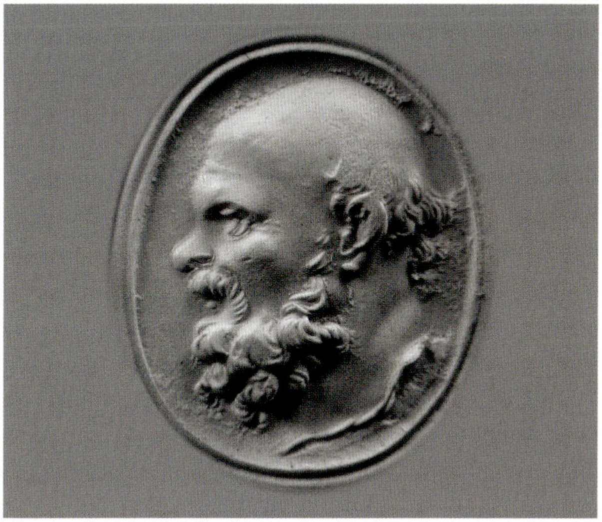

Portrait head of Socrates.

Compare Lang, *Wissen*, 59–64 and *Würzburg* nos 502–5.

Hellenistic. 2nd century BC?

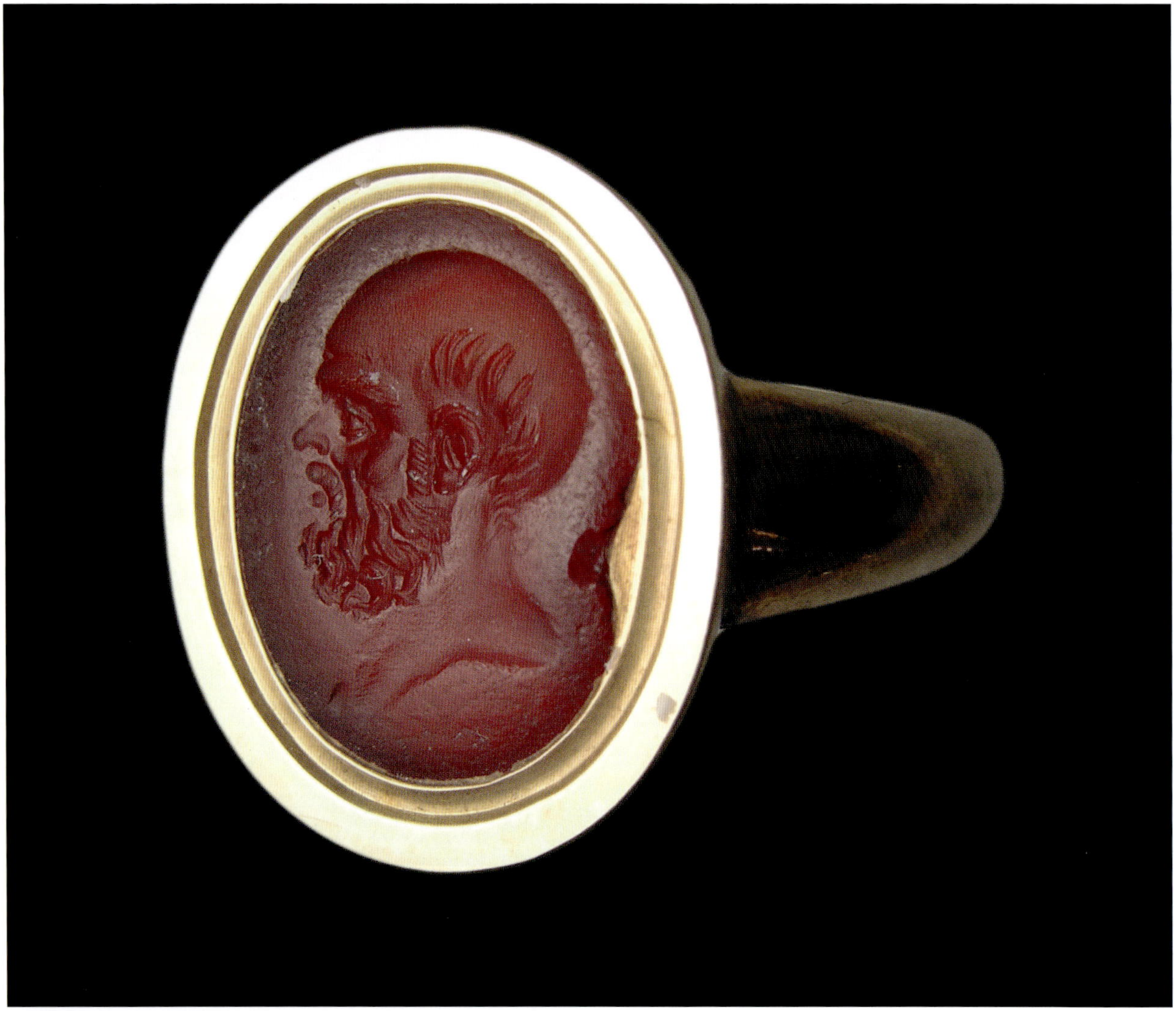

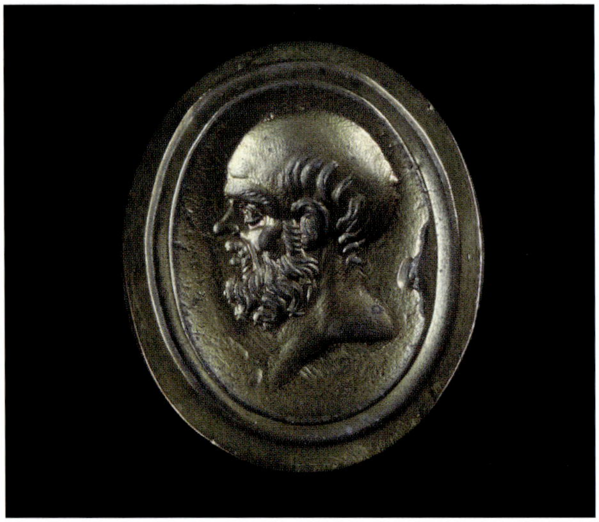

209

(10696) K162 (pl. 6)
Sard, chipped at the edge behind the neck, polished convex back, set on a plain gold ring
14 x 10

SG.Imp. 152; Inst.Imp. no. 108.

Head of Socrates?

Compare Lang, *Wissen*, 59–64 and *Würzburg* nos 501–5.

1st century BC.

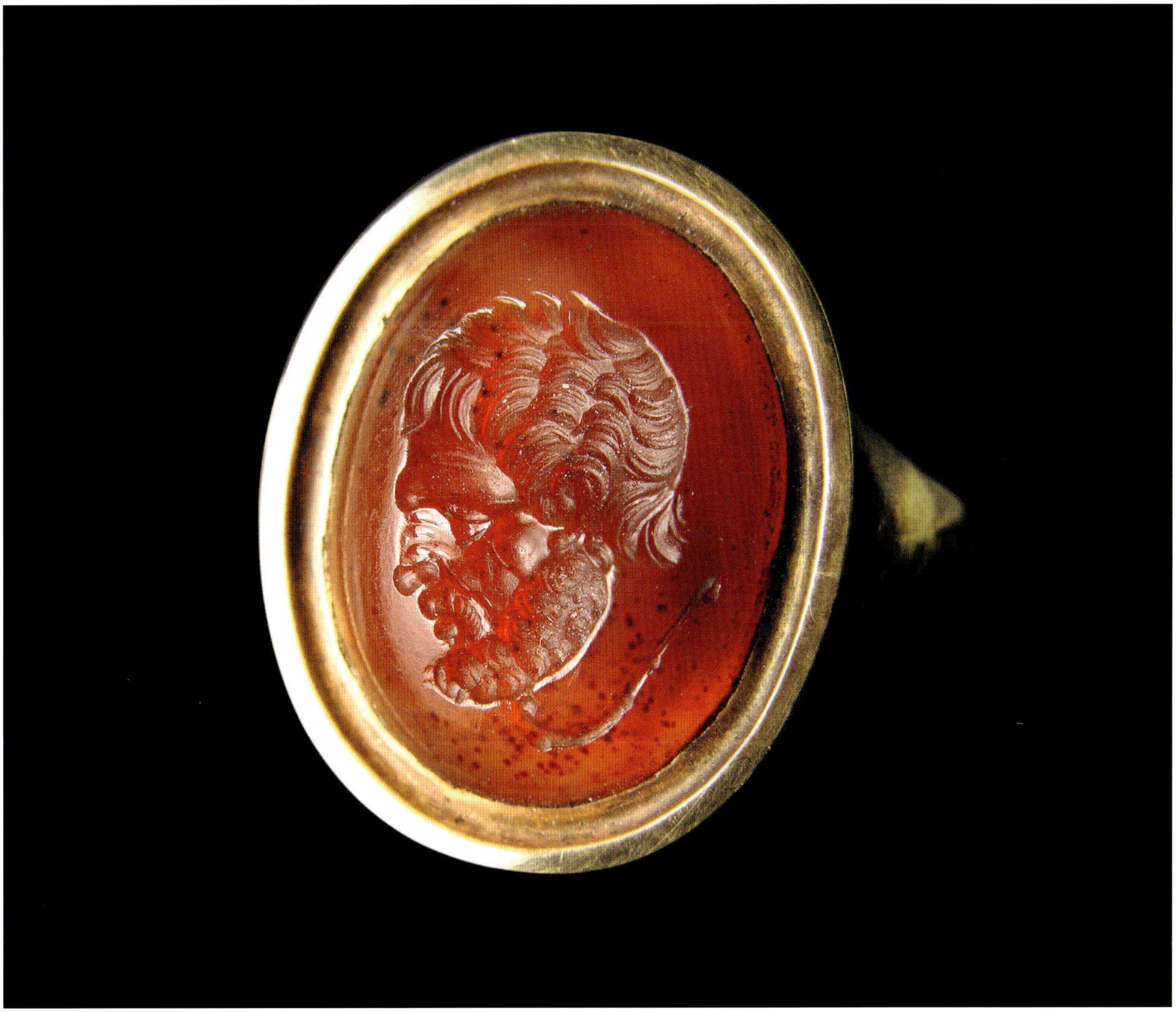

210

(10729) K191 (pl. 5)
Sard, flat polished back, set on a plain gold ring
14 x 10

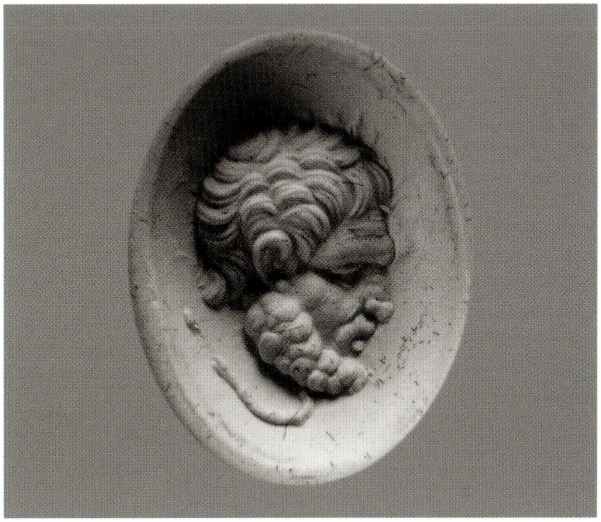

Head of a bearded man and pedum. Possibly a mask.

1st century BC.

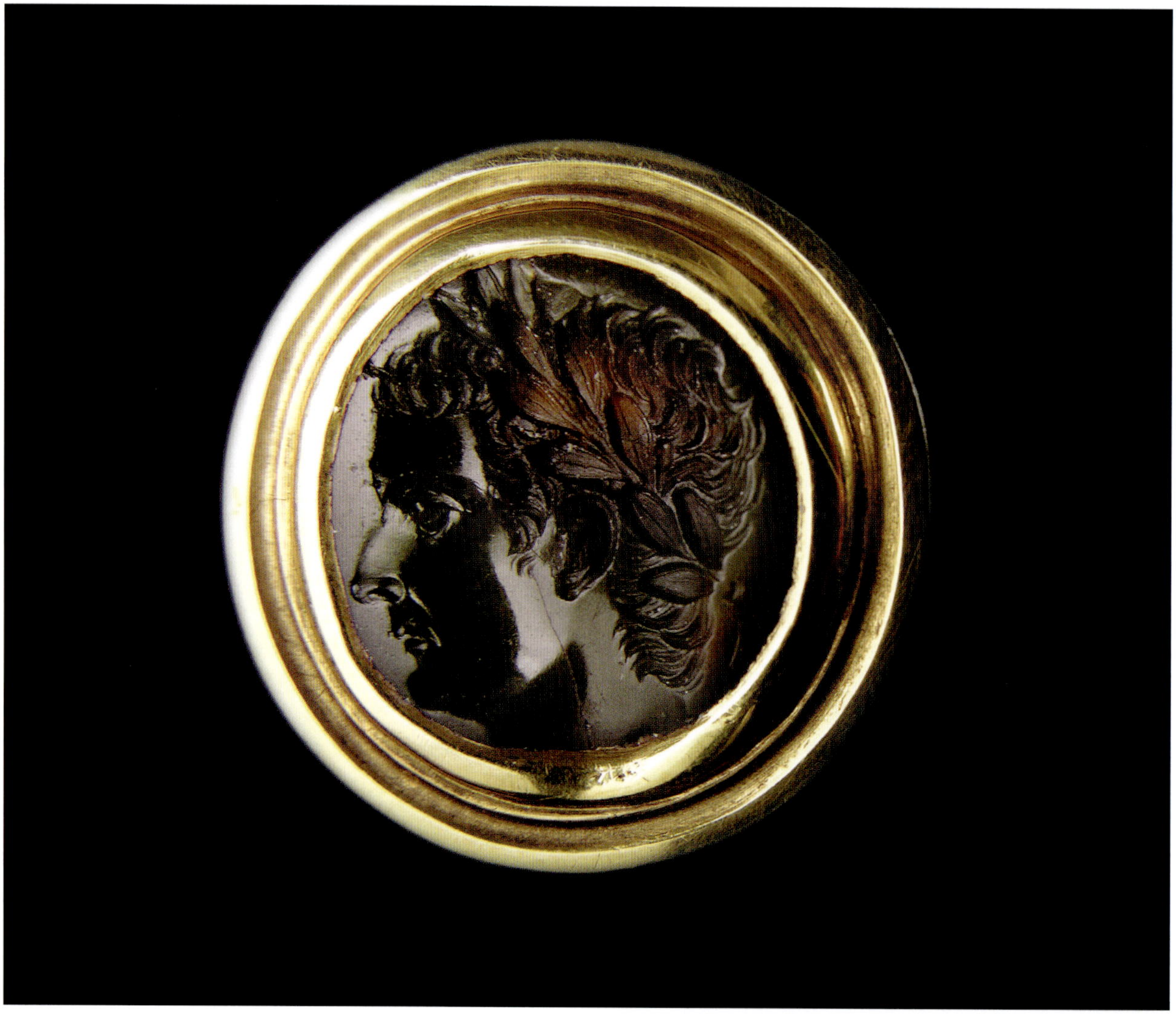

211

(10621) K83 (pl. 3)
Green jasper, set in a plain gold ring
12 x 11

SG.Imp. 88; Tassie 11189; Inst.Imp. no. 90; *AG* pl. 47.63.

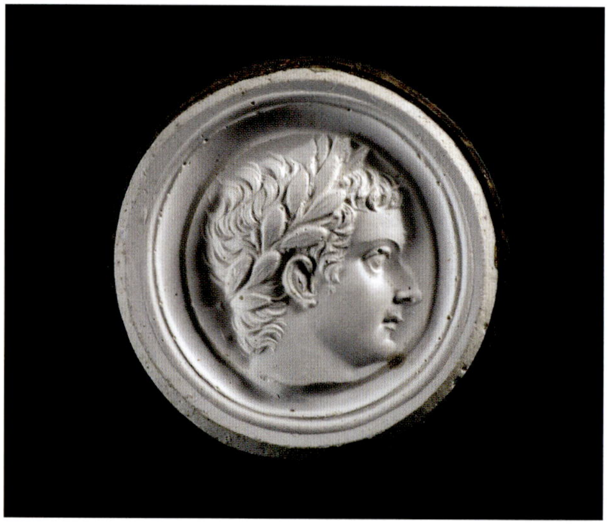

Laureate head of Tiberius.

AD 14–37.

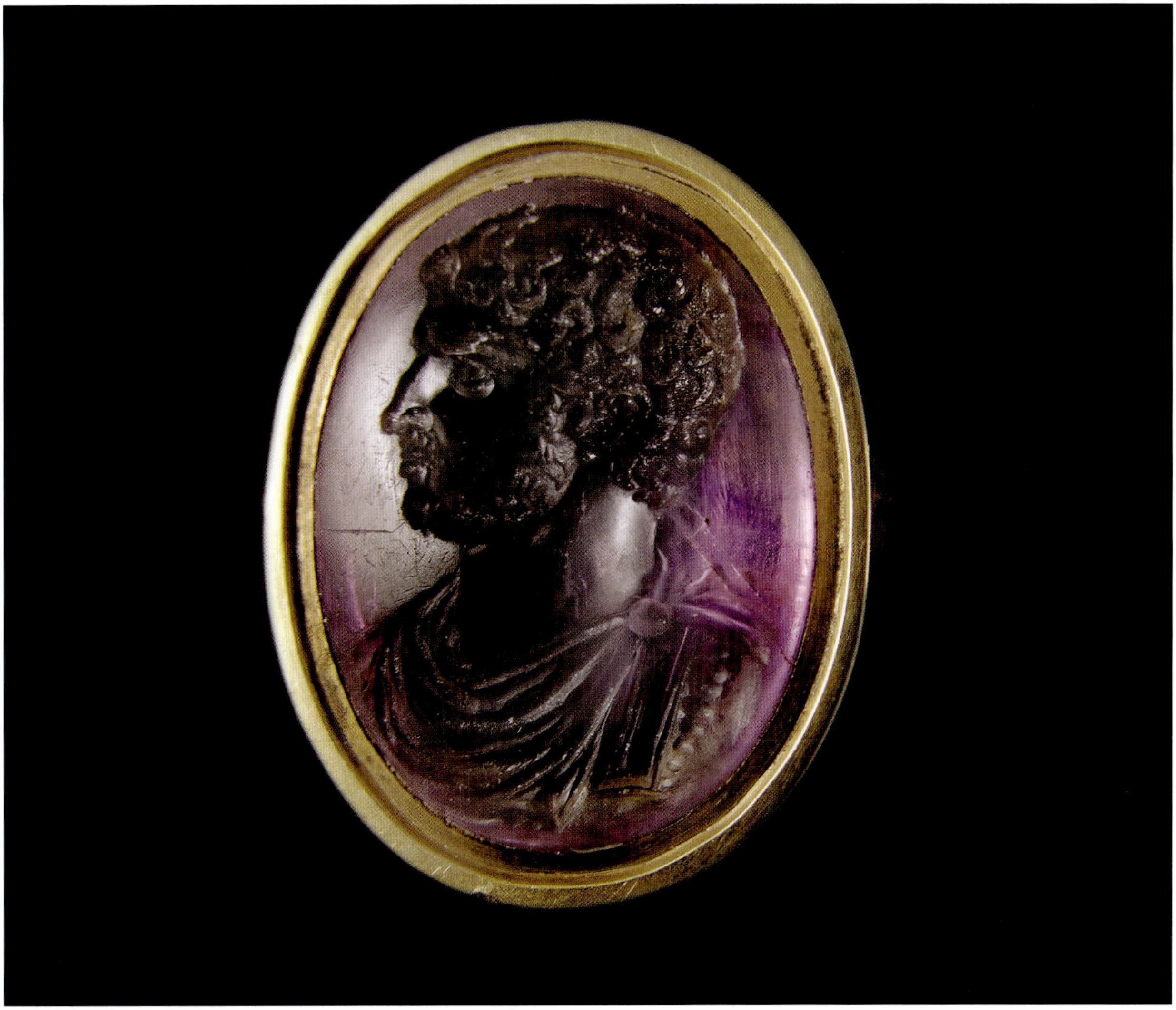

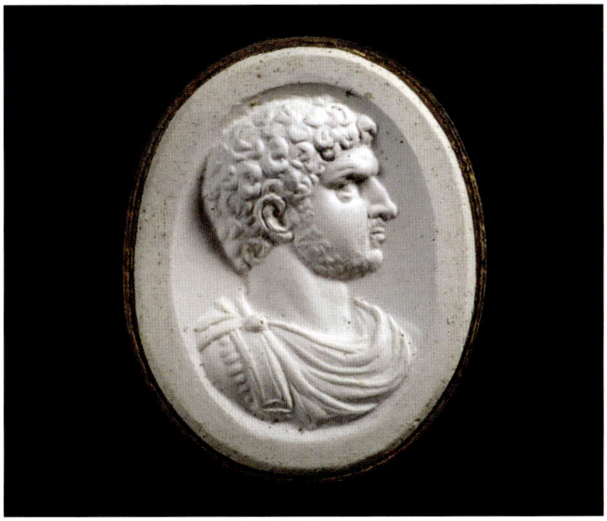

212

(10643) K105 (pl. 4)
Amethyst, polished convex back, set on a plain gold ring
21 x 15

SG.Imp. 174; Inst.Imp. no. 149.

Bust of Caracalla, Roman emperor (AD 198–217) wearing a cloak over armour. See also Tassie 12011-2.

Early 3rd century AD?

213

(10791)
Carnelian, polished convex back, set on a plain gold ring
18 x 12

Bust of a laureate bearded man, dressed, shoulder bared. Lucius Verus?

18th century.

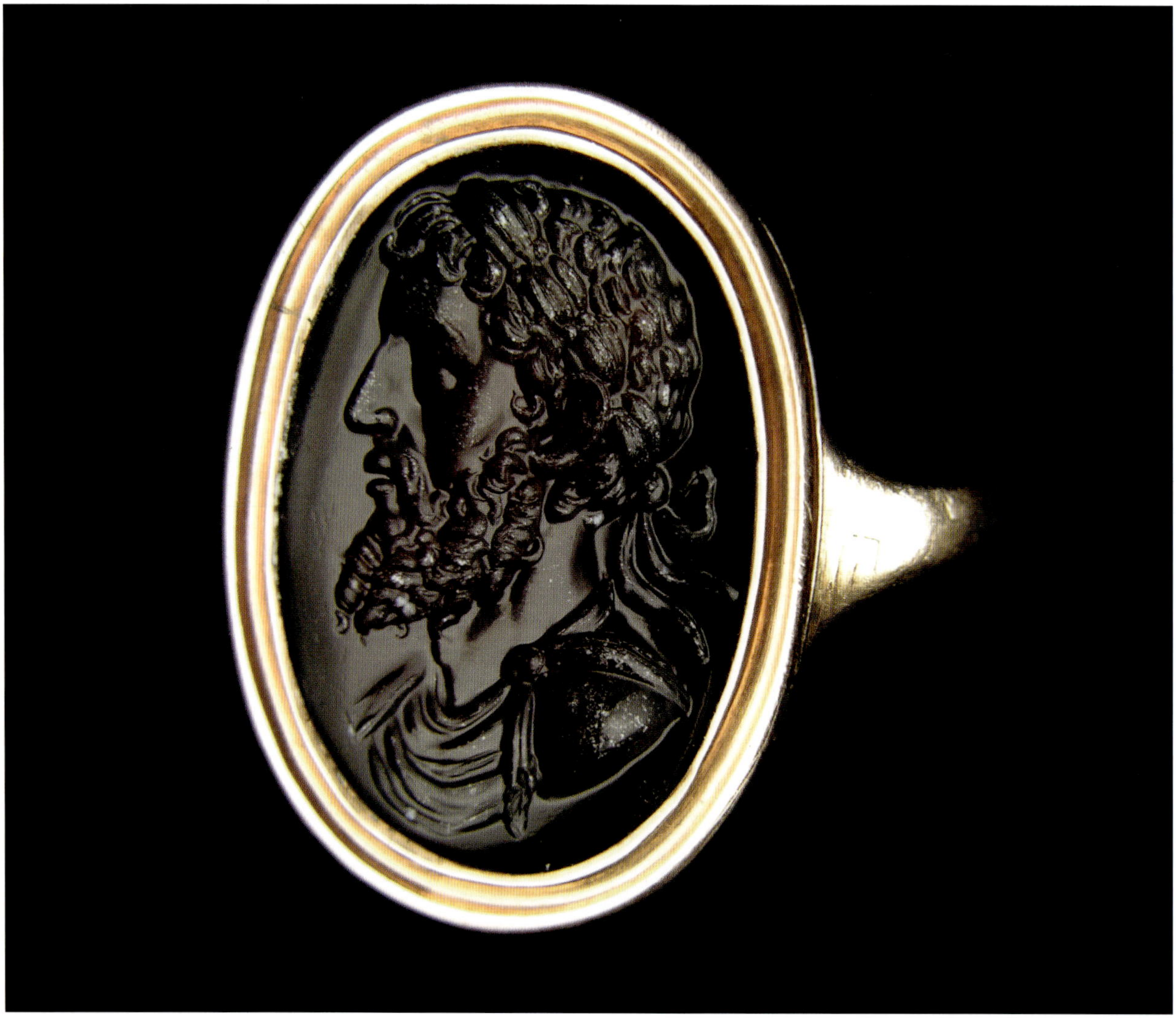

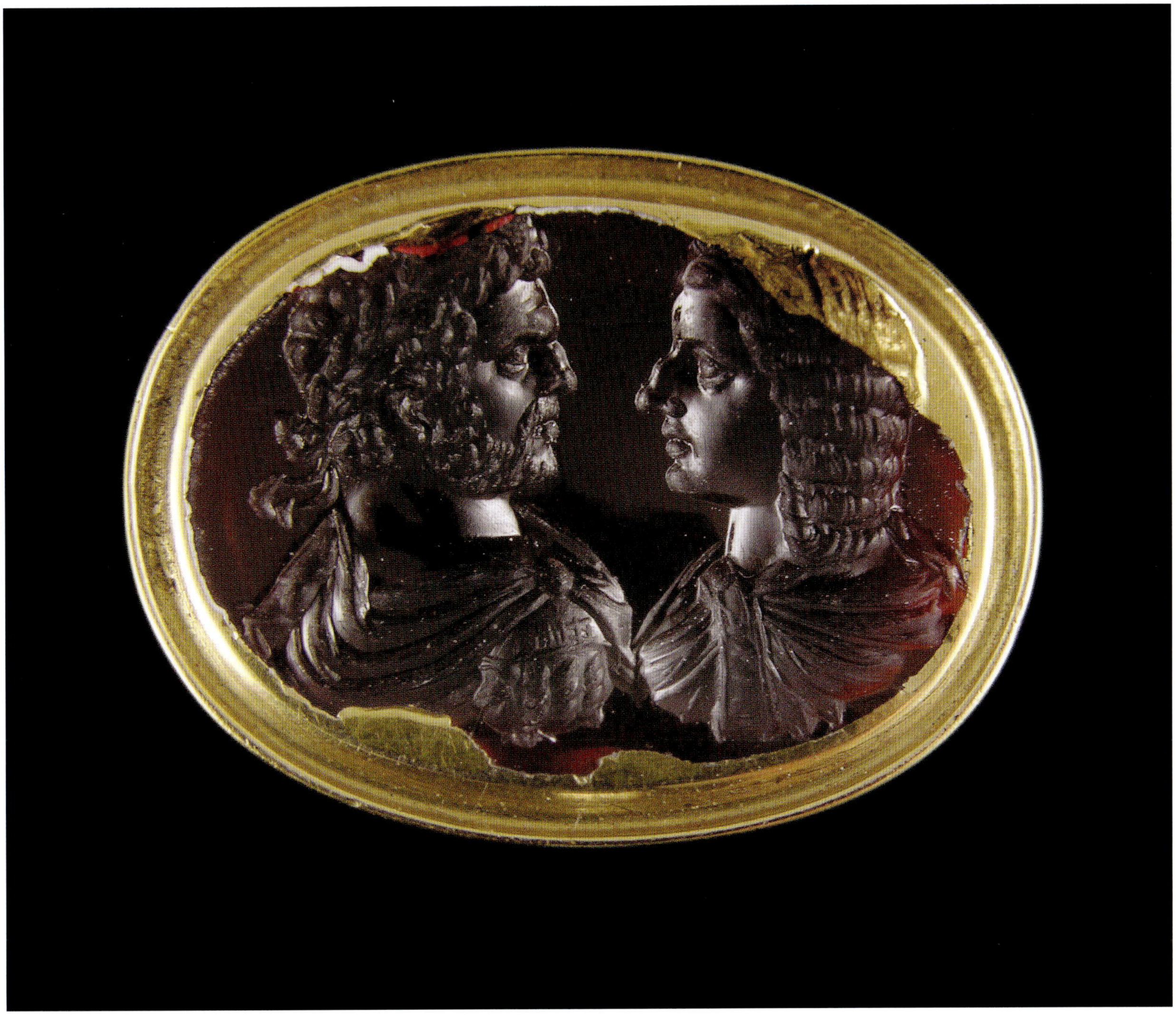

214

(10637) K99 (pl. 4)
Sard, polished flat back, set on a plain gold ring
18 x 13

Laureate bust of an emperor wearing a corselet, and of his consort, with a patterned border to her dress; probably Caracalla and Julia Domna.

3rd century AD.

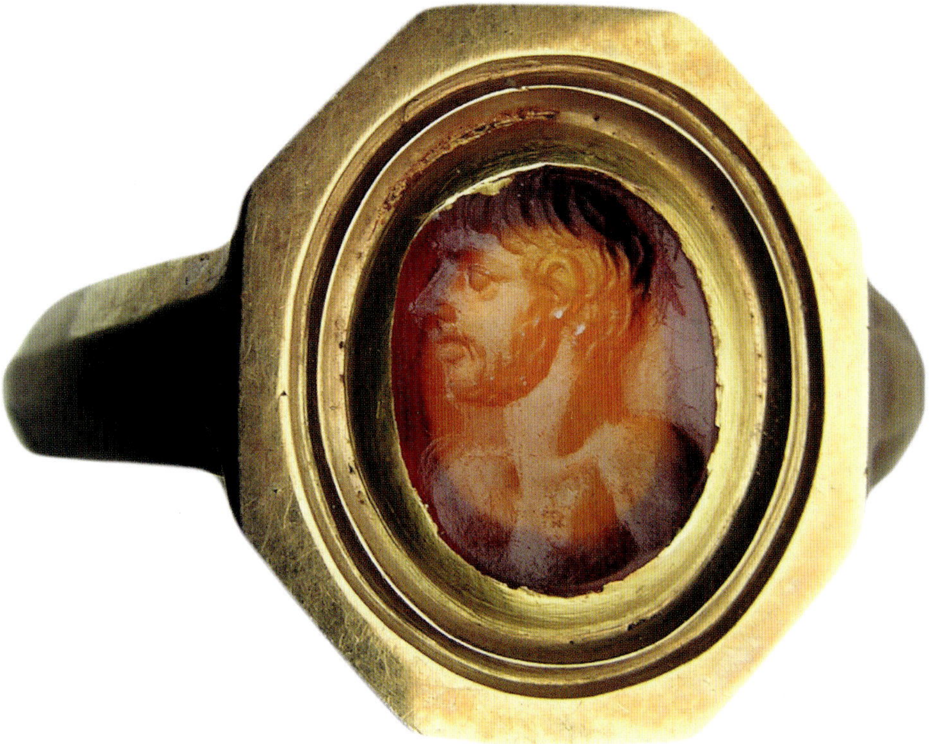

215

(10793)
Carnelian, polished flat back, set in a plain gold ring with octagonal bezel
7 x 6

Bust of a naked man with a short beard.

1st or 18th century AD?

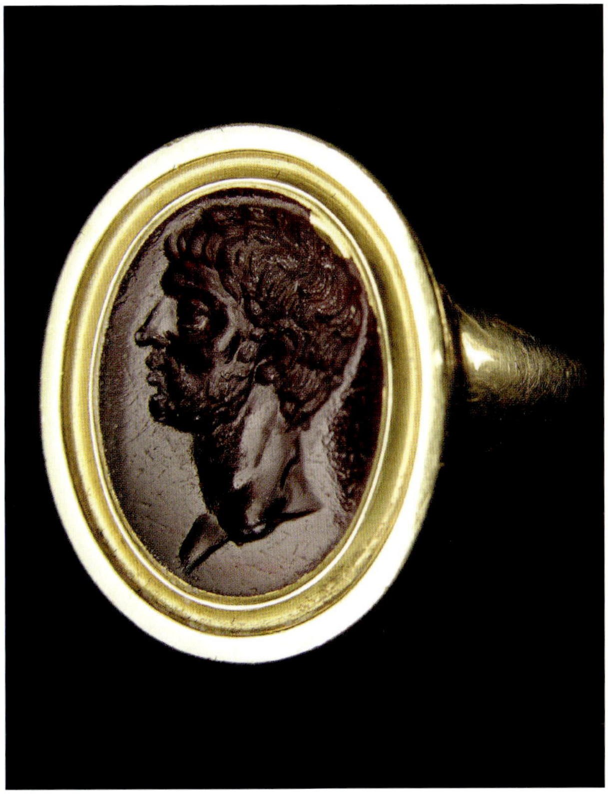

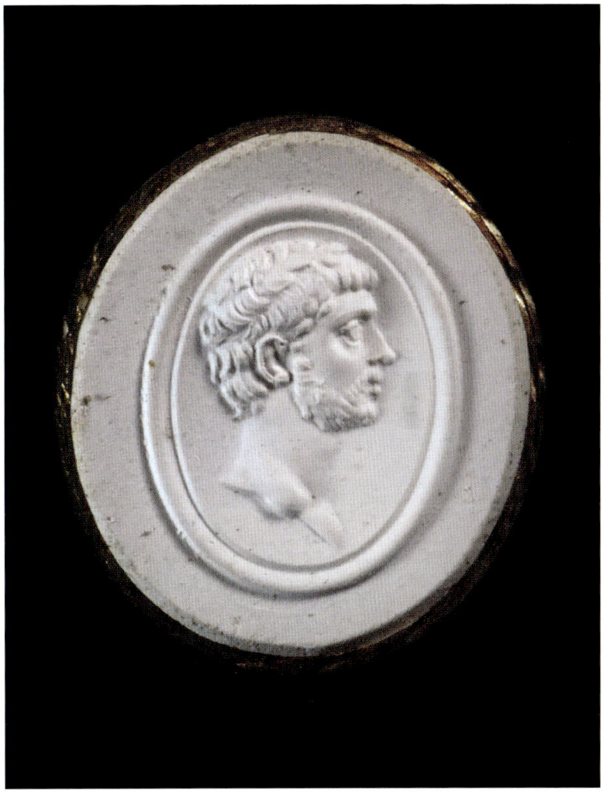

216

(10604) K66 (pl. 3)
Sard, polished convex back, set on a plain gold ring
13 x 9

SG.Imp. 171; Tassie 10645; Inst.Imp. no. 98; M.-L. Vollenweider, *Die Porträtgemmen der römischen Republik* (1972–4) 151, 162, 217, pl. 118. 2, 4.

Head of a bearded man.

Identified by Tassie and Knight as L. Junius Brutus.

Mid-1st century BC?

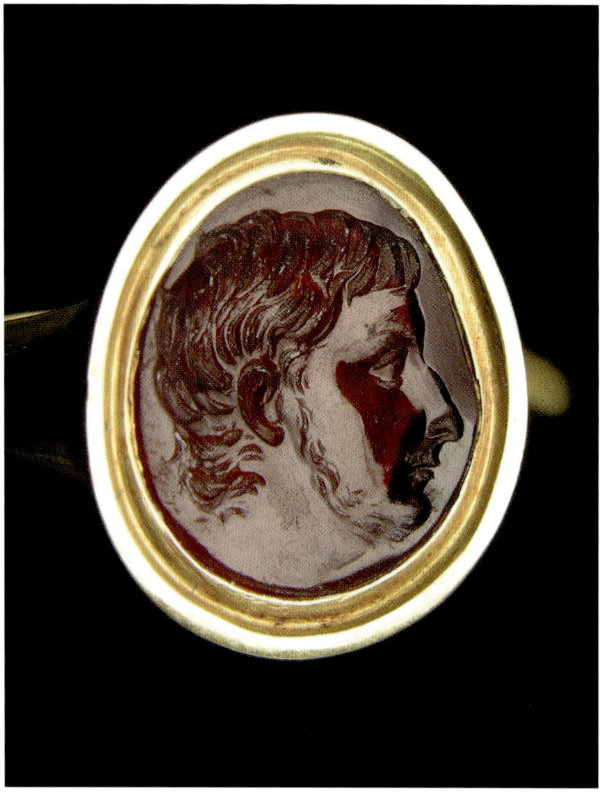

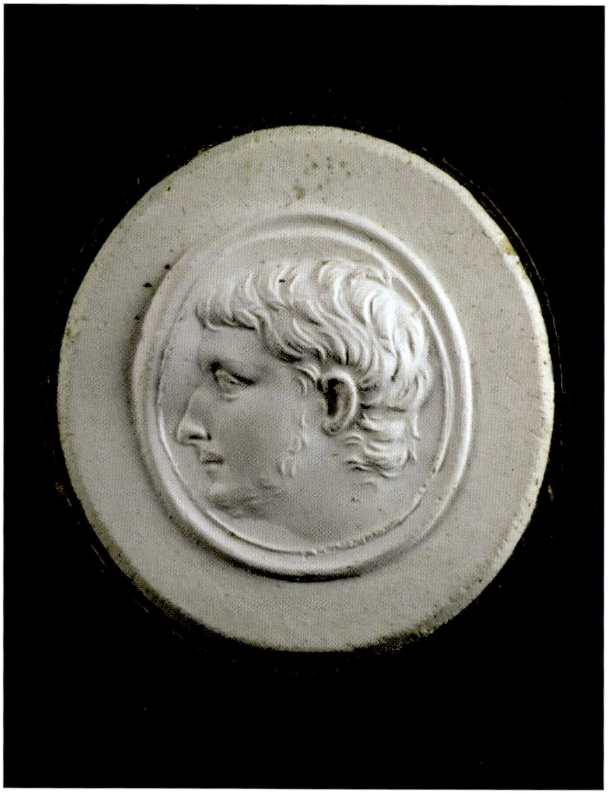

217

(10694) K156 (pl. 6)
Sard, polished flat back, set on a plain gold ring
13 x 11

SG.Imp. 3; Inst.Imp. no. 106.

Portrait head of Octavian wearing a mourning beard.

For the type see *Würzburg* no. 553; Pannuti, *Napoli* no. 225; *Marlborough* no. 743.

Late 1st century BC.

218

(10790)
Glass, unpolished flat back, set on a plain gold ring
15 x 15

Laureate head of Tiberius (14-37 AD). Cast from **211.**

18th century.

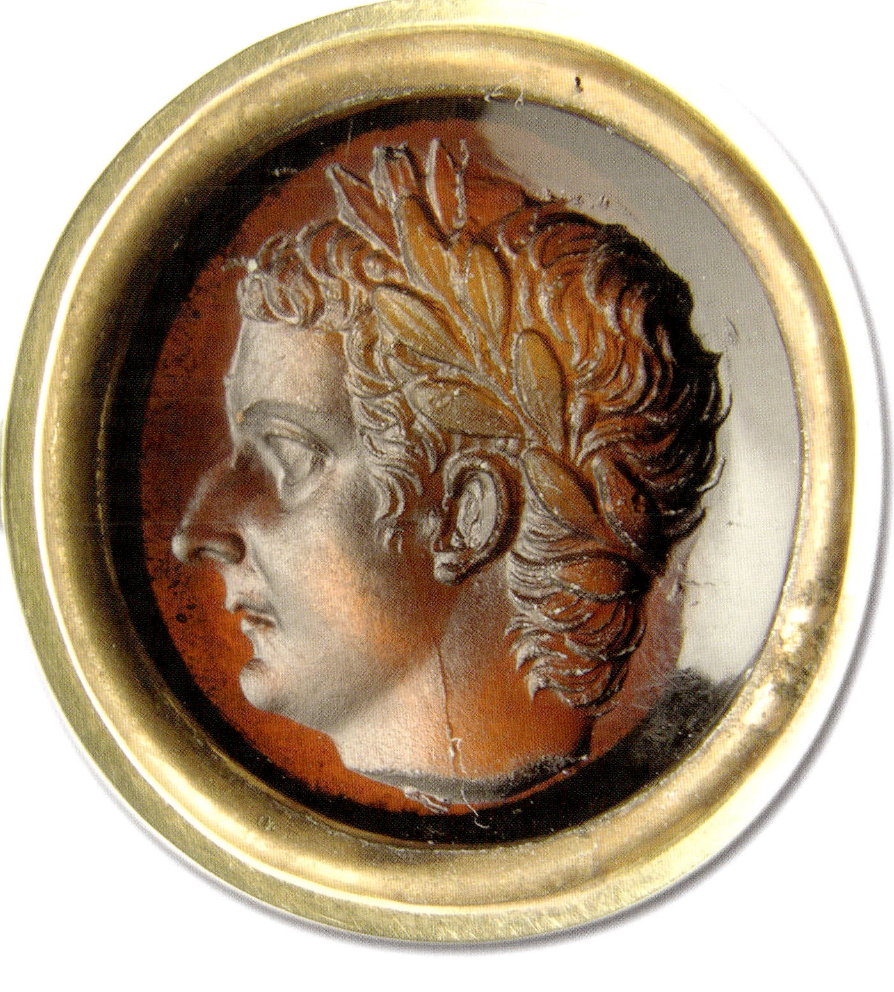

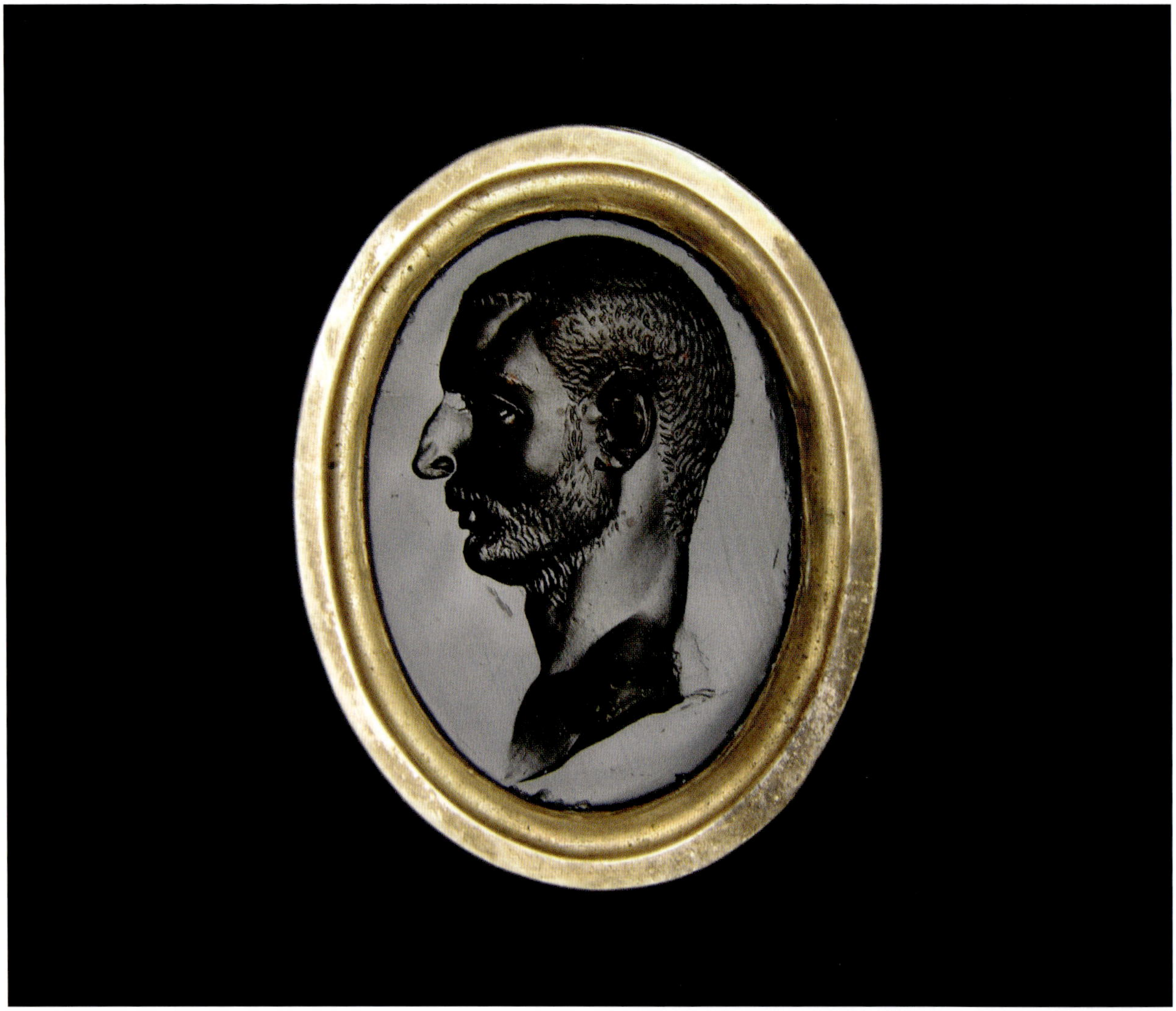

219

(10792)
Glass simulating sard, unpolished flat back, set in a plain gold ring
15 x 11

Head of a man with stubbly hair and beard (a copy of **221**).

18th century.

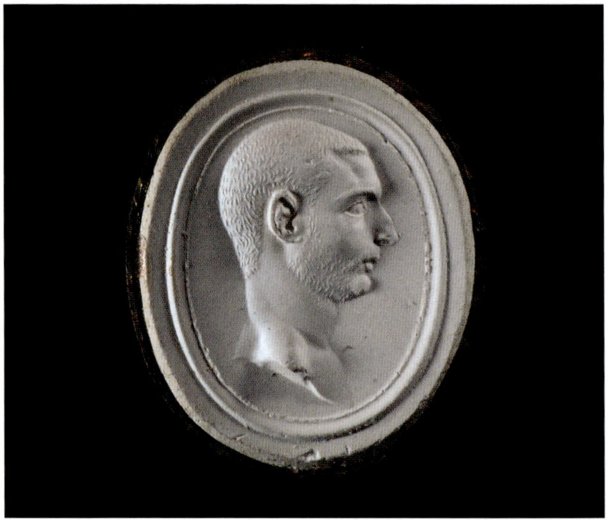

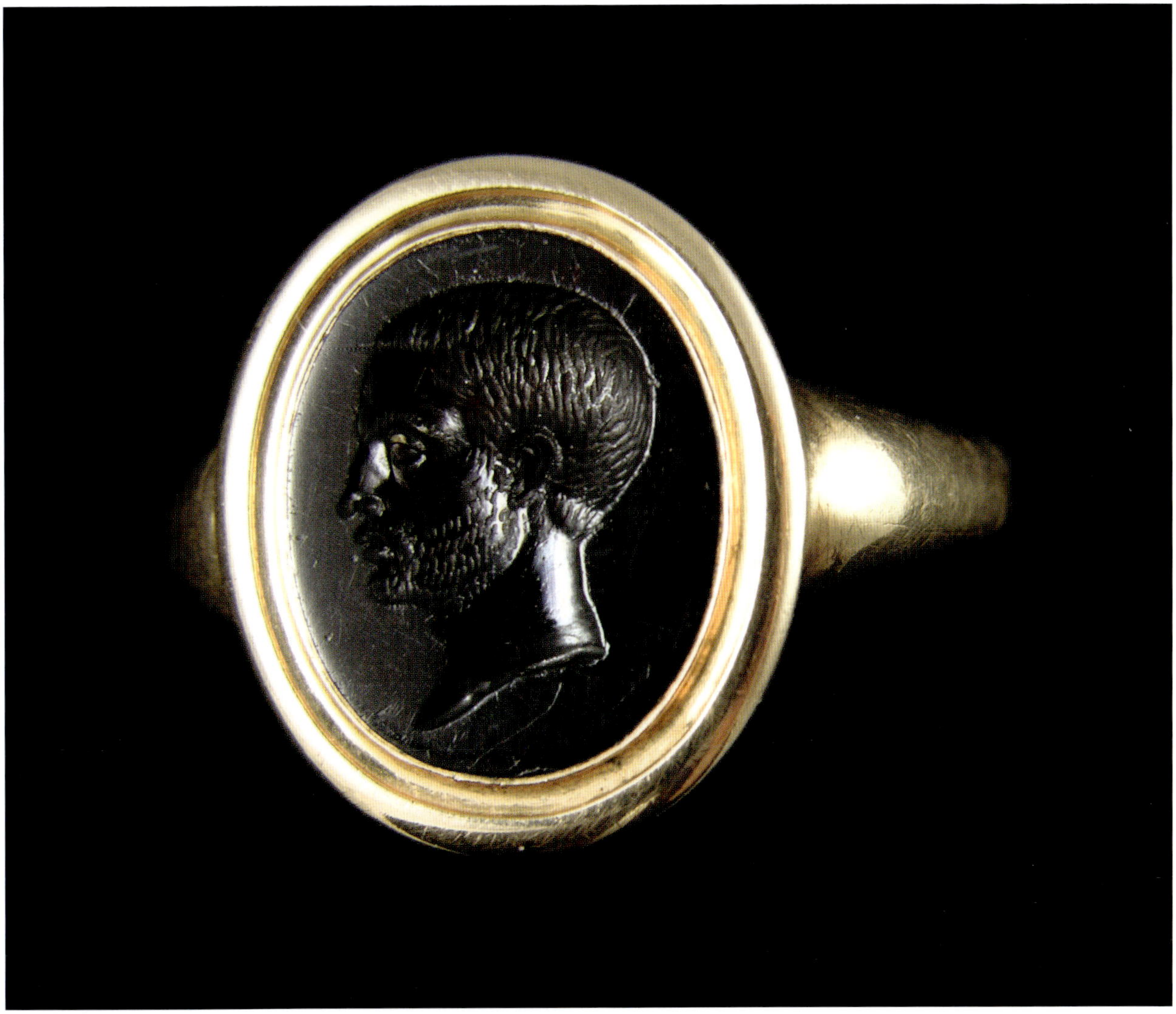

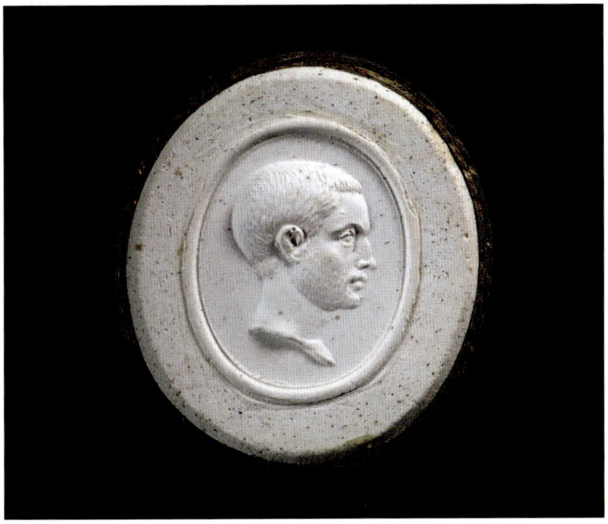

220

(10640) K102 (pl. 4)
Sard, flat polished back, set on a plain gold ring
11 x 9

SG.Imp. 165; Inst.Imp. no. 58.

Head of a man with short cropped hair (Knight – 'Maecenas', which is incorrect).

1st century BC.

221

(10697) K159 (pl. 5)
Grey/green jasper, polished flat back, set on a plain gold ring
16 x 12

SG.Imp. 92; Inst.Imp. no. 100.

Head of a man with closely cropped hair.

The type is as Paoletti I, IV.468 (Drusus major); rather similar to *Berlin* no. 224a; Spilsbury, no. 15. **219** is a copy.

1st century BC/AD.

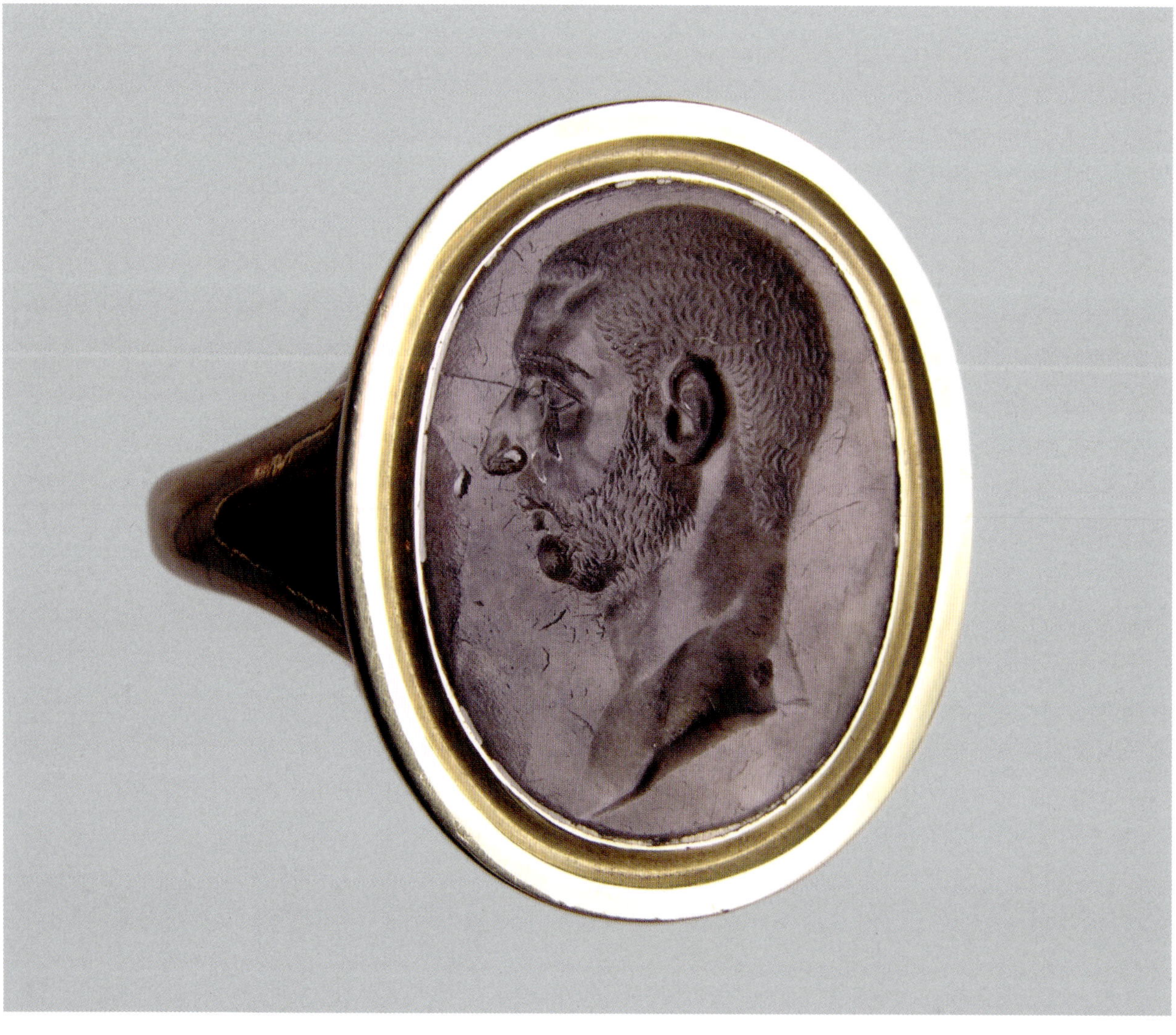

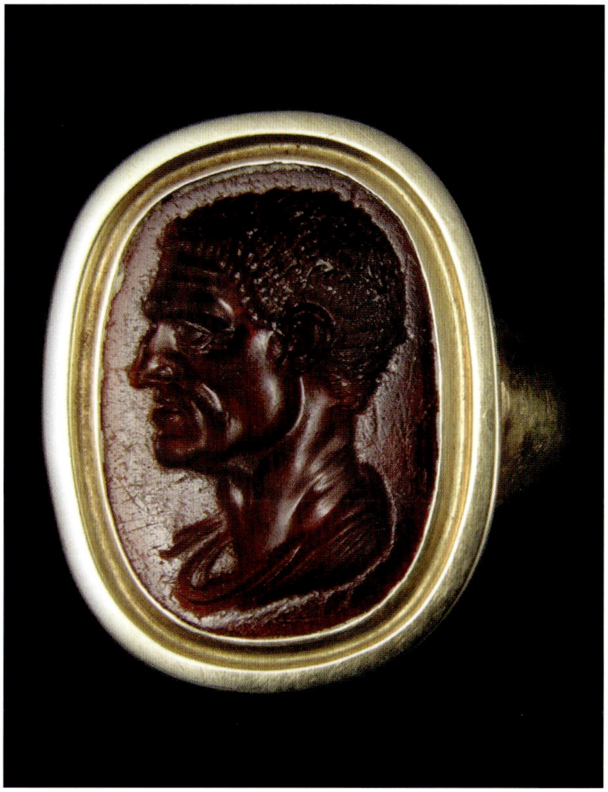

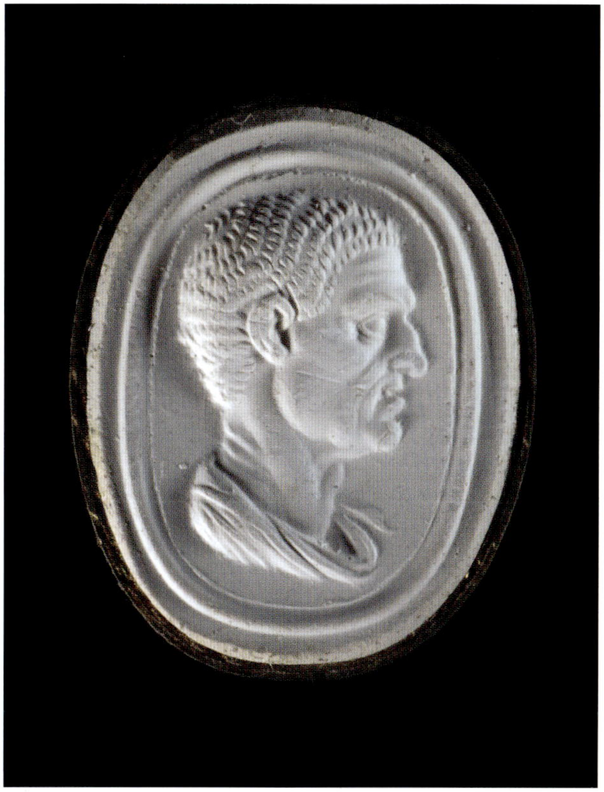

222

(10633) K95 (pl. 4)
Sard, polished flat back, set on a plain gold ring
15 x 10

SG.Imp. 99; Inst.Imp. no. 109.

Bust of a man. Possibly ancient.

1st century BC/AD?

223

(10695) K157 (pl. 6)
Sard, polished flat back, set on a plain gold ring
13 x 11

Head of a laureate man (Knight – 'Nero', of whom this is a possible version).

Mid-1st century AD.

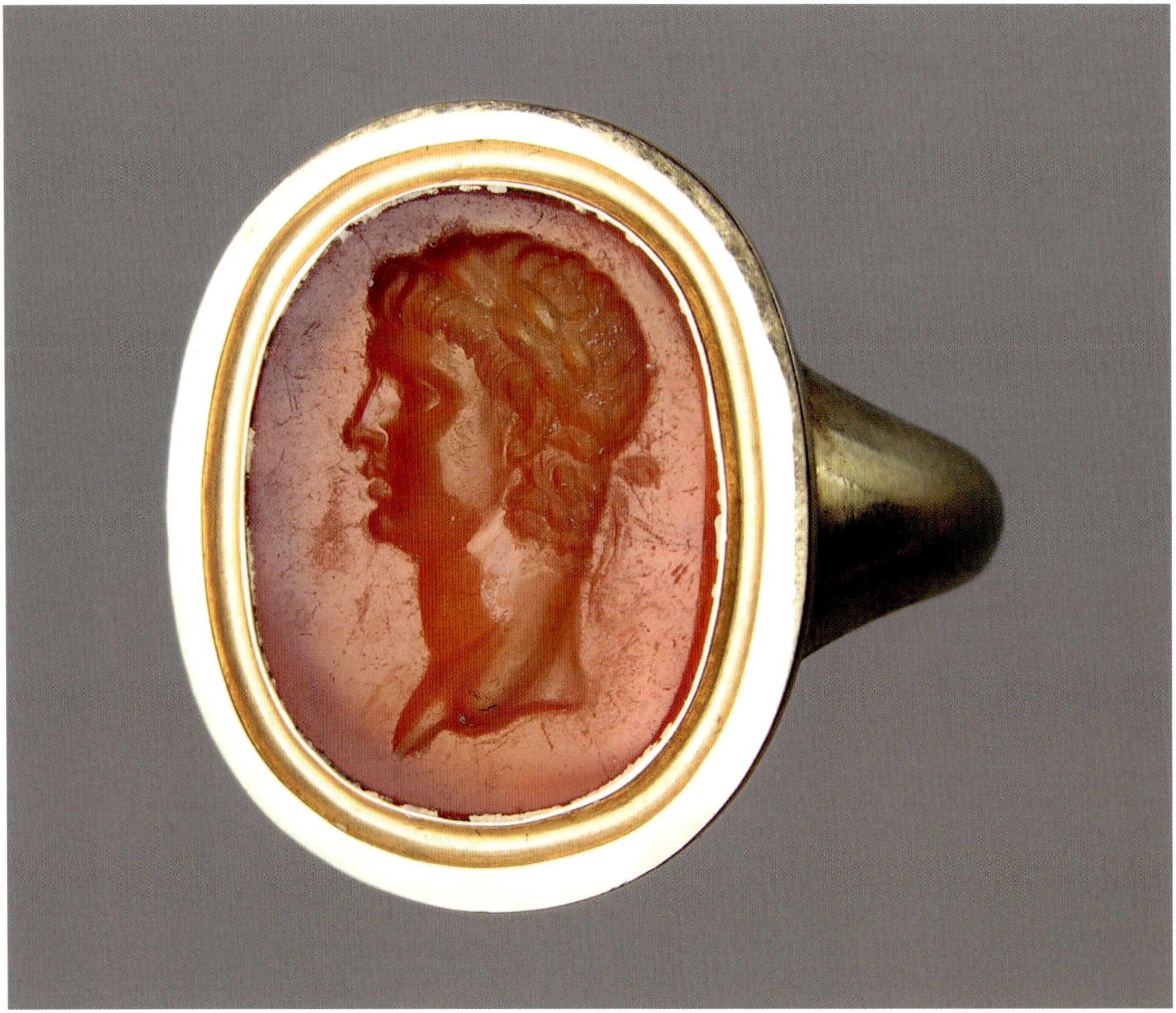

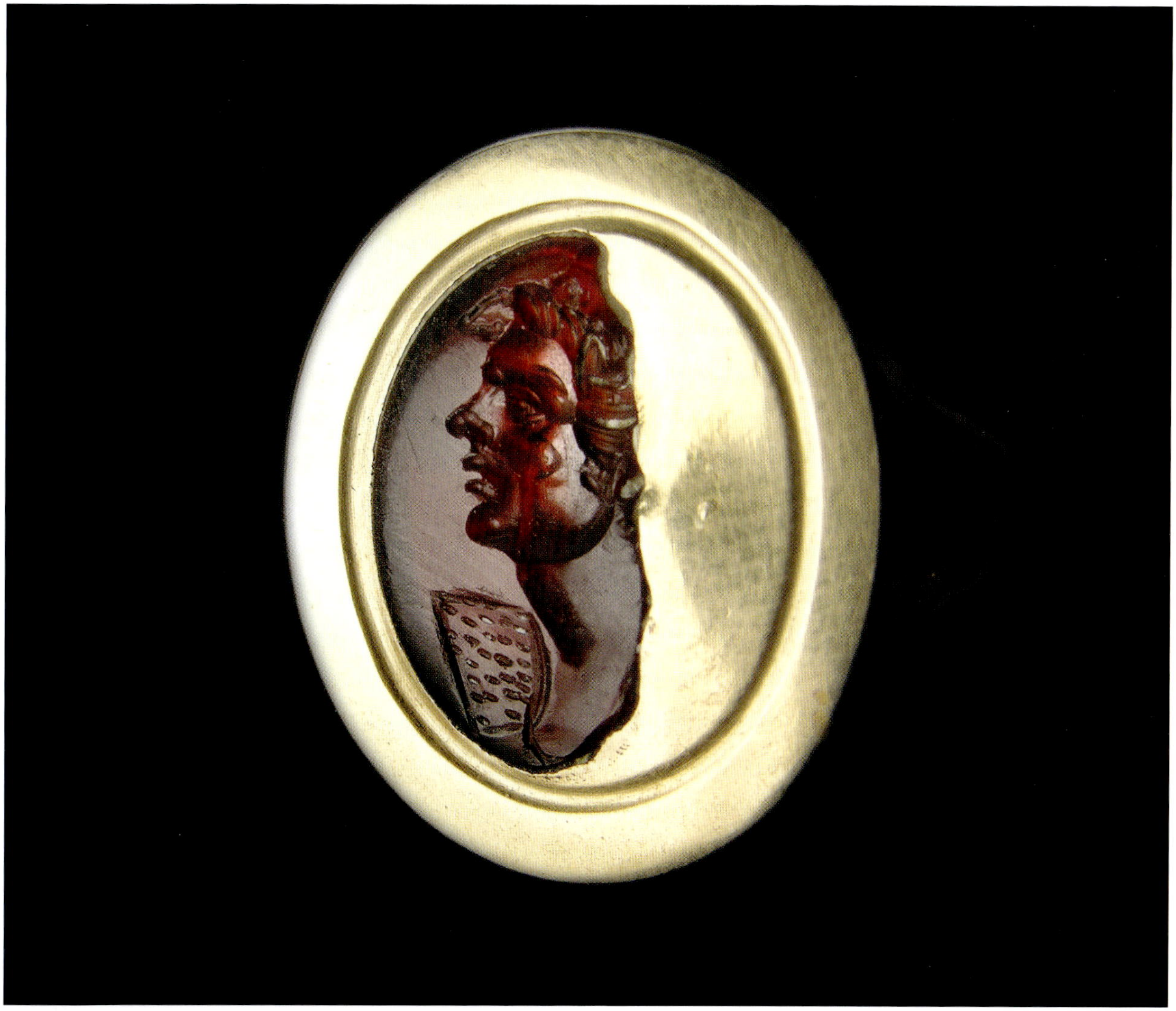

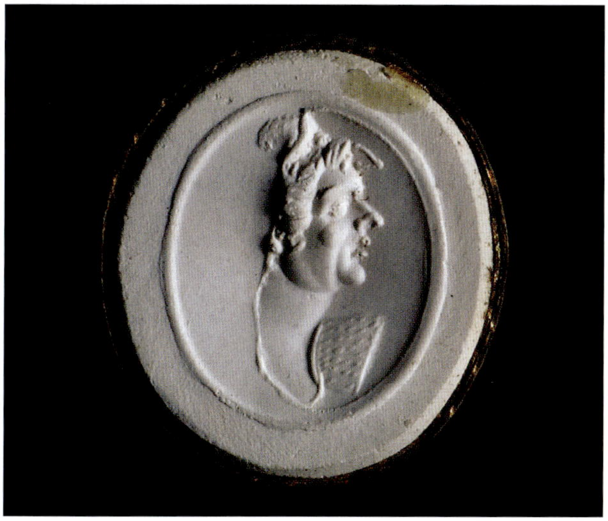

224

(10732) K194
Sard fragment, polished flat back, restored in gold and set on a plain gold ring
11 x 7

SG.Imp. 102.

Head of a young satyr with ivy wreath. The object at his shoulder was taken by Knight for a basket of grapes, but might be part of an animal skin he is wearing, the edge of which shows round his neck.

1st century BC/AD?

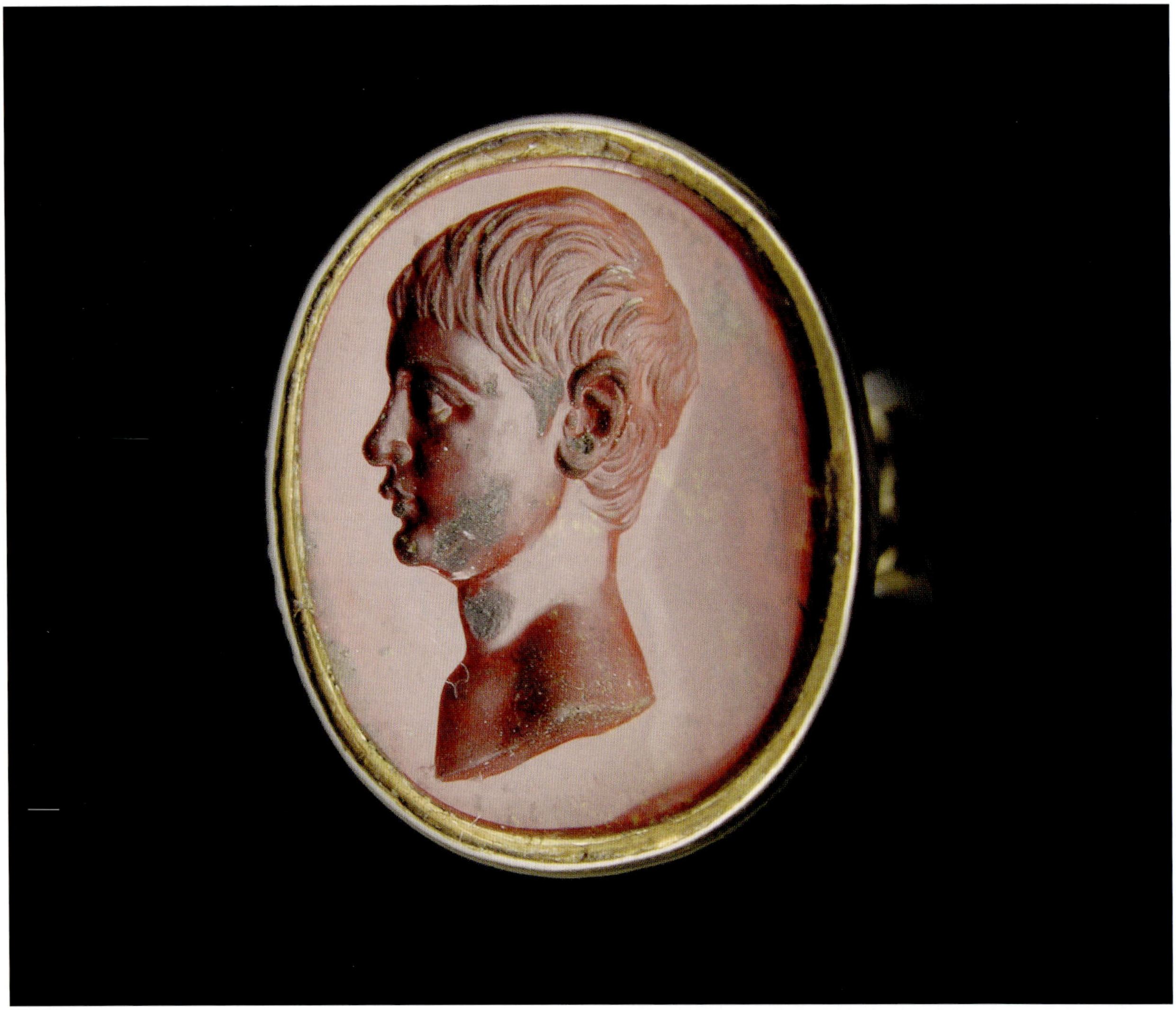

225

(10794)
Red jasper, set as a gold stamp with an ornate handle
18 x 16, height 31

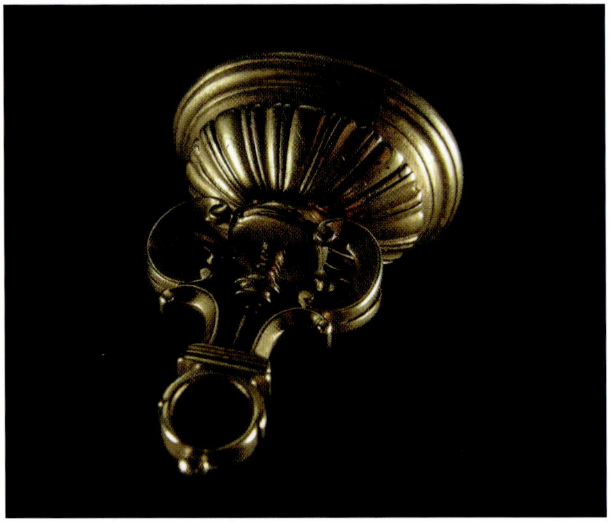

There is a drawing of the cameo original, labelled Britannicus, as property of the 1st Duke when known as Sir Hugh Smithson (see above, pp. XXII, XXVII).

Head of a boy.

1st century AD?

226

(10801)
Carnelian, polished flat back, set in a gold ring with triple-forked ends to the hoop
15 x 14

Head of Michelangelo(?), dress at the neck.

18th century.

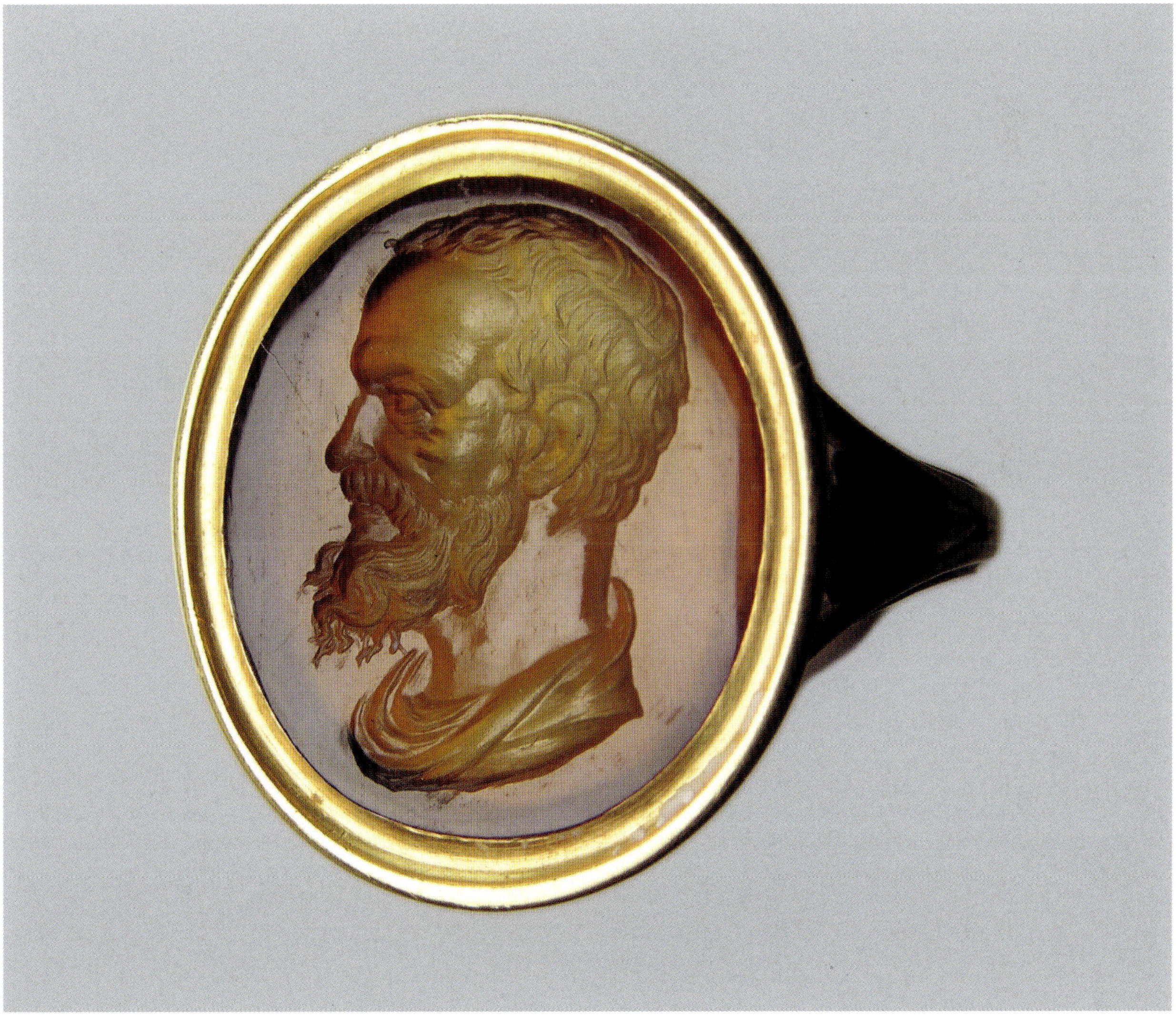

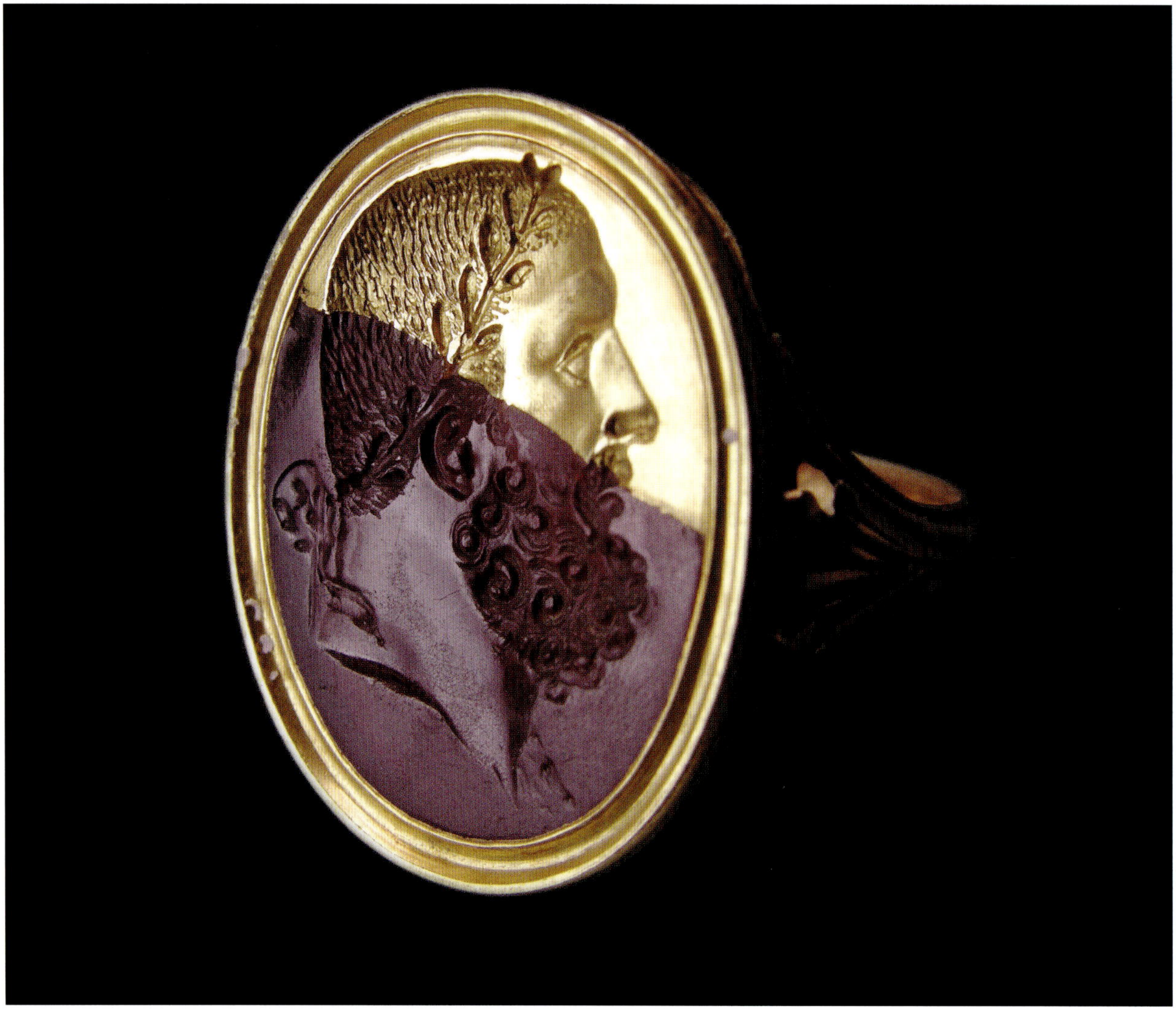

227

(10772)
Carnelian, fragment, the top half completed in gold, polished flat back, set on a gold ring with floral ends to the hoop
15 x 17

Head of Hercules, laureate, shouldering his club.

1st century BC/AD?

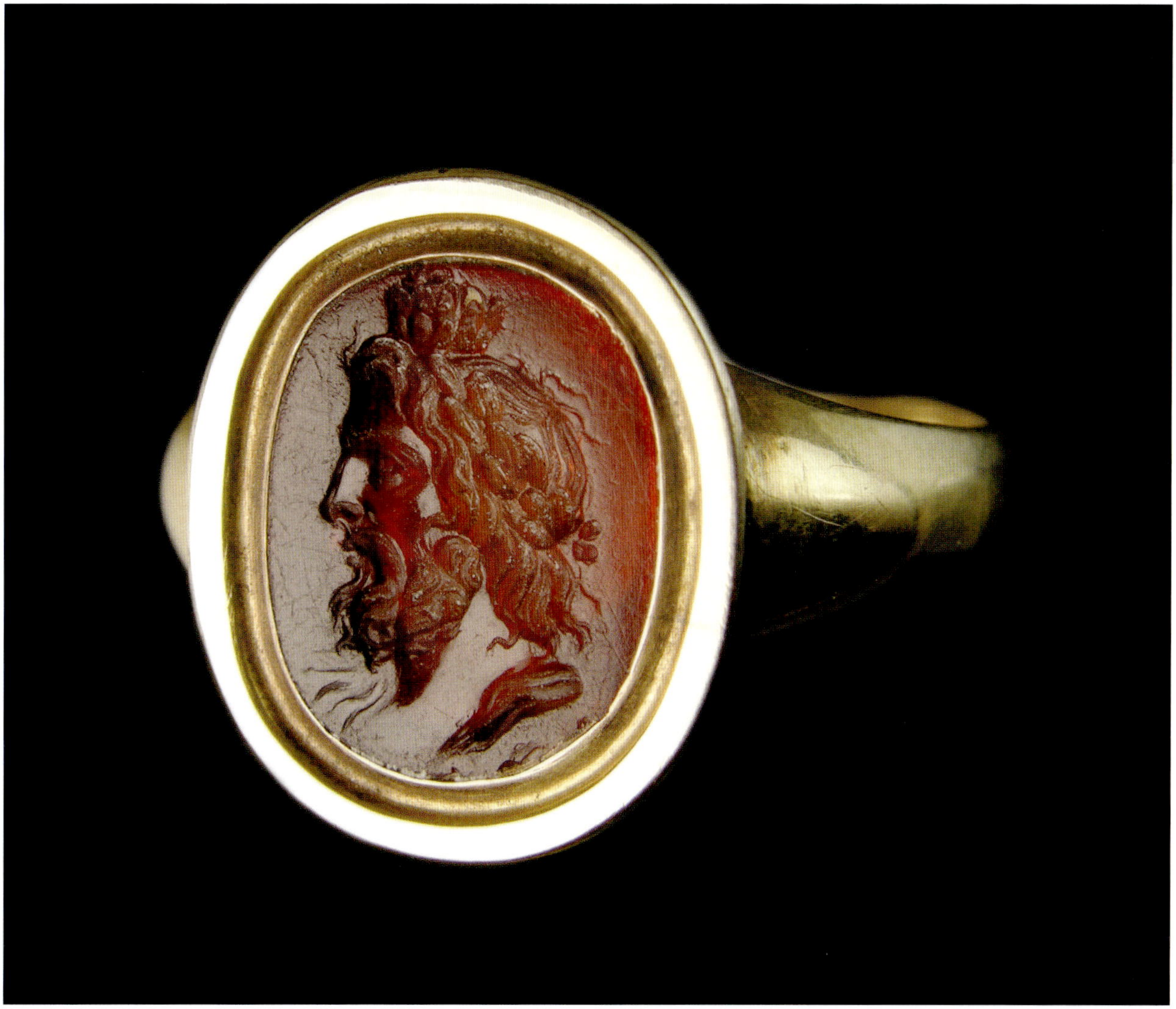

228

(10661) K123 (pl. 6)
Sard, unpolished flat back, set on a plain gold ring
11 x 9

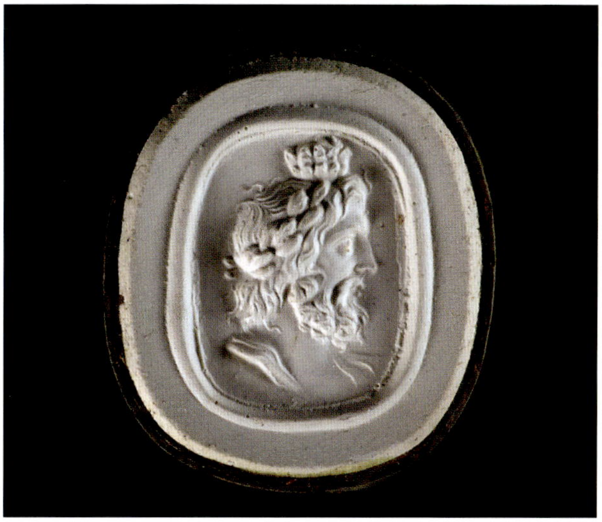

SG.Imp. 106; Inst.Imp. no. 102; Paoletti I, IV.130.

Bust of Jupiter Serapis, laureate, with a floral modius. The hair styled with an *anastole*.

This is Veymiers' type I.AA 1–92 (R. Veymiers, *Ἵλεως τῷ φοροῦντι. Sérapis sur les gemmes et les bijoux antiques* (Brussels 2009)).

2nd/1st century BC?

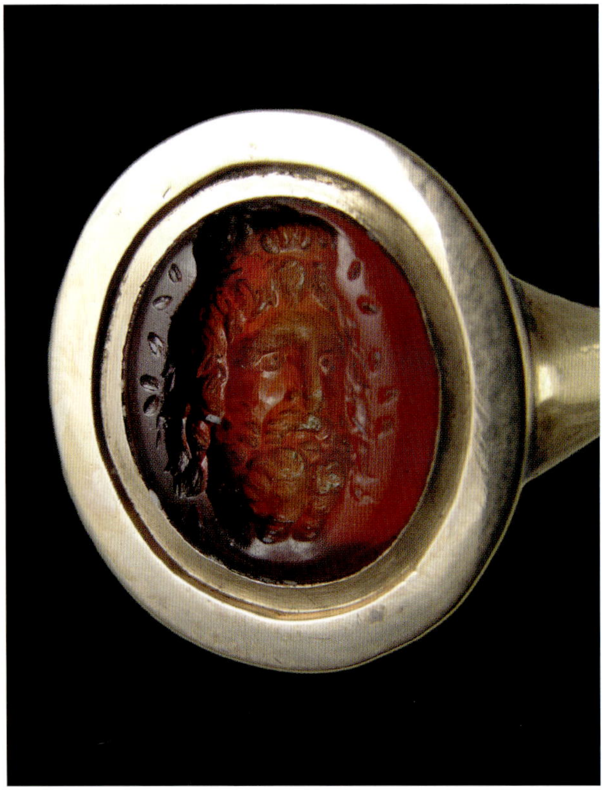
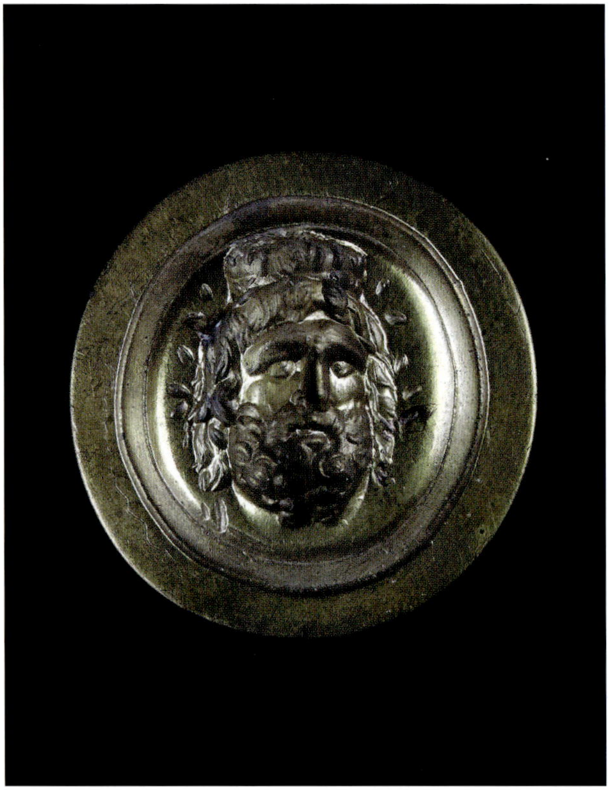

229

(10684) K146 (pl. 6)
Sard, polished flat back, set on a plain gold ring
11 x 10

SG.Imp. 115; Inst.Imp. no. 95.

Facing head of Jupiter Serapis with flowers or buds on his modius. Possibly radiate.

Compare R. Veymiers (op.cit., **228**), type I.AB and *Würzburg* no. 326.

1st century BC.

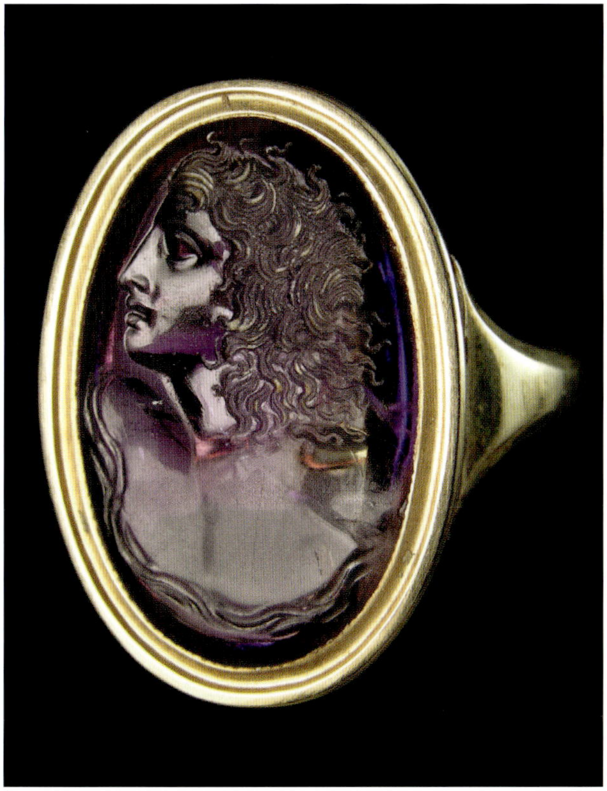

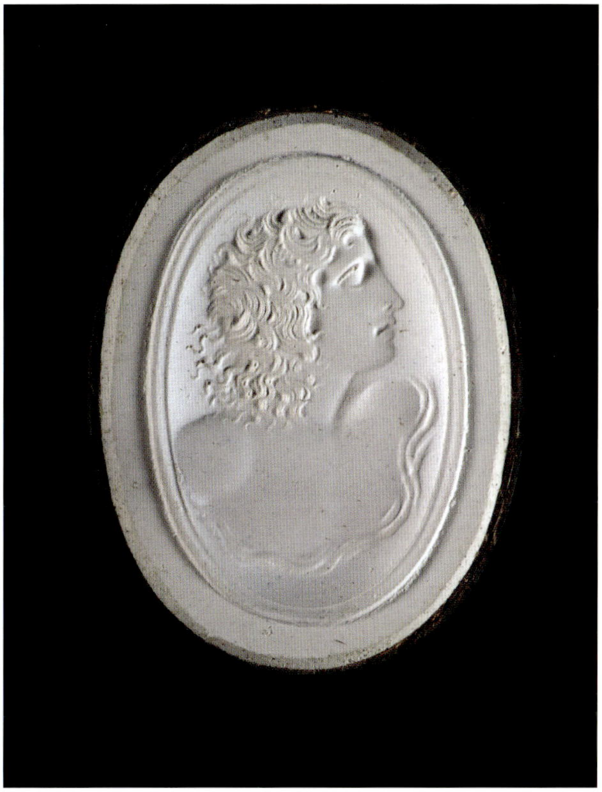

230

(10689) K151 (pl. 5)
Amethyst, convex back, set on a plain gold ring
13 x 22

SG.Imp. 49; Inst.Imp. no. 85.

The bust of Leander or a river god, swimming, waves at his chest.

The subject was much copied in the 18th century, symbolising the passionate lover ready to die by drowning rather than miss a meeting with Hero. See *Würzburg* no. 48; *Munich* I no. 496; *Hanover* no. 1773 (late copy); *London,* Dalton no. 744 (late copy). This is possibly the gem in the Duchess' Collection no. 31, of 'Kerry Stone'. County Kerry, Ireland, is a source for a variety of such quartzes.

2nd/1st century BC?

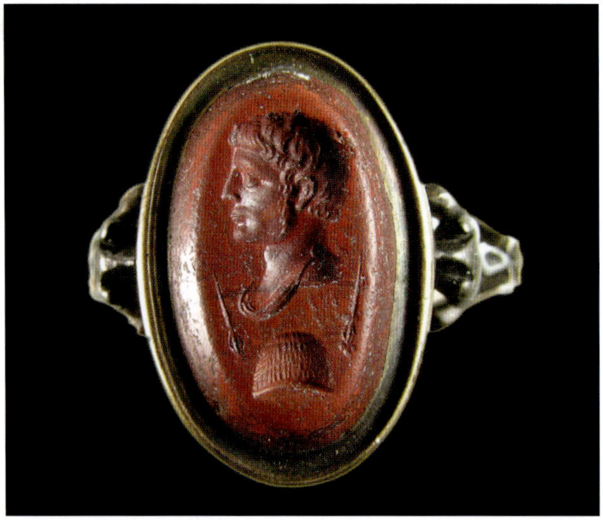

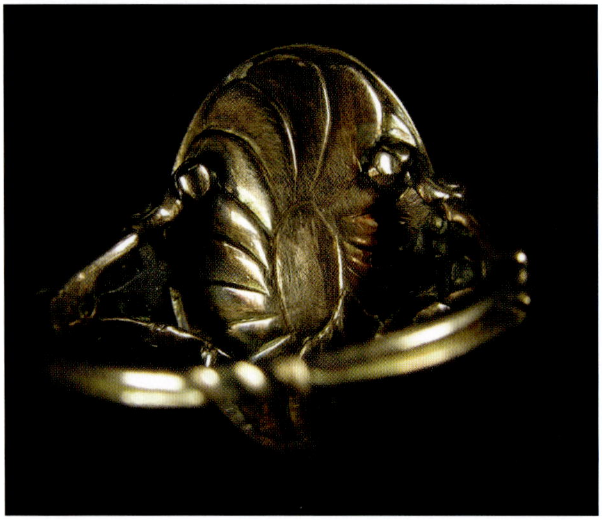

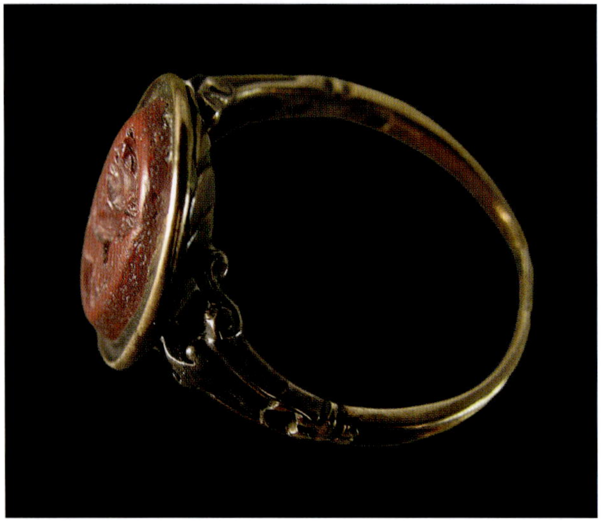

231

(10690) K152 (pl. 6)
Red jasper, set in a gold ring with forked ends to the hoop bearing fleurs-de-lys, the bezel back is scalloped
15 x 8

SG.Imp. 39; Inst.Imp. no. 78; *AG* pl. 47.37.

The bust of Brutus over the skin cap of Liberty and two daggers.

The attributes recall Brutus' role as Caesar's assassin; a popular ancient design much copied. Knight observes that the daggers are of Italian not Roman design. Though much rubbed, it is likely to be contemporary with its 18th-century ring setting. The subject was regarded by Republicans, such as Thomas Hollis (1720–74), as 'a sacred effigy, heroic virtue itself'.

18th century.

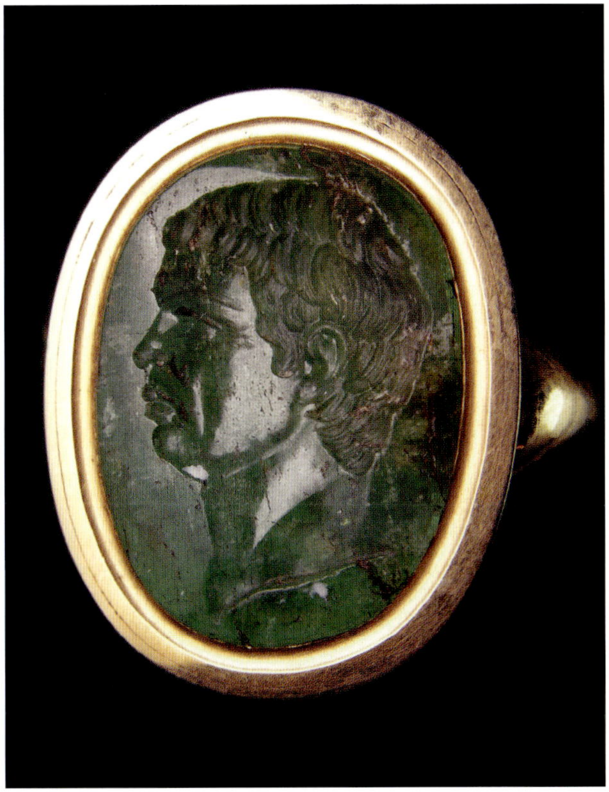

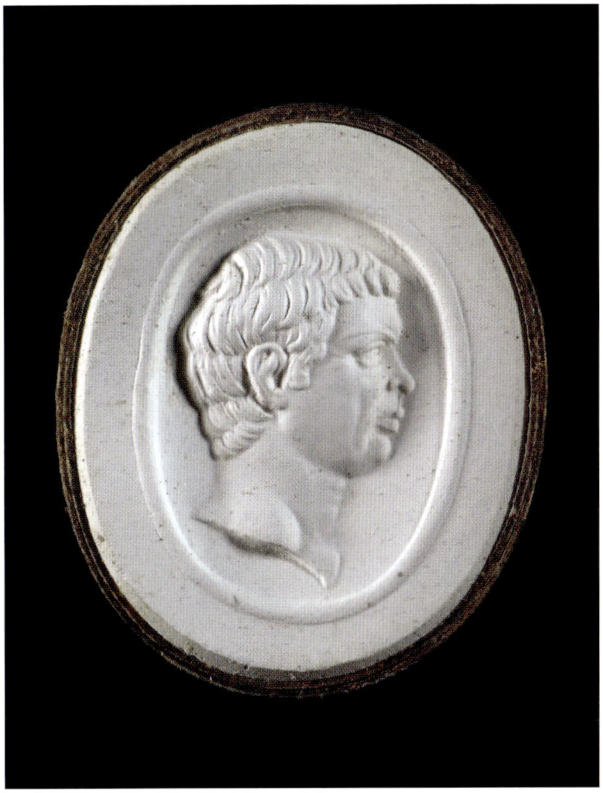

232

(10698) K160 (pl. 5)
Emerald, polished convex back, set on a plain gold ring
20 x 15

SG.Imp. 53; Inst.Imp. no. 83.

Portrait head of a man, possibly by Agathopous.
Cf. Vollenweider *Die Porträtgemmen der römischen Republik* (1972–4) pl. 112, 1.3

1st century BC?

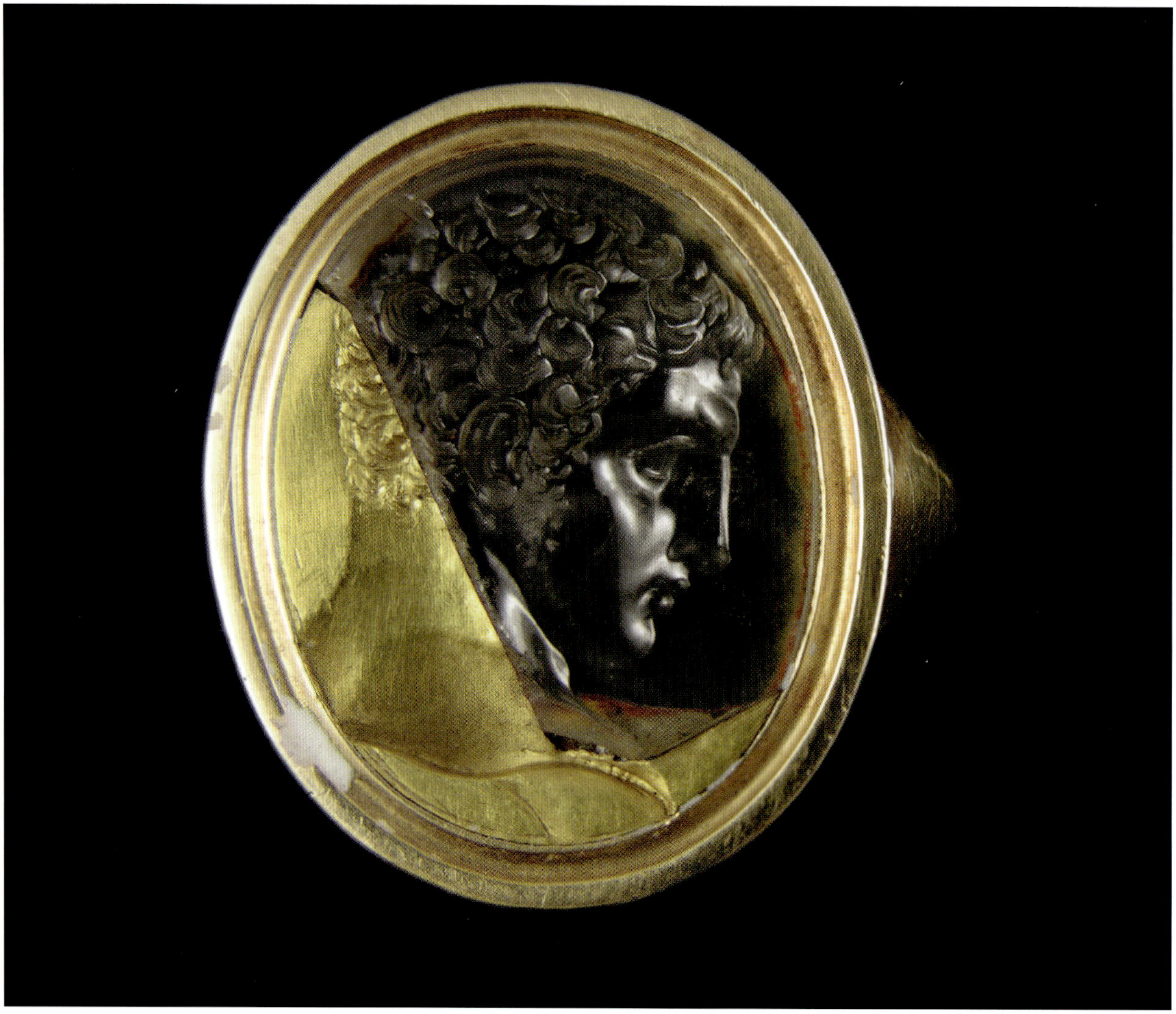

233

(10641) K103 (pl. 4)
Pale amethyst fragment, completed in gold, polished flat back, set on a plain gold ring
length 16

Head of youth, probably Hercules.

1st century BC/AD?

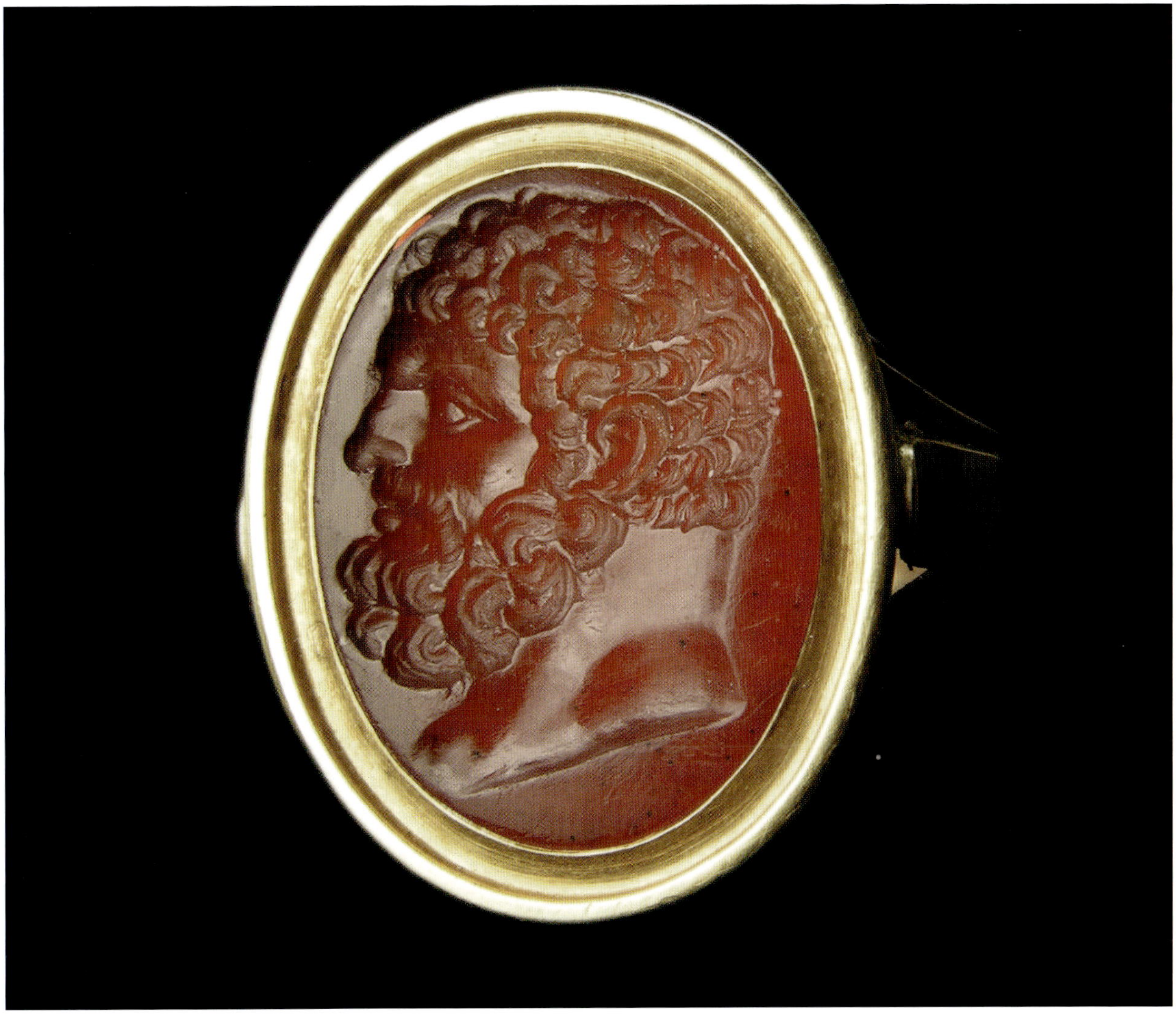

234

(10773)
Carnelian, polished flat back, set on a plain gold ring
15 x 1

Head of a bearded man. Hercules?

18th century?

235

(10777)
Amethyst, broken, polished flat back, set on a plain gold ring
18 x 15

A copy of our **91** (fragmentary head of Hercules or Omphale).

18th century.

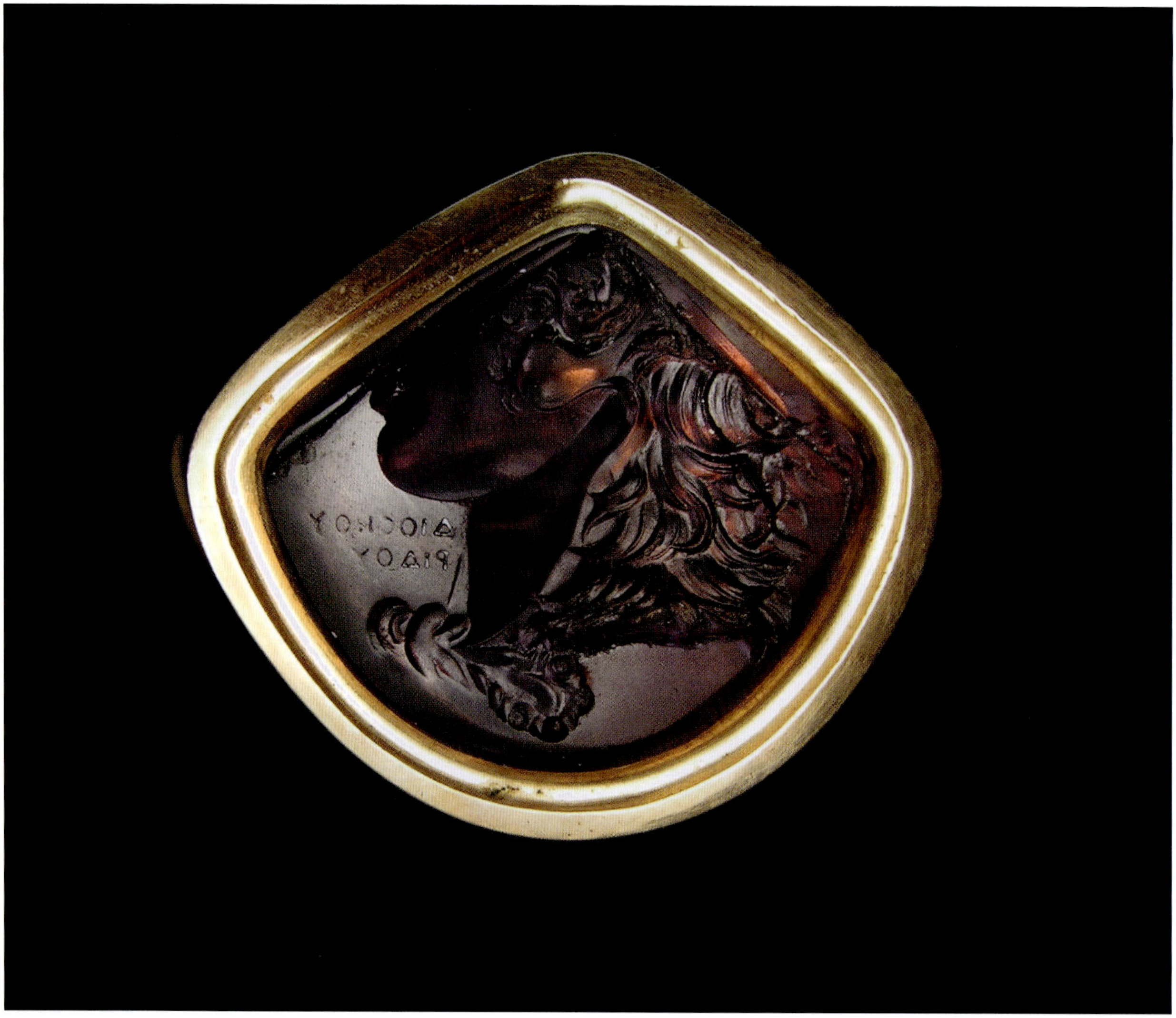

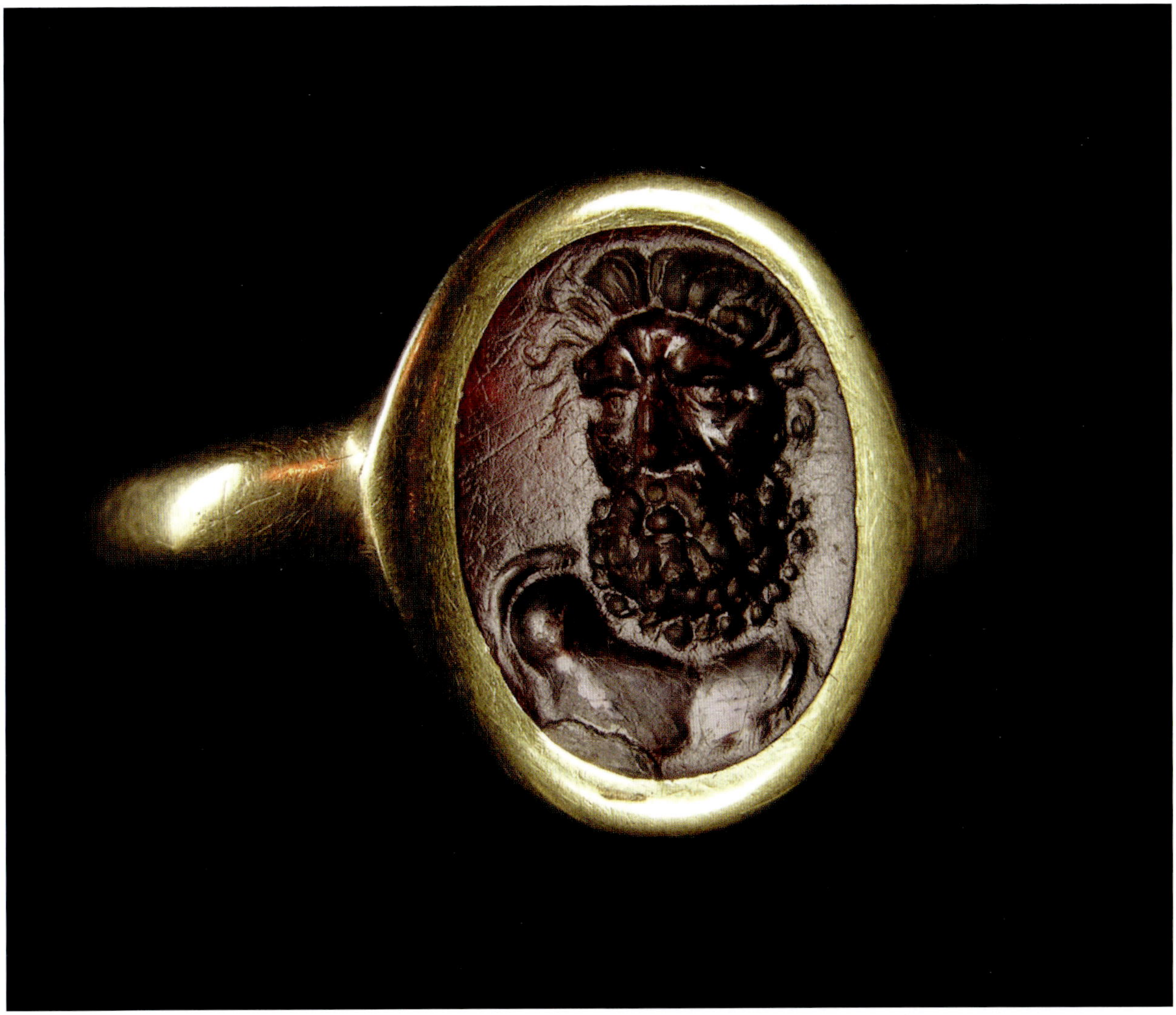

236

(10700) K158 (pl. 6)
Sard, polished flat back, set on a plain gold ring
11 x 9

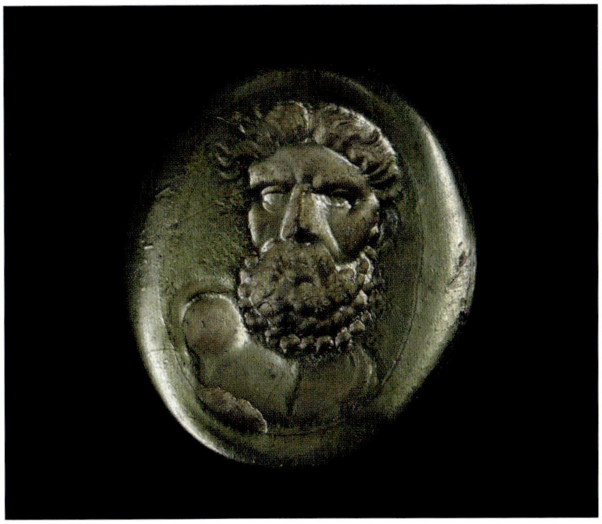

Inst.Imp. no. 89.

Facing head of Laocoon as on the sculpture group in the Vatican, a snake at his shoulder.

Compare *Marlborough* no. 359, which is a better copy, and Weber 1995, nos 301–2. The type was invented by Sirletti; see Paoletti II, VIII.149.

18th century.

237

(10800)
Rock crystal mounted in gold over gold foil, set on a gold ring with triple terminals to the hoop
15 x 12

Three-quarter bust of a man wearing a curly-brimmed helmet with knobbed top and short flowing crest. He has long hair, the bust is draped and he holds the end of a spear.

17th/18th century.

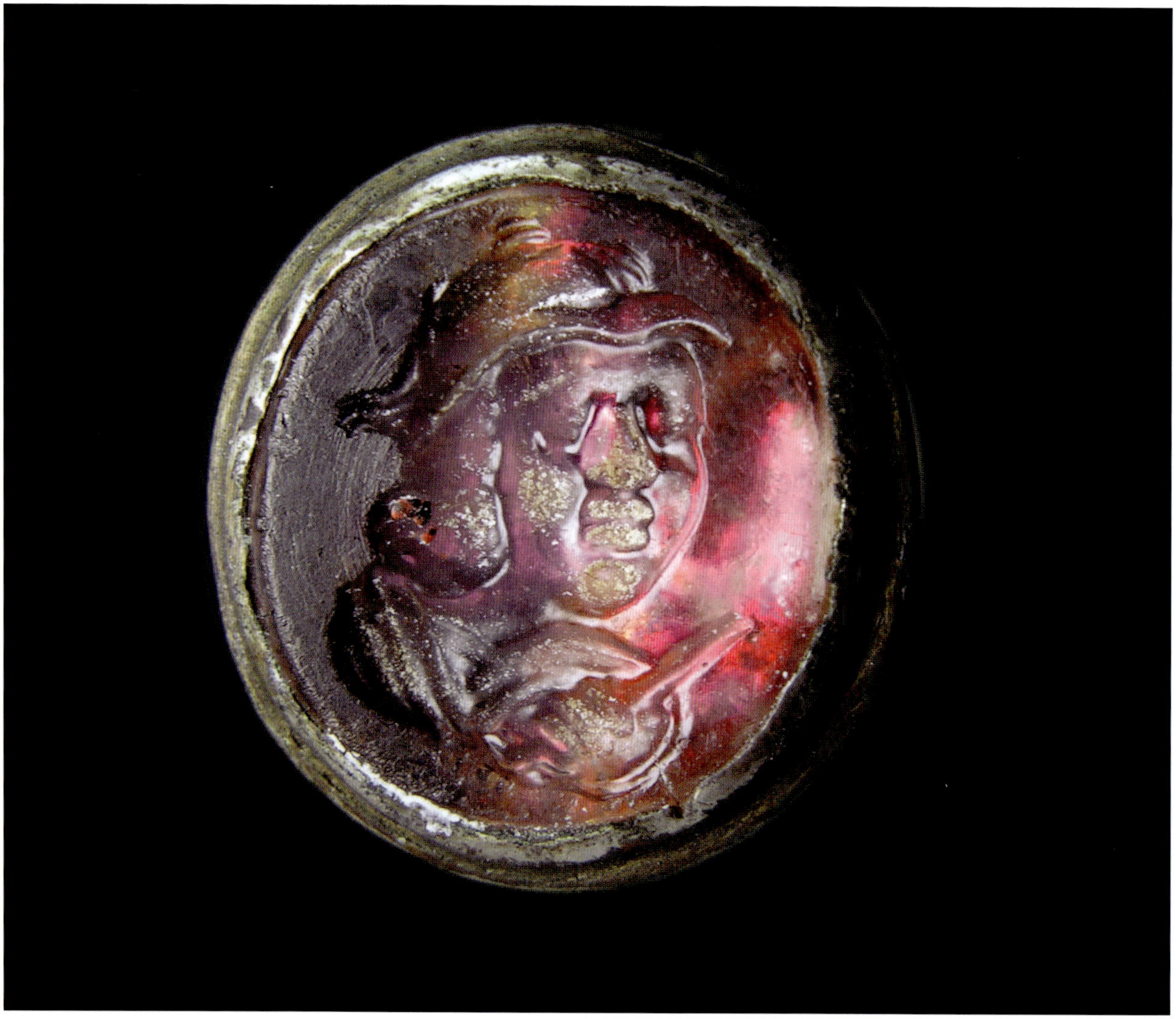

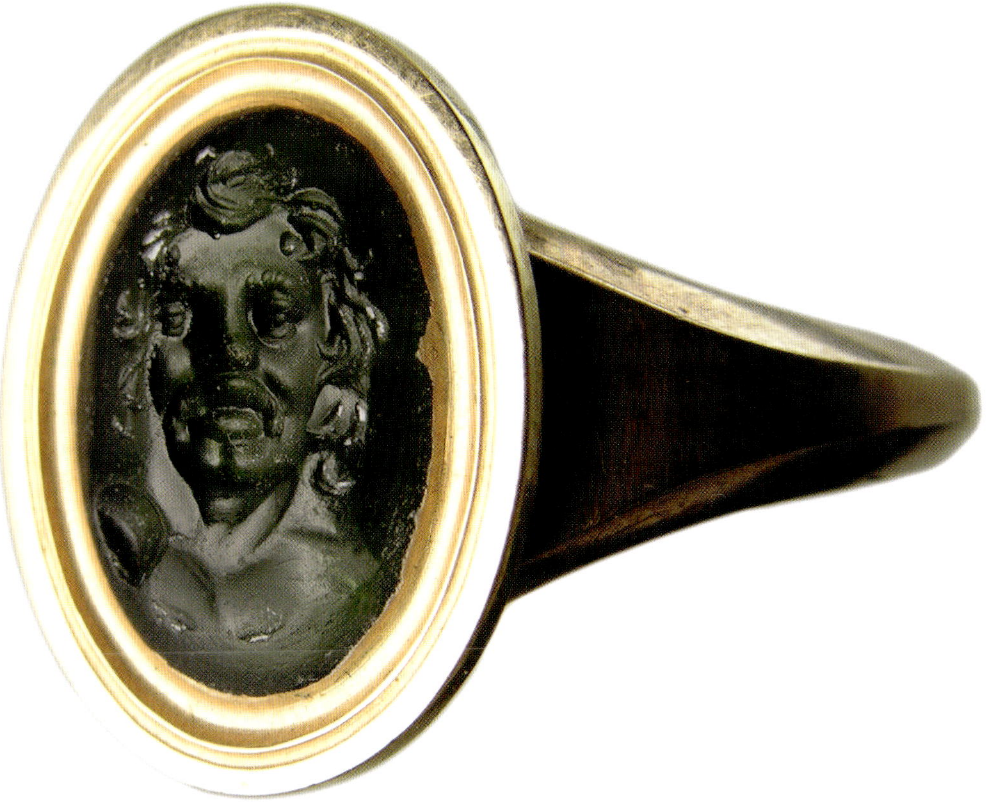

238

(10733) K195
Plasma, polished flat back, set on a plain gold ring
11 x 7

SG.Imp. 40; Inst.Imp. no. 86.

Facing bust of a man with wild hair and a drooping moustache.

18th century?

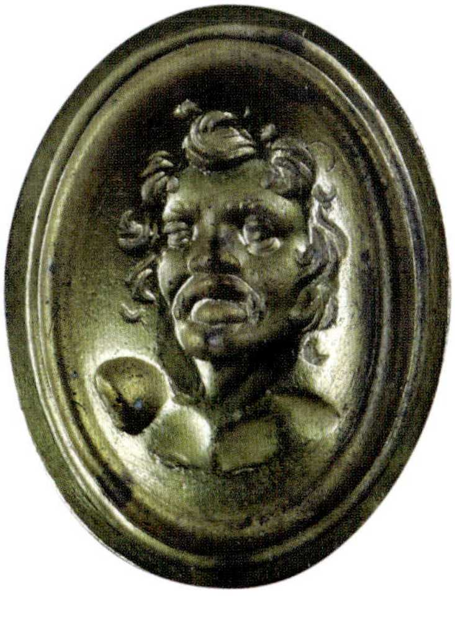

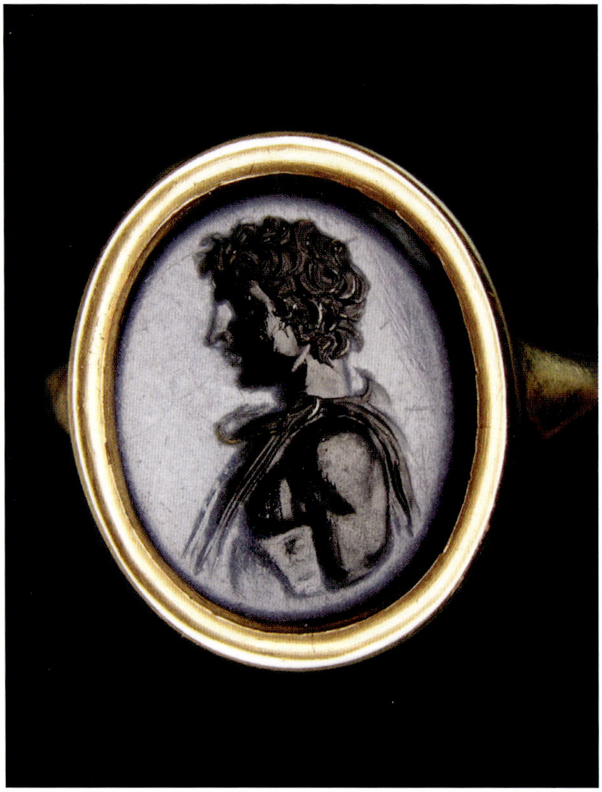

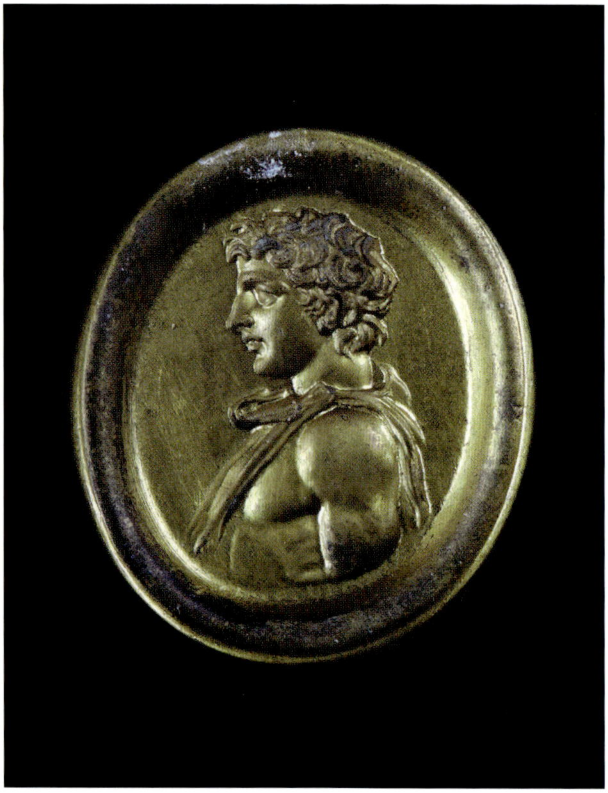

239

(10693) K155 (pl. 6)
Nicolo, polished flat back, set on a plain gold ring
16 x 12

SG.Imp. 103; Inst.Imp. no. 107; Paoletti I, III.204.

Bust of a youth wearing a cloak fastened around his neck, his ribs exaggerated.

M.L. Vollenweider (*Camées et Intailles,* I, no. 155) takes a similar figure for a Ptolemaic princess. 'Son of Antoninus Pius'(Stefanelli).

17th/18th century.

240

(10798)
Carnelian, polished flat back, set on a plain gold ring
19 x 15

Head of a balding man with heavy beard.

18th century?

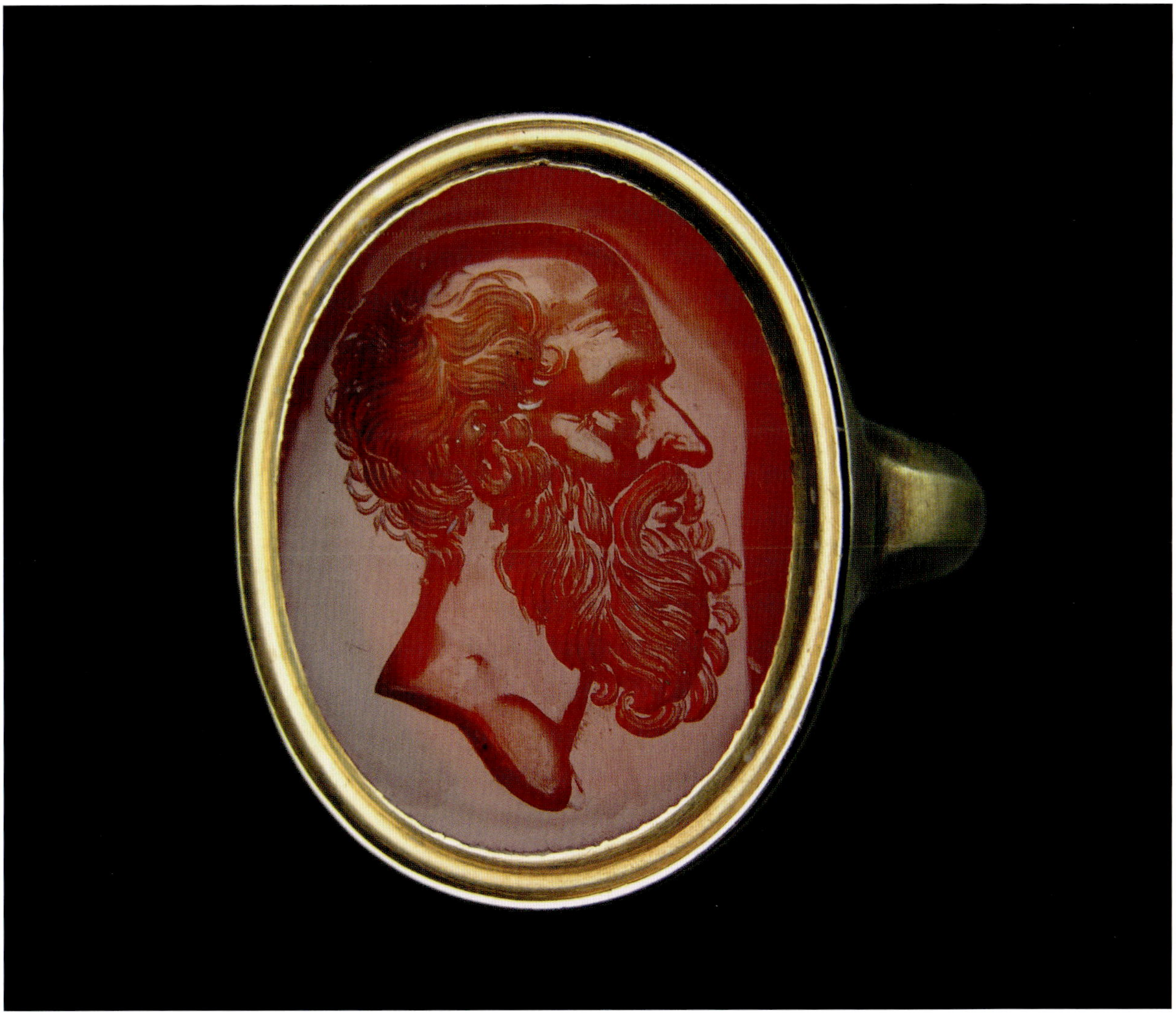

241

(10710) K172 (pl. 5)
Red jasper, a chip at the bottom restored in gold, unpolished flat back, set on a plain gold ring
8 x 7

SG.Imp. 59.

Head herm of a man wearing a fillet in his hair. Knight – 'Plato.' Probably an archaising bust of Bacchus; compare *Würzburg* no. 716.

1st century AD.

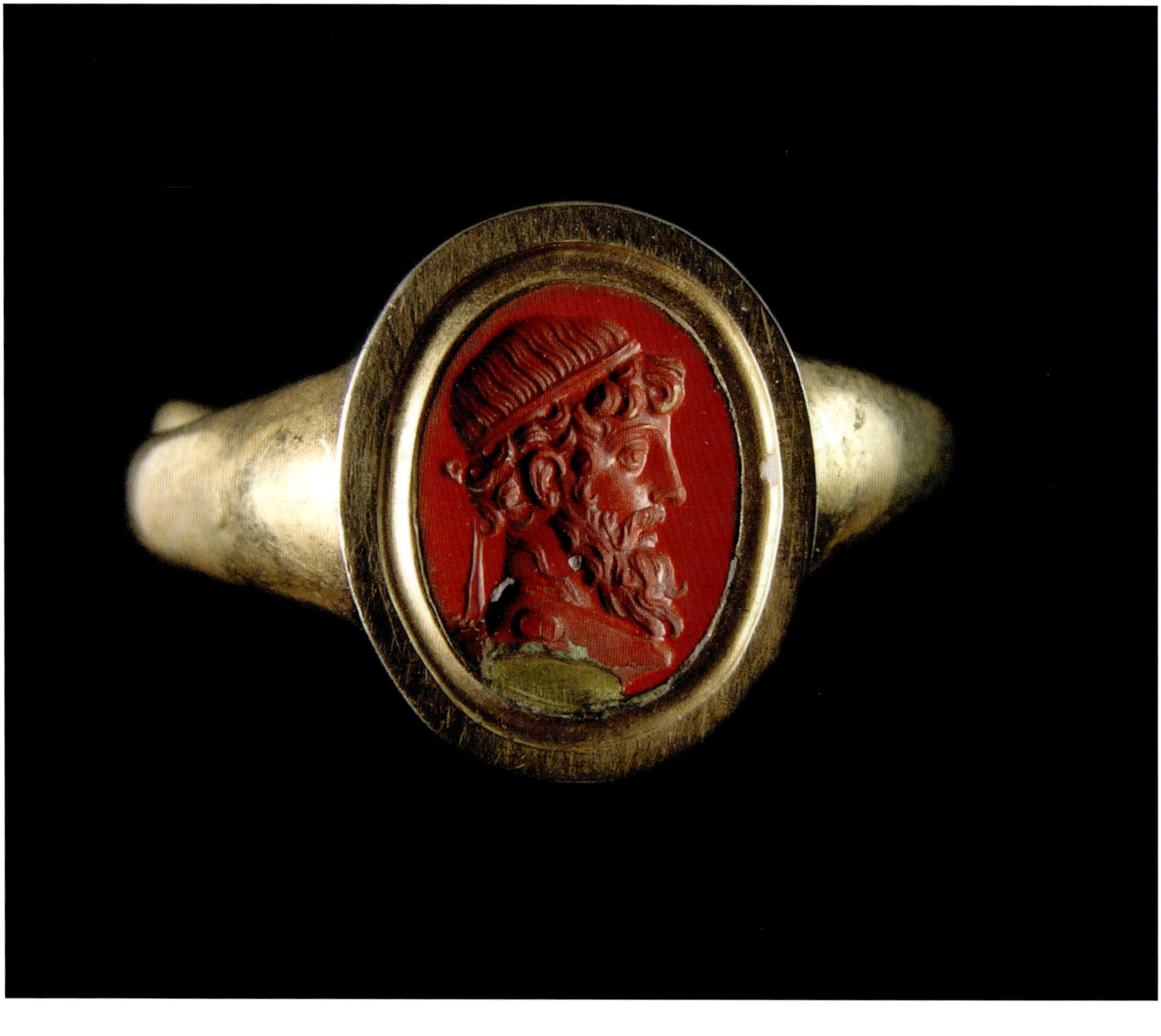

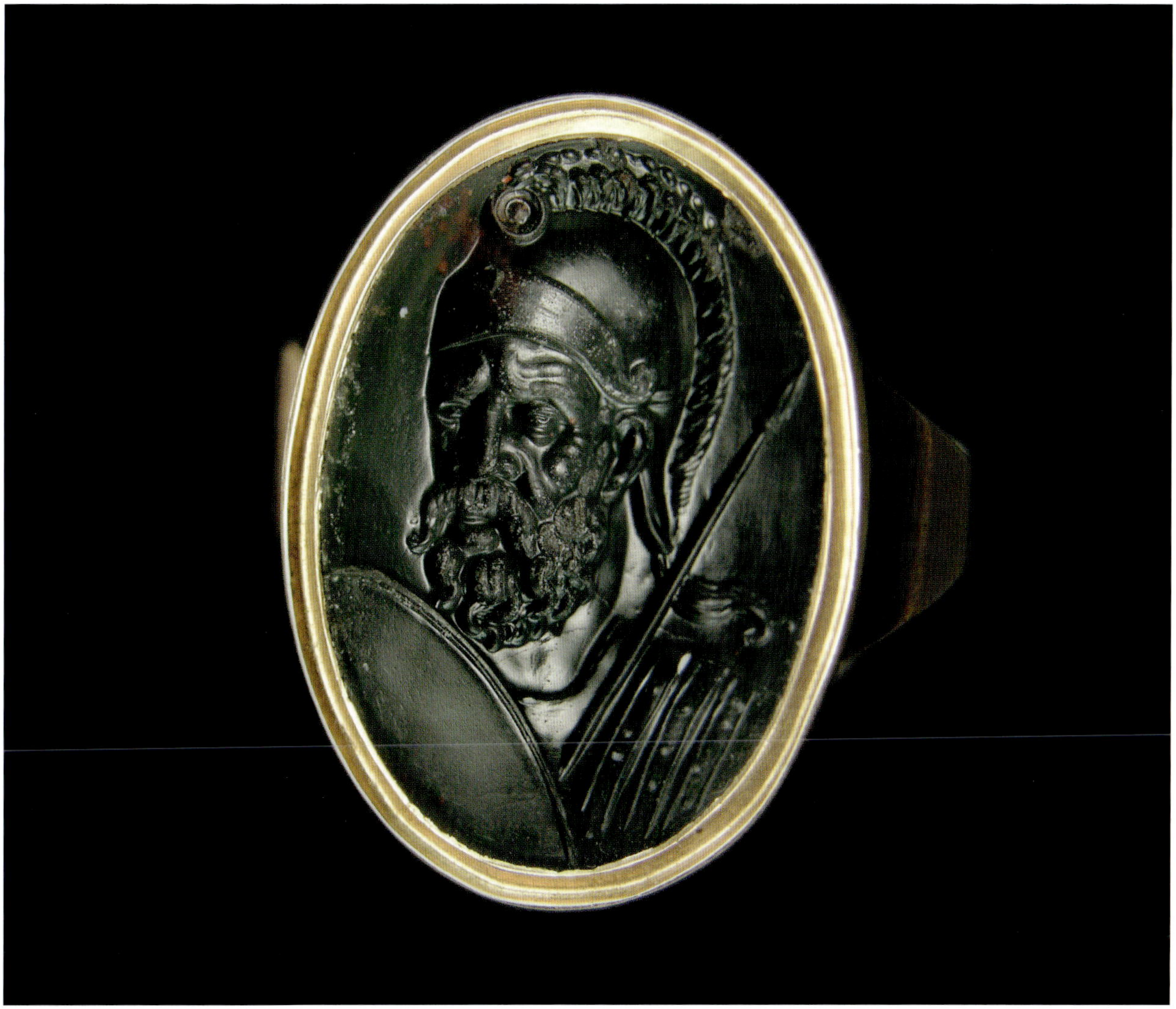

242

(10799)
Black jasper, polished convex back, set on a plain gold ring
22 x 17

Bust of an armed man with spear and shield.

This is the 'Hannibal' type, much copied. The version is very like Tassie 9608, Lippert II 280, for the elaboration of the helmet crest, but the necklet is slightly different.

17th/18th century.

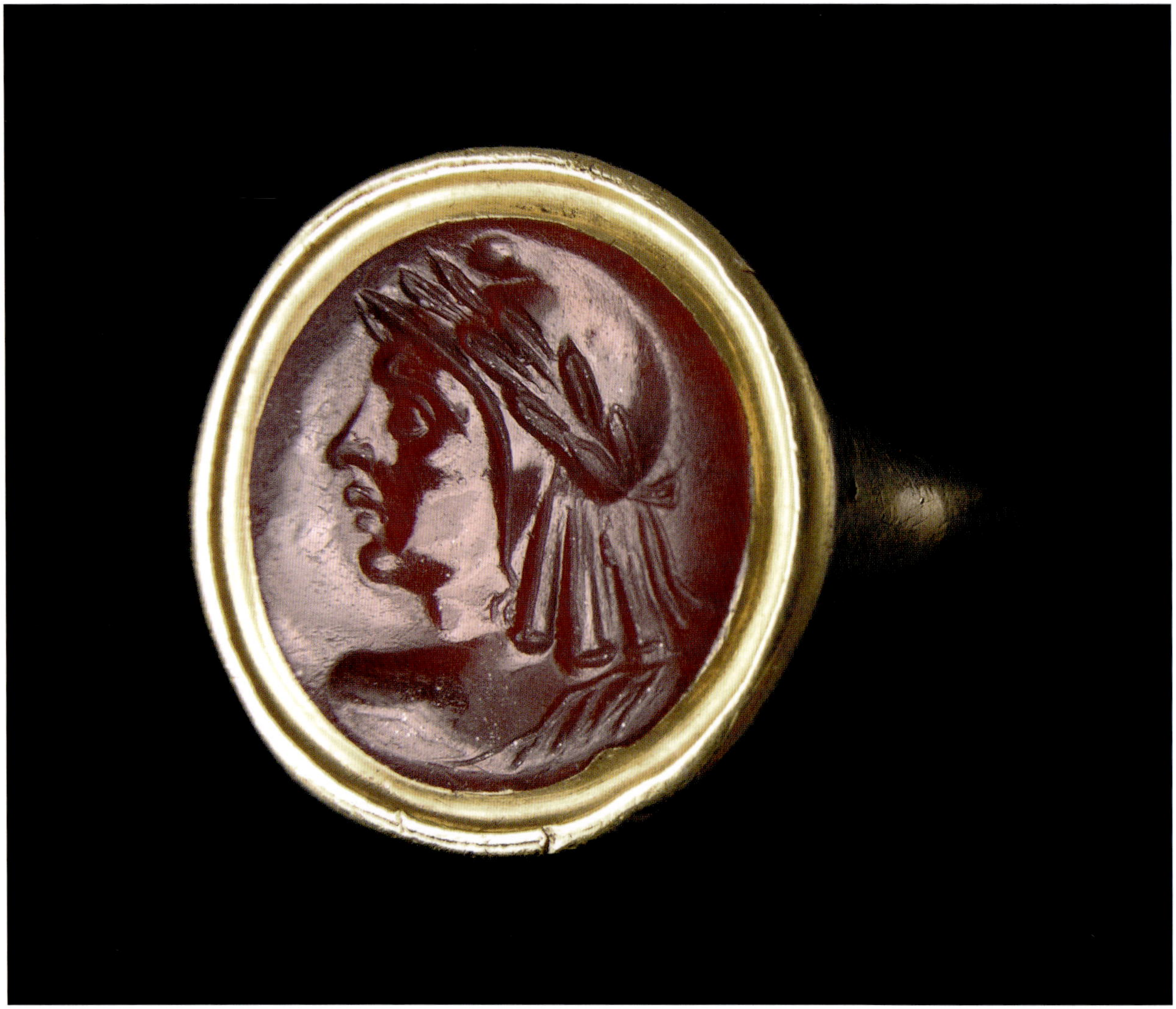

243

(10639) K101 (pl. 4)
Sard, polished flat back, set on a plain gold ring
12 x 12

SG.Imp. 52; Tassie 9724; Inst.Imp. no. 141.

Head of a laureate youth, one shoulder bared, wearing a version of a Phrygian cap with laurel wreath. Paris?

17th/18th century.

244

(10802)
Pale blue chalcedony, polished convex back, set on a plain gold ring
17 x 15

Head of a man, curly hair brushed back from the forehead and gathered at the nape, draped 'à l'antique.'

A portrait of the 1st Duke, and no. 45 in the 1st Duchess' Collection. Six copies in different coloured glass of this portrait were found when her tomb was opened in 1856 (see below, Glass Portraits). Kagan 2010, 155, suggests that, although unsigned, the engraving is close to the manner of Lorenz Natter.

18th century.

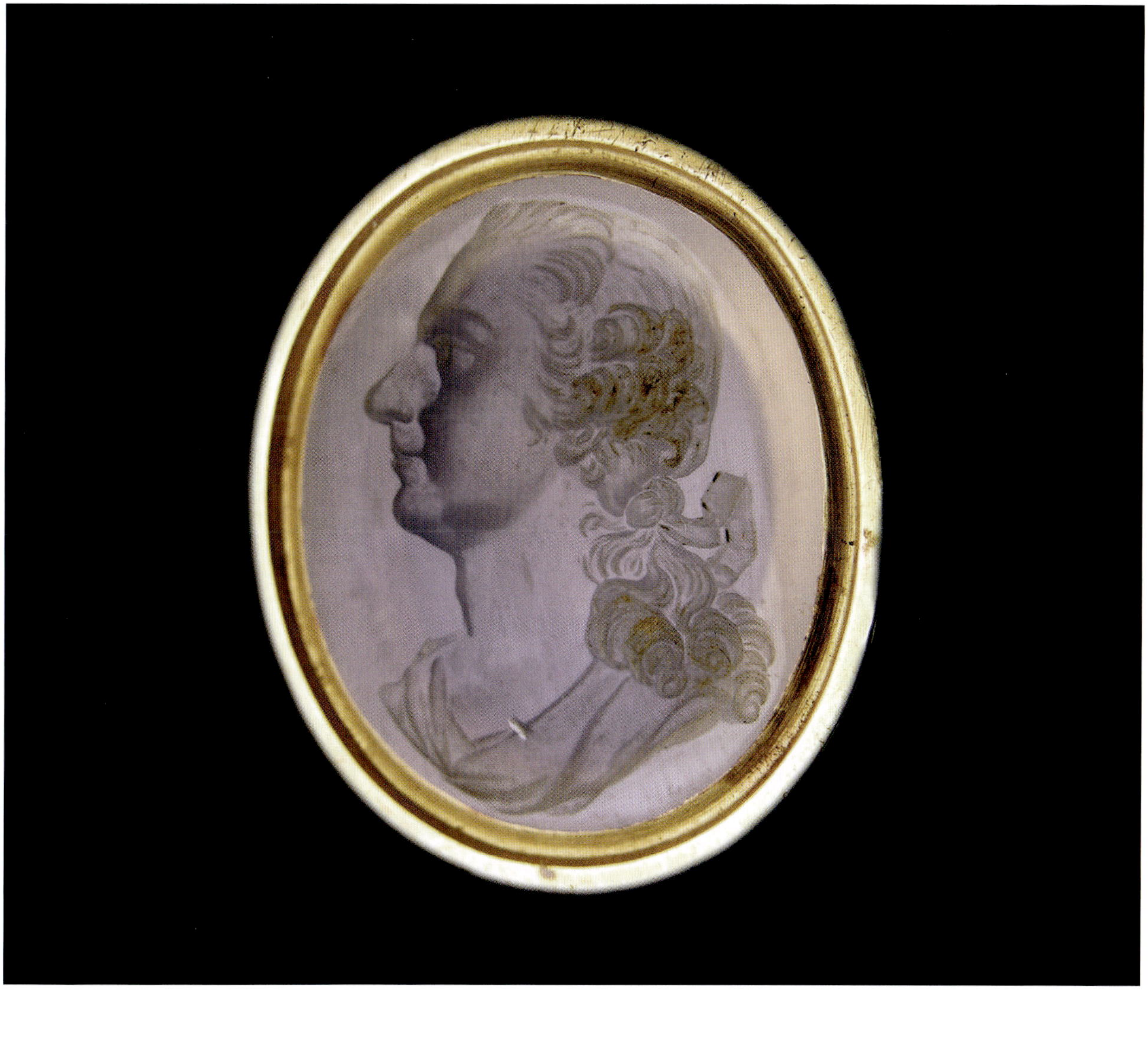

HEADS AND BUSTS, FEMALE

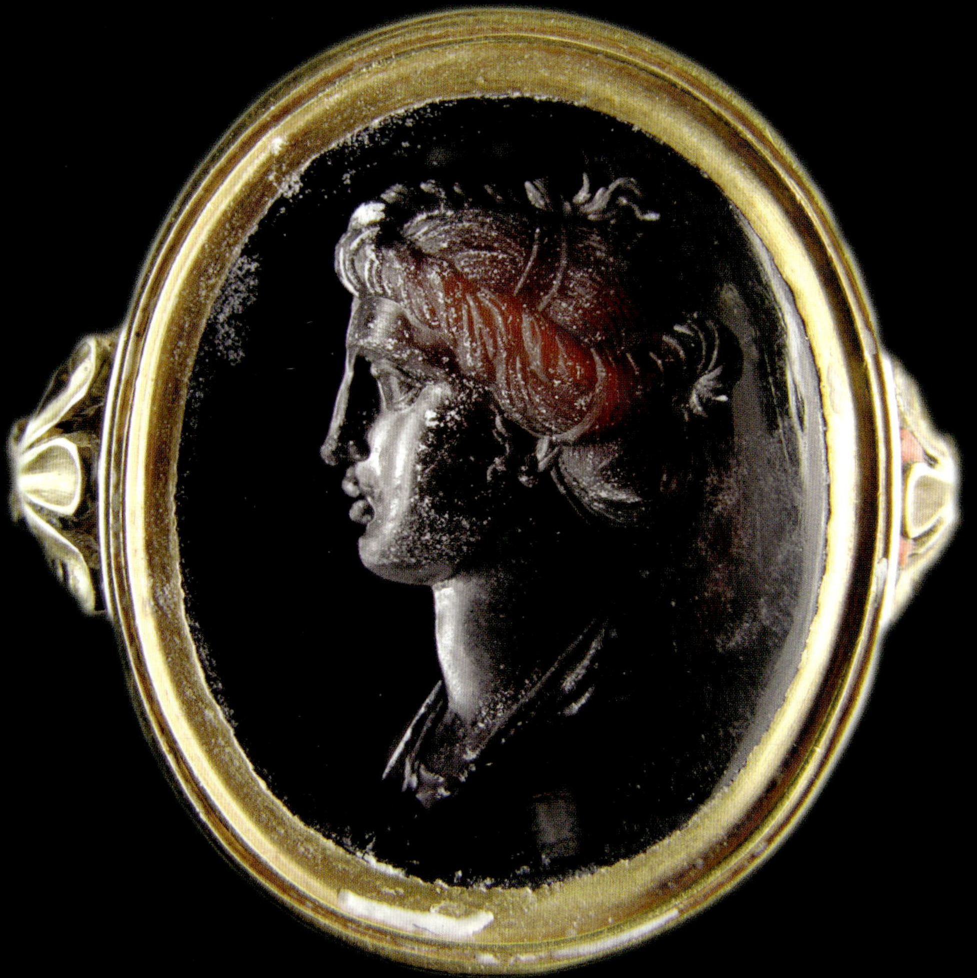

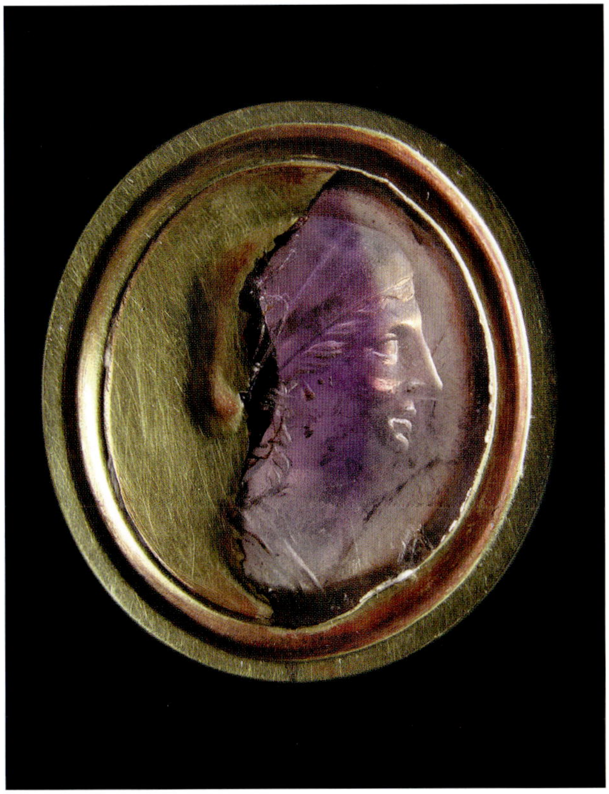

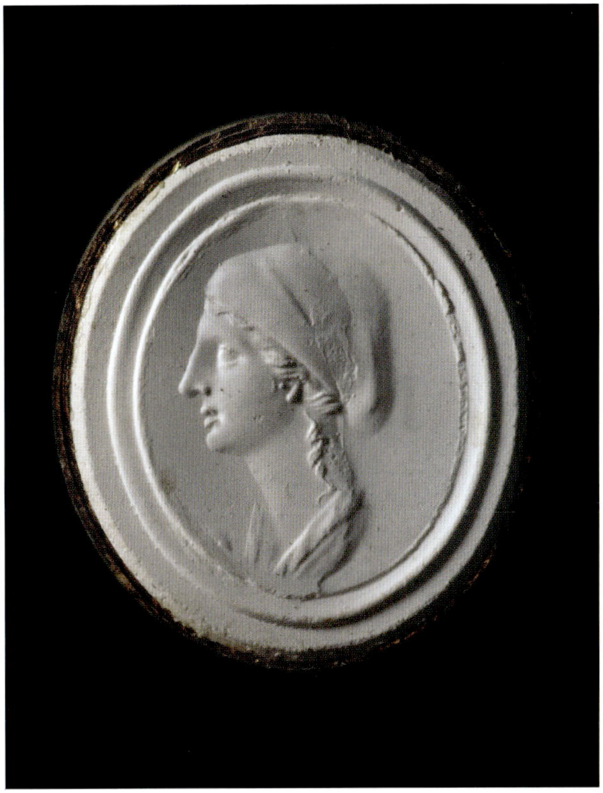

245

(10642) K104 (pl. 4)
Amethyst fragment, polished convex back, restored in gold and set in a plain gold ring.
length 15

SG.Imp. 7; Inst.Imp. no. 111; Paoletti I, IV.226. Plantzos 70 (18th century).

Head of a woman wearing a head-cloth.

On the type, its date and the possibility of a portrait of Arsinoe II, see *Marlborough* no. 769 and Plantzos 69–70. He groups our Beverley gem with other neoclassical versions; however, he did not have access to the original. Our **108** is a neoclassical copy.

2nd century BC?

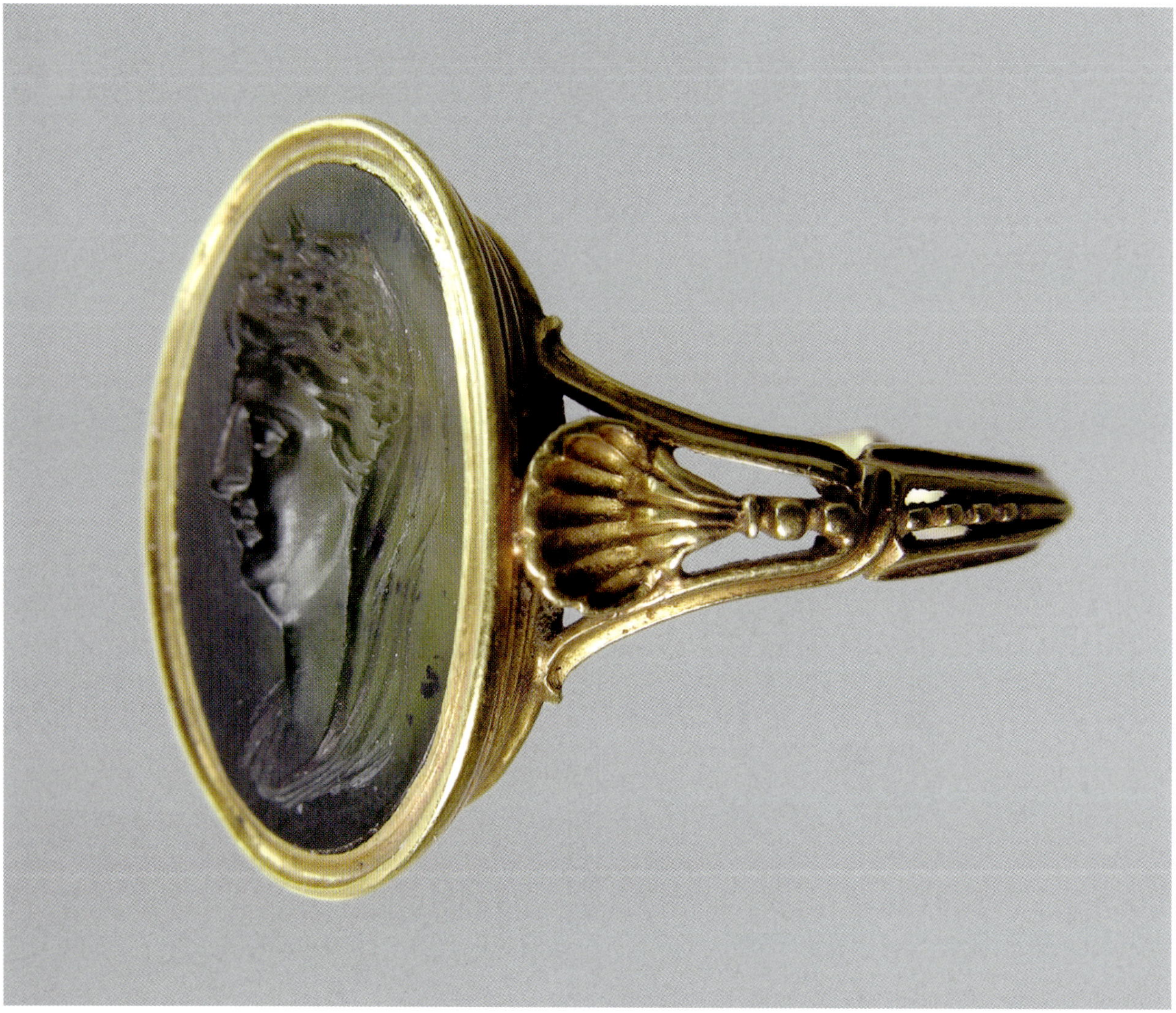

246

(10804)
Chrome chalcedony, polished flat back, set in a gold ring with shell terminals
15 x 10

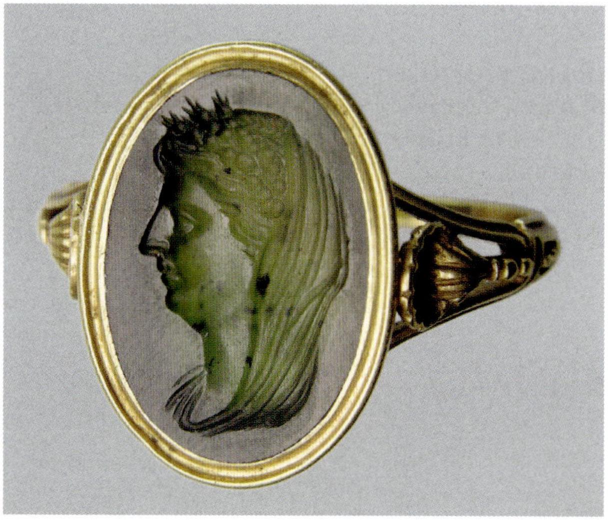

Veiled head of Livia as Ceres with corn heads as a crown.
Compare Giuliano, *Cammei* no. 155; *Würzburg* no. 581.

About AD 20.

247

(10627) K89 (pl. 3)
Sard, convex polished back, set on a plain gold ring
14 x 11

SG.Imp. 97; Tassie 11899; Inst.Imp. no. 97.

Bust of a woman, taken by Knight as Plotina, wife of Trajan.

1st century AD.

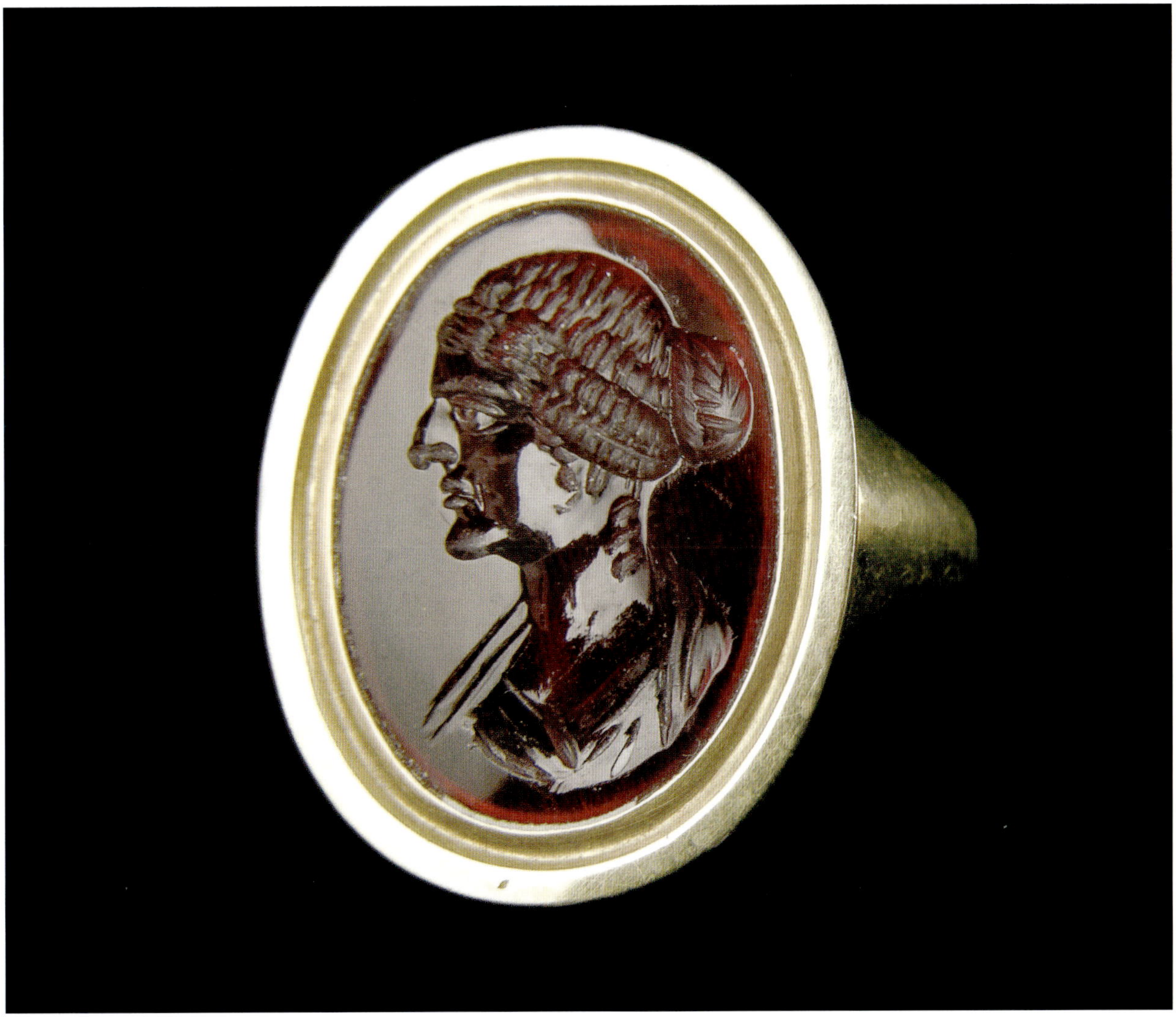

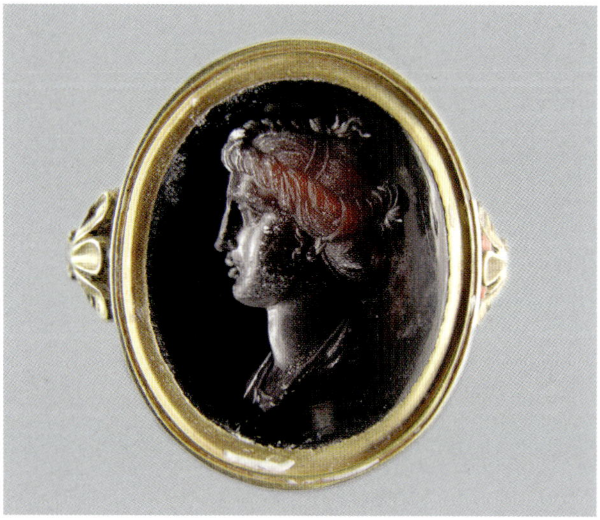

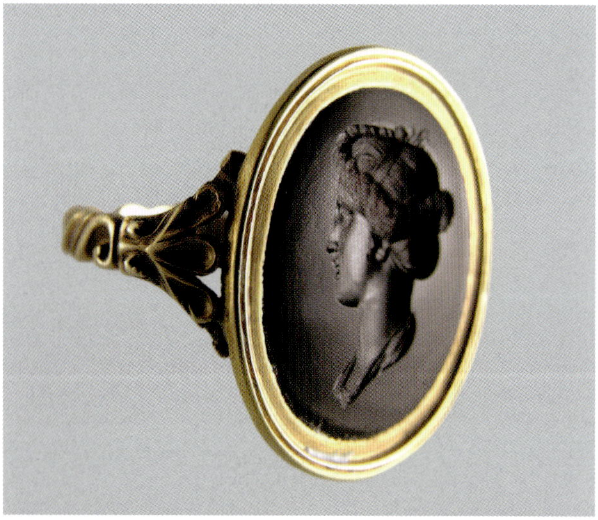

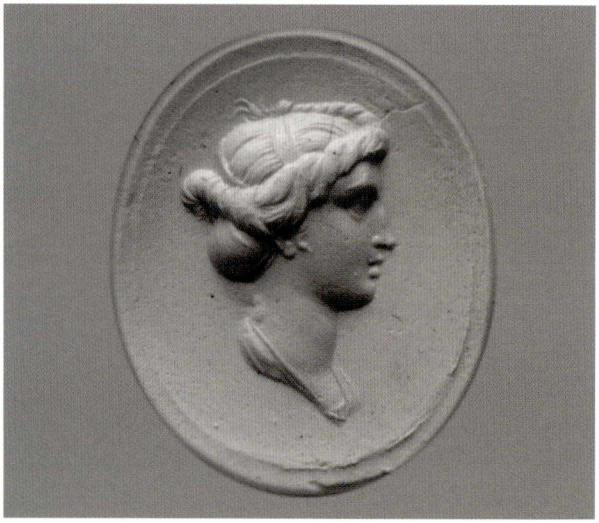

248

(10807)
Carnelian, polished flat back, set on a gold ring with leafy terminals to the hoop
16 x 13

Head of a woman, dressed at the neck, the back hair bound in a flat bun, a tress laid back over the top of the head, and a double diadem over the forehead hair.

18th century.

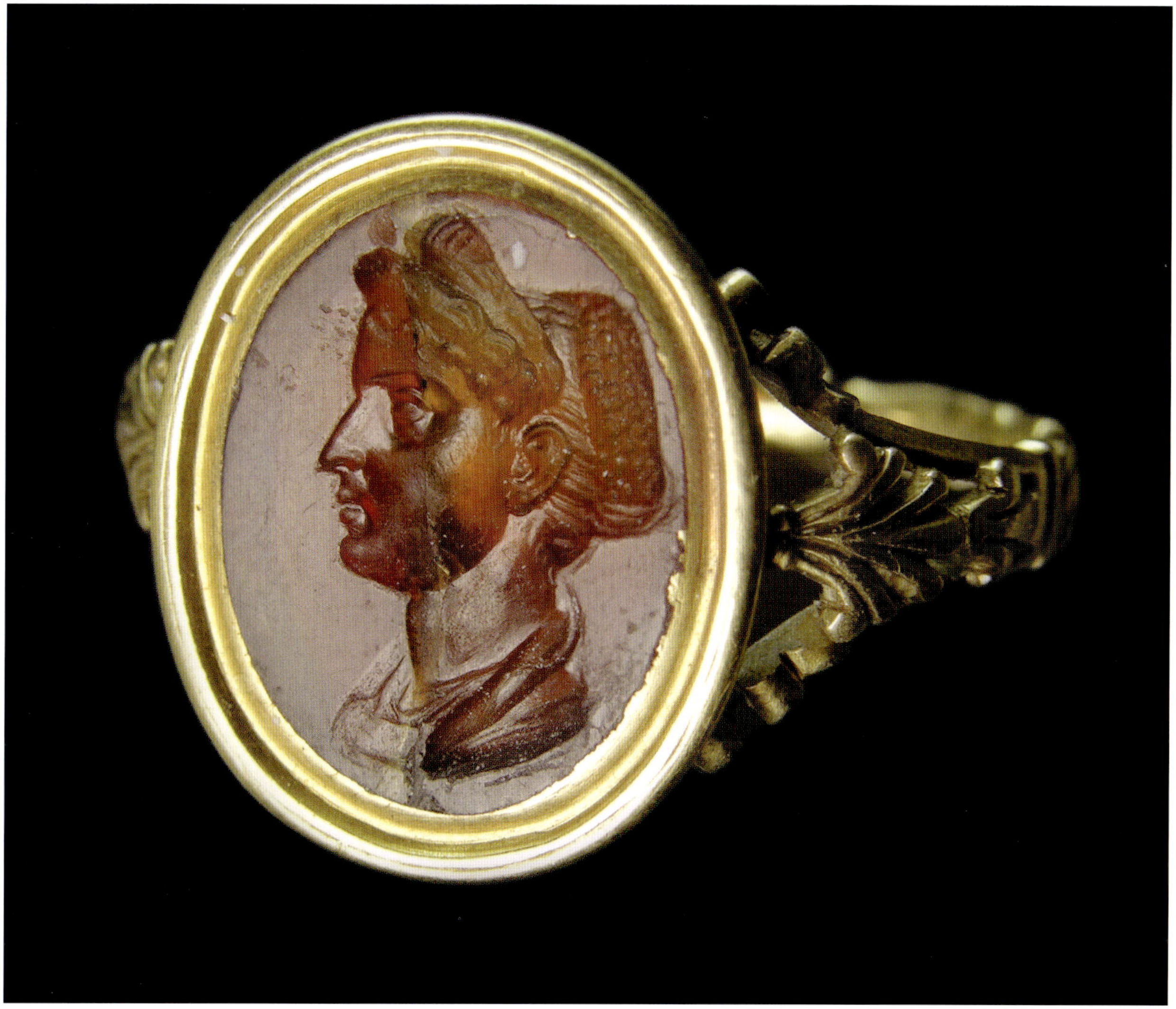

249

(10805)
Carnelian, polished flat back, set in a gold ring with floral terminals
12 x 9

Portrait of a woman, dress at her neck, the back hair bound in plaits and two rows of wavy hair over the forehead. Compare the heads, *Würzburg* pl.143.

2nd century AD.

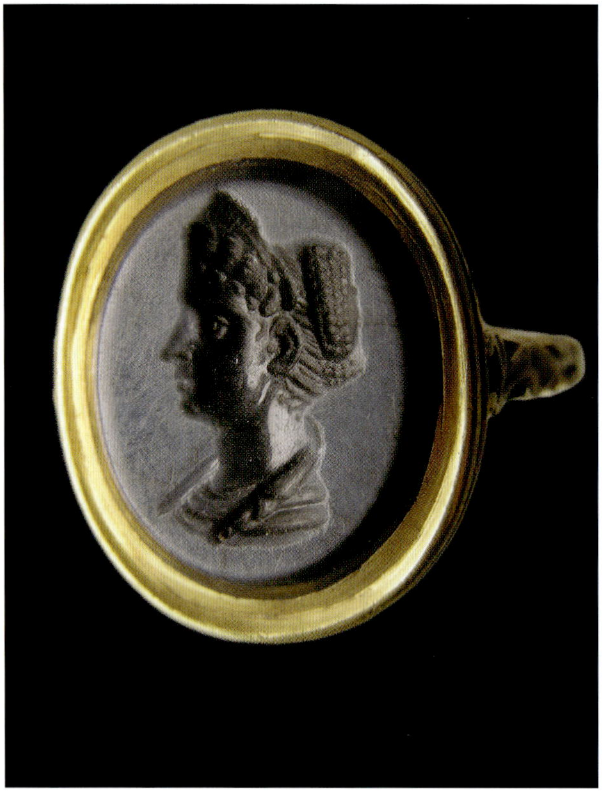 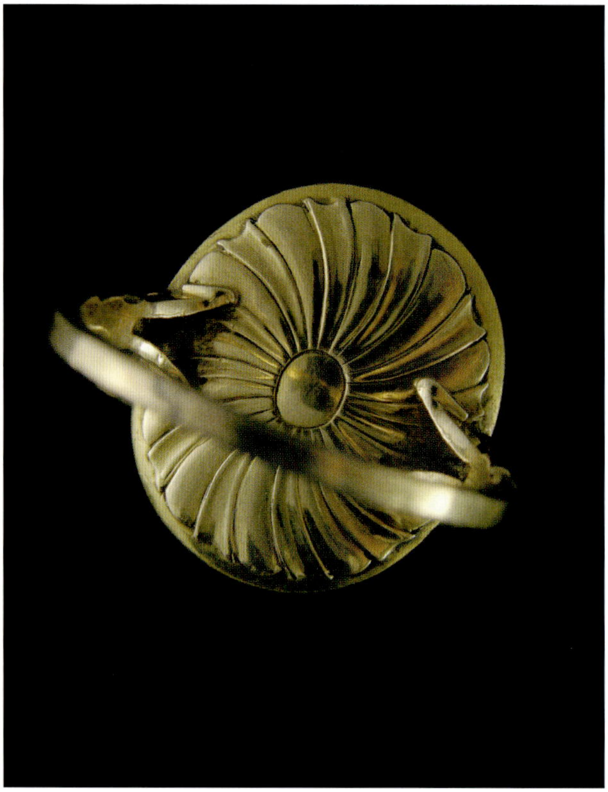

250

(10634) K96 (pl. 4)
Nicolo, set on a gold ring with leaves at the hoop ends and a spiral-fluted back
16 x 12

Bust of a woman wearing a tiara and with elaborately dressed hair.

This is a familiar type of the earlier 2nd century AD, not certainly identified. Compare *Würzburg* no. 820.

2nd century AD?

251

(10746) K208
Ruby, set in a gold ring with a steel bezel flanked by groups of three Cupids, one holding up two others who hold the bezel
9 x 6

Head of a woman or maenad with long hair, dressed in a bun, and wearing a vine wreath (?).

A note with the ring states: 'Ring set by Benvenuto Cellini.' Cellini was the master of figurative jewellery in the Renaissance, influencing the ring designs of Pierre Woeriot (*Livre des Anneaux* (Lyon 1561)) with bezels, as here, supported by groups of children, old men and young women.

16th century.

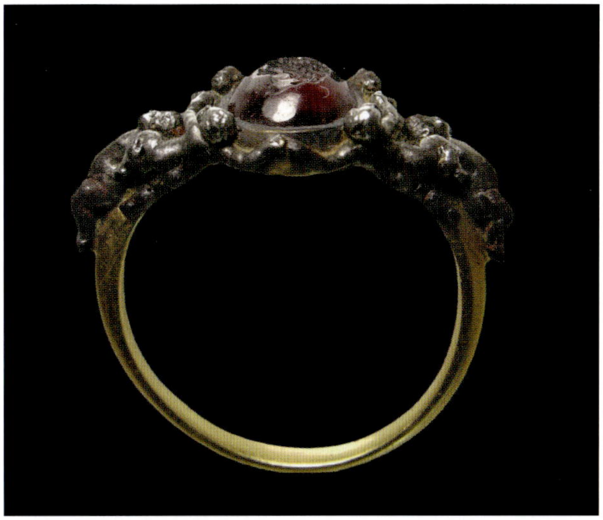

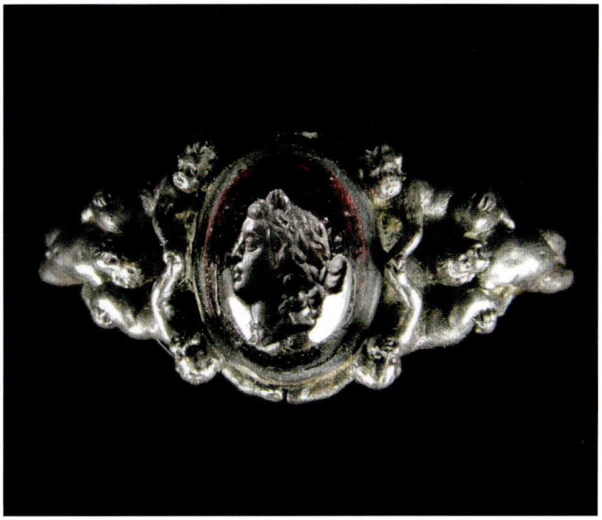

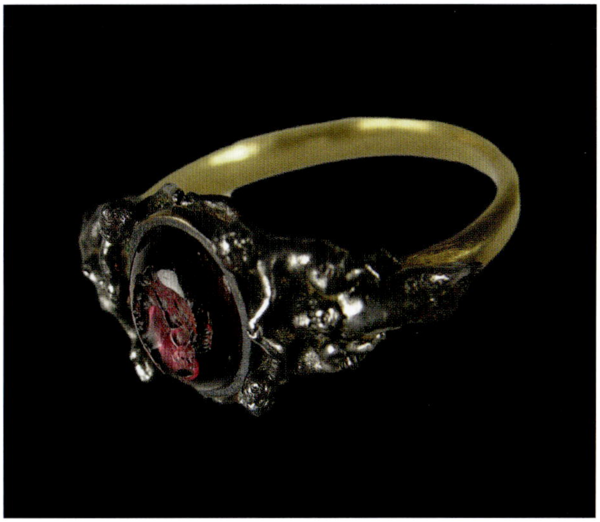

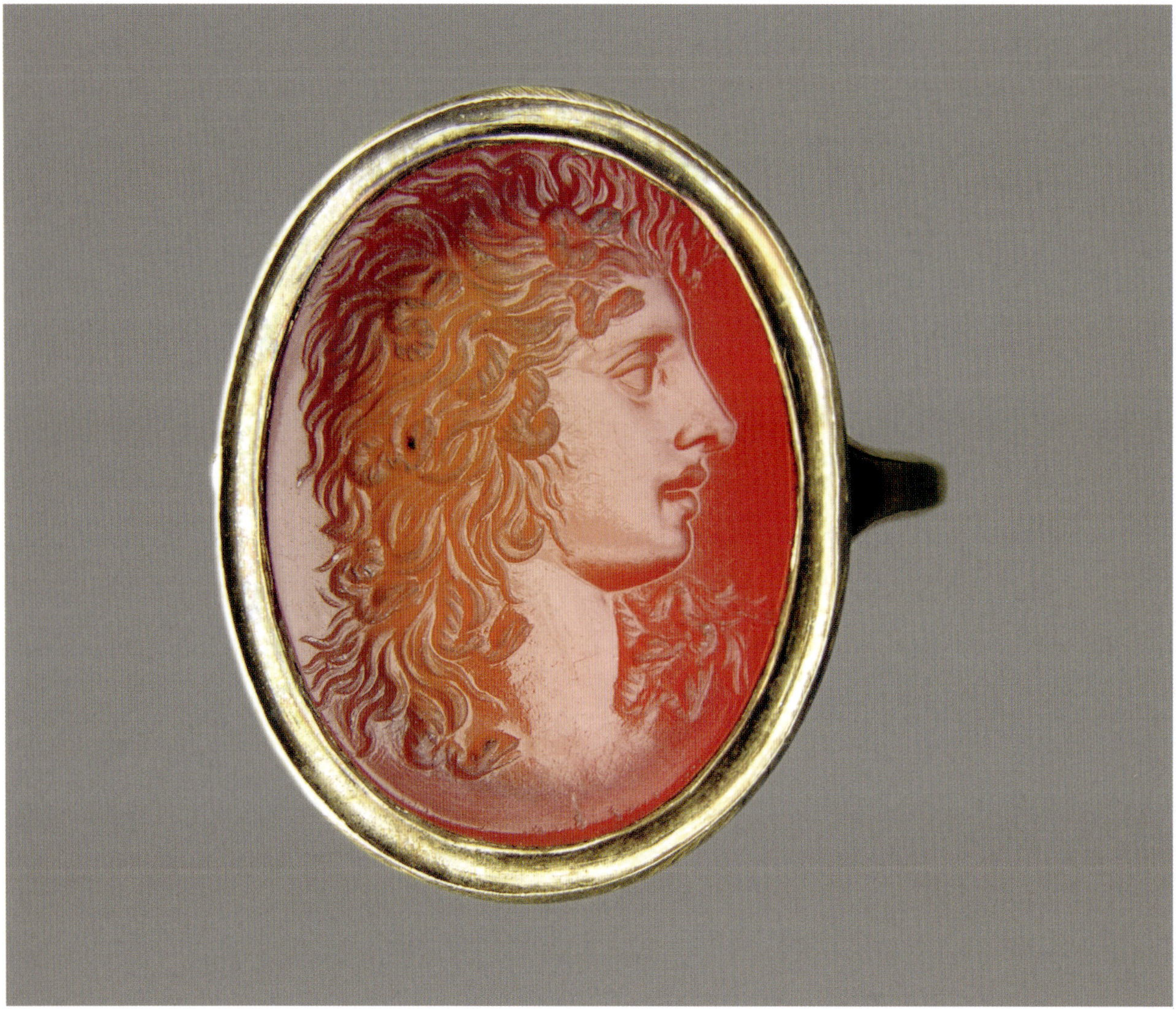

252

(10771)

Pale carnelian, polished flat back, set on a plain gold ring

18 x 14

Head of a maenad or Medusa – there are small snakes in the long locks of hair.

Although not signed, this could be the cornelian Medus(a), no. 48 in the Collection of the 1st Duchess, by Carlo Costanzi (1705–81). The head derives from the Medusa signed by Solon in the Strozzi Collection, which Costanzi copied on chalcedony in 1729 for the Cardinal de Polignac.

18th century.

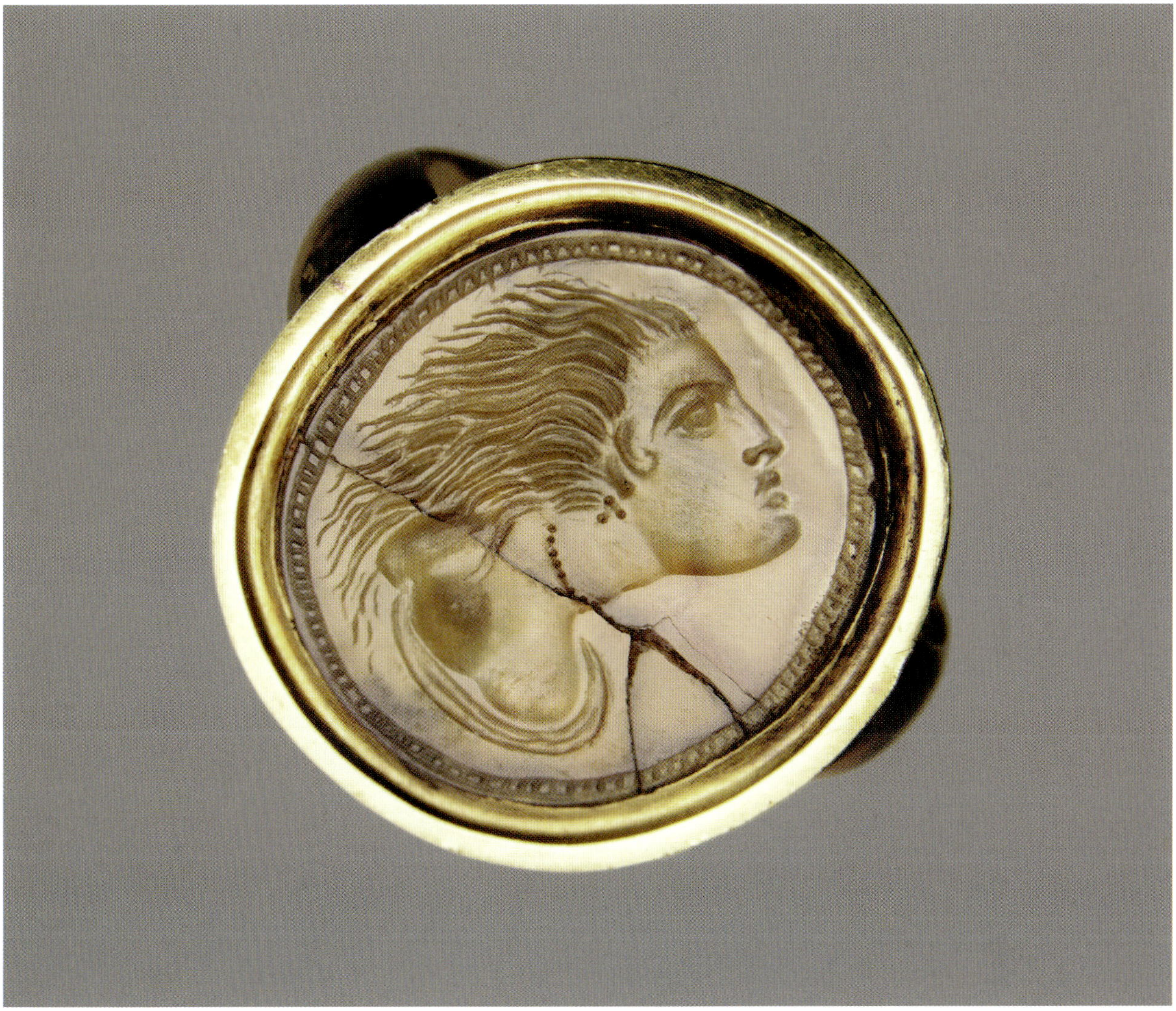

253

(10724) K186 (pl. 5)
Yellow jasper with clear layers above and below, polished flat back, set on a plain gold ring
18 x 16

SG.Imp. 37; Tassie 5008; Inst.Imp. no. 104; Paoletti I, II.157.

The head and shoulders of a woman with loose hair, wearing a necklet and earring, dress at her breast. Hatched border.

She is possibly meant for a maenad or even a swimming figure. 'Glauke, daughter of Kreon, killed by Medea' (Knight).

18th century.

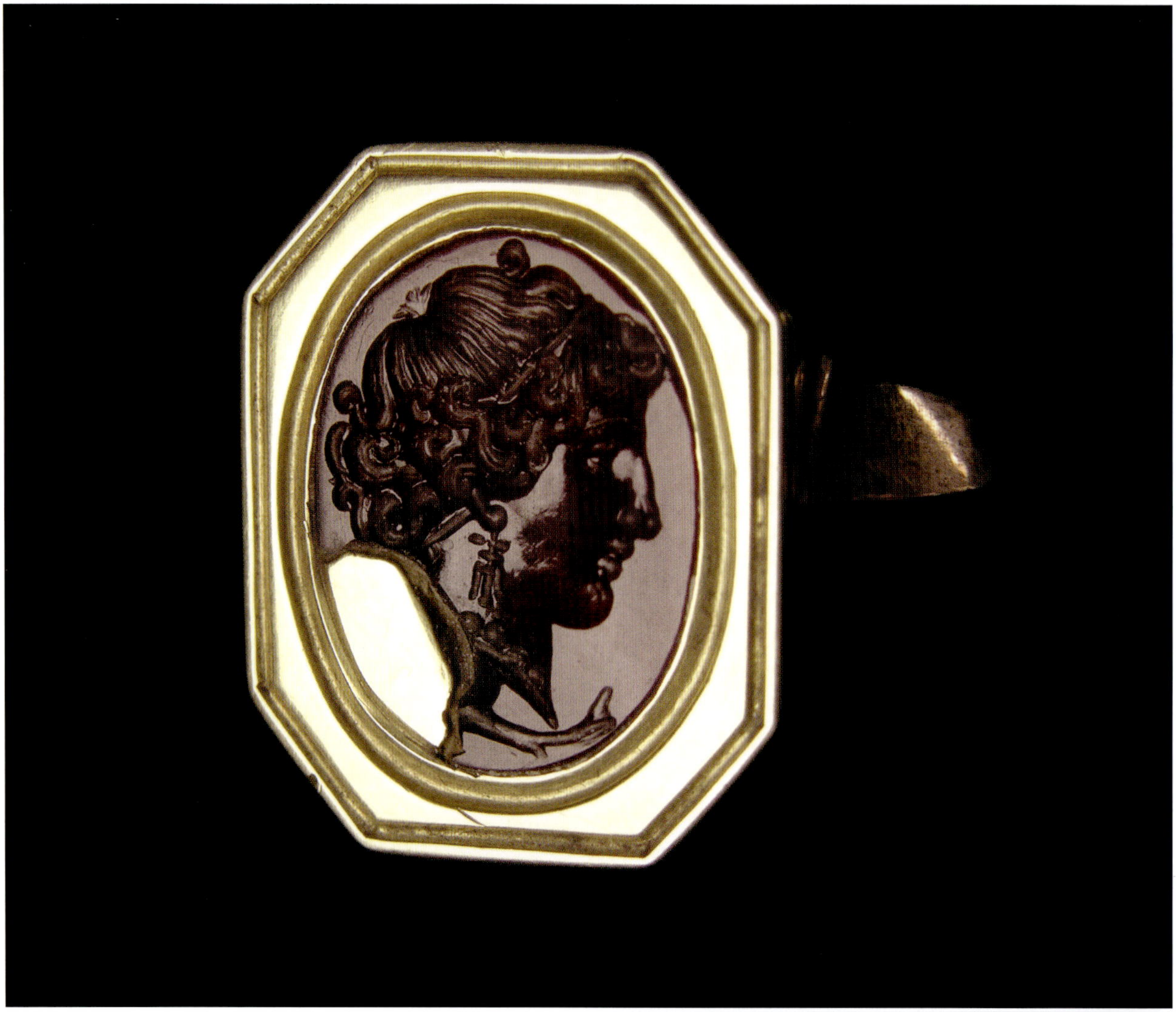

254

(10691) K153 (pl. 5)
Sard, set on a plain gold ring with octagonal bezel
14 x 11

SG.Imp. 5; Inst.Imp. no. 105.

The head of Arethusa (the head adopted from the coinage of Syracuse) wearing a hair band, necklet and earring. The part behind the neck restored in gold, concealing part of a dolphin which protrudes before her neck.

18th century.

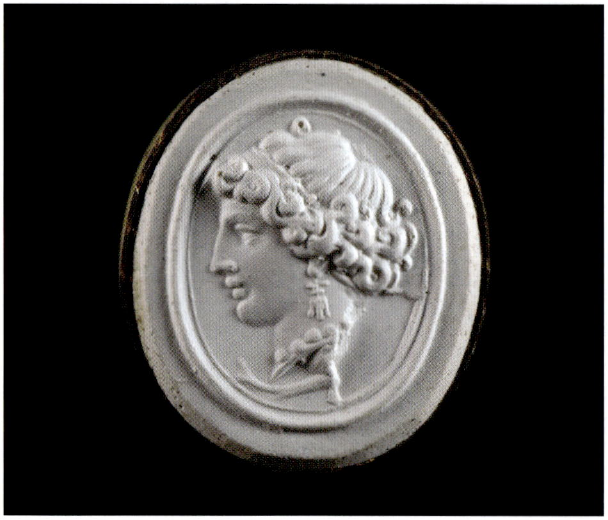

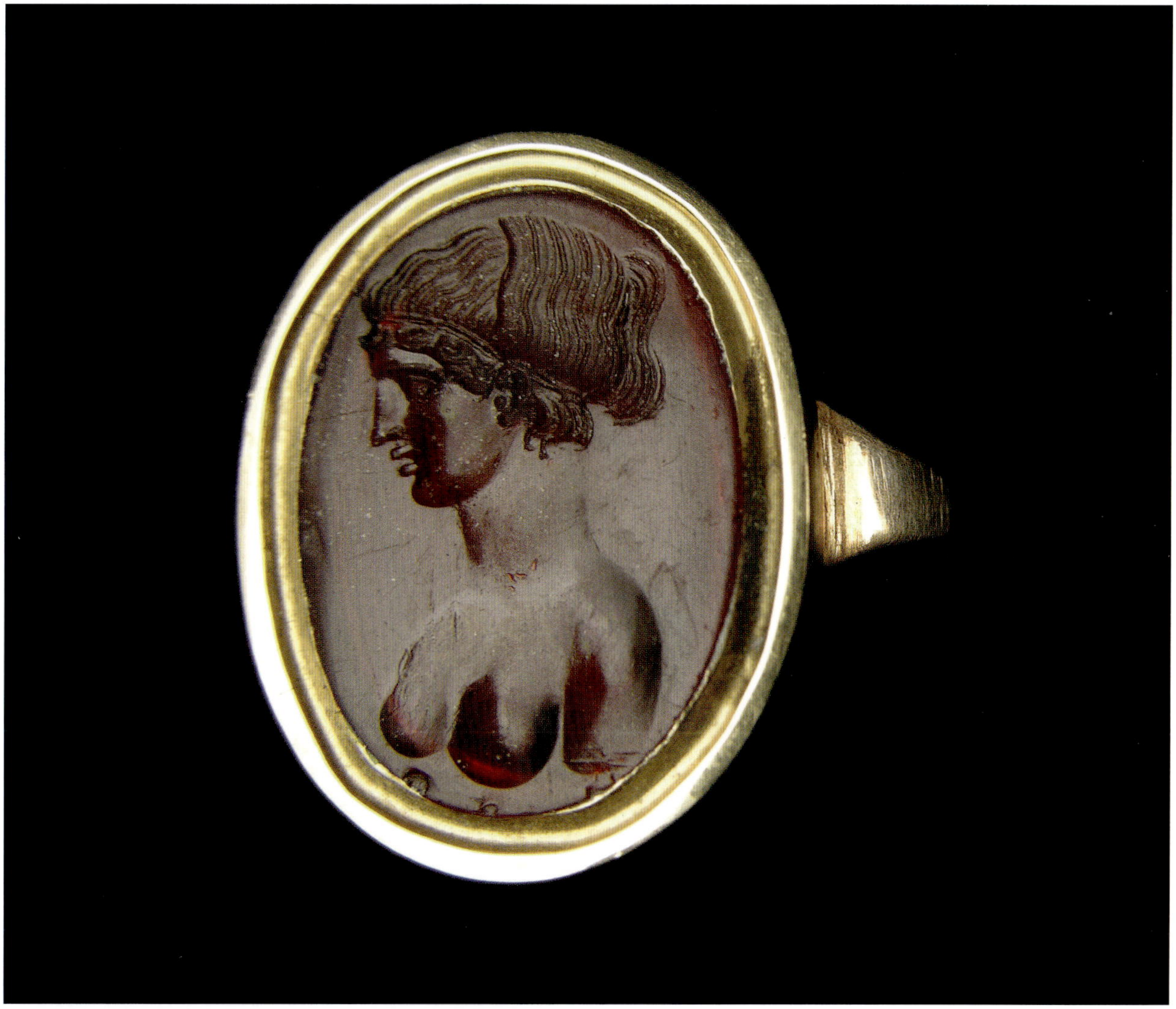

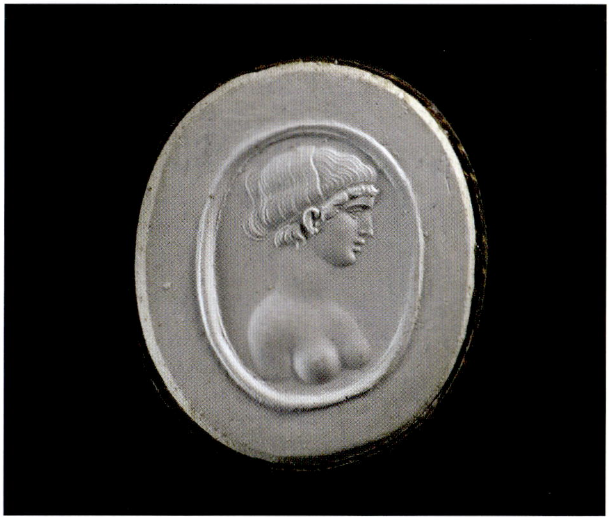

255

(10626) K88 (pl. 3)
Sard, polished flat back, set on a plain gold ring
15 x 12

SG.Imp. 81; Tassie 3417; Inst.Imp. no. 99.

Bust of a bare-breasted woman, her hair dressed in a roll.

Knight saw traces of an inscription below; possible traces of the tops of two letters (?ΠΙ).

18th century.

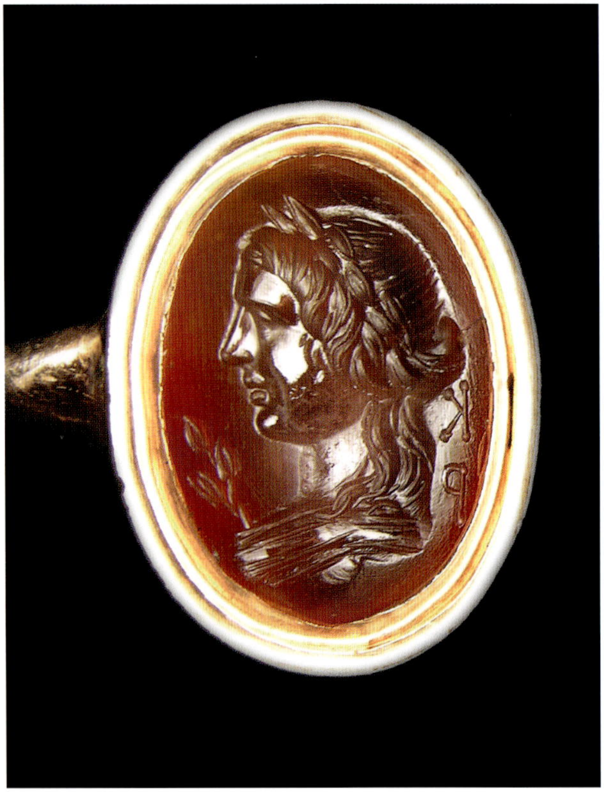
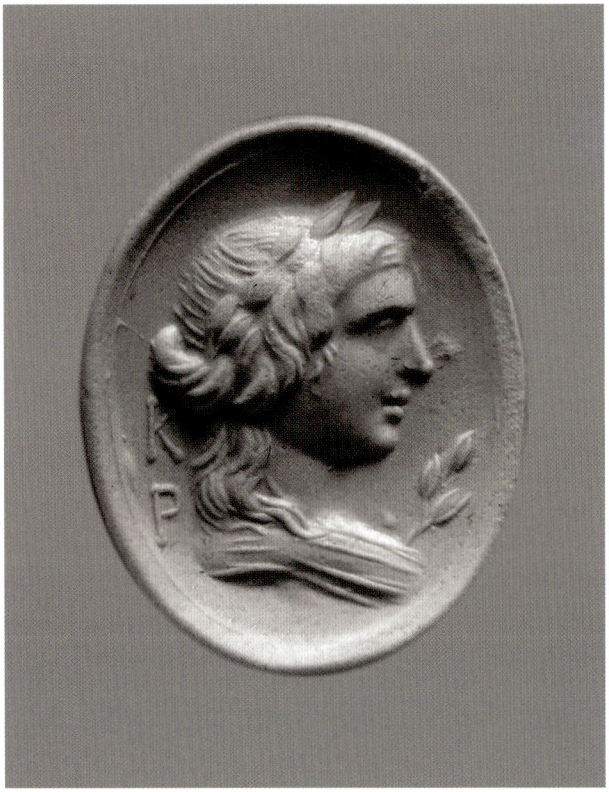

256

(10803)
Carnelian, polished convex back, set on a plain gold ring
13 x 10

Laureate bust of Apollo with long back hair, a sprig of laurel before him. Inscribed KP.

Perhaps a work by Gaspare Capparoni (1761–1808), copying a 4th-century BC type.

18th century?

ANIMALS AND MONSTERS

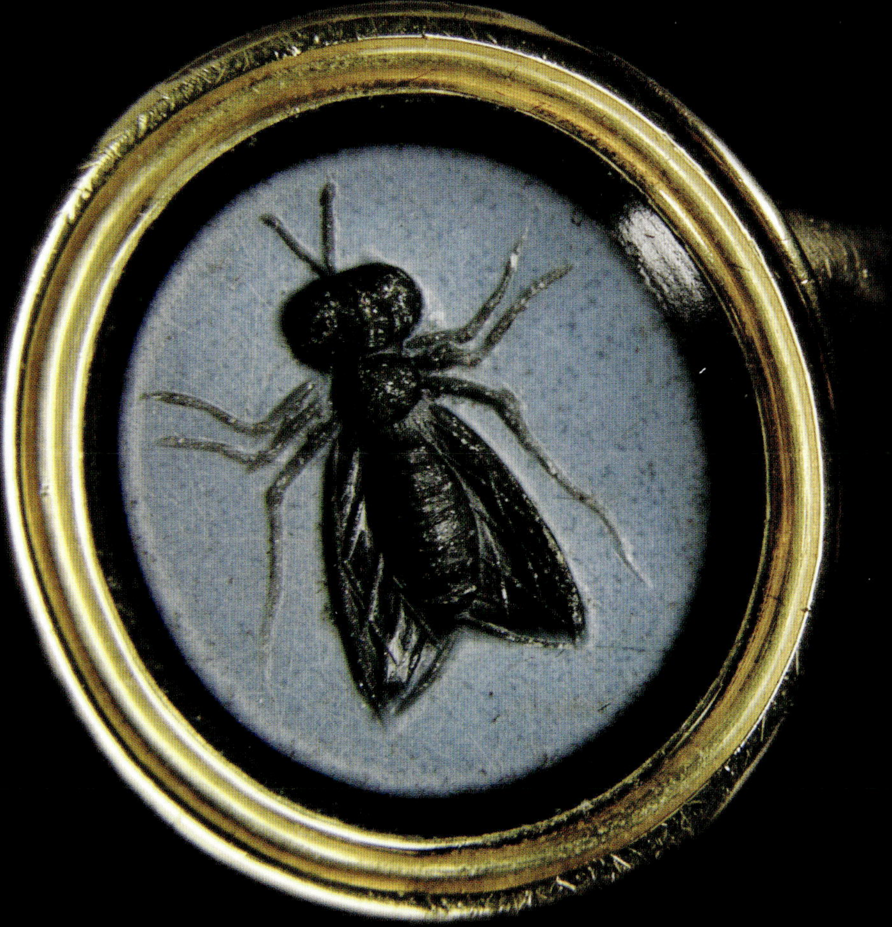

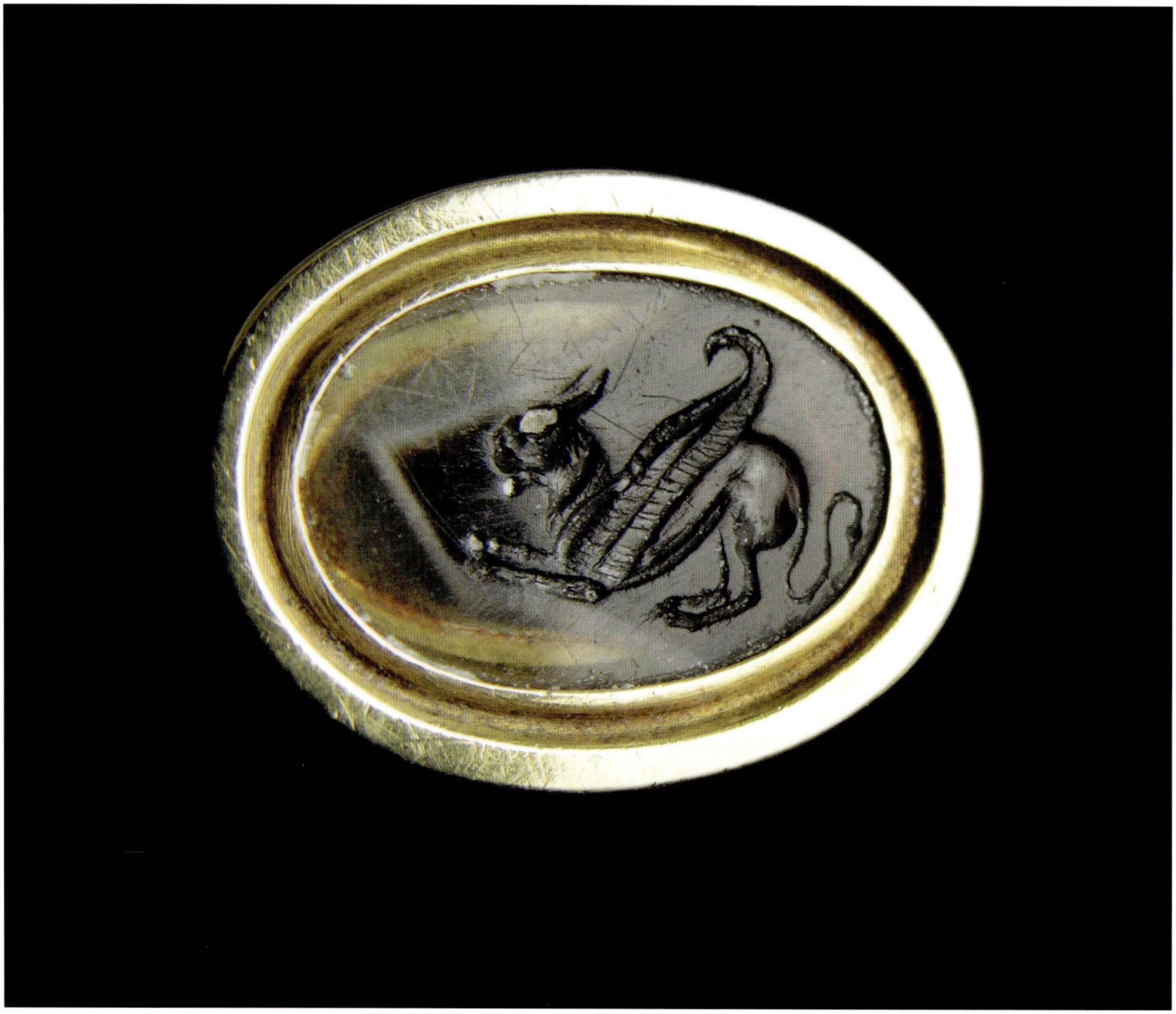

257

(10602) K64 (pl. 3)
Onyx, set in a plain gold ring
11 x 7

SG.Imp. 56; Tassie 146; Inst.Imp. no. 57; King 1872, pl. 56.8.

A winged panther or lynx crouching.
The feline type resembles *Würzburg* no. 34.

3rd/2nd century BC?

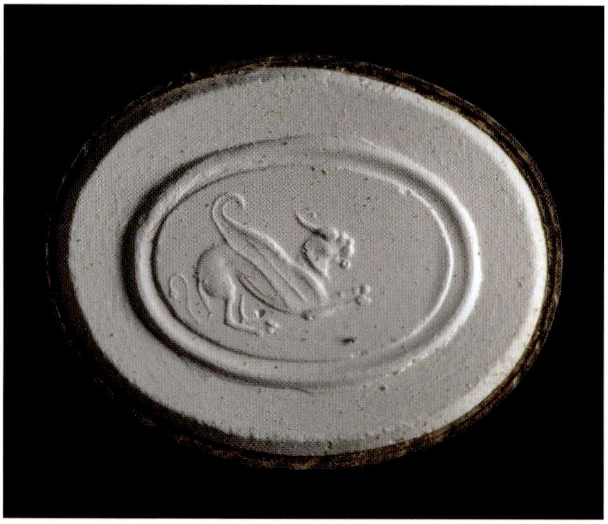

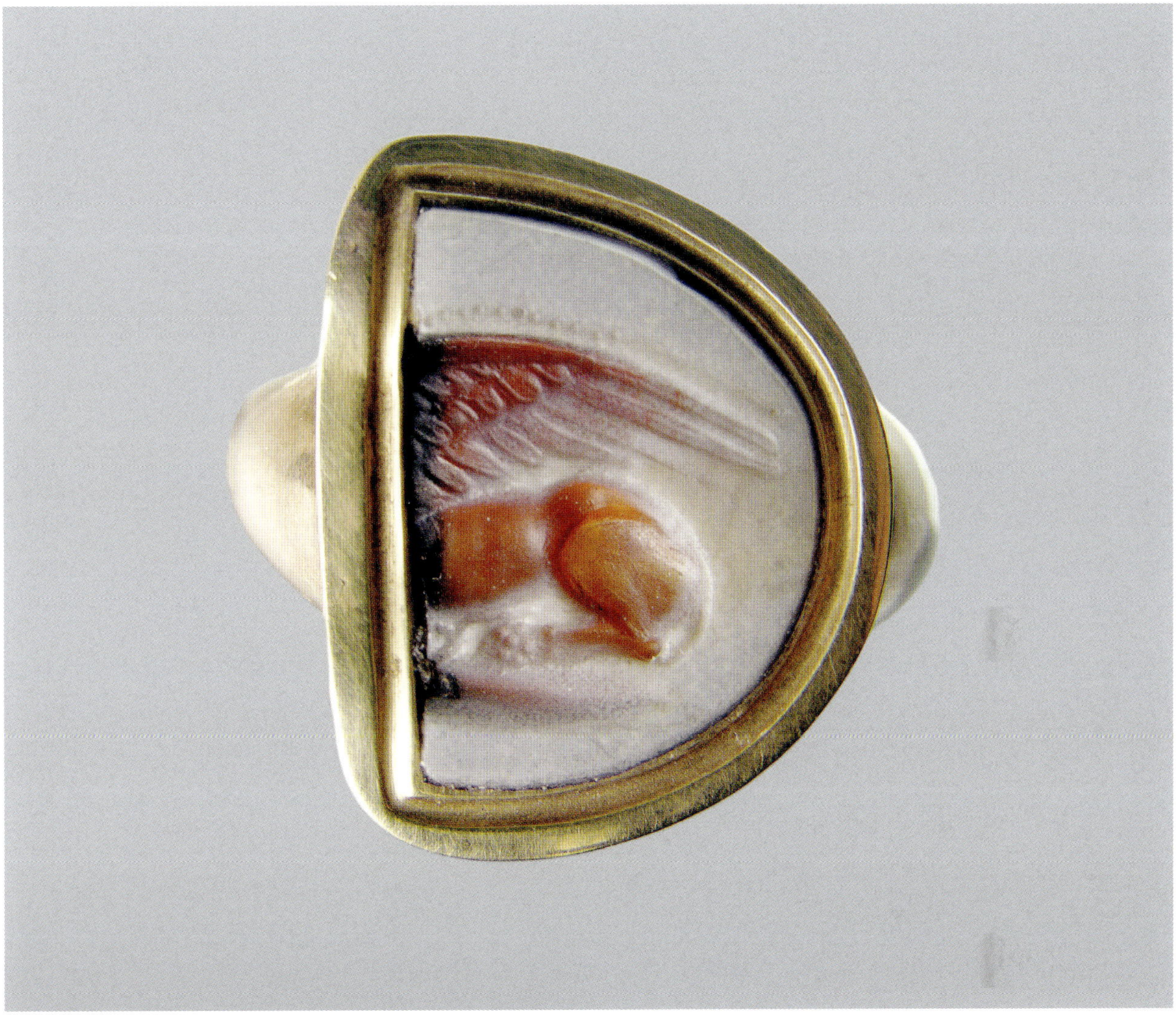

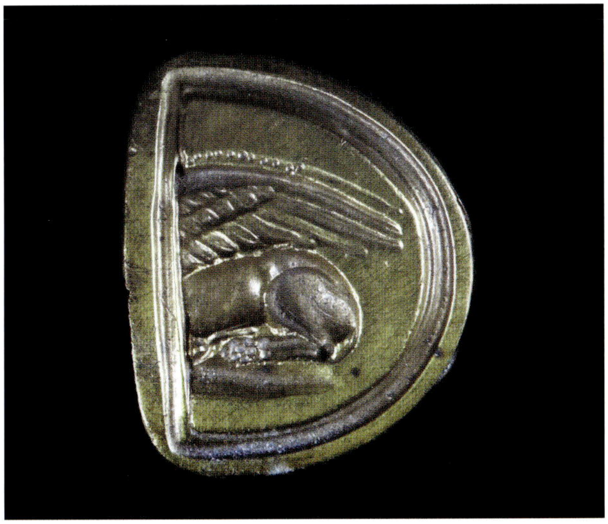

258

(10603) K65 (pl. 3)
Sardonyx fragment, white/reddish brown, polished flat back, set on a plain gold ring
13 x 10

A winged feline. Ground line.
Compare the last.

3rd/2nd century BC.

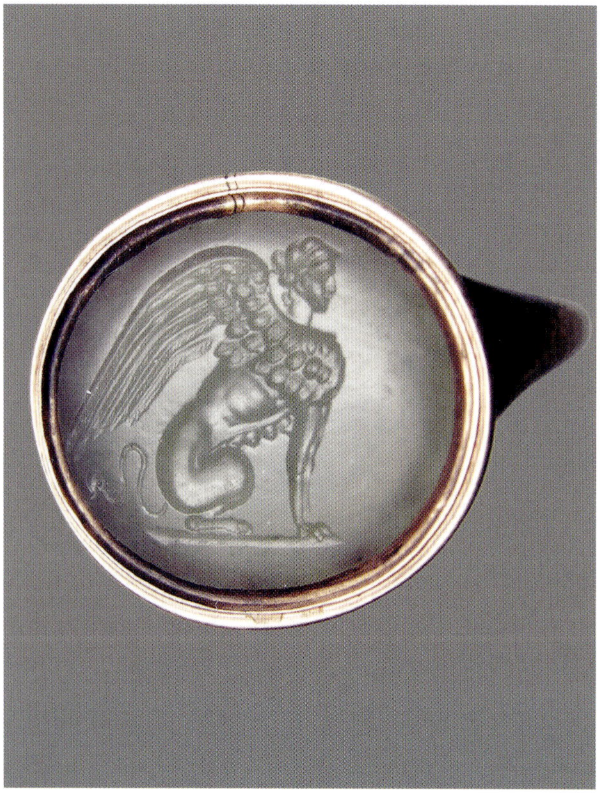

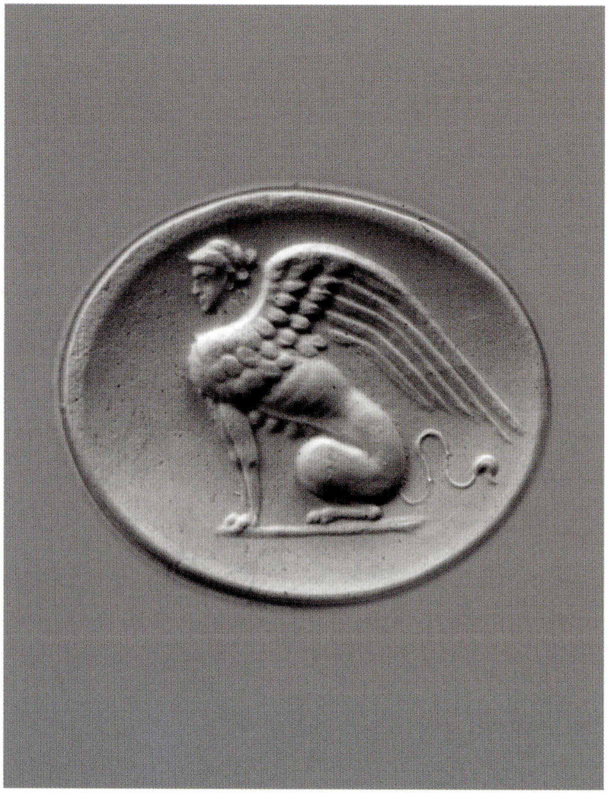

259

(10813)
Grey chalcedony, polished convex back, set on a plain gold ring
17 x 15

A seated sphinx. Ground line.
Paoletti I, IV.25 is closely comparable.

1st century BC?

260

(10599) K61 (pl. 3)
Sardonyx, black/white/brown, unpolished flat back, set on a plain gold ring
22 x 17

A hippocamp and a dolphin which holds its reins. An unusual combination with the dolphin in control.

2nd/1st century BC.

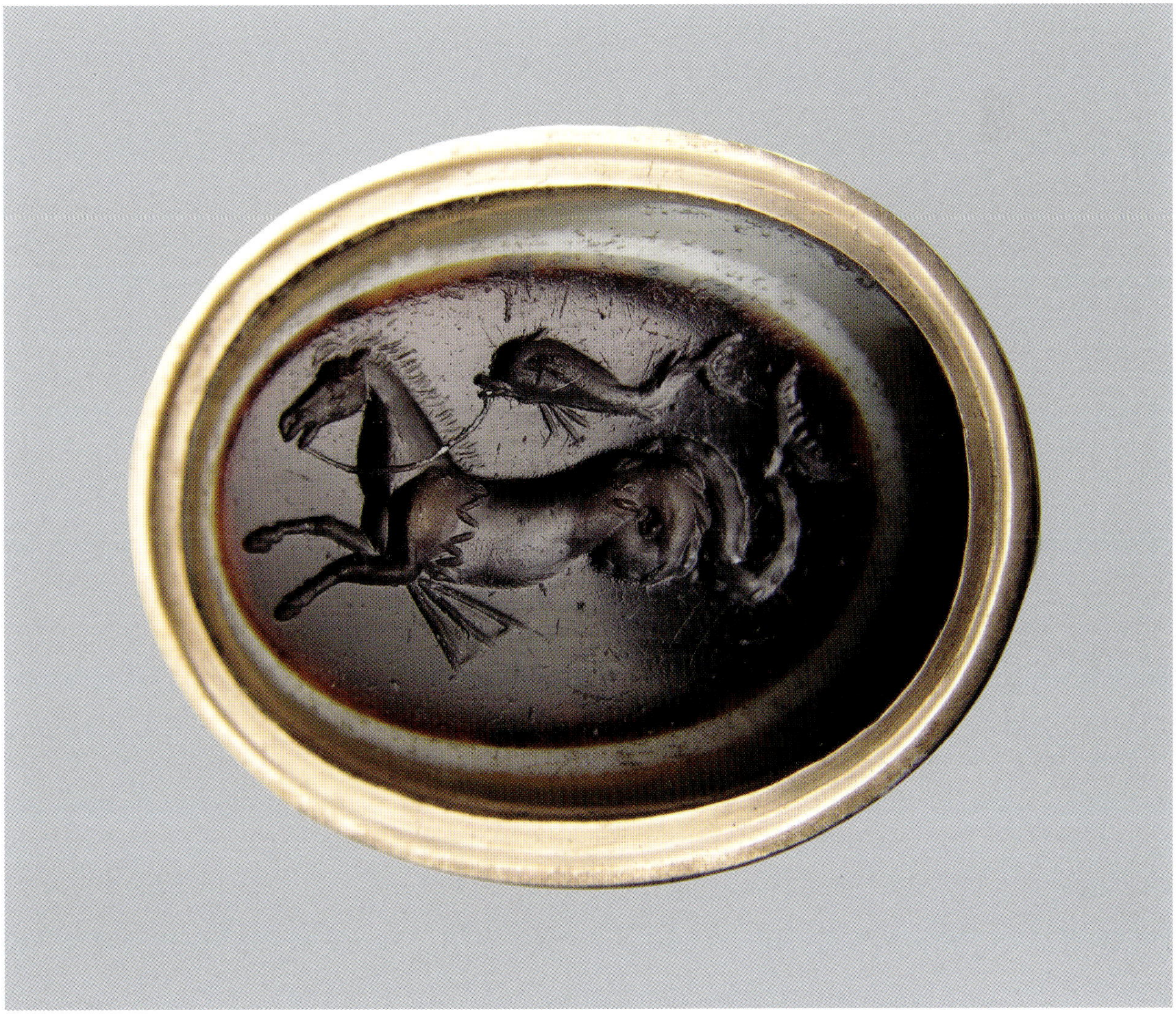

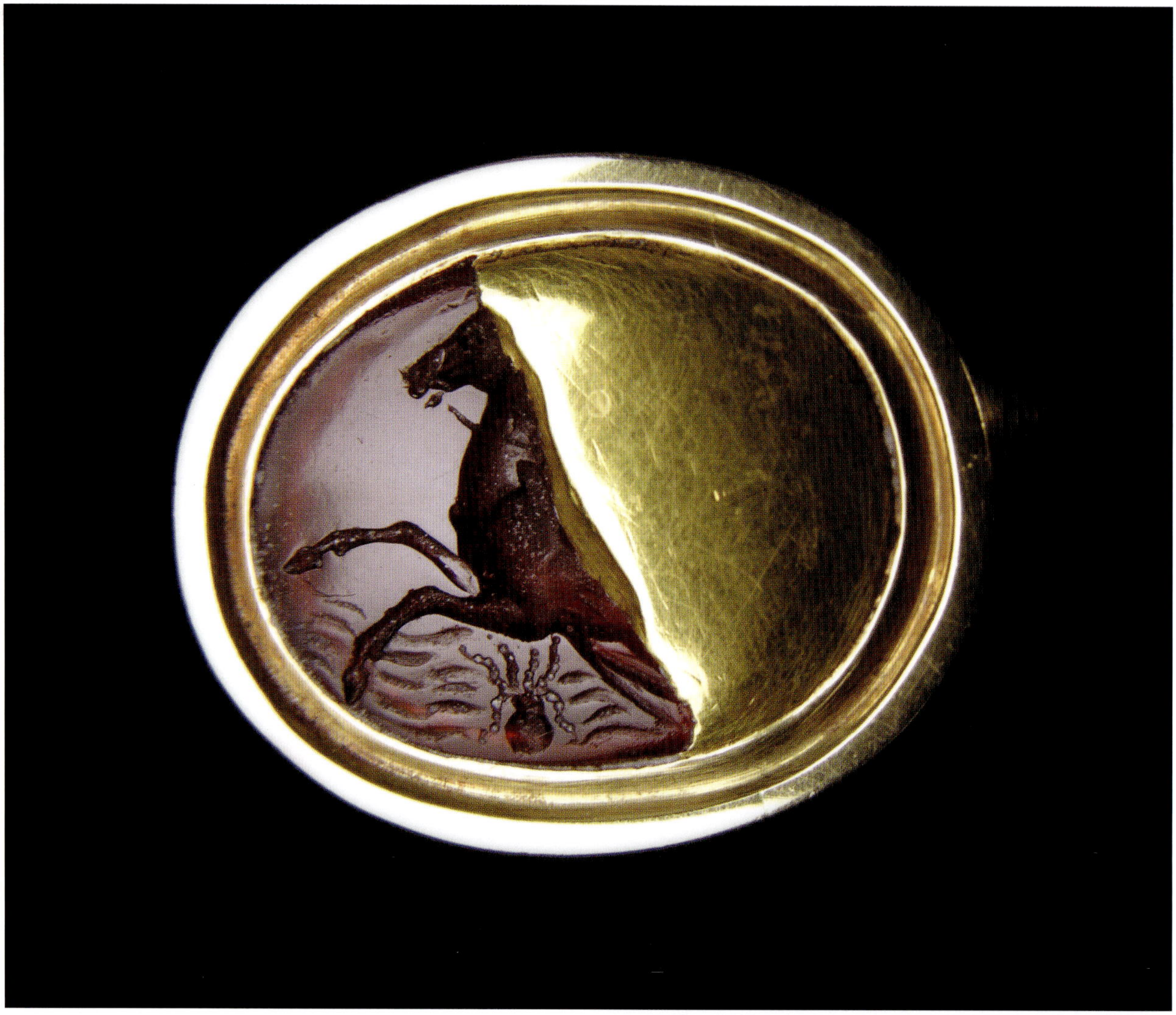

261

(10613) K75 (pl. 3)
Sard fragment restored in gold, polished flat back, set on a plain gold ring
height 12

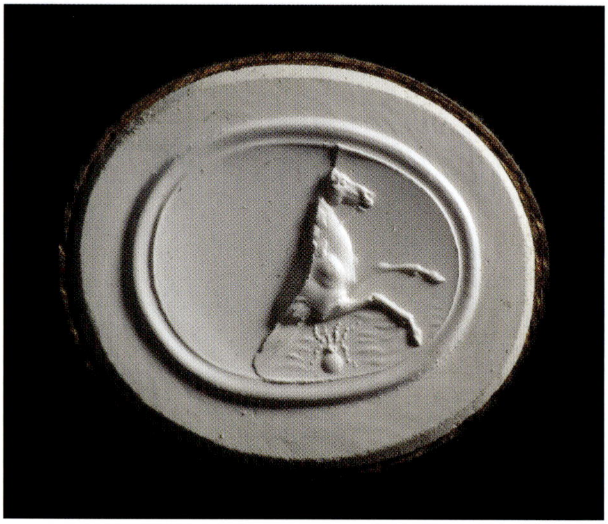

SG.Imp. 79; Tassie 2665; Inst.Imp. no. 158.

A bridled hippocamp in water, with an octopus.

For a complete Poniatowski Collection version see Paoletti I, III.530.

1st century BC/AD.

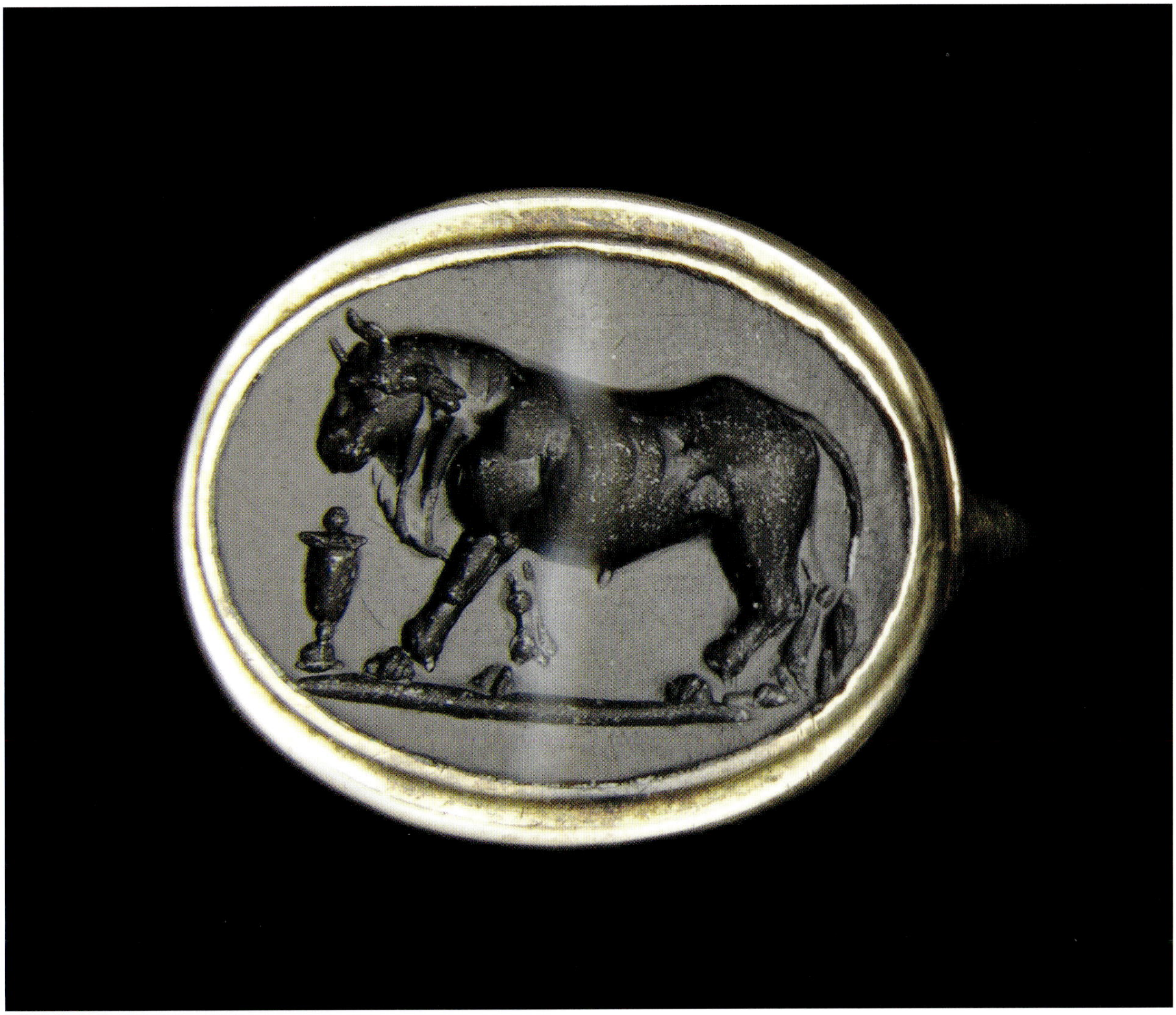

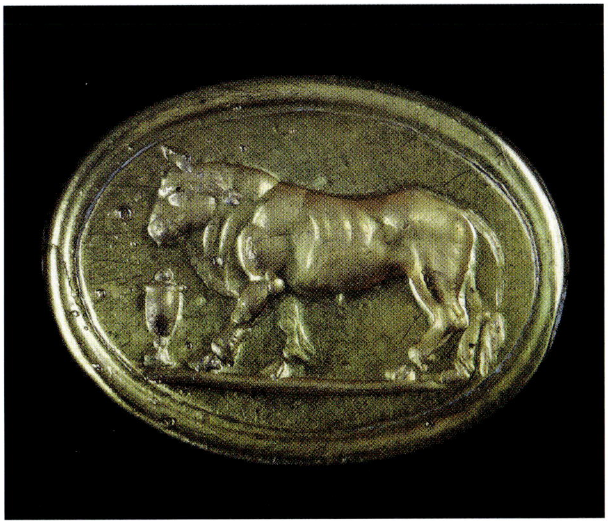

262

(10609) K71 (pl. 3)
Sardonyx, brown/white, polished flat back, set on a plain gold ring
13 x 10

A bull walking; a stemmed vase with knobbed lid before it. Ground line.

1st century BC/AD?

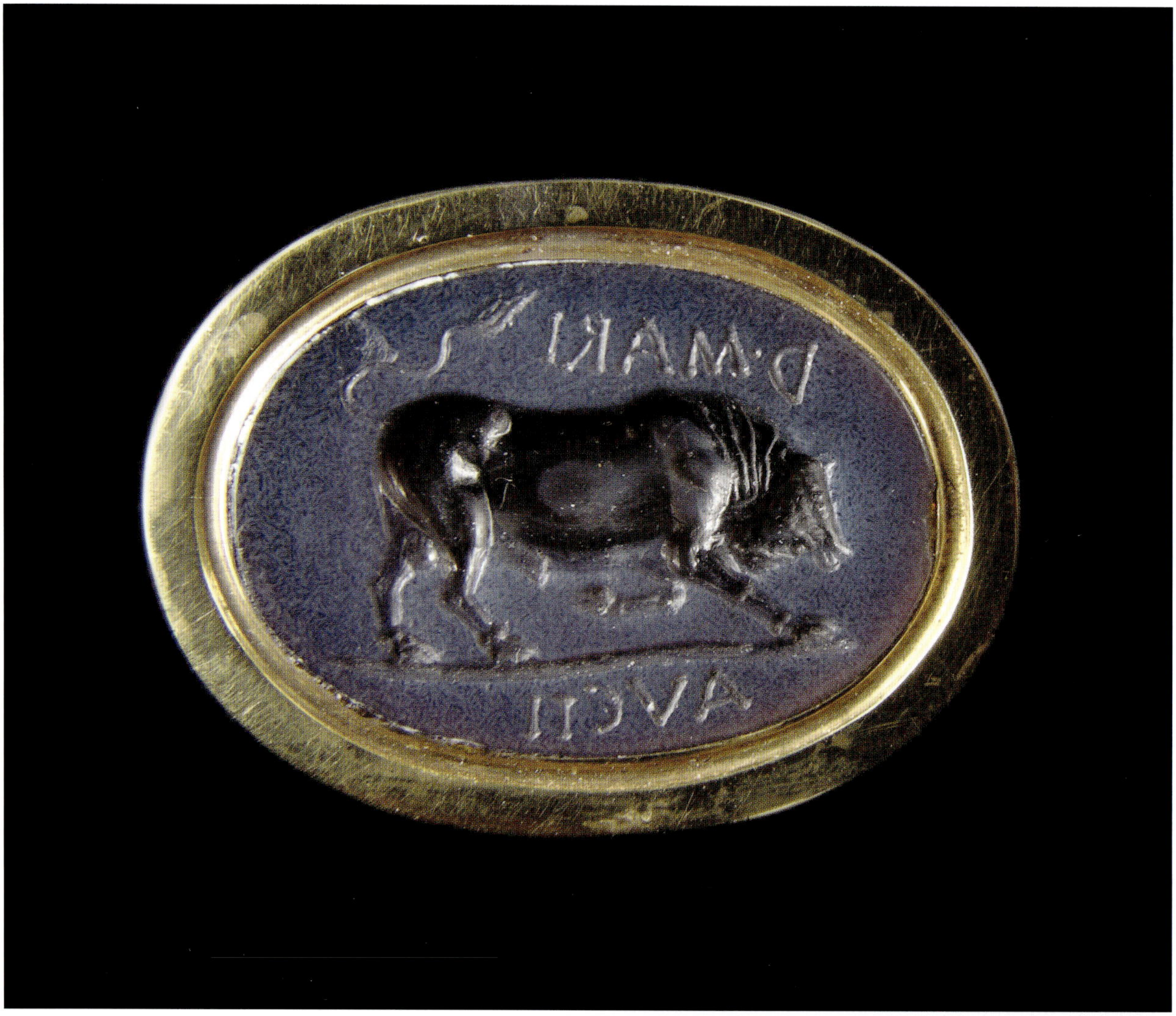

263

(10608) K70 (pl. 3)
Sard, polished flat back, set on a plain gold ring
18 x 13

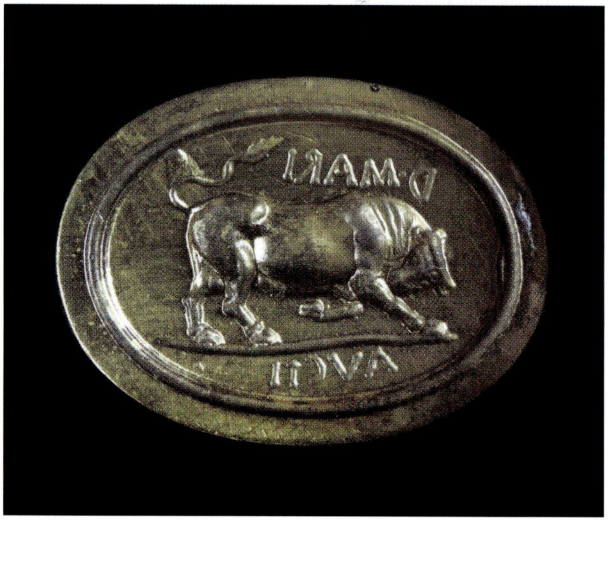

A charging bull. Ground line. Inscribed D.MARI AVCTI.
The type is as *Würzburg* no. 37, which is earlier.

1st century BC.

264

(10744) K206
Nicolo with bevelled edge, set in an ancient gold ring
11 x 13

Charlesworth, pl. 6.11.

A ram walking, a thistle before it. Ground line.

'The ring was found by a countryman at Maldon, Essex, who sold it to the first Lord Beverley' (Knight). See above, p.xxiv.

1st century AD.

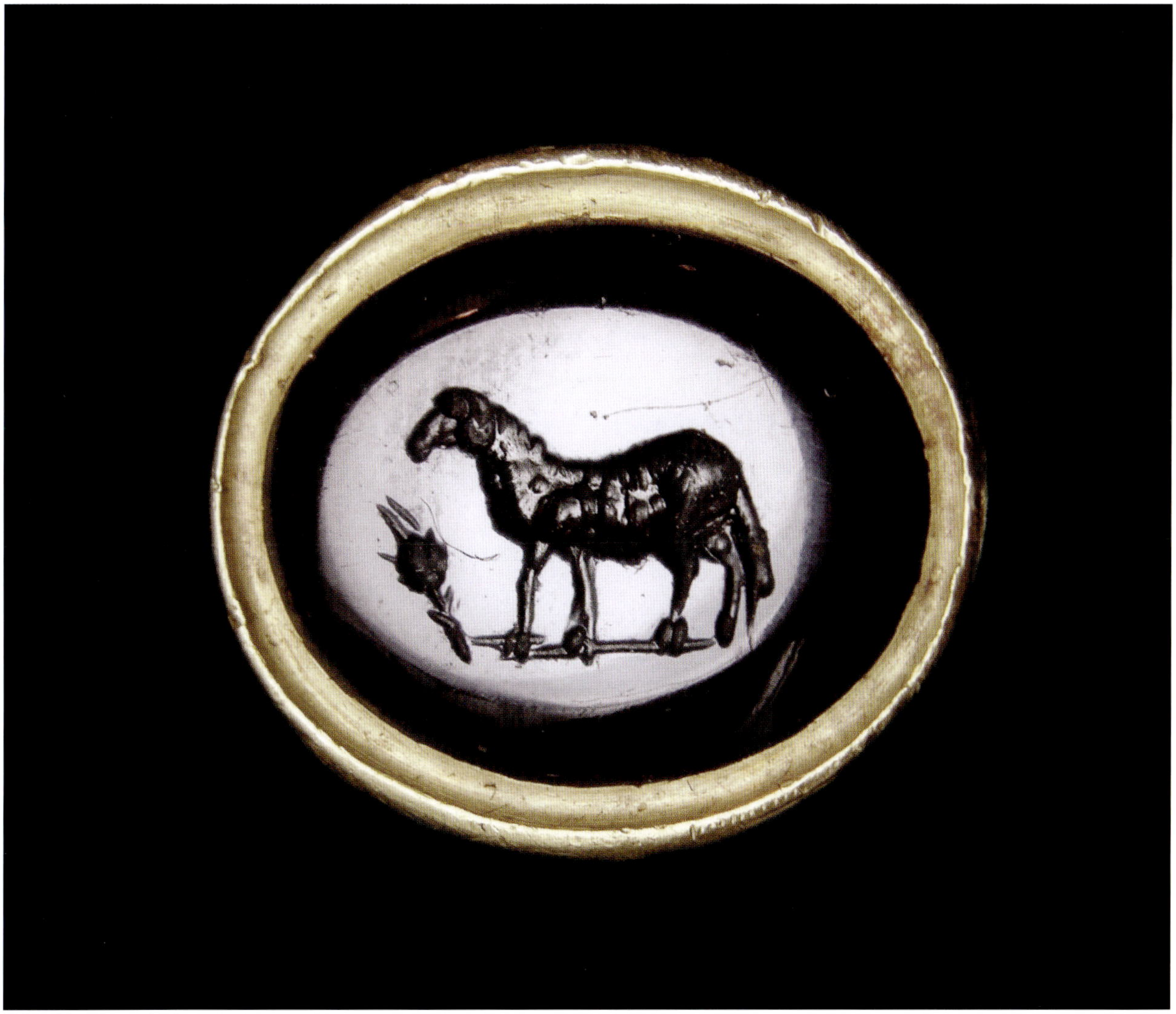

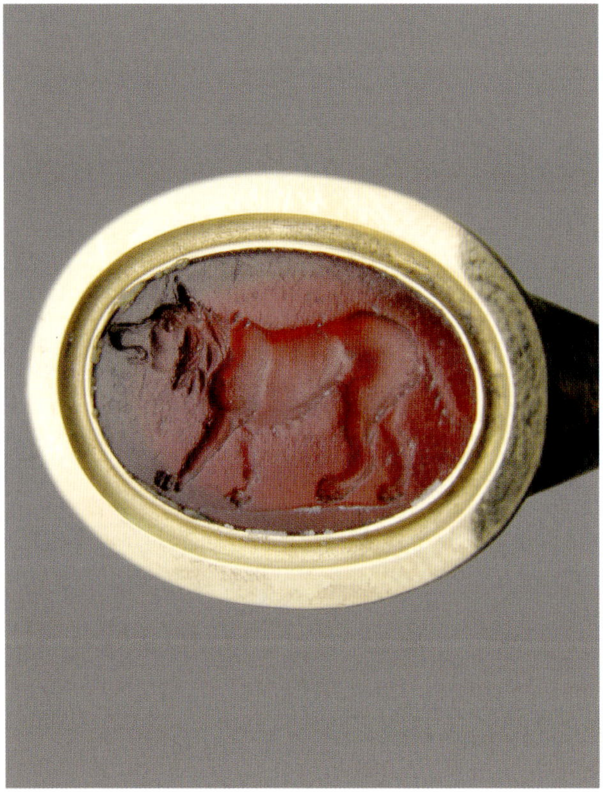

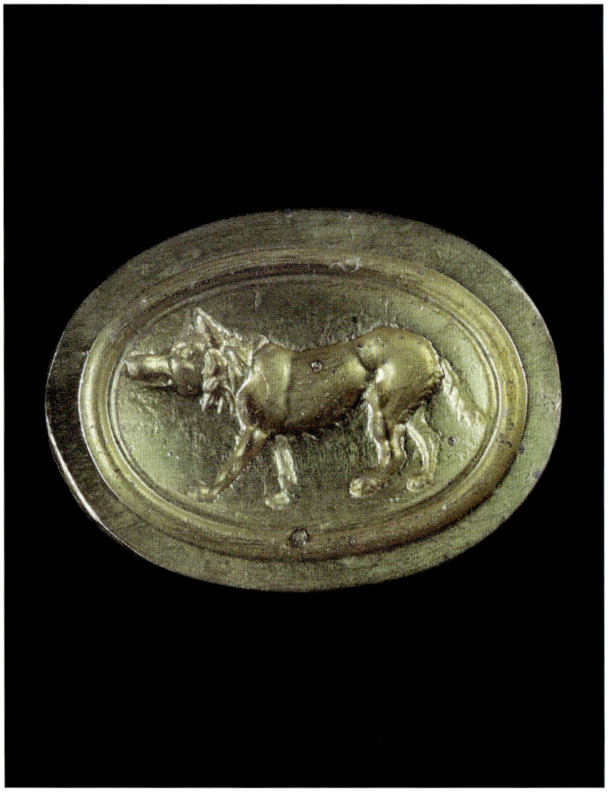

265

(10606) K68 (pl. 3)
Sard, polished flat back, set on a plain gold ring
112 x 7

A wolf walking. Ground line.

1st century BC/AD.

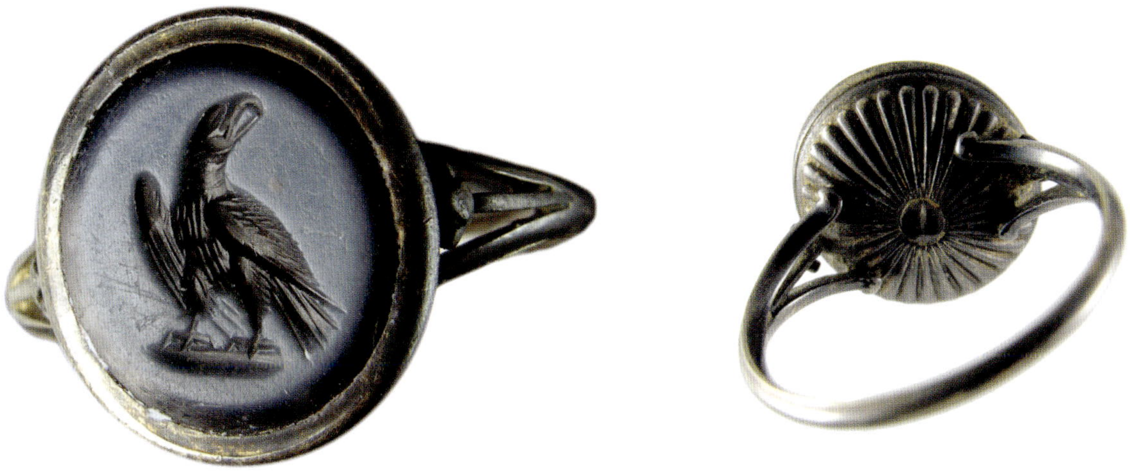

266

(10752)
Nicolo, set on a gold ring with floral terminals and a ribbed back
11 x 10

An eagle standing, head turned back. Short ground line.

1st/2nd century AD.

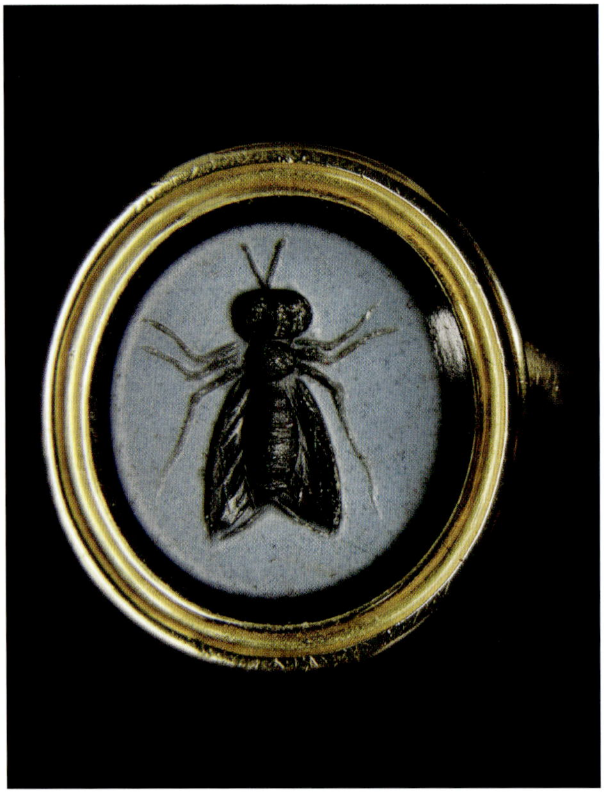

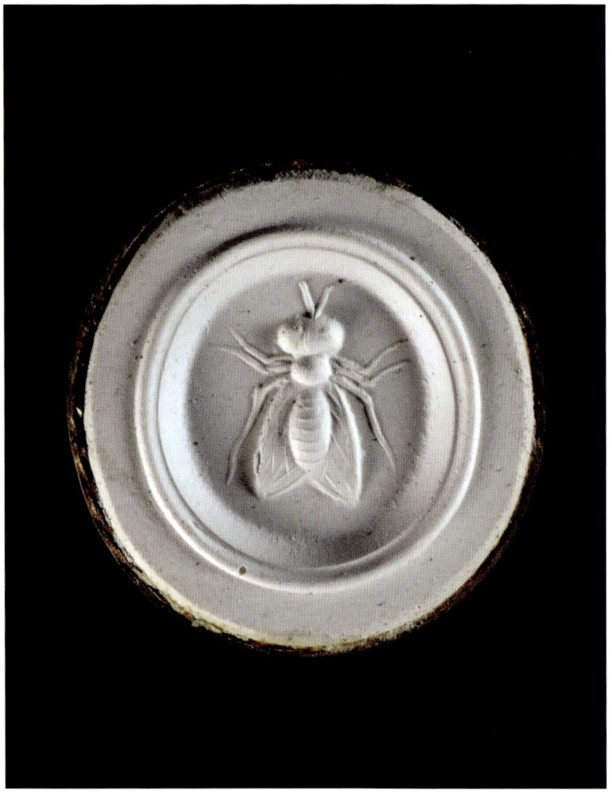

267

(10610) K72 (pl. 3)
Nicolo, polished flat back, set on a plain gold ring
11 x 8

SG.Imp. 144; Tassie 13322; Inst.Imp. no. 79;
AGE no. 254.

A fly.

1st century BC/AD.

268

(10785)
Nicolo, unpolished flat back, set on a plain gold ring
11 x 8

Tassie 13269.

A mouse holding an ear of corn or fruit. Inscribed TFM.

1st/2nd century AD.

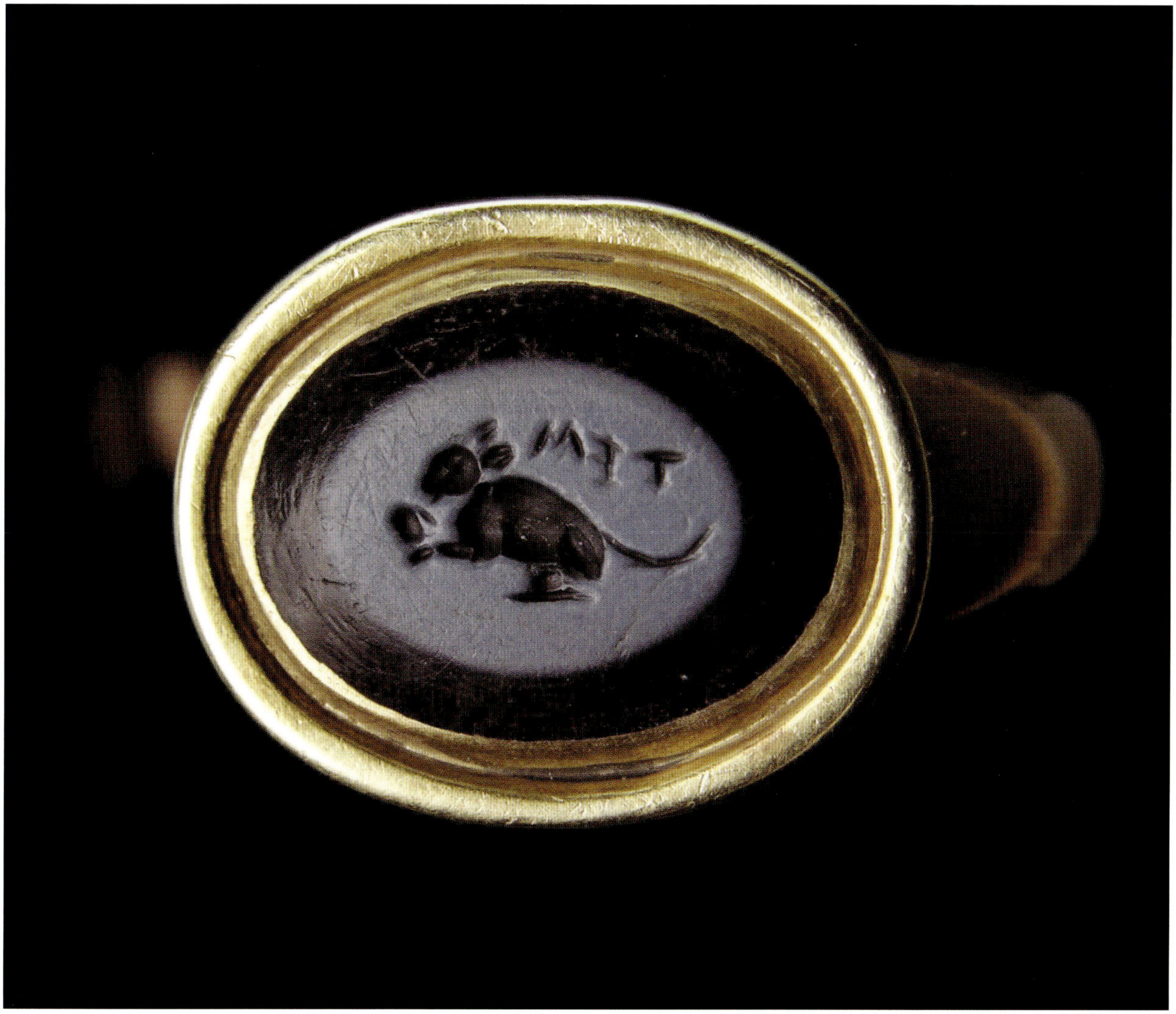

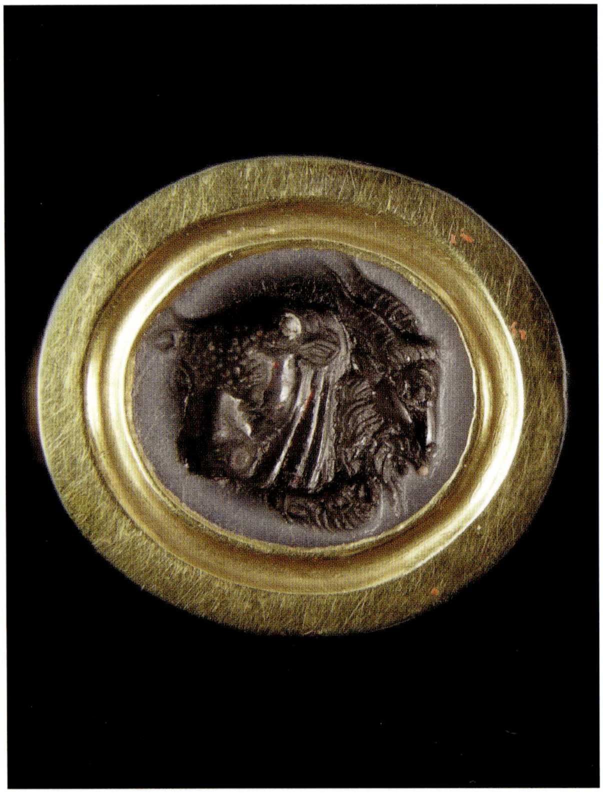

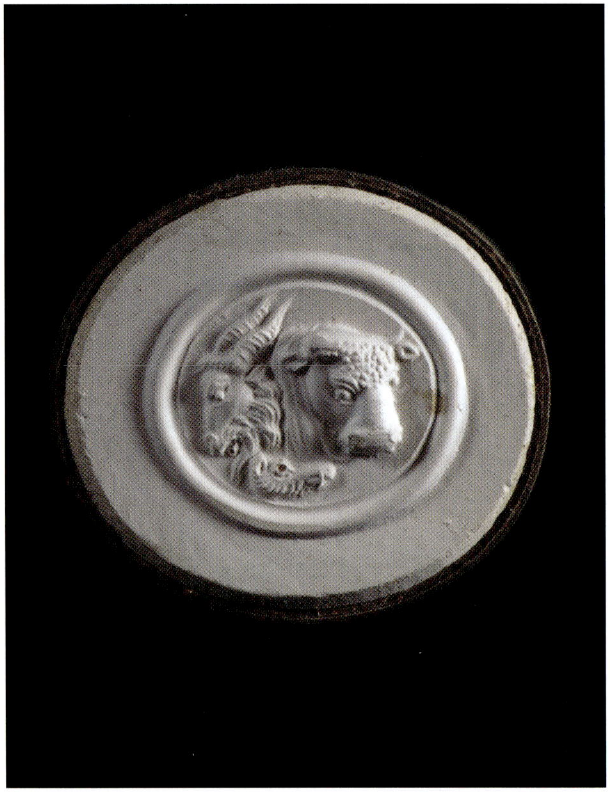

269

(10630) K92 (pl. 4)
Sardonyx, the surface pale, polished flat back, set on a plain gold ring
9 x 8

SG.Imp. 41; Tassie 13499; Inst.Imp. no. 76; Paoletti I, I.725.

A bull's, goat's and (small) ram's heads conjoined. A 'gryllus'.

1st century BC/AD.

MASKS AND OBJECTS

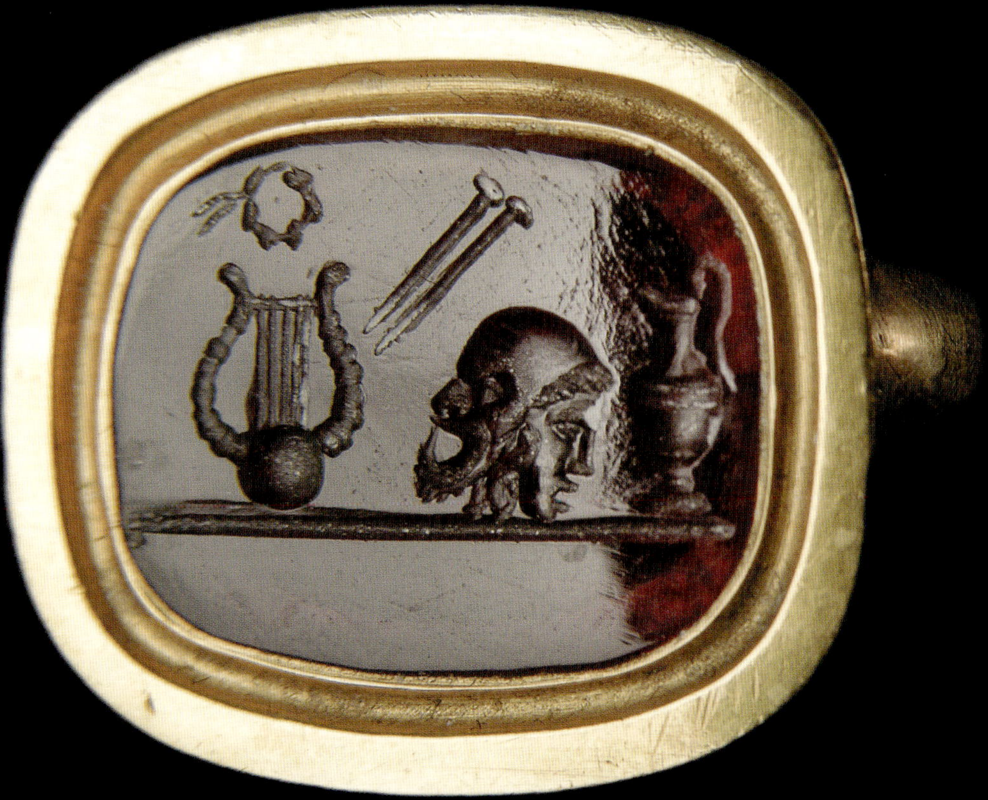

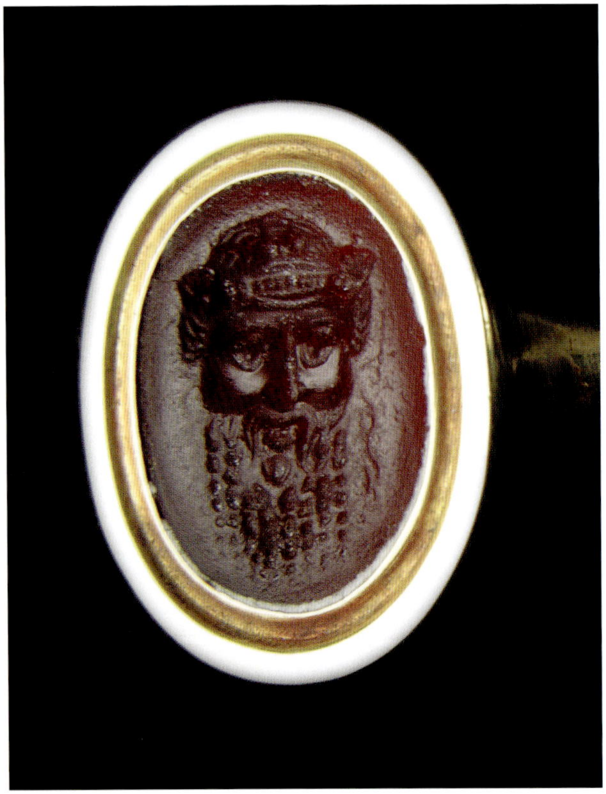

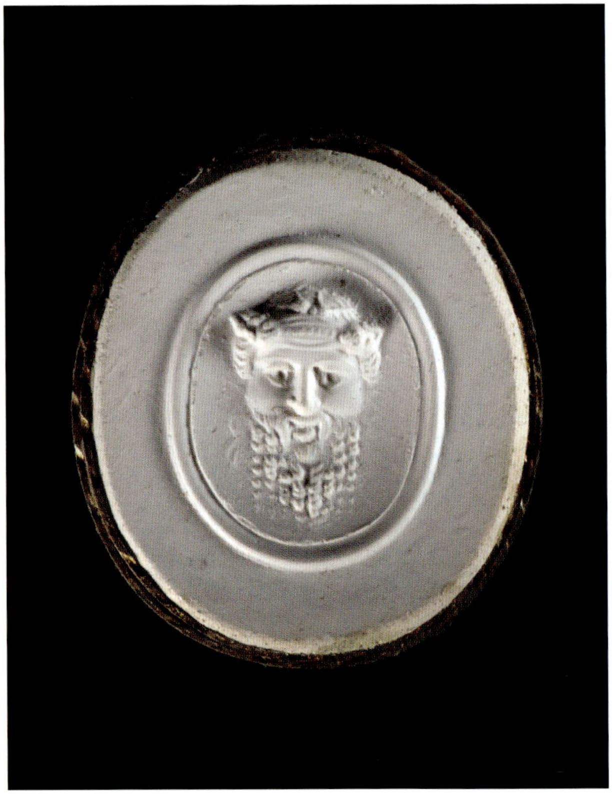

270

(10611) K73 (pl. 3)
Sard, polished flat back, set on a plain gold ring
18 x 11

SG.Imp. 105; Inst.Imp. no. 96.

The facing mask of bearded Bacchus wearing a dotted fillet with grape clusters.

On the type see *Wien* I no. 328, *Würzburg* no. 608.

1st century BC.

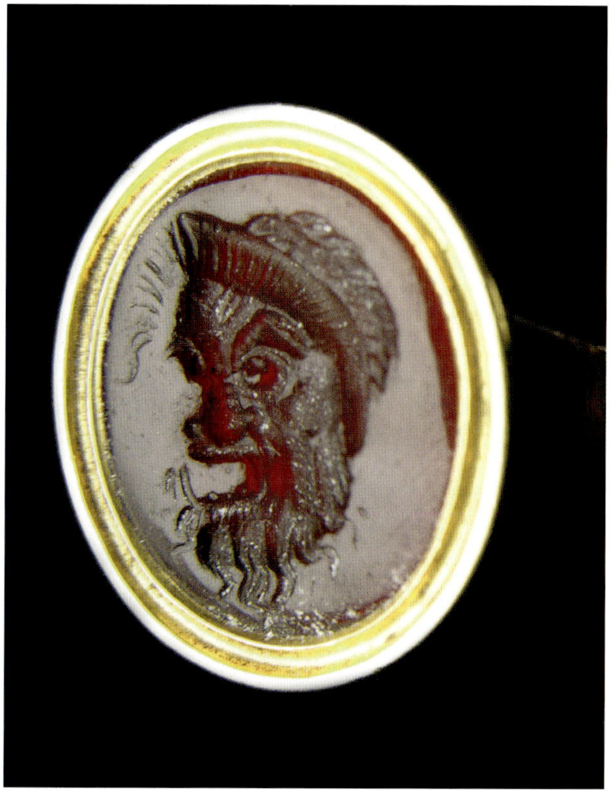

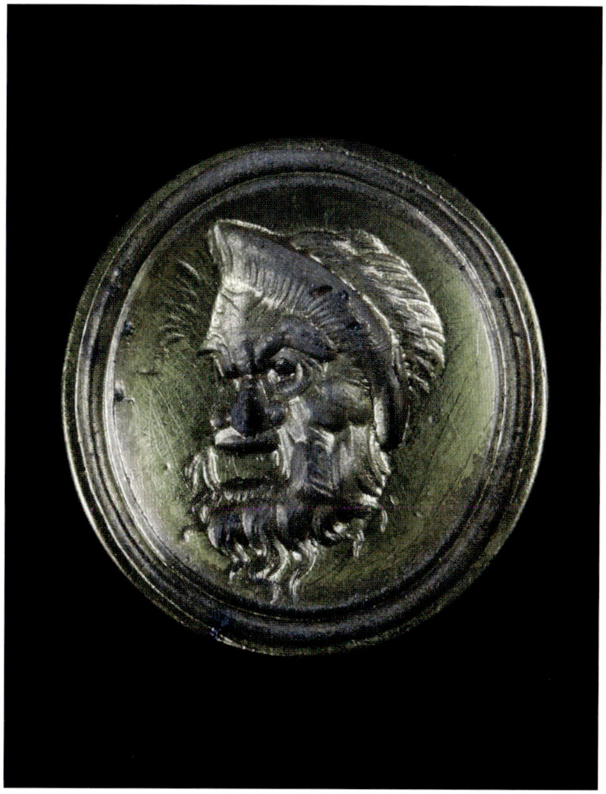

271

(10615) K77 (pl. 3)
Sard, polished flat back, set on a plain gold ring
12 x 10

King 1872, pl. 31.1; *King 1885*, pl. 62.4.

Three-quarter view of the mask of an old man.

1st century BC/AD.

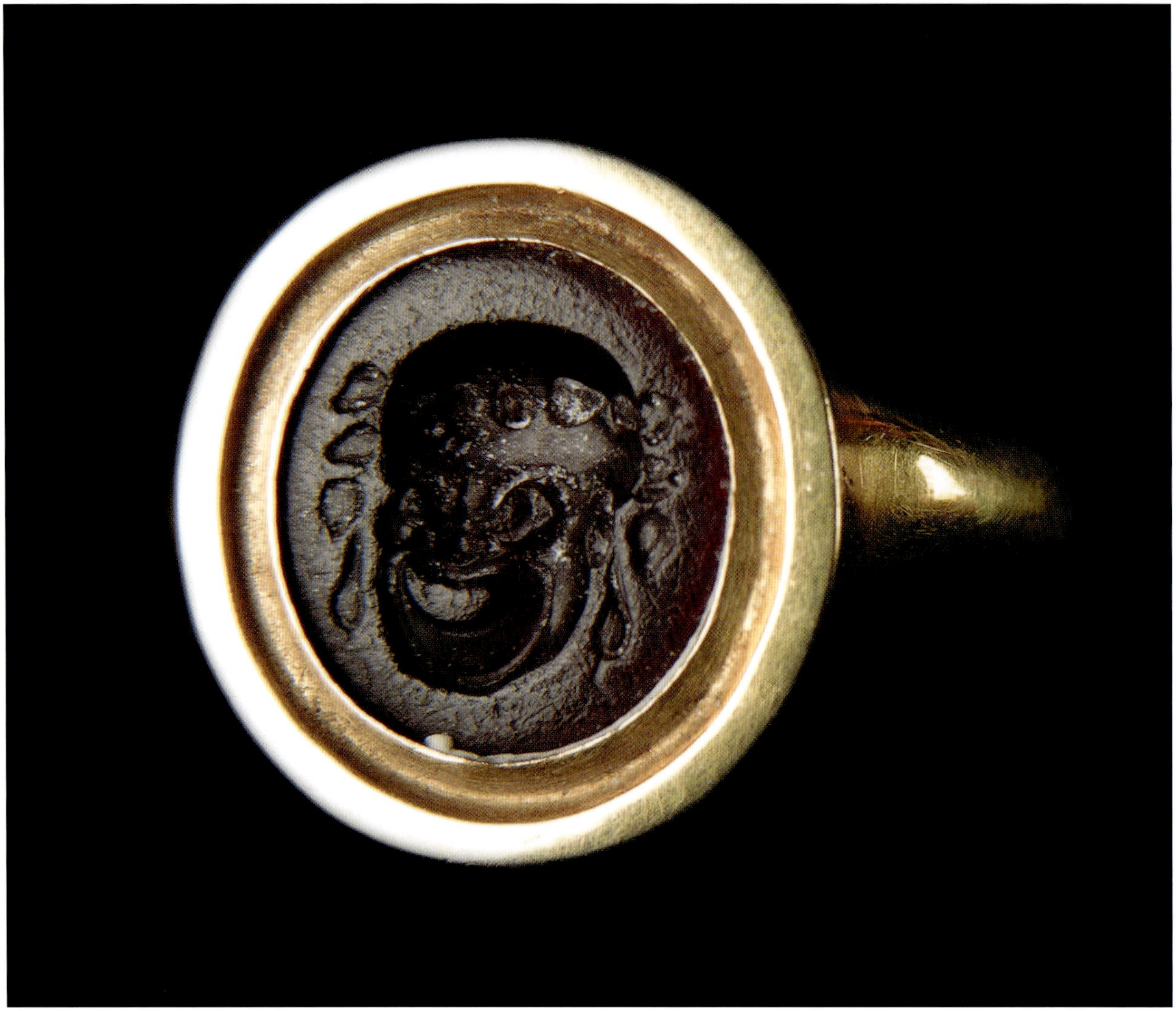

272

(10632) K94 (pl. 4)
Sard, polished flat back, set on a plain gold ring
9 x 8

SG.Imp. 133; Inst.Imp. no. 91.

An ivy-wreathed comic mask.

1st century BC/AD.

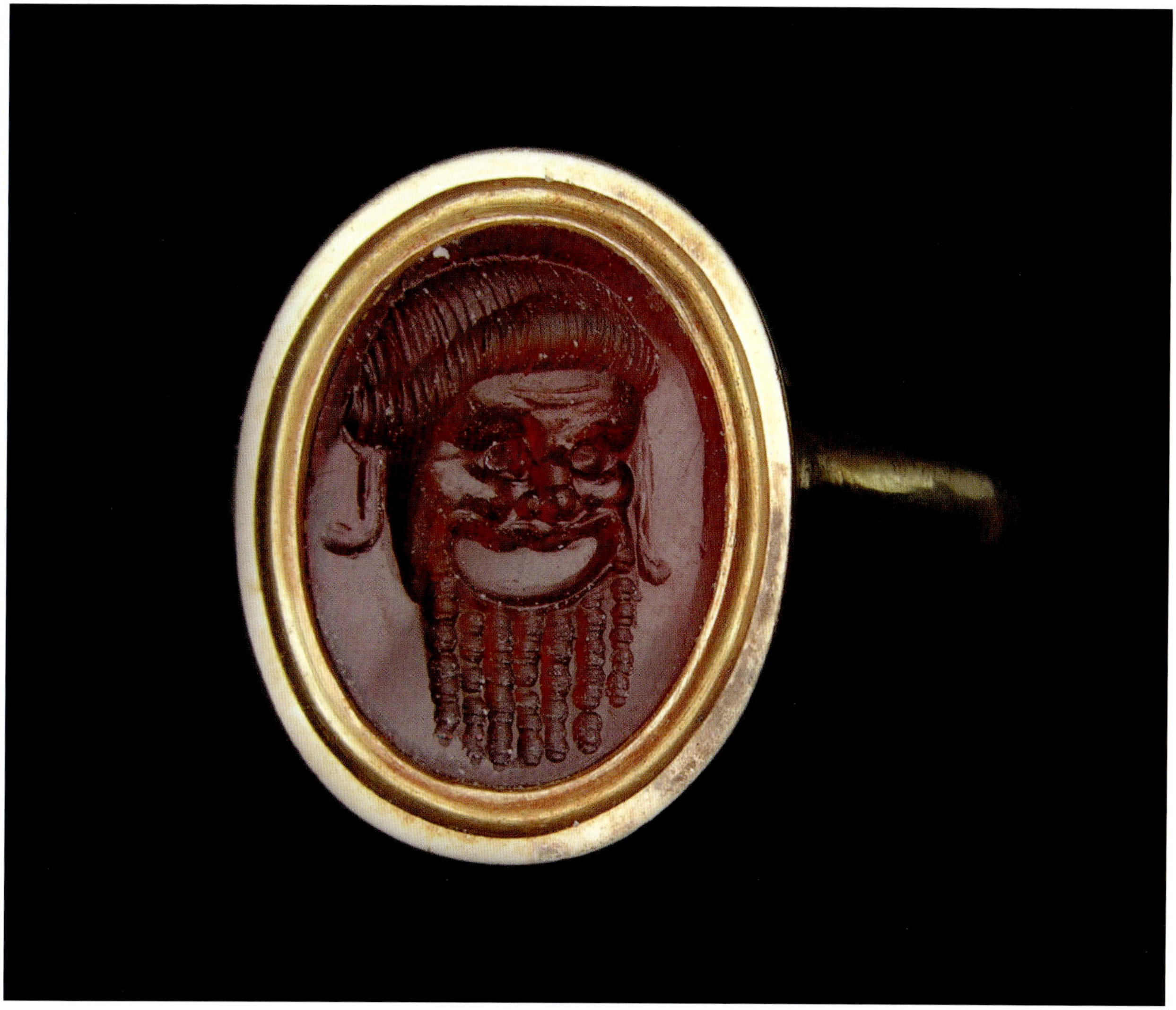

273

(10766)
Carnelian, polished flat back, set on a plain gold ring
12 x 9

Comic mask of a bearded head.
Compare *Würzburg* no. 610.

1st century BC/AD.

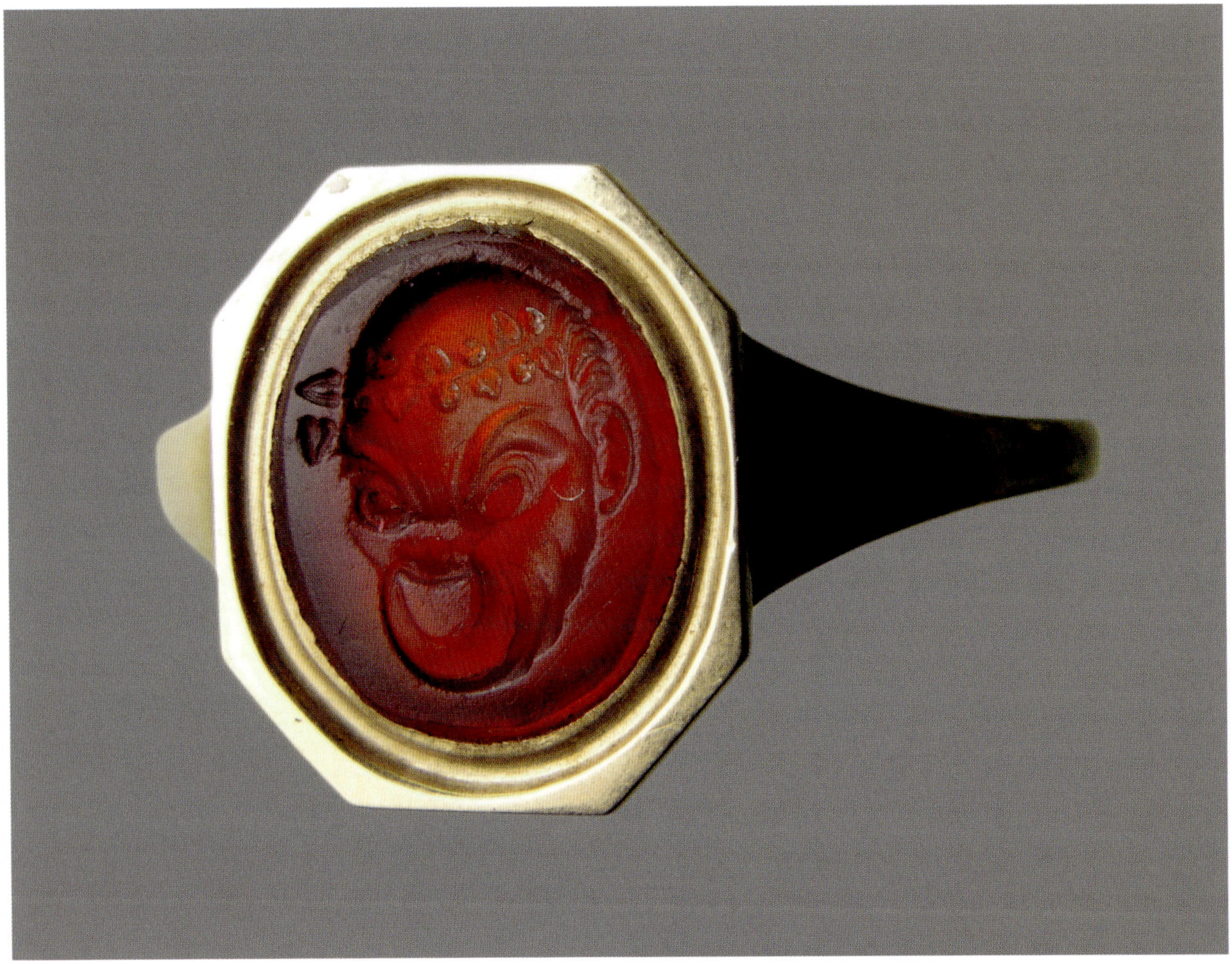

274

(10612) K74 (pl. 3)
Sard, polished flat back, set on a plain gold ring
10 x 8

SG.Imp. 113; Inst.Imp. no. 87.

An ivy-wreathed comic mask.

1st century BC/AD.

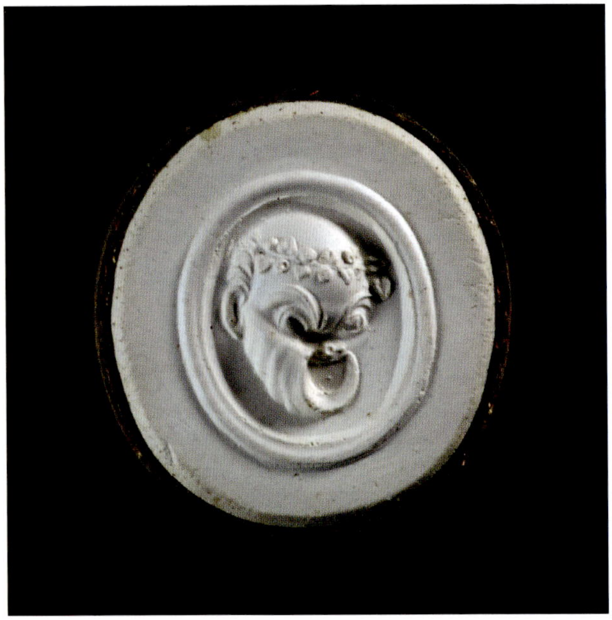

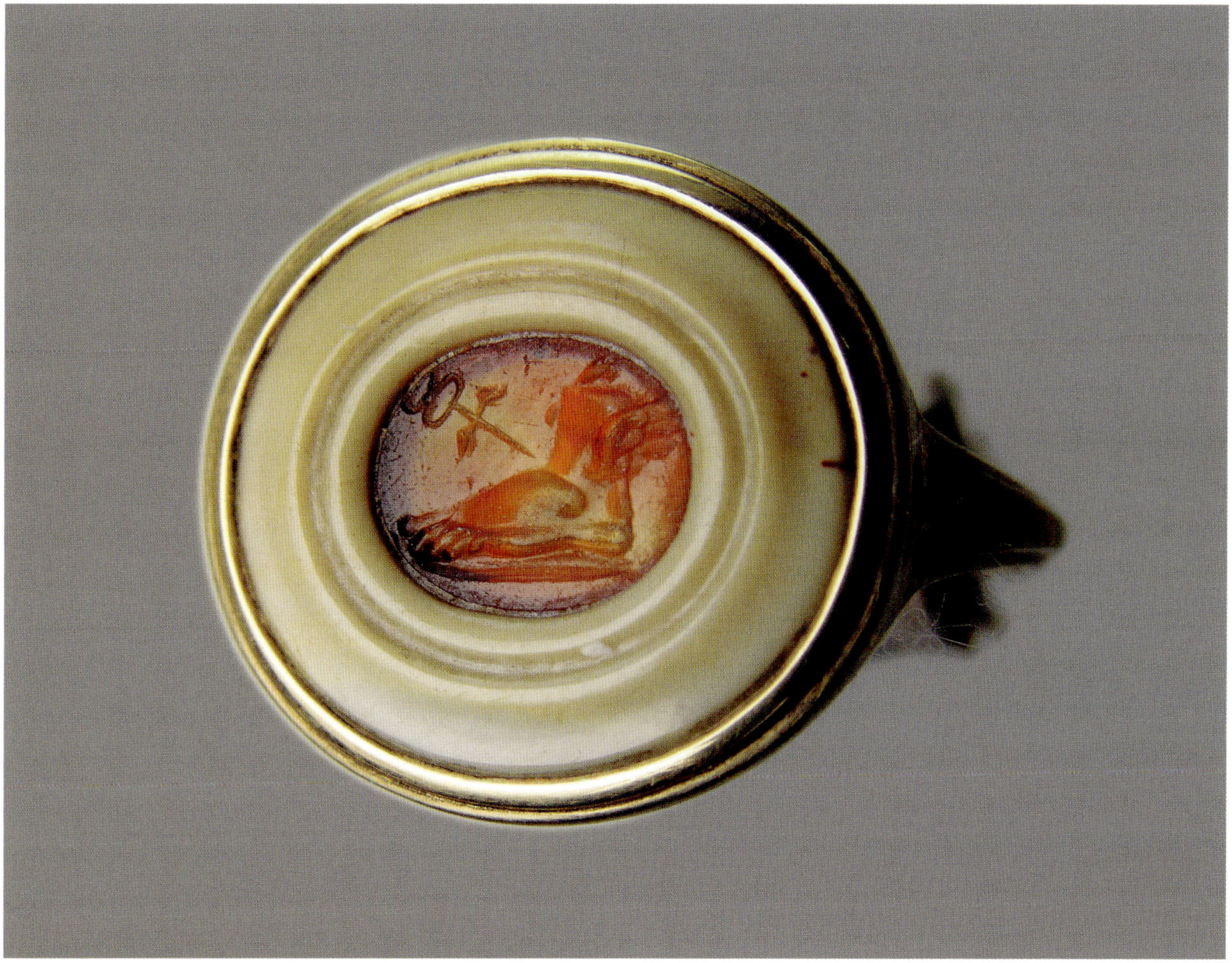

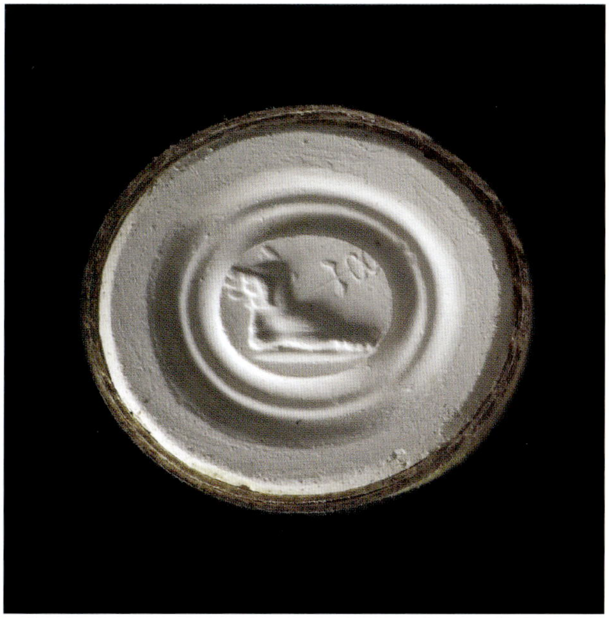

275

(10685) K147 (pl. 6)
Sard, polished convex back, set in an agate roundel on a plain gold ring
7 x 6

SG.Imp. 62; ?Tassie 2500 ('jacinth'); Paoletti I, I.265; Inst. Imp. no. 72.

A winged foot and the caduceus of Hermes/Mercury. Ground line.

Compare *Munich* 3, nos 2358, 3451; *Würzburg* no. 702; Spier, *Getty* no. 346 (winged boot). Knight suggests that it is the work of Louis Siries, but other gems signed by Siries do not have such wide borders.

18th century.

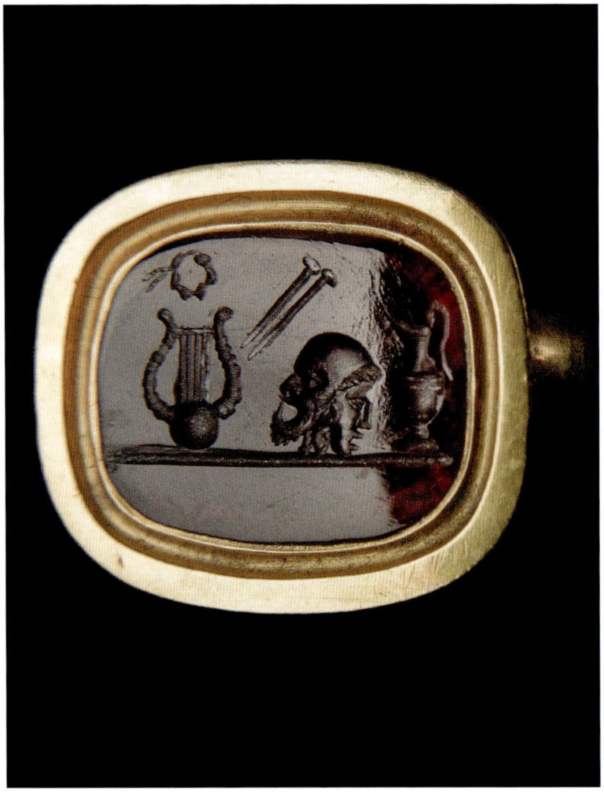

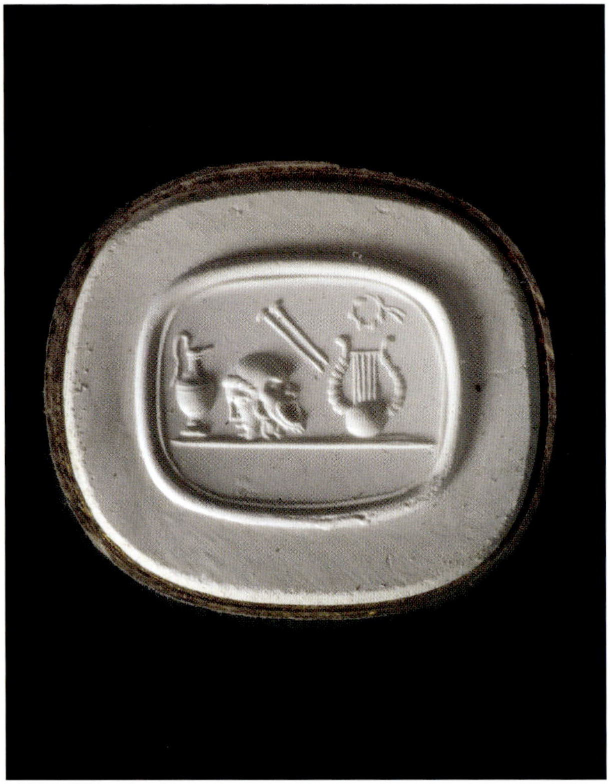

276

(10614) K76 (pl. 3)
Sard, polished convex back, set on a plain gold ring
12 x 10

SG.Imp. 54; Tassie 3623; Inst.Imp. no. 66.

A lyre, conjoined bearded (comic) and beardless (tragic) masks, a jug; above are a wreath and double pipes. Ground line.

A theatrical group. Ficoroni 1757, pl. 8, illustrates another sard with the group of a lyre, wreath, butterfly and jug, with a skull instead of masks and forceps instead of pipes.

1st century BC/AD.

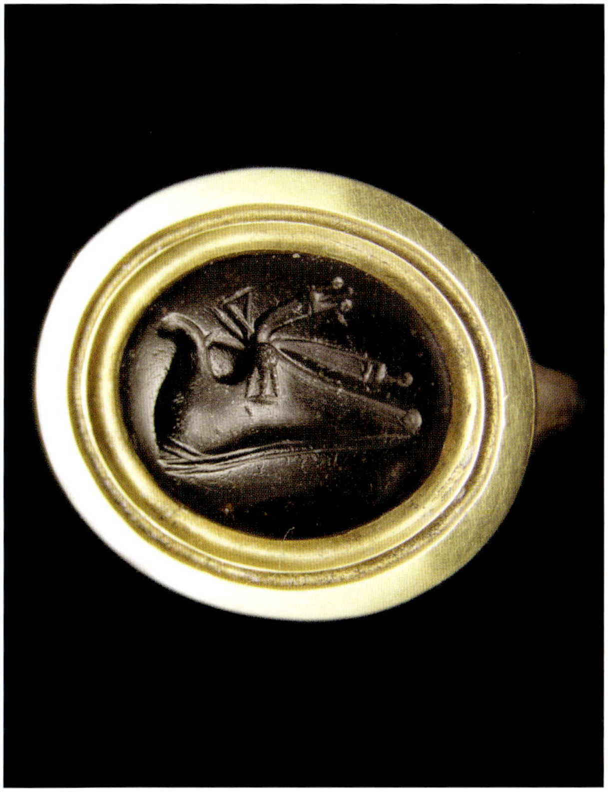

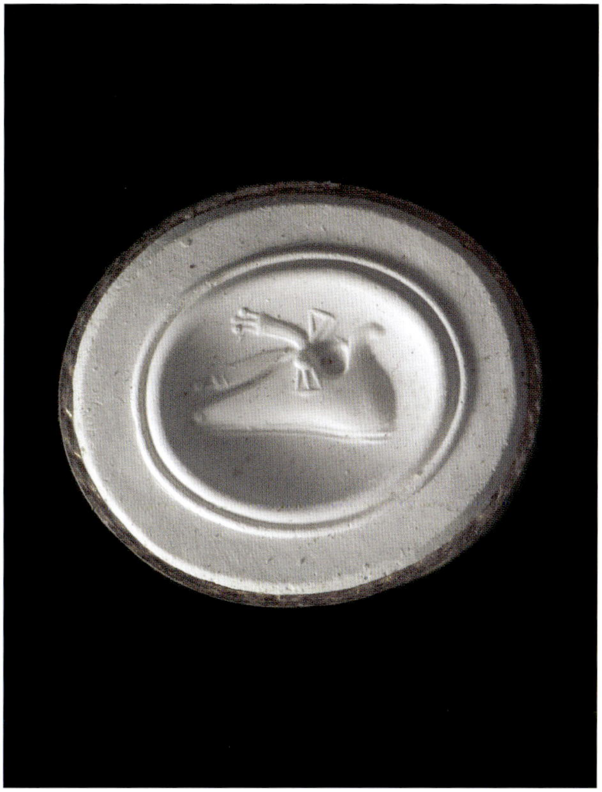

277

(10605) K67 (pl. 3)
Deep orange sard, polished flat back, set on a plain gold ring
12 x 10

SG.Imp. 148; Inst.Imp. no. 67; W.Tassie 2686.

A shoe tied with a bow, possibly the Roman *soccus*.
Compare *Hanover* no. 237; Lippold, pl. 98.10.
By Nathaniel Marchant.

18th century.

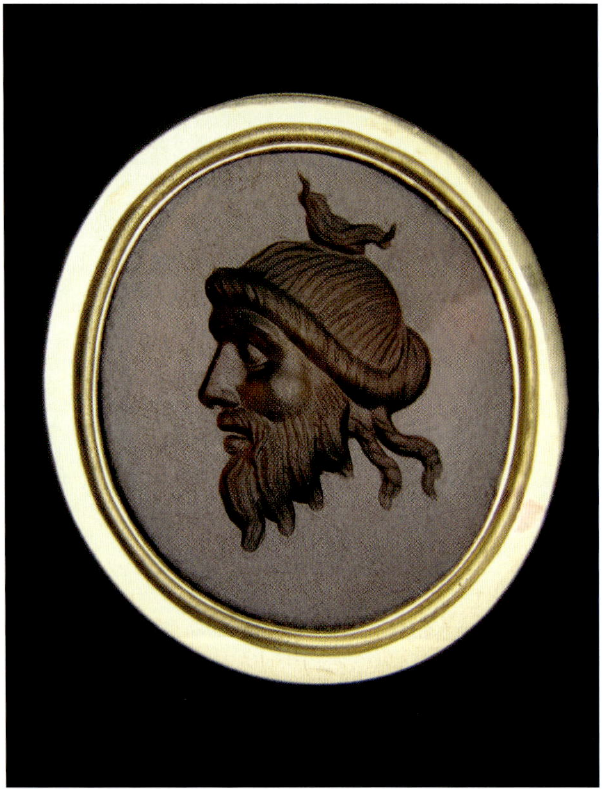

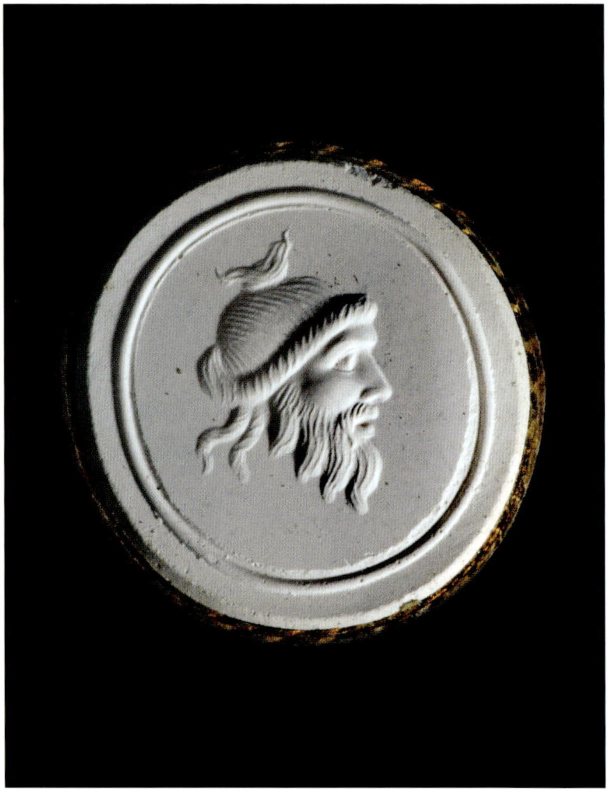

278

(10727) K189 (pl. 5)
Sard, polished flat back, set on a plain gold ring
18 x 14

SG.Imp. 1; Inst.Imp. no. 137.

Bearded head or mask with hair ends rolled and a knot of hair on the crown; broadly 'Bacchic'.

18th century.

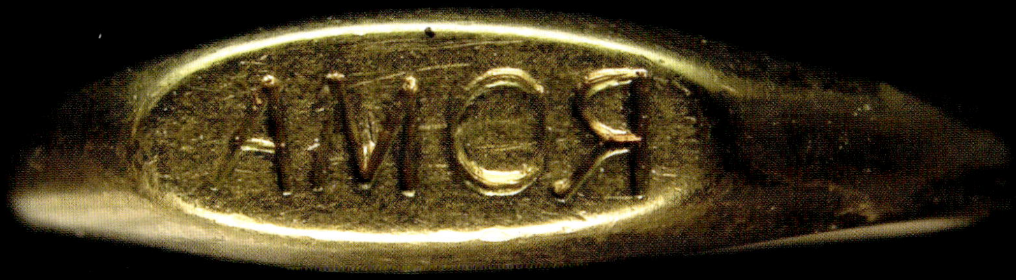

279

(10818)
Gold ring
19 x 19; bezel 12 x 3

Inscribed ROMA.

2nd/1st century BC or 19th century?

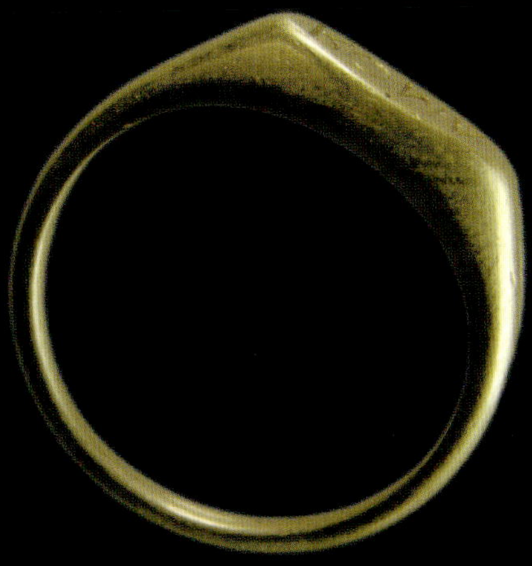

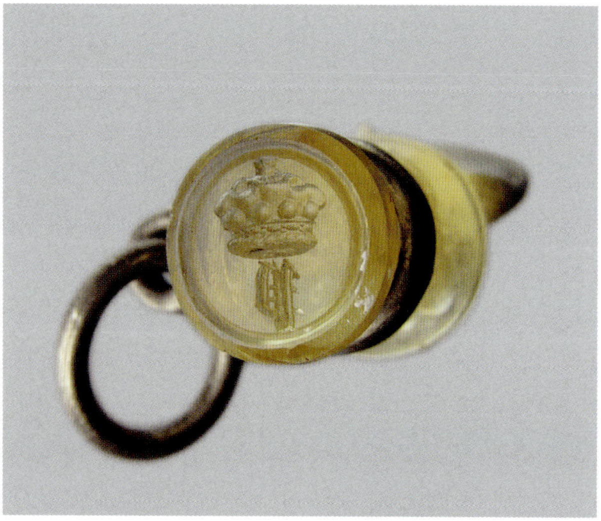

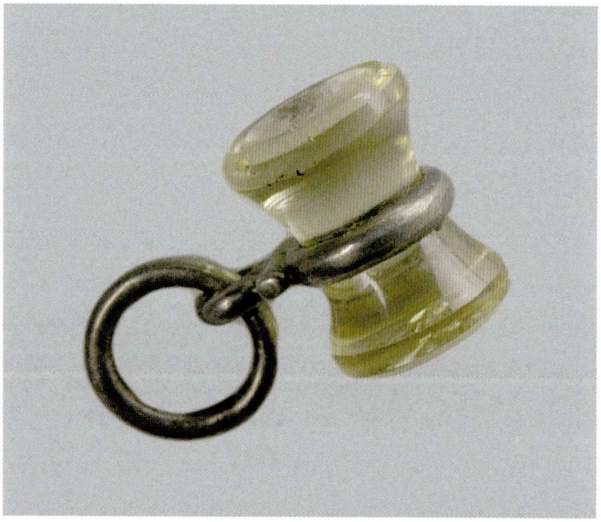

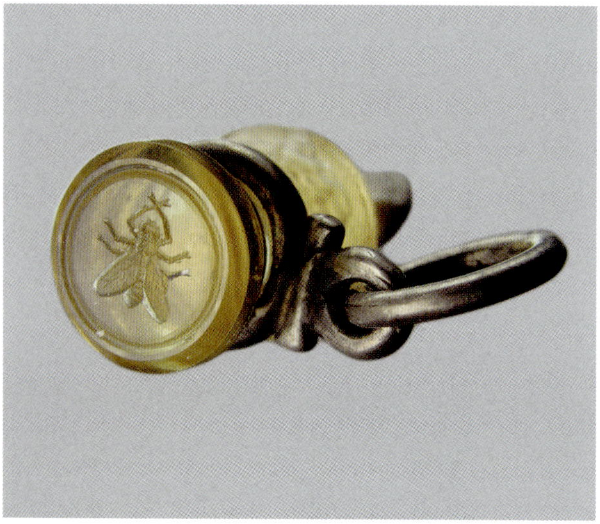

280

(10817)
Citrine biconical pendant, on a gold hoop pendant
7 x 7; length 11

A: crown; underneath, the letter P.
B: a bee.

The seal of Baron Percy (from 1792–1816), created Lord Prudhoe (1816–47), and then the 4th Duke (1847–65).

18th/early 19th century.

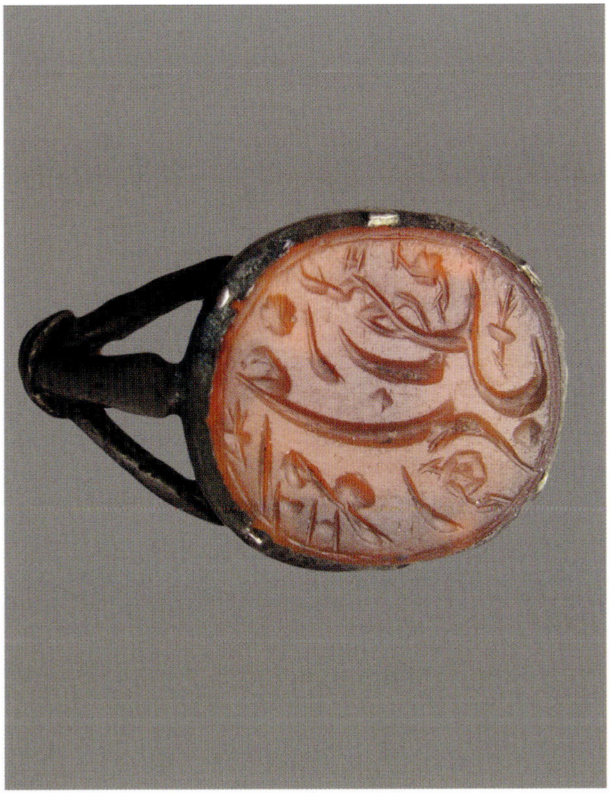

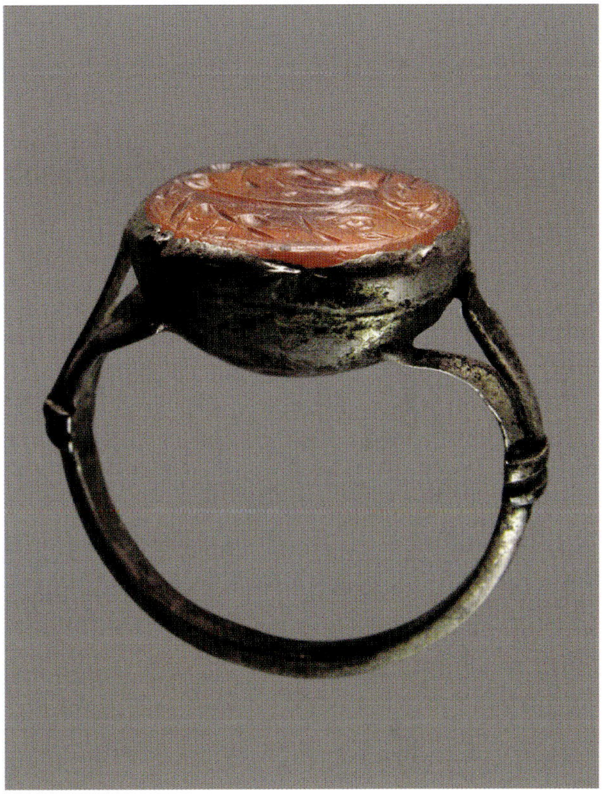

281

(10815)
Carnelian, set on a silver ring with triple-forked terminals
8 x 7

Arabic inscription 'Lord! Make smooth Umar's affairs 1016.' Ottoman, 1607–8.

There was a cornelian intaglio head of Abucher inscribed on the back 'in Arabic characters' in the 1st Duchess' Collection, no. 49.

Modern

THE EMPERORS NECKLACE

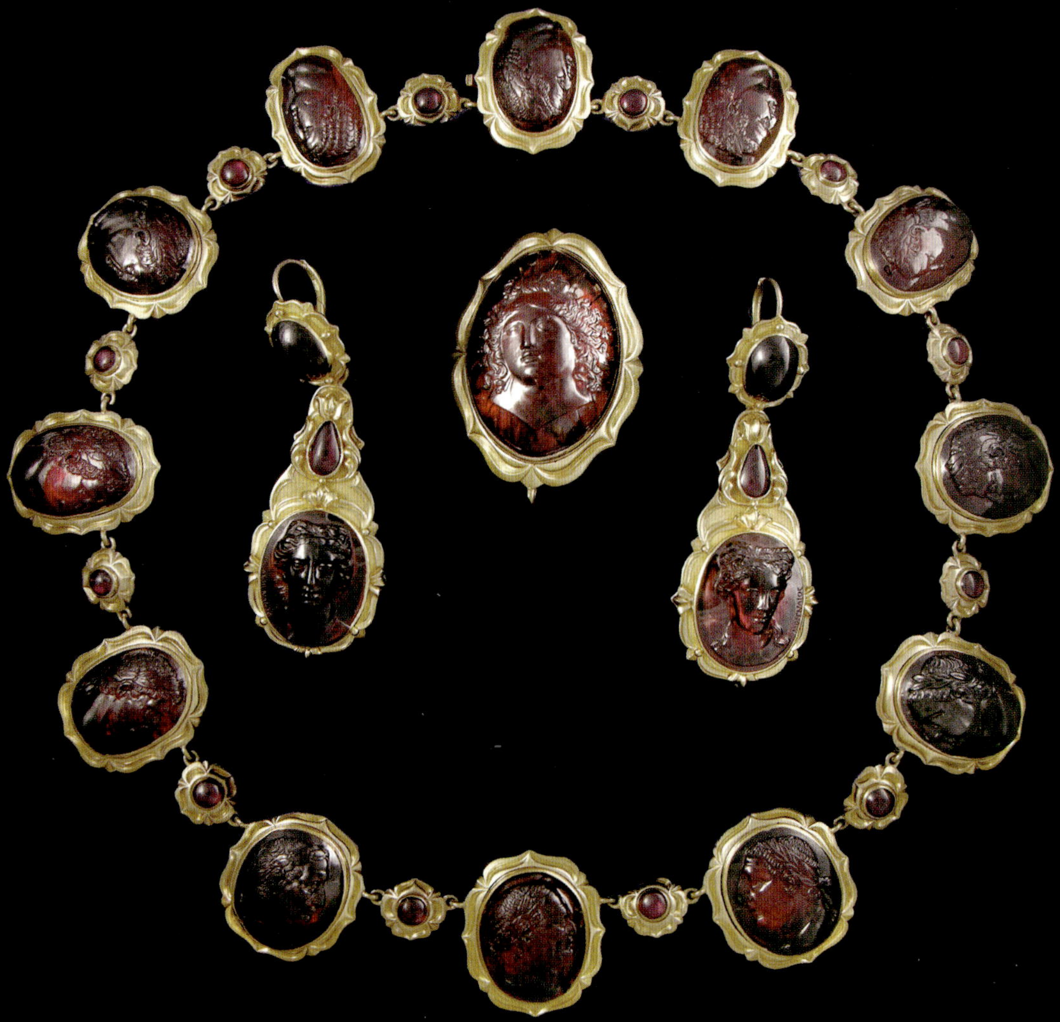

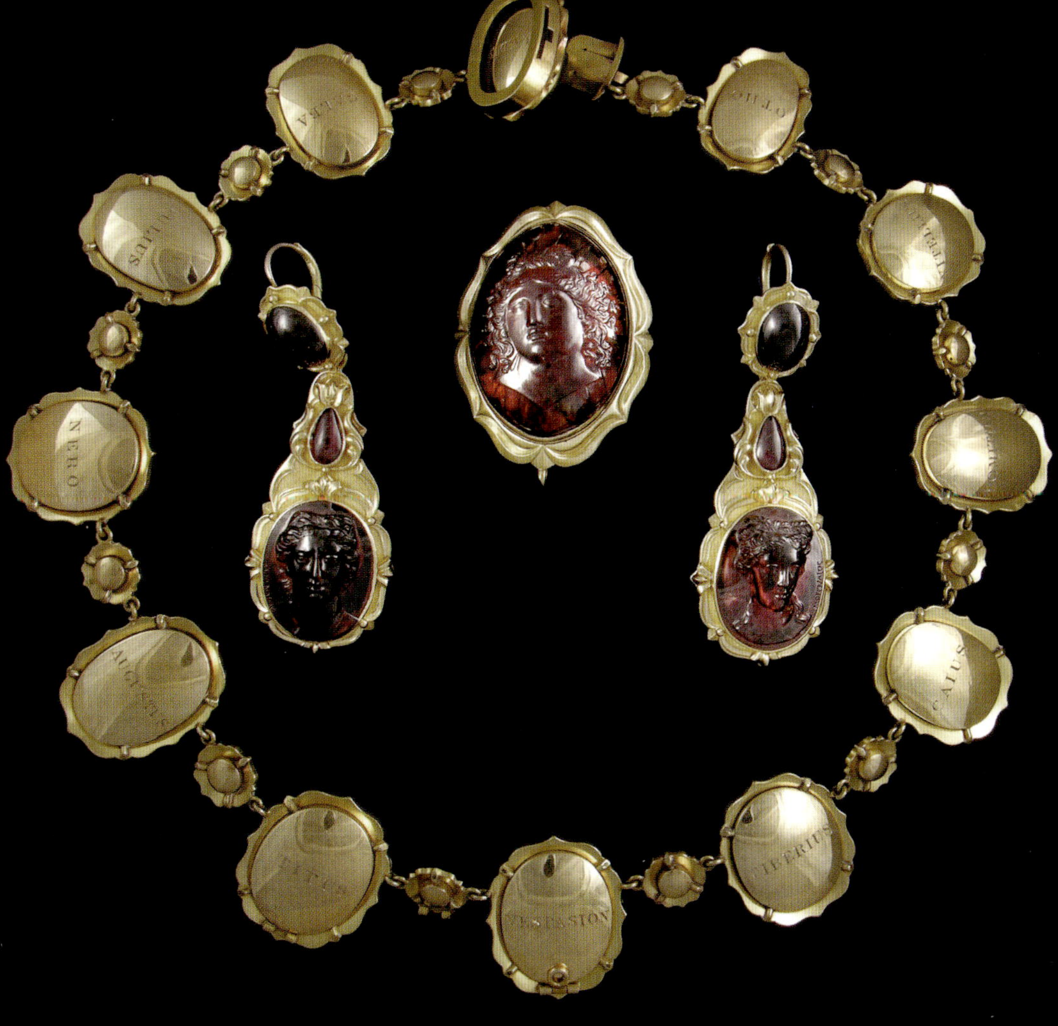

The necklace, brooch and earrings were acquired by Charlotte Florentia Clive, who married the 3rd Duke of Northumberland in 1817, and they are listed in the inventory of her jewels (1836).

AGE no. 26.

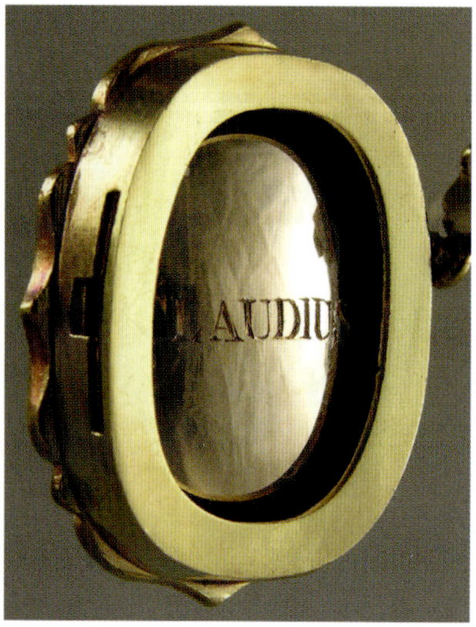
LAUDIU

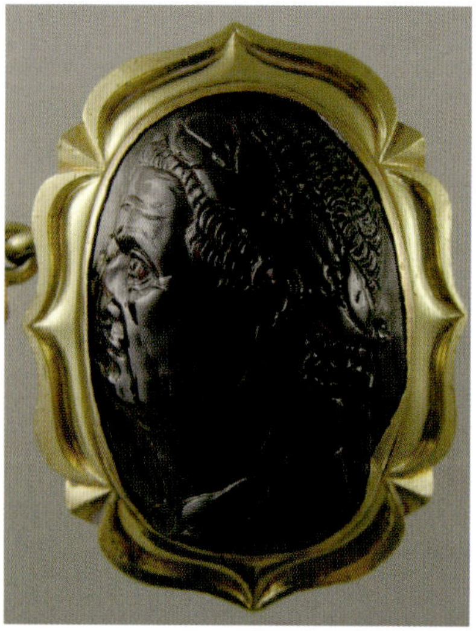

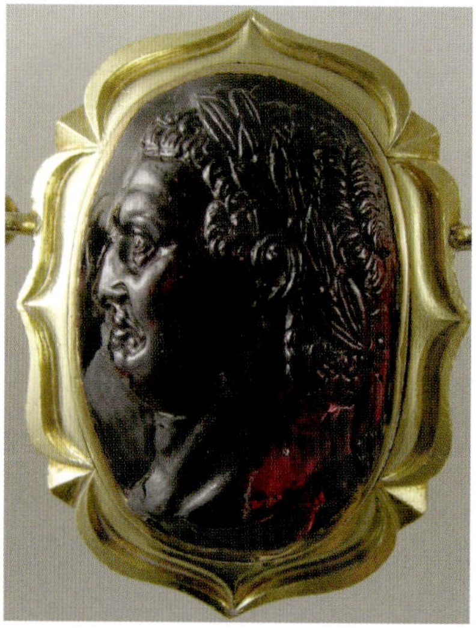

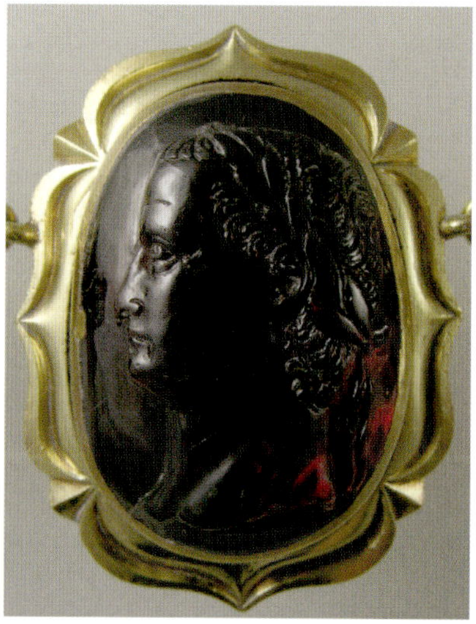

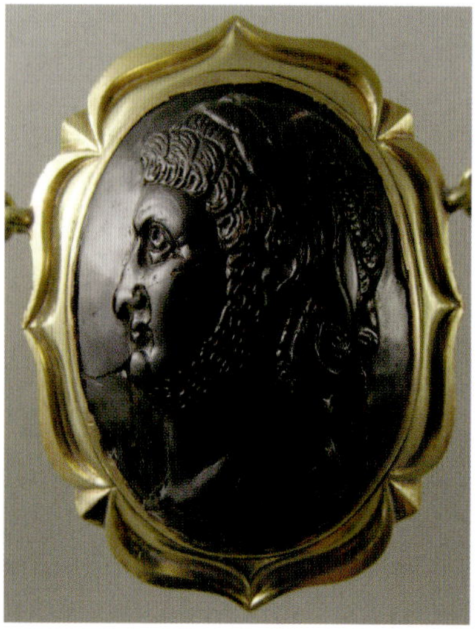

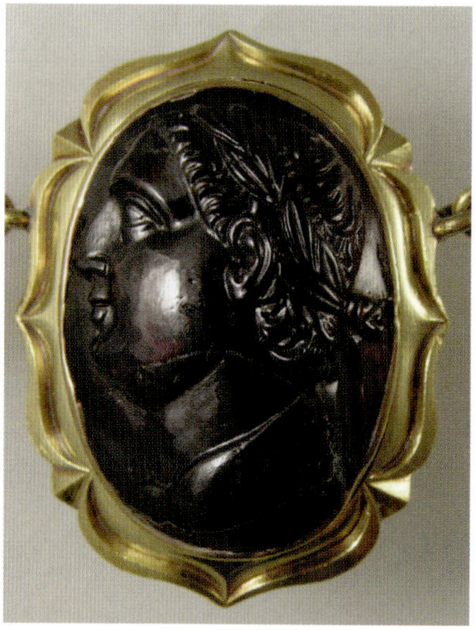

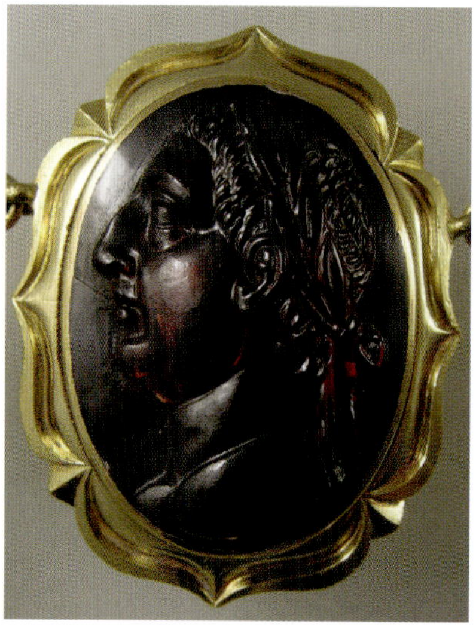

Garnet cameo portraits of the Twelve Roman Emperors (in the range 26–9 x 13–17) set in gold mounts decorated with flattened scrolls and divided by gold rosettes set with garnets. Their names are inscribed on their backs, now in the order:

Claudius, Galba, Julius, Nero, Augustus, Titus, Vespasian, Tiberius, Gaius, Domitian, Vitellius, Otho.

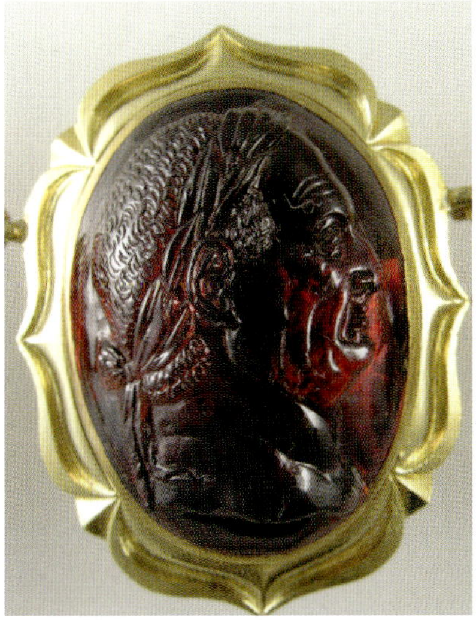
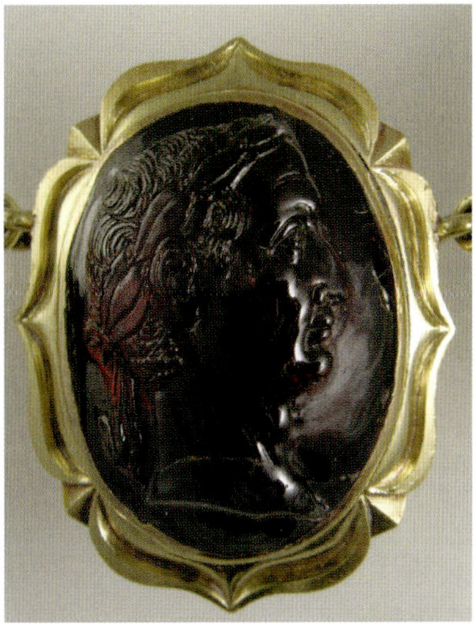
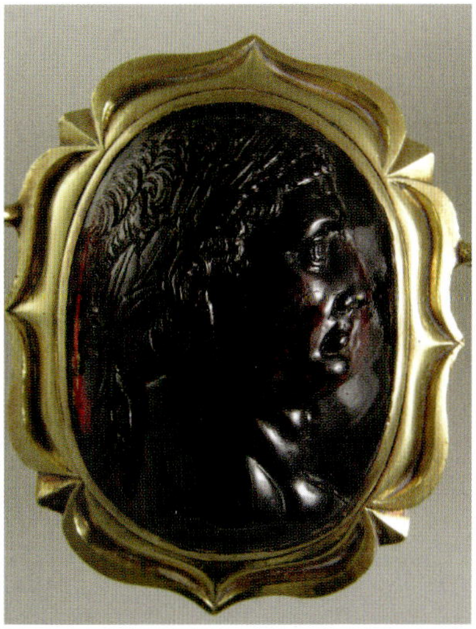
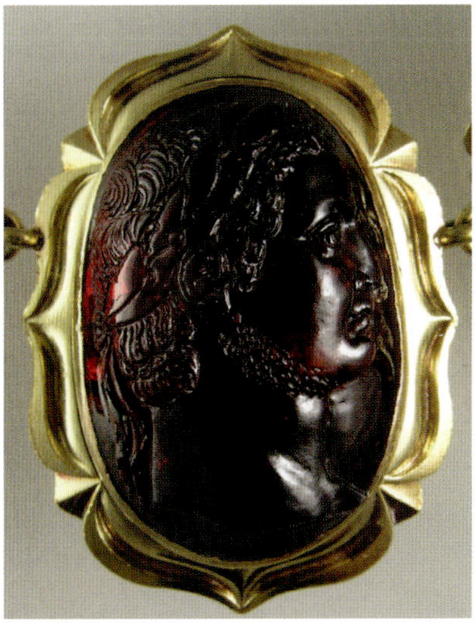
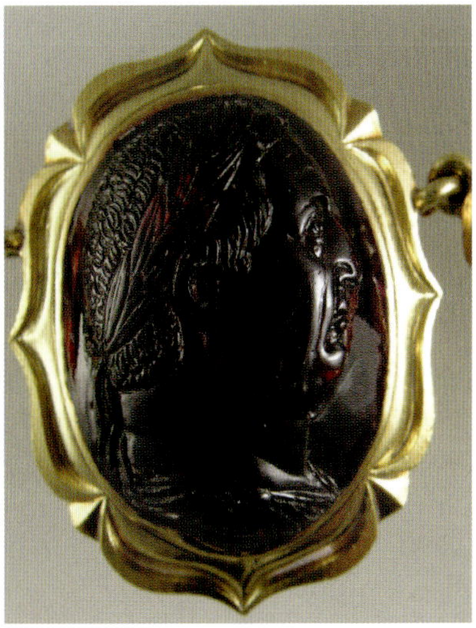
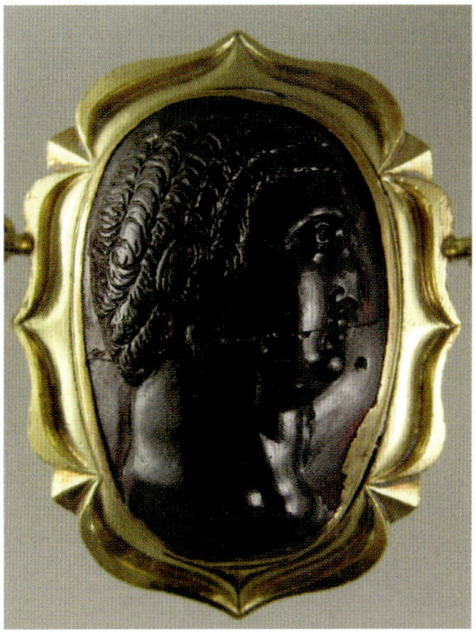

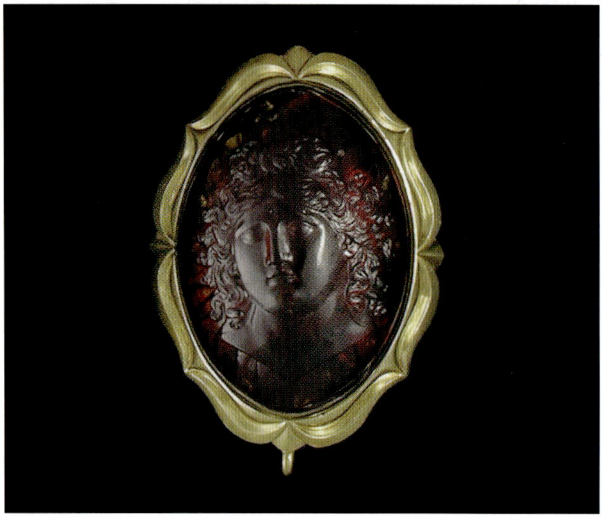

A brooch (43 x 32) with a garnet cameo showing the radiate head of the Sun. Set with a border of scrolls and leaves

A pair of earring pendants, each with the head of a Muse and inscribed in Greek – ΜΟΥΣΝΑΙΟΣ. Set in a border of scrolls and with a stippled ground.

Early 19th century.

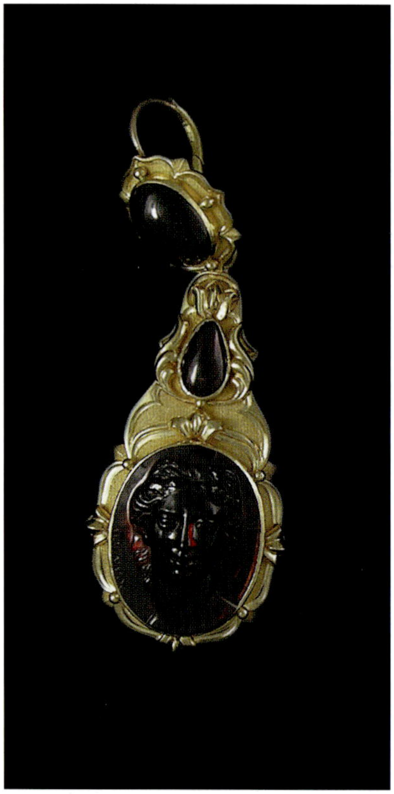

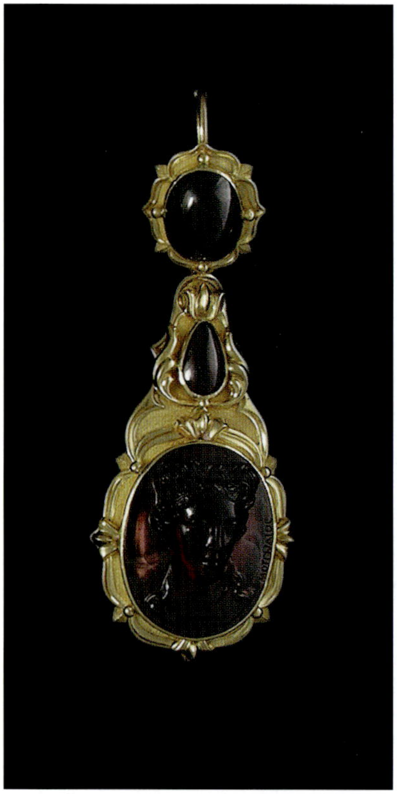

GLASS PORTRAITS

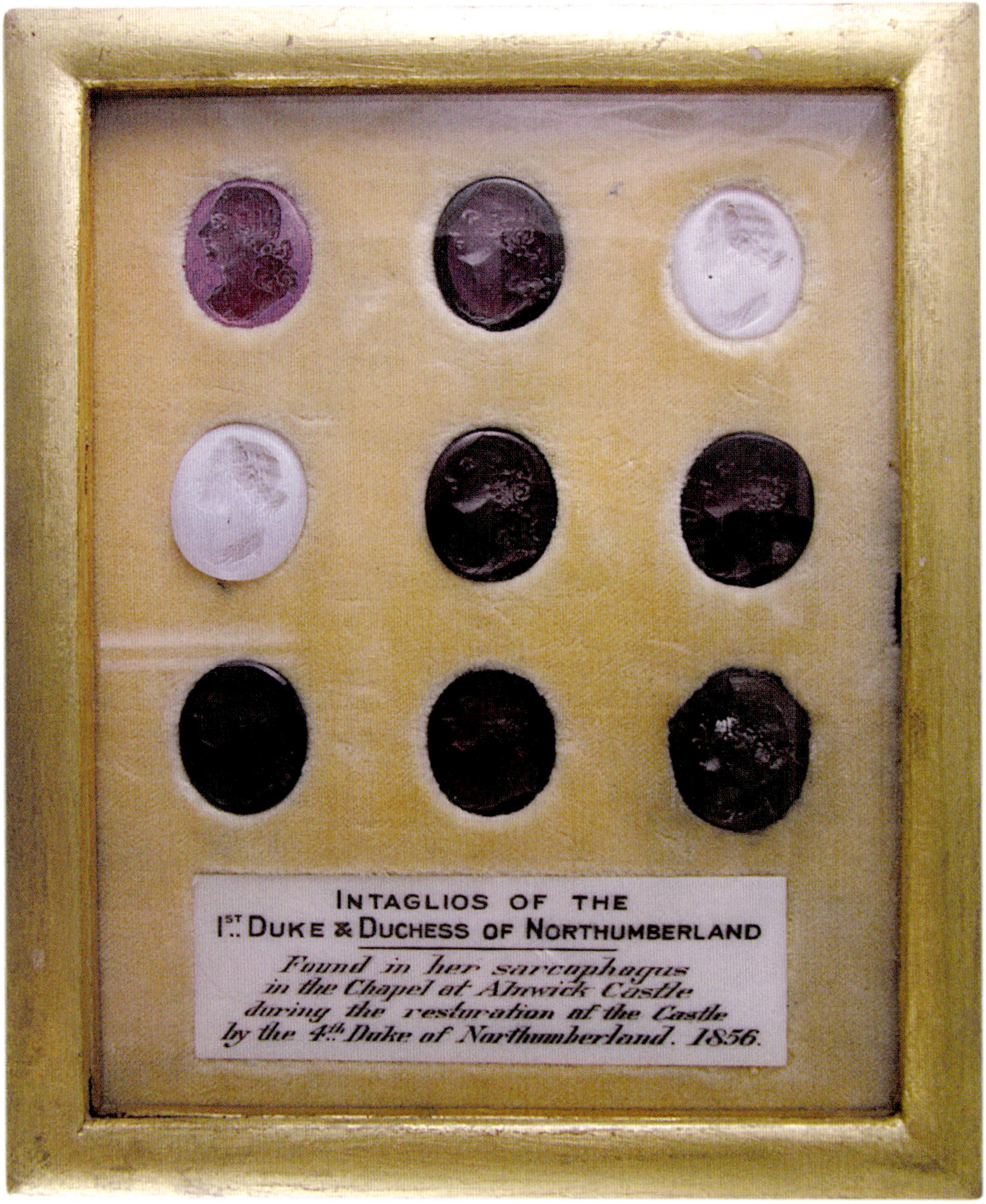
INTAGLIOS OF THE
1st. DUKE & DUCHESS OF NORTHUMBERLAND
Found in her sarcophagus
in the Chapel at Alnwick Castle
during the restoration of the Castle
by the 4th. Duke of Northumberland. 1856.

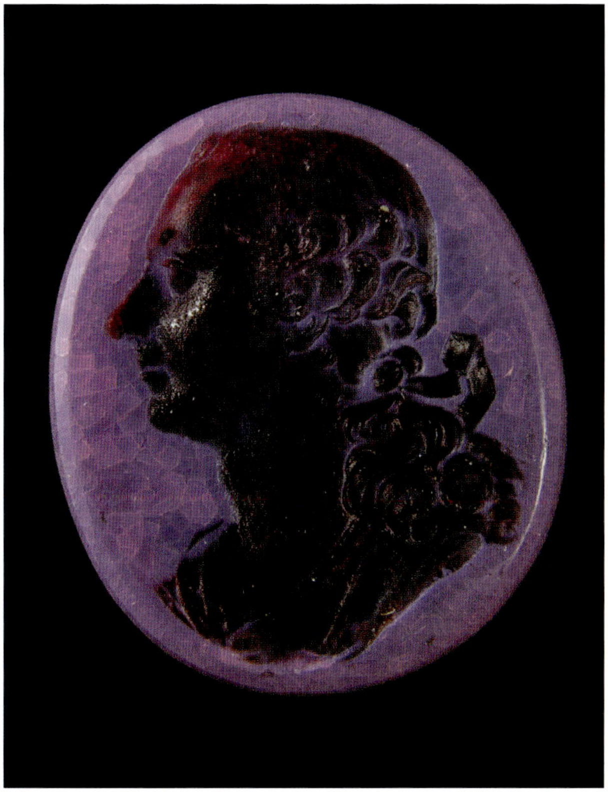 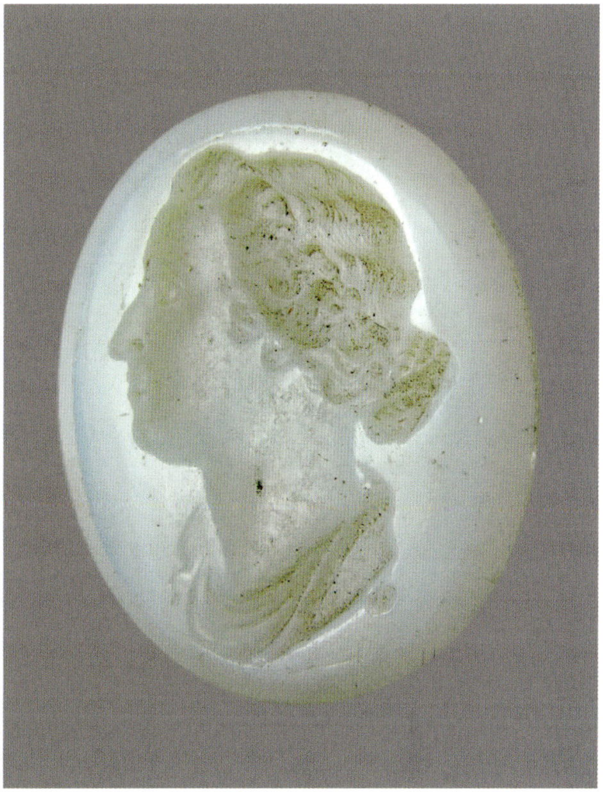

A box contains twelve coloured glass intaglio portraits (each 17 x 13) of the 1st Duke and Duchess. It is labelled:

> INTAGLIOS OF THE 1ST DUKE & DUCHESS
> OF NORTHUMBERLAND
>
> Found in her sarcophagus
> in the Chapel of Alnwick Castle
> during the restoration of the Castle
> by the 4th Duke of Northumberland in 1856

See our **244**.

TASSIE AND CATHERINE THE GREAT

James Tassie spent a while with Dr Quin of Dublin, who was perfecting a technique of creating glass paste impressions and casts of gems. Some of Quin's casts were in the 1st Duchess' collection. Tassie returned to London and began assiduously collecting casts which he listed in a catalogue in 1775 with 3,106 items, of which only one was a 'Percy' (no. 956). He moved to Scotland, continuing to collect, notably a large collection made by Baron Stosch in Italy. His second catalogue, of 15,800 items, was published in 1791 with descriptions by R.E. Raspe (also the creator of Baron Munchhausen). The Empress Catherine the Great of Russia, herself an almost obsessive collector of gems, was his patron. She had some knowledge of the Percy gems and desired to acquire 'the best' of them, which was achieved in 1786 by her agent in Britain, Count Semyon Vorontsov (Kagan, 156). She subsequently complained that she had not received 'the best', but the collection of 'Percy' gems in St Petersburg is distinguished, and the very best Beverley gems were the cameos from the Rohan-Chabot collection, which were acquired after 1786.[34]

As well as these 'Beverley Gems' no longer in Britain, there is a substantial number listed in Tassie's catalogue as belonging to the Beverley collection, which have not been found at Alnwick. There are also a few in 'Beverley' cast collections (Cades and SG.Imp.) but not so far identified in originals. A separate publication will present these pieces.

34. On Catherine and Natter, and on the alleged withholding of some Beverley gems, see E. Dmitrieva, Journal of the History of Collections 25 (2013) 79–81.

INDEXES

Index to Previous Collections

references are to the catalogue numbers

Index to Artists

including those named in discussions

Index to Subjects

List of Inscriptions

1 NASSARO
2 GIROMETTI
3 ΒΟΗΘΟΥ
4 ΘΑΜΥΡΟΥ
5 BHRINI
10 LAV.R.MED.
14 Γ
54 AB
55 Mrs Burrell. Aet. 89. Ob:16. Aug.1789.
80]ΔΙΟC
90 AVΛOV
91 ΔΙΟCΚΟΥ ΡΙΔΟΥ
92 ΑΠΟΛΛΩΝΙΔΟΥ
93 ΑΜΜΩΝΙΟΥ
94 ΒΟΗΘΟΥ
95 ΣΚΥΛΑΚΟ
96 ΣΚΥΛΑΚΟ
97 ΦΑΡΝΑΚΟΥ
98 ΦΑΡΝΑΚΗC ΕΠ.
99 ΓΝΑΙΟC
100 ΡΕΓΑ
101 MARCHANT F
102 MARCHANT
103 BURCH.INV
104 ΑΡΡΙΣ
105 L.N.
106 ΠΙΧΛΕΡ
107 ΠΙΧΛΕΡ
108 ΠΙΧΛΕΡ
109 ΠΑΣΑΛΙΑΣ=
110 CADES
111 WRAY FEC:
162 MARATHI
164 C·S·RIO
170 monograms of Δ and T, and O and Y
182 X·V·X, ΠΕΙ, ΟΙΝΗΡΟC
187 LME
195 ANTINOOC
197 I
235 copy of 91
255 ?ΠΙ
256 KP
263 D.MARI AVCTI
268 TFM
279 ROMA
280 P
281 Arabic
Emperors Necklace (names)

Pictorial Index

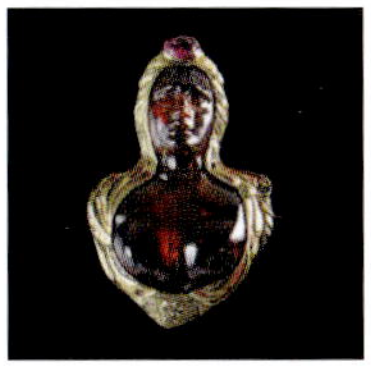

1. 4–5

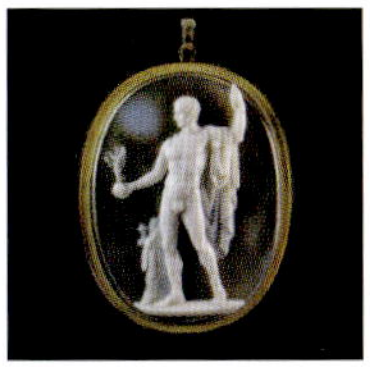

2. 6

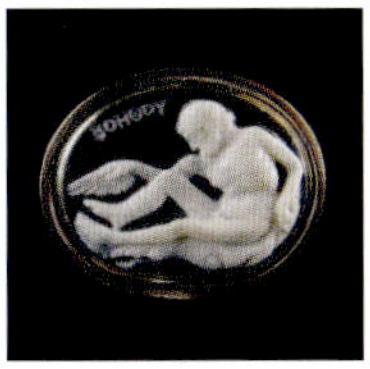

3. 7

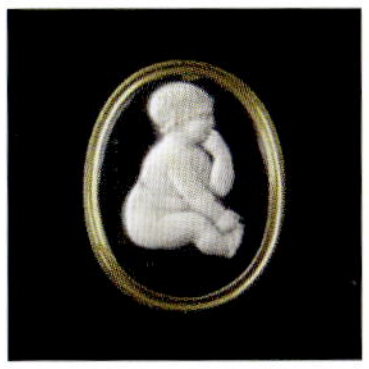

4. 8

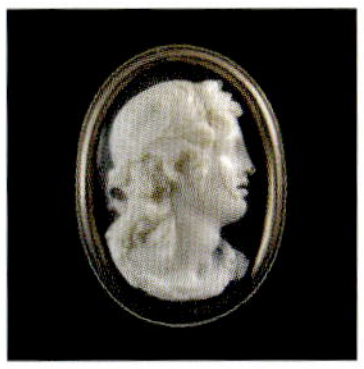

5. 9

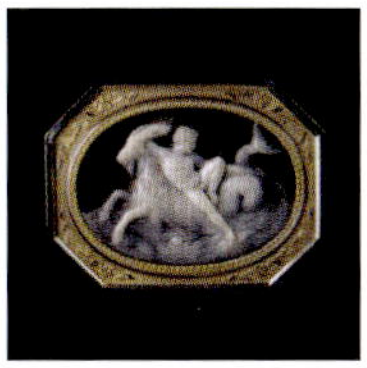

6. xxxii, 11

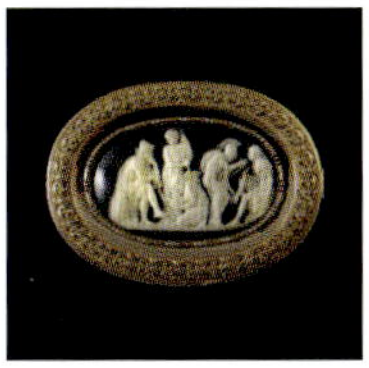

7. 12

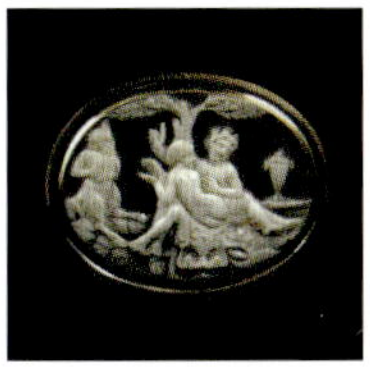

8. 13

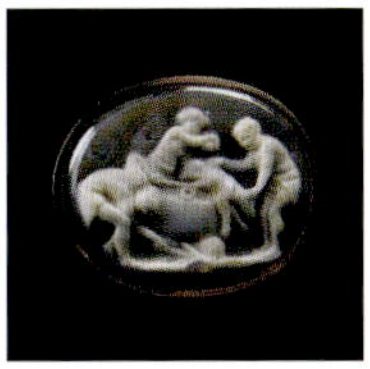

9. 14

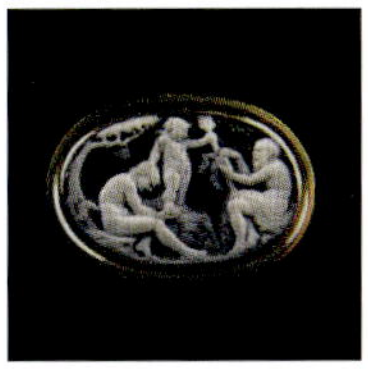

10. 15

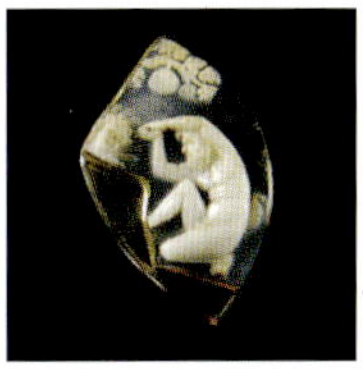

11. 16

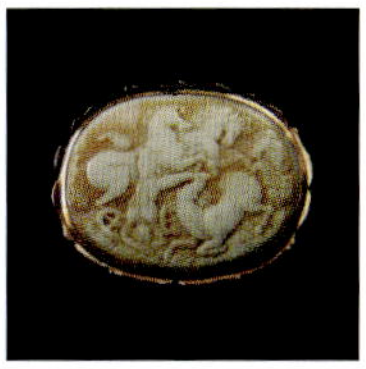

12. 17

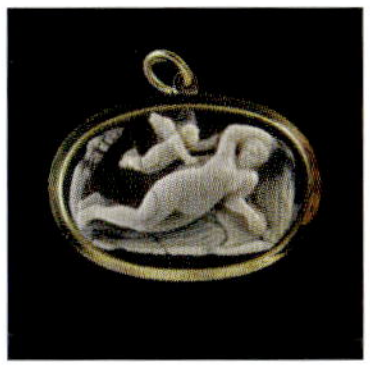

13. 18

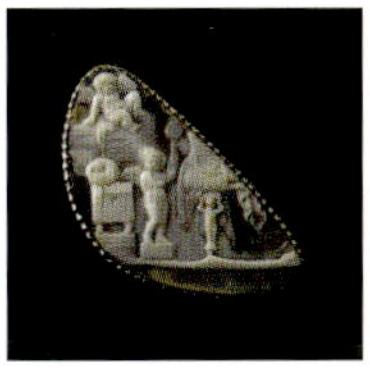

14. 19

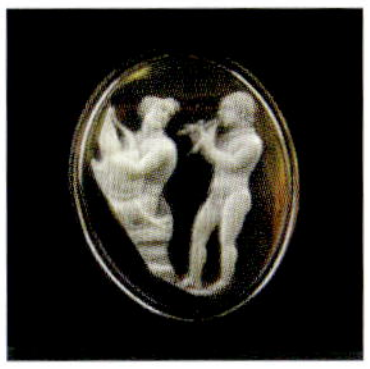

15. 20

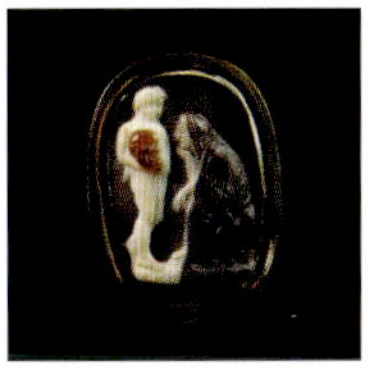

16. 21

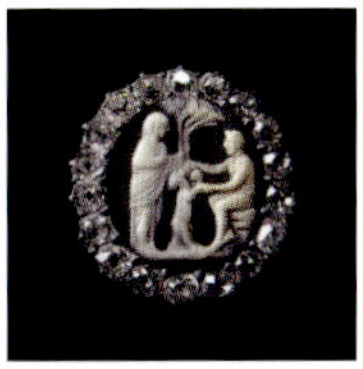

17. 22

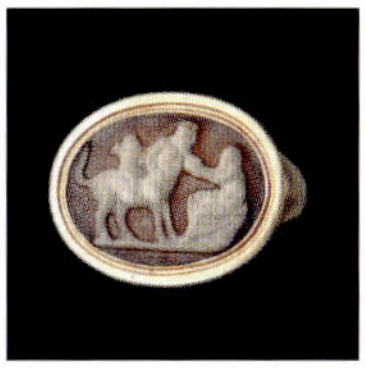

18. 23

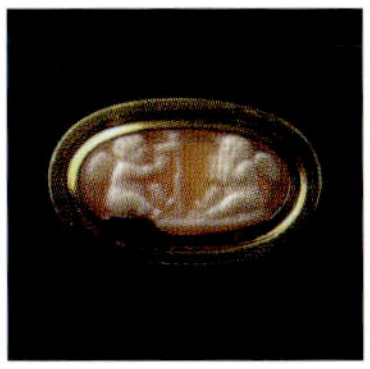

19. 24

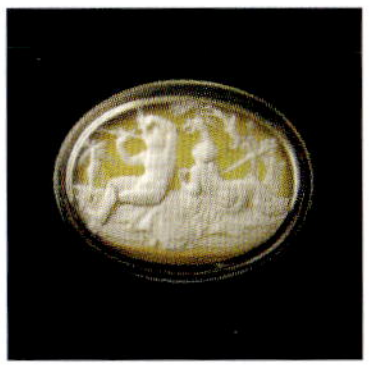

20. 10, 25

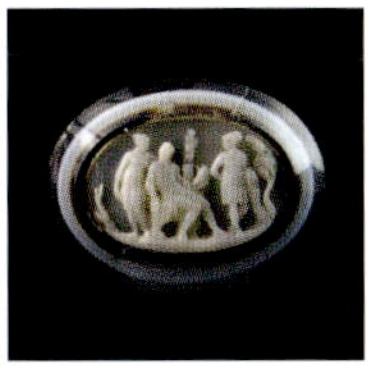

21. 26

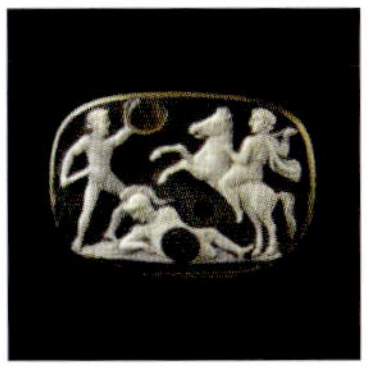

22. 27

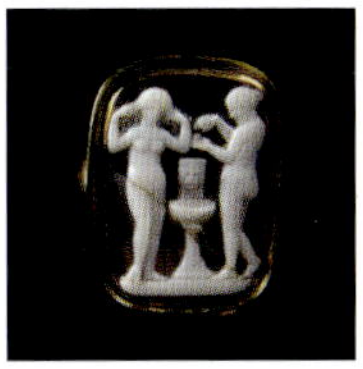

23. 28

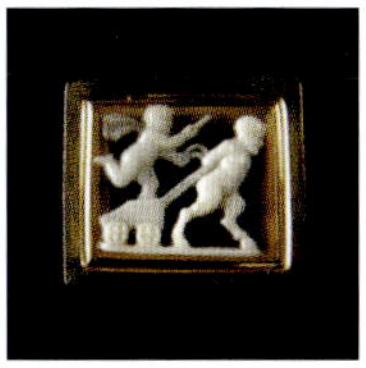

24. 29

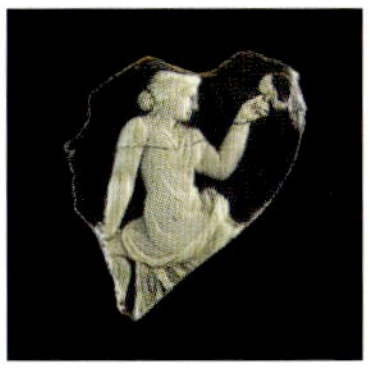

25. 31

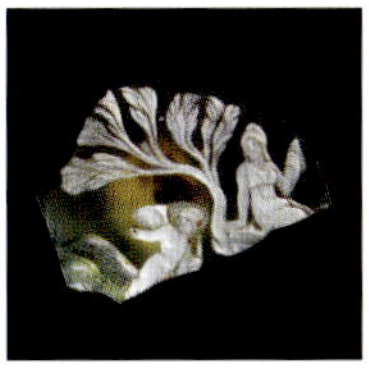

26. 30, 32

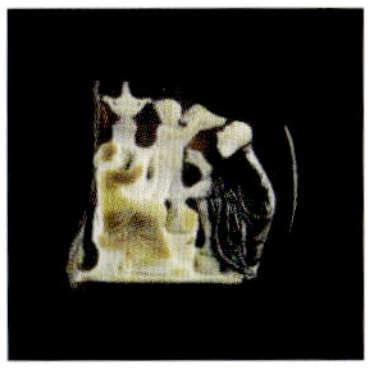

27. 33

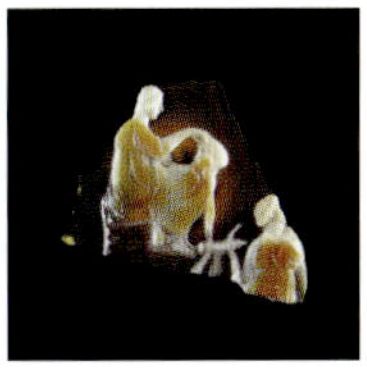

28. 34

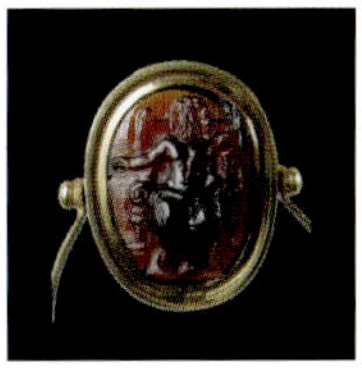

29. 36

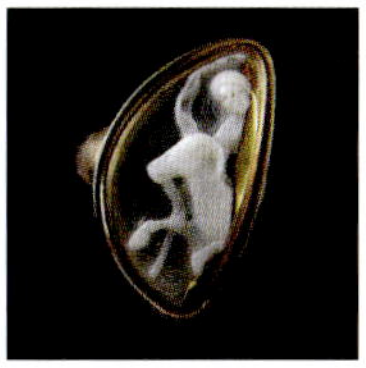

30. 37

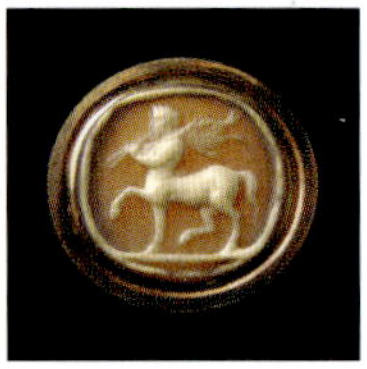

31. 38

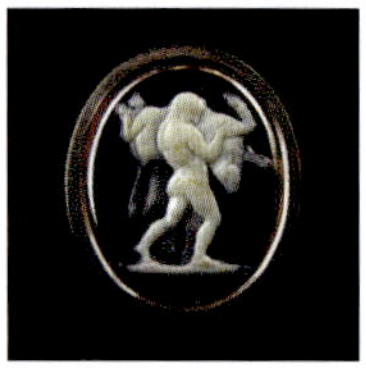

32. 39

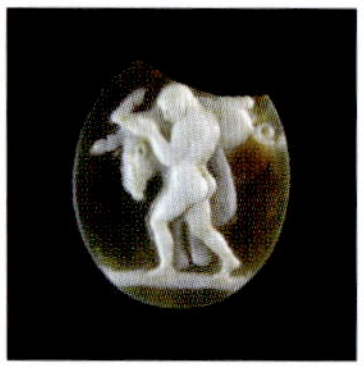

33. 40

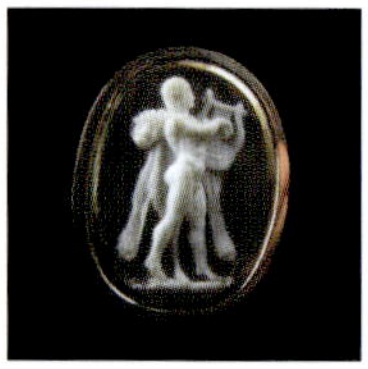

34. 41

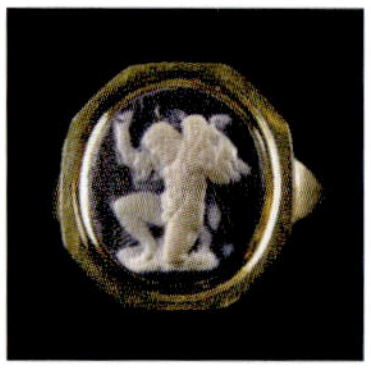

35. 35, 42

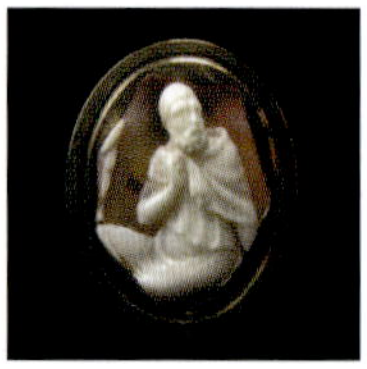

36. 43

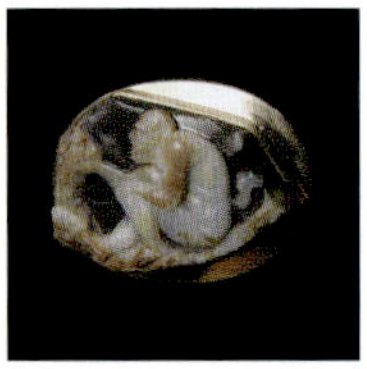

37. 44

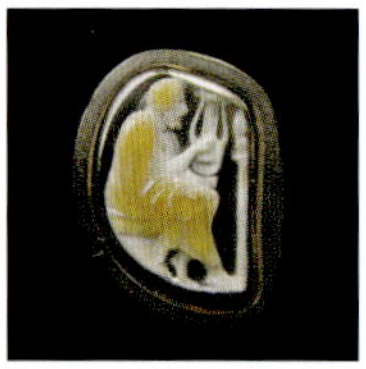

38. 45

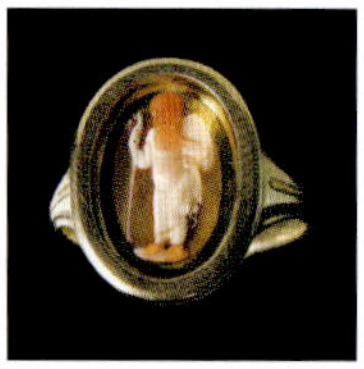

39. 46

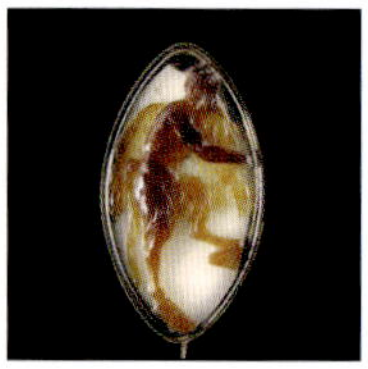

40. 47

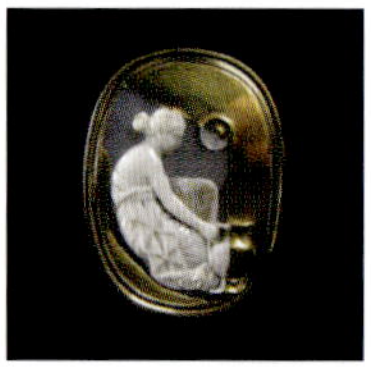

41. 48

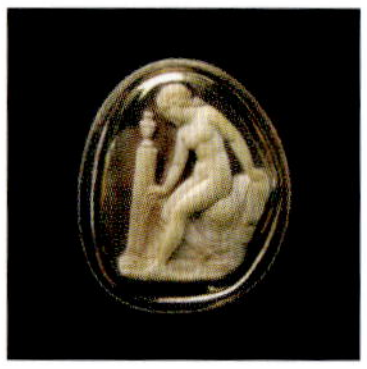

42. 49

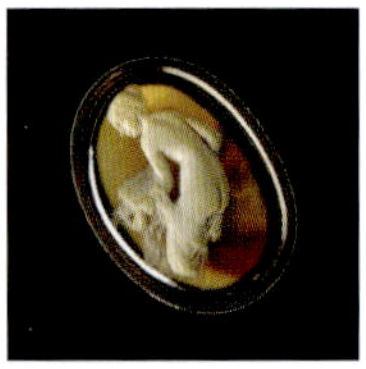

43. 50

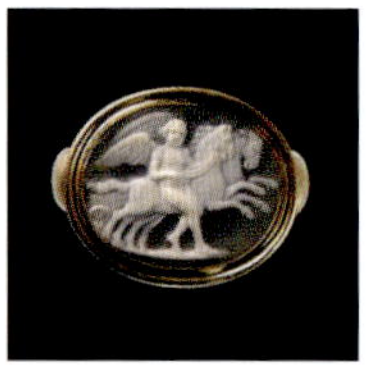

44. 51

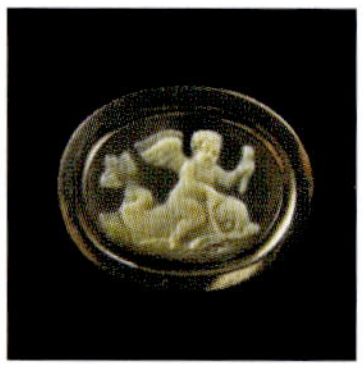

45. 52

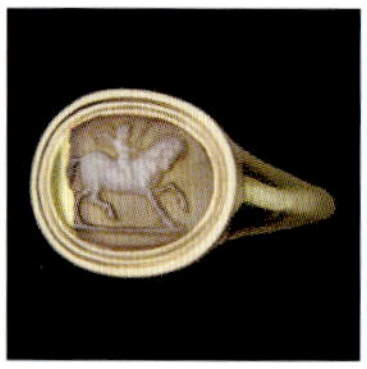

46. 53

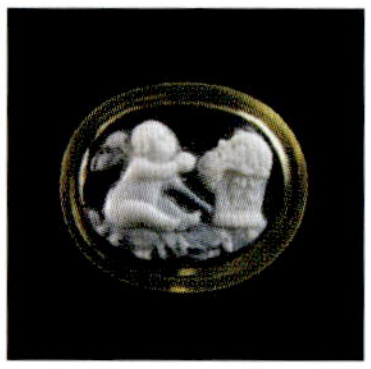

47. 54

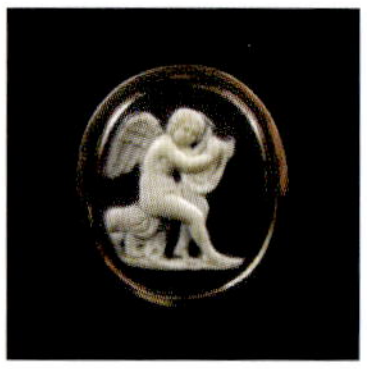

48. 55

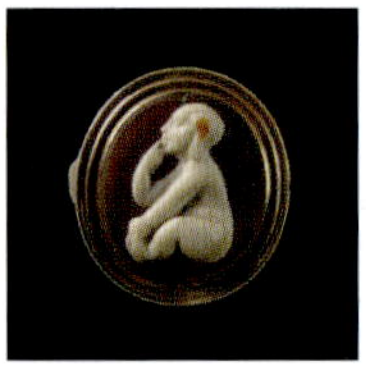

49. 56

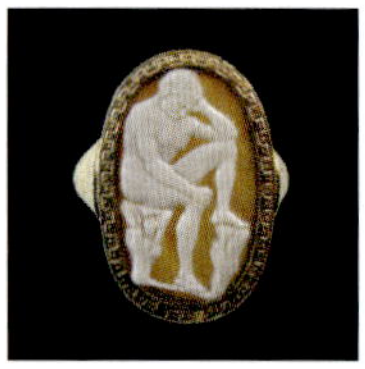

50. 56–7

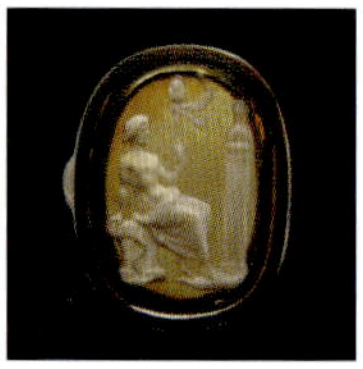

51. 58

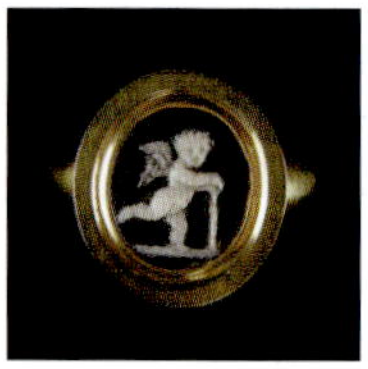

52. 59

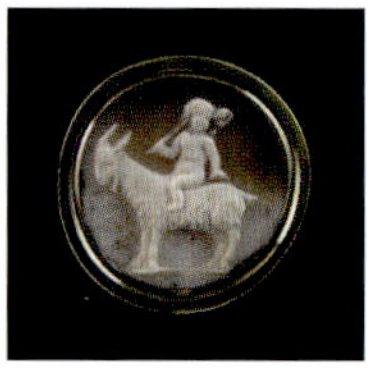

53. 60

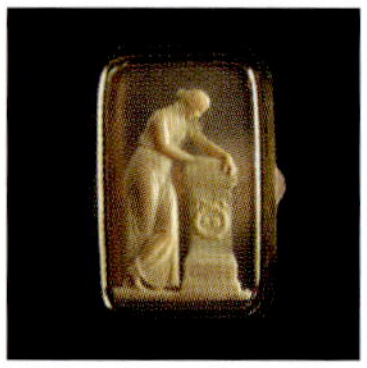

54. 60–1

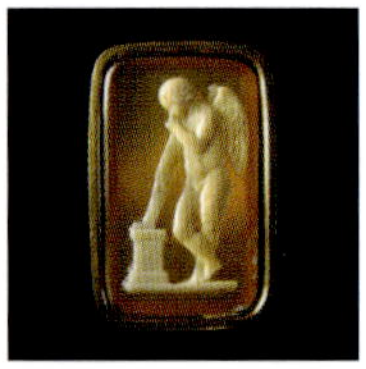

55. 62

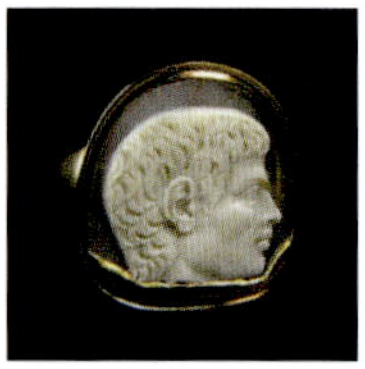

56. 64

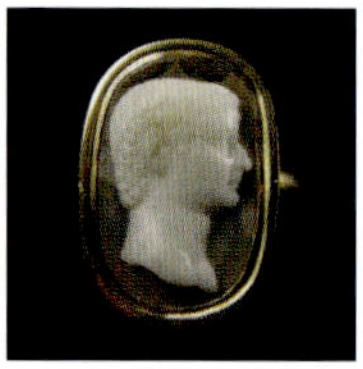

57. 65

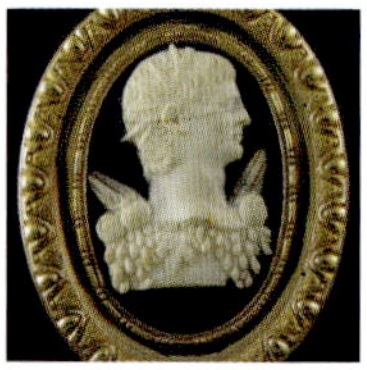

58. 66

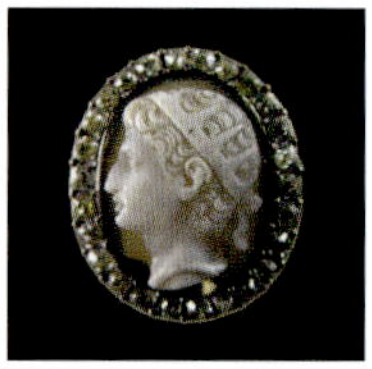

59. 67

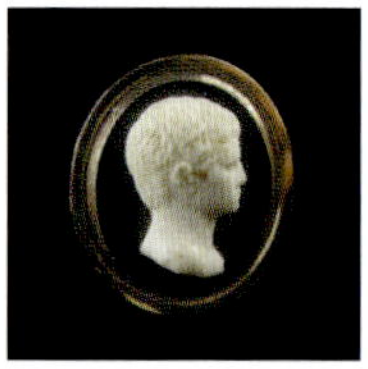

60. 68

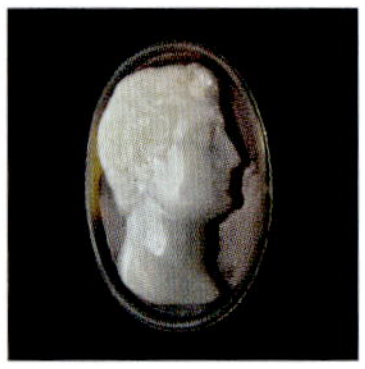

61. 69

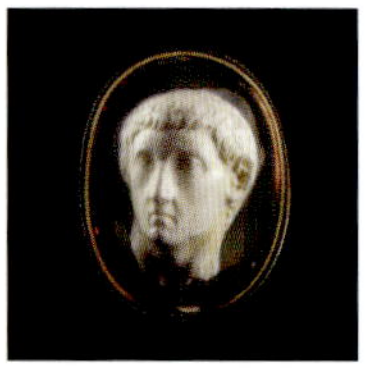

62. 70

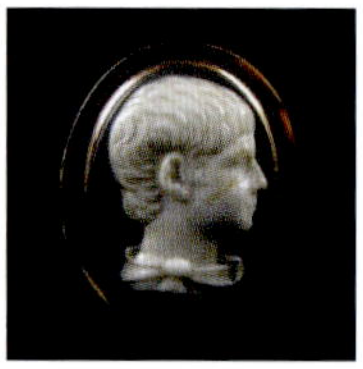

63. 71

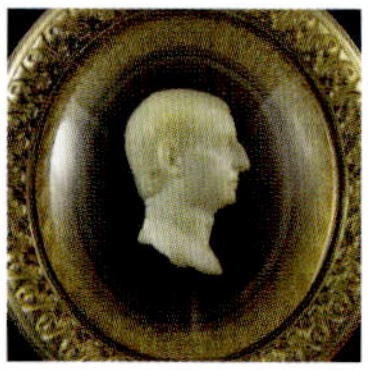

64. 72

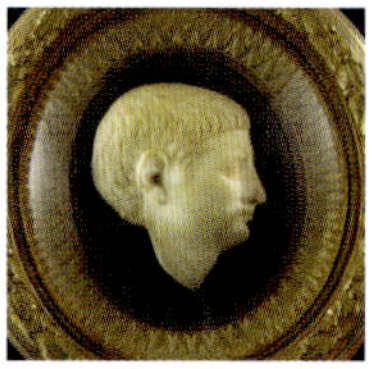

65. 73

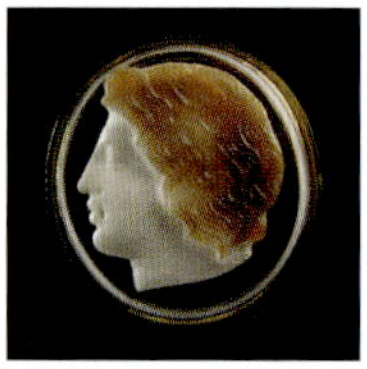

66. 63, 74

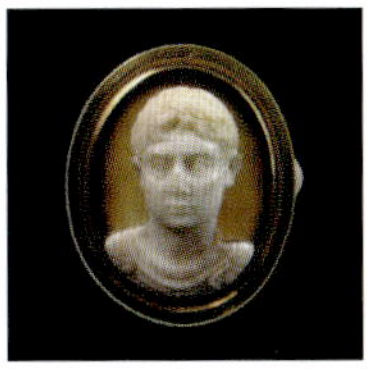
67. 75

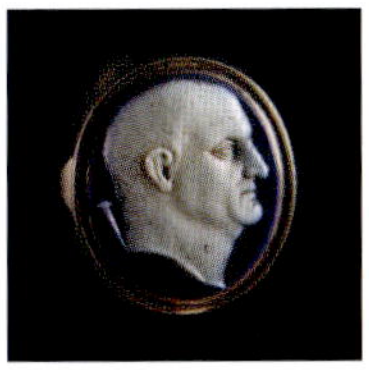
68. 76

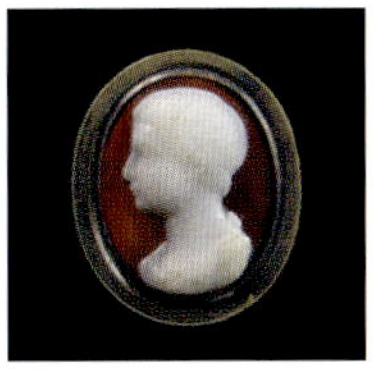
69. 77

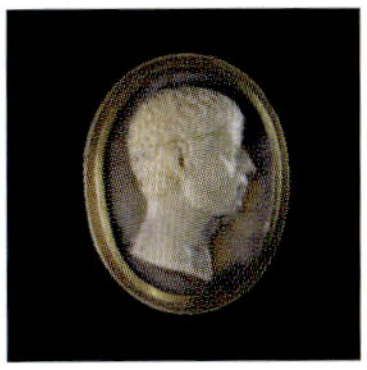
70. 78

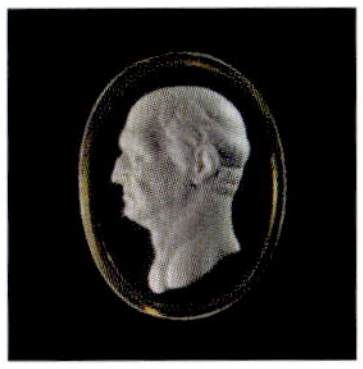
71. 79

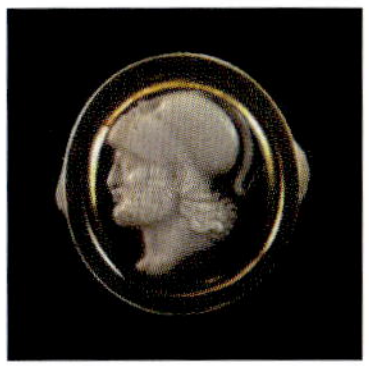
72. 80

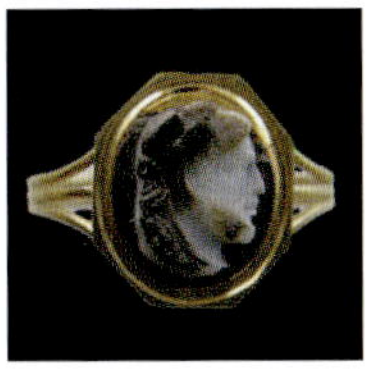
73. 81

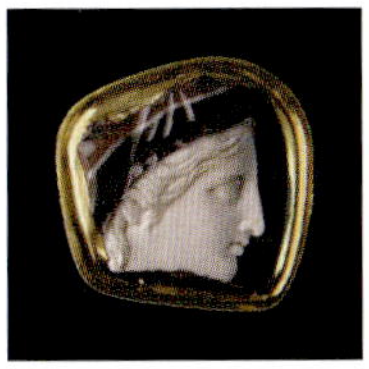
74. 82

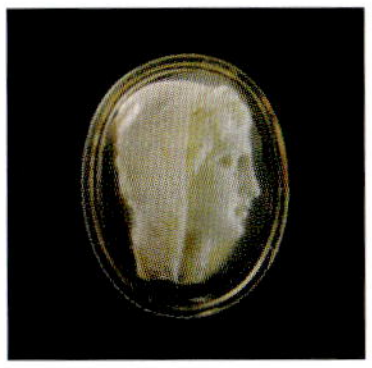
75. 83

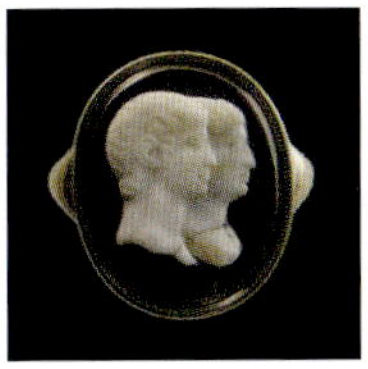
76. 84

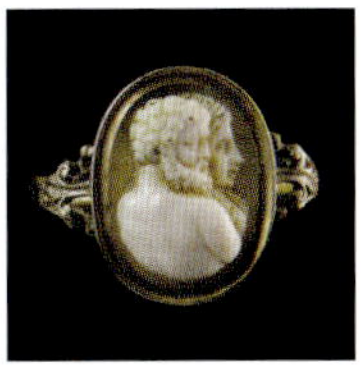
77. 85

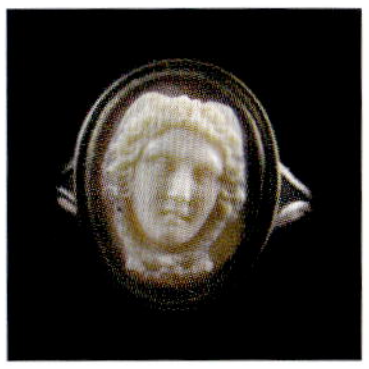
78. 86

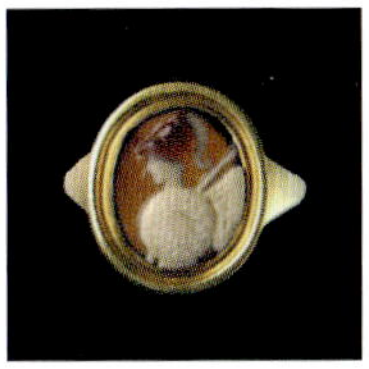
79. 87

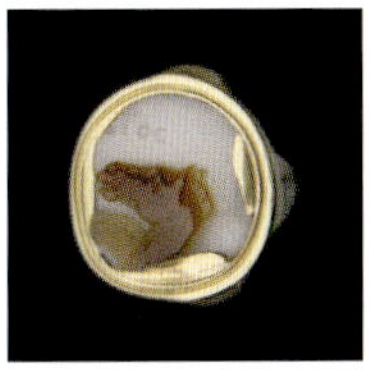
80. 89

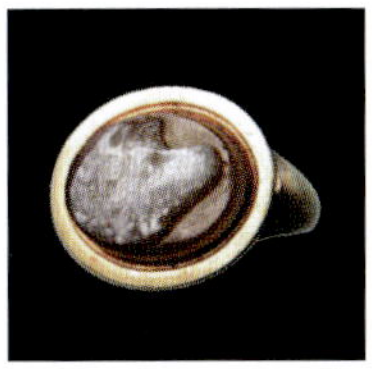
81. 90

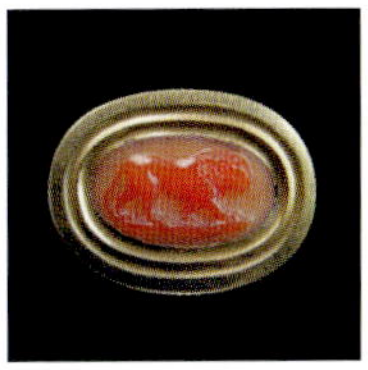
82. 91

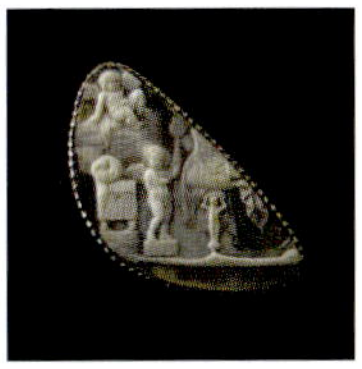
83. 92

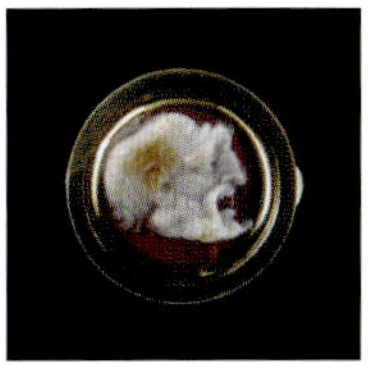
84. 93

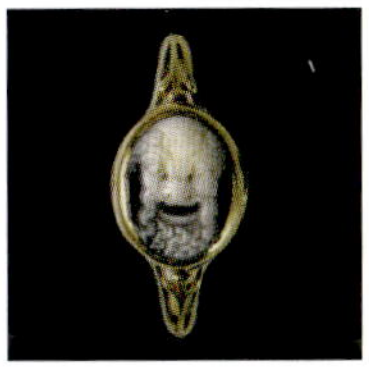
85. 94–5

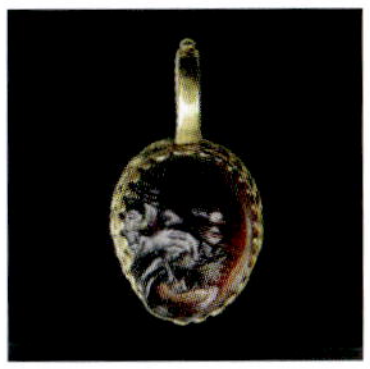
86. 95

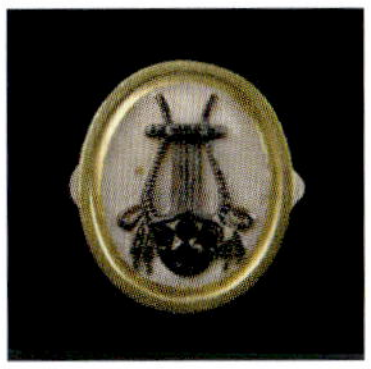
87. 88, 96

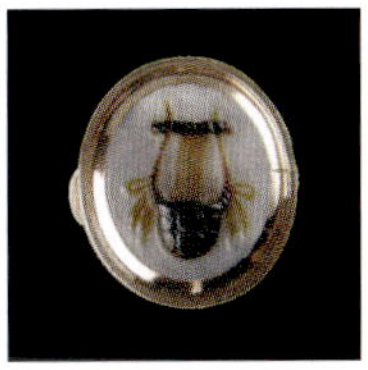
88. 97

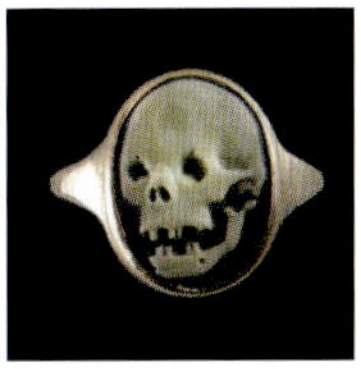
89. 98

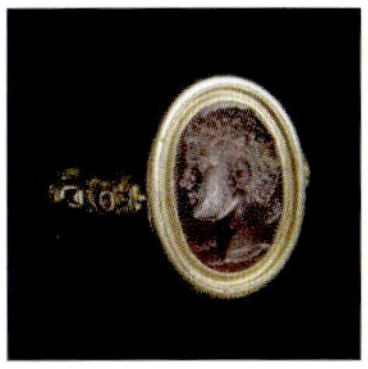
90. 100–1

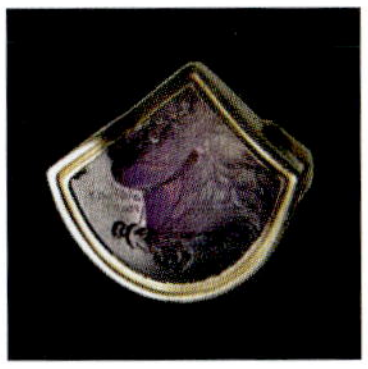
91. 102

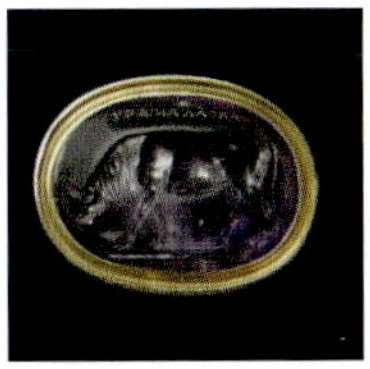
92. 103

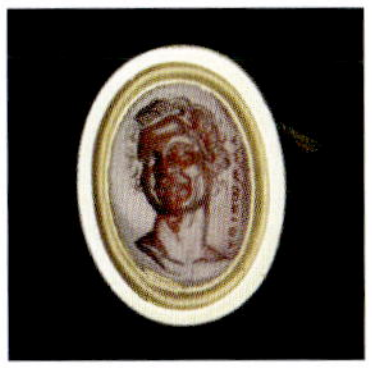
93. 104

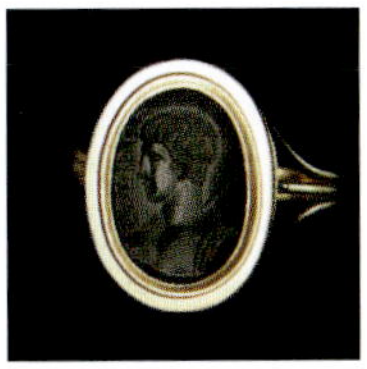
94. 105

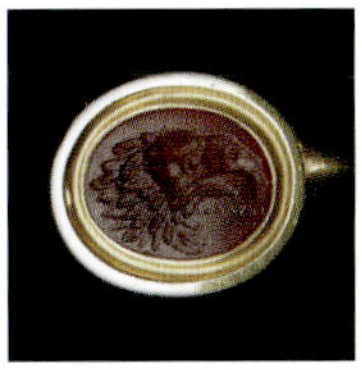
95. 106

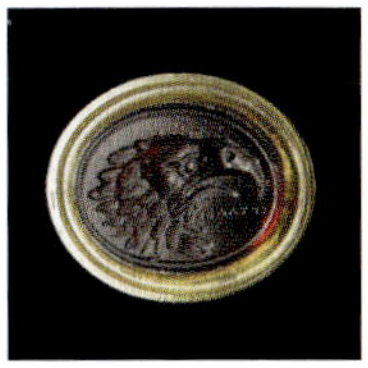
96. 107

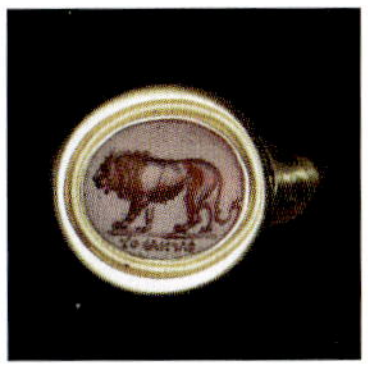
97. 108

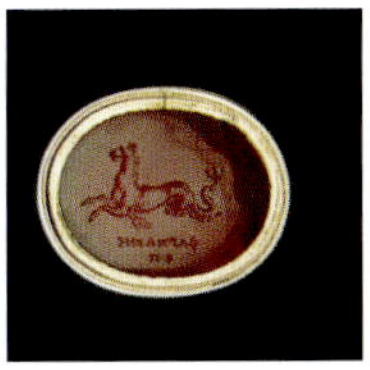
98. 109

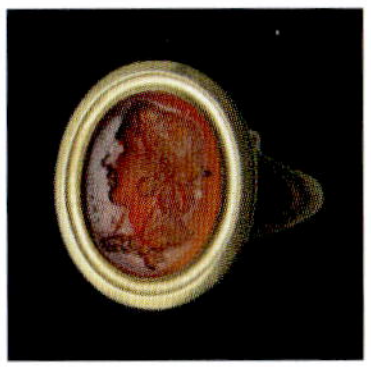
99. 110

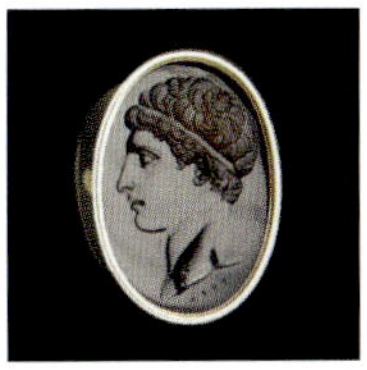
100. 111

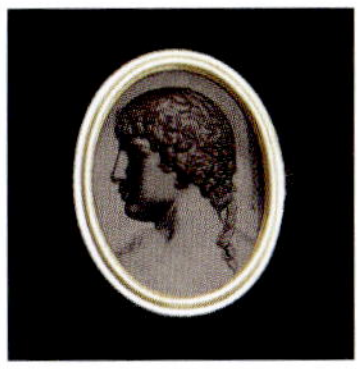
101. 112

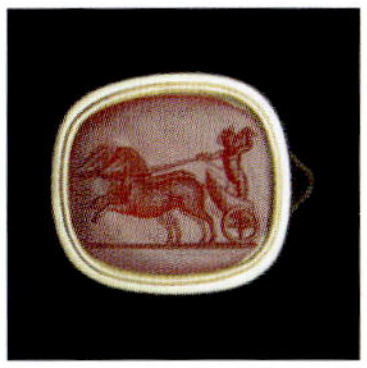
102. 113

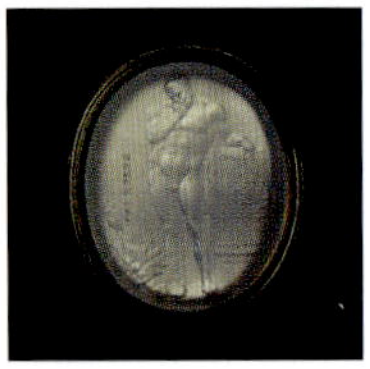
103. 114

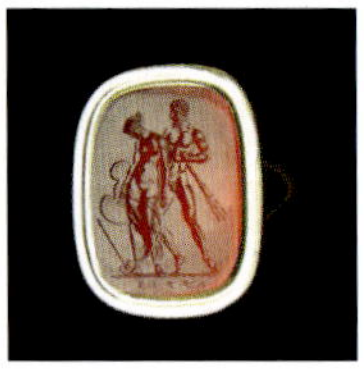
104. 115

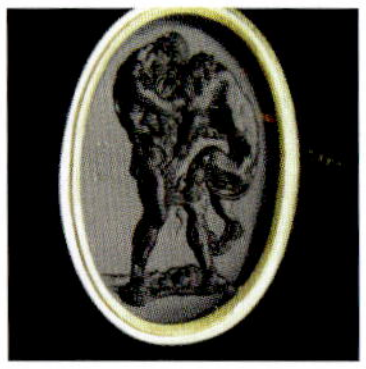
105. 116

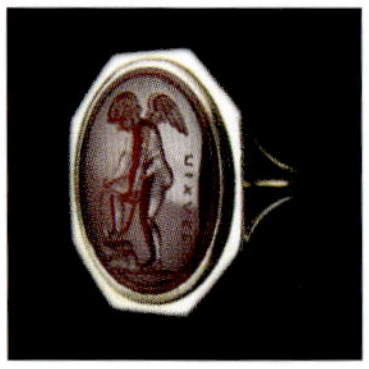
106. 117

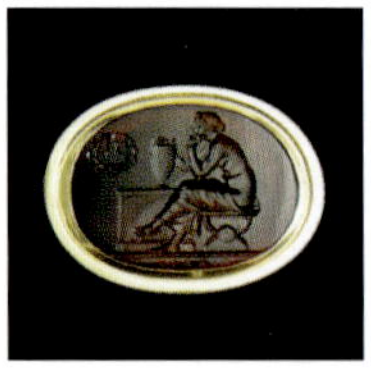
107. 118

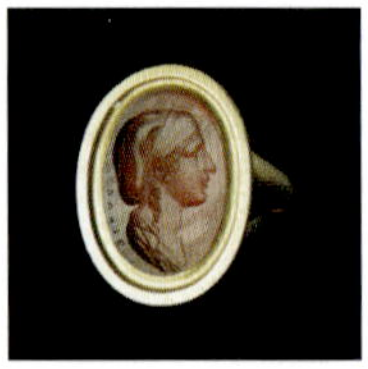
108. 119

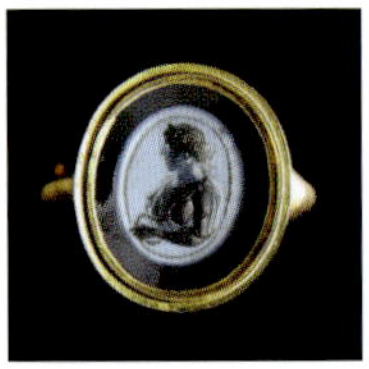
109. 120

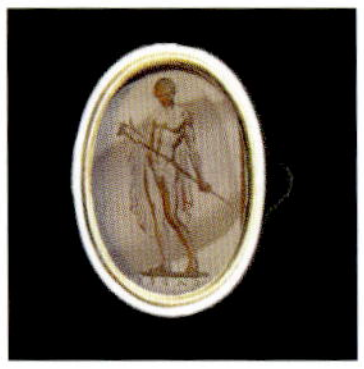
110. 121

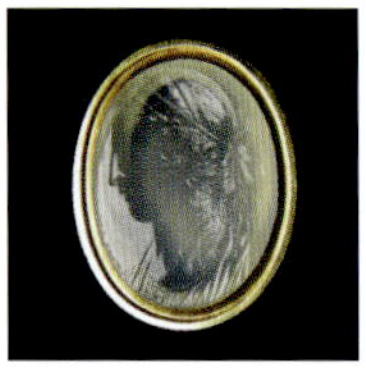
111. 122

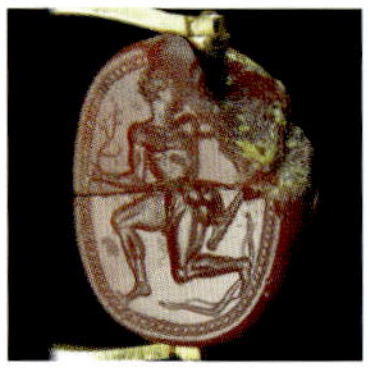
112. 124

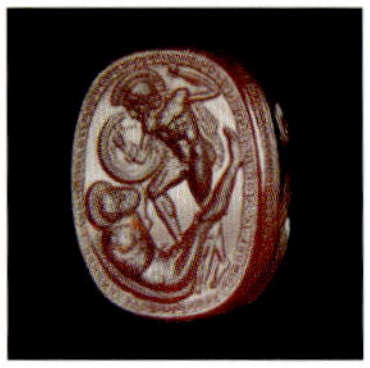
113. 123, 125

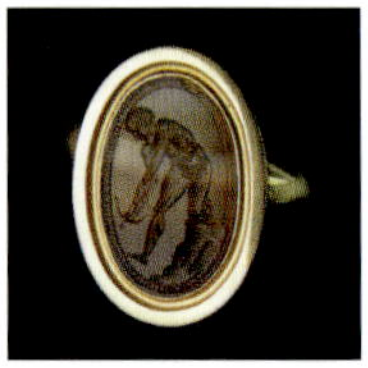
114. 126

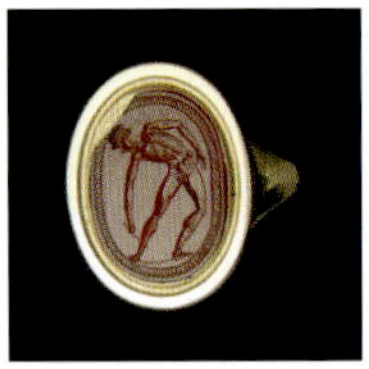
115. 127

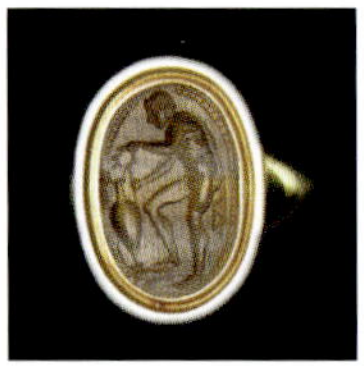
116. 128

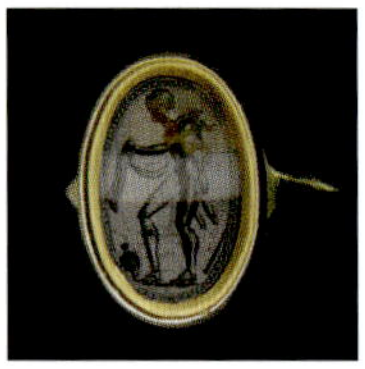
117. 129

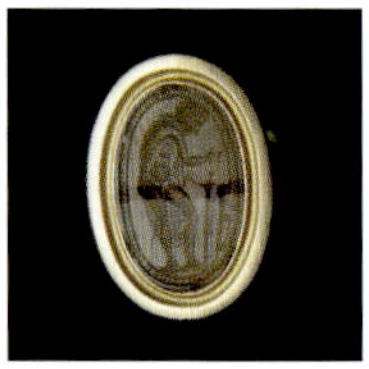
118. 130

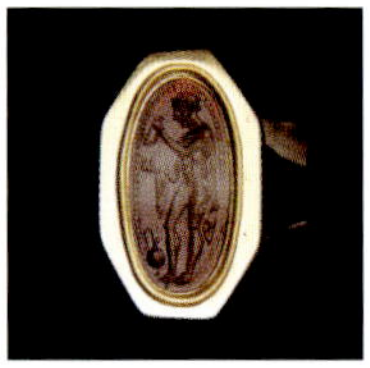
119. 131

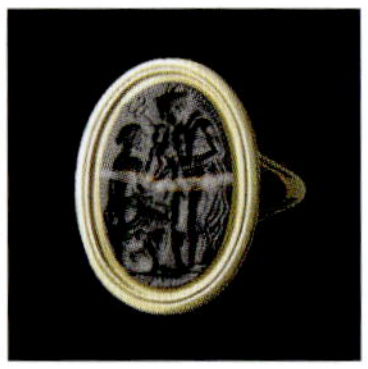
120. 132

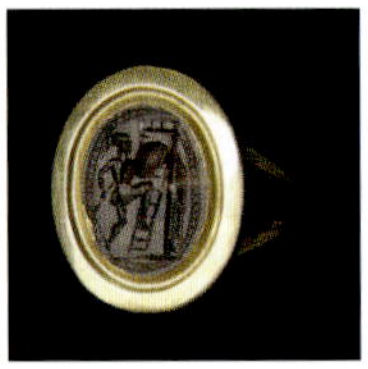
121. 133

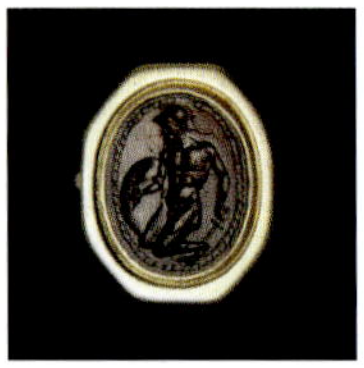
122. 134

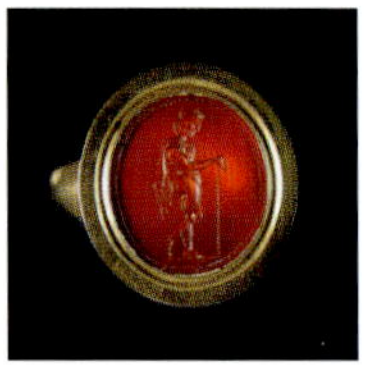
123. 135

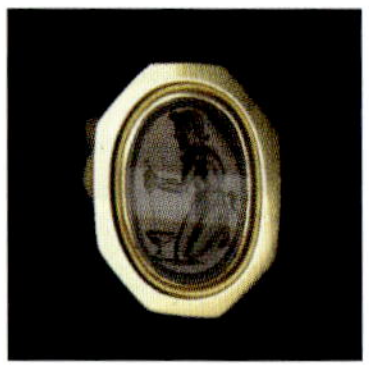
124. 136

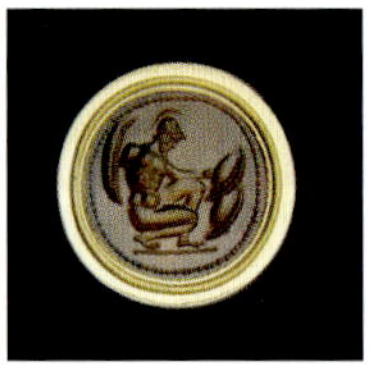
125. 137

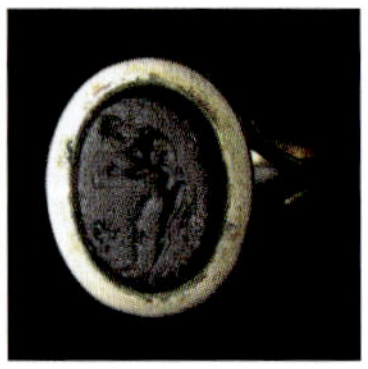
126. 138

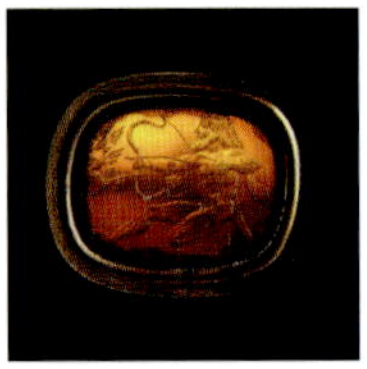
127. 139

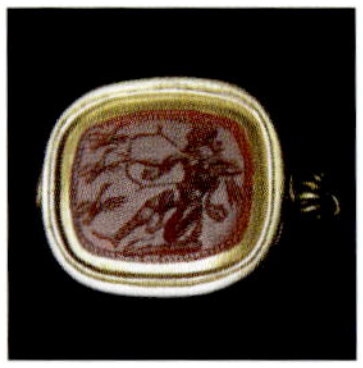
128. 140

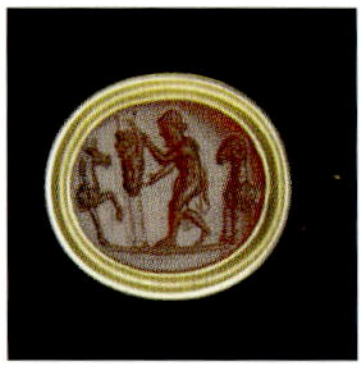
129. 141

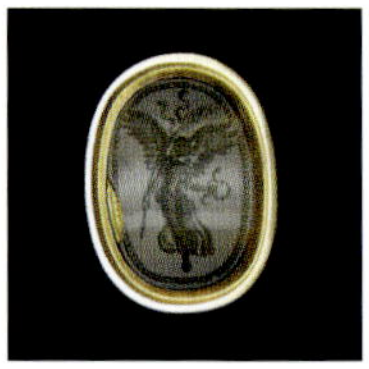
130. 142

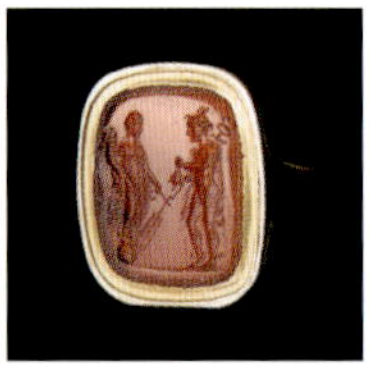
131. 143

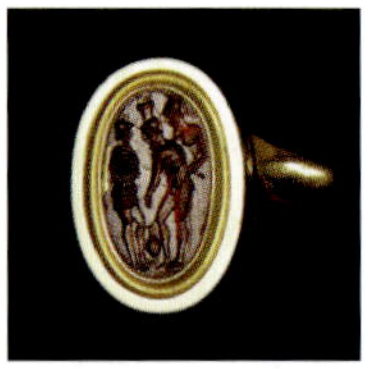
132. 144

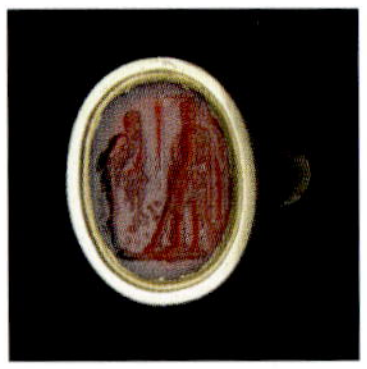
133. 146

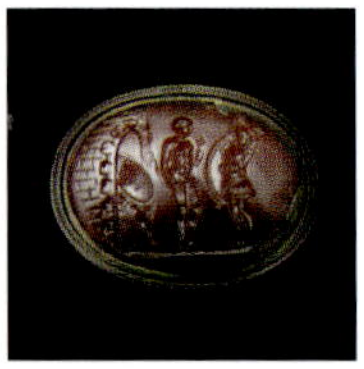
134. 147

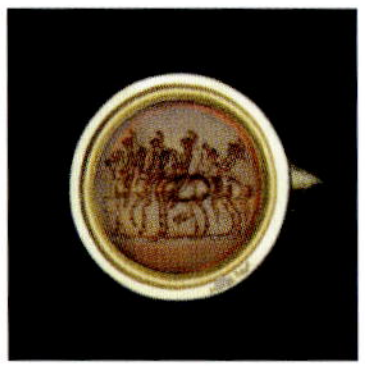
135. 148

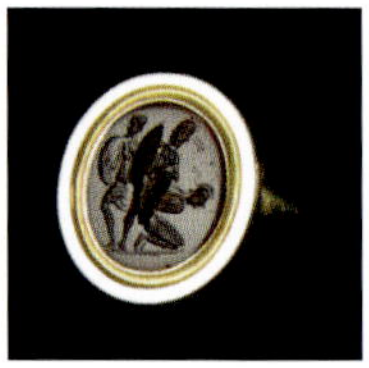
136. 149

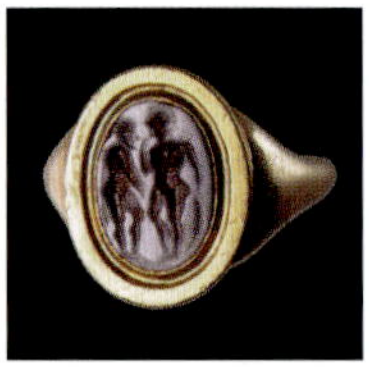
137. 150

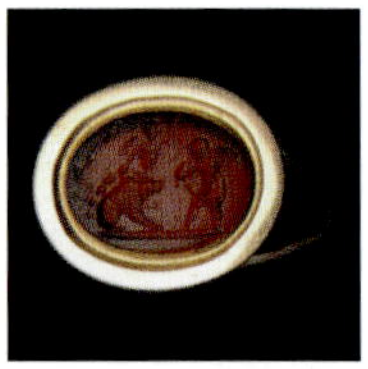
138. 151

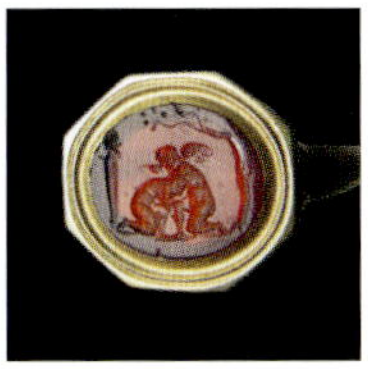

139. 152

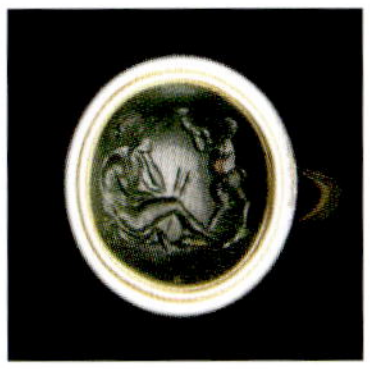

140. 153

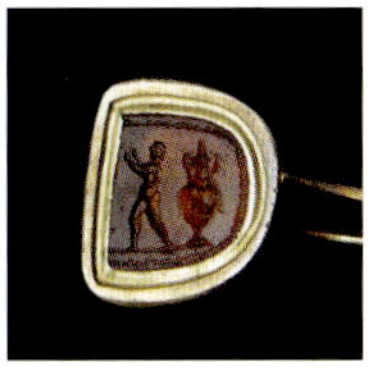

141. 154

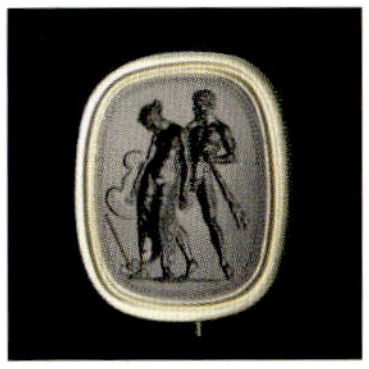

142. 2, 155

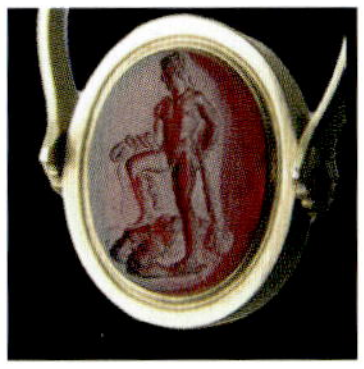

143. 156

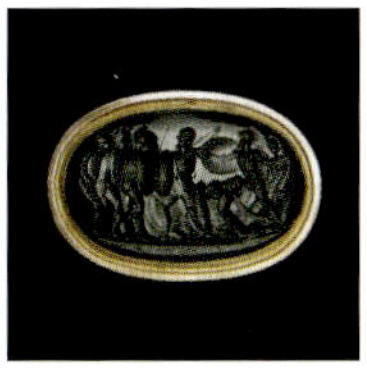

144. 145, 157

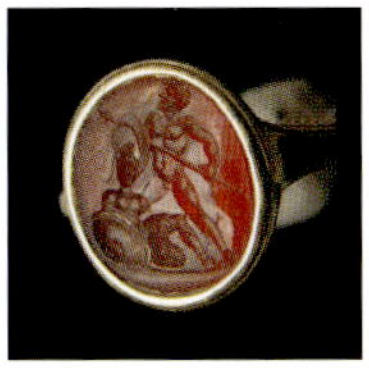

145. 158

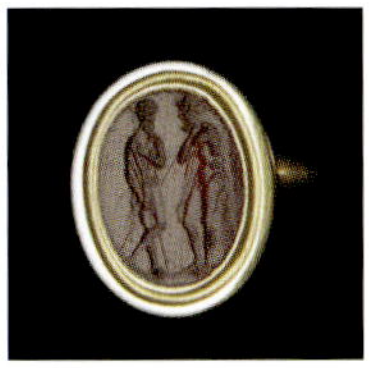

146. 159

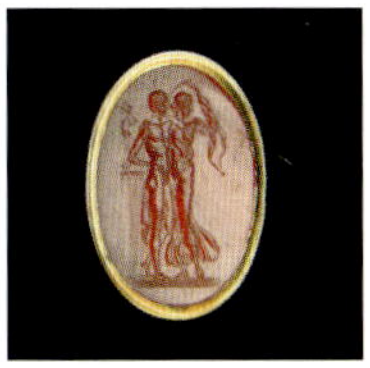

147. 160

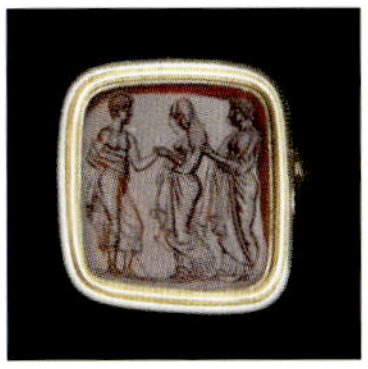

148. 161

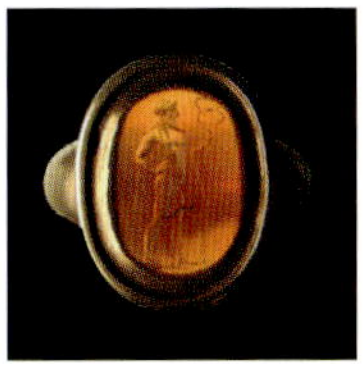

149. 163

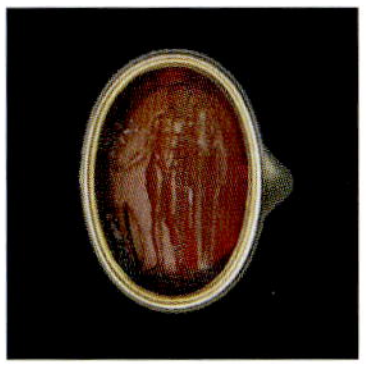

150. 164

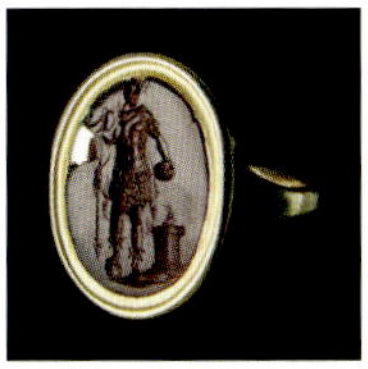

151. 165

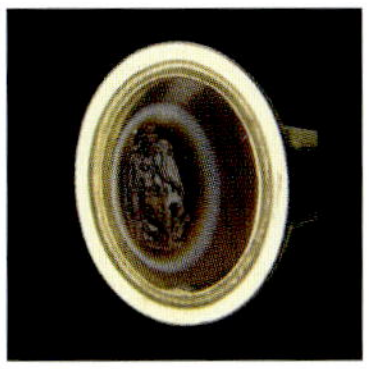

152. 166

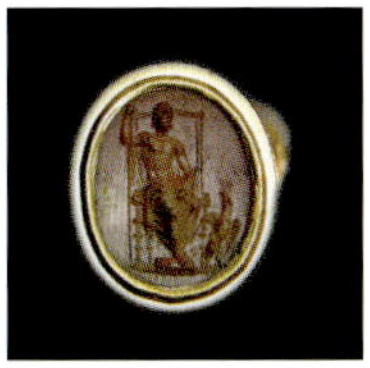

153. 167

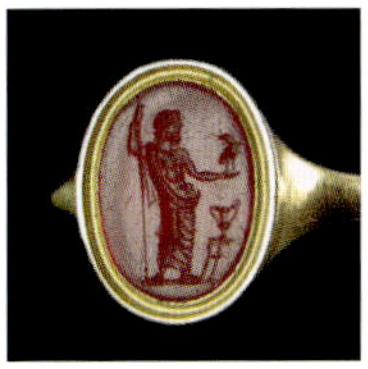

154. 168

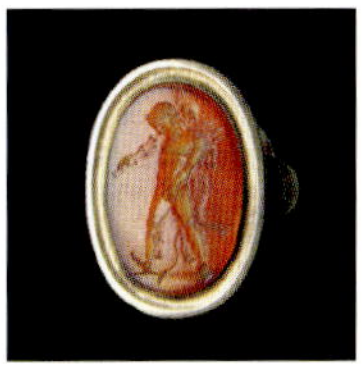

155. 169

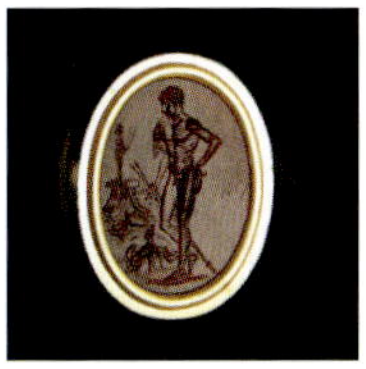

156. 170

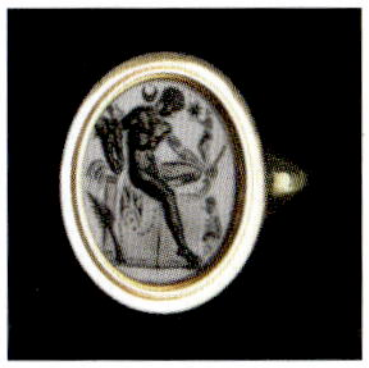

157. 162, 171

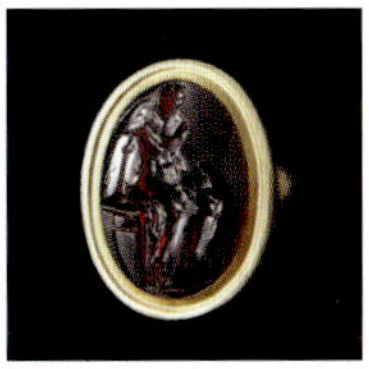

158. 172

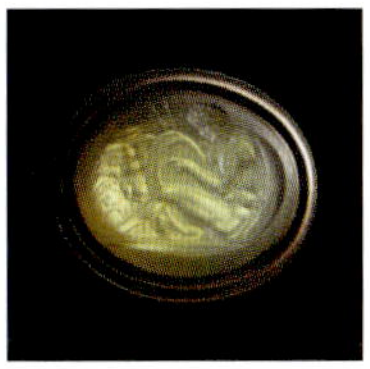

159. 173

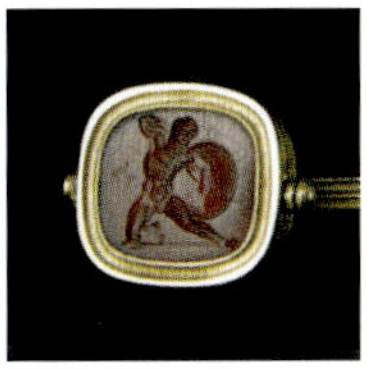

160. 174

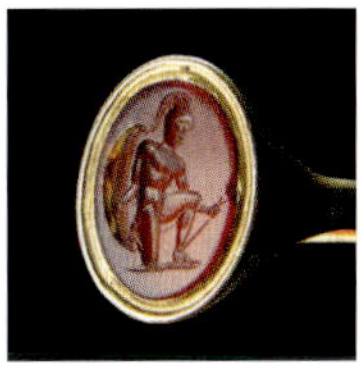

161. 175

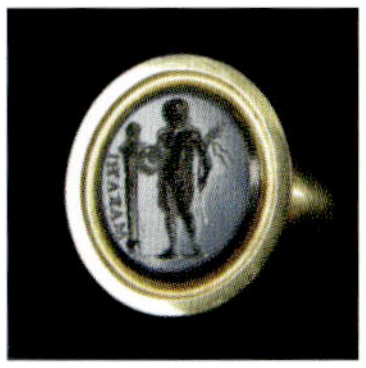

162. 176

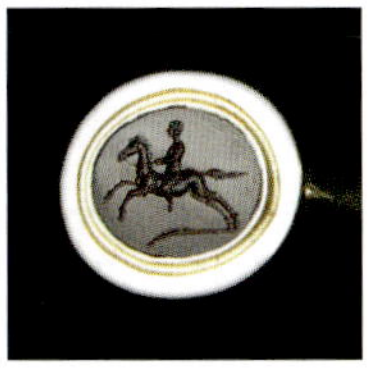

163. 177

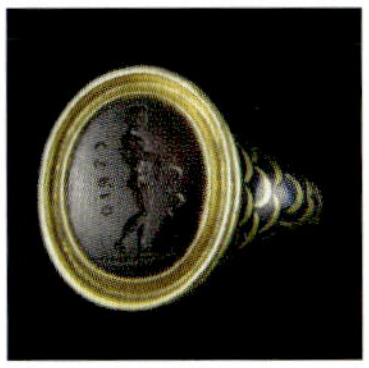

164. 178

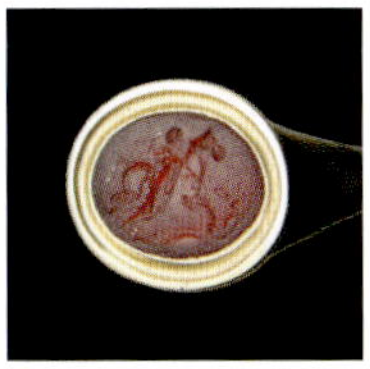

165. 179

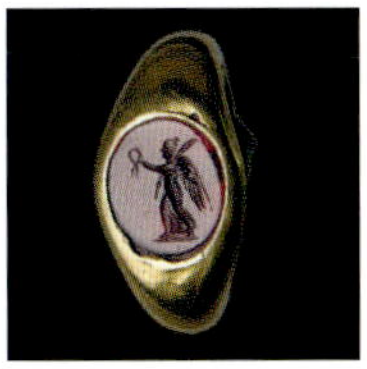

166. 180

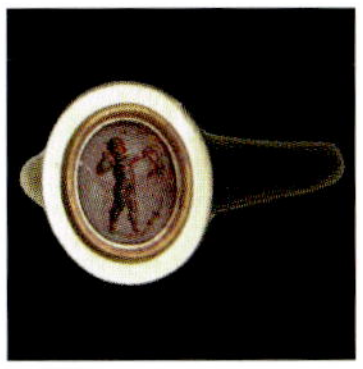

167. 181

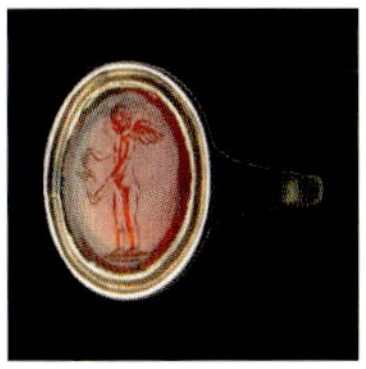

168. 182

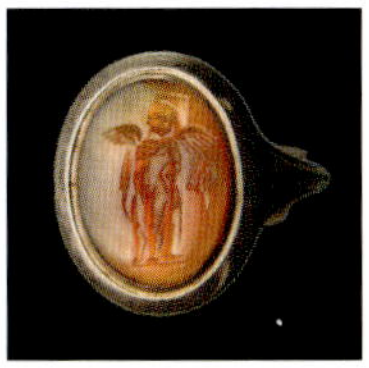

169. 183

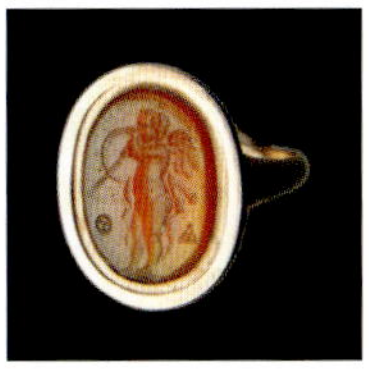

170. 184

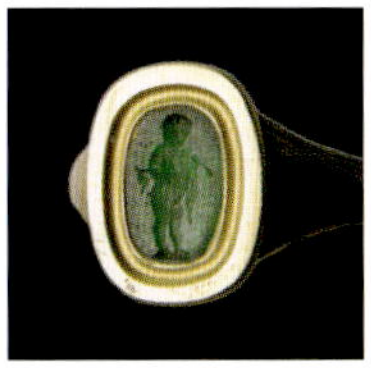

171. 185

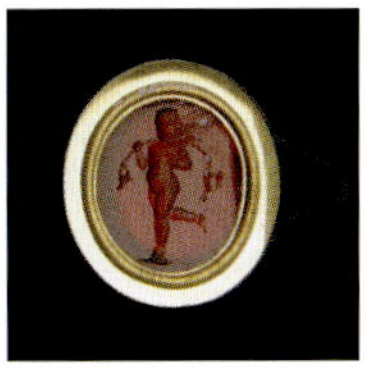

172. 186

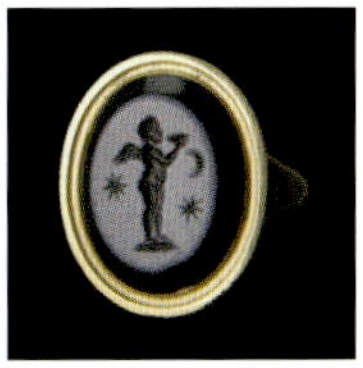

173. 187

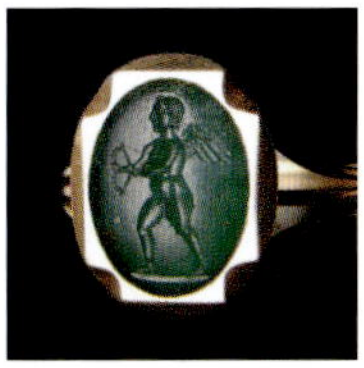

174. 188

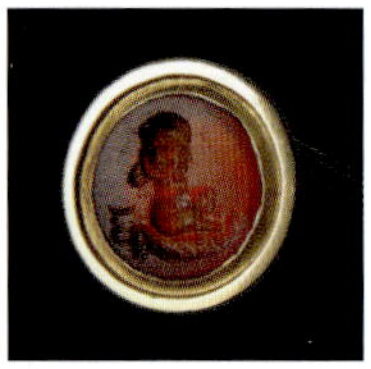
175. 189

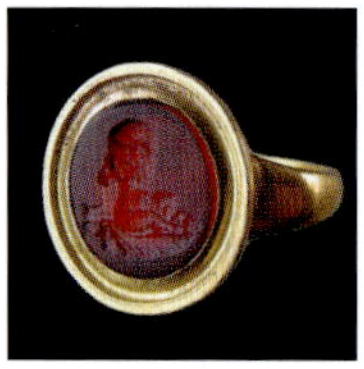
176. 190

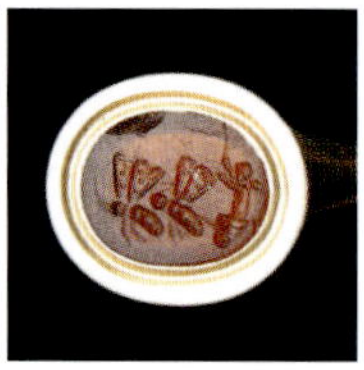
177. 191

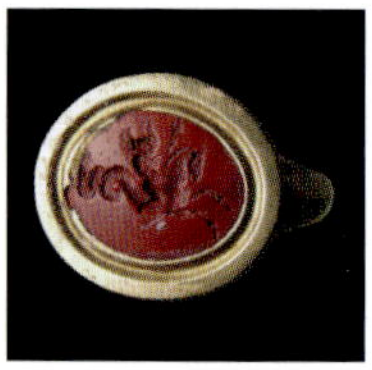
178. 192

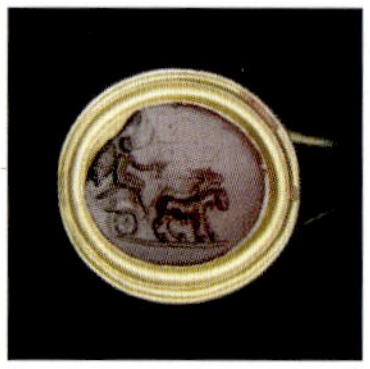
179. 193

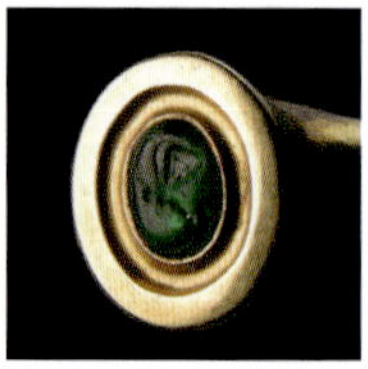
180. 194

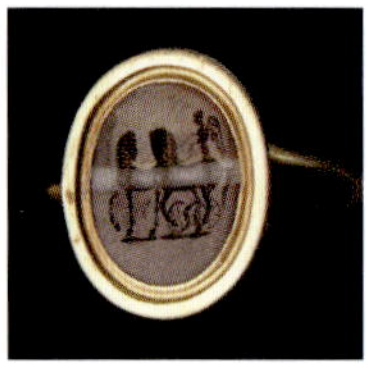
181. 195

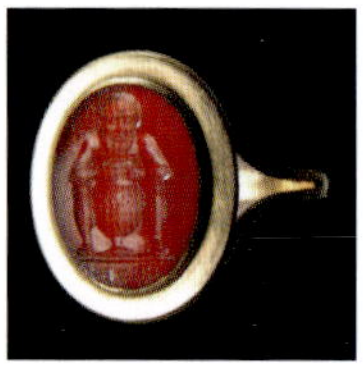
182. 196

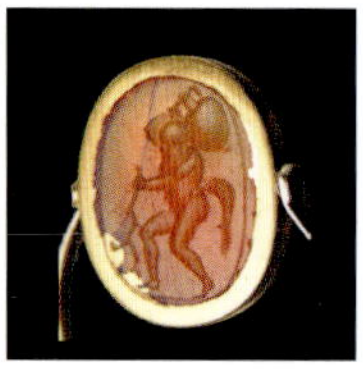
183. 197

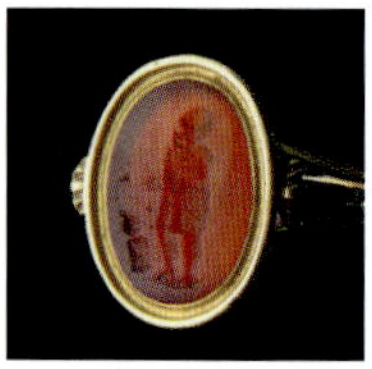
184. 198

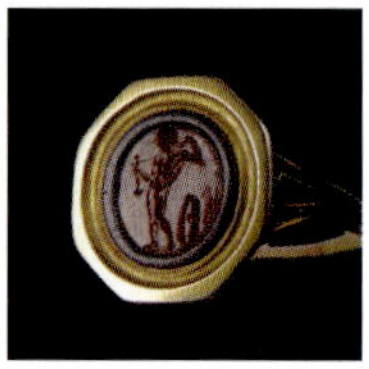
185. 199

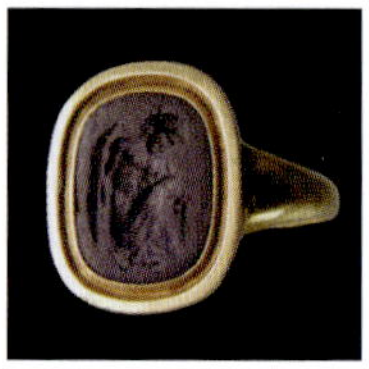
186. 200

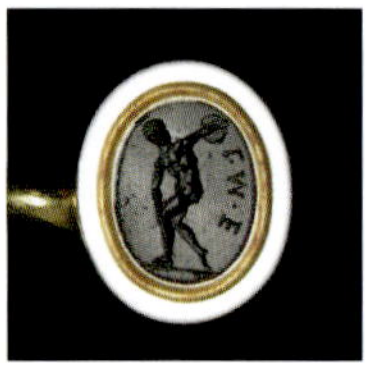
187. 201

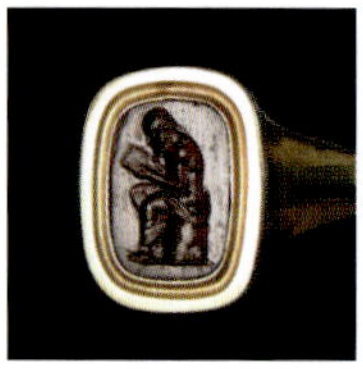
188. 202

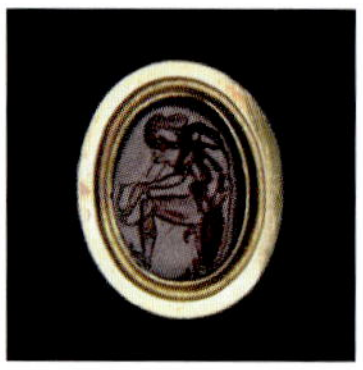
189. 203

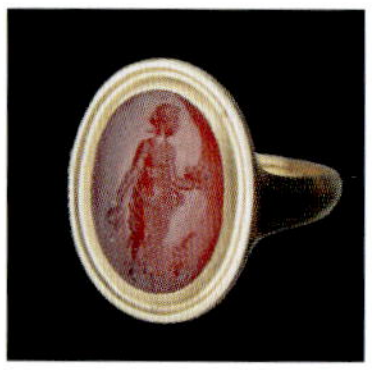
190. 204

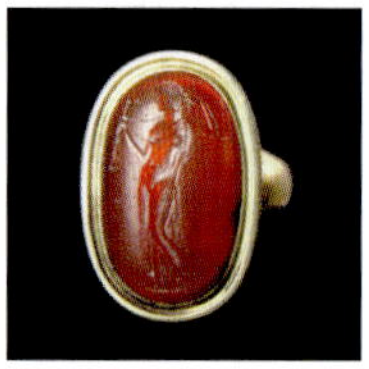
191. 205

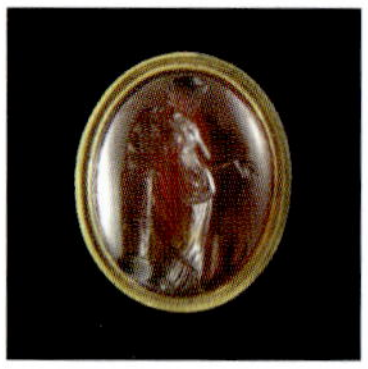
192. 206

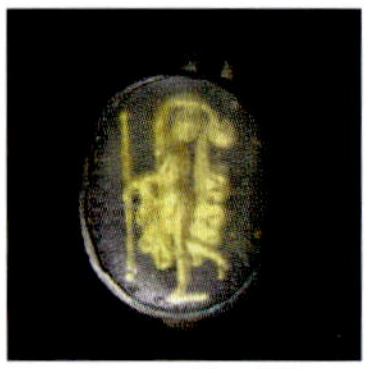
193. 207

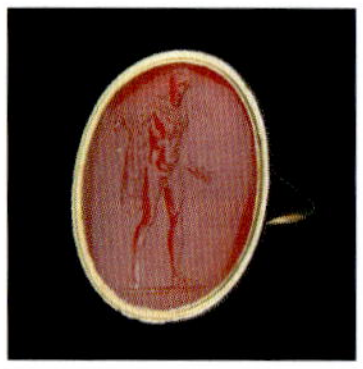
194. 208

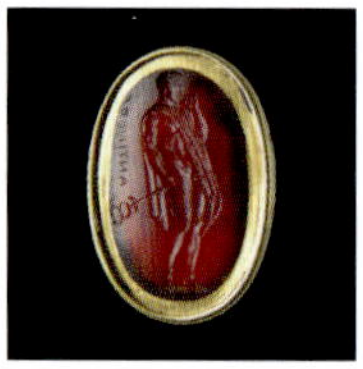
195. 209

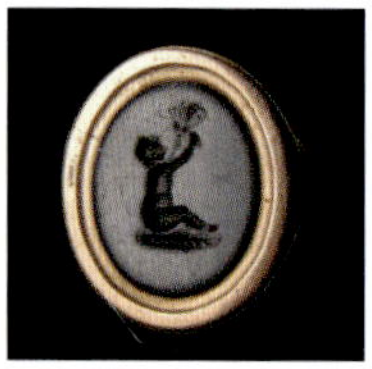
196. 210

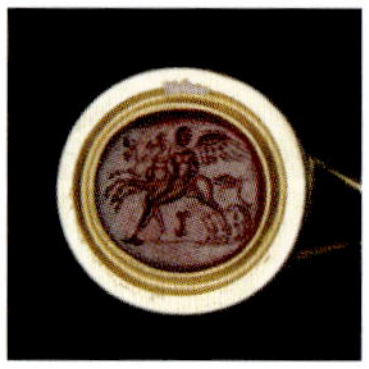
197. 211

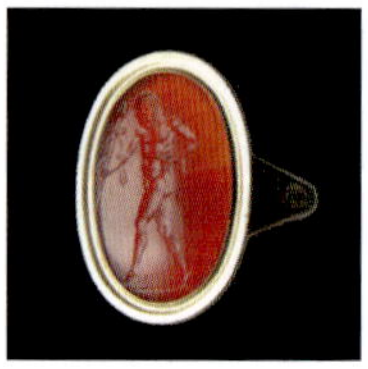
198. 212

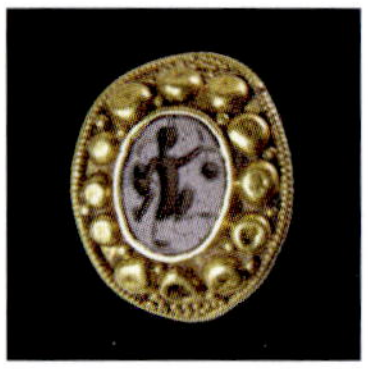
199. 213

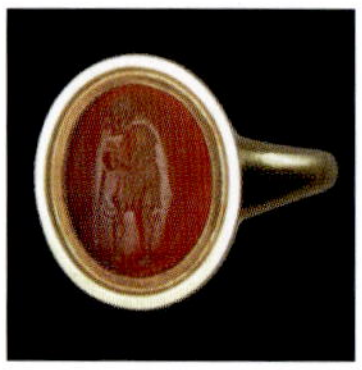
200. 214

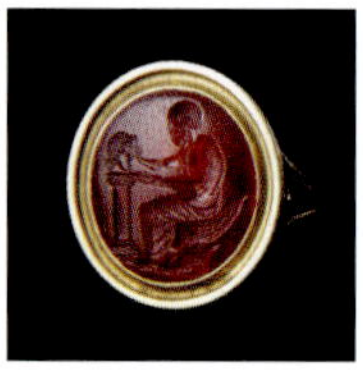
201. 215

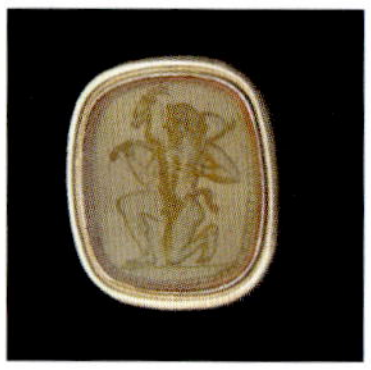
202. 216

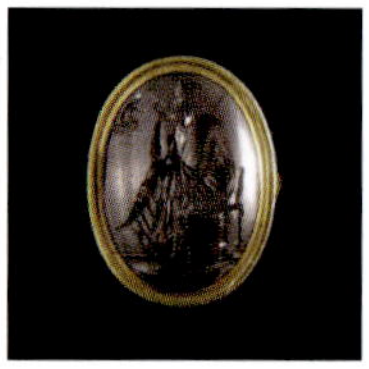
203. 217

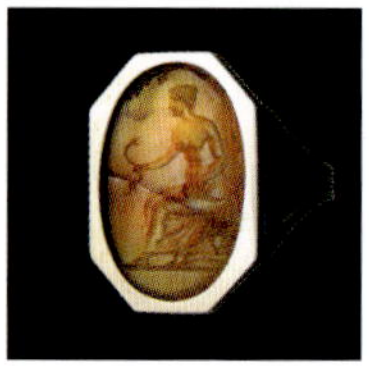
204. 218

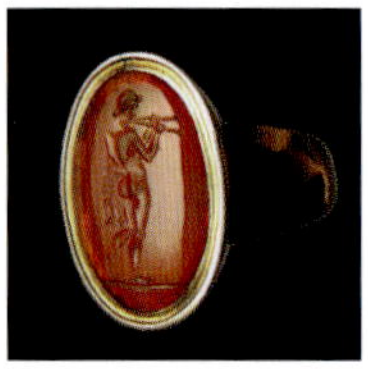
205. 219

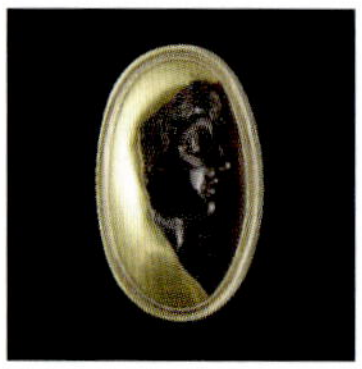
206. 221

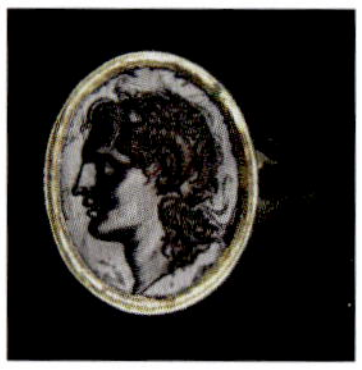
207. 222

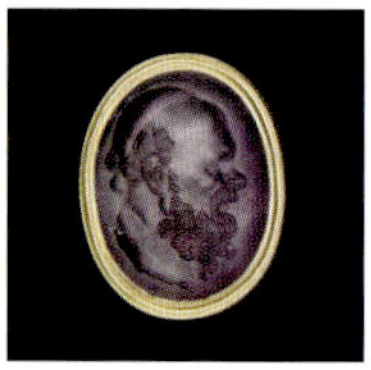
208. 223

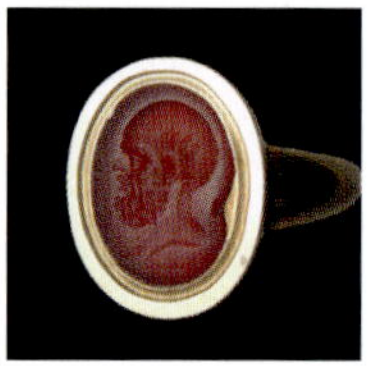
209. 224

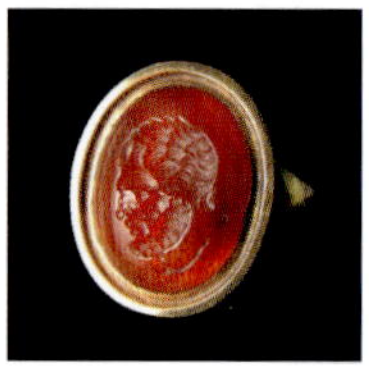
210. 225

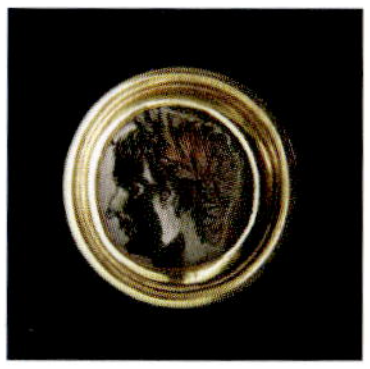
211. 226

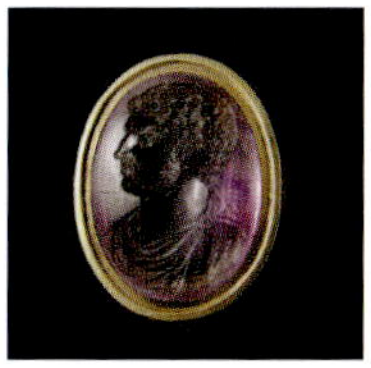
212. 227

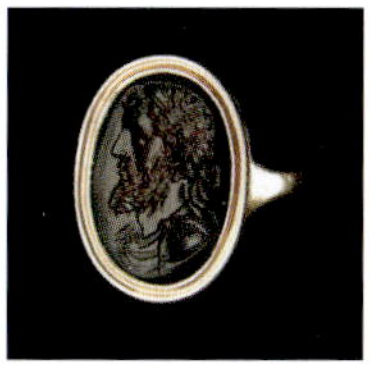
213. 228

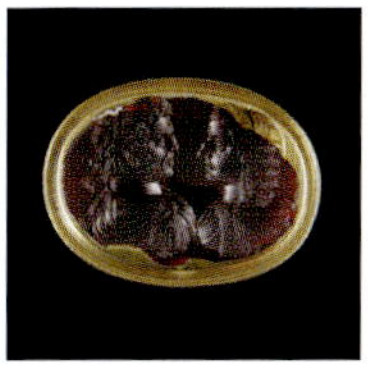
214. 229

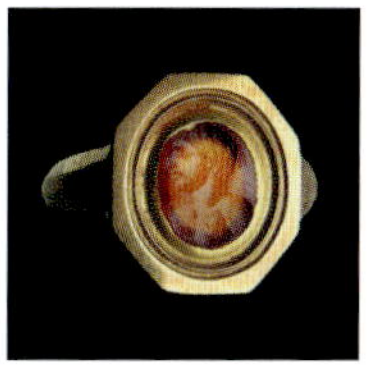
215. 230

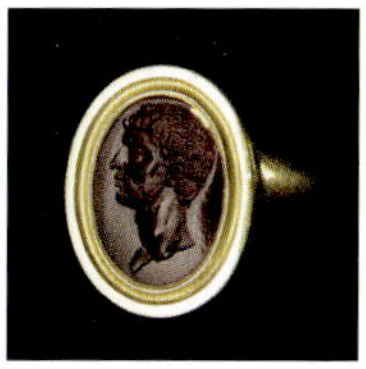
216. 231

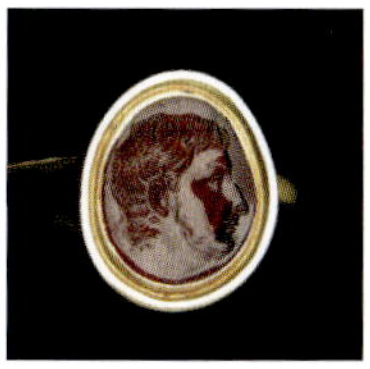
217. 232

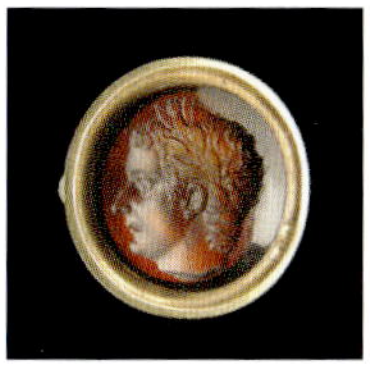
218. 233

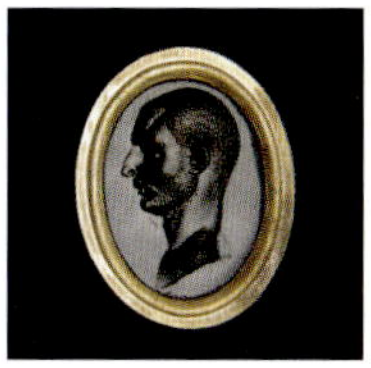
219. 234

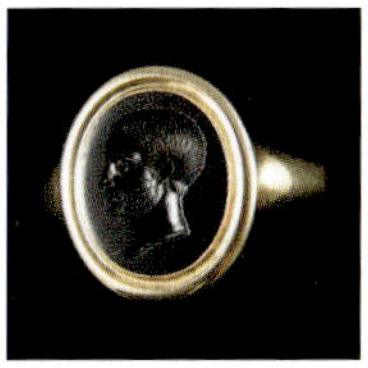
220. 235

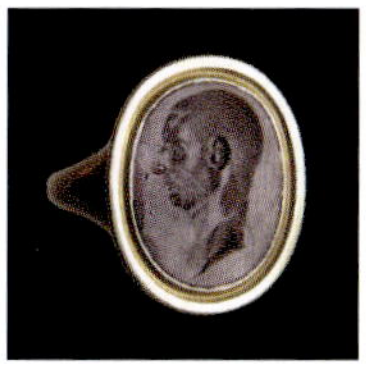
221. 236

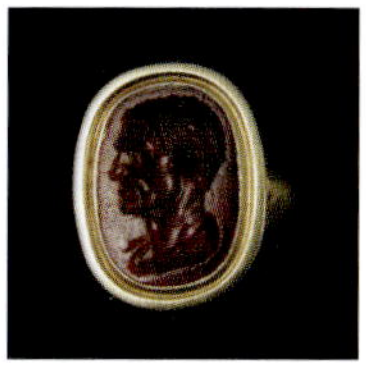
222. 237

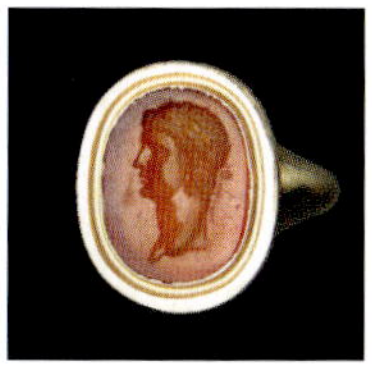
223. 238

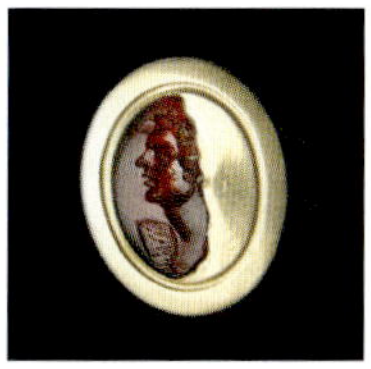
224. 239

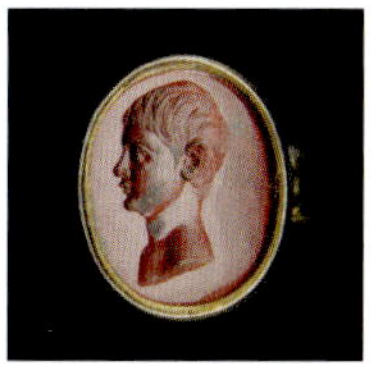
225. 240

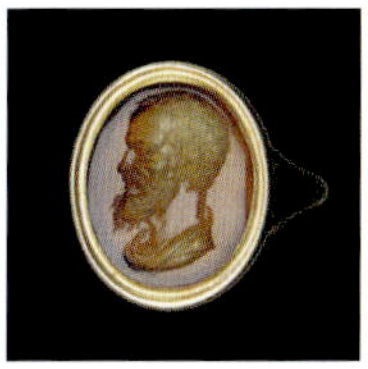
226. 241

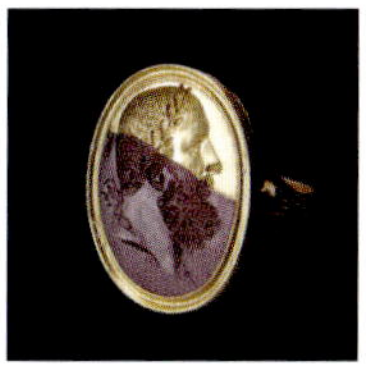
227. 242

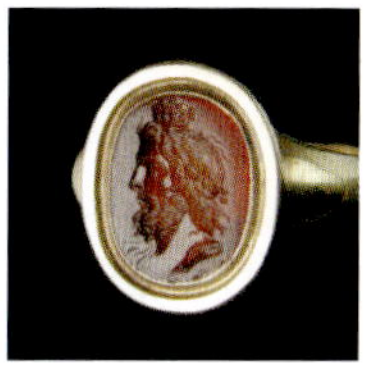
228. 243

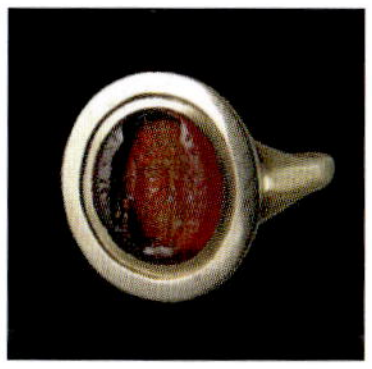
229. 244

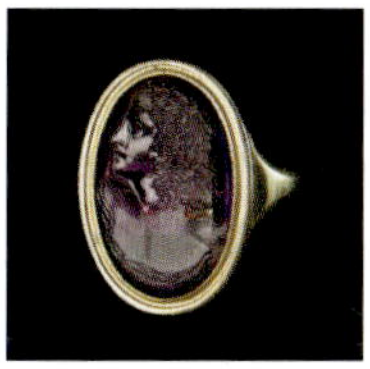
230. 220, 245

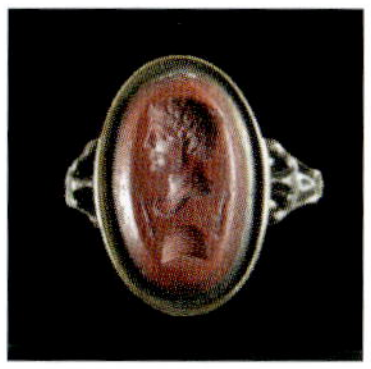
231. 246

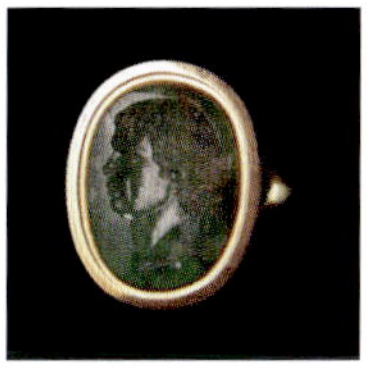
232. 247

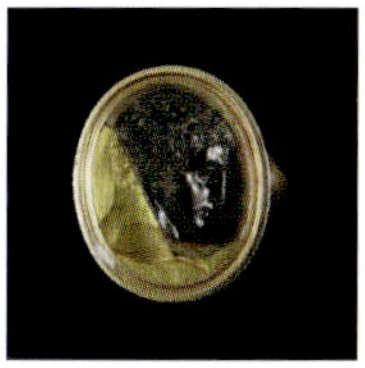
233. 248

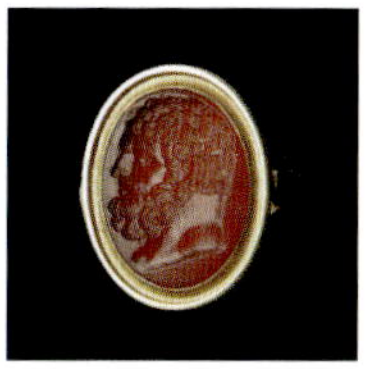
234. 249

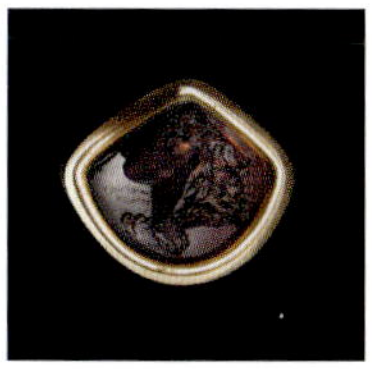
235. 250

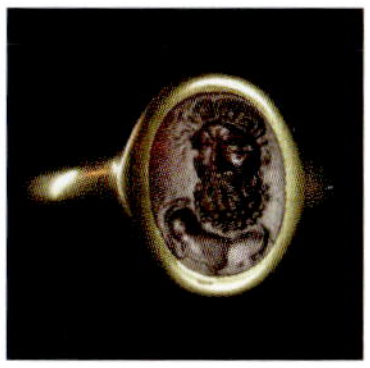
236. 251

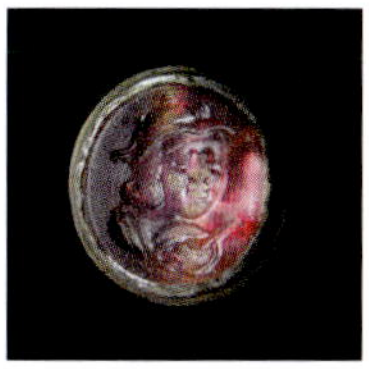
237. 252

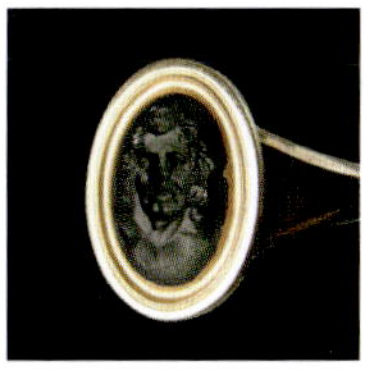
238. 253

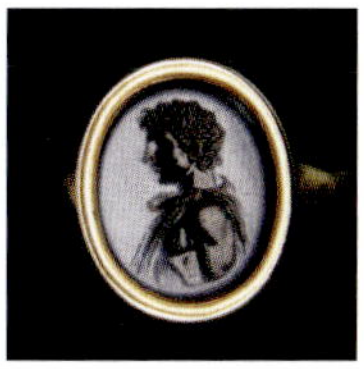
239. 254

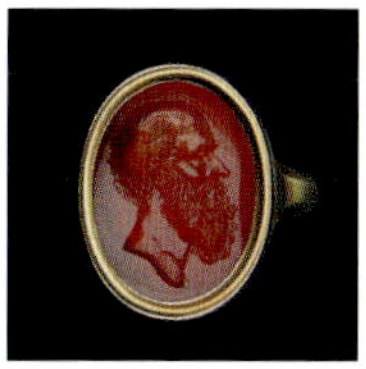
240. 255

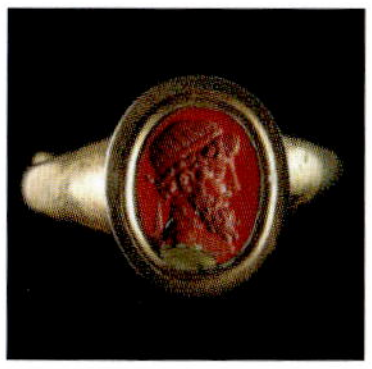
241. 256

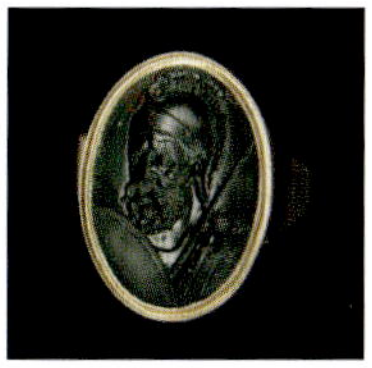
242. 257

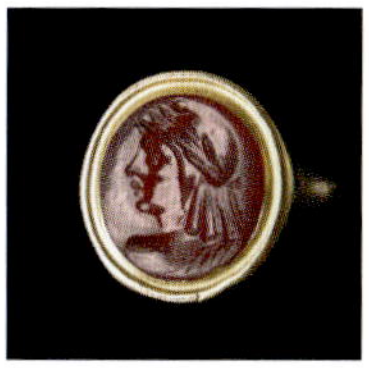
243. 258

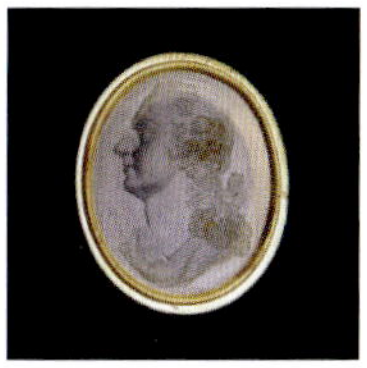
244. 259

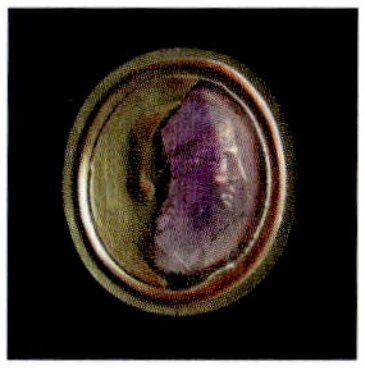
245. 261

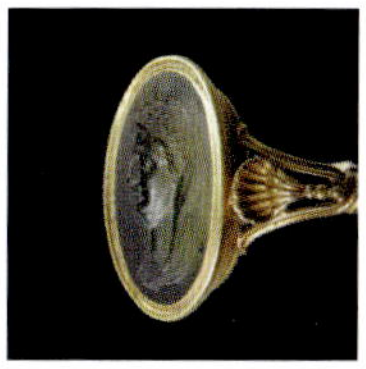
246. 262

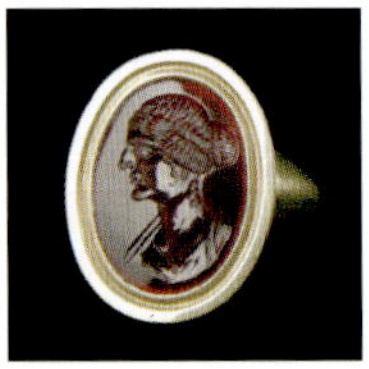
247. 263

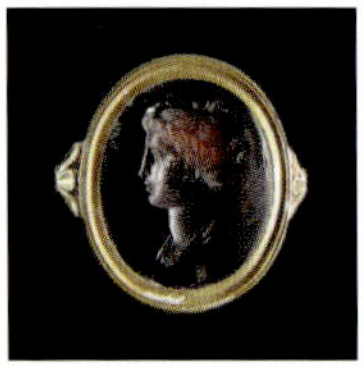
248. 260, 264

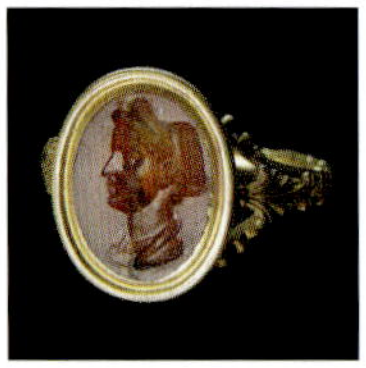
249. 265

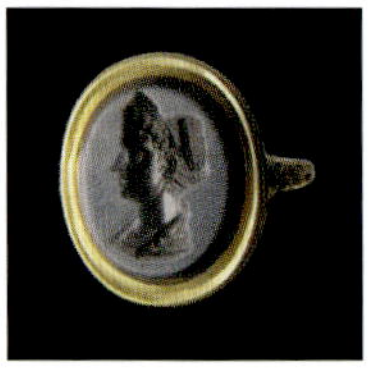
250. 266

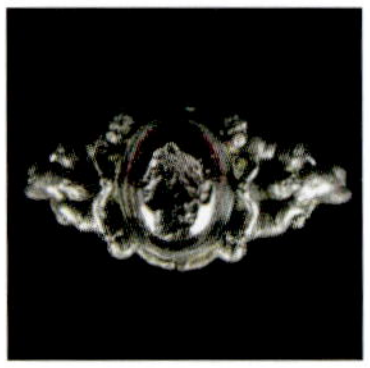
251. 267

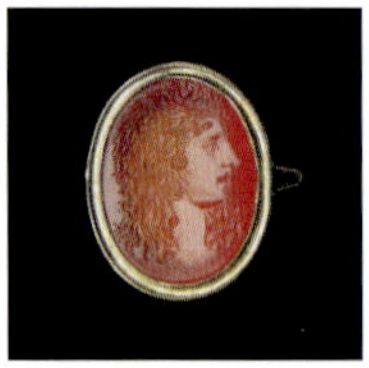
252. 268

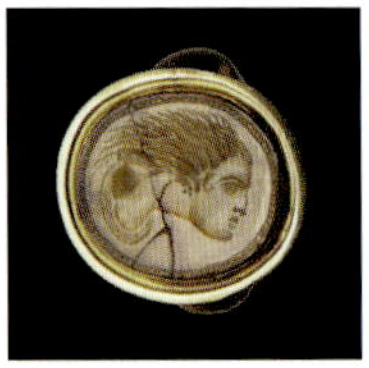
253. 269

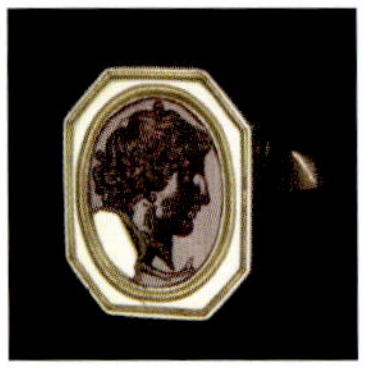
254. 270

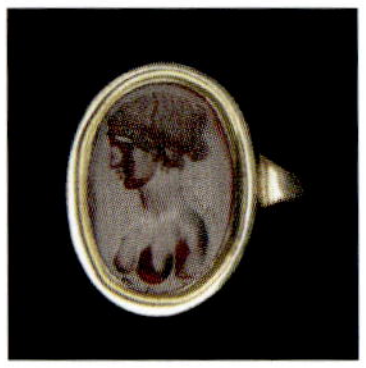
255. 271

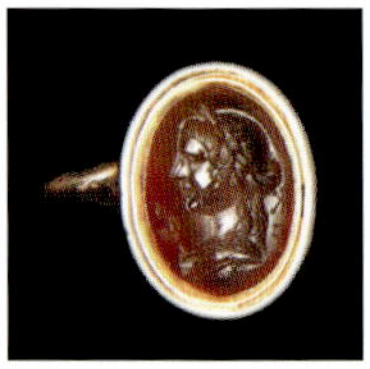
256. 272

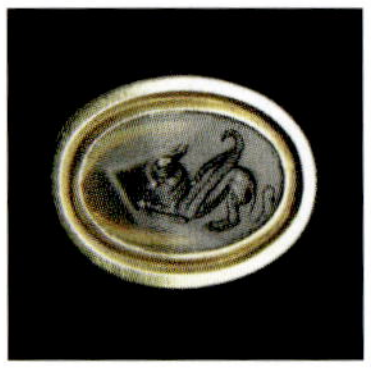
257. 274

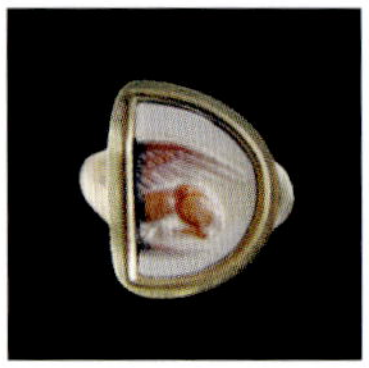
258. 275

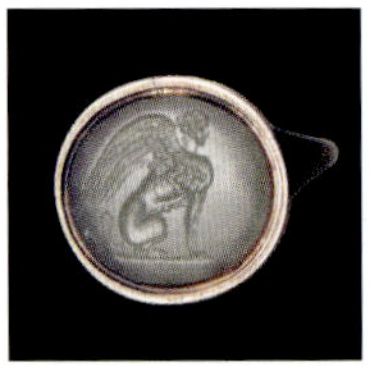
259. 276

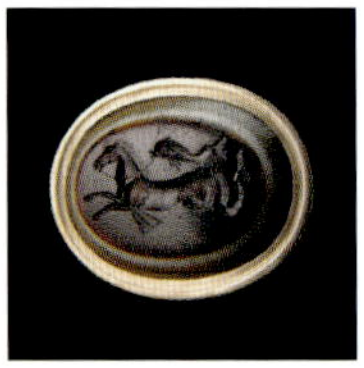
260. 277

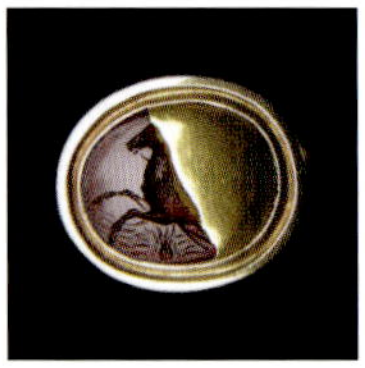
261. 278

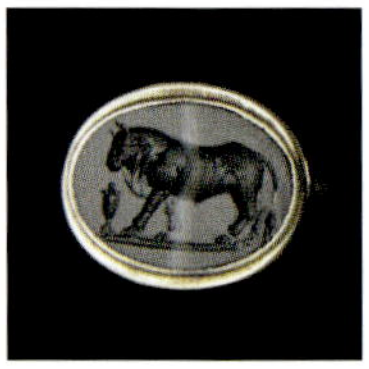
262. 279

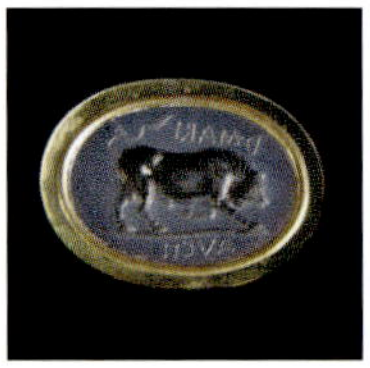
263. 280

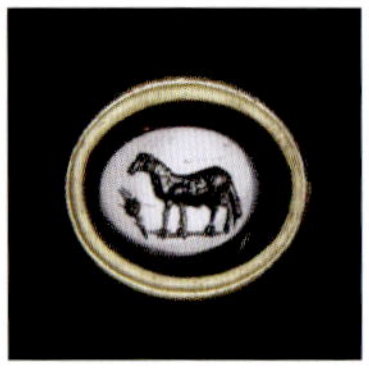
264. 281

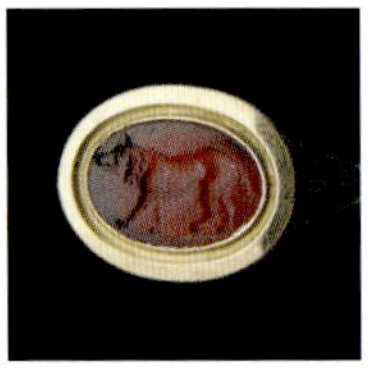
265. 282

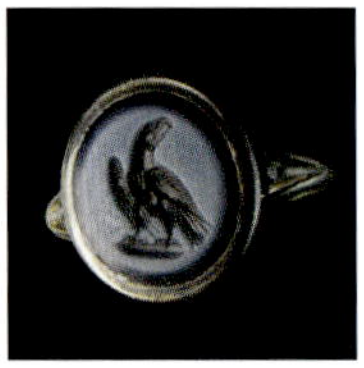
266. 283

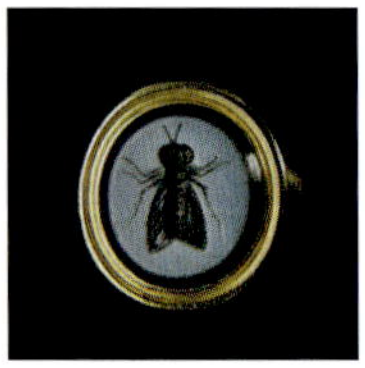
267. 273, 284

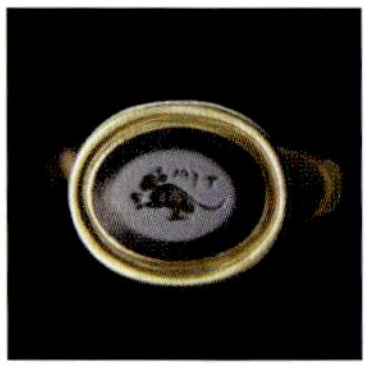
268. 285

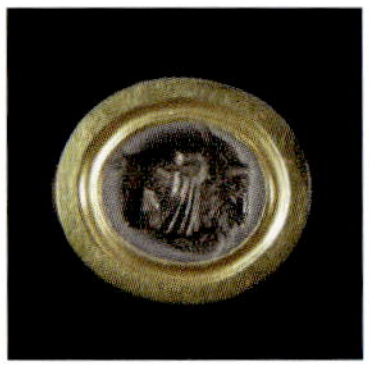
269. 286

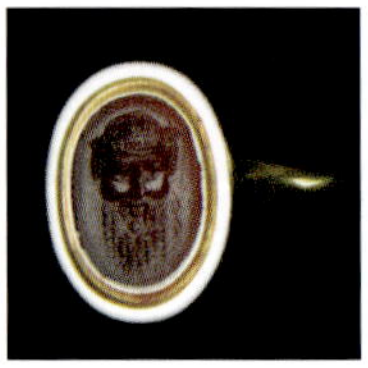
270. 288

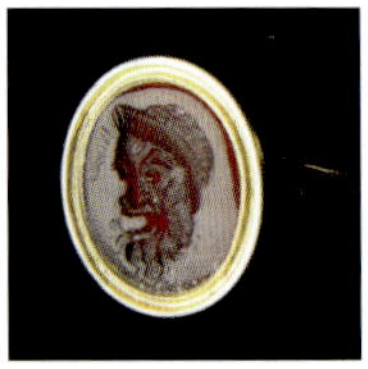
271. 289

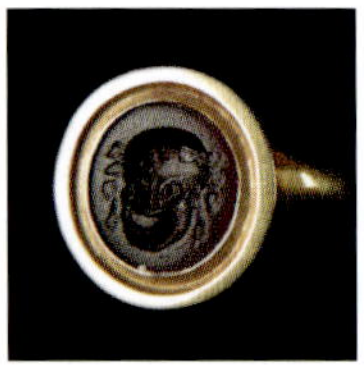
272. 290

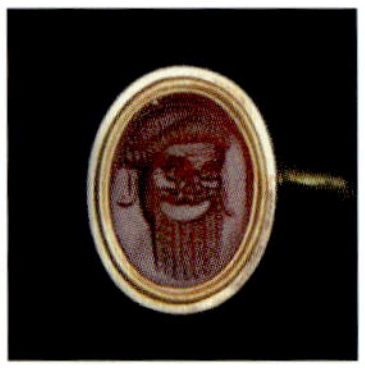
273. 291

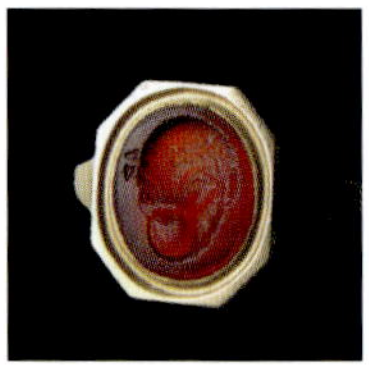
274. 292

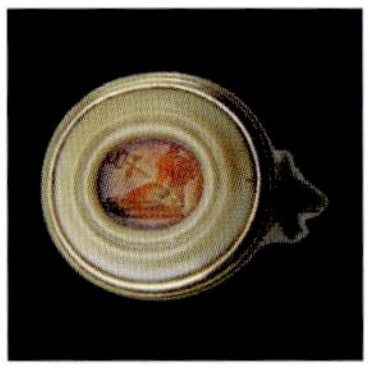
275. 293

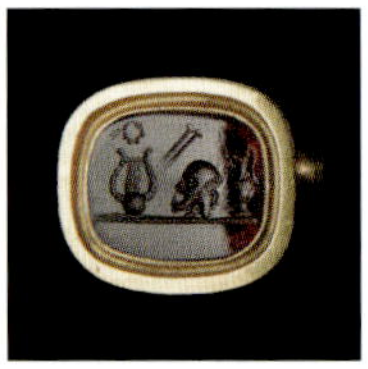
276. 287, 294

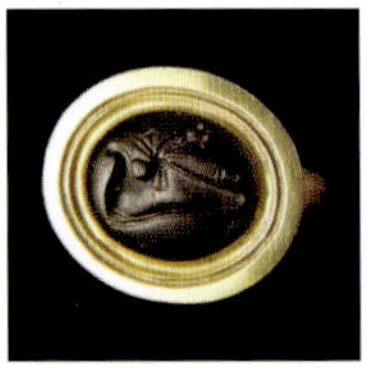
277. 295

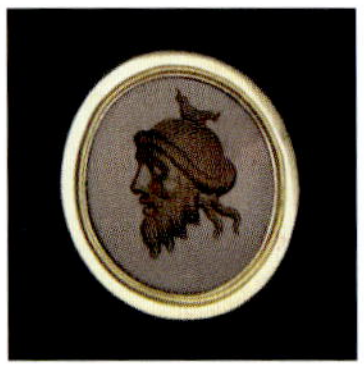
278. 296

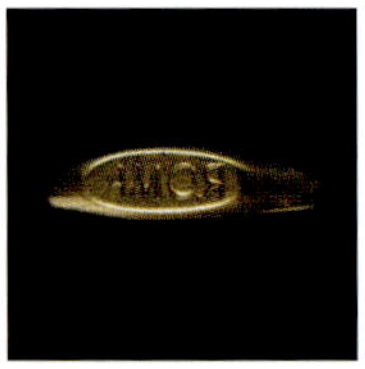
279. 297

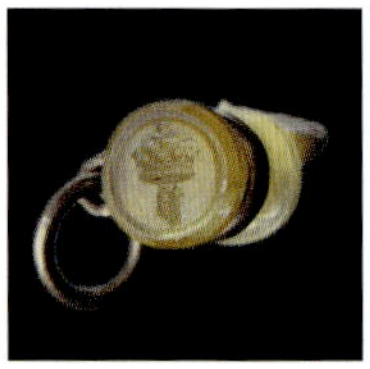
280. 298

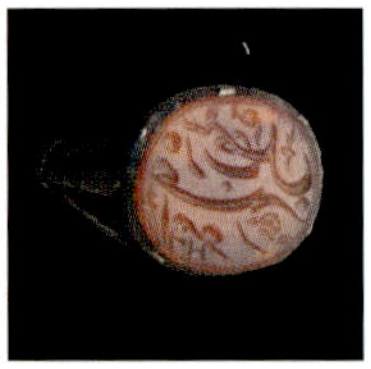
281. 299

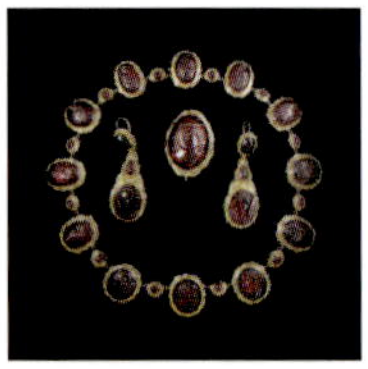
THE EMPERORS NECKLACE. 300